JEWISH WRITERS
OF LATIN AMERICA

LATIN AMERICAN STUDIES
VOLUME 9
GARLAND REFERENCE LIBRARY OF THE HUMANITIES
VOLUME 1794

LATIN AMERICAN STUDIES
DAVID WILLIAM FOSTER, *Series Editor*

THE CONTEMPORARY PRAXIS
OF THE FANTASTIC
Borges and Cortázar
by Julio Rodríguez-Luis

TROPICAL PATHS
*Essays on Modern
Brazilian Literature*
edited by Randal Johnson

THE POSTMODERN IN LATIN
AND LATINO AMERICAN
CULTURAL NARRATIVES
Collected Essays and Interviews
edited by Claudia Ferman

READERS AND LABYRINTHS
*Detective Fiction in Borges,
Bustos Domecq, and Eco*
by Jorge Hernández Martín

MAGIC REALISM
Social Context and Discourse
by María-Elena Angulo

RESISTING BOUNDARIES
*The Subject of
Naturalism in Brazil*
by Eva Paulino Bueno

LESBIAN VOICES
FROM LATIN AMERICA
Breaking Ground
by Elena M. Martínez

THE JEWISH DIASPORA
IN LATIN AMERICA
*New Studies on
History and Literature*
edited by David Sheinin
and Lois Baer Barr

JEWISH WRITERS
OF LATIN AMERICA
A Dictionary
edited by Darrell B. Lockhart

READERS AND
WRITERS IN CUBA
*A Social History
of Print Culture,
1830s–1990s*
by Pamela Maria Smorkaloff

Jewish Writers of Latin America
A Dictionary

Edited by
Darrell B. Lockhart

Garland Publishing, Inc.
New York and London
1997

Library of Congress Cataloging-in-Publication Data

Lockhart, Darrell B.
      Jewish writers of Latin America : a dictionary / [edited by] Darrell B.
Lockhart.
            p.   cm. — (Latin American studies ; 9) (Garland reference library
of the humanities ; vol. 1794)
      Includes bibliographical references and index.
      ISBN 0-8153-1495-7 (alk. paper)
      1. Latin American literature—Jewish authors—Biography—Dictionar-
ies.   2. Jewish authors—Latin America—Biography—Dictionaries.   I. Title.
II. Series.   III. Series: Garland reference library of the humanities ; vol. 1794.
PQ7081.3.L63   1997
860.9'8924'098—dc20   96-24191
                                                                   CIP

Printed on acid-free, 250-year-life paper
Manufactured in the United States of America

CONTENTS

Preface

Jewish Writers of Latin America: A Dictionary represents the first attempt, to my knowledge, to provide a comprehensive examination of Latin American Jewish writing. There is a dual purpose and underlying goal in presenting this volume to both the general and specialized reader. First, it is my intention that this compilation provide greater recognition of the vast contribution that Latin American Jewish writers have made to Latin American literature as a whole. Secondly, and perhaps more importantly, the aim is to stimulate further critical attention not only to the works and authors included here, but also to those who do not form part of this volume. It is my hope that this volume will serve as a valuable resource for the study of Latin American Jewish literature and open the doors of this body of writing to a wider audience.

Jewish Writers of Latin America: A Dictionary includes approximately 120 entries on authors who represent ten Latin American countries. The majority of authors included in the volume are associated with Argentina, Mexico, and Brazil, a fact that reflects the demographic reality of Latin America's Jewish communities. Likewise, it brings together the collective efforts of some fifty scholars committed to the advancement of Latin American Jewish studies.

In organizing the volume, each contributor was asked to provide a brief biographical sketch of the author (in some cases this has been difficult or even impossible to obtain), and then to discuss the author's work; focusing on issues and themes germane to Jewish identity and cultural tradition whenever possible. There were few stylistic or format restraints placed on the contributors, therefore the entries may differ in their approach, but each provides a general overview of the writer's works. The length of the entries was left to the discretion of each contributor, within certain parameters, in order to provide the best comprehensive coverage of the author.

The entries are organized alphabetically by the author's actual last name, or the last name of his or her pseudonym for which he or she is better known. Next to each author's name is the country with which he or she is associated as a writer and the year of birth. The country, however, is not necessarily their place of birth. For example, Ariel Dorfman was born in Argentina and now lives in the United States, but he is known as a Chilean writer. Therefore, the entry on him reads as follows: DORFMAN, ARIEL (Chile; 1942). Each contributor was asked to provide a complete bibliography of the author's works as well as criticism on their works. In the case of writers such as Clarice Lispector, for whom there are book-length bibliographies, the contributors were asked to provide a selective bibliography of criticism that in their judgement best represents the writer. The primary bibliographies include the author's works in their original language and, when available, in English translation only—the exception being works originally written in Yiddish and then translated into Spanish, wherein the Spanish edition is listed (this situation does not occur in the case of the Brazilian authors included). In the interest of space, translations into languages other than English have been excluded.

There have been a number of difficulties associated with compiling a dictionary such as this one. Regrettably there are at least as many authors left out of this volume as there are included in it. Constraints of both time and space have forced me to exclude many authors who merit greater attention. A secondary problem arose with efforts to locate critics who were willing and able to write entries. While I received an overwhelming response to my call for contributions, there were simply many more writers than there were contributors to take on the task of preparing the entries. I have attempted to include all the authors who are considered to be the major figures of Latin American Jewish writing as well introduce many lesser known writers. I am also very pleased that women writers figure prominently in the dictionary.

A central issue of concern in organizing *Jewish Writers of Latin America: A Dictionary* has been how to delineate the scope of the volume. The question was should it include only those writers whose works directly reflect a Jewish identity while excluding those whose works do not, notwithstanding their important and vast literary contributions to the respective national literary scene. Likewise, the question was raised as to whether a writer like Jorge Luis Borges, whose works contain a significant amount of what may be considered Jewish material and that many critics have analyzed from specifically Jewish perspectives, should be included. I arrived at the conclusion that the dictionary should in its totality be a critical sourcebook of Latin American Jewish writers and not just Jewish writing. While the main focus of the book is to define in what way Latin American Jewish writers directly reflect a Jewish identity in their works, I feel it equally important to include those whose work has greatly influenced Latin American socioliterary trends. By writers whose works directly reflect a Jewish identity I mean to say that their writing in large part deals with so-called Jewish concerns, which include but are not limited to the problematics of identity, assimilation, tradition, immigration, the Sephardic heritage of Latin America, Yiddishkeit, Judaism\Jewishness, self-hatred, anti-Semitism, the Holocaust, Zionism, and Israel.

Finally, I wish to acknowledge the individuals who have made this volume possible, first and foremost the contributors who embraced this project with enthusiasm and without whom it would not have become a reality. I am grateful and indebted to David William Foster who has been a constant source of support and encouragement and to Melissa Fitch Lockhart, not only for her editorial assistance but also for her patience and understanding. I also wish to acknowledge and extend my gratitude to Laurel Stegina at Garland for her excellent editing of the manuscript. Finally, this project was also made possible by a grant from the Rabbi Morris N. Kertzer Memorial Research Award at Arizona State University, and I am thankful for the enthusiasm with which the proposal was received.

Darrell B. Lockhart

Introduction

Darrell B. Lockhart

To consider Jewish writing as a subdivision of Latin American literature raises a series of complex questions regarding issues that range from the theorizing of identity, both individual and collective, to canon formation. Any approach to the subject of Jewish literature in general must take into account a number of theoretical, methodological, and ontological interpretive strategies in order to define it as a legitimate socioliterary phenomenon. The debate over precisely what elements contribute to the creation of a text that can be designated as Jewish has been going on for some time and promises to continue well into the future. The forum for these discussions has been dominated primarily by a focus on Jewish literature from the United States, Europe, and Israel. Such debate is fueled not only by differing ideological postures established along the lines of nationality, language, ethnicity, and religiosity, but also by the fact that the forces that guide social and literary criticism are constantly changing. In one of the more recent attempts to pinpoint the nature of Jewish literature Hana Wirth-Nesher, in a clever deployment of reader-response theory, places the bulk of responsibility on the recipient of a text when she states that a text's "characterization as Jewish will depend upon the reader and all of the circumstances of its reception" (5).

It is not insignificant that global debates have excluded Latin American Jewish writing as a viable contributor to the wider corpus of works. Such an exclusion directly signals the double marginalization of Latin American Jewish writers. On the grand scale they are marginalized with the rest of Latin America in both geographic and socioeconomic terms as inhabitants of Third-World nations. Furthermore, they exist on the fringes of a society in which the codes, values and mores of the dominant Luso- or Hispano-Catholic society maintain a strong, often nationalistic, cultural hegemony over alter/native identities that do not conform to the established paradigm. In addition, one can maintain that the Jewish woman writer is even further marginalized as a female, constrained by deep-rooted Latin American and Jewish patriarchal traditions. Likewise is the case for Jewish queer writers. Latin American national identities have traditionally been formed around the ideals of cultural homogeneity in which the collective takes precedence over the individual. Therefore, the dynamics of cultural inter-subjectivity, or the way in which the different and often disparate elements interact, are played out under the rubric of center versus margin. Jews, as ex/centric members of Latin American societies, occupy the position of the Other.

Latin American literature in general did not attract global consideration until the mid-1960s with the advent of the so-called Boom. Such writers as Julio Cortázar (1914-84), Gabriel García Márquez (1928), Carlos Fuentes (1928), Mario Vargas Llosa (1936), and José Donoso (1925) burst onto the international scene and focused the world's attention on the vast literary resources of Latin America. The exception to the previous statement is of course Jorge Luis Borges (1899-1986), whose works began to be noticed outside Argentina in the 1940s, mainly because of their universal appeal rather than for their regional particularism. Traditionally, the Latin American literary canon has been the domain of such consecrated national writers as those mentioned above. Only recently has the process of canon formation been called into question as critical attention has increasingly turned to the examination of subaltern literary voices. Most prominent in this movement has been the reassessment of women's writing. In the circles of academe there has been a concerted effort to promote Latin American women's writing to an English-reading public—the result of which has been the translation and publication of a large number of individual works and anthologies that have brought well-deserved international recognition to women writers. To a lesser extent, other marginal literatures such as Afro-Hispanic and/or Brazilian, indigenous, and gay and lesbian writing have achieved considerable notice. It is within this polyphonic chorus of marginalia that Latin American Jewish literature is situated, and from where any consideration of it as a valid discourse representative of a cultural identity must begin.

Critic Saúl Sosnowski, who has been instrumental in defining the parameters of Latin American Jewish literature, comments: "When in addition to Latin American one adds the defining term Jewish, it is easy to recall astonished gazes and conflicting images of the accepted and simple cliches for both" (1987; 299). This is a fundamental observation regarding the foundation from which Latin American Jewish literature springs, for it points to the lack of understanding about just how far-reaching and deeply entrenched the Jewish-Latin American relationship is. Nevertheless, it has only been in the past fifteen years that Latin American Jewish studies has evolved into a fully developed academic discipline. This has been achieved by the formation of such ground-breaking organizations as the Latin American Jewish Studies Association (LAJSA), which has attracted a large world-wide membership and has been instrumental in providing a forum and a network for the advancement and dissemination of research in all areas of concern to the history and culture of the Jewish communities of Latin America. Specific to literary studies, the Asociación Internacional de Escritores Judíos en

Lengua Hispana y Portuguesa (International Association of Jewish Writers in Spanish and Portuguese), which publishes the literary journal *Noaj* from its headquarters in Jerusalem, has been invaluable for its efforts to promote Jewish literature in Spanish and Portuguese. University curricula have also begun to reflect the growing interest in this area, as courses in Latin American Jewish literature and history are now being offered, though primarily as special topics courses.

A certain level of familiarization with the sociohistorical circumstances that gave rise to the presence of Jews in Latin America is essential to a comprehensive understanding of the forces that have shaped Latin American Jewish literature over the course of its development. It is not within the scope of this brief introduction to recount the details of the Jewish presence in Latin America, which spans a period of over five hundred years. Suffice to say that the history of mass immigration which gave rise to the present-day Jewish communities from Mexico to Argentina belongs to the twentieth century (see the history section in the selected bibliography). Consequently, the history of Jewish literature in Latin America begins in the twentieth century as well. This is not to say that there are no Jewish-authored texts in Latin America prior to this time. One of the earliest and most significant testimonies of Jewish life in colonial Latin America was left by Luis de Carvajal y de la Cueva (1539-91?). He and his family were persecuted and finally condemned by the Inquisition in Mexico for Judaizing—that is, secretly practicing the Jewish religion and customs. The nineteenth century saw the appearance of Jorge Isaacs (1837-95), who became one of the canonical Latin American authors, and whose novel *María* (1867) gained an immediate fame throughout the Spanish-speaking world that continues to this day. Nevertheless, Isaacs virtually stands alone as a nineteenth-century Jewish writer. Moreover, his own Jewish identity as well as the content of his work is rarely noted (see Doris Sommer's essay on Issacs in this volume and her "*María*'s Disease").

The figure of the Jew as literary device and romantic metaphor (Jew-as-object) in nineteenth- and early twentieth-century Latin American literature precedes the appearance of the genuine Jewish subject in literary texts. Some of the most obvious examples include the novel *La hija del judío* (1849) by Mexican author Justo Sierra O'Reilly (1848-1912) in which the Jewishness of the protagonist serves as a symbolic voice to promote anticlericalism. Latin American Modernism found the figure of the Jew useful for promulgating the ideals of societal advancement and progressive modernization that characterized the movement. Rubén Darío (1867-1916) and Leopoldo Lugones (1874-1938) both incorporated highly idyllic images of Jews as synedoches to demonstrate the benefits of programmatic immigration to Argentina (Senkman "La representación del judío").

Other important literary characterizations of Jews by non-Jewish writers sought quite a different goal. In Argentina, several blatantly anti-Semitic novels portrayed the Jew as a dangerous invader by utilizing popular negative stereotypes, informed in large part by the bogus *Protocols of the Elders of Zion*. Such texts as *La bolsa* (The Stockmarket; 1891) by Julián Martel (pseudonym of José María Miró [1867-96]) and the two-part *Kahal* and *Oro* (1935) by Hugo Wast (pseudonym of Gustavo Adolfo Martínez Zuviría [1883-1954]), director of the National Library, were widely circulated and read. They were primarily based on myths about Jewish schemes to take over the banks, control the stock market, and ultimately gain complete economic control of the country. Jewish conspiracy myths have survived and have informed the ideology of the extreme right in Argentina to the present day (Rock; Senkman *El antisemitismo*). The Jewish poet and dramatist César Tiempo (pseudonym of Israel Zeitlin [1906-80]) wrote a scathing response to Wast's caustic literature published as *La campaña antisemita y el director de la Biblioteca Nacional* (The Anti-Semitic Campaign and the Director of the National Library; 1935). In *El mal metafísico* (The Metaphysical Malaise; 1922) Manuel Gálvez (1889-1950), one of the major figures of the Argentine canon, propagates anti-Semitic stereotypes through the negative portrayal of Jews as poor, dirty, physically unappealing, conniving, morally corrupt, and as usurers.

Throughout Latin America non-Jewish writers have approached Jewish subjects with varying results. Mexican authors Carlos Fuentes and Homero Aridjis (1931) recall the expulsion of the Jews from Spain and the precarious existence of the *conversos* in the New World, Fuentes in *Terra nostra* (1975) and Aridjis in his two-volume historical narrative comprised of *1492: vida y tiempos de Juan Cabezón de Castilla* (*1492: The Life and Times of Juan Cabezón de Castilla*; 1985) and *Memorias del Nuevo Mundo* (Memories of the New World; 1988). Critic Seymour Menton found Aridjis's *1492* so authentically "Jewish" as to include it in his analysis of the Jewish Latin American historical novel. *Morirás lejos* (*A Distant Death*; 1967) by Mexican writer José Emilio Pacheco (1939) and *Vastas emoções e pensamentos imperfeitos* (Vast Emotions and Imperfect Thoughts; 1988) by Brazilian Rubem Fonseca (1925), are both texts by non-Jewish authors that approach the topic of the Holocaust. Likewise, author Carlos Heitor Cony (1926) of Brazil creates a Jewish protagonist and a Jewishly motivated plot in his 1967 novel *Pessach: a travessia* (Pessach: The Crossing) in which the main character undergoes a type of awakening regarding his Jewish identity. The novel speaks quite effectively to the issue of assimilation and it parallels the marginal condition of Jewishness with political opposition during a time of military dictatorship in Brazil, both of which run counter to official conceptions of the national character.

Finally, as a non-Jewish author, Jorge Luis Borges must be considered as unique among the previously mentioned writers. It is not difficult to sustain the notion of Borges as one of the most Jewish of Latin American authors. His intense interest in and study of Judaica led him to write a significant portion of his literature which is not only thematically, but more significantly is structurally or stylistically Jewish. His emphasis on Kabbalistic thinking, Jewish mysticism and mythology, as well as his focus on the power of the written word, hidden meanings, and textual labyrinths single him out as a Jewish writer par excellence. Various critics have cogently investigated these elements in Borges's works toward a delineation of the writer's uniquely Jewish perspective (Alazraki; Aizenberg; Sosnowski *Borges y la Cábala*; Solotorevsky).

The foregoing observations regarding non-Jewish writers who write "Jewish" texts lead to an important critical question. What is it that renders a text "Jewish?" Certainly, it is not the mere fact that an author can be identified as a Jew. Such reductionist labelling serves little purpose and indeed is counterproductive. It places restrictions on writers whose works as a whole surpass or are not limited to an identifiable connection with Judaic tradition. Furthermore, it seemingly establishes the precedence of Jewish over Latin American identity and transforms the hyphen that joins the two together into an instrument of separation. Some authors do not adhere to a Jewish identity, either ethnically or religiously. Many Latin American Jewish intellectuals have embraced Marxism in lieu of Judaism as a means of mediating cultural identity. This is not an uncommon practice, as Mark Shechner explains with regard to American Jewish writers: "It is not mistaken to regard Marxism, at a certain moment of its penetration into Jewish existence, as a substitute Judaism, endowed with all the powers once possessed by halakhic or Orthodox Judaism for interpreting the world, dictating principles, forming character, and regulating conduct" (8). Uruguayan author and social critic Egon Friedler recently questioned the ideological foundation of this practice among Latin American Jewish intellectuals, particularly as it relates to Jewish identity.

The interpretation of identity is a highly personal one that occurs on an individual level. Therefore, it is for each author to decide what being Jewish means for him or her and how it will be enacted in the process of daily living. Others choose not to incorporate Jewishly defined elements, at least overtly, into their works. Indeed, so-called Jewish texts often form only a minimal part of a given writer's entire *oeuvre*, which more often deals with the complexities of

Latin American reality. Moreover, the Jewish perspective is never separate from the larger social environment, but instead provides for the possibility of a dialogic discourse of alterity. Jewishness, then, is not necessarily a self-evident component of a text. Nevertheless, returning to the question of the author, there is a significant distinction to be made. Non-Jewish authors write *about* the periphery, while Jewish authors are relegated to the position of writing *from* the periphery. So, while Borges or any other may be able to write *like* a Jew in terms of style or theme, they cannot write *as* a Jew. Latin American Jewish authors, on the other hand, write both as Jews and as Latin Americans as they draw on two cultural and historical sources for their writing, each an integral part of their identity.

In spite of the problematics surrounding the characterization of Jewish writing as a subcategory of Latin American literature, one cannot overlook the fact that as a corpus of works, texts written by Jewish authors work in conjunction to forge a Latin American Jewish discourse. As authors bring to the page, and thereby to the scrutiny of the reading public, topics of Jewish concern within a Latin American context, they provide a unique lens through which to view their individual societies. The forces that shape these authors' texts may include, in part, issues pertaining to Jewish identity such as immigration, assimilation, acculturation, religious and ethnic identity, language, Zionism, anti-Semitism, and Judaic tradition, as well as Latin American sociopolitical realities like authoritarianism, economic underdevelopment, and nonpluralistic societies. Each of these topics may be approached from and motivated by different viewpoints and/or opposing ideological stances, but together they constitute the artistic expression of a shared Jewish collective social reality as experienced throughout Latin America. However, one must be careful not to conceive of Latin America as a single geographical space in which the Jewish experience unfolds, even within the boundaries of a single country. The cosmopolitan environment of a city like Buenos Aires informs the Jewish writer's worldview in a way that is substantially different from one who wrote as an immigrant farmer in the interior of the country. Likewise, it is just as dissimilar to the writer in Mexico City, Caracas, or São Paulo, where differences derive from distinct historical, linguistic, and cultural circumstances.

As a vehicle for a culturally specific discourse, though not necessarily a homogeneous one, Latin American Jewish writing constitutes a socioliterary phenomenon that exercises and contributes to the creation of cultural identity. Also, as a social text marked by its decentered marginal status as a minority discourse, Jewish writing serves an important function as a countervoice to official discourse. Latin American Jewish writing, like other minority literatures, endures as a contestatory response to the hegemonic telling of social history. Jewish writers offer a reversion of events and challenge the facticity and authority of the established canon as the authentic voice of Latin America. This does not imply that they seek to demarcate a new set of truths, but rather to question the process by which accepted truths have been established as such.

Contemporary critical theories associated with postmodernism and postcolonialism readily lend themselves to the analysis of Latin American Jewish literature. It may at first seem contradictory to think of this writing in postmodernist terms inasmuch as this seems to indicate a break with tradition, the negation of the master narrative, and the denial of historical authority, all of which results in the apparent dissolution of textual coherence. Nevertheless, there are convincing arguments for viewing Jewish literature as abiding, at least in part, to the posturing of postmodern textual practices.

Norman Finkelstein has aptly described the influence of postmodernism on several major American and European Jewish intellectuals, and his discussion is equally germane to the situation of contemporary Latin Americans. He begins his assessment by stating that postmodernism has failed to attract what he terms "self-conscious" Jewish writers and intellectuals—those who ascribe to a Jewish identity—because they tend to adhere to history and cultural metanarratives of Jewish tradition. However, this fact, he goes on to state, does not prevent Jewish intellectuals from being affected by the postmodern world in which they live and operate. He utilizes Jacques Derrida's concept of *différance* to point out that this fundamental component of postmodernist ideology "speaks directly to Jewish intellectuals' self-conception, their understanding of their obviously vexed Jewish identity and the role they play in the greater drama of culture at large" (15-16). Similarly, in *A Poetics of Postmodernism* Linda Hutcheon theorizes postmodern narrative as what she calls "historiographic metafiction," defined as texts that are "both intensely self-reflexive and yet paradoxically also lay claim to historical events and personages" (5). She cogently explicates how postmodern thought has led to a valuing of the margins as a result of the disintegration of the center (see especially chapter 4, 57-73). What these critics have in common and what they share with others is their reliance on Derrida's *différance* as the basis for an advantageous marginal position from which to speak. This concept has most recently been applied specifically to the context of Latin American Jewish writing by Nelson H. Vieira, who relies heavily upon *différance* as the guiding ideologeme in establishing the theoretical framework of his analysis of Brazilian Jewish literature. He relates Derrida's suitability to his study in the following way.

> Derrida's ideas and expositions are especially relevant to my
> discussion because he demonstrates how Judaic hermeneutics
> reflect his own stress upon the importance of textuality and
> writing and how différance relates to philosophy and literature
> as well as to power, knowledge, and politics. (41)

The privileging of the margins has produced an inversion of the hegemony maintained by colonial Luso- and/or Hispano-centric totalizing discourse.
Contemporary Latin American Jewish discourse, then, is fashioned out of the
postmodern conception of identity formation based on difference as opposed to
conformity. The clarifying term "contemporary" must be used here since early
manifestations of Jewish writing operated on the hope of inclusion, before the
realization that exclusionary practices would systematically relegate it to a marginal status. Finkelstein, though referring to the subjects of his study, makes an
important observation that can equally be applied to Latin American writers.

> Through the assertion of difference, Jewish intellectuals reveal
> their historical—or better, counterhistorical—aspect. Secular,
> largely assimilated, they speak of culture and to culture, know-
> ing all the while that culture itself can be understood as a play
> of differences. Yet they do not dissolve completely into this
> play of differences [...] They cleave to the narratives of cul-
> ture, including that of Judaism itself—a narrative of difference
> from which they are free to speak. (17)

This assessment also signals the role, or one could even say the responsibility, of Jewish authors as creators of culture and keepers of collective memory. Yosef Hayim Yerushalmi also seems to ascribe to these notions when he
declares "it would appear that even where Jews do not reject history out of hand,
they are not prepared to confront it directly, but seem to await a new, metahistorical myth, for which the novel provides at least a temporary modern surrogate"
(98). This in turn reverts back to Hutcheon's conceptualization of historiographic
metafiction as a means of "rethinking and reworking the forms and contents of
the past" (5). In this way many Latin American Jewish authors not only break
with conventional modes of literary creation, but they also undertake a process
of de/scribing the nature of contemporary Latin American and/or Jewish identity.
Jewish writing reveals itself as postcolonial discourse in the way in which aspects
of the texts that characterize them as marginal increasingly become superimposed on the values and traits of the center. For example, this is most readily

apparent in works that incorporate multiple linguistic encodements and culturally specific referents that function doubly as the signifier and the signified within a given context. One of the more common narrative strategies employed by authors is to create polyphonic texts by including words, phrases, and expressions in Jewish languages like Yiddish, Hebrew, and Ladino, as well as national languages that signal origin such as Russian, Polish, or Arabic. By doing so, the author resists homogenization by the dominant culture symbolized by the monolingually-restricted canon and the consequent loss of an alter/native identity.

This leads to the characterization of much of Latin American Jewish literature as being essentially dialogic in nature. Mikhail Bakhtin's concept of the dialogic imagination neatly applies to the vast majority of Jewish-authored texts in Latin American literature. The interaction of different narrative voices, languages, points of view, and the semiotic connotations embedded in utterances, all contribute to the heteroglossia of a given text (Bakhtin *The Dialogic Imagination*). At the core of Bakhtin's theory is the notion that language is the primary motivator of and vehicle for the transmission of ideology, or what Fredric Jameson would call the "political unconscious" of a text. The protagonist of the Latin American Jewish novel often functions as the mediator of multiple voices who may or may not aid the reader in sorting out the myriad layers of meaning that constitute the heteroglossic strata of the text. This textual dialogue between center and margin is one of the defining features of Latin American Jewish literature.

While sociohistorical circumstances specific to individual countries have influenced Jewish writing within national boundaries, as a whole Jewish literature has evolved through a series of basically common stages throughout Latin America over the course of the twentieth century. Any discussion of the development of this literature into an identifiable socioliterary phenomenon as it is today must begin in Argentina with Alberto Gerchunoff (1884-1950). Argentina, as home to the world's fifth-largest Jewish population, consequently produces the overwhelming majority of Jewish literature in Latin America. Two recent bibliographic publications illustrate the enormity of the Argentine Jewish literary community: David William Foster's and Naomi Lindstrom's primary bibliography of works by over three hundred writers "Jewish Argentine Authors: A Registry," and the two-volume biobibliographical source book *Escritores judeo-argentinos: bibliografía 1900-1987* (Jewish-Argentine Writers: A Bibliography 1900-1987; 1994), compiled by Ana E. Weinstein and Miryam E. Gover de Nasatsky, which lists over two hundred authors.

Gerchunoff is generally perceived to be the forefather of Jewish literary tradition in Argentina, and by extension in the whole of Latin America. His 1910

Los gauchos judíos (*The Jewish Gauchos of the Pampas*), which can be read either as a novel or as a collection of interrelated short stories, is widely considered to be the urtext of Latin American Jewish literature. It was written on commission from Leopoldo Lugones, who encouraged Gerchunoff to provide a specifically Jewish work as part of the cultural festivities in celebration of the Argentine Centennial. Gerchunoff was driven by a strong desire to assimilate into Argentine society and he viewed the nation as a literal Promised Land in which the Jew could find earthly and spiritual redemption from the hardships of Eastern Europe and Russia. He was the first, and one of the few, Jewish writers to gain acceptance into mainstream Argentine literature, and by extension society. His writing—first and foremost *Los gauchos judíos*—has become normalized into the Argentine literary canon to such a point that he no longer represents a problem, as a Jewish writer, within a predominantly Hispano-Catholic literary tradition. This is the case largely because of his engagement in a life-long program of identity formation by which he consciously and energetically sought to forge a nonthreatening identity as an Argentine of Jewish descent. A central part of such a process of self-identification was Gerchunoff's insistence on language—in this case Spanish—as the vehicle by which he constructed his personal and his cultural identity. Although *Los gauchos judíos* endures as his most familiar work, and it is still the most-read work by a Jewish author in Argentina, he wrote over twenty other books.

Contemporary critics such as David Viñas, Saúl Sosnowski, and Gladys Onega have found ample reason to criticize *Los gauchos judíos* for its idyllic, glossed-over representation of the early immigrant experience at the turn of the century. In sum, they reproach the author's motivation for writing a work that would gain him favor with the established conservative literary and political power centers of the country. Naomi Lindstrom approaches the text from a different optic, insightfully analyzing the influence of Eastern European Jewish thought in the author's narrative. Leonardo Senkman and Beatriz Stambler are the two critics who have most thoroughly analyzed Gerchunoff's contribution to Argentine literature. Senkman apportions a significant part of his book *La identidad judía en la literatura argentina* (1983) to the examination of Gerchunoff's works. He focuses primarily on Gerchunoff's effort to legitimize the Jewish presence in Argentina by recalling the Sephardic past of the Iberian peninsula in literature, language, and culture in the hope of establishing a Hispano-Jewish commonality. Stambler's *Vida y obra de Alberto Gerchunoff* (1985) is the most complete study to date on Gerchunoff's literary corpus as a whole. These different critical approaches and interpretations provide an idea as to the multiplicity of meanings found in the text and also of the sociopolitical motivations underlying it.

Gerchunoff's influence as an author and journalist has impacted subsequent generations of writers in Argentina, both Jewish and non-Jewish alike. The first generation of Jewish writers to succeed Gerchunoff included Samuel Eichelbaum (1894-1967), Enrique Espinosa (pseud. of Samuel Glusberg; 1897-1987), Carlos Grünberg (1903-68), Lázaro Liacho (1897-1969), and César Tiempo, all of whom reached a level of relatively lasting fame owed, at least in part, to the door opened to them by the efforts of Gerchunoff. Several authors of this generation, namely Grünberg and Espinosa, continued to seek official acceptance into Argentine society by insisting on the building of the Hispano-Sephardic cultural bridge. Curiously, all of these authors were of Ashkenazic origin with no real ties to Sephardic tradition or culture.

Contemporary heirs of Gerchunoff often portray the Jewish experience in Argentina with a perspective 180 degrees from that of *Los gauchos judíos*. Mario Szichman most readily comes to mind as an author who represents the anti-Gerchunoff figure, with all the parricidal implications the term connotes. His saga of the Pechof family—(*La crónica falsa* [The False Chronicle; 1969], revised in 1972 as *La verdadera crónica falsa* [The True False Chronicle]; *Los judíos del Mar Dulce* [The Jews of the Fresh-Water Sea; 1971]; *A las 20:25 la señora entró en la inmortalidad* [*At 8:25 Evita Became Immortal*; 1981])—depicts a very different reality for the Jews of Argentina. In spite of his (in)version of Gerchunoff's original model, however, *Los gauchos judíos* is incontrovertibly the master narrative that informs Szichman's trilogy.

Generally speaking, Latin American Jewish literature can be grouped into three generational periods. The first represents the generation in which authors focus thematically on the experience of immigration. Feelings of alienation in a new country, nostalgia for the old country, the desire to gain acceptance while maintaining Jewish cultural identity, the depiction of economic hardship and the strife of establishing roots in a foreign land are all common themes to this generation of writers. The second phase is carried out primarily by the children of immigrants who, as first-generation Latin Americans, feel a closer bond to the dominant culture than to the traditions, languages, and religious identity of their parents. Literature of this generation is characterized by interfamilial conflict brought on by issues of rapid assimilation, intermarriage, loss or shunning (depending on the perspective) of traditional values in favor of blending into the dominant society. Second-generation authors also tend to openly confront matters that directly affect them as Jews such as anti-Semitism, and as citizens and full participants in national politics. With the realization that as

Jews they are granted at best second-class citizenship within Luso- and Hispano-Catholic societies, these writers no longer are concerned with not offending those in power. Instead, they boldly assert their alterity and they challenge hegemonic versions of Latin American cultural identity. Third- and fourth-generation writers, almost exclusively secular and completely assimilated, often seek a return to and recovery of Jewish identity by salvaging the remnants of their ethnoreligious heritage through literature. Many write texts based on family genealogy and history in an attempt to preserve and/or restore cultural memory. The narrative of nostalgic remembrance is common, often told through the voice of a child narrator. The literary text becomes an exercise of self-identification as authors attempt to blend their Jewish past with their Latin American present in such a way as to fuse the two elements into a single identity.

The number of works that attempt to give expression to the devastation of the Holocaust is quite limited relative to the enormous quantity of texts that comprise the Latin American Jewish literary corpus. Most provide fictional accounts of how Jewish communities dealt with the effects of the Holocaust and its aftermath specific to the context of Latin American societies. Texts range from the allegorical to fictionalized accounts of survival and endurance. The majority of authors that deal with the topic include it as but one element of a given text rather than as the central theme. Argentines Bernardo Verbitsky (1907-79), Bernardo Kordon (1915), and especially Simja Sneh (1914), a Holocaust survivor, stand out as authors who have given expression to this greatest of Jewish tragedies. Sneh, incidentally, also survived the terrorist bombing of the AMIA (Asociación Mutual Israelita Argentina [Argentine Jewish Mutual Association]) building in July of 1994 in which nearly one hundred people fell victim to a virulent act of anti-Semitism. In Brazil, both Zevi Ghivelder (1934) and Eliezer Levin (date unknown) have written novels with significant content relating to the Holocaust.

The Latin American Jewish historical novel is a prevalent form of narrative among contemporary writers. Such works tend to be rather lengthy narrations in which authors combine fiction with historical fact, and often with a good deal of fantasy. Common to this type of text is the reaffirmation of the Jewish presence as part of the ethnic and cultural heritage of Latin America by creating narratives that conform to what Hutcheon designated as historiographic metafiction and what Yerushalmi termed the novelistic metahistorical myth. As counterversions of official discourse these novels represent a direct challenge to the center in their brazen attempt to rewrite the historico-cultural memory of Latin America. They harken back to Sepharad, the Expulsion of the Jews from Spain, and the colonial era in Latin America. Likewise, they are populated by heroic protagonists who overcome persecution, survive in exile, and maintain the integrity of their Jewish identity. Notwithstanding their focus on the past, many times these novels speak directly to the present. The themes of the Inquisition, persecution, and exile parallel the reality of contemporary Latin Americans living under fascist military regimes. Some of the most exemplary of these texts include *Aventuras de Edmund Ziller en tierras del Nuevo Mundo* (Adventures of Edmund Ziller in the Lands of the New World; 1977) by Pedro Orgambide (1929), *Identidad* (Identity; 1980) by Antonio Elio Brailovsky (1946), *La gesta del marrano* (The Epic Song of the Jew; 1991) by Marcos Aguinis (1935) in Argentina; *A estranha nação de Rafael Mendes* (*The Strange Nation of Rafael Mendes*; 1983) by Moacyr Scliar (1937) in Brazil; *Tierra adentro* (Homeward Bound; 1977) by Angelina Muñiz-Huberman (1936) in Mexico; and *Colombina descubierta* (Discovered Colombine; 1991) by Alicia Freilich Segal (1939) in Venezuela.

Israel and Zionism, as a political movement and ideology of the national resurrection of the Jewish people, have had a wide-reaching and lasting effect on Latin American Jews. Zionism was embraced by many as a way to express a nonreligious Jewish identity, and in fact became the religion of the majority of Latin American Jews. It allowed them to demythify their Jewishness in religious terms and align themselves politically as Jews to the new Jewish homeland. This, of course, stimulated a great deal of mistrust against Jews as questions of dual loyalty were raised. Israel and Zionism as literary motifs figure most prominently in the literature of Argentina and Brazil, and to a lesser extent in Mexico. Poetry proved to be the preferred genre for singing praises of Zion and celebrating the creation of the Jewish state, although the themes also appear in narrative and essay.

Theater, as a literary genre and mode of artistic and cultural expression, is able to reach a large number of people simultaneously and directly. Yiddish theater troupes thrived in Argentina during the first part of the twentieth century and enjoyed considerable success in Brazil and Mexico as well, due to the larger populations and the organization of the Jewish communities. Although the heyday of Yiddish drama faded, the tradition of the theater survived through a number of Jewish dramatists who have achieved national and international recognition for their works, and several have been major influences in defining and developing the nature of Latin American theater. They bring to the stage the reality of the Latin American Jewish experience and provide an important medium for the dissemination and continuance of cultural diversity. Samuel Eichelbaum, Osvaldo Dragún (1929), Ricardo Halac (1935), Germán Rozenmacher (1936-71), Jorge Goldenberg (1941) and Diana Raznovich (1943) in Argentina, Isaac Chocrón (1930) and Elisa Lerner (1932) in Venezuela, Samuel Rovinski

(1932) in Costa Rica, and Sabina Berman (1954) in Mexico have all been instrumental in shaping theatrical traditions and form in their respective countries. Women writers deserve a special mention for their extensive and highly innovative contributions to Latin American Jewish literature. They provide a unique perspective on both the Jewish and Latin American traditions. In Mexico, women writers constitute the overwhelming majority of Jewish authors and their literature ranks with that of the best in the country. Brazilian Clarice Lispector (1926-77) is easily the most well-known and widely read woman writer from Latin America. Although her works do not reflect any overt treatment of Jewish themes, several critics have recently approached her writing as revealing a Jewish sensibility in her style and creative process (Vieira; Wengrover; Schiminovich). Likewise is the case of the controversial Argentine poet Alejandra Pizarnik (1936-72) (Goldberg). Writers like Marjorie Agosín (1955) from Chile, Teresa Porzecanski (1945) from Uruguay, Alicia Steimberg (1933), Silvia Plager (1942), and Cecilia Absatz (1943) from Argentina, Sabina Berman, Margo Glantz (1930), Esther Seligson (1941), Angelina Muñiz-Huberman and Sara Levi Calderón (1942) from Mexico contribute to the making of a Jewish feminist discourse in Latin American literature as they write against patriarchal tradition while affirming a strong Jewish identity.

While the thematics of Jewishness continue to dominate Jewish writing in Latin America, there is an increasing number of authors who are beginning to surpass theme to concentrate on Judaic substance. Put differently, in some instances their writing represents an evolutionary change described by Irving Howe as a "transition from Jewishness as experience to Jewishness as essence" (70); that is, texts that contain Jewish metaphysical content, Kabbalism, a reliance on Hebraic hermeneutics, an emphasis on textual interpretation, Midrashic commentary, Talmudic exegesis, and the power of the written letter and word. This does not mean that writers replicate these styles of writing, but that their literature draws on and is informed by these traditionally Jewish modes of scriptural production and thought. This type of writing, represented by authors like Mario Satz (1944), and Marcos Ricardo Barnatán (1946) adds a new dimension to Latin American Jewish literature.

While Jewish authors have made significant contributions to Latin American literature, they continue to remain on the margins of what is considered to be the canon. Most are not widely read, even within their own countries. The few who have gained international recognition—Clarice Lispector, Moacyr Scliar, Humberto Costantini (1924-87), Isaac Goldemberg (1945) to name a few—represent but a small fraction of the hundreds of authors who have joined voices to produce the socioliterary manifestation of Latin American Jewish identity. When one peruses the many dictionaries, encyclopedias, histories, anthologies, and bibliographies of Latin American literature, one of the most striking features common to them all is the resounding echo of absence created by the underrepresentation of Jewish authors. Their voices speak to us from the margins and challenge us to read Latin America from their alter/native perspective.

Works Cited

Aizenberg, Edna. *The Aleph Weaver: Biblical, Kabbalistic, and Judaic Elements in Borges*. Potomac, MD: Scripta Humanistica, 1984.

Alazraki, Jaime. *Borges and the Kabbalah and Other Essays on His Fiction and Poetry*. Cambridge: Cambridge UP, 1988.

Aridjis, Homero. *Memorias del Nuevo Mundo*. México, D.F.: Diana, 1988.

—. *1492: vida y tiempos de Juan Cabezón de Castilla*. México, D.F.: Siglo XXI, 1985.

Bakhtin, Mikhail. *The Dialogic Imagination*. Trans. by Caryl Emerson and Michael Holquist. Austin: U of Texas P, 1990.

Carvajal, Luis de. *The Enlightened: The Writings of Luis de Carvajal, el Mozo*. Trans., ed., intro., and epilogue by Seymour Liebman. Preface by Allan Nevins. Coral Gables: U of Miami P, 1967.

—. *Procesos de Luis de Carvajal (el Mozo)*. México: Talleres Gráficos de la Nación, 1935.

Cony, Carlos Heitor. *Pessach: A Travessia*. Rio de Janeiro: Civilização Brasileira, 1975.

Finkelstein, Norman. *The Ritual of New Creation: Jewish Tradition and Contemporary Literature*. Albany: SUNY Press, 1992.

Fonseca, Rubem. *Vastas emoções e pensamentos imperfeitos*. São Paulo: Schwartz, 1988.

Foster, David William, and Naomi Lindstrom. "Jewish Argentine Authors: A Registry," parts 1 and 2, *Revista interamericana de bibliografía/Inter-American Review of Bibliography* 41.3 (1991): 478-503; 41.4 (1991): 655-82.

Friedler, Egon. "Jewish Latin Intellectuals and the Leftist Seduction." *Midstream* 40.1 (1994): 15-16.

Fuentes, Carlos. *Terra nostra*. Barcelona: Seix Barral, 1975.

Gálvez, Manuel. *El mal metafísico*. Buenos Aires: Espasa-Calpe Argentina, 1962.

Gerchunoff, Alberto. *Los gauchos judíos*. La Plata, Argentina. J. Sesé, 1910.

Goldberg, Florinda F. *Alejandra Pizarnik: "Este espacio que somos."* Gaithersburg, MD: Hispamérica, 1994.

Howe, Irving. "Response to Ted Solotaroff: The End of Marginality in Jewish Literature." In *The Writer in the Jewish Community: An Israeli-North American Dialogue.* Ed. Richard Siegel and Tamar Sofer. Cranbury, NJ: Associated University Presses, 1993. 67-71.

Jameson, Fredric. *The Political Unconscious: Narrative as a Socially Symbolic Act.* Ithaca: Cornell UP, 1982.

Martel, Julián. *La bolsa.* Buenos Aires: Plus Ultra, 1975.

Menton, Seymour. "Over Two Thousand Years of Exile and Marginality: The Jewish Latin American Historical Novel." In his *Latin America's New Historical Novel.* Austin: U of Texas P, 1993. 138-62.

Onega, Gladys. *La inmigración en la literatura argentina, 1880-1910.* Buenos Aires: Galerna, 1969.

Pacheco, José Emilio. *Morirás lejos.* México, D.F.: Joaquin Mortiz, 1967.

Rock, David. "Antecedents of the Argentine Right." In *The Argentine Right: Its History and Intellectual Origins, 1910 to the Present.* Ed. Sandra McGee Deutsch and Ronald H. Dolkart. Wilmington, Delaware: Scholarly Resources, 1993. 1-34.

Schiminovich, Flora. "Lispector's Rethinking of Biblical and Mystical Discourse." In *Tradition and Innovation: Reflections on Latin American Jewish Writing.* Ed. Robert DiAntonio and Nora Glickman. Albany: SUNY Press, 1993. 147-55.

Senkman, Leonardo. *La identidad judía en la literatura argentina.* Buenos Aires: Pardés, 1983.

—. "La representación del judío en el discurso literario latinoamericano." In *El imaginario judío en la literatura de América Latina: visión y realidad.* Ed. Patricia Finzi, Eliahu Toker, and Marcos Faerman. Buenos Aires: Shalom, 1992. 76-83.

Senkman, Leonardo, comp. *El antisemitismo en la Argentina.* 2nd ed. Buenos Aires: Centro Editor de América Latina, 1989.

Shechner, Mark. *After the Revolution: Studies in the Contemporary Jewish American Imagination.* Bloomington: Indiana UP, 1987.

Solotorevsky, Myrna. "The Model of Midrash and Borges's Interpretative Tales and Essays." In *Midrash and Literature.* Ed. Geoffrey H. Hartman and Sanford Budick. New Haven and London: Yale UP, 1986. 253-64.

Sommer, Doris. "*María*'s Disease: A National Novel (Con)founded." In her *Foundational Fictions: The National Romances of Latin America*. Berkeley/Los Angeles: U of California P, 1991. 172-203.

Sosnoswki, Saúl. *Borges y la Cábala: la búsqueda del verbo*. Buenos Aires: Pardés, 1986.

—. "Latin American-Jewish Writers: Protecting the Hyphen." In *The Jewish Presence in Latin America*. Ed. Judith Laiken Elkin and Gilbert W. Merkx. Boston: Allen & Unwin, 1987. 297-323.

Stambler, Beatriz Marquis. *Vida y obra de Alberto Gerchunoff*. Madrid: Albar, 1985.

Szichman, Mario. *A las 20:25 la señora entró en la inmortalidad*. Hanover, NH: Ediciones del Norte, 1981.

—. *La crónica falsa*. Buenos Aires: Jorge Alvarez, 1969.

—. *Los judíos del Mar Dulce*. Buenos Aires/Caracas: Galerna/Síntesis 2000, 1971.

—. *La verdadera crónica falsa*. Buenos Aires: Centro Editor de América Latina, 1972.

Tiempo, César. *La campaña antisemita y el director de la Biblioteca Nacional*. Buenos Aires: Mundo Israelita, 1935.

Vieira, Nelson H. *Jewish Voices in Brazilian Literature: A Prophetic Discourse of Alterity*. Gainesville: UP of Florida, 1995.

Viñas, David. *Literatura argentina y realidad política: apogeo de la oligarquía*. Buenos Aires: Siglo Veinte, 1975.

Wast, Hugo. *Kahal*. Buenos Aires: Editores de Hugo Wast, 1935.

—. *Oro*. Buenos Aires: Editores de Hugo Wast, 1935.

Weinstein, Ana E., and Miryam Gover de Nasatsky, comps. *Escritores judeo-argentinos: bibliografía 1900-1987*. 2 vols. Buenos Aires: Milá, 1994.

Wengrover, Esther. "La ética cabalística de Clarice Lispector." In *El imaginario judío en la literatura de América Latina: visión y realidad*. Ed. Patricia Finzi, Eliahu Toker and Marcos Faerman. Buenos Aires: Shalom, 1992. 143-47.

Wirth-Nesher, Hana, ed. *What Is Jewish Literature?* Philadelphia/Jerusalem: The Jewish Publication Society, 1994.

SELECTED BIBLIOGRAPHY

LITERARY ANTHOLOGIES

Cien años de narrativa judeoargentina 1889-1989. Buenos Aires: Milá, 1990.

Crónicas judeoargentinas/1: los pioneros en ídish 1890-1944. Buenos Aires: Milá, 1987.

Kalechofsky, Robert, and Roberta Kalechofsky, eds. *Echad: An Anthology of Latin American Jewish Writings.* Marblehead, MA: Micah Publications, 1980.

Feierstein, Ricardo, comp. *Cuentos judíos latinoamericanos.* Buenos Aires: Milá, 1989.

Gardiol, Rita, ed. and trans. *The Silver Candelabra and Other Stories: A Century of Jewish-Argentine Literature.* Pittsburgh: Latin American Literary Review Press, 1997.

Glickman, Nora, and Gloria F. Waldman, eds. and trans. *Argentine Jewish Theatre: A Critical Anthology.* Lewisburg: Bucknell UP, 1996.

Stavans, Ilán, ed. *Tropical Synagogues: Short Stories by Jewish-Latin American Writers.* New York: Holmes & Meier, 1994.

Yiddish 8.3-4 (1992), special issue, *Argentine Jewish Writing: Translations.* Joseph C. Landis and Nora Glickman, eds.

CRITICISM
Books/Periodical Sources

AMIA (Asociación Mutual Israelita Argentina)/Comunidad Judía de Buenos Aires. *Pluralismo e identidad: lo judío en la literatura latinoamericana.* Buenos Aires: Milá, 1986.

Barr, Lois Baer. *Isaac Unbound: Patriarchal Tradition in the Latin American Jewish Novel.* Tempe, AZ: Center for Latin American Studies, Arizona State University, 1995.

DiAntonio, Robert, and Nora Glickman, eds. *Tradition and Innovation: Reflections on Latin American Jewish Writing.* Albany: SUNY Press, 1993.

Finzi, Patricia, Eliahu Toker, and Marcos Faerman, eds. *El imaginario judío en la literatura de América Latina: visión y realidad.* Buenos Aires: Shalom, 1992.

Folio 17 (1987), special issue, *Latin American Jewish Writers.* Judith Morganroth Schneider, guest ed.

Igel, Regina. *Imigrantes judeus / escritores brasileiros (o componente judaico na literatura brasileira).* Forthcoming, 1997.

Lindstrom, Naomi. *Jewish Issues in Argentine Literature: From Gerchunoff to Szichman*. Columbia: U of Missouri P, 1989.

Noaj (formerly *Noah* [Jerusalem]). 1987-. Journal of the Asociación Internacional de Escritores Judíos en Lengua Hispana y Portuguesa.

Senkman, Leonardo. *La identidad judía en la literatura argentina*. Buenos Aires: Pardés, 1983.

Sosnowski, Saúl. *La orilla inminente: escritores judíos argentinos*. Buenos Aires: Legasa, 1987.

Vieira, Nelson H. *Jewish Voices in Brazilian Literature: A Prophetic Discourse of Alterity*. Gainesville: UP of Florida, 1995.

Yiddish 9.1 (1993), special issue, *Argentine-Jewish Writing: Critical Essays*. Nora Glickman, ed.

Articles

Aínsa, Fernando. "La tierra prometida como motivo en la narrativa argentina." *Hispamérica* 18.53-54 (1989): 3-23.

Aizenberg, Edna. "Las peripecias de una metáfora: el sefaradismo literario judeo-argentino." *Noaj* 7-8 (1992): 54-59.

—. "Latin American Jewish Writing." *Contemporary Judaism* 28 (Spring 1974): 66-72.

—. "Sephardim and Neo-Sephardim in Latin American Literature." *Sephardic Scholar Series* 4 (1979-1982): 125-32.

DiAntonio, Robert. "Aspects of Contemporary Judeo-Brazilian Writing." In his *Brazilian Fiction: Aspects and Evolution of Contemporary Narrative*. Fayetteville/London: U of Arkansas P, 1989. 113-18.

—. "Redemption and Rebirth on a Safe Shore: The Holocaust in Contemporary Brazilian Fiction." *Hispania* 74.4 (1991): 876-80.

—. "Resonances of the Yiddishkeit Tradition in the Contemporary Brazilian Narrative." In *Tradition and Innovation: Reflections on Latin American Jewish Writing*. Ed. Robert DiAntonio and Nora Glickman. Albany: SUNY Press, 1993. 45-60.

Foster, David William. "Argentine Jewish Dramatists: Aspects of a National Consciousness." *Folio* 17 (1987): 74-103. Also in his *Cultural Diversity in Latin American Literature*. Albuquerque: U of New Mexico P, 1994. 95-150.

Friedman, Edward H. "Theory in the Margin: Latin American Literature and the Jewish Subject." In *The Jewish Diaspora in Latin America: New Studies on History and Literature*. Ed. David Sheinin and Lois Baer Barr. New York: Garland, 1996. 21-31.

Gardiol, Rita. "Argentina's Jewish Poets." *Yiddish* 9.1 (1993): 44-71.

—. *Argentina's Jewish Short Story Writers.* Muncie, IN: Ball State University, 1986.

—. "Jewish Writers: An Emerging Force in Contemporary Argentine Literature." *Hispanófila* 91 (1987): 65-76.

Glickman, Nora. "The Jewish White Slave Trade in Latin American Writings." *American Jewish Archives* 34.2 (1982): 178-89.

—. "Jewish Women Writers in Latin America." In *Women of the Word: Jewish Women and Jewish Writing.* Ed. Judith R. Baskin. Detroit: Wayne State UP, 1994. 299-322.

Horn, José. "Los nuevos escritores judíos de la Argentina." *Judaica* (Buenos Aires) 70 (1939): 123-29.

Igel, Regina. "La inmigración judía en la ficción de Brasil." *Judaica latinoamericana: estudios histórico-sociales II.* Asociación Israelí de Investigadores del Judaísmo Latinoamericano. Jerusalem: Editorial Universitaria Magnes, Universidad Hebrea, 1993. 265-74.

—. "O tema do Holocausto na literatura brasileira." *Noaj* 6 (1991): 55-65.

Kleiner, Alberto, comp. *La temática judía en el teatro argentino.* Buenos Aires: Polígono, 1983.

Krauze, Ethel. "Los escritores mexicanos judíos." *Noaj* 3.3-4 (1989): 96-100.

Lindstrom, Naomi. "Oral Histories and the Literature of Reminiscence: Writing Up the Jewish Argentine Past." In *The Jewish Diaspora in Latin America: New Studies on History and Literature.* Ed. David Sheinin and Lois Baer Barr. New York: Garland, 1996. 89-100.

—. "Problems and Possibilities in the Analysis of Jewish Argentine Literary Works." *Latin American Research Review* 18.1 (1983): 118-26.

Lipp, Solomon. "Israel and the Holocaust in Contemporary Spanish-American Poetry." *Hispania* 64 (1982): 536-43.

—. "Jewish Themes and Authors in Contemporary Argentine Fiction." In *El Cono Sur: dinámica y dimensiones de su literatura.* Ed. Rose S. Minc. Upper Montclair, NJ: Montclair State College, 1985. 49-55.

Menton, Seymour. "Over Two Thousand Years of Exile and Marginality: The Jewish Latin American Historical Novel." In his *Latin America's New Historical Novel.* Austin: U of Texas P, 1993. 138-62.

Muñiz-Huberman, Angelina. "De las tinieblas a la luz. La historia de la literatura judeomexicana." *La jornada semanal* (Mexico) 285 (27 Nov., 1994): 32-35.

Nesbit, Louis. "The Jewish Contribution to Argentine Literature." *Hispania* 33.4 (1950): 313-20.

Sadow, Stephen, A. "Judíos y gauchos: The Search for Identity in Argentine-Jewish Literature." *American Jewish Archives* 34.2 (1982): 164-77.

Schallman, Lázaro. "El judaísmo y los judíos a través de las letras argentinas." *Comentario* 48 (1966): 113-24.

—. "El tema judío en la poesía argentina." *Comentario* 11.38 (1964): 72-79.

Schwartz, Kessel. "Antisemitism in Modern Argentine Fiction." *Jewish Social Studies* 40.2 (1978): 131-40.

—. "The Jew in Twentieth-Century Argentine Fiction." *The American Hispanist* 3.19 (1977): 9-12.

Senkman, Leonardo. "De la legitimación del israelita argentino a la asunción de la identidad en algunos escritores judeoargentinos." In *El Cono Sur: dinámica y dimensiones de su literatura*. Ed. Rose S. Minc. Upper Montclair, NJ: Montclair State College, 1985. 56-71.

—. "Jewish Latin American Writers and Collective Memory." In *Tradition and Innovation: Reflections on Latin American Jewish Writing*. Ed. Robert DiAntonio and Nora Glickman. Albany: SUNY Press, 1993. 33-43.

Sosnowski, Saúl. "Contemporary Jewish-Argentine Writers: Tradition and Politics." *Latin American Literary Review* 6.12 (1978): 1-14.

—. "Latin American-Jewish Writers: Protecting the Hyphen." In *The Jewish Presence in Latin America*. Ed. Judith Laiken Elkin and Gilbert W. Merkx. Boston: Allen & Unwin, 1987. 297-323. Also as "Escritores judeo-latinoamericanos: el guión protector." *La orilla inminente: escritores judíos argentinos*. Buenos Aires: Legasa, 1987. 15-36.

—. "Latin American Jewish Literature: On Ethnic and National Boundaries." *Folio* 17 (1987): 1-8. Originally in Spanish as "Literatura judeo-latino-americana: sobre fronteras étnicas y nacionales." *Punto de vista* (Buenos Aires) 7.25 (1985): 17-19.

—. "Latin American Jewish Writers: A Bridge Toward History." *Prooftexts* 4.1 (1984): 71-92.

Stavans, Ilán. "América Latina y su pluma judía." *Revista hispánica moderna* 63.1 (1990): 114-17.

—. Introduction to *Tropical Synagogues: Short Stories by Jewish-Latin American Writers*. New York: Holmes & Meier, 1994. 1-38.

—. "Jewish Writers in Latin America." *Midstream* 34.6 (1988): 51-53.

Vieira, Nelson H. "Judaic Fiction in Brazil: To Be and Not To Be Jewish." *Latin American Literary Review* 14.28 (1986): 31-45.

——. "Outsiders and Insiders: Brazilian Jews and the Discourse of Alterity." In *The Jewish Diaspora in Latin America: New Studies on History and Literature*. Ed. David Sheinin and Lois Baer Barr. New York: Garland, 1996. 101-16.

——. "Post-Holocaust Literature in Brazil: Jewish Resistance and Resurgence as Literary Metaphors for Brazilian Society and Politics." *Modern Language Studies* 16.1 (1986): 62-70.

Winter, Calvert, J. "Some Jewish Writers of the Argentine." *Hispania* 19.4 (1936): 431-36.

Bibliographies

Foster, David William, and Naomi Lindstrom. "Jewish Argentine Authors: A Registry," parts 1 and 2, *Revista interamericana de bibliografía/Inter-American Review of Bibliography* 41.3 (1991): 478-503; 41.4 (1991): 655-82.

Weinstein, Ana E., and Miryam E. Gover de Nasatsky, comps. *Escritores judeoargentinos: bibliografía 1900-1987*. 2 vols. Buenos Aires: Milá, 1994.

LATIN AMERICAN JEWISH HISTORY

Avni, Haim. *Argentina and the Jews: A History of Jewish Immigration*. Trans. by Gila Brand. Tuscaloosa: U of Alabama P, 1991.

——. *Argentina y la historia de la inmigración judía (1810-1950)*. Buenos Aires: AMIA/Comunidad Judía de Buenos Aires/Hebrew University of Jerusalem, 1983.

——. *Mexico: Immigration and Refuge*. Washington, D.C.: Woodrow Wilson International Center for Scholars, 1989.

Beller, Jacob. *Jews in Latin America*. New York: Jonathan David, 1969.

Bergstein, Nahum. *Judío: una experiencia uruguaya*. Montevideo: Fin de Siglo, 1993.

Bohm, Gunter. *Historia de los judíos en Chile*. Santiago: Andrés Bello, 1984.

——. *Judíos en el Perú durante el siglo XIX*. Santiago: Universidad de Chile, 1985.

Elkin, Judith Laiken. *Jews of the Latin American Republics*. Chapel Hill: U of North Carolina P, 1980.

Elkin, Judith Laiken, and Gilbert W. Merkx, eds. *The Jewish Presence in Latin America*. Boston: Allen & Unwin, 1987.

Glickman, Nora. *La trata de blancas. Regeneración: drama en cuatro actos de Leib Malaj*. Trans. of *Regeneración* from Yiddish by Nora Glickman and Rosalía Rosembuj. Buenos Aires: Pardés, 1984.

Kleiner, Alberto, comp. *Inmigración judía a Uruguay, Perú y Paraguay: informe presentado en Argentina por la Sociedad de Socorro a los judíos de habla alemana.* Buenos Aires: Instituto Hebreo de Ciencias, 1988.

Krause, Corinne A. *Los judíos en México: una historia con énfasis especial en el período de 1857-1930.* Trad. Ariela Katz de Gugenheim. México, D.F.: Universidad Iberoamericana, 1987.

Lesser, Jeffrey. *Welcoming the Undesirables: Brazil and the Jewish Question.* Berkeley: U of California P, 1994.

Levine, Robert M. *Tropical Diaspora: The Jewish Experience in Cuba.* Gainesville: UP of Florida, 1993.

Mirelman, Víctor A. *En búsqueda de una identidad: los inmigrantes judíos en Buenos Aires, 1890-1930.* Buenos Aires: Milá, 1988.

Nassi, Mario. *La comunidad ashkenazi de Caracas: breve historia institucional.* Caracas: Unión Israelita de Caracas, 1981.

Porzecanski, Teresa, comp. *Historias de vidas de inmigrantes judíos al Uruguay.* Montevideo: Kehila, Comunidad Israelita de Uruguay, 1986.

Seligson Berenfeld, Silvia. *Los judíos en México: un estudio preliminar.* México, D.F.: Cultura SEP, 1983.

Trahtemberg Siederer, León. *La inmigración judía al Perú, 1848-1948: una historia documentada de la inmigración de los judíos de habla alemana.* Lima: n.p., 1987.

Weisbrot, Robert. *The Jews of Argentina: From the Inquisition to Perón.* Philadelphia: Jewish Publication Society of America, 1979.

Wolff, Martha, and Myrtha Schalom, eds. *Judíos y argentinos: judíos argentinos.* Buenos Aires: Manrique Zago, 1988.

Zago, Manrique, ed. *Pioneros de la Argentina, los inmigrantes judíos [Pioneers in Argentina, the Jewish Immigrants].* Buenos Aires: Manrique Zago, 1982.

Zárate Miguel, Guadalupe. *México y la diáspora judía.* México, D.F.: Instituto Nacional de Antropología, 1986.

ABSATZ, CECILIA (Argentina; 1943)

Cecilia Absatz was born and raised in Buenos Aires, where she continues to reside. She studied philosophy at the University of Buenos Aires and soon after initiated a successful career in advertising, publishing, and journalism beginning in the mid-1960s. Absatz worked as an editor for and eventually became director of the magazine *Status*, a *Playboy*-style publication for men. She also has worked for a variety of other magazines and newspapers (*Claudia*, *Vosotras*, *Somos*, *La Nación*) in the capacity of editor or columnist. In addition, Absatz has written several television film scripts and she is a professional translator.

As an author, Absatz maintains a low profile within Argentine literary circles. In interviews, she has expressed a certain degree of reluctance toward literary success, or what is perceived as such, stating that she views success as a "risk" (Lóizaga 10). More directly she contends, "The worst thing that can happen to a writer or a literary generation is to be successful. When I see that all published books are systematically around six hundred pages long, I feel distrust because I can see business looming behind it" (Flori, "Cecilia Absatz" 206). Clearly then, as an author Absatz does not engage in writing as a commercial venture. Instead, she describes writing in very personal terms as a survival technique: "Writing is my salvation. I'm a marginal being and I don't belong to any type of structure, so when I feel the world is collapsing around me, the only thing that can save me is to sit down and write" (Flori, "Cecilia Absatz" 208).

Absatz's first published book, *Feiguele y otras mujeres* (Feiguele and Other Women; 1976), contains a novella "Feiguele" and six short stories, which all revolve around the other women mentioned in the title. The thematic common denominator contained in all the stories of this collection is the characters' efforts to forge a space for female identity within (masculine) Argentine society. *Feiguele* was banned in Argentina by the military government just three months after its publication. The rationale given was that it was immoral in content, but Absatz attributes its proscription to the military's persecution of the publishing house (Ediciones de la Flor), not as a direct threat to herself (Flori, "Cecilia Absatz" 205). She did not leave the country during the years of the dictatorship (1976-83), as did many other writers and intellectuals. While she continued to write throughout this period, her next book was not published until 1982, when the grip of the military regime was already beginning to loosen.

"Feiguele," the novella that opens the book, is the story of a young girl growing up in Buenos Aires within a middle-class family of Polish-Jewish immigrants. It is narrated in the first person by the young Feiguele, who recounts approximately one year in her life. To a certain extent, the text is autobiographical. One finds episodes in the book that correlate directly to revelations about her own family that Absatz has disclosed in interviews. For instance, Feiguele states that her father never spoke Spanish, only Yiddish, even after having lived in Argentina for forty years (39). Similarly, Absatz states that her own father never spoke Spanish at home, even though he knew how (Flori, "Cecilia Absatz" 210). From this and other examples one may draw the conclusion that the story draws heavily upon the author's own experience, even though it is not a story about her own life. The tone of the story is established in the opening lines, which read, "Me llamo Feiguele y soy muy gorda. Tengo catorce años, y aunque ustedes se rían, conozco bastante del dolor del mundo" (My name is Feiguele and I am very fat. I'm fourteen years old, and although you may laugh, I know plenty about the pain of the world [7]). Feiguele, like many teenagers, is consumed with conflicting emotions, angry, and very insecure. She is self-conscious about her weight, her appearance and her Jewishness. She views her father's stubborn adherence to Yiddishkeit (his newspapers, radio shows, and insistence on speaking only Yiddish) as an anachronism, which she finds both annoying and endearing. Feiguele's name sets her apart, labels her as different. She is constantly subjected to odd looks and even laughter when she is introduced, and she must repeatedly pronounce and/or spell out her foreign-sounding name for others. Absatz endows her character with an acerbic wit and a knack for sarcasm that she wields with great expertise. Feiguele turns the ostracism and rejection of her peers into a means of independence. Most significantly, she discovers—as her friends do not—a sense of empowerment that comes from surviving on one's own, rather than becoming dependent on male companionship. Her rejection of the ideals that men (or adolescent boys) place on women (or adolescent girls) frees her to pursue her own interests. Nevertheless, this does not prevent Feiguele from feeling the emotional pain brought on by her so-called friends' nonacceptance of her.

The other stories in the book portray equally strong female characters. In contrast to Feiguele, though, the "other women" in the subsequent stories are more mature. As adult women, they are in search of success in their professional lives and happiness in their private lives, which at times prove to be incompatible aspirations. Absatz's characters seldom achieve the ideal situation, but it is the struggle or the search as a means that is more important than the end. The stories are feminocentric in nature; they spring from the very core of female identity. The dynamics of the male-female relationship are central to these urban tales of women who find themselves at pivotal moments in their lives. Furthermore, the stories take on an erotic dimension afforded by the often sexually aggressive behavior of the protagonists (and herein lies the so-called immorality for which the book was censored). These metropolitan heroines, in the course of their daily lives, challenge the obstacles placed before them by a patriarchal, machista, society. Through the stories, Absatz speaks out against the victimization and stereotyping of women, and the constraints placed on them by the institution of marriage. In texts following *Feiguele*, such as the short story "El descubrimiento de Barracas" (The Discovery of Barracas; 1984 [published in two different anthologies of Argentine erotic literature]), Absatz continues to make use of eroticism as a means of female empowerment and liberation.

Although her characters tend to be Jewish, specifically Jewish themes are not the focal point of Absatz's writing. Rather, her stories and characters can be seen as representative of the degree to which Argentine Jews have assimilated into the dominant culture, to the point of being only nominally Jewish. Her short story "Rosenberg" published in *Buenos Aires: una antología de nueva ficción argentina* (Buenos Aires: An Anthology of New Argentine Fiction; 1992), exemplifies this tendency. It is the uneventful story of a Buenos Aires journalist by the name of Rosenberg who dreams of more exotic places than the dreary atmosphere of his office. His boss sends him on an assignment—authorizing his full access to the expense account—to gather important, and somewhat secret information about the visit of an American dignitary. He easily obtains the information with one phone call, but the story ends with him boarding a plane to Bogotá for a vacation at the expense of his employer. There is nothing specifically Jewish about the story, save the protagonist's name. Nevertheless, it is indicative of the extent to which Argentine Jews have come to form part of the middle class, with all the drudgery that such an inclusion entails: a dead-end job, a failed marriage, a drab existence. The text is unique to Absatz's literary corpus in that the protagonist is a man. The author quite effectively portrays a genuine (as opposed to satiric) male perspective as Rosenberg relates to the reader—of whom he is very aware—the events that led up to his "free" vacation.

The novel *Té con canela* (Cinnamon Tea; 1982) is Absatz's second book. It received favorable reviews, although it was largely misunderstood by the critics and the public alike, mostly because it does not conform to the traditional parameters of novelistic discourse. It is composed of a series of disjointed narrative fragments and the author calls the book a "tribute to television" (Flori, "Cecilia Absatz" 211). The novel is structured around the interior ruminations of the protagonist who, in the midst of an emotional crisis, locks herself up in her apartment over a long holiday weekend to reevaluate her life. *Té con canela* is particularly suited to demonstrating, within the artistic space of literature, the process of self-identification that women undertake. The protagonist embarks on an interior journey of self-discovery in which she constructs an identity based on her qualities as individual, discarding the labels that society has placed on her as a woman. The novel also contains the characteristic sardonic humor and eroticism that inform Absatz's writing.

The novel *Los años pares* (The Even-Numbered Years) was published in 1985. In terms of style, it is much more conventional than *Té con canela* in that it follows a traditional plot line. There is an undercurrent of intrigue that links the text to the narrative genre of detective fiction and that keeps the story flowing. The novel is circular in structure, beginning in 1980, then moving to 1976, 1978, and finally back to 1980. These dates situate the novel during the period of the most virulent oppression of the military dictatorship, which serves as the backdrop for the novel. The narration begins with the protagonist, Clara, an Argentine Jew, having difficulties as she tries to renew her national identity card; an act that from the beginning establishes the issue of identity as central to the text. Through a series of events Clara (whose last name significantly is Auslender, German for "foreigner") meets Eric, who is from Holland, and a relationship ensues. Clara is confronted with several different issues of identity. In order to resolve the question of her identity card she must travel to the interior of the country. Once surrounded by the largely indigenous and creole population of the interior of the country, she is compelled to come to terms with her own European ancestry. The larger issue for Clara, however, is that of her identity as a woman, and her independence. This is the theme that has most attracted critics to the novel, and the way in which Absatz so eloquently presents the topic makes the text especially accommodating to feminist theoretical models (Flori; Gimbernat González). Notwithstanding the fact that all of Absatz's works readily lend themselves to a feminist reading, the author herself denies writing as a feminist. She has rather forthrightly stated that "El feminismo es como la política, no tiene nada que ver con la literatura" (Feminism is like politics, it has nothing to do with literature [Lóizaga 15]).

Absatz's latest novel, *¿Dónde estás amor de mi vida, que no te puedo encontrar?* (Where Are You Love of My Life, that I Cannot Find You?; 1995), is based on the television miniseries she scripted by the same title. The miniseries was directed by the well-known Argentine filmmaker Juan José Jusid, who had also made the feature film version in 1992. The story revolves around the production of a radio program from which the novel takes its title. The original idea was Jusid's, as Absatz makes clear on the title page with the clarifying statement, "Sobre una idea de Juan José Jusid" (Based on the idea of Juan José Jusid). Octavio Luz, a famous radio personality, and Liliana Milman, a psychoanalyst, host a call-in radio show that caters to the lonely and lovelorn inhabitants of the Buenos Aires metropolis. In contrast to the author's previous works, *¿Dónde estás amor de mi vida?* is written with a decidedly less somber outlook. Composed some thirteen years after the end of the military dictatorship, the novel is not charged with references to political violence and repression nor is it formulated around narrative postulations of identity formation. It narrates the foibles, perserverance and ingenuity of human nature through the optic of a wide gamut of characters representative of different generations and social classes. This fictional microcosm provides a contemporary view of daily life in Buenos Aires as it focuses on personal relationships that are both platonic and amorous. Lonely callers reach out to the program in search of help in finding if not a soulmate at least a companion. The novel advances by narrating the circumstances of several love stories, both failed and successful, which tend to be overdetermined by romantic clichés that make an appeal for soap-opera passion. Nevertheless, trite sentimental formulas, or parodies of them, are superseded by the down-to-earth depiction of the characters as real and feeling individuals who confront each day in search of meaningful emotional contact. The separate episodes are connectd by the core story of the relationship between the two radio hosts themsleves, which evolves from friendship to the awakening of requited romantic love. Absatz's characteristic humor and irony fill the pages of this entertaining text that engages the attention of the reader from the onset. The women in the novel continue to be the type of strong, independent individuals found in the previous texts.

Absatz's other recent work is not fiction, but a collection of essays titled *Mujeres peligrosas: la pasión según el teleteatro* (Dangerous Women: Passion According to the Soap Operas; 1995). It consists of a series of essays in which the author reflects on Argentine popular culture—more specifically, how it is influenced by United States popular culture—, the roles of women, feminist issues, and passion as it is played out on television and in literature. Absatz not only discusses and compares Argentine, Mexican, Brazilian, and American soap operas, but she also examines contemporary American situation comedies such as *Murphy Brown* and *Roseanne*, both very popular in Argentina, in her analysis of the ever-changing public roles and images of women in/on television. Likewise, she draws upon a wide range of literary texts from Latin America, Europe and the United States in order to delineate and define a variety of women's issues. What is most amazing about *Mujeres peligrosas* is the way in which Absatz is able to coordinate such a diverse assortment of popular culture artifacts (a small sampling includes the rock lyrics of Pink Floyd, *The Simpsons*, the fiction of Stephen King, *Apocalypse Now*, Susan Faludi's *Backlash* [1991], Marta Lynch's novels, Verónica Castro, and *Simplemente María)* in order to compose a coherent, entertaining, and fascinating analysis of the situation and image of contemporary women.

6 ABSATZ, CECILIA

PRIMARY BIBLIOGRAPHY
Creative Writing
Los años pares. Buenos Aires: Legasa, 1985.

"A Ballet for Girls." Trans. by H. Ernest Lewald. In *The Web: Stories by Argentine Women.* Ed. and translated by H. Ernest Lewald. Washington, D.C.: Three Continents Press, 1983. 155-61.

"El descubrimiento de Barracas." In *Cuentos eróticos.* Enrique Medina, et al. Buenos Aires: Eryda, 1984. 43-48. Also in *Antología del erotismo en la literatura argentina.* Comp. Francisco Herrera. Buenos Aires: Fraterna, 1990. 18-24.

¿Dónde estás amor de mi vida, que no te puedo encontrar? Buenos Aires: Espasa Calpe/Seix Barral, 1995.

Feiguele y otras mujeres. Buenos Aires: Ediciones de la Flor, 1976.

"Las flores rojas de los semáforos." *Puro cuento* 3.17 (1989): 42-43.

"Rosenberg." In *Buenos Aires: una antología de nueva ficción argentina.* Ed. Juan Forn. Barcelona: Anagrama, 1992. 145-54.

Té con canela. Buenos Aires: Sudamericana, 1982.

"Zapateo americano,""Balance del ejercicio."*Hispamérica* 15.45 (1986): 123-27.

Nonfiction
Mujeres peligrosas: la pasión según el teleteatro. Buenos Aires: Planeta, 1995.

SECONDARY BIBLIOGRAPHY
Criticism
Flori, Mónica. "Cecilia Absatz." In her *Streams of Silver: Six Contemporary Women Writers from Argentina.* Lewisburg, NJ: Bucknell UP, 1995. 185-213. (Critical essay on Absatz's work followed by an interview.)

—. "Identidad y discurso de la femineidad en *Los años pares* de Cecilia Absatz." *Explicación de textos literarios* 22.2 (1993-94): 87-97.

Gimbernat González, Ester. "En los nones de *Los años pares.*" In her *Aventuras del desacuerdo: novelistas argentinas de los 80.* Buenos Aires: Danilo Albero Vergara, 1992. 94-99.

Kreimer, Juan Carlos. "Mate con ginseng." Rev. of *Té con canela. Humor* (Buenos Aires) 2 Dec., 1982: 117-18.

Roffé, Mercedes. Rev. of *Feiguele y otras mujeres. Repertorio latinoamericano* 3.24 (1977): 9.

Villordo, Oscar Hermes. "Cecilia Absatz: el mundo de la mujer." *Cultura de la Argentina contemporánea* 4.28-29 (1988): 40-42.

Interviews

Fingueret, Manuela. "Ser escritoras argentinas y judías." *Nueva Sión* 623 (7 Sept., 1985): 20-21.

Flori, Mónica. "Alicia Steimberg y Cecilia Absatz: dos narradoras argentinas contemporáneas." *Chasqui* 17.2 (1988): 83-92.

Lóizaga, Patricio J. "Cecilia Absatz: 'La literatura nunca está en crisis.'" *Cultura de la Argentina contemporánea* 6.31 (1989): 8-15.

Roffé, Reina. "No nos interesa coleccionar amantes." *Crisis* 55 (87): 52.

Darrell B. Lockhart

AGOSÍN, MARJORIE (Chile; 1955)

Spanning poetry, fiction, literary criticism, and the editing of anthologies, the work of Marjorie Agosín engages concerns representative of many Latin American Jewish women writers today. Her recurring themes include the experiences of love and loss, the struggle for human rights, and the attempt to represent feminine experience from within. Her poetry and prose poetry reveals a remarkable range, veering from satires on the hypocrisies of social identity to lyrical exploration of the elaborate codes of intimate relationships, with forays into a variety of rich, sensual, descriptive topics: the experience of the body, the sea, the countryside. Agosín's self-identification as a Chilean and a Jew have been central aspects shaping the more recent (post 1988) publications in fiction and nonfiction which have added to the already considerable reputation that she enjoyed as a poet. From at least the mid-1980s Marjorie Agosín has emerged as one of the leading voices of Latin American feminism in the United States.

Born of Chilean parents in Bethesda, Maryland, in 1955, Marjorie Agosín was raised in Chile. Her maternal grandfather was born and raised in Vienna, which he had left "for the love of a cabaret dancer," according to Agosín, in the mid-1920s. His having escaped Europe prior to the rise of Nazism enabled him to help subsequent refugees establish themselves in Chile. Agosín's other grandparents and greatgrandparents, also from Vienna and Odessa, similarly belonged to that minority within a minority, of German-speaking European and Eastern European Jews, whose children were Chilean citizens. Because Agosín attended Santiago's remarkable Insituto Hebreo for her primary as well as secondary schooling she grew up speaking both Hebrew and Spanish. Her parents lived in one of Santiago's older neighborhoods, Nuñoa, close to sites such as the Carabineros school, the Pedagogical Institute, and the commercial district of Irrarrázabal Street. For large portions of every summer she went with her family to live by the rocky shore south of Valparaíso and Pablo Neruda's (1904-73) Isla Negra, and marine imagery consequently pervades Agosín's poetry and prose. When Agosín was in her teens, rumors of an impending coup led her immediate family (her father was a doctor and biochemist) to move to the United States in what they expected to be a fairly short-term arrangement. Once the seriousness of the 1973 military takeover became evident, her family settled in the state of Georgia, where Agosín studied philosophy as an undergraduate. She went on to take a Ph.D. in literature from Indiana University: her doctoral dissertation concentrated on the work of Chilean writer María Luisa Bombal (1910-80). Agosín has been teaching in the Department of Spanish and Portuguese at Wellesley College for the past fifteen years, where she is currently an associate professor. Married, with two children, Agosín is a US citizen, but she spends part of every year with members of her family in Chile.

Agosín's earliest publications were in poetry: *Conchalí* (1980) is a book of poems named for the old Jewish cemetery in Santiago, where some of Agosín's uncles are buried. *Brujas y algo más/Witches and Other Things* (1984) enjoyed good sales and critical success: this interesting collection of poems indicates Agosín's playfulness, multi-levelled use of language, and the interest in esoteric knowledge which is a persistent theme for Chilean women writers, from early twentieth-century theosophists, up through the poet and Nobel Laureate Gabriela Mistral (1889-1957), to the popular novelist Isabel Allende (1942).

As a poet one of Agosín's commitments is to the expression of love, be it erotic or filial. Her poetry details what she calls the "gestures" of love; irony and self-mockery often co-exist with the strongest nostalgia. Much of her poetry, criticism, and prose poetry takes human rights as its primary concern, but this too is founded in what could be termed a vatic vocation. The compulsion to bear witness to suffering comes first, almost involuntarily, its form and shape fast on the heels of the urge to speak and write.

A number of Agosín's books are organized around recounting women's resistance to the tyranny of the military dictatorships ruling Argentina and Chile in the 1970s and the 1980s. She has described the ordeal of Renée Epelbaum, a central figure in the Argentine Mothers of the Plaza de Mayo movement, with whom Agosín lived for several months (see *Mothers of the Plaza de Mayo* [1989]). After having described in non-fiction prose the Mothers' attempts to obtain information about their children who were "disappeared" during the so-called Dirty War conducted by the Argentine military against its own people,

Agosín went on to write poetry based on the experience of the Mothers, in the book *Circles of Madness* (1992). Still another book, *Scraps of Life* (1987), details the work of the Chilean *arpilleristas*, women who with their needles described the day-to-day lives of the families of persons who had been disappeared or held as political prisoners. As with other Chilean writers, politics has had a direct and immediate impact on Agosín's subject matter. At a time when the military dictatorships governing the writer's native Chile as well as neighboring Argentina made it difficult for many writers to survive, Agosín was able to take advantage of her freedom, as an American citizen, to return to Argentina and Chile and to chronicle the efforts of the opposition. She offers invaluable documentary commentaries on the lives of women who suddenly found themselves projected into the political realms, by virtue of disappearances and murders of their husbands and children.

Feminism is key to Agosín's continuing, compassionate articulation of the lives of the women who are in one way or another outsiders. Much of Agosín's work focuses on the perspectives of individuals whose every existence challenges and points up the limitations which "good society" imposes. Exiles, recluses, and seeming madwomen are prominent in her catalogue of heros. These may be figures such as Anne Frank (1929-44), whose writings are a touchstone in Agosín's work, appearing in *Zones of Pain/Las zonas del dolor* (1988), as well as in her most recent collection, *Sagrada memoria: reminiscencias de una niña judía en Chile* (*A Cross and a Star: Memoirs of a Jewish Girl in Chile*; 1994). This latter book, told from the perspective of the writer's mother, is a fascinating historical document, beginning in family history but going far beyond that, including memories of the various Indian and mixed-blood women who worked in her parents' and grandparents' houses. It includes as well harrowing accounts of the popularity of Nazism among the German enclaves of Southern Chile, and the day-to-day experiences of the children of the four Jewish families of Osorno, Chile, who on being excluded from the Catholic and German schools, attended the local schools with the Indians.

Much of Agosín's work approximates the genre of testimonial literature, popular throughout the eighties, yet what is most original in her writing emerges from her differences from this form. A problematic of testimonial literature is the sense that a privileged speaker has appropriated another person's otherwise silent voice to her own, so that instead of "giving voice" to those who suffer, the writer/editor actually confirms the muteness of the person who is being "spoken for." Agosín, on the other hand, never represents herself as "speaking for" another. Rather, she engages in what could be termed a duet, which conjoins her own awareness of suffering with another's. What emerges is less an artificially constructed unified single voice, than a litany of voices that includes the dead and the living, the poet and the mourners, Jews, Gentiles, Indians, and the children of Nazis, to name just a few. This technique is especially interesting in Agosín's most recent work *La felicidad* (*Happiness*; 1991) and *Sagrada memoria*, in which the history of Latin American Jews is more deliberately and openly engaged. She has thus moved beyond the lamentation for the missing, to celebrate the victorious men and women of the past, of Chile's tiny minority of Jews (some 20,000 in 14 million) who survived, often alongside and within the atmosphere that was during the Second World War strongly pro-German. If there is anyone whose language is capable of expressing the tremendous daily paradox involved when those whose parents escaped the Holocaust find that their neighbors are followers of Adolf Hitler, Augusto Pinochet, or Jorge R. Videla, it is Marjorie Agosín.

PRIMARY BIBLIOGRAPHY
Creative Writing

Las alfareras. Santiago: Cuarto Propio, 1994. English version as *Women in Disguise: Stories*. Trans. by Diane Russell-Pineda. Falls Church, VA: Azul Editions, 1996.

Brujas y algo más/Witches and Other Things. Trans. by Cola Franzen. Pittsburgh: Latin American Literary Review Press, 1984.

Circles of Madness:Mothers of the Plaza de Mayo/Círculos de locura: Madres de la Plaza de Mayo. Trans. by Celeste Kostopulos-Cooperman. Photographs by Alicia D'Amico and Alicia Sanguinetti. Fredonia, NY: White Pine Press, 1992.

Conchalí. New York: Senda Nueva de Ediciones, 1980.

Dear Anne Frank: Poems. Bilingual edition trans. by Richard Schaaf. Washington, D.C.: Azul Editions, 1994.

La felicidad. Santiago: Cuarto Propio, 1991. English version as *Happiness*. Trans. by Elizabeth Horan. Fredonia, NY: White Pine Press, 1993.

Hogueras. Santiago: Editorial Universitaria, 1986.

Hogueras/Bonfires. Trans. by Naomi Lindstrom. Tempe, AZ: Bilingual Press/ Editorial Bilingüe, 1990.

"A Huge Black Umbrella." Trans. by Lori M. Carlson. In *Where Angels Glide at Dawn: New Stories from Latin America*. Ed. Lori M. Carlson and Cynthia L. Ventura. New York: HarperCollins, 1990. 99-104.

"My Stomach," "What We Are," "Penis." Trans. by Daisy C. de Filippis. In *Pleasure in the Word: Erotic Writings by Latin American Women*. Ed. Margarite Fernández Olmos and Lizabeth Paravisini-Gebert. Fredonia, NY: White Pine Press, 1993. 46-49.

Sagrada memoria: reminiscencias de una niña judía en Chile. Santiago: Cuarto Propio, 1994. English version as *A Cross and a Star: Memoirs of a Jewish Girl in Chile.* Trans. by Celeste Kostopulos-Cooperman. U of New Mexico P, 1995.

Sargazo=Sargasso: poemas. Trans. by Cola Franzen. Fredonia, NY: White Pine Press, 1993.

Toward the Splendid City. Trans. by Richard Schaaf. Tempe, AZ: Bilingual Press/Editorial Bilingüe, 1994.

"When She Showed Me Her Photograph," "Memorial," "The Most Unbelievable Part," "Disappeared Woman V," "Seven Stones," "Language." Trans. by Celeste Kostopulos-Cooperman and Cola Franzen. In *These Are Not Sweet Girls: Poetry by Latin American Women.* Ed. Marjorie Agosín. Fredonia, NY: White Pine Press, 1994. 239-44.

Women of Smoke/Mujeres de humo. Trans. by Naomi Lindstrom. Pittsburgh: Latin American Literary Review Press, 1988.

Zones of Pain/Las zonas del dolor. Trans. by Cola Franzen. Fredonia, NY: White Pine Press, 1988.

Nonfiction

La literatura y los derechos humanos. San José: EDUCA, 1989.

The Mothers of Plaza de Mayo (Línea Fundadora): The Story of Renée Epelbaum 1976-1985. Trans. by Janice Molloy. Stratford, Ontario, Canada: Williams-Wallace Publishers, 1989.

Pablo Neruda. Trans. by Lorraine Ross. Boston: Twayne, 1986.

Scraps of Life: The Chilean Arpilleras: Chilean Women and the Pinochet Dictatorship. Trans. by Cola Franzen. Trenton, NJ: Red Sea Press, 1987.

Silencio e imaginación: metáforas de la escritura femenina. México, D.F.: Katún, 1986.

Tapestries of Hope, Threads of Love: The Arpillera Movement in Chile, 1974-1994. Albuquerque: U of New Mexico P, 1996.

Violeta Parra: Santa de Pura Greda. Inez Dolz Blackburn, co-author. Santiago: Planeta, 1988.

Women of Smoke: Latin American Women in Literature and Life. Trans. by Janice Molloy. Trenton, NJ: Red Sea Press, 1989.

Editions

A Dream of Light and Shadows: Potraits of Latin American Women Writers. Albuquerque: U of New Mexico P, 1995.

Landscapes of a New Land: Short Fiction by Latin American Women. Buffalo: White Pine Press, 1989.

María Luisa Bombal: apreciaciones críticas. Co-edited with Elena Gascón Vera and Joy Renjilian Burgy. Tempe, AZ: Bilingual Press/Editorial Bilingüe, 1987.

Secret Weavers: Stories of the Fantastic by Women of Argentina and Chile. Assistant editor Celeste Kostopulos-Cooperman. Fredonia, NY: White Pine Press, 1992.

Surviving Beyond Fear: Women, Children, and Human Rights in Latin America. Asst. to the editor Monica Bruno. Fredonia, NY: White Pine Press, 1993.

These Are Not Sweet Girls: Poetry by Latin American Women. Fredonia, NY: White Pine Press, 1994.

SECONDARY BIBLIOGRAPHY
Criticism

Coddou, Marcelo. "Marjorie Agosín pide hablar en medio de un ahuecado silencio." *Veinte estudios sobre la literatura chilena del siglo veinte.* Santiago: Monografías del Maitén/Instituto Profesional del Pacífico, 1989. 103-12.

Franzen, Cola. "Marjorie Agosín: A Portrait. Introduction and Poems." *Mundus-Artium: A Journal of International Literature and the Arts* 15.1-2 (1985): 54-57.

Frey, Melissa A. "Transcending Wounds: Images of Women's Bodies in the Poetry of Marjorie Agosín." Unpublished thesis, Princeton University, Princeton, NJ, 1991.

Horan, Elizabeth. "Prelude to a Literary Alliance." In *Happiness.* Trans by Elizabeth Horan. Fredonia, NY: White Pine Press, 1993. 13-26.

Scott, Nina. "Marjorie Agosín as Latina Writer." In *Breaking Boundaries: Latina Writings and Critical Readings.* Ed. Asunción Horno-Delgado, et al. Amherst: U of Massachusetts P, 1989. 235-49.

Travniceck, Odile. "El reconocimiento de una presencia activa: un poema de Marjorie Agosín." *Ventanal: Revista de creación y crítica* 12 (9187): 92-97.

Umpierre, Lus-María. "La ansiedad de la influencia en Sandra María Esteres y Marjorie Agosín." *Revista chicano-riqueña* 11.3-4 (1983): 139-47.

Villegas Morales, Juan. "Agosín: The Road to Transgression." In *Hogueras/Bonfires.* Trans. by Naomi Lindstrom. Tempe, AZ: Bilingual Press/Editorial Bilingüe, 1990. 1-7.

—. "Marjorie Agosín: desde la antipoesía al feminismo y la ironización del discurso patriarcal." *El discurso lírico de la mujer en Chile: 1975-1990.* Santiago: Mosquito Editores, 1993. 143-50.

Interviews

Mujica, Barbara. "Marjorie Agosín Weaves Magic with Social Vision." *Américas* 45.1 (1993): 44-49.

Elizabeth Rosa Horan

AGUINIS, MARCOS (Argentina; 1935)

A versatile man accomplished in music and medicine as well as literature, Marcos Aguinis has written everything from novels and short stories to essays on art, psychology, sociology, and literary criticism. He has also lectured on these various topics in Buenos Aires, Rosario, Córdoba, and Mendoza in Argentina; Madrid, Barcelona, Seville, and Málaga in Spain, and Frankfurt and Bonn in Germany. A concert class pianist, a sometime composer, and eventually a medical doctor, psychoanalyst, and neurosurgeon by training, Aguinis, was born in Córdoba, Argentina where he grew up, excelling in both music and art during his adolescent years. At the National University in Córdoba, however, drawn to medicine because of its humanistic value, he elected to study medicine and graduated in 1958 with degrees in Medicine and Surgery. Aguinis's intense interest in the ancient physician and humanist Maimónides led him to research and write *Maimónides, un sabio avanzado* (Maimónides, a Prescient Scholar; 1963) and *Maimónides, sacerdote de los oprimidos* (Maimónides, Priest of the Oppressed; 1963), well received biographical studies about the ancient scholar whom he considered an enduring model of humanity and inspiration for scientists and scholars.

Interested in psychiatry but appalled at the way patients suffering mental illnesses were treated, Aguinis turned to the newer studies of neurology and neurosurgery because they seemed to offer possible solutions to some mental problems. A scholarship to study neurology at the school of medicine in Buenos Aires was followed by additional scholarships for advanced training in France and Germany. In Paris, the rigors of his training eventually diverted him from his cherished musical ambitions, although not from his love of writing.

Seeing the many refugees in Germany, the young student became interested in Europe's refugee population and collected information and articles about
them. From this concern for refugees grew a desire to understand Arab-Israeli
differences which eventually led him to write *Los refugiados* (The Refugees;
1969), a curious novel in which he, a Jewish author, narrates the story of a
Palestinian protagonist in first person. Because both Jewish and Arab sources
which Aguinis researched offered nothing more than propaganda to support their
views, the author sought more substantive understanding. "To find valid arguments" he told one interviewer, "I tried to put myself on the Palestinian's side,
to show his emotion, his loyalty and the suffering that surely saddened his days"
(Paley Francescato, "Entrevista" 121). His thoroughness as a researcher led Aguinis to study not only historical works but even the Koran to better understand
and interpret the mental framework and attitudes of his characters. In preparation
for several years because it encountered numerous publication delays the novel
appeared shortly after the Six Days War and was met with mixed reviews. Some
considered it antisemitic, some, pro-Arab and many, nonplussed, simply refused
to promote it. Aguinis's justification for his approach was, quite forthrightly, that
he had striven to clarify the arguments of both sides in a way that had not been
done heretofore.

Refugiados is the story of a Palestinian refugee interning in neurosurgery
in Germany, who meets and falls in love with Miriam, a young Jewish woman,
when he operates on and saves the life of her adopted father injured in an automobile accident. Miriam, like him, a medical scholarship student, happens to be
also a survivor of Auschwitz. She understands his sense of isolation and alienation and their ensuing love enables them to understand and bridge the differences separating them. Her assassination at the hands of a Nazi, who has assumed a false identity in Freiberg and fears that she may recognize and expose
him brings an element of suspense and intrigue to the novel. It also brings the
Palestinian protagonist to a realization of the destructive effects of hate. Although
based upon some implausible coincidences, the novel effectively presents one of
Aguinis's basic concerns—the problem of individual and group identity—and
succeeds in conveying his intrinsic faith that humanity supersedes nationalism
and that love and understanding can overcome prejudice and hate.

On his return to Argentina after this training, the young doctor established a thriving neurosurgical practice, married, had several children, and continued to write. His persistent humanistic interests, however, led him to continue
seeking to penetrate the human mind through means other than analysis or surgery. Some years later, despite the responsibilities of marriage and four children,
Aguinis decided to leave his practice to study psychoanalysis in the belief that

it would synthesize his varied interests and enhance his insights as an author. This real life interest in understanding the human psyche is consistently reflected in Aguinis's writing.

Both his scientific background and natural inclination seem to have made Marcos Aguinis an avid and exact researcher, who writes with equal authenticity of his Catholic characters in *La cruz invertida* (The Inverted Cross; 1970 [a novel which earned him Spain's prestigious Premio Planeta award the same year]) as he had about his Palestinian protagonist previously. In *La cruz*, the story of an idealistic young priest turned activist by his empathy for a group of student revolutionaries, Aguinis graphically depicts the repressive measures used by both the church and an indeterminate Latin American government against the liberal cleric and his student flock. The novel struck a resounding chord in Spain, Argentina and other countries where church and state authority had historically oppressed ordinary people seeking to liberate themselves from pervasive moral and political control. The thoroughness of Aguinis's research on the structure and beliefs of the Catholic Church and his insightful observations of Argentina's predominantly catholic culture brought an authenticity to the novel that caused many critics to believe it was written by either a fallen-away priest or seminarian, or a disillusioned convert to Catholicism.

In *Cantata de los diablos* (Devils' Cantata; 1972), Aguinis describes with insight and mordant humor the frustrations besetting a young writer from Leobuco, an insignificant town of the interior, when he tries to have his historical novel about the town published in the capital. He depicts the town fathers as derided, ridiculed and rebuked for their pretentiousness in financing the book, shows how the investigation of a funding scam led to arrests of some of the town's leading citizens and the young author's falling out with his father which finally caused him to leave home.

Aguinis's intimate knowledge of abnormal psychology and the world of medicine lends almost frightful authenticity to his novel *La conspiración de los idiotas* (A Conspiracy of Idiots; 1979) as the author puts himself inside the person of Natalio Comte, a paranoid salesman for a pharmaceutical company. At first the protagonist seems normal as he denounces bad medical practice and the abuses of medication. It is only as the novel progresses and Comte accuses his long-suffering wife of infidelity with a doctor friend and sees plots in every innocent word or gesture that the reader gradually becomes aware of the existence and extent of the protagonist's psychotic paranoia. Through a tortuous web of mental processes and theories, Comte gradually arrives at the conclusion that the *homúnculos* (dwarfs, midgets, mongoloids and other mentally retarded persons) have formed a world wide conspiracy to gain control. He believes that they talk a secret language using signs, sounds, gestures, etc. not because they are mentally retarded but because they don't want to be understood by non-members of their conspiracy. With repugnantly warped pseudo-lucidity and deviously grotesque persistence Comte first sets about forming a friendship with a small retarded boy, and then, later to seduce a retarded twenty-year-old girl to "learn their secrets." In the last chapter, the demented protagonist coldly plans to blow up part of the colony for retarded children and people. Aguinis's protagonist, sly, conniving, meticulous, apparently logical, is successfully presented from *within*. Aguinis manages to guide the reader inside the mind of his protagonist, a creation he admits inspired repugnance even in him, its author (Paley Francescato, "Entrevista" 129). Describing this work in an interview, Aguinis explained that he had written it partly as a parable of the illogical world that Argentina had become under Perón and the military, attempting to show that, like his protagonist, he too had lived in an climate of paranoid fear of persecution (Paley Francescato, "Entrevista" 130).

Less successful as a novel was *El combate perpetuo* (Perpetual Combat; 1981 [a reedition of *Brown*; 1977]), a somewhat lifeless historical novel or biography of Admiral Guillermo Brown, father of the Argentine navy, written on commission, for the occasion of the 200th anniversary of Brown's birth. Possibly because he felt compelled by history and tradition to treat Brown as a hero, Aguinis never manages to really "get inside" this character but merely describes him moving stiffly through life and a series of essentially unappreciated, heroic deeds. Carefully researched and succinctly narrated, the novel describes the sharp vicissitudes that affected the subject's life and career, but lacks dialogue, feeling, and passion. The General's personality is not sufficiently developed for him to emerge as a person. While Brown's real life abounded in conflict (war, battle, storms, disease, treachery, love, abandonment, honor and despair) all this is presented in a curiously impersonal, factual and unemotional narrative manner. Perhaps because the work was based on a historical character and historical fact and rather than emanating from the writer's own imagination, the author felt compelled to describe the life he had researched rather than to create (or recreate) the personality who had lived that life.

In *Profanación del amor* (Profanation of Love; 1982), Aguinis's protagonist, Felipe, is an ordinary forty-something individual for whom after a lifetime of complaint, socially acceptable behavior yields to the liberating temptations aroused by his emotional and physical desire for Tesi, his best friend's wife. Amusing at first, the author's description of Felipe's forced renunciation of Tesi subtly turns to criticism of a social structure that condemns him to a life entirely circumscribed by the expectations of others. The author almost clinically chronicles Felipe's progress from initial temptation to subsequent rationalizations, guilt, anxiety, self-deception and cowardice. Felipe's Tía (Aunt) Mercedes embodies all the social and religious arguments opposing his attempt to disregard accepted mores as she brings to bear all the arms of religion and superstition to weigh upon him. Felipe's ultimate ignoble renunciation of Tesi and his resignation to the inevitable grayness of his prescribed life style are summed up in his final words: "Me siento condenado. Peor: condenado y resignado a la condena" (I feel condemned. Worse: condemned and resigned to the condemnation [324]).

Although Aguinis professed to believe that Jewish authors express themselves best when **not** explicitly writing of Jewish themes, his most recent novel, *La gesta del marrano* (Acts of a Jew; 1993), clearly shows the author's growing preoccupation with his Jewish history and heritage. A well researched historical novel, *Gesta* narrates the saga of two *marranos* (a derogatory term literally meaning "pig," but commonly used in Spanish as a synonym for "Jew") a father and son, each struggling to live according to his conscience in a world dominated by the fears and suspicions of the omnipresent and all-powerful Inquisition. Aguinis shows how historical protagonist, Francisco Maldonado da Silva, a gentle, scholarly, noble-minded sixteenth-century Portuguese Jewish physician inexorably falls into the clutches of the Inquisition despite fleeing Portugal for Brazil and then Peru. He intertwines Francisco's story with that of the work's true protagonist, Francisco's son, Diego Nuñez da Silva who defies the Inquisition by making the "gesta" or gesture of the title, a defiant acknowledgement of his Jewishness, a suicidal affirmation of his right to freedom of conscience.

While Aguinis at times overdoes his depiction of the venality, avarice, concupiscence and fanaticism of some of the religious or Inquisition characters, the over-all thoroughness of his research and understanding of both the Christian and Jewish perspectives and his evidently deep feeling for his subject results in a powerful portrayal of the indomitable human spirit. The substantive theological arguments, both Catholic and Jewish, which Aguinis develops as both Diego and selected church fathers argue their opposing causes, seem to reflect the author's own search for universal truths, as he weighs arguments for and against the beliefs and sophistries of both sides.

In addition to his novels, Aguinis has published several books of essays. *Carta esperanzada a un general* (Hopeful Letter to a General; 1983) is a book length essay. Rather than a series of letters, however, it is more of a series of observations, commentaries and personal ruminations addressed to the general, in which the author analyzes and dissects traditional military mentality up to the present day, both in a general, historical mode, and also as it has specifically affected Argentina. He observes, thoughtfully, almost gently "General, . . . usted es un parásito. . . no es la fuerza, sino la habilidad para habernos mantenido en el engaño durante centurias, habernos inducido a metabolizar la ficción de su importancia. Pero. . . no lo culpo de esta mentira. No la inventó usted, sino que la inventamos entre nosotros. . . en nuestro desamparo, inventamos a los militares para calmar el miedo" (General. . . you are a parasite. . . it's not your power, but your ability to have continued to deceive us over the centuries, to have induced us to have metabolized the fiction of your importance. But. . . I don't blame you for this lie. You didn't invent it, but we who invented it among ourselves. . . in our forsakenness we invited the military to calm our fears [14]). He notes that the rigorous education and authoritarian training of the military preclude humor, introspection, creativity, and independence in order to inculcate such blind obedience, conformity, rigidity, and loyalty to the military clan and superiors that any observation or admission of defects are precluded. He comments that "tres profesiones mantienen una relación particularmente intensa con la muerte: . . . el médico la combate, el sacerdote la endulza, y el militar la produce" (three professions maintain a particularly intense relationship with death: . . . the doctor fights it, the priest sweetens it, and the military man produces it [139]). Comparing the military man's attachment to the service with a child's attachment to its mother, Aguinis observes that it is equally absurd to expect either dependent to criticize what nurtures it (158) and finally concludes that violence is as necessary as oxygen to perpetuate the military for "sin violencia en el mundo, no habría militares" (without violence in the world, there would be no military [127]).

El valor de escribir (The Courage to Write; 1985) is a collection of some of Aguinis's published and unpublished essays in which the author discusses a variety of topics indicative of his wide-ranging interests. Some essays discuss the importance of words to articulate man's relation with the universe, the power of written words to preserve and document these concepts or the "valor de escribir" sometimes needed to overcome fear, caution, and self-interest to publish one's written words. One essay comments on the concept of so-called best sellers noting that they are produced as much by skillful marketing as by public popularity and notes that quantity should not be equated with quality. Others discuss the work of contemporary writers like Bernardo Verbitsky (1907-79) and Jorge Luis Borges (1899-1986) or the works of a variety of classical and contemporary artists and musicians noting that genius and madness are frequently associated. Some essays may have been speeches presented to special groups (such as his fellow neurosurgeons), others deal with myths by or about Jews or Jewish traditions. He writes ironically of the "book of the year" (The National Constitution); describes the private professor-run "underground universities" that maintained education despite the official closure of established universities;

decries the ease with which public opinion can be manipulated and reminds the reader that it is not enough to be free to stop being a slave, one must begin to speak out. Finally, Aguinis expresses a note of hope: repression is giving way in Argentina, order is being restored, democracy, though imperfect, is taking hold and must be fostered dynamically, without violence, the country must learn to tolerate differences of opinion.

In *Un país de novela* (A Land of Fiction; 1988) Aguinis provides an excellent review of Argentine history from indigenous, precolonial times to the present along with insightful observations into the Argentine character from a clearly personal but insightful point of view. The melancholy fatalism and the ironic humor expressed in the tangos; the concept of "quien no es vivo es zonzo" (whoever is not clever is a dunce) resulting in a systematic violation of law; the chaotic political swings from democracy to military dictatorships; the significance of the valiant, loyal, independent gaucho, Martín Fierro, hero of the famous literary work by the same name that most Argentines recognize as representative of their collective identity—all are treated in this collection of essays. Aguinis concludes that the Argentina people carry in their hearts has, in fact, ceased to exist. It has been replaced by a new reality which he urges his readers to accept as better than their long history of oppressive political hypocrisy. Ever the optimist, Aguinis claims that Argentines now understand the causes of their crises. By correcting corruption, they are learning to resolve rather then merely confront their country's problems; they are beginning to see small successes and to be more truly free.

A fourth volume of essays, *Elogio de la culpa* (In Praise of Guilt; 1993), is an innovative text which follows the style of Erasmus's (1466-1536) *The Praise of Folly* (1509). Aguinis attempts to literally unveil the hidden meanings of guilt, following the metaphor of Salomé's Dance of the Seven Veils.

Beside these novels and essays, Aguinis also has published three volumes of short stories of uneven length and quality ranging from five to twenty pages. Although his stories are interesting and varied, they are sometimes stilted, forced, or obscure, as if the author is trying too hard to be as cerebral as Borges or is striving too hard for a surprise ending. Aguinis's tales often reflect the author's own interests in medicine, psychology, psychoanalysis, or music. *Importancia por contacto* (Importance by Contact; 1983), a book of seven short stories could well be subtitled "Variations on the Theme of Jonas." Each is preceded by a brief but appropriate quotation from the Book of Jonas hinting at the story line. All of the stories in this collection are written in a vigorous, lively style that conveys an element of suspense and makes the reader think. Their topics range from the humorous to the discomfiting, from psychological investigation to social criticism. We read of the family hounded out of their apartment by the alarmed neighborhood consortium after they had received a threatening anonymous letter; the grave digger who helps business along with a bit of cyanide; the generous, but insecure individual who aspires to impress others with the importance of his contacts; the two friends who having parted ways after an early commitment to Zionism—one going to a kibbutz, the other into a successful business career—meet after many years, only to upbraid each other; the resentful partner of an architectural firm who plots the destruction of his erstwhile partners or the bright idealistic young aide to the director of a civic organization who quits, overwhelmed with disillusionment by the vacuous self-serving of the organization, its members and directors.

A second collection of short stories, published as *Operativo siesta* (Working Siesta; 1978), is noteworthy for the variety of its tales, each qualified by a parenthetical description following its title: "oddities," "romance," "nightmare," "mischief," "elegy," etc. Highly original, the stories vary from humorous or pathetic to ironic and moralistic as they describe an impotent young husband erroneously accused of attempting to cover up an incestuous relationship with his well-meaning mother-in-law when her supposed corpse surprises thieves by emerging from a catatonic state; a mischievous child who places his infant brother in a path of oncoming traffic, convinced that the magic shoe on which he rested the baby will safely waft him aloft at the onslaught of traffic; the reunion of three brothers whose dreams of glory and world travel have gone awry; the priest who announces the miracle of finding a small casketful of gold coins and gems beneath the Virgin's alter, and refuses to believe they have been stolen from the bedroom of the town's exemplary young widow; the blue-eyed mistress who arrives unannounced at the home of her fifty-year-old lover pretending to be his visiting cousin from Mexico and is dearly bought off—only to have the real cousin destroy the charade; the young couple whose gynecologist only pretends to perform three abortions in three months because his young client is so determined not to have children; the uncomprehending Jewish child who believed that local officials were planning to honor his father when in fact they had come to burn him at the stake; the aspiring writer whose supportive wife dies after reading the letter announcing that his third book of poems has been accepted for publication or the exacting piano teacher whose stellar student, obsessed with her drive for perfection, immolates herself on the day of her debut.

The stories from these two books along with two other stories that had appeared separately, "La torre de amor" (The Tower of Love) and "Sebastian" were republished in a third volume entitled *Y la rama llena de frutos* (And the Branch Full of Fruit; 1986). In "La torre" a son torches his family home after realizing that his dying father's feverish ramblings about fertile Gods visiting his wife in the mansion's tower have revealed the questionable truth of his paternity. In "Sebastian," an autopsy reveals the intriguing discovery that the protagonist had seemed to be an incompetent idiot only because his senses were crossed: he had heard with his eyes and seen with his ears.

In addition to his literary production, Aguinis has published more than thirty-five scientific articles in professional journals in France, Austria, Spain and Argentina and served for ten years as editor of a medical journal *Anales de la Clínica Regional del Sud*, (Annals of the Southern Regional Clinic). In recent years he has become increasingly active in national affairs, serving first as Assistant Secretary of State for Cultural Affairs, then as Secretary from 1983 to 1987. As Secretary he created PRONDEC (Programa Nacional de Democratización de la Cultura), an altruistic program he headed until 1989 and whose history and achievements are recorded in a collection of essays entitled *Memorias de una siembra* (Recollection of a Seed; 1990) which he edited.

Aguinis has been honored not only with literary awards but also with the Annual Silver Plaque of the EFE Spanish World News Agency, (EFE signifies literally, the Spanish spelling for the letter "F" which was used here to represent three "F's": Franco, Faith and Falange.), for his contributions to Hispanic language and culture. He has been designated a Knight of Arts and Letters by France; won the National Prize in Sociology; been awarded the University Reform Award by Argentine universities and even been nominated for UNESCO's Award for Peace Education.

PRIMARY BIBLIOGRAPHY
Creative Writing

Brown. Buenos Aires: Delegación de Asociaciones Israelitas Argentinas, 1977.
Cantata de los diablos. Barcelona: Planeta, 1972.
El combate perpetuo. (Reedition of *Brown*). Buenos Aires: Planeta, 1981. Also, Buenos Aires: Sudamericana, 1995.
La conspiración de los idiotas. Buenos Aires: Emecé, 1979.
La cruz invertida. Barcelona: Planeta, 1970.
La gesta del marrano. Buenos Aires: Planeta, 1991.
"The Homage." *Present Tense* 2.4 (Summer 1975): 42.
Importancia por contacto. Buenos Aires: Planeta, 1983.
Operativo siesta. Buenos Aires: Planeta, 1977.
Profanación del amor. Barcelona: Planeta, 1982.
"Profeta en Nínive." In *Cuentos judíos latinoamericanos*. Ed. Ricardo Feierstein. Buenos Aires: Milá, 1989. 114-33.

Refugiados. Buenos Aires: Losada, 1969, 1970, 1976.

"Short Story Contest." Trans. by Norman Thomas di Giovanni and Susan Ashe. In *Celeste Goes Dancing and Other Stories: An Argentine Collection.* Ed. Norman Thomas di Giovanni. San Francisco: North Point Press, 1990. 75-84.

Todos los cuentos. Buenos Aires: Sudamericana, 1995.

Y la rama llena de frutos. Buenos Aires: Sudamericana/Planeta, 1986.

Nonfiction

Carta esperanzada a un general: puente sobre el abismo. Buenos Aires: Sudamericana/Planeta, 1983.

La cuestión judía vista desde el Tercer Mundo. Río Cuarto: Librería Superior, 1974. Also, Buenos Aires: Centro Cultural I. L. Peretz, 1986.

"De la legitimación apologética a la crítica reparadora." *Hispamérica* 14.42 (1985): 57-64.

Elogio de la culpa. Buenos Aires: Planeta, 1993.

"Hopeful Letter to a General: A Fragment." Trans. by David William Foster. *The Massachusetts Review* 27.3-4 (1986): 712-21.

Judaísmo y psicoanálisis. Buenos Aires: Fundación Tzedaka, 1993.

Maimónides: sacerdote de los oprimidos. Buenos Aires: Ediciones Biblioteca Popular Judía, 1976.

Maimónides, un sabio avanzado. Buenos Aires: Editorial Iwo, 1963.

Un país de novela: viaje hacia la mentalidad de los argentinos. Buenos Aires: Planeta, 1988.

"La perpetua tensión entre institución y creador." In *El imaginario judío en la literatura de América Latina: visión y realidad.* Buenos Aires: Grupo Editorial Shalom, 1990. 172-73.

El valor de escribir. Buenos Aires: Sudamericana/Planeta, 1985.

Editions

Memoria de una siembra. Buenos Aires: Planeta, 1990.

SECONDARY BIBLIOGRAPHY
Criticism

Aizenberg, Edna. "Las peripecias de una metáfora: el sefaradismo literario judeoargentino." *Noaj* 6.7-8 (1992): 54-59.

Avellaneda, Andrés. "El análisis del autoritarismo en el ensayo argentino contemporáneo: notas sobre *Carta esperanzada a un general* de Marcos Aguinis." *Hispanic Journal* 6.2 (1985): 187-97.

Foster, David William. "Argentine Sociopolitical Commentary, the Malvinas Conflict, and Beyond: Rhetoricizing a National Experience." *Latin American Research Review* 22.1 (1987): 7-34.

Najenson, José Luis. Rev. of *La gesta del marrano. Noaj* 6.7-8 (1992) 152-53.

Paley Francescato, Martha. "Marcos Aguinis: A Controversial Argentine Jewish Writer." *Folio* 17 (1987): 57-63.

—. "Prólogo." *Y la rama llena de frutos.* Buenos Aires: Sudamericana/Planeta, 1986. 9-16.

Sarrocchi Carreño, Augusto César. "*Camisa limpia* y *La gesta del marrano*: dos voces para una misma problemática." *Revista signos* (Chile) 25.31-32 (1992): 155-65.

Schneider, Judith Morganroth. "Marcos Aguinis: Shifting Lines of Difference Between the Other and the Self." In *Tradition and Innovation: Reflections on Latin American Jewish Writing.* Ed. Robert DiAntonio and Nora Glickman. Albany: SUNY Press, 1993. 135-46.

Schraibman, José. Rev. of *La gesta del marrano. Hispamérica* 21.63 (1992): 89-91.

Senkman, Leonardo. "Crónica de un palestino: la identidad gemela de la pareja judeo-árabe." In *La identidad judía en la literatura argentina.* Buenos Aires: Pardés, 1983. 395-99.

Sloer de Godfrid, Fanny Norah, and Edda Lucchesi de Ramacciotti. "El judaísmo subyacente en la obra de Marcos Aguinis." *Ensayos sobre judaísmo latinoamericano.* Proceedings of the V Congreso Internacional de Investigadores sobre Judaísmo Latinoamericano, Buenos Aires, 14-19 August, 1989. Buenos Aires: Milá, 1990. 353-65.

Weinstein, Ana E., and Miryam E. Gover de Nasatsky, comps. *Escritores judeo-argentinos: bibliografía 1900-1987.* 2 vols. Buenos Aires: Milá, 1994. I.25-31.

Interviews

Lóizaga, Patricio. "Marcos Aguinis." In his *La contradicción argentina.* Buenos Aires: Emecé, 1995. 13-41.

Moncalvo, Mona. "Marcos Aguinis." In her *Entrelíneas: confesiones y opiniones de once escritores en diálogo con Mona Moncalvo.* Buenos Aires: Planeta, 1993. 13-31.

Paley Francescato, Martha. "Entrevista con Marcos Aguinis." *Revista de estudios hispánicos* 19.1 (1985): 117-38.

Rita Gardiol

BARNATÁN, MARCOS RICARDO (Argentina; 1946)

Marcos Ricardo Barnatán was born in Buenos Aires in 1946 into a Sephardic family of Hispano-Syrian origin. In 1965, his family left Argentina and relocated in Madrid. Barnatán is prolific, with credentials in scholarly writing, poetry, and fiction. He has published editions on works as diverse as *Gilgamesh*, Manuel Mujica Láinez's (1910-84) novel *Bomarzo* (1962), and Jorge Luis Borges's (1899-1986) *Narraciones* (Narrations; 1988); the introduction to Bernard-Henri Lévy's (1948) *El diablo en la cabeza* (*Diable en tête*; 1985); and anthologies of the Beat Generation and Hispanic erotic poetry. His compilation of *Poesía erótica castellana (del siglo X a nuestros días)* (Erotic Castillian Poetry [from the 10th Century to the Present]; 1974) includes *jarchas* (i.e. Spanish poetry written in Hebrew or Arabic), the passage on "las dueñas chicas" (short women) from the *Libro de buen amor* (The Book of Good Love; 1343?) by Arcipreste de Hita (1283?-1350?), the Marqués de Santillana's (1398-1458) "Serranilla de la Finojosa" (Poem of the Good Woman from Finojosa), Santa Teresa's (1515-82) "Vivo sin vivir en mí" (I Live Without Living in Me), and San Juan de la Cruz's (1542-91) "Cántico espiritual" (Spiritual Canticle); in addition, there are selections from Sor Juana Inés de la Cruz (1542-91), Francisco de Quevedo y Villegas (1580-1645), José Martí (1853-95), Ramón del Valle-Inclán (1866-1936), and Rubén Darío (1867-1916). Barnatán also included his own poem "Erótica," written in English. *Las metáforas de Eduardo Sanz* (Eduardo Sanz's Metaphors; 1976) is a study of that contemporary Spanish artist's work and is rich in pictures of the paintings and in quotations from such writers as Oscar Wilde (1854-1900), Samuel Beckett (1906-89), and of course, Borges. *Fernando Savater contra el Todo* (Fernando Savater Against Everything; 1984) is an extended interview with the intellectual about his life as well as philosophy, literature, and theatre. *Acontecimientos que cambiaron la historia* (Events that Changed History; 1975) contains such diverse subjects as "Los mitos originarios" (Myths of Origin [Adam and Eve, Moses, Buddha]); "Estrellas y serpientes" (Stars and Serpents [Columbus, Copernicus]); "Los tiempos modernos" (Modern Times [American Independence, the French Revolution, Marx and Marxism]); and "El espejo del presente" (Mirror of the Present [October Revolution, 23 August 1944, Picasso, Surrealist Art]). *La Kábala: una mística del lenguaje* (Kabbalah: Mystical Language; 1974) gives the numerical equivalents of the letters of the Hebrew alphabet and explains the relationship of the Hebrew letters to the plants and to the symbology of Tarot cards. In addition to the edition of *Narraciones*, Barnatán has written four books on Borges, whose influence is evident throughout the literary production of his disciple. In the works of both writers, there are labyrinths; Jewish mysticism, such as Kabbalah and Zohar; erudition in the historical and mythological allusions; the creation of not only literary characters, but of bibliographies of those characters; the use of poetry in works of prose; and Argentina as subject matter.

El horóscopo de las infantas (The Princesses' Horoscope; 1988) is a collection of stories written by Barnatán between 1980-88 and derives from his reading of Borges and Vladimir Nabokov (1899-1977); the title comes from a poem by José María Eguren (1874-1942), a Peruvian poet. One of the stories is "Fragmentos del diario de David Jerusalem" (Fragments of David Jerusalem's Diary), to whom Borges makes reference in his short story "Deutsches Requiem." According to Barnatán's note, Jerusalem, a poet, was killed by the Nazis in 1943 and his work is collected in a bilingual English-Yiddish version presumably published in New York in 1957 (the only reference to David Jerusalem in bibliographical archives appears under Barnatán's name). References to Nazis already appeared in the novel El laberinto de Sión (The Labyrinth of Zion; 1971), which he began writing twenty years before Horóscopo.

Barnatán's earliest writing is in poetry. He published Acerca de los viajes (On Travels) in 1966. Its subject matter is largely traditional—nature, the sea—but the ideas are not. "Buenos Aires tras la niebla" (Buenos Aires Behind the Mist), begins with a quotation from Borges. Nostalgia for his native city will be a theme in the recent novel, Con la frente marchita (With a Wrinkled Brow; 1989). His Tres poemas fantásticos (Three Fantastic Poems; 1967) are "Alucinación junto al Manzanares" (Hallucination by the Manzanares River), "El anáfora funesta del divino veneno" (The Ill-fated Anaphora of Divine Poison), and "Asamblea de brujas" (Gathering of Witches); and Muerte serena (Serene Death; 1970) contains four poems, one with a reference to labyrinths. El oráculo invocado. Poesía (1965-1983) (The Oracle Invoked: Poetry; 1984) combines in a single volume the poems which appeared originally in separate collections: Los pasos perdidos (Lost Footsteps; 1968), El libro del talismán (The Book of the Talisman; 1970), Arcana mayor (Greater Secret; 1973), and La escritura del vidente (The Prophet's Writing; 1979). Some of the poems in Los pasos perdidos are rich in Jewish content. "Visión de Canaán" (Vision of Canaan) is a meditation on the ancient cities of Israel; Jerusalem, Jericho, Jenin, Nablus, Hebron, and Masada. "Luminarias de Januca" (Chanukah Candles) is a reflection on the Jewish diaspora. "La ofrenda de Ahína" (The Offering of Ahina) treats the offerings in the Holy Temple; and "La casa de Dios" (The House of God) describes the Morning Service with the reading from the Torah in the synagogue: each morning is a renewal of the Covenant. The poem's refrain is "nunca desamparé al pueblo mío" (I shall never abandon my people). "Cuando el cuerpo de Israel salió disuelto en humo" (When the Body of Israel Went Up in Smoke) offers the Jewish People the assurance that there is always light for them behind the cloud of smoke. "Oración en Venecia" (Prayer in Venice) is a plea to Hashem to hear the voice of the just after the horrors of the ovens and the crematoria. The final selection, "El oráculo invocado (1979-1983)" includes a poem called "Borges." Finally, there is *Cinco poemas de David Jerusalem* (Five Poems by David Jerusalem; 1986), composed by Barnatán.

Barnatán has written four works which he calls novels. In her essay "Barnatán: joven, brillante novelista" (Barnatán: Young, Brilliant Novelist) in the collection *Yo amo a Columbo* (I Love Columbo; 1979) Elisa Lerner (1932) opines that one word describes *El laberinto de Sión*: "precocidad" (precociousness). She identifies not only "el universo borgiano" (Borges's universe), but also a Proustian influence. She sees, too, that "su condición de judío prefigura todo drama. Acaso define su precocidad" (his condition as a Jew prefigures every act. Perhaps defines his precociousness [328]). He also shows a profound sensitivity throughout *Laberinto* about Jewish history and Law as well as Germany and the Nazis. His second novel is *Gor* (1973). Barnatán reveals in *La escritura del vidente* that the title *Gor* has kabbalistic, numerical value. He uses as his point of departure the letters aleph, mem, and shin. Aleph=Germen primero y único (first and only germ); mem=Orgía fecunda y líquida (fecund and liquid orgy); shin=Renueva todo lo que existe (renews everything that exists). *Diano* (1982) is the third part of the trilogy which contains *Laberinto* and *Gor*. It is a story of love and death and is characterized by wordplay and contains no capital letters. Barnatán, like the Spanish writer Miguel de Unamumo (1864-1936), calls his characters *agonistas* (agonizers).

While his novelistic trilogy contains erudition and games that border on pretention (or *precocidad*), *Con la frente marchita* follows the format of a traditional novel. It is a semi-autobiographical work about a Jewish writer, who, after twenty years in Madrid returns to his native Buenos Aires. Once again there are many religious and literary references to Kabbalah; to labyrinths; to Borges and covertly to the latter's short story "Emma Zunz." The character in the story denies that the work is autobiographical and insists that it only tells the story of an author, whose obligation it is to write a great novel.

PRIMARY BIBLIOGRAPHY
Creative Writing
Acerca de los viajes. Madrid: Pájaro Cascabel, 1966.
Ante mí: poesía del hombre mutable. Buenos Aires: Nuevo Hombre, 1964.

Arcana mayor. Madrid: VISOT, 1973.

Cinco poemas de David Jerusalem. Madrid: Tapir, 1986.

Con la frente marchita. Barcelona: Versal, 1989.

Diano. Madrid: Júcar, 1982.

La escritura del vidente. Barcelona: La Gaya Ciencia, 1979.

Gor. Barcelona: Barral/Hispánica Nova, 1973.

El horóscopo de las infantas. Madrid: Dragón, 1988.

El laberinto de Sión. Barcelona: Barral/Hispánica Nova, 1971.

El libro del talismán. Madrid: Azur, 1970.

Muerte serena. Málaga: Cuadernos de María Isabel, 1970.

El oráculo invocado: poesía (1965-1983). Madrid: Visor, 1984.

Los pasos perdidos. Madrid: Ediciones Rialp, 1968.

Tres poemas fantásticos. Málaga: Librería Anticuaria El Guadalhorce, 1967.

Nonfiction

Acontecimientos que cambiaron la historia. Planeta: Barcelona, 1975.

Borges. Madrid: EPESA, 1972

Borges. Barcelona: Barcanoca, 1984.

Conocer Borges y su obra. Barcelona: DOPESA, 1978.

Fernando Savater contra el Todo. Madrid: Anjana, 1984.

Jorge Luis Borges. Madrid: Júcar, 1972

La Kábala: Una mística del lenguaje. Barcelona: Barral, 1974.

Las metáforas de Eduardo Sanz. Madrid: Rayuela, 1976.

Editions

Antología de la "Beat Generation." Barcelona: Plaza y Janés, 1970.

Narraciones/Jorge Luis Borges. Madrid: Cátedra, 1988.

Poesía erótica castellana (del siglo X a nuestros diás). Madrid: Júcar, 1974.

SECONDARY BIBLIOGRAPHY

Aizenberg, Edna. "*El laberinto de Sión*: Barnatán's Borgesian Quest for Sephardic Identity." *Yiddish* 9.1 (1993): 9-18.

Lerner, Elisa. "Barnatán: joven, brillante novelista." In her *Yo amo a Columbo o la pasión dispersa.* Caracas: Monte Avila, 1979. 327-29.

Lindstrom, Naomi. "Marcos Ricardo Barnatán: The New Novel as Access to Kabbalah." In her *Jewish Issues in Argentine Literature: From Gerchunoff to Szichman.* Columbia, MO: U of Missouri P, 1989. 130-45.

Senkman, Leonardo. *La identidad judía en la literatura argentina.* Buenos Aires: Pardés, 1983. 342-44, 399-400.

Dennis A. Klein

BERMAN, SABINA (Mexico; 1954)

Sabina Berman, along with Angeles Mastretta (1949) and Laura Esquivel (1950), are part of a flowering of Mexican women writers which began in the 1960s. Many of Berman's literary predecessors and contemporaries—Margo Glantz (1930), Angelina Muñiz (1937), Esther Seligson (1941), Gloria Gervitz (1943)—are daughters of East European Jewish immigrants. Berman began her career as a film scriptwriter with *La tía Alejandra* (Aunt Alejandra; 1979) written with Delfina Careaga. In 1988 she published *Lunas* (Moons), an experimental collection of poetry which was lyrical and erotic in style. But even in her poetry Berman was striving for a tridimensional, theatrical effect. The poems of *Mariposa* (Butterfly; 1974) show a deliberate break in chronology, as they leap between realism and the fantastic in an attempt to follow the disorderly rhythm brought about by drug consumption.

Berman's major and most successful production is in the theater, where she examines Mexico's culture and folklore, as she strives to integrate experiences of the past to achieve a better understanding of the present. Propelled by the rebellious spirit of the sixties, she deconstructs both official history and national myths, providing her own original versions.

The successive changes in titles that Berman's plays have undergone over the years, also reflect significant thematic, stylistic, and structural revisions. Her initial monologue *Esta no es una obra de teatro* (This is Not a Play; 1975) became *Un actor se repara* (An Actor Corrects Himself). *Bill*, which won her the first Premio Nacional de Teatro (National Theatre Award) in 1979, changed to *Yankee*. *Un buen trabajador del piolet* (A Good Ice-Pick Worker; 1979) became *Rompecabezas* (Puzzle), and *Marranos* (1983), which also won the National Theatre Award, became *Anatema* (Anathema) and later *Herejía* (Heresy).

For Berman, theater is a social spectacle. It is also the natural stage for producing dramatic stories out of legends and real history. Such is the case of *La maravillosa historia del chiquito Pingüica* (The Marvelous Story of Little Pinguica), which was first produced in 1983—a humorous play based on the Mayan legend of the *Popol Vuh*, the Mayan Bible.

In writing *Aguila o sol: historia de la conquista del imperio azteca* (Eagle or Sun: History of the Conquest of the Aztec Empire; 1988), she attempted to chronicle Mexico's history from its origins to the destruction of the Aztec civilization. The play deals with the fear of failure that pursues all Mexicans.

Here Berman defies the European version of history and casts doubt on the myths based on patriarchal images.

Directed to a young audience, *Aguila o sol* integrates the dramatic tradition of the farce with Indian codes, and uses linguistic anachronisms and surrealist devices. She also displays some characteristics of the comic strip—billboard titles and humorous interjections. The style is also eclectic in that it combines techniques of social realism with those of street theater and satire. The American critic Sandra Cypess does not regard this as a shortcoming (cf. *La malinche in Mexican Literature*). It is one of the work's strongest features, since it reveals the conflicts that unravel from the conquest itself. Cortés is depicted as a feeble-minded, grotesque figure, whose unintelligible Spanish requires an interpreter. Ironically, his lover, Doña Marina/La Malinche, translates Cortés's words to a Hispanic audience into a bastardized language that further stresses his limitations, and makes the public identify with the vanquished Indian: La Malinche embodies a new Mexican idiosyncracy composed of a blend of cultures. She is not depicted as a traitor, since her own people are also to blame for their defeat: the Tlazcaltecas, ancient enemies of the Aztecas take sides with the Spaniards and submit to them.

Paradoxically, Moctezuma is the main exponent of *malinchismo*, a deference to foreigners and a rejection of one's native culture. Obsessed with the theological meaning of events, he believes that Cortés is the god Quetzacoatl making his prophesied return. He welcomes the invaders, offers them the treasures of his empire, and submits without a struggle. *Aguila o sol* implies that both patriarchal systems—the Indian and the Spanish—ought to be subverted.

The confrontation of cultures and of historical periods—a constant feature in Berman's plays—is related to her own origins: a descendent of Austrian and Polish-Jewish immigrants, she was brought up in a milieu that exposed her to various languages and cultures. Her family dynamics permeates her entire work. At the same time, Berman is intent on understanding her Mexican heritage, both immediate and remote.

Berman's political theatre is also her most intimate and audacious. The tone of *Muerte súbita* (Sudden Death; 1988) is tragicomic. Ostensibly, it centers on the relationship of a couple determined to inhabit a house which is about to tumble down. Upon the arrival of a stranger, everything in the house is destroyed. The building represents Mexico in decay: there is no one there to save it.

Bill is similar to *Muerte súbita* in its treatment of the clash of cultures and the ambiguity of sexual relations. It tells of a Vietnam veteran in Mexico who believes he sees the Virgin of Guadalupe holding baby Jesus in her arms.

Pretending to be a builder, he gains entrance to the woman's house and ends up shooting her husband. On a metaphorical level, *Bill* is about the cultural clash between two bordering countries: the United States and Mexico. The Yankee, defeated in Vietnam, travels to Mexico in search of stability in a new country. He enters a stranger's house to fix it, but invades it instead.

By choosing to write about particular historical events, Berman explores her own Eastern European roots and presents them to her generation. *Rompeca-bezas* (Puzzle) dramatizes patricide—in a figurative sense—from several angles. It describes the gruesome assassination of Leon Trotsky who was killed in 1940 by a blow to his head with an ice pick. Berman began to write this play after being a television witness to several other assassinations: The Kennedys, Martin Luther King Jr., Anwar Sadat, and attempts on the lives of Ronald Reagan and the Pope. Berman interprets patricide as a call to action for her generation. Coming of age after the wave of student revolts of the late sixties, when the hippie age was fading, Berman found herself disenchanted with contemporary politics and ideologies. Patricide was viewed by her as a desperate gesture to fend off despair and nihilism.

Berman's defiance of authority, her skeptical view of history, and her criticism of established institutions, is best represented in her play *Herejía*, which relates to her own ancestry and to her perception of the Jew as a wanderer and a rebel. This epic play exhibits different types of Jewish identity. Jews are pulled by the temptation to submit to Catholic religion and to save their lives and property. But they are also subject to a deep-seated love of Jehovah, their own God. Set in the seventeenth century, *Herejía* depicts a situation of extreme tension, when the Holy Inquisition was at the height of its tyranny. Based on a celebrated Inquisition trial, and inspired by the autobiography of Luis de Carvajal, *Herejía* explores the causes of the exodus of the Carvajal family from Spain, their prosperity in Mexico, and finally their fall when accused of being secret Jews disguised as Catholics. In the style of the Passover Haggadah, Berman characterizes different types of Jews and explores the religious preferences of each, by placing them at a crossroads. Don Luis de Carvajal is the atheist, the individualist, whose mission is to survive during times of intolerance. Luis de Carvajal, El Mozo, is the Jew who delves deep into the words of the Torah to experience God. From this perspective, he observes the closeness of his own religion to Catholicism. Agustín de Carvajal, a Dominican friar, is the Jew brought up as a Catholic to preserve his Jewish blood, lest his family be annihilated. Finally, Jesús Baltazar is a Christian who became a Jew: "que se hizo judío por bien comerciar y por judío terminó hecho ceniza" (for succeeding in business, and for being a Jew, [he] ended up in ashes [*Teatro de Sabina Berman* 167]).

This treatment of an ideological polemic—by casting doubt on what appears to be true—is characteristic of Berman's dramaturgy. Her most recent example being *Entre Villa y una mujer desnuda* (Between Villa and a Naked Woman; 1993), a comedy that reveals her skepticism about the legacy of the Mexican revolution and about the futility of such vast human sacrifice. Pancho Villa is depicted here as the *gran macho* of the Mexican Revolution and as the alter ego of the protagonist. Berman establishes parallels by having the ghost of Pancho Villa interrupt the action and advise Adrián, his modern counterpart, that in order to be a so-called real man he has to be a consummate *chingón* (son-of-a-bitch) and violate everyone's rights.

Villa returns to the world of the living to spread his machista legacy. Just as he proves to be impotent in the end, trying to shoot a cannon and failing, Adrián, the modern biographer displays his failure in his pathetic relationship with women. Berman offers an alternative version of masculinity, more in keeping with the concept of gender as an aspect of personality, combined in different ways within each man and woman. The new man is presented in the person of Ariel, who is driven by a need to explore all the aspects of his character.

Berman had previously analyzed the polarities of the sexes in *El suplicio del placer* (The Torment of Pleasure; 1992), where she redefined the limits of the genders. El (He) and Ella (She) shared a false moustache that allowed them to experiment with alternative realities, giving her masculine traits and him feminine traits.

Berman's first novel, *La bobe* (Yiddish for The Grandmother; 1990), is mostly impressionistic. Here the confrontation between logic and the experience of religion is embodied in the relationship between the grandmother and the narrator-protagonist. The latter is a young Mexican searching for revelations from her past, which only her grandmother can transmit. The Bobe is a kind of anachronism: she is a Viennese aristocratic Jew who lives in Mexico, but disassociates herself from Mexico's culture and society. To the granddaughter the old woman has the gift of alchemy, which enables her to transform the everyday into the sacred. The child's mother, on the other hand, has acculturated into Mexican life. Without rejecting either world, the child finds a synthesis that is based on the mystical perception of an infinite, eternal light—the *Ein sof*, symbolized in simple acts that are sacralized and turned into celebrations. This is the message that the girl gathers from her daily contact with her mother and her grandmother. Narrated exclusively in women's voices, *La bobe* provides the reader with a historical trajectory of Mexican Judaism over the course of this century, as it moves from orthodoxy to atheism, and from there to a more universal world view.

PRIMARY BIBLIOGRAPHY

El árbol de humo. México: Consejo Nacional para la Cultura y las Artes, 1994.

Amante de lo ajeno. México, D.F.: Planeta, 1994.

Bill. In *Más teatro joven.* Ed. Emilio Carballido. México, D.F.: Editores Mexicanos Unidos, 1982. 123-71. Also, *Avanzada: más teatro joven de México.* Ed. Emilio Carballido. México, D.F.: Editores Mexicanos Unidos, 1984. 113-61.

La bobe. México, D.F.: Planeta, 1990.

Los dientes. Tramoya 39 (1994): 123-34.

En el nombre de Dios. Tramoya 32 (1993): 26-58.

Entre Villa y una mujer desnuda. México, D.F.: Sociedad General de Escritores de México, 1993. Also, México, D.F.: El Milagro, 1994.

Entre Villa y una mujer desnuda; Muerte súbita; El suplicio del placer. México, D.F.: Gaceta, 1994.

El gordo, la pájara y el narco. México, D.F.: Fonca, 1994.

Un grano de arroz. México, D.F.: Seix Barral, 1994.

Lunas. México, D.F.: Katún, 1988.

La maravillosa historia del chiquito Pingüica. México, D.F.: Editores Mexicanos Unidos, 1984.

Muerte súbita. México, D.F.: Katún, 1988.

Poemas de agua. México, D.F.: Shanik, 1986.

El polvo del tiempo. Tramoya 9 (1987): 98-113.

Rompecabezas. México, D.F.: Oasis, 1982.

El suplicio del placer (also includes *El gordo, la pájara y el narco*). México, D.F.: Conaculta, 1994.

Teatro de Sabina Berman (contains *Yankee [Bill]; Rompecabezas; Herejía; Aguila o sol; El suplicio del placer; Esta no es una obra de teatro [Un actor se repara]*). México, D.F.: Editores Mexicanos Unidos, 1985.

Volar. México, D.F.: Posada, 1987.

SECONDARY BIBLIOGRAPHY
Criticism

Burgess, Ronald D. *The New Dramatists of Mexico, 1967-1985.* Lexington, KY: UP of Kentucky, 1991. 80-91.

—. "Sabina Berman's Act of Creative Failure: *Bill.*" *Gestos* 2.3 (1987): 103-13.

Cortés, Eladio. "Sabina Berman." *Dictionary of Mexican Literature.* Ed. Eladio Cortés. Westport, CT: Greenwood Press, 1992. 87-88.

Costantino, Roselyn. "El discurso del poder en *El suplicio del placer* de Sabina Berman." In *De la colonia a la postmodernidad: teoría teatral y crítica sobre teatro latinoamericano.* Ed. Peter Roster and Mario Rojas. Buenos Aires: Galerna/IITCTL, 1992. 245-52.

—. "Resistant Creativity: Interpretative Stategies and Gender Representation in Contemporary Women's Writing in Mexico." Ph.D. diss., Arizona State University, Tempe, 1992.

—. "Sabina Berman." In *Latin American Writers on Gay and Lesbian Themes: A Bio-Critical Sourcebook.* Ed. David William Foster. Westport, CT: Greenwood Press, 1994. 59-63.

Cypess, Sandra Messinger. "Ethnic Identity in the Plays of Sabina Berman." In *Tradition and Innovation: Reflections on Latin American Jewish Writing.* Ed. Robert DiAntonio and Nora Glickman. Albany: SUNY Press, 1993. 165-77.

—. *La Malinche in Mexican Literature.* Austin: U of Texas P, 1991. 133-37.

Guerra, Humberto. "Judíos en la Nueva España: recreación dramática de Sabina Berman." In *América-Europa. De encuentros, desencuentros y encubrimientos (memorias del II Encuentro y Diálogo entre dos Mundos: 1992).* México, D.F.: Universidad Autónoma Metropolitana, 1993. 208-11.

Lockhart, Darrell B. "Growing Up Jewish in Mexico: Sabina Berman's *La bobe* and Rosa Nissán's *Novia que te vea.*" In *The Other Mirror: Women's Narrative in Mexico, 1980-1995.* Ed. Kristine L. Ibsen. Westport, CT: Greenwood, 1997. 159-74.

Magnarelli, Sharon. "Tea for Two: Performing History and Desire in Sabina Berman's *Entre Villa y una mujer desnuda.*" *Latin American Theatre Review* 30.1 (1996): 55-74.

Nigro, Kirsten. "Sexualidad y género: la mujer como signo en el teatro latinoamericano." In *Semiótica y teatro latinoamericano.* Ed. Fernando de Toro. Buenos Aires: Galerna/IITCTL, 1990. 257-66.

Ochoa, Hermida, and Alejandro E. T. "Entre lo crudo y los amaneceres: introspección al teatro de Sabina Berman." *Teatro de Sabina Berman.* México, D.F.: Editores Mexicanos Unidos, 1985. 5-10.

Interviews

Ramírez, Luis Enrique. Two part interview with Sabina Berman. *La Jornada* 22 Feb., 1995: 25; *La Jornada* 23 Feb., 1995: 27.

Nora Glickman

BIBLIOWICZ, AZRIEL (Colombia; 1949)

Azriel Bibliowicz was born in Bogotá in 1949. He earned his Ph.D. in sociology from Cornell University and currently resides in Bogotá where he works as a journalist and university professor. As a sociologist Bibliowicz has authored a number of volumes and articles dealing with Colombian society, in particular issues concerning children.

Bibliowicz's first, and currently only, work of fiction is his rather intriguing novel, *El rumor del astracán* (The Rustle of Astrakhan; 1991). The novel was on the best-seller list in Colombia for several weeks and met with wide critical and public acclaim. It is essentially a historical text which recounts the Jewish immigrant experience in the Bogotá of the 1930s. The text is divided into "sequences" which provide cinematographic portrayals of the characters and the events which shape their lives and design their destinies. The story revolves around the lives of Jacob and Saúl who leave their native village in the Old World to make it in America. They initially plan, as did so many immigrants, to amass a small fortune and return in two years time. Of course, they both end up settling in Bogotá. Through connections with relatives, Saúl arranges a wife for Jacob. Ruth, once arriving in America, becomes one of the novel's main characters. She struggles for independence, and eventually is able to gain both intellectual and sexual liberation, although she also strives to maintain her Jewish religious heritage. The author unfolds a variety of problems that the characters must deal with, including issues of assimilation and anti-Jewish sentiment within a strongly Catholic environment. Saúl seeks to assimilate quickly in order to fit in more easily and thereby earn a better living. He soon learns that he can make more money by selling scented pictures of Catholic saints than he can selling clothes and household items. The rather large Jewish community is portrayed as being close knit and willing to give a helping hand to the newcomers. Jacob struggles to remain a pious man and dreams of opening a religious book store with texts in Yiddish and Hebrew.

One of the more fascinating intertextual allusions in the novel is to the famous Argentine Jewish writer Alberto Gerchunoff (1884-1950) through the fictional character of Moisés Gerchunoff. Moisés is presented as a Jewish agricultural pioneer who settled the colony of Moisesville, Argentina. He tells the Colombian Jews stories of Jewish gauchos of the Argentine pampas and the story of the Baron Mauricio de Hirsch. Moisés is travelling through Latin America collecting funds for the establishment of a Jewish state in Palestine. The majority, mostly the men, are highly suspicious of him, mainly because he is highly secularized, as is evident in his interest in creative literature as opposed to Jewish religious writing. Through Moisés Gerchunoff, Bibliowicz tells of the long history of the Jewish presence in Latin America beginning with the arrival of Columbus, and more specifically the long history of a Jewish presence in Colombia. Bibliowicz is careful to develop his story from the perspective of many different members of the Jewish community, both men and women, pious and secular, and even children. The young boy Gershon provides an ample view into his own world at school as he tries to fit in and struggles against cultural barriers ranging from accusations of being a Christ killer hurled at him by his schoolmates, to the humiliation of being laughed at for being circumcised.

Ruth is perhaps the most interesting of the characters. She undergoes a complete transformation as a person and liberation as a woman. Her father originally forbade her to leave for America to marry Jacob, certain that she was being beguiled into the infamous white slave trade of Buenos Aires. At first Ruth is happy with her new life in Bogotá with Jacob, but she soon realizes that she is still confined to the demands of her husband. Under the excuse of having to earn money to bring her younger brother to Colombia she begins to work for David, a wealthy Jewish merchant and, as she discovers, dealer in contraband. She takes pride in her work as a window dresser and seamstress and she attracts more business for the store. David begins to rely on her for advice and a relationship sparks between them. She unwittingly becomes involved in his scheme of illegally importing astrakhan pelts hidden within teddy bears. The two end up consummating their adulterous affair amid a pile of gutted teddy bears and their illegal lambskin stuffing. Ruth is torn between the religious tradition of Jacob and her family, and her new-found sexual and intellectual liberation achieved through David. David admires her business sense and intelligence, while Jacob constantly berates her for thinking she knows about anything other than the kitchen. The affair is revealed and in the end Jacob dies, ironically in the Synagogue, at the hands of David. The death is described as an accident to the officials since the Jews want no trouble with the police. Many of the sequences revolve around Jewish holidays narrated in very descriptive terms, which are most likely intended to shed light on them for the non-Jewish Colombian reader. It is really quite surprising how completely Bibliowicz has been able to illustrate Jewish life in Colombia during the period. Indeed, the text can be considered as a kind of Colombian *Hester Street*.

An interesting comparison can be made between Jorge Isaacs's (1837-95) *María* (1867), in which a Jewish girl had to change her name and assume a Christian identity in order to live comfortably in nineteenth-century Colombia, and Bibliowicz's characters who are able to openly express their Jewishness. They speak mainly Yiddish among themselves in the streets, businesses, and the barbershop (a favorite gathering spot in the novel) of Bogotá, much to the consternation of the local citizens who repeatedly question why they don't speak "Christian" (i.e., Spanish).

El rumor del astracán is an important text within contemporary Colombian literature as it virtually stands alone as the standard bearer of Jewish literature in that country. One hopes that Bibliowicz will continue to write fiction, and that his text will serve to inspire more literature by Jewish writers in Colombia to be published.

PRIMARY BIBLIOGRAPHY

El rumor del astracán. Bogotá: Planeta, 1991.

SECONDARY BIBLIOGRAPHY

Schraibman, José. Rev. of *El rumor del astracán. Hispamérica* 20.58 (1991): 154-55.

Siemens, William L. Rev. of *El rumor del astracán. Chasqui* 22.2 (1993): 184-85.

Darrell B. Lockhart

BLAISTEN, ISIDORO (Argentina; 1933)

Isidoro Blaisten was born in Concordia, Entre Ríos, on January 12, 1933. His surname is actually Blaistein, but in 1980 the author modified the spelling. His books, therefore, can be found under both spellings. Among other occupations he has worked as a journalist, photographer, and director of literary workshops. He is, of course, also a prolific writer, mostly of short stories. Many of his stories have been translated into English, French and German, and Blaisten has been the recipient of various literary awards and honors.

Early in his career Blaisten was a frequent participant in intellectual gatherings and circles. His first poems were published in leading literary journals such as *El escarabajo de oro* (The Golden Scarab), directed by writer Abelardo Castillo (1935). Within this environment his talent quickly began to be recognized. *Sucedió en la lluvia* (It Happened in the Rain; 1965), a collection of poetry, was his first published work in book form. It won him an award from the Fondo Nacional de las Artes (National Foundation for the Arts).

His first volume of short stories, *La felicidad* (Happiness), appeared in 1969. The collection contains some truly exceptional stories, and the book was well received by critics and the public alike. "El tío Facundo" ("Uncle Facundo") is a particularly disquieting tale about a family that kills an uncle who comes to visit and buries him in a cement wall. It was originally published in the journal *Sur* (South) the year prior to its inclusion in this volume. Another outstanding story is "Los tarmas" (The Termites), about a family who crashes wakes in order to scam the grieving relatives of the deceased. Both stories are indicative of the often absurd characteristics that will define Blaisten's later narrative.

La salvación (Salvation; 1972) was the author's next collection of short fiction in which the two previously mentioned stories are repeated along with eight new tales, and in fact, it can be considered as the continuation of the previous volume. The most praised stories from the collection include "Mishiadura en Aires" (Misery in Buenos Aires), "Victorcito, el hombre oblicuo" (Little Victor, the Oblique Man), and "La salvación" (Salvation), the story that gives the volume its title. Blaisten's generous and hilarious humor brought an all-too-infrequent freshness to the literature of the time. Blaisten's characters have in common their status as what one can identify as the typical schlemiel. One man suffers *mishiadura* (misery and bad luck) because he has the misfortune of belonging to the zodiacal sign of Aries, another finds himself constantly presented with twisted problems and convoluted situations, while a third desperately seeks salvation. These three characters provide a type of sociological cross section of the Argentine urban middle class. Blaisten very effectively portrays the marginated first and second generation immigrant who desires above all else to make it in America, but whose social upward mobility is hampered by societal constraints.

Blaisten has often described his work as constituting a way of organizing chaos, and he views humor as one stage of desperation. He employs his acerbic wit to tenderly caricature the impossible dreams of the anonymous inhabitants of the city. The depiction of absurd urban vicissitudes parodies the disenchantment and insignificant destinies of the city dweller. Blaisten's stories mask a reality marked by migrations and languages of diverse origins where the past has been lost by uprooting and the future is uncertain. The author's use of humor is also a remedy against futile self-commiseration.

El mago (The Magician; 1974) is a collection of short stories and mini-stories, some of them only a few lines long. With *El mago* Blaisten began to formalize his ludic writing style, the result of which is a raw humor that utilizes contrasting linguistic registers, parodic situations, uncommon rhetorical formulations, and lexical freedom.

Blaisten began to enjoy real literary success beginning in 1980, following the publication of his book *Dublín al sur* (South Dublin), which remained a bestseller for several years to follow. The volume is, among other things, a satire of the relationship between literary creation and the mass media. It was translated into French in 1989 and the title story has also been translated into English. As a consequence of *Dublin*'s success, the Buenos Aires publishing house Emecé began to publish one of Blaisten's books every year: *Cerrado por melancolía* (Closed on Account of Melancholy) in 1981, *Cuentos anteriores* (Previous Stories), in 1982 and *Anti-conferencias* (Antilectures) in 1983. Emecé has continued to publish reprints of practically all Blaisten's books.

Cerrado por melancolía contains many biographical elements from the author's own life. It is, in part, the story of the bookstore that he personally ran for seven years on the corner of San Juan and Boedo, a neighborhood steeped in the mythology of the tango. Prior to being a bookstore owner, Blaisten worked as a photographer, taking pictures of people for a fee in the plazas of Buenos Aires.

Anti-conferencias is also highly autobiographical. It contains a variety of anecdotes, ideas, and memories that came about as the result of a series of lectures Blaisten gave at the Sociedad Hebraica Argentina, one of the major Jewish associations in Argentina. The book represents a departure from narrative as the author focuses on creating texts that are much more essayistic in nature. Texts like "Dinero y creación" (Money and Creation) and "Para qué sirve un poeta" (What Good Is a Poet) were widely read and were quickly picked up as models for a new genre that existed somewhere between essay and narrative.

While Blaisten's writing contains only scattered references to a specifically Jewish cultural identity, several of his stories do revolve around Jewish characters and include intimations of Jewish tradition. The story "Violín de fango" (The Mud Violin [written in 1977 and included in *Dublín al sur*]) revolves around the protagonist, Samuelito Socolivsky, an actor and tango singer who goes by the stage name of Nacho Mendoza. Samuelito emulates Agustín Magaldi, a gallant tango star from the 1940s who discovered Eva Perón, and he himself becomes quite famous. "Violín de fango" is in essence a parody, but it does demonstrate the easy assimilation of the Jewish community into Buenos Aires society and the inevitable syncretism that was produced in the new generations. In the story "Lotz no contesta" ("Lotz Makes No Reply") the character Pecheny awakes early one morning with the premonition that his neighbor and lifetime friend, Lotz, has died. His feeling is confirmed when he hears Lotz's wife scream from across the garden fence.

In 1985 Blaisten published a new collection of stories, *A mí nunca me dejaban hablar* (They Never Let Me Speak), followed by *Carroza y reina* (Carriage and Queen) in 1986. The latter received the prestigious Municipality of Buenos Aires literary award and the Faja de Honor (Sash of Honor) granted by the Sociedad Argentina de Escritores (Argentine Writer's Guild). The story "Permiso, maestro" (May I, Master) represents the maturity of the work. In the story Blaisten manipulates two distinct levels of language, corresponding to contrasting characters. The first is a retired Harvard professor, and the second is the neighborhood butcher. It is a highly ironic detective story in which the butcher is a writer and the Harvard professor turns out to be a murderer. The story, armed with Borgesian symmetries—a writer to whom one may say Blaisten is paying homage—presents an almost perfect narrative structure.

Blaisten's next volume of writing, *Cuando éramos felices* (When We Were Happy; 1992), is autobiographical, as the author allows himself to nostalgically reminiscence on days gone by. The work is similar to *Anti-conferencias* in that the texts are written in that undefined genre between narrative and essay. The reader is taken to Concordia, Blaisten's birthplace. His father, a native of Odessa, settled in one of the agricultural colonies established in Argentina at the turn of the century. As a young boy Blaisten moved to the tenement housing in the Barrio Almagro of Buenos Aires with his family: his five older sisters, his widowed mother, his sister the seamstress and brother-in-law the surveyor, and his two older brothers. His brother Enrique was killed by the Nazis in 1945 on the Avenida de Mayo. Also included in *Cuando éramos felices* is the text "De San Telmo a Jerusalén" (From San Telmo to Jerusalem; originally written in 1984). It is based on the author's trip to Israel when he was invited to participate in the first conference for Jewish writers from Latin America, Spain, and Portugal.

One of the least known aspects of Blaisten's work is his poetry. He has always written poetry and continues to do so, yet he has not published any of his poems since *Sucedió en la lluvia*, and, in fact, he refuses to do so. Blaisten's work can be read as being the continuation of the expressionism of Roberto Arlt (1900-42) and the ludic style of Julio Cortázar (1914-84). The stories in Blaisten's most recent collection, *El acecho* (The Ambush; 1995), can be classified as detective fiction and they are connected by the theme of murder.

PRIMARY BIBLIOGRAPHY

El acecho. Buenos Aires: Emecé, 1995.
A mí nunca me dejaban hablar: antología de cuentos. Buenos Aires: Sudamericana, 1985.

Anti-conferencias. Buenos Aires: Emecé, 1983. 3rd ed., 1986.

"Carpe Diem." Trans. by Norman Thomas di Giovanni and Susan Ashe. *Winter's Tales*. (New Series, 7) Ed. Robin Baird-Smith. New York: St. Martin's Press, 1991. 293-301.

Carroza y reina. Buenos Aires: Emecé, 1986.

Cerrado por melancolía. Buenos Aires: Editorial de Belgrano, 1981. 2nd ed., 1985. Also, Buenos Aires: Emecé, 1993.

Cuando éramos felices. Buenos Aires: Emecé, 1992.

Cuentos anteriores. Buenos Aires: Editorial de Belgrano, 1982. 2nd ed., 1984.

Dublín al sur. Buenos Aires: El Cid, 1980. 3rd ed., 1984. Also, Buenos Aires: Emecé, 1992.

La felicidad. Buenos Aires: Galerna, 1969.

"Lotz Makes No Reply." Trans. by Norman Thomas di Giovanni and Susan Ashe. In *Celeste Goes Dancing and Other Stories: An Argentine Collection*. Ed. Norman Thomas di Giovanni. San Francisco: North Point Press, 1990. 35-43.

El mago. Buenos Aires: Ediciones del Sol, 1974.

El mago: nueva versión. Buenos Aires: Emecé, 1993.

La salvación. Buenos Aires: Centro Editor de América Latina, 1971.

Sucedió en la lluvia. Buenos Aires: Stilcograf, 1965.

"South Dublin." Trans. by Norman Thomas di Giovanni and Susan Ashe. *Winter's Tales* (New Series, 6) Ed. Robin Baird-Smith. New York: St. Martin's Press, 1993. 115-34.

"Uncle Facundo." Trans. by Cynthia Ventura. In *The Faber Book of Contemporary Latin American Short Stories*. Ed. Nick Caistor. London/Boston: Faber and Faber, 1989. 3-11. Also translated by Alberto Manguel in *Tropical Synagogues: Short Stories by Jewish-Latin American Writers*. Ed. Ilán Stavans. New York: Holmes & Meier, 1994. 50-57.

SECONDARY BIBLIOGRAPHY
Criticism

Gardiol, Rita. *Argentina's Jewish Short Story Writers*. Muncie, IN: Ball State University, 1986. 30-33.

Heker, Liliana. "*La felicidad*, de Isidoro Blaisten." *El escarabajo de oro* 40 (1969): 20-21.

Lynch, Marta. "Una carta viva [a Isidoro Blaisten]." *Davar* 124 (1970): 47-50.

Sneh, Simja. "En torno de una mesa redonda." *Raíces* 23 (1970): 52-55.

Medrano, Martha. *"Carroza y reina."* *Letras de Buenos Aires* 16 (1986): 81-83.

Weinstein, Ana E., and Miryam E. Gover de Nasatsky, comps. *Escritores judeo-argentinos: bibliografía 1900-1987.* 2 vols. Buenos Aires: Milá, 1994. I.80-85.

Interviews

Halperín, Jorge. "Charla con el escritor Isidoro Blaisten sobre la realidad, la fantasía, la poesía y la locura." *Clarín [Opinión]* July 24, 1994: 20-21.

"Isidoro Blaisten." In *Encuesta a la literatura argentina contemporánea.* Buenos Aires: Centro Editor de América Latina, 1982. 205-10.

Isod, Liliana. "Cerrado por melancolía." *Mundo Israelita* 3229 (Nov. 25, 1985): 9.

Lóizaga, Patricio J. "Isidoro Blaisten: la reivindicación del lenguaje." *Cultura de la Argentina contemporánea* 3.14 (1986): 6-11.

Morever, Rubén C. "Isidoro Blaisten: no existe una temática judía en la literatura." *La luz* 1357 (1984): 16.

Ploshchuk, Ariel. "Dialogando con Isidoro Blaisten: un replanteo para forjar la nueva interrelación de intelectuales judíos y la comunidad." *Mundo Israelita* 3030 (Dec. 12, 1981): 5.

Cristina Guzzo

BORINSKY, ALICIA (Argentina; 1946)

Poet, novelist, literary critic, professor, scholar: Alicia Borinsky carries on her various careers with aplomb and distinction. She has published five books of criticism, along with numerous articles in scholarly journals, three volumes of poetry, and a novel. A second novel has been completed. She is one of the most versatile and active members of a new generation of scholar-writers who find no conflict between creative and critical writing, but instead believe that each informs and enlivens the other. All of her writing can be characterized as nontraditional. Her criticism offers a clue as to her interests and inclinations: Macedonio Fernández (1874-1952), Jorge Luis Borges (1899-1986), Julio Cortázar (1914-84), Manuel Puig (1929-90), Adolfo Bioy Casares (1914), Jean Rhys (1894-1979), María Luisa Bombal (1910-80), but also Miguel de Cervantes Saavedra (1547-1616), Pedro Calderón de la Barca (1600-81), Lewis Carroll

(1832-98), and other innovative, experimental writers of their time, those who dared to take risks, as she herself does.

She was born in Buenos Aires in 1946 in the midst of a family and community of Eastern European Jewish exiles who had fled the Nazis in Poland and the pogroms in Russia. At the time Buenos Aires was a city of immigrants from many different countries. As new arrivals took on a new language and customs, they also set about to forge new identities and to realize plans, projects, and dreams frustrated and abandoned in their countries of origin. The resulting society was a heady and volatile mix of politics, culture, arts, a particularly propitious time for literature. By the beginning of the century the important innovative currents of literature and art from Europe and North America had been absorbed by Latin American writers, the Argentinian authors in particular, giving rise to the remarkable creative surge that continues to this day. As it happens, it was also in 1946 that Juan Perón was elected president of Argentina for the first time, ushering in the phenomenal movement known as Peronism, still a force in Argentinian politics and still exerting a hold over the Argentine imagination. Alicia Borinsky grew up in the heyday of that highly emotional atmosphere.

She received her schooling in Buenos Aires, was awarded a degree as Maestra Normal (indicates graduation from a teacher's college with certification as a teacher) in 1964, then studied at the Universidad de Buenos Aires from 1965-1967, where she concentrated on modern literatures and philosophy. One of her professors at the University was Borges who introduced his students to the work of Macedonio Fernández; both were to have a lasting impact on Borinsky's thinking and her work. Following yet another military coup in 1966, the fourth during her time there, she left Argentina to continue her studies at the University of Pittsburgh where she received her Master of Arts degree in Hispanic Languages and Literatures in 1968 and her Doctor of Philosophy degree in 1971; her doctoral dissertation was titled *Macedonio Fernández y la nueva novelística* (Macedonio Fernández and the New Novel).

She began teaching as a graduate assistant at the University of Pittsburgh in 1968, then taught at Johns Hopkins University from 1970-1980, before joining the Department of Modern Foreign Languages at Boston University in the fall of 1980 where she is now professor of modern foreign languages and literature. She has lectured at many universities in the United States, Argentina, Mexico, and Spain, given a number of readings of her creative work, and been a visiting professor at both Washington University in St. Louis and at Harvard.

Alicia Borinsky began to write poetry and stories very early. Drawn from the first to work that blurs the boundaries between genres and upsets traditional narrative and chronological order, she searches for means to capture the intricate, chancy nature of daily life, to reveal it in full, with its dark underside, contradictions, and petty shameful corners along with the fun, vigor, joy. This many-faceted aspect gives her work an intense immediacy, an energetic jolt, and a disturbing edge. In her writing, as in life, everything is flux, unstable, subject to imminent change. The feeling of excitement and heightened unease that some of her work engenders resembles the atmosphere of certain dreams when we find ourselves suddenly on stage in the middle of a performance, unready and often inappropriately dressed, and realize we are also expected to play a part. To compare Borinsky's writing to a theatrical production is quite fitting; her work is dramatic and she employs many techniques used in drama, such as speaking directly to readers, involving them in the action, using asides to let us in on little secrets or to skip over events and blocks of time. In her novel *Mina cruel* (*Mean Woman*; 1989) there are many notes and letters addressed to the reader. A typical one says, "There's no need for me to dwell on what we know already" (49). Or ". . . Father Gabriel. . . didn't know, as we do, that the most important thing in this life is to be nice and warm in a cozy bed, with familiar smells, a friendly pillow and feet snug beneath the blanket" (134).

One of the most constant and engaging elements of her work is her humor which comes from many directions. She uses it to talk about things so searing they could not be approached in any other way. She surprises by unexpected juxtapositions; ludicrous and outrageous events are made believable through inventive detail and a straightforward style, as in fairy tales. The characters blurt out what everyone feels or thinks but would not dare say; reveal the games we play with ourselves and with each other, the laughable airs we put on. Another element worth mentioning in her work is the ongoing dialogue with other writing, often charged with ironical, parodical, and satirical overtones. Images and echoes constantly spark and arc to and from other works, adding yet another facet to her literary complex.

Borinsky's critical and creative writings share many of the same characteristics: particularly the inclusion of the reader in the reading, which in her case, is always a quest. There is also a similar dramatic quality. We are not only given a lucid outline of the "play," meet the members of the cast, see snippets of scenes, but we are taken backstage and shown the machinery that creates the illusion. As always when considering works of art, there is a hiatus between the tools and artisanry necessary to produce it and the finished work. Art happens in that interval when something intangible is added causing a transformation to take place. It takes a leap of the mind, the imagination to bridge the gap. Borinsky is singularly astute at finding the strands, hints, and clues that delineate those intangibles.

Her approach to criticism is well stated in her introduction to *Intersticios* (Interstices; 1986), which includes chapters concerning work of Cervantes, Vicente Huidobro (1893-1948), Octavio Paz (1914), Juan Gelman (1930), Alberto Girri (1919), Adolfo Bioy Casares, Gabriel García Márquez (1928), Julio Cortázar, and María Luisa Bombal. She describes the relationship between the authors treated as resembling the connecting threads to be found in the contents of Joseph Cornell's boxes, "conciliation of newspaper fragments, dusty pharmaceutical bottles, remains of experiments that do not want to be entirely erased; in the subterranean order of Cortázar's almanacs; in the modest insistence of philosophy in so many of Discépolo's tangos" (9). She continues: "What does a discourse offer whose parodoxical objective is to show the dismemberment of its parts? A measured dose of freedom where the theoretical perspective appears as fissure. . . I intend the literary theory as *effect* in a reader deliberately open to the celebrations of chance, militant against the authoritarianisms that divide creation from criticism, the theory from its multiform mirages" (9).

Theoretical Fables (1993), which concerns many of the same authors, takes a broad view of contemporary Latin American fiction, while going beyond the well-known litany of its attributes, ("its self reflexivity, its playful relationship to history and the everyday, frequently woven into extravagantly complicated plots. . ." [ix-x]) to ponder other aspects, particularly "its lucidity about the workings of language, and its ability to invoke, in various ways, a region not *beyond* literature, but *through* literature. . ." (ix-x), an area where meaning may (or may not) be found, but what does indeed occur is the "uncovering of a path toward the intuition of its message" (ix-x).

Borinsky's writing cannot be pigeon-holed. She is light-hearted and witty but also dead serious. Her concerns are the eternal ones: the search for identity (identities), the relationship between men and women; sexuality; the nature of love and friendship, the self; hope, betrayal, fear, and death; the pleasures of art; instability and uncertainty, political and otherwise. She asks the questions but does not try to provide all the answers. Her work invites re-reading and further reading. For writer and reader, the quest goes on.

PRIMARY BIBLIOGRAPHY
Creative Writing
Mina cruel. Buenos Aires: Corregidor, 1989. English version as *Mean Woman.* Trans. by Cola Franzen. Lincoln: University of Nebraska Press, 1993.

Mujeres tímidas y la Venus de China. Buenos Aires: Corregidor, 1987. English version as *Timorous Women.* Translation by Cola Franzen. Peterborough, England: Spectacular Diseases Press, 1992.

La pareja desmontable. Buenos Aires: Corregidor, 1994. Translation by Cola Franzen in progress.

Sueños del seductor: novela vodevil. Buenos Aires: Corregidor, 1995.

La ventrílocua y otras canciones. Buenos Aires: Cuarto Poder, 1975.

Nonfiction

Epistolario de Macedonio Fernández. Buenos Aires: Corregidor, 1976.

Intersticios: estudios críticos de literatura hispana. Veracruz, Mexico: Universidad Veracruzana, 1986.

Macedonio Fernández y la teoría crítica: una evaluación. Buenos Aires: Corregidor, 1987.

Theoretical Fables: The Pedagogical Dream in Latin American Fiction. Philadelphia: University of Pennsylvania Press, 1993.

Ver/Ser Visto: notas para una analítica poética. Barcelona: Bosch, 1978.

SECONDARY BIBLIOGRAPHY

Franzen, Cola. "Introduction." *Mean Woman.* Trans. by Cola Franzen. Lincoln: University of Nebraska Press, 1993. vii-xiv.

—. "Translator's Note." In *Timorous Women.* Trans. by Cola Franzen. Peterborough: Spectacular Diseases Press, 1992. 3-4.

Gimbernat González, Ester. "La proliferante expectativa de lo implícito: *Mina cruel.* In her *Aventuras del desacuerdo: novelistas argentinas de los 80.* Buenos Aires: Danilo Albero Vergara, 1992. 301-12.

Graves, James. "Mean Woman." *Bostonia.* Boston University, Fall, 1993. 79-80.

Jamison, Barbara. "Autumn of the Patriarchs." *The Nation* (New York: The Nation Company, Inc.) 257.21 (Dec. 20, 1993): 775-77.

Cola Franzen

BORTNIK, AÍDA (Argentina; 1942)

One of Argentina's foremost writers, Aída Bortnik was born in Buenos Aires in 1942. She began her career as a journalist, although since 1972 she has been a playwright, film director, and screenwriter. When her life was threatened during the military dictatorship (1976-83), she moved to Spain, where she lived for three years and worked for Spanish television. Her unpublished plays include *Soldados y soldaditos* (Soldiers and Little Soldiers; 1972), *Tres por Chéjov* (Three for Chekhov; 1974), inspired by characters and situations in the works of Anton Chekhov (1860-1904), and *Dale nomás* (Go Ahead; 1975).

As a screenwriter Bortnik wrote *La tregua* (The Truce; 1974), based on a novel by Uruguayan author Mario Benedetti (1920), and *Una mujer* (A Woman; 1975), inspired by one of Bortnik's own short stories and adapted as a screenplay in collaboration with fellow Argentine Osvaldo Soriano (1943). Other original screenplays include *Crecer de golpe* (Growing Up at Once; 1977), a free adaptation from a novel by Argentine writer Haroldo Conti (1925-79), *Volver* (Coming Back; 1983), *La historia oficial* (The Official Story; 1983), *Pobre mariposa* (Poor Butterfly; 1986), *Old Gringo* (1989), based on the novel by Mexican author Carlos Fuentes (1928), and *Tango feroz* (Savage Tango; 1993), an Argentine-Spanish coproduction in collaboration with Marcelo Piñeyro. Bortnik's latest screenplay is *Caballos salvajes* (Wild Horses; 1994).

Bortnik is the recipient of numerous prestigious awards, among them an Oscar for *La historia oficial*, the Academy Award for Best Foreign Film of 1983; Best Argentine Screenplay 1976-80, and Primer Premio Nacional Argentores (First Place National Prize of the Argentine Writers' Guild), 1981. *Pobre mariposa* received the prize for Best Screenplay at the Caracas Cinema Festival in 1987. At present Bortnik divides her time between Argentina, the United States, and England, where she lectures, teaches, and writes plays and screenplays.

The film *La isla* (The Island; 1979) became an immediate success in Buenos Aires, in spite of the repressive climate of the late 1970s. The metaphor of insanity that runs through this play applies not only to those confined to a psychiatric institute, but to their friends and relatives as well.

Aída Bortnik is interested in exploring the correspondence between the internal development of a character and the impact external events have on that character. The women she creates emerge from their passive, conventional roles when political events disrupt their accustomed values and life styles. They are forced to become heroines who pursue the truth with passion and ferocity.

La historia oficial exposes the sickness of a society that succumbs to extortion and to lies. It is an indictment of political repression. The film traces the journey of Alicia, a woman who adopts a child during the years of the so-called *Proceso* (the name given to the military dictatorship), and refuses to acknowledge that her child belonged to a disappeared couple. At a critical moment she realizes that although the acceptance of the facts may destroy her, she cannot deny it to herself or to others. Alicia represents the majority of Argentines dwelling in the largest social stratum: the middle class.

Papá querido (Dear Dad) opened in 1981 as one of the twenty-one plays that promoted national theater in a movement called Teatro Abierto (Open Theater), a collective creation by dramatists that put the military government under scrutiny. Bortnik considers *Papá querido* an aesthetic and ideological synthesis of all she has written before and after. Paradoxically, the father comes alive more strongly in the minds of his children after his death, when they gather for the reading of his last will and testament. The dialogue among the brothers—who meet for the first time on that occasion—stands as a warning against the easy betrayal of one's own ideals.

Although the portrayal of the Jew has been mostly implied and indirect rather than deliberate in Bortnik's work, her Jewish sensitivity and her inheritance can be traced in some of her characters, particularly those of *Pobre mariposa*. Here she juxtaposes the personal history of her protagonist with the social and political history of her country. Clara Marino strives to save the memory of her father and will not allow his death to be dismissed. Searching into his past, she becomes attached not only to his books and typewriter, but to his social and political conscience as well. Clara discovers, in spite of herself, a sensitivity to the Jewish part of her identity.

From her private investigation she determines that her father did not suffer a heart attack—as stated in the official report—but that he was murdered when he was about to disclose the list of Nazi criminals who had entered Argentina illegally after World War II.

Clara discovers the conflict within the Jewish branch of her family when she witnesses the internal disagreements between Zionists and Communists and between traditional and liberal Jews. As the title *Pobre mariposa* suggests, Clara's doubts regarding her identity bring her closer to the light; they burn her wings and consume her in an anonymous, insignificant death. When she is about to pass on her father's list of Nazis, Clara is murdered by an allegedly stray bullet in a street demonstration, on October 17, 1945—the day of Juan Perón's coup d'état.

Like *Papá querido*, *Pobre mariposa* stands as a metaphor for the meaning of freedom and for the denial of unbearable political truths. Brought up from age ten by her mother's Catholic conservative family, Clara prefers to ignore the political upheaval brewing in her country and believe the radio announcements which affirm that calm reigns in the country. Only at her father's death, when she begins to reexamine her own past, she realizes that what she had once considered Jewish paranoia was, in fact, recognition of real anti-Semitism and that her own ignorance of Jewish customs has alienated her from other Jews. Like Alicia of *La historia oficial*, Clara is all alone in her search for knowledge. Each time she is shaken by a painful truth, she abandons her passive role and takes action.

Bortnik contends that Clara's road is that of Oedipus, because it finally ends in tragedy; but it is also the product of memory of a newly acquired heritage—a Jewish heritage. Bortnik suggests that the vicissitudes her ancestors suffered when they immigrated to Argentina are far from over. Each generation has been put to the test and it is precisely this consciousness of material and physical precariousness that gives Bortnik's protagonist spiritual strength.

As in the rest of Bortnik's work, *De a uno* (One by One; 1983), which was presented in the 1983 cycle of Teatro Abierto, uses allegorical and surrealistic artifices; easily encoded by the intelligent public but not by the censors. Ostensibly, the play deals with the conventional life of a middle-class family.

Nora Mazziotti observes how Bortnik gives new meaning to regional, romantic comedies by ritualizing family activities: sitting around the table for a typical Sunday lunch that stretches over a period of eight years—coinciding with the duration of the national dictatorship. Whereas at the typical lunch table a family discusses social and political issues, in this get-together the preparation of the meal, and the setting of the table appear as distorted ceremonies.

In *De a uno* Bortnik's image of the family comes close to those of contemporary dramatists Roberto Cossa (1934), Ricardo Halac (1935), Germán Rozenmacher (1936-71), and Ricardo Monti (1944) in its deliberate absence of affection and solidarity between the characters. What Bortnik adds to her play is the family's complicity of silence and its blind submission to the dictatorial politics enveloping it.

Bortnik selects particularly visual and auditory images to illustrate how Sunday rituals gradually break down. The music, for example, suffers distortions: the Creole waltz, usually associated with nostalgia and idealized versions of daily life, becomes a muffled scream, an inhuman howl.

Another distorted image is that of the table. Its size, normally set in accordance with the number of children living in the family, here becomes immense and overbearing, a collective tomb. The table is used as an ominous place covering the dissenters, and thus fostering an association with the disappearance of people and the loss of values that characterizes the period under scrutiny. In this fashion, Bortnik transforms daily events into horrific figures.

Each family member opts for negation and concealment; each is isolated in speeches and actions that don't concern the others. The family's submission to dictatorial power is evidenced by its inability to admit any knowledge about the kidnappings. They are prisoners of terror who abide by the slogan that "silence means health" and choose to isolate themselves. The father, who imposes his will arbitrarily around the house, seals its doors and windows with tape, he says, to block out the noise and everything else. The mother immures herself in domestic chores; the children are urged to keep silent and to know their place. The grandfather—to whom no one pays attention—reports obliquely and with the same impersonal tone all outside communiques, whether they are news of the military Junta or a soccer match.

There is no more affection or sharing left in this family. The message of the play is expressed by one of the characters, before he is forced into exile: "no se puede vivir sin testigos y sin memoria" (You cannot live without witnesses, without memory [72]). Through the actions of one family, Bortnik encapsulates what she meant about generations of Argentines who learned at great cost that morality and ethics cannot be transmitted or propagated or imposed by force.

By setting the play against the backdrop of a repressive climate, the metaphor of denial gains further strength. It extends to Argentine society at large, which reproduces official rhetoric and chooses to ignore the truth. Bortnik's creative production depicts commonplace situations that turn out to represent moral choices. Hence her use of daily family events to signify the importance of personal commitment to freedom, and of the need for people to participate collectively in shaping their society.

PRIMARY BIBLIOGRAPHY

"Celeste's Heart." Trans. by Alberto Manguel. In *Tropical Synagogues: Short Stories by Jewish-Latin American Writers*. Ed. with introduction by Ilán Stavans. New York: Holmes & Meier, 1994. 95-97.

De a uno. Hispamérica 15.43 (1986): 57-72.

Domesticados. Buenos Aires: Argentores, 1988.

La historia oficial: libro cinematográfico. Buenos Aires: Ediciones de la Urraca, 1985.

La isla. In *Guiones cinematográficos: Aída Bortnik, La isla; Mario Reynoso, Allá lejos y hace tiempo*. Buenos Aires: Centro Editor de América Latina, 1981. 119-242.

Papá querido. In *Teatro Abierto 1981: 21 estrenos argentinos*. Buenos Aires: Banco Credicoop Cooperativo Limitado, 1981. 11-20. 2nd ed. Buenos Aires: Corregidor, 1992. 13-26. Also in *Teatro breve contemporáneo argentino*. Buenos Aires: Ediciones Colihue, 1989. 23-38.

Pobre mariposa (fragments). In *Cien años de narrativa judeoargentina 1889-1989*. Ed. Ricardo Feierstein. Buenos Aires: Milá, 1987. 330-43.

"Por la vida," "El corazón de Celeste," "Buscando." In *Cuentos judíos latinoame-*
ricanos. Ed. Ricardo Feierstein. Buenos Aires: Milá, 1989.159-64.
Primaveras. Buenos Aires: Teatro Municipal General San Martín, 1985. Also in
Teatro argentino contemporáneo: antología. Madrid: Centro de Documentación Teatral, Ministerio de Cultura; Sociedad Estatal Quinto Centenario; Fondo de Cultura Económica, 1992. 889-950.

SECONDARY BIBLIOGRAPHY
Criticism

Brocato, Carlos A. "*La historia oficial*." *Nueva presencia* 457 (April 4, 1986):
4-6.
Foster, David William. "*The Official Story (La historia oficial)*: Truth and Con-
sequences." In his *Contemporary Argentine Cinema*. Columbia, MO: U
of Missouri P, 1992. 38-54.
Giella, Miguel Angel. "*Papá querido* de Aída Bortnik." In his *Teatro Abierto*
1981: teatro argentino bajo vigilancia. Buenos Aires: Corregidor, 1992.
67-74.
Glickman, Nora. "Discovering Self in History: Aída Bortnik and Gerardo Mario
Goloboff." In *The Jewish Diaspora in Latin America: New Studies on*
History and Literature. Ed. David Sheinin and Lois Baer Barr. New
York: Garland, 1996. 61-73.
Graham-Jones, Jean. "Decir 'no': el aporte de Bortnik, Gambaro y Raznovich al
Teatro Abierto '81." In *Teatro argentino durante el proceso 1976-1983*.
Ed. Juana A. Arancibia and Zulema Mirkin. Buenos Aires: Vinciguerra,
1992. 181-97.
Mazziotti, Nora. "Lo cotidiano enrarecido: *De a uno*, de Aída Bortnik." In *Tea-*
tro argentino durante el Proceso: 1976-1983. Ed. Juana A. Arancibia
and Zulema Mirkin. Buenos Aires: Vinciguerra, 1992. 91-97.
Priamo, Luis. "El cine y el proceso, una nueva lectura de *La historia oficial*."
Nueva presencia 425 (Aug. 23, 1985): 12-16.
Ramsey, Cynthia. "*The Official Story*": Feminist Re-visioning as Spectator Re-
sponse." *Studies in Latin American Popular Culture* 11 (1992): 157-69.
Roffo, Analía. "El tiempo y las apuestas vitales." In *Teatro argentino contem-*
poráneo: antología. Madrid: Centro de Documentación Teatral, Ministe-
rio de Cultura; Sociedad Estatal Quinto Centenario; Fondo de Cultura
Económica, 1992. 883-87.
Staif, Kive. "Democracia y cultura (*Primaveras*)." *Teatro: Teatro Municipal*
General San Martín 19 (1984): 2-3.

Weinstein, Ana E., and Miryam Gover de Nasatsky, comps. *Escritores judeo-argentinos: bibliografía 1900-1987*. 2 vols. Buenos Aires: Milá, 1994. I.86-89.

Zayas de Lima, Perla. *Diccionario de autores teatrales argentinos 1950-1990*. Buenos Aires: Galerna, 1991. 50-52.

Interviews

Glickman, Nora. "Entrevista con Aída Bortnik." New York: 17 May, 1994, unpublished.

Hendel, Noemí. "Develar todas las respuestas posibles: pluralismo e identidad." *Nueva Sión* 643 (Aug. 23, 1987): 19-23.

Matar, Beatriz. "Una conversación con Aída Bortnik, autora de *Primaveras*." *Teatro: Teatro Municipal Gneral San Martín* 19 (1984): 34-46.

Meson, Danusia L. "*The Official Story*: An Interview with Aída Bortnik." *Cineaste* 14.4 (9186): 30-35.

Morero, Sergio. "La autora." *Primaveras*. Buenos Aires: Teatro Municipal General San Martín, 1985. 9-24.

Nora Glickman

BRAILOVSKY, ANTONIO ELIO (Argentina; 1946)

Antonio Elio Brailovsky, born December 17, 1946 in Buenos Aires, is a complex personality. He has earned his living as a journalist, a political economist, a civil servant for the Municipality of Buenos Aires, and as a professor of Natural Resources at the University of Buenos Aires. In 1990 he was appointed Professor at Belgrano University. He is also a historian, an ecologist, and a writer. Even this last activity alone is many-faceted. He has written non-fiction (books and essays on history, economics, and ecology), and fiction (short stories and novels).

As early as 1969 Brailovsky (at the age of 23) had a political essay published: "Cuestionamiento de la Argentina contemporánea" (A Questioning of Contemporary Argentina) in the book *México y Argentina vistos por sus jóvenes* (Mexico and Argentina As Seen by Their Youth).

Brailovsky's historical survey of the Argentine economy, especially the financial crises the country has undergone, *Historia de las crisis argentinas* (History of the Argentine Crises; 1982), went through five editions. It might seem incredible to an American public that a book on an academic and seemingly dry subject like economics could be of sufficient interest to a general public as to merit being practically a best-seller. There are two reasons for the popularity of this book: (1) the run-away inflation Argentina suffered during the 1980s gave rise to a profound, almost obsessive, interest in the economy, (2) in this book Brailovsky's imagination and artistry—using novels, speeches, and newspaper articles as sources—blur the line between essay and fiction, science and art, the technical and the literary.

While describing the manner in which natural resources were used throughout Argentine history, as well as suggesting improvements, he theorizes that each society has its own peculiar relationship with nature, rationally using certain resources, abandoning others, pillaging or destroying still others, depending on the type of society.

His essay on political economy and the environment, "Política ambiental de la Generación del 80" (Environmental Policies of the Generation of 1980) included in the volume *Tres estudios argentinos* (Three Argentine Studies; 1981), is an important contribution to studies on the manner in which the ecology of Argentina has been affected by economic activity.

In 1983 two essays were published: *Los empleados públicos* (Public Servants), and *El Riachuelo*, an ecological history of an area of the port district of Buenos Aires. In 1988 the University of Buenos Aires published two more studies by Brailovsky: *El agua en Buenos Aires* (Water in Buenos Aires), an ecological essay, and *El negocio de envenenar* (The Poison Business), an investigative politico-ecological essay.

Brailovsky's artistic abilities as well as the more intimate nature of his personality can be more readily observed in his works of fiction. His first novel, *Identidad* (Identity; 1980), was awarded First Prize in the novel category that year by the Coca-Cola Company's Argentine branch. It is also the work of fiction in which the author's Jewish identity can most clearly be examined. The exact nature of Brailovsky's Jewish identity, as expressed in this novel and in his own comments on it, however, is not easy to pin down.

Identidad deals with a group of crypto-Jews who, sometime after 1492, set out, ostensibly like Cortés, Pizarro and all the other Spanish *conquistadores* and settlers, to conquer and settle territory in the New World. Once at sea, they openly revert to Judaism, change their assumed Christian-Spanish names back to their original Hebrew ones, and ban the use of the Spanish language in favor of Hebrew. Like Cortés, they destroy their ship upon reaching land; however, unlike Cortés, they do so in order not to be discovered by the Spaniards. They form a

Jewish kingdom in the most inaccessible reaches of the Mexican jungle, after conquering the natives and converting them to Judaism.

These elements of the novel are intertwined with those that deal with the twentieth-century descendants of the conquerors and the conquered: Hebrew-speaking Indians of the Jewish religion who live in villages deep in the jungle. These Jewish Indians fervently await the Messiah who will lead them to the Promised Land. By our own day, some of them desert the village to follow a Mexican politician whom they believe to be the Anointed One, while others leave to see the wonders of Mexico City, and still others join Mexican illegal immigrants on the trip to the Promised Land of California. One group is brought to Israel where they are mistakenly believed to be part of a hoax on the part of a politician.

This beautiful novel—in which the sixteenth-century founders of the Jewish kingdom communicate with their twentieth-century descendants, in which spoken words become visible and palpable, in which several characters see their own souls reflected in other characters' eyes—is filled with magic realism. It is also a rather pessimistic view of Jewish destiny. The founder of the kingdom becomes a tyrant, there are growing indications that the establishment of the Jewish kingdom is a quixotic, even futile, enterprise, and by the present day, the people are abandoning their villages and their heritage.

In spite of the obvious Judaic aspects of the plot, book reviews of the novel in Argentina often overlook the Jewish element. The title of Omar Borré's review is "*Identidad* conforma una bella crónica americanista" (*Identidad* Offers a Beautiful Americanist Chronicle), thereby referring only to a historical novel concerning the New World. Yet, within the review itself Borré alludes to "un pueblo que un día se echó a andar por el mundo con la historia del mundo bajo los brazos" (a people that one day began to roam the world, carrying the history of the world with them [Borré 6]). The Jewish content is obvious in the body of the review, since the plot summary about the Jewish kingdom is given.

Brailovsky's own comments on *Identidad* reveal an ambiguity in the author's mind concerning the meaning of the work, as well as an ambivalence toward his relationship with the Jewish world. In an interview he maintained that *Identidad* metaphorically represents the Argentine (not the Jewish) experience (Zlotchew, "Opresión . . ."). He affirmed that the negatively portrayed Jewish kingdom is only a pretext for displaying his loss of faith in Argentine society during the 1970s (Zlotchew, "Antonio Elio Brailovsky").

Brailovsky composed the book during a period of terror in Argentina. He wrote it in order to vent his feelings about what was occurring, but his mental health could not tolerate using present-day Argentina as the location of this terror; it was too close to him. Therefore, he placed it at arm's length: in Spain and Mexico in the sixteenth century (Zlotchew, "Antonio Elio Brailovsky"). Still, when pressed, Brailovsky does link the novel to Jewish history: "The persecuted repeat the history of their persecution; sometimes they learn how to persecute; other times they only change persecutors. The destiny of the Jews is incessant dispersion, failure in the quest for a Promised Land . . . or a Messiah who never arrives . . ." (Personal letter to Zlotchew). He even makes this link personal: "Besides, there is something else: the quest for my own roots" (Zlotchew, "Antonio Elio Brailovsky" 56).

Brailovsky's other books of fiction—historical novels containing strong social commentary—have no obvious Jewish references. *El asalto al cielo* (Assault on Heaven; 1985) takes place in France during the suppression of the Commune. *Tiempo de opresión* (Time of Oppression; 1986) refers to the forced labor of Indian workers in the silver mines of Bolivia and of their ill-fated rebellion in the eighteenth century. His novel, *Esta maldita lujuria* (This Cursed Lasciviousness; 1992) is an hallucinatory account—from the superstitious and fevered point of view of one of the colonists—of events during the Spanish colonization of the New World. It was awarded the Casa de las Américas prize (the Latin American equivalent to the Pulitzer). A group of Brailovsky's short stories are gathered in the collection titled, *Libro de las desmesuras* (Book of Excesses; 1984). His most recent novel, *Me gustan sus cuernos* (I Like Your Horns; 1995), blends the past with the present in an erotically-charged detectivesque story about secret documents and the Spanish Inquisition. The book belongs to the erotic literature series *La Sonrisa Vertical* (The Vertical Smile) published by Tusquets in Barcelona.

PRIMARY BIBLIOGRAPHY
Creative Writing

El asalto al cielo. Buenos Aires: Sudamericana/Planeta, 1985.
"Ecclesiastes." Translation of "Eclesiastés" (chapter 18 of *Identidad*). Trans. by
        Clark M. Zlotchew. *Webster Review* 12.2 (Fall 1987): 30-41.
Esta maldita lujuria. La Habana: Casa de las Américas, 1990. Also, Buenos
        Aires: Planeta, 1992.
Identidad. Buenos Aires: Sudamericana, 1980.
Libro de las desmesuras. Buenos Aires: Celtia, 1984.
Me gustan sus cuernos. Barcelona: Tusquets, 1995.
"El nombre." In *Cuentos judíos latinoamericanos*. Ed. by Ricardo Feierstein.
        Buenos Aires: Milá, 1989. 229-36.
Tiempo de opresión. Buenos Aires: Belgrano, 1986.

Nonfiction

El agua en Buenos Aires. Buenos Aires: Universidad de Buenos Aires, 1988.

"Cuestionamiento de la Argentina contemporánea." In *México y Argentina vistos por sus jóvenes*. México, D.F.: Siglo XXI, 1969. 13-75.

La ecología en la Biblia: un análisis del vínculo con la naturaleza en el texto bíblico. Buenos Aires: Planeta Tierra, 1993.

Los empleados públicos. Buenos Aires: Centro Editor de América Latina, 1983.

Historia de las crisis argentinas. Buenos Aires: Belgrano, 1982.

Introducción al estudio de los recursos naturales. Buenos Aires: Universidad de Buenos Aires, 1987.

"Política ambiental de la Generación del 80." In *Tres estudios argentinos*. Buenos Aires: Sudamericana, 1981. 287-364.

El Riachuelo. Buenos Aires: Centro Editor de América Latina, 1983.

SECONDARY BIBLIOGRAPHY
Criticism

Borré, Omar. "*Identidad* conforma una bella crónica americanista." Rev. of *Identidad*. *Convicción* (March 8, 1981).

Case, T. E. Rev. of *Esta maldita lujuria*. *World Literature Today* 67.1 (Winter 1993): 155.

Goldberg, Florinda F. Rev. of *Me gustan sus cuernos*. *Hispamérica* 24.72 (1995): 112-15.

Moledo, Leonardo. "Premios de un concurso." Rev. of *Identidad*. *Clarín* (March 19, 1981): n.p.

Modern, Rodolfo. "La novela rigurosa escrita con gran talento narrativo." Rev. of *Identidad*. *La Gaceta* (May 29, 1981): n.p.

Reati, Fernando. "Posse, Saer, Di Benedetto y Brailovsky: deseo y paraíso en la novela argentina sobre la Conquista." *Revista de estudios hispánicos* 24.1 (1995): 121-36.

Senkman, Leonardo. *La identidad judía en la literatura argentina*. Buenos Aires: Pardés, 1983. 466-67.

Zlotchew, Clark M. "Problematic Identity in Antonio Elio Brailovsky's *Identidad*." *Modern Jewish Studies Annual VIII* (special publication of *Yiddish*) 9.1 (1993): 111-21.

—. "La Segunda Jerusalem de la Nueva Sefarad de las Indias: *Identidad* de A.E. Brailovsky." *Noaj* 6.7-8 (1992): 96-105.

Interviews

Zlotchew, Clark M. "Antonio Elio Brailovsky." In *Voices of the River Plate: Interviews with Writers of Argentina and Uruguay*, by Clark M. Zlotchew. San Bernardino: Borgo Press, 1995. 51-66. Originally in Spanish as, "Entrevista con Antonio Elio Brailovsky." *Alba de América* 5.8-9 (1987): 371-83.

—. "Opresión, libertad y la magia: entrevista con Antonio Elio Brailovsky." *Hispania* 71.3 (1988): 595-97.

Clark M. Zlotchew

BUDASOFF, NATALIO (Argentina; 1903-81)

Natalio Budasoff was born in Russia in 1903. His family emigrated to Argentina in 1914 where they settled in one of the agricultural colonies of the Entre Ríos province established by Baron Mauricio Hirsch. In his prologue to Budasoff's collection of plays, Antonio Portnoy provides a brief biography of the author in which he describes the hardships of life in the agricultural settlements and the author's eventual transition to urban life. A particularly trying time for family came in the early 1930s in the form of massive swarms of locusts. The insects plagued farmers for several consecutive years, destroying crops and forcing many into bankruptcy which led to the abandonment of the colonies. It apparently left such a profound impression on Budasoff that he wrote a study about the devastating economic effects of the insects and proposed ways to rid the country and the continent of this plague of Biblical proportions. The book, titled *La langosta: un mal nacional y sudamericano* (The Locust: A National and South American Affliction; 1946), was lauded by public officials, legislators, and scientists (Portnoy 10). According to Portnoy, Budasoff's early texts were written in Yiddish and remain unpublished (12). His first published work in Spanish was a collection of poems titled *Elevación* (Elevation; 1945). In 1935 Budasoff was forced to move to Buenos Aires as a result of the dire economic situation. He found employment as the administrator of the Hospital Israelita (Jewish Hospital). Budasoff's rural upbringing and his work in the health care field form the thematic basis of his literary corpus.

Budasoff's *Teatro* (Theater; 1950) is a collection of five plays; two full-length and three one-act pieces. As a dramatist, Budasoff made no lasting impact on Argentine theater. In fact his works, like the author himself, have been relegated to a position of almost complete obscurity. Although he belongs roughly to the same generation as Samuel Eichelbaum (1894-1967), he lacks the creative depth and insight that led the latter to become one of the foremost Argentine dramatists of his time. Nevertheless, Budasoff's works do merit some credit if only on a thematic basis. The first play of the collection, *Espigas en flor* (Ripening Wheat; written in 1935), takes place in the early agricultural settlements. The action revolves around the struggle of an extended Jewish family of three generations to cope with the hardships of eking out a living from the land. In the first act the father and son are embroiled in an argument over whether they should risk purchasing a tractor. Budasoff also introduces two outside characters, Giacomini and Ramírez, who respectively represent the presence of Italian and Spanish immigrants who add to the diverse social make-up of the rural province. There seems to be a conscious effort on the part of the playwright to recreate authentic rural speech patterns, but he does so rather unconvincingly. This is mainly evident in the fact that he indiscriminately alternates his use of the second-person pronoun *tú* (you) and corresponding verb conjugations with those of the native Argentine *vos*. Likewise, his excessive use of overly emotive, at times even inane, dialogue distracts from the potentially engaging premise of the play. Budasoff does not attempt to portray rural life as a joyful existence in the new Promised Land. In fact, his depiction presents quite the opposite view as his family must deal with drought, insect plagues and unrelenting rain. Nevertheless, the play does reveal an abiding connection to and respect for the earth, both as a source of spiritual renewal and as the unforgiving wielder of nature's power. Budasoff's tellurism can be directly correlated to the ideals of the Haskalah, or Jewish Enlightenment. One of the major tenets of which is the belief in the possibility of spiritual redemption through contact with nature and labor on the land. The family in the play, however, finds few redeeming qualities in the land. By the end the grandparents die and the family is forced to sell their property and auction off their belongings.

In the second play, *Feria medicinal* (Medical Fair) Budasoff moves from the rural agricultural backdrop to the environment of the Buenos Aires medical community. Obviously, his experience as a hospital administrator gave him the thematic grounding for this play that posits two generations of doctors at opposites ends of the medical ethics spectrum. A demanding senior physician struggles to impress upon a group of young residents the importance of the medical and emotional aspects of patient care and to instill in them a professional attitude in tune with the Hippocratic oath. After one of the young doctor's negligence causes the unnecessary death of a patient he is dismissed from the hospital staff.

He finds work in a clinic, but does little to change his professional demeanor. In the end justice is served when a young woman comes to see him under the guise of an appointment but whose purpose is to kill him in order to avenge her husband and child who suffered under the doctor's care. Like the previous play, *Feria medicinal* offers little as a dramatic work but it is interesting for its representation, albeit exaggerated, of the medical community of the 1930s.

The three short plays that make up the rest of the collection are of only minimal interest. Like the previous two, they take place in both rural and urban medical environments. Of the three, *Comisión Main-Hider Bichi-Bay* (Main-Hider and Bichi-Bay Commission) merits mention for its satirical style that distinguishes it from the other plays.

In addition to poetry and drama, Budasoff also wrote a collection of short stories titled *Lluvias salvajes* (Savage Rains; 1962). It is unquestionably the author's most accomplished work. The stories can be grouped with a number of other works that appeared in the 1960s and which sought to describe the early immigrant experience; for instance, the novels *Dios era verde* (God Was Green; 1963) and *Pueblo pan* (People of Bread; 1967) by José Chudnovsky (1915-66), and *Cuentos criollos con judíos* (Creole Stories with Jews; 1967) by Pablo Schvartzman (1927). As in his plays, Budasoff does not present an idyllic view of life in the rural settlements. Rather, his stories are filled with grief, misfortune, and a good deal of violence. His protagonists tend to be obstinate, petty, cruel, unforgiving, and vengeful. The Jewish colonists are often at odds with the cold-hearted administrators of the Jewish Colonization Association or with neighbors, both Jewish and non-Jewish. The collection of seven stories opens with "Motl Katarinschik," the tale of a stubborn father who physically and emotionally abuses his young sons. His obdurate pride leads to a disastrous wagon wreck while crossing a river that results in the death of the horses and a narrow escape for himself and his sons. As he begins to weigh the consequences of his mulish behavior he suffers an emotional breakdown brought on by guilt, anger, and shame. The story "La muerte de Rodolfo Wladimiroff" (The Death of Rodolfo Wladimiroff) is one of the best of the collection. In it a new parish priest begins to stir up anti-Semitic sentiments among the locals by inciting them with accusations against the Jews as Christ killers, the cause of hunger and pestilence, and he gets a big laugh from his parishioners when he tells them that Jews don't eat pork because their God is a swine (39-40). The fact that he makes his priest a German immigrant leads one to question whether or not Budasoff was unwilling to portray native Argentines as anti-Semites. The protagonist of the story is portrayed as a skilled horseman, completely at home on the Argentine pampa. He is, in effect, the embodiment of the *gaucho judío* (Jewish gaucho) first presented by Alberto Gerchunoff (1884-1950). When Rodolfo Wladimiroff attempts to recover some stolen animals from a creole neighbor he is violently attacked and stabbed to death before he has a chance to defend himself. In "Butzecul" two close friends, a Jew and a non-Jew, are first presented as inseparable but their friendship quickly dissolves over their competition to win the heart of a local girl. Butzecul is forced to kill Goya, the son of Spanish immigrants and his best friend, in self-defense. He goes to prison for his crime and on release his mother pleads with him to flee to escape the revenge that Goya's family has promised to exercise. The other stories present similar situations which invariably end in disaster. For example, a drunken politician beats his wife to death, a young boy is brutally killed as the result of feud, and a shooting accident profoundly affects the relationship between two brothers. Budasoff makes an even greater effort here than he did is his plays to recreate authentic creole speech by effecting orthographic changes to many words and by employing archaisms that are reminiscent of the language found in *Martín Fierro* (1872), the classic work of gaucho literature by José Hernández (1834-86). However, what most grips the reader in these stories is the author's attention to graphic violence that seems to originate at the most basic instinctual level of the protagonists' psyche.

PRIMARY BIBLIOGRAPHY
Creative Writing
Elevación. Buenos Aires: Mosaicos, 1945.
Lluvias salvajes. Buenos Aires: Mosaicos, 1962.
Teatro. Prólogo de Antonio Portnoy. Buenos Aires: Mosaicos, 1950.
Nonfiction
La langosta: un mal nacional y sudamericano. Buenos Aires: Mosaicos, 1946.

SECONDARY BIBLIOGRAPHY
Pavlotzky, José. Rev. of *Lluvias salvajes. Davar* 96 (1963): 134-36.

Darrell B. Lockhart

CALNY, EUGENIA (Pseud. of Fany Eugenia Kalnitzky de Brener; Argentina; 1929)

Eugenia Calny is an extremely prolific author whose works are important within the realm of contemporary Jewish-Argentine writers because they display a feminist, Jewish approach to tradition and politics in Argentina. Her writing spans the genres of novel, poetry, drama, and children's literature. Through this variety of expression emerges an author who is obviously an astute observer of her time. Perhaps one of her more revealing statements appears in the book entitled *El unicornio celeste y el caballito con alas* (The Celestial Unicorn and the Little Winged Horse; 1984), where in essence she states that she has turned away from the confines of adult literature. Her imagination, she says, preferred and even required the limitless world of infantile and adolescent literature. Eugenia Calny has published seven books aimed at an adult audience and various juvenile works which include storybooks for young readers such as *Osobel y la fantasía* (Osobel and the Fantasy; 1977) and *Conejita Blanca y el viaje a la luna* (White Bunny and the Voyage to the Moon; 1976), as well as those directed at a more mature following including, *El congreso de los árboles* (The Congress of the Tress; 1979) and the aforementioned *El unicornio celeste*. These texts, which use rituals, religion, myths, polemics, and art would provide an interesting study of symbolic interpretation in Argentine children's literature.

La madriguera (The Hideaway; 1967) is a four-act play which examines Jewish identity and the role of women within the Argentine social structure and the literary canon. The characters of this drama are participants at a retreat who are expected to create papers in their respective fields in an ambience of silence and solitude. The irony lies in the fact that in 1967 existing governmental controls had already exiled many of the best writers and Jews in particular, to physical and mental spaces of silence. It also becomes apparent as the play progresses that these participants have been closely studied and selected for this bizarre experience and that all have signed a contract stating that they will tacitly support the findings of the judge.

The judge and the doctor, a psychiatrist, are the characters who exercise the greatest amount of authority, followed in succession by an old man who is a writer, the young writer Leo who is Jewish, Ana a typical young, educated Argentine from whom the feminine aspects of this work radiate, and Celeste who is there to accommodate the guests in any way possible. It is evident that Celeste has been tortured and abused by the judge.

The judge, the doctor, and the old writer represent the existing social and political order of Argentina in the late 1960s. The judge maintains dictatorial control over the group and the doctor always supports his decisions. Both characters are able to name individual studies and rules and regulations by their clausal names and numbers. The old writer has been awarded titles and prizes in his field. As the play closes, the old writer and the doctor are the first to come forward with their completed works.

Leo, as is the case with many other Jews of his generation, views his religious ambiguity as both a strength and a weakness. He states that he is against all that divides, classifies, and limits, but his actions throughout the play show that he plays both sides of the fence. His treatment of both Ana and Celeste reveals above all else that he, like most Jewish men, sees women as inferior, and primarily as sex objects. He does, however, confide in both these female characters. One way he does this is to reveal to them his immigrant's dream (29).

The dream consists of a celebration of brotherhood where Ukrainians, Yugoslavs, Italians, Spaniards, Armenians, and Israelis, among others, are all Argentines, and more importantly, none is able to declare himself more Argentine than the other. During one of the panel meetings, the doctor and judge express their gratitude for the studies conducted on humans at Nuremberg. Leo reacts crazily and is given a sedative by the doctor. Even in this state it is easy for Leo to draw the parallels between these men of authority and the Nazis. It is Ana who stays with Leo because as a woman she has also suffered from oppression and understands his pain. Leo tells Ana that he is indeed of the chosen race: chosen to suffer. That Leo and Ana share the misery of oppression is significant. Calny is demonstrating that women, like Jews, were repressed during this period of Argentine history. Argentine Jewish women, therefore, embodied an amplified status of those forces that were viewed as subversive and dangerous to the existing order. As the play closes Leo and Celeste elect to stay behind at the retreat after the others have left. Celeste begs Leo to finish an ancient Hebrew tale which he had begun earlier, but Leo pleads with her to pardon him from completing it. Although he wishes to escape from the past and begins feverishly typing a work entitled "Pudor para el dolor" (Shame for the Pain) it is evident that both he and Celeste have accepted their inferior positions within the hierarchy. When Leo asks Celeste, who is off to town for provisions, how she knows he'll be there when she returns, she replies that he is free, but that they are both prisoners of their world.

Las mujeres virtuosas (Virtuous Women; 1967) is a compilation of individual women's stories that contains very few overt Jewish references, but rather prefers to focus on the struggles which face modern women. Each vignette is separately titled followed by a particular female character's name which appears in parenthesis. This, in effect, is the entire tone of the book as the title characters assume subservient positions within the story. The reader is introduced to various women confined by their societal roles, prejudged by both male and female counterparts as inferior, and imbued by a self-effacing complacency to their predetermined destinies. More often than not in these stories it is the matrilineal line which perpetuates their misery and enables the masculine characters to retain their positions of authority outside the household realm. The most pertinent Jewish theme, which appears in the chapter "Los duendes (Magdalena)" (The Goblins [Magdalena]), treats the pitfalls of intermarriage and is dismissed quickly although it is explored extensively in her next book *Clara al amanecer* (Clara at Dawn; 1972).

The final chapter entitled "Calle abajo... (Violeta)" (Down the Street [Violeta]), might be considered the title story since it contains direct references to the title of the book. In this final story the reader meets Violeta, spurned by the fellow women of her town to the point of banishment. She becomes a nurse-maid to Oscar, the male protagonist of the story. Violeta, after reading many historical anecdotes, concludes that all women who have attained immortality through fame are specifically lacking in virtue. With the possible exception of Madame Curie, she believes that most of these women achieved greatness by being inspirational in some man's life and not through inspiring their own personal accomplishments. Violeta herself had fallen for a poet once, who left her with nothing but his debts. The poet likened her to a boat, and it is easy to extend this idea to many of the other female protagonists of this compilation of short stories. These women are vessels which carry their men either sexually, ideologically, or physically to a specific destination without ever being allowed to develop their own separate journeys. They are often left floating at the harbor while their men enjoy what the port has to offer. Ironically, it is Oscar's meddling mother who from her position in the kitchen is described by the author as virtuous. Thus Calny, in her role as literary mother, has identified in various ways the confusing ideologies that confront modern women.

In her subsequent book, *Clara al amanecer*, the title character Clara is a young Jewish woman struggling with her paradoxical Argentine existence. In the first paragraph of the book, Clara describes herself as sterile even though she may not be, and she considers this condition synonymous with her anguish. She has known about anguish throughout her entire life, eating, drinking, and breathing the atrocities of her ancestors' past which have been kept alive mostly through tales told by her mother and grandmother. In this town survivors of the Holocaust, especially the women, perpetuate their misery, and are unable to embrace their new country.

Clara is suffocated and confused by the incongruous nature of her life and that of her predecessors. She falls in love with Aníbal, a young professional who is not Jewish. Aníbal leaves Argentina to find better work in Canada. He never sends for Clara as he promised, and she loses his baby due to prematurity at birth. At the behest of her family, she agrees to marry Saúl, a much older Jewish doctor. The disequilibrium between Clara and Saúl demonstrates the generational rift that divides many of her fellow Jewish compatriots. She is able to weed out what is important to her from the past, while the older generations of Jews cling to and even thrive on their past misfortunes. Family bonds, for Clara, become chains from which she struggles to break free. She seems to be the only guest at a party able to see that the son who has left home to make a life of his own did not occasion the death of his ninety-year-old father by doing so.

There are many tender, ironic twists in this story. Clara is easily accepted by the non-Jewish family of Aníbal and feels comfort in their joyous familial gatherings. Nonetheless, she heeds her family's advice to return to her own kind after the execution of Adolf Eichmann, the Nazi war criminal, provokes a resurgence of anti-Semitism in Argentina. Clara, for the first time, feels fear in her own country. She refers to the doctor to who she marries as Dr. Grim, since he reminds her of the brothers Grimm. Although she does not love him, she understands him, for he has suffered, as she believes she has. Nevertheless, she is also attracted to his childlike personality and good-natured disposition. These traits directly oppose Clara's pessimism, which she believes she was born with. Her mother and grandmother along with the chronic anti-Semitism of her countrymen and women have perpetuated Clara's melancholia by not permitting her to break free from their sorrowful past.

Nevertheless the author continues to point out that certain men and women have tried to reinvent their existence. When a homosexual man marries a straight woman, with no apparent knowledge of his sexual orientation, it is Clara who rebukes the marriage as destined to fail. Saúl, on the other hand, with his fairytale optimism exclaims that all must be given their opportunity. Another woman of the town, Fermina, went to Israel in search of the Promised Land. She grew thin in the desert, along with her cattle, before their return to Argentina. As the book ends, Clara is hospitalized after two hours of hemorrhaging. It is then that she realizes that she must overcome her fatigue and depression to explore all the possibilities that life has to offer. However, she still fantasizes that Aníbal, like the Jewish vision of the Promised Land, will bring her inner peace and solve all her problems. The reader is left doubtful that she will ever realize her potential.

Her next book, *La tarde de los ocres dorados* (The Golden Ochre Afternoon; 1978) is another compilation of short stories which are individually subtitled in parentheses. These stories explore a diverse spectrum of women and their individual concerns. The title story is perhaps the most significant for identifying the overall meaning of the book. In the chapter "La tarde de los ocres dorados (Elvira)," the story progresses as Elvira, an elementary school teacher, begins to feel condemned to forever playing her role as schoolmarm, be it in school or in the town plaza. Former students continually enter her life in search of the same reassuring hand that she had given them in their formative years. Like a mother, she remembers each one, although she is repulsed by the association of mother-hood and her vocation. Nevertheless, in this story, as in others, feminine and maternal leitmotifs surface repeatedly. For years Elvira has looked in vain for financial support to change the school's location. She calls this fight a sterile one; a fight to which she has become accustomed. Ironically she achieves a new locale through a repositioning of her own, as she becomes literary mother to a whole town.

When a rebellious ex-student comes to live with her, Elvira decides that writing is her path to freedom and enlightenment. Much to her own surprise and that of the town, her poem is published in the local paper. The butcher is so stunned that he doesn't know how to react, but his wife finds Elvira's poetry very moving. Calny seems to be emphasizing the misunderstanding by the com-munity of the feminine voice and the particular ability of women to totally comprehend one another. Like Calny herself, Elvira penetrates all literary bound-aries by writing poetry, essays, stories, and critical commentaries. Elvira gains much notoriety and is perplexed by her own success outside the confines of her small town. She is now assaulted by the continuous flow of student writers who come to call at her house.

The rebellious young girl returns to Elvira's house about the same time that a young man arrives carrying many personal manuscripts which he wants Elvira to read. The girl has changed and while she may still be considered rebel-lious, her marginal behavior is easily contained. It becomes apparent to the reader that Elvira's success parallels this girl's life. Elvira's once potent desire to manipulate the system has been castrated by her permitted entry into it. She now views the young man as a rival, because his real talent threatens her current position of power. Although this story does not deal directly with Jewish themes, there are passages which suggest that grim reminders of past injustices must permeate modern life in order to activate change, as in the case of the young girl who carries on the legacy of her ex-lover who threw himself from a window.

The story "La noche de los recuerdos (Ana y Kata)" (The Night of Memories [Ana and Kata]), directly addresses the generational and societal gap of Argentine Jewry. Two Jewish families habitually play cards in order to forget and escape the hardships endured by the couples in their real lives. One evening when the cards cannot be found they are all forced to confront the banality of their acts in the face of the world surrounding them. The tension begins to rise, especially between the two women. Kata's son is living and working in a kibbutz where his life is threatened daily due to Arab-Israeli hostilities. Ana, whose child Jaime has already died just a few kilometers from the kibbutz, doesn't understand why Kata laments to the extent that she does, since Kata's son is still alive. When the conversation turns even more political, the men express their doubts that Golda Meir is able to control such a volatile situation. The women then regain their solidarity defending the female prime minister. The men go off to neighboring apartments in search of a deck of cards and not so innocently end up in the apartment of a beautiful young artist. The women are aghast and the argument ensues as the night progresses. When the Beresteins finally decide to go home, Kata is almost hysterical with anger towards her friends and her husband as well. These two Jewish couples have built their lives around routine. The dullness of their daily existence is a thin shell that shatters at the smallest deviation from the norm, exposing the frail and tenuous positions that they occupy in the modern world.

Cuentos bíblicos y cuentos de la diáspora (Biblical Tales and Tales of the Diaspora; 1985) is a book of short stories that echoes the past while often dealing with modern Jewish or feminist themes. In the opening story "Adán" (Adam), we find Adam posing many historical questions and comments to God, who remains reticent throughout the narrative. Adam bluntly states that he assumes total responsibility for disobeying the Lord's wishes and that he will not blame Eve as others have traditionally done. He also questions God's decision not to punish the angels for their role in the Garden of Eden and wonders why only he and Eve were dealt with harshly. His ending lines chastise God for bringing him into the world as an adult, for not giving him a mother, and for never allowing him to be a child.

In "La sentencia bíblica" (The Biblical Sentence), God, in need of some relaxation, asks an angel to read something to him from the library. The angel chooses a version of the Bible which God has never read. When he reads the part that says that women will give birth in pain, God is incredulous. The angel tells him that all the versions contain the same decree. God says that he never meant it to be painful in any way except that the woman would be emotionally distressed due to her attachment to the child that grew within her. The angel then asserts that it must be a printing error, or an error in translation or interpretation. God leaves the library wondering how many other errors there are which have been taken as the literal and gospel truth.

Both "La fábula" (The Fable) and "Fantasía" (Fantasy) deal with desires to create new histories for Jews. In the first story Padre Torquemada (the infamous Grand Inquisitor who himself was of Jewish descent) tries to convince the King and Queen of Spain to fabricate a story that excludes the Jews from historically significant roles in the Spanish empire. While the monarchs are impressed with the idea, they ironically cannot quite accept that anyone would believe such a tale. The second story shows how Jewish immigrants have recreated their own reality not only by reinventing their existence in the New World, but also by concocting historical fantasies. Both these vignettes show how a lack of written modern Jewish history has enabled people to fill in the empty spaces without any consideration given to truth or accuracy. A similar transgression can be found in the book *La torre de babel* (The Tower of Babel; 1987). In the part entitled "El último tren" (The Last Train) there is a mixture of characters from history, literature, and fantasy who embark on a journey in order to abandon their native Russia. Although written for young adults its treatment of historical figures who appear in other segments, such as Sor Juana Inés de la Cruz (1651-95) and Alfonsina Storni (1892-1938), can attract older readers as well.

Calny's book of poetry *La clepsidra* (The Clepsydra; 1989) treats varying themes from existential solitude to lost love and passion. Many of the individual poems might be interpreted as typically Jewish, demonstrating confusion and alienation, but they also often contain references of love or foreign countries that are incompatible with this particular religious thematic. In the poem "Síntesis" (Synthesis), the author writes of having to mature from within, to know her roots and walk naked before she is able to rule her own life. Although this is mainly a feminist voice, it does deal with confronting the past and stripping away her current trappings in order to gain a better understanding of herself. In "Precipicios" (Precipices), Calny begins the poem stating that she loves precipices and says perhaps that it is because she learned to live at their edge. Jews have learned to live on the cultural edge; however, her religious references here are to Zen Buddhism. "La welwitschia" tells of the South African plant that grew in the desert, but whose roots walk miles and miles away searching for water to quench its thirst. Calny says she understands this plant, "Te comprendo, amiga vegetal y solitaria" (I understand you, my solitary plant friend [19]), that has come so far in order to survive, but the verses that end this poem express the search for love, not religious freedom.

The one poem that is rich in Jewish imagery is entitled "Ancestros" (Ancestors). It speaks of the phantoms that come to life in her memory, in her blood, and of all those who battled in varying countries and times. She writes of her family and Russia, and the train that was either to save them or take them to their deaths; of a father whose hand she never held, of a mother who was once so beautiful, and of a grandfather whose eyes reflect the dark nature of the cossacks. Calny likens her life to an uncontrollable horseback ride, with the brand of death on the animal's rump . She joins and disjoins herself from her ancestors, these strange people who although they speak another language, she can nevertheless understand. In the poem's final verses she reveals that she is more a fictitious character, a ghost, than a real person. Like another Jewish Argentine author, Alejandra Pizarnik (1936-72), the lines between real life and fiction blur. Poetry is the defining expression. The poem "La imaginación" (Imagination), supports the freedom associated with poetic creation. As in her statement from *El unicornio celeste y el caballito con alas* this poem exalts the limitless, unrestrained force of words that operate under no time frame and do not necessarily adhere to any predetermined spirituality. She juxtaposes heaven and hell, sanity and dementia to prove that all these realms must be untethered for true artistic freedom. Calny, like many Jewish women authors, is struggling to shape the particulars of her existence. This self-understanding is paramount to achieving literary identity. Her self-exile to children's literature is unfortunate for adult readers. The subversive humor and irony that permeate her books could help to educate the unenlightened.

PRIMARY BIBLIOGRAPHY
Creative Writing
El agua y la sed. Buenos Aires: Stilcograf, 1964.

"La batalla (Lila)." *39 cuentos de vanguardia.* Comp. Carlos Mastrángelo. Buenos Aires: Plus Ultra, 1985. 93-101.

"Campamento minero." *Trece cuentos argentinos.* Buenos Aires: Instituto Amigos del Libro Argentino, 1965. 29-36.

Clara al amanecer. Buenos Aires: Crisol, 1972.

La clepsidra. Buenos Aires: Ediciones Centro Cultural Corregidor, 1989.

"El concierto." *40 cuentos breves argentinos del siglo XX.* Comp. Fernando Sorrentino. Buenos Aires: Plus Ultra, 1977. 58-62.

Cuentos bíblicos y cuentos de la diáspora. Buenos Aires: Instituto de Intercambio Cultural y Científico Argentino Israelí, 1985.

"El hombre que pudo elegir." In *17 cuentos fantásticos argentinos del siglo XX.* 2da ed. Comp. Fernando Sorrentino. Buenos Aires: Plus Ultra, 1979. 145-52.

La madriguera. Buenos Aires: Instituto Amigos del Libro Argentino, 1967.

Las mujeres virtuosas. Buenos Aires: Instituto Amigos del Libro Argentino, 1967.

"El río..." *Selección de cuentos.* Buenos Aires: Hoy en la Cultura, 1966. 67-71. Also in *Ficción* 10 (1957): 43-45.

"Siesta." *Diez cuentistas argentinas.* Comp. Ernest H. Lewald. Buenos Aires: Riomar, 1968. 27-34. English version as "Siesta." Trans. by H. Ernest

Lewald. In *The Web: Stories by Argentine Women*. Ed. H. Ernest Lewald. Washington, D.C.: Three Continents Press, 1983. 119-24.

La tarde de los ocres dorados. Buenos Aires: Marymar, 1978.

"La Welwittschia." *Pájaro de fuego* 3.21 (1979-80): n.p.

Children's Literature

Los años de colores. Buenos Aires: Norte, 1990.

Conejita blanca y el viaje a la luna. Buenos Aires: Plus Ultra, 1976.

El congreso de los árboles. Buenos Aires: Plus Ultra, 1979.

Cuentos para soñar despierto. Buenos Aires: Magisterio del Río de la Plata, 1987.

Cum, el joven guerrero celta. Buenos Aires: Braga, 1991.

"Los escarabajos y el gato Sitehevisto-nomeacuerdo." *Piolín de barrilete*. Buenos Aires: Leo Lee, 1985. 68-72.

Gatimoreno y los molinos de viento. Buenos Aires: Plus Ultra, 1987.

Gato rayado y ratoncito lector. Buenos Aires: Plus Ultra, 1981.

La gaviota perdida. Buenos Aires: Plus Ultra, 1978.

La góndola y sus hermanos barcos. Buenos Aires: Plus Ultra, 1987.

Historias de ositos. Buenos Aires: Plus Ultra, 1979.

"Ingenuote tímidus, el zorrito." *Amistad, divino tesoro*. Buenos Aires: Orión, 1980. 94-110, 124.

Lágrimas de cocodrilo. Buenos Aires: Plus Ultra, 1987.

El leoncito que quería ser famoso. Buenos Aires: Plus Ultra, 1985.

Morrongo, el gato sin botas y otros cuentos. Buenos Aires: Guadalupe, 1978.

Osobel y la fantasía. Buenos Aires: Sigmar, 1977.

Poemas gatunos. Buenos Aires: Plus Ultra, 1986.

La torre de Babel. Buenos Aires: Guadalupe, 1987.

Totó, el zorro y la fiebre del oro en California. Buenos Aires: Sudamericana, 1984.

El unicornio celeste y el caballito con alas. Buenos Aires: ACME, 1984.

"La Welwittschia." *Pájaro de fuego* 3.21 (1979-80): n.p.

SECONDARY BIBLIOGRAPHY

A.C. "*La tarde de los ocres dorados*, de Eugenia Calny." *Pájaro de fuego* 12 (1979): 20.

Bonome, Rodrigo. "*Las mujeres virtuosas*, de Eugenia Calny." *Bibliograma* 40 (1968): 25-26.

Lipp, Solomon. "The Literary World of Eugenia Calny." *Folio* 17 (1987): 64-73.

Marsky. "*La gaviota perdida* de Eugenia Calny." *Mundo Israelita* 2837 (April 8, 1978): 11.

Mego, Elsa Ofelia. "El agua y la sed." *Señales* 123 (1960): 15-16.

Pirovano, Nélida. "*Conejita Blanca y el viaje a la luna*: Cuentos para los más pequeños." *Bibliograma* 54-55 (1977): 46.

Schon, Isabel. "Eugenia Calny." In *Contemporary Spanish-Speaking Writers and Illustrators for Children and Young Adults*. Ed. Isabel Schon with the collaboration of Lourdes Galvaldón de Barreto. Trans. by Jason Douglas White. Westport, CT: Greenwood Press, 1994. 45-46.

Tapia, Atols. "*El agua y la sed*, por Eugenia Calny." *Ficción* 29 (1961): 144-45.

Weinstein, Ana E., and Miryam Gover de Nasatsky, comps. *Escritores judeo-argentinos: bibliografía 1900-1987*. 2 vols. Buenos Aires: Milá, 1994. I.104-109.

Susan Romain Speirs

CHEJFEC, SERGIO (Argentina; 1956)

Chejfec, about whom biographical information is unavailable, has published three novels. *Lenta biografía* (Slow Biography; 1990) introduces a significantly new dimension in Argentine ethnic literature without abandoning customary themes. The work's title is to be taken literally: through various figures of discourse reiteration, the narrator offers an extremely, almost maddeningly morose account of his attempts to uncover his father's Old World past. He knows that his father is the only survivor of a Polish family destroyed by the Nazis, that he was once a shoemaker (although he has become a carpenter in Argentina), that he made it to Argentina after the war, and that he does not want to talk about the past. By listening in over the years on the meandering weekend discussions of his father and his friends in Yiddish (conversations that are themselves marked by a morose recurring circularity), by reading the signs of his father's many silences, by interpreting the protocols of his chessmanship, and by gingerly approaching him directly on the matter, usually with little result.

The product of these efforts is less the coherent story he is seeking and more an image of the process of encodement by which individuals, lost in a monstrous world, explain their existence and the daily course of events. Built around a story told by an individual about another individual (*el perseguido*—one who is pursued/persecuted) who has, in turn, told about certain events of suffering and deprivation, the narrator constructs a text that is more the biography of himself as a witness to forms of cultural processing than it is the biography of his father he set out to reconstruct. The point is not so much that there is no story to uncover, but rather how the process of cultural encodement both impedes the discovery of what is taken to be the "truth" and serves, in the face of the overwhelming oppressiveness of daily life, to provide a texture of (inter)communication for individuals essentially lost in the morass of history.

Lenta biografía, while at the same time confirming the abiding themes of Jewish immigrant writing in the Americas, provides an excellent example of the function of narrative, on the level of literary writing as well as within the context of natural discourse, not just to give meaning to human experience but, perhaps of greater importance, to provide a materiality for day-to-day existence while confronting all of its horrors.

Chejfec's second novel is, to a great extent, the liquidation of the Argentine Jewish Novel, even if his first novel examined in depth the immigrant experience. In a certain sense, *Moral* (1990) is an antinovel, in the sense that it defies being read as one is accustomed to reading a narrative, especially if it brings with it references to lived sociohistorical experience. Samich is indeed a marginal immigrant, although there is no specific reference to his ethnic or religious culture, except for allusions to his anticlericalism. But he is an immigrant in Buenos Aires as an impulse refugee, so to speak, from Catamarca, having simply decided one day to migrate to the capital. He is marginal through a series of choices: he lives in a modest house in a nondescript (and unidentified) Buenos Aires suburb, where, in defiance of the hard-work ethic of his neighbors, he is a Poet. However, he is an illiterate poet, with no formal literary training and, apparently, the inability to make any sense of the literary tradition. He gathers around himself a few stray individuals who venerate him, but it is clear that this is far from the nucleus for new innovations in the long-standing Argentine tradition of "neighborhood" culture. Samich touts a principle of dispersion, which is indeed the basis of Chejfec's novel: the sensation of recursive digressions that provide a cumulative mosaic of pointlessness. This may certainly be an accurate image of Samich's life, and in the process of implicitly rejecting the concept of transcendent signifiers what the novel does is evacuate of any meaning the triangular narrative conjunction of immigrant antihero, the circumstance of momentous cultural conflict, and the hostile environment in which it is worked out, whether tragically, comically, or pathetically. Thus, if *Moral* (the title is ambiguous in its dual evocation of morals—the word as feminine in Spanish—and of the mulberry tree under whose sparse shadow at the back of Samich's house he and his followers on occasion gather—the word as masculine in Spanish) is a repudiation of the mythopoteic Creole project evoked in Leopoldo Marechal's 1948 *Adán Buenosayres*, it is also the seeming negation that there are any Master Narratives of the Jewish experience in Argentine left to tell. At best, Samich is a parody of the century of such narratives, and the very fact that the novel appears almost to be written to end up unread constitutes the cancellation of even the integrity of his role at that level. Samich—and it is worth noting that Chejfec's third novel will be dedicated to Luisa Samich—belongs to an alternate tradition of Argentine poetry, that of writers who essentially never published during their lifetime. The paradigm here is Macedonio Fernández (1874-1952), one of Borges's mentors, and includes the eccentric novelist Juan Filloy (1894) and Jacobo Fijman (1898-1970), who was in and out of insane asylums and who at one point converted to Catholicism.

El aire (The Air; 1992) indicates that Chejfec has indeed set aside the treatment of Jewish themes in his writing. The novel covers approximately a week in the life of Barroso, who has been abandoned by his wife. While there is no indication that she has left him permanently, the impact on his daily life is as though she has. The disruption of her disappearance brings Barroso back into intimate contact with his own psyche and forces him to scrutinize the routines and ceremonies of his life. Roaming through metropolitan Buenos Aires, a city he senses to be vaguely ominous, Barroso seems to perceive a gradual coming apart of the social pact. It is unclear whether his sense of a threatening collapse of urban civic life is a consequence of the psychological blow of his wife's disappearance or whether her decision is a correlative or a symptom of the social malaise Barroso identifies. *El aire* is an interesting, if undistinguished, example of a sort of postmodern urban writing in which in a minimalist fashion the decline of the urban core is represented, although it never seems to matter much to anyone. There is a long tradition of Argentine writing in which the map of the Buenos Aires megalopolis is more than just the stage for human events, becoming rather a powerful semiotic correlative, in authors as diverse as Roberto Arlt (1900-42) and Eduardo Mallea (1903-82), Ernesto Sabato (1911) and Leopoldo Marechal (1900-70), Enrique Medina (1937) and Marta Lynch (1929-85). In a certain sense, *El aire* invites a reading in terms of current socioeconomic realignments in Argentina, characterized both by aggressive multinationalization and the abandonment of the central urban core, but more than anything else it demonstrates the author's apparent disinterest in pursuing anything resembling ethnic identity—which is, to be sure, itself superfluous in the urban setting posited by the novel.

PRIMARY BIBLIOGRAPHY

El aire. Buenos Aires: Aguilar, Altea, Taurus, Alfaguara, 1992.

"El extranjero." *Noaj* 9 (1993): 40-46. Also, *Punto de vista* (Argentina) 16.45 (1993): 6-11.

Lenta biografía. Buenos Aires: Puntosur Editores, 1990.

Moral. Buenos Aires: Puntosur Editores, 1990.

SECONDARY BIBLIOGRAPHY

Criticism

Aizenberg, Edna. "*Lenta biografía*: el *jad-gadyá* pos-holocáustico, pos-colonial de Sergio Chejfec." *Noaj* 6 (1991): 51-54. Expanded English version as "*Lenta biografía*: Chejfec's Post-Holocaust, Postcolonial *Had Gadya*." In *The Jewish Diaspora in Latin America: New Studies on History and Literature*. Ed. David Sheinin and Lois Baer Barr. New York: Garland, 1996. 53-60.

Foster, David William. Rev. of *Lenta biografía*. *World Literature Today* 65.2 (1991): 274.

Interviews

Saavedra, Guillermo. "Sergio Chejfec: la lenta moral del relato." In his *La curiosidad impertinente: entrevistas con narradores argentinos*. Buenos Aires: Beatriz Viterbo, 1993. 141-53.

David William Foster

CHIROM, PERLA (Argentina; 1937)

Perla Chirom was born in Mar del Plata, Argentina in 1937. She received a law degree from the Universidad de Buenos Aires in 1965 and taught at the Facultad de Derecho (College of Law) until 1975. Beginning in 1979 she has been involved in organizing and directing literary workshops in Buenos Aires. She has also worked as a consultant for the literary journal *Puro cuento*, directed by fellow author Mempo Giardinelli (1947). Chirom has written one full-length novel, but she has mainly concentrated her writing on the short story genre.

Her first collection of stories, *Cuentos con abogados* (Stories with Lawyers; 1969), reflects her education as an attorney. The first three stories are linked by the common denominator of uncertainty or anxiety on the part of the narrator, who in each case is a newly graduated lawyer or has just set up practice. In other instances the theme of corruption in the legal system is presented with particular irony, as is the case in the story "Cómo ser un buen testigo" (How To Be a Good Witness), in which a man is paid to give false testimony at a trial, and who in the end turns out to be the perpetrator of the crime.

Perhaps the most intriguing aspect of this collection is the author's incorporation of elements of the fantastic which are woven into the texts. The fantastic in Argentine women's writing has a rather long history that dates back to mid-nineteenth-century author Juana Manuela Gorriti (1818-92) and continues with twentieth-century writers Silvina Ocampo (1906-94), Luisa Mercedes Levinson (1914-89), Elvira Orpheé (1930), Olga Orozco (1920), and Angélica Gorodischer (1929), among many others. Perla Chirom's early short stories can be easily identified as continuous with the tradition of fantastic literature in Argentina. Stories in which common people are confronted with uncommon occurrences lead the reader to question the limits of reality. For example, a man whose vision slowly changes until the only color he is able to see is gray, the color that best suits his profession, in "El color del tiempo" (The Color of Time). In "Tiempo intermedio" (Intermediate Time), a man experiences an alternate plane of reality while waiting to meet someone in the halls of the court building. "¿Será Justicia?" (Can It Be Justice?) is a rather comical tale in which a statue of Justice comes to life and shows up in the narrator's apartment. She convinces the lawyer-narrator to buy her some clothes that would enable her to go out onto the street unnoticed. The story traces her adventures through the streets of Buenos Aires as she goes from place to place pointing out injustices and commenting on how those in power use her name in order to commit the greatest injustices of all. The humorous tone of the story does not diminish the indictments made by the author on the social inequities to be found in Buenos Aires society.

Chirom's second collection of stories, *El deseo sin amor* (Desire Without Love), was published in 1980. In the ten years since the author's first publication one can note a significant change in tone and style. The sociopolitical realities of Argentina under the military dictatorship known as the Proceso de Reorganización Nacional (Process of National Reorganization [1976-1983]) are strongly felt throughout the stories of *El deseo*. The unifying theme is that of exile; in particular its effects on both those who stayed in the country and those who left. A strong element of nostalgia coupled with an overwhelming sense of despair characterizes these stories and makes them almost painful to read. Acts of love are carried out almost methodically, driven by habit, not by passion. The stories, set in Buenos Aires, contain an abundance of geographic markers (street names, parks, landmarks, cafes, businesses, etc.) that are readily recognizable to any inhabitant of the city and create as much a sense of familiarity as of strangeness. These stories relate the experience of exile from the perspective of those left behind while a number of stories recount the experience of exile as lived in Barcelona, Madrid, or Paris.

Chirom's third collection of short stories, *En la fiesta* (At the Party), was published in 1984, one year following the country's return to democracy. The title story describes the woman narrator's anxiety at a party to which she has been invited. None of the characters are given any names, but are merely referred to as the host, the lawyer, the actress, the poet. Shortly after arriving the woman notices that the hem of her dress is coming unravelled. As it progressively becomes more noticeable her anxiety level increases simultaneously until reaching a state of panic. The majority of the stories concentrates on the psychological motivations of the characters. The theme of exile is again recurrent throughout the collection, with two of the stories from *El deseo sin amor* included. The last three stories are grouped together under the title "Pequeña familia, pequeña historia" (Small Family, Small History). They represent Chirom's most overt treatment of Jewish themes in her writing.

These three stories were reissued by Editorial Milá in 1991 as one volume with the same title, *Pequeña familia, pequeña historia*. The stories are preceded by a brief introduction written by Ricardo Feierstein (1942), and Chirom has also added what she calls a "Relato a manera de prólogo" (A Tale in the Way of a Prologue). The volume contains old photographs of what one assumes are Chirom's immigrant grandparents and which on a much smaller scale allow for a comparison with Mexican writer Margo Glantz's (1930) illustrated novel *Las genealogías* (*The Family Tree*; 1981). Within the text itself, however, the photograph figures rather prominently as a medium by which family history, memory, and Jewish identity are remembered and preserved. In her prologue-style "Relato" Chirom recounts the story of Jewish immigration to Argentina, the process of assimilation, and the return to a Jewish identity because, as she explains, "la tradición era la manera de salvarse, de pertenecer" (tradition was a way to save yourself, to belong [23]). The three stories are connected by the presence of the same characters, photos and objects, such as an old samovar, a family heirloom brought to Argentina by the grandparents. The first story, "Abuela Clara" (Grandmother Clara), is narrated by a woman named Isabel and is set in 1980. She has left Argentina to live in Mexico, in exile. She speaks of long trips, deaths, and disappearances. As she is unpacking boxes in her new home she comes across a box of old photographs that lead her to reminisce about the past. She states that she invokes the past in order to better deal with the present (28). One of the photos is of her Abuela Clara, taken shortly after her arrival in Buenos Aires from Kiev. She remembers her grandmother as at last being free from the pogroms and persecution of Russia, however, not entirely free. A single Jewish woman in Buenos Aires had few options. She marries and makes many sacrifices so that one day her children or grandchildren will be able to study and have a better life. "Abuelo Víctor" (Grandfather Victor) tells of the grandfather's arrival in Argentina in 1910 singing anti-Czarist songs, with one particular line about the "chancho burgués" (bourgeois pig) being repeated throughout the story. He had every intention of returning to Kiev one day. In Argentina he becomes active in the Socialist party and his political activities are intertwined with his religious ones. There is a photo of him taken during the Semana Trágica (Tragic Week) of 1919, also known as the Argentine pogrom in which many Jews were killed in an uprising. Víctor grows old in Argentina and somewhat embittered as he realizes that none of his younger family members have ever joined in his causes. The last story, "La tía" (The Aunt), is a brief and tragic portrayal of the tragedy of the military dictatorship. The family has met together and is looking at old photographs, commenting and laughing until a picture of Aunt Eugenia appears. The room goes silent as the photo brings painful memories to the fore. The unidentified narrator recalls Eugenia's past, her childhood, marriage, and children, but sadly states that since 1976 nothing has been the same (42). Her son Luis was "disappeared" by the military and the remark is made that the last time anyone saw Eugenia was on the television with some other women who had white handkerchiefs on their heads; an obvious allusion to the Mothers of the Plaza de Mayo.

Chirom's first and only novel to date, *Nostalgia del último domingo de verano* (Nostalgia for the Last Sunday of Summer; 1988) takes up some of the topics found in *El deseo sin amor* and *En la fiesta*. It is essentially a novel of exile and its psychological impact. The book takes its title from the date on which a group of friends meets one Sunday in March 1976. The obvious referent, although never overtly stated, is that this is the last day of normality prior to the military coup of March 1976, an event which irrevocably and permanently altered Argentine culture and society. This was the last time the narrator saw her lover, who says he's leaving for Europe. The novel consists mainly of a series of interior monologues, letters, and diary entries that trace the protagonist's search for her exiled lover, from whom she never hears again. She is haunted by his memory and cannot overcome her loss or the uncertainty surrounding his disappearance. She consults a fortune teller who advises her to travel to Russia and Europe. There is a passing reference to the protagonist's Jewish identity as she visits Kiev, the city from which her grandparents emigrated. She visits the

synagogue where her grandfather worshipped and discovers bread like her grandmother used to bake in Argentina in a bakery. She travels to Paris to visit a
friend exiled there and she spends quite a lot of time in Italy where she meets
a young Uruguayan, also exiled. Each letter that she receives she expects to be
from Joel and at each corner she hopes to see his face. Finally, she returns to Argentina without having found even a sign of him. Temporally, the novel covers
the entire period of the dictatorship and the return to democracy. It ends with the
protagonist attending a wedding with the same group of friends that had met on
that Sunday in March 1976.

Perla Chirom's writing is a telling testimony of Argentine reality of the
past two decades. Her narrative forms part of a large corpus of works by Argentine writers who have attempted to give witness to the tragedy occasioned by the
so-called *Proceso*.

PRIMARY BIBLIOGRAPHY

Cuentos con abogados. Buenos Aires: Ediciones Argentinas, 1969.
El deseo sin amor. Buenos Aires: Rodolfo Alonso, 1980.
En la fiesta. Buenos Aires: Losada, 1983.
Nostalgia del último domingo de verano. Buenos Aires: Galerna, 1988.
Pequeña familia, pequeña historia. Buenos Aires: Milá, 1991.

SECONDARY BIBLIOGRAPHY

Feierstein, Ricardo. "La literatura de la memoria." In *Pequeña familia, pequeña
    historia*. Buenos Aires: Milá, 1991. 5-6.
Gimbernat González, Ester. "*Nostalgia del último domingo de verano*: La pere-
    grina de nostalgias." In her *Aventuras del desacuerdo: novelistas argen-
    tinas de los 80*. Buenos Aires: Danilo Albero Vergara, 1992. 103-7.

                                                            Darrell B. Lockhart

CHOCRÓN, ISAAC (Venezuela; 1930)

Isaac Chocrón is one of the most important figures in Venezuelan literature, excelling as a playwright and novelist, as well as a literary critic. The son
of a Jewish family, Chocrón received his first years of education within both the
Jewish and Catholic religions in Venezuela, and later received a Protestant educa-

tion when at fifteen he was sent to study at a military academy in the United States. Chocrón continued his education in the United States and in 1952 he earned a Bachelor of Arts from Syracuse University. From Syracuse he went on to Columbia University, where he earned a Masters degree in International Studies in 1954. He later (1959-60) did postgraduate work in economic development at Manchester University.

In Venezuela Chocrón's never-tiring labors have earned him a solid reputation within the field of Venezuelan theater. Together with his activities as playwright and novelist during a period of thirty-seven years, the author has also held administrative positions within some of the country's institutions that have notably contributed to the development of Venezuelan theater. Chocrón has been the president of a theater group called El Nuevo Grupo (The New Group), president of the Venezuelan Association of Theater Professionals, president of the National Theater Council, and vice-president of the Teatro Juvenil de Venezuela (Venezuelan Youth Theater). Furthermore, the author has been a professor of a seminar on Latin American theater and in the Master's Program in Latin American literature at Simón Bolívar University, a professor at the Escuela de Arte de la Universidad Central de Venezuela (School of Art of the University of Central Venezuela), the director of the theater workshop of the Rómulo Gallegos Center for Latin American Studies, and a professor of the National School of Theater. Added to all these activities is the fact that Chocrón, as a excellent representative of Venezuelan theater, is constantly being invited to lecture at conferences and visiting faculty positions at different universities in the United States.

As a writer, Chocrón began his career in 1956 with his novel *Pasaje* (Passage), a work in which a certain topic stands out, among others, that will characterize his later works: the presentation of individuals who feel like foreigners within their own country, and even within their own family nucleus. Following *Pasaje*, the first Festival of Venezuelan Theater took place (1959) in which Chocrón participated with his first play titled *Mónica y el florentino* (Mónica and the Florentine). From 1959 to the present Chocrón has continued writing to such an extent that his literary production includes seventeen plays, an opera libretto, "Doña Bárbara" (1967), an ensemble of texts of the play entitled *Teresa* (1982), seven novels, and various essays and critical articles. His latest dramatic text titled *Escrito y sellado* (Written and Sealed) was presented on the Caracas stage in April and May 1993.

One of the objectives of Chocrón's theater is to orient the reader/spectator toward social awareness through the use of certain techniques or dramatic strategies. His personal style and influence on national theater have led critics to refer to Chocronian technique. In his first two works, *Mónica y el florentino* and *El quinto infierno* (The Fifth Inferno; 1961), for example, the elements of the written or performed text foreshadow a type of presentation that follows the standards of realist theater. In the case of *El quinto infierno* the playwright introduces a symbolic element that breaks with realism: an immense glass wall that functions as both a window and a mirror. The audience is lead to believe that it has a privileged view—as an observer through a window—of all the family's actions upon which the work centers. However, in reality Chocrón makes the audience arrive at the conclusion that what it saw in the dramatic presentation was a reflection of itself. In *Amoroso o una mínima incandescencia* (Loving or a Minimal Incandescence; 1961), techniques belonging to the Theater of the Absurd are utilized in order to present the relationship between the characters to the reader/spectator. In *Asia y el Lejano Oriente* (Asia and the Far East; 1966), as likewise in *Okey* (1969), Chocrón approaches one of his favorite themes, referring to the world as a great market where everything can be bought or sold. Thus in *Asia y el Lejano Oriente* he presents a town enraptured in a kind of game in which the people sell their own country to a foreign consortium. In this work Chocrón utilizes techniques borrowed from Brechtian theater. With the use of these techniques it is hoped that the reader/spectator, in a critical and objective way, will evaluate the events that have been presented on stage, reflect on them and take his/her critique beyond the stage. In *Tric-Trac* (1967), the dramatic action occurs in a children's park and the scenery consists solely of a cage constructed from scaffolding, on which ten characters identified only by a number worn on their chest, strike up a game that permits them to give expression to the different problems that afflict them in their daily lives. Chocrón's desire to utilize different methods in his dramatic works has led him to a process of experimentation that manifests itself quite well in *Alfabeto para analfabetos* (Alphabet for Illiterates; 1973). The work refers to language itself and its innovation lies in the fact that letters and words are used as basic elements of the dramatic structure. Through the use of an uninterrupted verbal game, which includes the use of choruses and kinesthetic elements, the characters take a journey through the twenty-eight letters in the Spanish alphabet. In *Simón* (1983), the titles given to the four scenes that divide the play correspond to the four movements of Beethoven's *Eroica*. It is necessary to point out that although the dramatic action has as its focal point two historical figures, Simón Bolívar and Simón Rodríguez, neither of the two is presented in their condition as national heroes. The fundamental idea is to project on the stage the sincere friendship that in real life united the two characters. The subject of friendship is also presented in another play titled *Mesopotamia* (1980). Together with his technique, there is another characteristic of Chocrón's works: the act of raising questions without giving solutions. The emphasis falls on the process by which the reader/spectator's attitudes are manipulated, his/her vision oriented, and his/her imaginative faculties stimulated in order to make him/her a dynamic collaborator in the interpretation of the text.

It is only natural that Chocrón project his Jewish identity as the subject matter of some of his plays. Using memory as a base, the dramatic action in *Animales feroces* (Fierce Animals; 1963), and in *Clípper* (1987), revolves around the personal relationships among the members of two families of Sephardic origin. In *Clípper* the problem of generational conflict is posed: the parents as immigrants from Casablanca and Melilla, have arrived in America to settle and make their lives in a social, religious, and cultural environment that is not their own. Their primary desire is to maintain their identity and their tradition as Jews, but the children do not want to be like their parents and do not desire to act according to the social and religious rules that their elders try to impose on them. This generates a conflictive situation between parents and children, and as a consequence disagreements in the home are made manifest principally in the rebellious attitude of the children. In spite of the existing quarrels, the relationships among the family members in *Clípper* are not of a destructive nature, rather an atmosphere of affection among the characters in presented. This is contrary to what occurs in *Animales feroces* in which the characters are tense, confused, and unhappy. They attack each other verbally, accuse and criticize one another, and at times criticize Jewish religious practice. What is projected, then, is not the image of a united family, but rather a group of animals that, like wild beasts, attempts to devour each other. When the play was performed it gave rise to a wide variety of opinions and provoked a certain uproar among the members of the Jewish community. As a consequence it was necessary that the author insert a personal declaration in the program in which he asserted his adherence to a Jewish identity. This declaration has been reproduced in an article titled "Tu boca en los cielos" (Your Mouth in Heaven; 1985). *Clípper* and *Animales feroces* may be considered to have particular value to a Jewish audience for the obvious Jewish thematic content that both contain, however, they are also both valuable to a non-Jewish Venezuelan public because they present an image of a component of Venezuelan society that forms part of the country's social identity. What is presented on stage in these two plays could just as well occur in any family, regardless of religious identity.

Chocrón has also written seven novels, his latest is *Toda una dama* (All Lady; 1988). Many of the themes presented in his dramatic texts are also common to his novels. *Pájaro de mar por tierra* (Landlocked Seagull; 1972) can be characterized as epistolary in nature, in which the author makes his presence very clear. Through letters and interviews the life of the main character comes to be known; he is confused and without direction in life but attempts to get to know himself. In *Se ruega no tocar la carne por razones de higiene* (Please Don't Touch the Meat for Reasons of Hygiene; 1970), the narrative voice and the voices of the two characters work together to establish an effective means of narrative communicaton. *Cincuenta vacas gordas* (Fifty Fat Cows; 1980), is a mystery novel in which the protagonist is the unwilling witness of a crime. Through a first-person narrative she combines descriptions of what she saw, with memories of her childhood and her personal life as an adult. The narration also covers fifty years of political life in Venezuela. *Señales de tráfico* (Traffic Signals; 1972), is a chronicle that covers different themes with no connection to each other but in total form a series of topics that concern the contemporary individual. The themes are grouped under the following titles: travels, cities, deeds, people, books, film, and theater. Within Chocrón's novelistic production, *Rómpase en caso de incendio* (Break Glass in Case of Fire; 1975), is the only novel that explicitly contains a Jewish theme. The main body of the novel is made up of letters that the principal character, a Sephardic Venezuelan, sends to Chocrón himself, and other friends. After the death of his loved ones in Caracas, the protagonist, left alone and feeling to a certain degree alienated in his own country, embarks on a voyage to Madrid, Melilla, and Tangier with the objective of coming to terms with his roots and possibly in this way achieving a sort of spiritual peace.

Although not all of Chocrón's works openly deal with obvious Jewish themes, as is the case with *Clípper*, *Animales feroces*, and *Rómpase en caso de incendio*, the author in his labors as playwright and novelist, very much in his own style, and preoccupied with the problems that concern all human beings, focuses in his works—either as a fundamental or secondary theme—on the different problems of contemporary man, some of which can be said to go hand in hand with the Jewish condition. In his novels and plays his varied subject matter includes relates to uprootedness, loneliness, the lack of identity, family relationships, feeling out of place, rebellion against the establishment, the conflicts within groups of marginated or alienated persons within society caused by sexual or religious preferences or their condition of being emigrants/immigrants, power, friendship, anguish due to death and the passage of time, the interior emptiness of the characters, the desire to move up the social scale in search of a better standard of living, lack of direction or objectives in life, the chosen family versus the inherited family, Venezuela and its people, the use of language, lack of communication, the buying and selling of material objects as well as of human beings (in a world where money, material things, and luxury are worth more than personal relationships and the feelings derived from such relationships). All of these varied subjects are related to the type of character that Chocrón creates, since according to him characters "surgen de experiencias personales, observaciones que él hace, y son todos compuestos de gente que él conoce, con un poquito de inventado" ("surface from personal experiences, observations that he makes, and they are all composed of people that he knows, with a little invention" [Larson, "Entrevista" 119]).

PRIMARY BIBLIOGRAPHY
Creative Writing

Alfabeto para analfabetos. Caracas: Fundarte, 1980.

Amoroso o una mínima incandescencia. Caracas: Ediciones Teatro de Arte Caracas, 1962.

A propósito de triángulo (3ra parte de *Triángulo*). Caracas: Editorial Tierra Firme, 1962.

Asia y el Lejano Oriente; Tric-Trac. Caracas: Ediciones del Rectorado de la Universidad de los Andes, 1966.

Cincuenta vacas gordas. Caracas: Monte Avila, 1980.

Clípper. In *Teatro venezolano contemporáneo: antología*. Madrid: Centro de Documentación Teatral, Ministerio de Cultura; Sociedad Estatal Quinto Centenario; Fondo de Cultura Económica, 1991. 333-99.

Clípper; Simón. Caracas: Alfadil, 1987.

Color natural. Caracas: Grupo Montaña, 1968.

Doña Bárbara (libreto de ópera con arreglo musical de Caroline Lloyd). Caracas: Instituto Nacional de Cultura y Bellas Artes, 1967.

Escrito y sellado. Caracas: Ex Libris, 1993.

Mónica y el florentino. Caracas: Monte Avila, 1980.

Pájaro de mar por tierra. Caracas: Tiempo Nuevo, 1972.

Pasaje: un relato. Caracas: Monte Avila, 1956.

La Pereza domina Timbuctú. In *Los siete pecados capitales*. Manuel Trujillo, et al. Colección Teatro. Caracas: Monte Avila, 1974. 51-73.

El quinto infierno. Caracas: Ediciones Zodíaco, 1961.

Rómpase en caso de incendio. Caracas: Monte Avila, 1975.

Señales de tráfico: relatos. Caracas: Monte Avila, 1972.

Se ruega no tocar la carne por razones de higiene. Caracas: Tiempo Nuevo, 1970.

Solimán el magnífico. Caracas: Monte Avila, 1992.

Teatro I: Okey; La revolución; El acompañante. Caracas: Monte Avila, 1981.

Teatro II: Animales feroces; La máxima felicidad; Mesopotamia. Caracas: Monte Avila, 1984.

Teatro III: Mónica y el florentino; El quinto infierno; Amoroso o una mínima incandescencia. Caracas: Monte Avila, 1987.

Teatro IV: Asia y el Lejano Oriente; Tric-Trac; Alfabeto para analfabetos. Caracas: Monte Avila, 1990.

Teatro V: Simón; Clípper; Solimán el Magnífico. Caracas: Monte Avila, 1992.

Teresa. (Ensamblaje de textos por Isaac Chocrón llevado a escena por El Nuevo Grupo), 1982.

Toda una dama. Caracas: Alfadil Ediciones, 1988.

Nonfiction

Maracaibo 180°. Caracas: Ediciones Centro de Bellas Artes, 1978.

Nueva crítica de teatro venezolano. Caracas: Fundarte, 1981.

El nuevo teatro venezolano. Caracas: Oficina Central de Información, 1966.

El teatro de Sam Shepard: de imágenes a personas. Caracas: Monte Avila, 1991.

"Ser judío sefardí venezolano." *El Universal* 20 junio 1983: A1.

Sueño y tragedia en el teatro norteamericano. Caracas: Alfadil Ediciones, 1984.

Tendencias del teatro contemporáneo. Caracas: Monte Avila, 1968.

Tres fechas claves del teatro contemporáneo venezolano. Caracas: Fundarte, 1979.

"Tu boca en los cielos." *Hispamérica* 4.2 (1985): 65-71.

SECONDARY BIBLIOGRAPHY

Criticism

Aizenberg, Edna. "Sephardim and Neo-Sephardim in Latin American Literature." *The Sephardic Scholar* 4 (1979-1982): 125-32.

Azparren Giménez, Leonardo. "Isaac Chocrón: en busca de las pistas perdidas." *El teatro venezolano y otros teatros.* Caracas: Monte Avila, 1978. 107-28.

—. *"La revolución." Imagen* 38 (1972): 3.

Araujo, Elizabeth. *"Clípper* de Chocrón ganó unánimemente". *El Nacional* 25 Feb., 1988: C14.

Castillo, Susana. *El desarraigo en el teatro venezolano: marco histórico y manifestaciones modernas.* Caracas: Ateneo de Caracas, 1980. 85-122.

Cortés, Adriana. "La intimidad de Chocrón en *Clípper." 2001* 22 marzo 1987: 359.

Durbin, Joyce Lee. *La dramaturgia de Isaac Chocrón.* Ph.D. dissertation, Texas Tech, 1988.

Foster, David William. *Gay and Lesbian Themes in Latin American Writing.* Austin: U of Texas P, 1991. 51-55.

Friedman, Edward. "The Beast Within: The Rhetoric of Signification in Isaac Chocrón's *Animales feroces.*" *Folio* 17 (1987): 167-83.

——. "Cherchez la femme: El lector como detective en *50 vacas gordas* de Isaac Chocrón." *Discurso literario* 4.2 (1987): 647-56.

——. Playing with Fire: The Search for Selfhood in Isaac Chocrón's *Rómpase en caso de incendio.*" *Confluencia* 3.2 (1988): 27-37.

——. Rev. of *Clipper/Simón. Chasqui* 17.2 (1988): 142-43.

Giella, Miguel Angel. "Chocrón o la vocación teatral." *Primer acto: cuadernos de investigación teatral* 235 (1990): 98-101.

Hernández, Gleider. "El Bolívar de Isaac Chocrón." *Confluencia* 3.2 (1991): 39-46.

——. "Isaac Chocrón: lo histórico y lo antihistórico." In *Actas del IX Congreso de la Asociación Internacional de Hispanistas, I & II.* Ed. Sabastian Neumeister. Intro. Dieter Heckelmann and Franco Meregalli. Frankfurt: Vervuert, 1989. 559-66.

——. *Teatro: tres dramaturgos venezolanos de hoy: R. Chalbaud, J. I. Cabrujas, I. Chocrón.* Caracas: Ediciones El Nuevo Grupo, 1979. 93-133.

Jiménez, Maritza. "Chocrón: Soy un pez raro." *El Nacional* 30 octubre 1988: C1.

Klein, Dennis A. "The Theme of Alienation in the Theatre of Elisa Lerner and Isaac Chocrón." *Folio* 17 (1987): 151-66.

Larson, Milagro. "El lector/espectador frente a las estrategias dramáticas en obras selectas de Isaac Chocrón." Ph.D. dissertation, Arizona State University, 1991.

Mannarino, Carmen. "Chocrón o la palabra intencionada." *Imagen* 100.78 (1991): 10-11.

——. "Retrato de familia [*Clípper*]." *Teatro venezolano contemporáneo: antología.* Madrid: Centro de Documentación Teatral, Ministerio de Cultura; Sociedad Estatal Quinto Centenario; Fondo de Cultura Económica, 1991. 325-31.

Nigro, Kirsten. "A Triple Insurgence: Isaac Chocrón's *La revolución.*" *Rocky Mountain Review* 35.1 (1981): 47-53.

——. "Gringo on the Latin American Stage." *Ideas 192* 1.2 (1988): 81-89.

Rivera, Francisco. "Tres textos de Isaac Chocrón." *El Nacional* (Séptimo Día, papel literario) 4 febrero 1973: 9.

Rotker, Susana. *Isaac Chocrón y Elisa Lerner: los transgresores de la literatura venezolana.* Caracas: Fundarte, 1991.

Sosnowski, Saúl. "*Clípper*, de Isaac Chocrón: salida internacional." *Ensayos sobre judaísmo latinoamericano*. Buenos Aires: Milá, 1990. 417-24.

Torres, Víctor F. "Chocrón, Isaac." In *Latin American Writers on Gay and Lesbian Themes: A Bio-Critical Sourcebook*. Ed. David William Foster. Westport, CT: Greenwood, 1994. 110-15.

Ulive, Ugo. "*Solimán el magnífico* en la obra de Chocrón." *Conjunto* 90-91 (1992): 43-45.

Vestrini, Miyo. *Isaac Chocrón frente al espejo*. Caracas: Editorial Ateneo de Caracas, 1980.

Younoszai, Barbara, and Rossi Irausquin. "Not Establishing Limits: The Writing of Isaac Chocrón." *Inti: revista de literatura hispánica* 37-38 (1993): 155-61.

Interviews

Delgado, Carmen. "Entrevista en dos actos a un provocador: Isaac Chocrón." *El Nacional* 29 junio 1969: B8.

Larson, Milagro. "Entrevista con Isaac Chocrón." *Confluencia* 6.2 (1991): 117-25.

Senkman, Leonardo. "Entrevista a Isaac Chocrón: el misterio de la familia que heredamos." *Noah* 1.1 (1987): 79-82.

Waldman, Gloria. "An Interview with Isaac Chocrón." *Latin American Theatre Review* 11.1 (1977): 103-09.

Milagro Larson

CHUDNOVSKY, JOSÉ (Argentina; 1915-66)

José Chudnovsky was born in 1915 in the Argentine province of Entre Ríos, the principal region of the Jewish agricultural settlements founded by Baron Mauricio Hirsch. Chudnovsky's two novels, *Dios era verde* (God Was Green; 1963), and *Pueblo pan* (People of Bread; 1967), are largely biographical and based on the immigrant experience of his family. Both novels draw heavily on the figure of Chudnovsky's father who earned himself a considerable reputation as an educator (Senkman). Each novel is prefaced with an enthusiastic prologue by Guatemalan writer and Nobel laureate Miguel Angel Asturias (1899-1974).

In contrast to *Pueblo pan*, *Dios era verde* deals only obliquely with any specific Jewish theme. Indeed, any mention of Jewishness only comes after the first half of the novel. The text is interesting for its setting in the northeastern province of Chaco, an unusual backdrop for the novel of Jewish immigration. The book is narrated by the young protagonist whose nickname is Pajarito de Plomo (Little Leaden Bird). Asturias finds symbolic significance in the name in that it connotes both permanence and flight (*Dios era verde* 11). The novel follows the young narrator's experiences growing up in the rural Argentine outback. He comes to understand and respect the land as he learns from his father and older brother as well as from their neighbors. The novel may be considered a *bildungsroman* narrative as it traces the young hero's development into manhood at the tutelage of his more experienced elders. Pajarito describes life on their humble dairy farm in almost tedious detail. He is often impatient and critical of his father's frequently failed projects, which include chicken raising, cotton growing, dairy farming, silage processing, and growing bananas. He has very little communication with his father, Abraham, and finds it difficult to relate to him. His father speaks to him of the pogroms in Russia, of attending the cheder, and of teaching the Talmud. Abraham sees his son growing up entirely as an Argentine, outside of Jewish tradition. He inquisitively ponders "¿acaso puedo hablarte como a un judío?" (can I even speak to you as a Jew? [135]). His father desperately wants Pajarito to study, but the boy finds the local school too demanding and intimidating and soon drops out. Throughout the novel the reader gets the distinct impression that Pajarito is headed for better things yet it is not until the final three chapters that he leaves the family farm to get an education in Buenos Aires. After spending several trying years he returns home to Chaco to finds things just as he left them, or worse. He only stays for a visit and it is on the train back to Buenos Aires that he finally gains an understanding of who his father is and his relationship with him through some old letters. In the letters Abraham reveals his sentiments toward Judaism. He expounds on his disbelief in God in spite of his pious upbringing. Abraham proclaims Nature to be his god, and that God is to be found in all that is green and springs from the earth, not in the tattered pages of the Talmud.

One of the more telling episodes of the book is to be found in the protagonist's preoccupation with his appearance. It is quite clear that Pajarito is worried about looking Jewish. One day he suddenly realizes that his face is changing, more specifically that his nose is growing. He is horrified that the bridge of his nose seems to be swollen, and he can recognize his father's nose emerging from his face. In a desperate attempt to stop the physical transformation of his nose he decides to tightly bind it to impede the growth. Inspired by the Chinese custom of binding feet, he binds his nose while on his daily milk route from farm to farm, taking the apparatus off when he meets up with someone.

Pueblo pan is Chudnovsky's definitive text. It can be considered as a historical novel that recounts the story of Jewish colonization on the Argentine pampas. In contrast to Alberto Gerchunoff's (1884-1950) rather glossed over version of events in his *Los gauchos judíos* (1910), *Pueblo pan* is much more realistic in its portrayal of the immigration experience. The author not only relates the many hardships and trials that the colonists had to endure, but he also quite frankly discusses the corruption within the Jewish Colonization Association; in spite of the fact that Chudnovsky viewed the Association with the utmost regard as a means of Jewish progress. Highly evident in Chudnovsky's writing is the influence of Eastern European Jewish thought, in particular the ideals of Haskalah, or the Jewish Enlightenment. This in part explains Chudnovsky's insistence on the Jew's physical and spiritual ties to the land in an effort to renew his connection with Nature. The text continually makes an effort to sort out the problematics of being Jewish in Argentina: wholeheartedly embracing the new country and its customs, while at the same time being very committed to specifically Jewish ways of being, primarily through Jewish social movements and ideological beliefs. In essence this meant to be civically Argentine, and spiritually and culturally Jewish. A common idea set forth by Haskalah was to be Jewish at home and a common man in the street. This type of existence was found to be possible and desirable in Argentina, which many considered to be a new Jewish homeland.

Pueblo pan contains a constant flow of real life figures who appear on its pages as characters. Politicians, authors, ideologues, philanthropists, famous pioneer colonists, all come together to give the text a certain quality of historical verity. The narrative body of the text is separated by sections of interior monologue by the narrator/author in which he ponders his existence as a Jew, and as a Jew in Argentina. Chudnovsky's novel is quite possibly the most complete and honest fictional account of early Jewish immigration to the agricultural colonies of Argentina.

Aside from his two novels, Chudnovsky also wrote a rather interesting short story that was published posthumously in the journal *Davar*. "Tel Jay, el Monte de la Vida," (Tel Jai, the Mount of Life) was inspired by the author's trip to Israel in 1963. The story revolves around two central themes: the Holocaust and the edification of the state of Israel. It is structured around the visit of a Jewish couple from South America to their relatives in Israel. The visiting cousins spark old memories of the Holocaust in Itka, a survivor of the Nazi terror. She recounts the horrifying time spent in the concentration camp; how she escaped death numerous times until the Russians finally liberated them and they were able to emigrate to Palestine. Itka's story is told with incredible detail and emotion. The story is framed by testimonies that speak to the necessity of Israel as a safe haven, a home of their own, so that Jews never have to find themselves at the mercy of other nations. Judaism is described as being second to Israelism. Israel for the Jews of Poland was like "Dios, lejano, invisible" (God, distant, invisible [29]). The symbol of Israel's strength is defined by the Israeli characters of Mount Tel Jai, which gives the story its title. The hill was defended by a small number of Jews who gave their lives to preserve the Jewish state of Israel against the Arab armies.

Chudnovsky also published two volumes of poetry in Buenos Aires: *Motivos íntimos* (Intimate Motives; 1950), and *Pasos en el alma* (Steps in the Soul; 1952). Unfortunately, the author's poetry has gone virtually unnoticed, and he continues to be remembered for his narrative works.

PRIMARY BIBLIOGRAPHY

Dios era verde. Prologue by Miguel Angel Asturias. Buenos Aires: Goyanarte, 1963. 2d ed. Buenos Aires: Plus Ultra, 1965.

"Israel, miel y sal." *Nueva Sión* 415 (Oct. 1, 1965): 16.

Motivos íntimos. Buenos Aires, n.p., 1950.

Pasos en el alma. Buenos Aires: n.p., 1952.

Pueblo Pan. Prologue by Miguel Angel Asturias. Buenos Aires: Losada, 1967.

"Tel Jay, el Monte de la Vida." *Davar* 415 (1966): 18-30.

SECONDARY BIBLIOGRAPHY

Pavlotzky, José. "*Dios era verde*." *Davar* 103 (1964): 146-48.

Poletti, Syria. "*Pueblo pan*." *Davar* 116 (1968): 153-54.

Senkman, Leonardo. "Chudnovski [sic] y la colonización judía." *La identidad judía en la literatura argentina*. Buenos Aires: Pardés, 1983. 79-98.

Schwartz, Kessel. "The Jew in Twentieth-Century Argentine Fiction." *The American Hispanist* 3.19 (1977): 9-12.

Tapia, Atols. "*Dios era verde*." *Bibliograma* 29 (1964): 23-24.

Weinstein, Ana E., and Miryam E. Gover de Nasatsky, comps. *Escritores judeo-argentinos: bibliografía 1900-1987*. 2 vols. Buenos Aires: Milá, 1994. I.127-29.

Darrell B. Lockhart

COHEN, MARCELO (Argentina; 1951)

Marcelo Cohen, a writer, translator, journalist, and literary critic was born in Buenos Aires in 1951. After having abandoned graduate studies in literature, Cohen worked as a journalist in Buenos Aires until he emigrated to Barcelona, Spain, where he has resided since 1975. There he began his career as a translator, which he has alternated with journalism and fiction writing. He has published in the Barcelona journal *El viejo topo* (The Old Mole), the Madrid newspaper *El País* (The Country) and the cultural supplement of the newspaper *La vanguardia* (The Vanguard) on topics of literature and cultural politics. Since 1990, his articles also have been published in the newspapers *El País* of Montevideo and *Clarín* (The Clarion) of Buenos Aires, as well as the Argentine journal *Diario de poesía* (Poetry Newspaper). In 1980 he co-founded the literary journal *Quimera* (Hallucination) and the Montesinos publishing house. He has translated the works of Jane Austen (1775-1817), Robert Louis Stevenson (1852-94), Henry James (1843-1916), F. Scott Fitzgerald (1896-1940), John Dos Passos (1896-1970), T. S. Eliot (1888-1965) and James Ballard (1930), among others. He has also translated works from Catalan, Italian and Portuguese. He is currently the editor of Spanish language narrative for the Anaya and Mario Muchnik publishing house. He has participated in a variety of academic activities which include seminars, round tables, and conferences. He was writer in residence at the Maison des Ecrivians étrangers et Traducteurs de Saint-Nazaire, whose publishing house, Arcane 17, has announced the publication of the translation of his short novel *Inolvidables veladas* (Unforgettable Evenings; 1993), not yet published in Spanish. He was a grant recipient of The British Centre for Literary Translation, University of East Anglia, Norwich, England, for his translation of *Titus Alone* (1994) by Mervyn Peake (1911-68).

Cohen's literature is representative of another facet of the dissolution of geographic and literary boundaries characteristic of the literature of this fin de siècle. His novels and short stories alike are structured upon three spaces that interact and feed off of one another: the space of the futuristic, counterutopian tale; a localist subject matter, populated by Buenos Aires characters, in the style of Jorge Luis Borges (1899-1986) in his "El hombre de la esquina rosada" ("Streetcorner Man") or the early texts of Julio Cortázar (1914-84); and the universe of interpersonal relationships, characteristic of the psychological narrative. None of these nuclei in Cohen's writing is developed independent of the others, although in some of his short stories a single space tends to dominate almost completely. One element that is central to the construction of the futuristic story in Cohen's work is the positioning of his stories within syncretic, postnational geographies. The territories in which his stories take place are organized with different criteria than those of the modern nation. They are purely fictional places like Lorelei in *El oído absoluto* (The Perfect Pitch; 1989) or Bardas de Kramer in *Insomnio* (Insomnia; 1986), or chaotic continental conglomerations as in "Donde se realizan los sueños" (Where Dreams Come True [*El buitre en invierno*]). These places correspond to forms of government with high concentrations of power, which make the decisions of the individuals who inhabit them trivial by comparison. As soon as the individual alters the course that has been preset for him (even when he is part of the power structure), violence rears against him in its worst form. The characters are bound to these geographies, without freedom of movement (*El oído absoluto* or *El testamento de O'Jaral* [The Testament of O'Jaral; 1995]), or they amble about unnamed or ghostly territories (*El país de la dama eléctrica* [Electric Lady Land; 1984] or "La ilusión monarca" [The Monarch Illusion; in *El fin de lo mismo*]). In this postnational, postpolitical and postindustrial imaginary of Cohen's stories, technological advances are rarely mentioned, constituting nothing more than another means of oppression and disorientation for the characters. Another frequent topic in Cohen's stories is found in the presence of radical social changes taking place in the communities described. These changes render invalid certain cultural molds or idiosyncracies. The pain that the characters feel when faced with these circumstances instills in them a condition of maladjustment, which is presented not as a handicap but as a strategy of survival; for example in "El instrumento más caro de la tierra" (in the book by the same title) or "Visita de médico" (Doctor's Appointment; in *El buitre en invierno*)

In terms of language, Cohen proposes a defamiliarization of the literary phrase, imagery and metaphoric word play, in search of verbal independence. The result of this attempt is a descriptive language in which associations are unexpected, at times avant-garde, although in general with a mark that distinguishes his writing. He disarms the traditional, logical, association already established in the language, to propose another, improbable and seldom used. One of the most reiterated mechanisms in this style is imprecision: once the image or even the action is established, language disrupts them, negates them, and therefore impedes them from taking definite shape. Careful attention to verbal construction is essential to the creation of Cohen's literary imagery. Things are described fundamentally through verbs and adjectives which are often contradictory to the object they describe. In this way, as the text advances it constantly discredits itself. This procedure is particularly apparent in the dynamic of the characters' interaction. Misunderstandings and extreme superficiality surround these individuals, whose encounters are by definition always incomplete and emphatically declared as being undesired and unnecessary. Many of the events occur as if by the imposition of circumstances or due to the lack of a more active or aggressive attitude toward reality. This and other distancing techniques of literary language produce a disconcerting effect, that because of its imprecision becomes sometime circular and difficult to understand. Furthermore, Cohen wields diverse linguistic registers in his characters' speech; for example, the constant archaisms of one of the characters in *El sitio de Kelany* (The Site of Kelany; 1987); the language of the foreigner who has learned Spanish, and that of translations by characters in *Insomnio*; the neologisms of a fictional popular language in, for example, *El país de la dama eléctrica* or *El testamento de O'Jaral.*

Cohen published his first collection of short stories, *Los pájaros también se comen* (Birds Are also To Be Eaten; 1975), in Argentina. This volume (that Cohen tends not to include in his bibliography) contains a memorable story that demonstrates one of the trends in the author's early writing style. This type of writing has much in common with earlier literature of social realism in Argentina, and surfaces surreptitiously in Cohen's later works. The story, "La casa de la calle Andonaegui" (The House on Andonaegui Street), rewrites the traditional account of Jewish immigration to Buenos Aires with great originality and a critical eye. While Cohen has reflected on his Jewish identity in subsequent texts, he has not done so in such a direct manner. In *Insomnio*, for example, the protagonist contemplates his Jewish condition, admitting that his ethnic origins hold many ghostlike elements. The object that unites the characters of this novel is the Bible (although the protagonist declares his lack of basic knowledge of the sacred book). The story is replete, nevertheless, with numerous quotes from Ecclesiastes and the Song of Songs.

In *El instrumento más caro de la Tierra* (The Most Expensive Instrument on Earth; written between 1976 and 1979, published in 1982), themes revolve around the reflection on a new reality imposed on Argentina by the military coup of 1976. The narrative texture of this collection is constituted by questions such as the rupture of many of the national cultural traditions at the hands of the political authoritarianism of the dictatorship, the military repression and its consequences, and the misfortune of exile. Also present is the mythic "Villa Canedo," a space that represents one and all the *barrios* (neighborhoods) of Buenos Aires, and that appears frequently in Cohen's narrative.

The collection of short stories *El buitre en invierno* (The Vulture in Winter; 1984) presents an emblematic overlapping of the three narrative spaces described in Cohen: the cultural tradition of Buenos Aires (the machista fraternity among men, the culture of the bars and card games) frozen in virtual spaces to which one can always return ("Donde se realizan los sueños), or of those in which one is oppressively held captive ("Visita de médico"), in spite of the fact that the world has become a radically different space (the space of the counterutopian future). "Solo contra los marcianos" (Alone Against the Martians) is an excellent example of Cohen's psychological narrative vein.

El fin de lo mismo is a series of what Cohen calls "novelatos" (a combination of the forms of the novel [novela] and short story [relato]). These texts contain topics that are particular to the short story but are structured with formal traits of the novel (chapters, digressions, change in point of view). In all the stories of this collection, but particularly in "La ilusión monarca" (The Monarch Illusion), "Lydia en el canal" (Lydia in the Canal, and "Volubilidad" (Volubility), Cohen explores a narrative situation that is dear to him: the characters, in the style of the black novel, are isolated by a particular consciousness of themselves and the world that surrounds them. Nonetheless, in contrast to what occurs in the genre of detective fiction—of significant incidence in Cohen's writing—the characters do not attract the sympathy or interest of those around them, but rather different degrees of indifference or animadversion.

Cohen's first novel, *El país de la dama eléctrica*, is unique in Spanish language literature for the way in which it explores the universe of a young rock musician. Once again, a postnational geography places the mythical Buenos Aires neighborhood in contact with a European island. In *El oído absoluto* this postnational locality—the so-called city/cultural complex of Lorelei, built as a postindustrial recreational and tourist mecca—constitutes the foundation on which the story is built. Also central to the text is the encounter between a father who has been largely absent from his daughter's life, and the daughter. The combination of two heterogenous ideas for the construction of a story is, for Cohen, one of the frequent mechanisms that he uses in the construction of his plots (Domínguez 6; Saavedra 91). In the novel Cohen includes direct references to the reader and to the act of writing without detracting from the fundamental narrative aspect of the novel. Cohen has stated on more than one occasion that it is not only the act of narrating that legitimates a text; it is also necessary to establish a proposal of what literature is through the activity of narration. Efforts of this sort can be seen in this novel, as in many of his other works, but they are without a doubt especially important to the fabrication of the *El testamento de O'Jaral*.

Insomnio is a novel that operates within the boundaries of at least two different genres: the detective novel and fantastic literature. As an autonomous and absolutely chaotic territory, Bardas de Kramer, built from nothing and returned to nothing once its economic sources run out, provides a space for the development of intrigue in the style of a detective novel. This syncretic territory is an exemplary product of globalization: images connected with Europe and the United States are superimposed on street names that evoke Buenos Aires. Dreams are an important element in the novel; dreams that anticipate, contradict or tell the story in a different form.

El sitio de Kelany has powerful connections with the mystery novel. Even though the majority of the text seeks to cultivate a psychological story—characters that confront their weaknesses in their struggle for an amorous encounter—the plot is based on mystery and the search for its revelation in the characteristic context of narrative described as postnational, postindustrial and postpolitical.

El testamento de O'Jaral, stemming from a similar narrative universe, proposes a revision of the debate on utopian struggles. The characters of the novel discuss the political forms of participation of guerrilla groups and messianic leaders, at the same time that a reflection on the task of the writer as a utopia (fiction) builder is being elaborated. The novel may be defined as an examination of the human behavior of taking on tasks, tasks of salvation for others, for humanity, or those that seek to overcome the smallness of man. The senselessness of human life, the omnipotence of Those Above it All (the powerful of the world as they are referred to in the text), the imperious necessity of the individual to construct an identity in spite of it all, are themes of the many political-ideological discussions between the characters. A similar instance is the intense interior debate that the protagonist, O'Jaral, maintains within himself. However, the main crux of the novel is the topic of literature itself: debates about writing, translation, cultural industry, and artistic creation in general are intertwined in the narrative design.

Cohen also has published a work about Siddharta Gautama (*Buda* [Buddha; 1990]). The book, which is an accessible and detailed study, has been characterized by the author as a compromise between the publishing house's objectives and a private interest in the subject.

PRIMARY BIBLIOGRAPHY
Creative Writing

El buitre en invierno. Barcelona: Montesinos, 1984.

El fin de lo mismo. Buenos Aires: Anaya & Mario Muchnik/Alianza, 1992.

Insomnio. Barcelona: Muchnik, 1986; Buenos Aires: Paradiso, 1994.

El instrumento más caro de la Tierra. Barcelona: Montesinos, 1981.

El oído absoluto. Barcelona: Muchnik, 1989.

El país de la dama eléctrica. Buenos Aires: Bruguera, 1984.

Los pájaros también se comen. Buenos Aires: Boedo, 1975.

El sitio de Kelany. Barcelona: Muchnik, 1987; Buenos Aires: Ada Korn, 1987.

El testamento de O'Jaral. Madrid: Anaya & Mario Muchnik, 1995.

Nonfiction

Buda. Barcelona: Lumen, 1990.

SECONDARY BIBLIOGRAPHY

Criticism

Franco L., Luisa. "Pesquisas personales" (*El sitio de Kelany*). *Punto de vista* (Argentina) 11.32 (1988): 28-29.

Freidemberg, Daniel. "Vivir sin futuro" (*Insomnio*). *Clarín (Cultura y Nación)* June 5, 1986: 7.

—. "Marcelo Cohen: el malestar en la literatura." *Clarín (Cultura y Nación)* February 4, 1993: 2-3.

Montaldo, Graciela. "*El país de la dama eléctrica*, de Marcelo Cohen." *Punto de vista* 23 (1985): 37-39.

Interviews

Domínguez, Nora. "Marcelo Cohen. Almagro, verano de 1993." *Primer plano* (Buenos Aires) 19 Dec., 1993: 6-7.

Saavedra, Guillermo. "Marcelo Cohen. Los espacios imaginarios del narrador." In his *La curiosidad impertinente*. Buenos Aires: Beatriz Viterbo, 1993. 79-93.

Speranza, Graciela. "Marcelo Cohen." In her *Primera persona: conversaciones con quince narradores argentinos*. Buenos Aires: Norma, 1995. 67-84.

Claudia Ferman

COHEN, SANDRO (Mexico; 1953)

Sandro Cohen was born in Newark, New Jersey, in 1953. Since 1973 he has lived in Mexico and in 1982 he received his Mexican citizenship. He holds a Masters degree in Hispanic literature from Rutgers University, and in Mexico he completed his doctorate at the Universidad Nacional Autónoma de México. He is currently a professor and researcher at the Universidad Autónoma Metropolitana-Azcapotzalco (UAM). As part of his university career Sandro

Cohen has coordinated a literary criticism workshop at the UAM and a poetry workshop in Oaxaca. Cohen also belongs to the editorial board of the journal *Sin embargo* (However) and of the publishing house, La Máquina Eléctrica. He has worked as a contributor to the newspaper *Excélsior* and has published a great number of essays in the most well-known journals, newspapers, and literary supplements of the country such as the aforementioned *Excélsior* and *Proceso* (Process), *Revista de la universidad* (University Journal), and *Vuelta* (Turn).

Aside from his current career in education, Cohen works as a critic, translator, and essayist. He has published a collection of *crónicas* (short essay/journalism pieces) under the title *Pena capital: crónicas urbanas* (Mexico City Sorrow: Urban Chronicles; 1991), which consists of a series of short sketches that appeared previously in *UnoMásUno* and describe the inhabitants of Mexico City and their lives as lost souls in the immense capital.

However, in literary circles, Sandro Cohen is better known for his poetry. His published collections in this genre include *De noble origen desdichado* (Of Unfortunate Noble Origin; 1979), *A pesar del imperio* (In Spite of the Empire; 1980), *Los cuerpos de la furia* (Bodies of Fury; 1983), and *Línea de fuego* (Line of Fire; 1989). It is precisely in his poems where Cohen examines Jewish themes. In *De noble origin desdichado* the poet finds a large part of his inspiration in historical and biblical events and characters: Abraham, heretics, floods, promised lands, exile, Mount Sinai, and gas chambers are recurrent themes throughout the poems of this collection. Cohen ponders "Cómo esconder el legado sombrío/en siglos de todos mis nombres./El Dios de mi sangre es dios de la horca,/la cámara de gas/y la leyenda en mis oídos sobrevivientes" (How to hide the somber legacy/in the centuries of all my names./The God of my blood is the god of the noose,/the gas chamber/and the legend in my survivor's ears [51]). The poet remembers his tradition and through his poetry is a participant in the collective memory of the Jewish people that possesses no geographical border, the universal Jew.

In *A pesar del imperio* Cohen begins to introduce the subjects of love, amorous passion, paternal feeling, hunger; topics that will be markedly present in subsequent works. However, in the midst of this new subject matter Cohen continues to interject certain aspects of Jewish tradition. Indeed, the poet recalls his ancestors, his great-grandfather an "embrión de su anglohablante esperanza de salir" (embryo of his anglophone hope of leaving [17]) who emigrated from Russia to the land of salvation, America. Included in this collection of poems, although to a lesser degree, are biblical themes and characters such as Joshua, the battle of Jericho, and exile.

Finally, in *Los cuerpos de la furia* and *Línea de fuego* Cohen seems to focus exclusively on one experience and one existential search in which he treats topics of love, individual solitude, the destiny of the body, and death. Undoubtedly, Sandro Cohen is a literary figure who represents a facet of the Jew in exile. His poetry is of exquisite expressiveness. Each work consists of an equal balance of biblical, Classical, Helenic, and modern themes. Sandro Cohen is exile personified, through his poetry and his words he flies to faroff lands, the promised land, his promised land.

PRIMARY BIBLIOGRAPHY
Creative Writing
A pesar del imperio. México, D.F.: UNAM, 1980.
"Al indígena no lo visitó el ángel." *Desde Bet-El* Octubre 1991: 5.
Autobiografía del infiel. México, D.F.: Oasis, 1982.
Los cuerpos de la furia. México, D.F.: Katún, 1983.
De noble origen desdichado. México, D.F.: La Máquina Eléctrica, 1979.
Línea de fuego. México, D.F.: INBA/Ediciones Armella, 1989. Select poems in English translation by M. B. Jordan in *Ruido de sueños, Noise of Dreams*. Selection and Translation by El Grupo Tramontano-The Tramontane Group. México, D.F.: El Tucán de Virginia, 1994. 68-71.
Nonfiction
"La ética judía en tres poemas cristianos." *La presencia judía en México: Memorias*. México, D.F.: Coordinación de Difusión Cultural de la UNAM, 1987. 51-62.
"Los intelectuales judíos en México." *Desde Bet-El* Noviembre 1991: 4-5.
Pena capital: crónicas urbanas. Cuadernos de Malinalco, Estado de México, 1991.
Anthologies
Antología poética de poesía norteamericana. México, D.F.: Casa del Tiempo-/UAM, 1981.
El asidero de la zozobra: antología poética de Guillermo Fernández. Jalisco: Departamento de Bellas Artes del Gobierno de Jalisco, 1983.
Bonifaz Nuñó para jóvenes. México, D.F.: Instituto Nacional de Bellas Artes, 1989.
Breve antología poética de Elías Nandino. México, D.F.: Domés, 1983.
Palabra nueva: dos décadas de poesía en México. México, D.F.: Premià, 1981.

SECONDARY BIBLIOGRAPHY

Bonifaz Nuñó, Rubén. "Sandro Cohen: la rabiosa pasión de ser." *Excélsior* 14 Jan., 1984: 4C.

Campos, Marco Antonio. "De la Torre, Cohen, marginales." *Proceso* 24 Nov., 1980: 52-55.

"El poeta Sandro Cohen presentará su libro hoy (*De noble origen desdichado*)." *Excélsior* 22 Nov., 1979: 13C.

Quirarte, Vicente. "El cuerpo encarcelado: *Los cuerpos de la furia*." *Casa del tiempo* 36 (1983): 78-79.

Rev. of *Los cuerpos de la furia. Proceso* 4 June, 1984: 60-61.

Ronquillo, Víctor. "Sandro Cohen y *Los cuerpos de la furia*." *El nacional* 27 Oct., 1983: sección 3a, 4.

Vázquez, Jaime. "Los mejores autores de 1983 aquí: Puga, Giardinelli, Monsreal, Carballido, Montes de Oca, Lizalde, Illescas, Pacheco, Paz y Otros." *Excélsior* 31 Dec., 1983: 4C.

Daniela Schuvaks

COSTANTINI, HUMBERTO (Argentina; 1924-87)

Humberto Costantini was born on April 8, 1924 in Buenos Aires. His father, an Italian Jew of Sephardic heritage, had immigrated to Argentina in 1905. He was educated as a veterinarian and conducted rather extensive research in the area of immunology. With the military coup of Juan Perón in 1943, Costantini became active in anti-Peronist politics. As a writer he belongs to the generation of 1950. It was during that decade when his early texts—published in journals and periodicals—began to earn him a reputation. Costantini, like Pedro Orgambide (1929) and David Viñas (1929), seeks to portray the contemporary sociopolitical reality of Argentina. Indeed, his works constitute a literary history of Argentina through several periods of social, political, and economic upheaval. The most recent military dictatorship, known as the Proceso de Reorganización Nacional (Process of National Reorganization), which lasted from 1976 to 1983, had a profound effect on Costantini's personal and professional life. As the result of life-threatening circumstances in Buenos Aires, he went into exile in Mexico, where he remained until 1984. While in Mexico, Costantini wrote his most memorable works, which won him worldwide acclaim. His books have been translated into English, Hebrew, German, and Russian, and they have sold over a million copies in the former Soviet Union (Orgambide, "Humberto Costantini" 75). Costantini also received a variety of different literary prizes, the most important of which was the Casa de las Américas award (the Latin American Pulitzer) in 1979 for his novel *De dioses, hombrecitos y policías* (*The Gods, the Little Guys and the Police*). He died June 7, 1987 following a long battle with cancer.

Costantini's first book was a short-story collection titled *De por aquí no más* (Just from Around Here; 1958). It reflects the author's early years growing up on the outskirts of Buenos Aires. The stories, which depict the lives of a wide variety of *porteños* (inhabitants of Buenos Aires), follow the realist narrative and are told in a genuinely colloquial language. One story in particular from the collection stands out, however, for its theme and universal appeal. The story reveals early in Costantini's career the profound influence of his Italian Sephardic ancestry. "Don Iudá" is in part the tale of the protagonist Don Iudá, a tailor who lived in Lucena, a town in southern Spain. It is narrated by an individual who states that he is Iudá's nephew and who begins by portraying the tranquil, friendly atmosphere in the Jewish sector of the small Spanish town. However, the story is quickly transformed into a tale of terror. The narrator tells of the violent attack on the Jewish neighborhood that occurred a few days after Pessach in the year 1108. Homes were burned and people killed, but Don Iudá saved himself by submitting to a forced baptism. The story quite realistically presents a rather common occurrence in Jewish history. Nevertheless, what makes it so interesting is the complete dissolution of time wherein the same characters and situations resurface throughout history. The narrator himself states that he gets confused when telling this story because the facts become muddled with the circumstances surrounding the attack in Russia eight-hundred years later, or in Poland forty years after that. The narrator, then, becomes a mythological wandering Jew who is present at all these instances in Jewish history. Likewise, in the end he states that his uncle Iudá lived another three-hundred years in Lucena until March 31, 1492, the date the Jews were expelled from Spain. "Don Iudá" is also included in *Una vieja historia de caminantes* (An Old History of Travellers; 1967).

Costantini's next short-story collection, *Un señor alto, rubio, de bigotes* (A Tall Blond Man with a Mustache; 1963), clearly established Costantini as a writer. The title story is infused with an element of the fantastic. It revolves around a man who is desperately seeking a job interview. He frantically prepares to meet with the interviewer, but is constantly referred to someone else. Finally, he is told to go see a Mr. Otero, described as a tall blond man with a mustache.

When he ultimately meets Otero he quickly discovers that something is very amiss. The ambivalent end leaves the reader guessing whether Otero was really God, who had come to relieve the man of his worldly cares.

Una vieja historia de caminantes is in reality a compilation of former texts with some additional new stories. The story "Una vieja historia de caminantes" in one of Costantini's most complex. As in "Don Iudá," the author takes the reader back in history to a specifically Jewish setting. In this case the story is set in and around Jerusalem and is told by a travelling merchant, a contemporary of Jesus Christ. The merchant describes Jesus as a radical and rebellious Jew who boldly speaks out against authority, too boldly in the view of the narrator, who repeatedly states that his words and actions are going to get him killed. Costantini includes several famous episodes in Jesus's life such as the triumphal entry into Jerusalem and the cleansing of the Temple. He also describes the apostles, and not only Judas Iscariot, as self-serving traitors. Iosef de Rama (Joseph of Aramea), Iudá (Thadeus), Iudá (Judas Iscariot), Bar-Talmai (Bartholomew), and Iojanán (John) all appear in the story. By describing Jesus as a radical Jewish thinker rather than the founder of Christianity, Costantini assumes an ideological posture of defiance with regard to the Hispano-Catholic hegemony of Argentina.

Háblenme de Funes (Tell Me about Funes; 1970), *Bandeo* (Fed Up; 1975), and *En la noche* (At Night; 1985) are all short-story collections in which Costantini continues his tradition of social dissent combined with humor, popular culture, and at times shocking reality. Music plays a very important role in many of Costantini's stories and poems (many of which are composed as tangos or milongas, the two most typical and/or traditional Argentine musical forms). The story "Háblenme de Funes" consists of an intricate cacophony of voices (in fact the story is subtitled "Relato con voces" [Story with Voices]) and musical instruments. They are the voices of different orchestra members who briefly tell of their experience with a man named Funes. Significantly the name reminds the reader of "Funes el memorioso" ("Funes the Memorious") by Jorge Luis Borges (1899-1986). *En la noche* was Costantini's last collection of short stories. As a whole the book speaks out against not only the violence of the *Proceso* but against the violence of authoritarianism in general.

Costantini published two collections of poetry: *Cuestiones con la vida* (Issues with Life; 1966 [the 1986 edition is enlarged and includes the posterior volume]) and *Más cuestiones con la vida* (More Issues with Life; 1974). Thematically his poetry is an extension of his narrative. Themes of exile, loss, nostalgia, violence, and music dominate the volumes. One of his most intimate poems, certainly in terms of Jewish identity, is "Eli, Eli, lamma sabactani" (My God, My God, Why Hast Thou Forsaken Me [*Cuestiones con la vida*, 1986: 77-79]). The emotionally charged verses delineate the different aspects of his identity (Sephardic, Italian, and Latin American). Written as a prayer to God, the poem invokes the author's Italian-Jewish heritage by conjuring up visions of scenes in turn-of-the-century Turin, words in Hebrew and Italian. The poet expresses his current Latin American reality as superimposed on his Jewish identity forged over centuries of family history in Italy.

The novel *De dioses, hombrecitos y policías* is without doubt Costantini's most well-known work. Its translation into English and other languages brought the author to the attention of the world and also served to educate that vast reading audience about the tragedy and violence of the military dictatorship in Argentina. The story is loosely based on a historical event; the action taken by the military following the death of general Esteban Cáceres Monié in a guerrilla attack in 1975. Paramilitary forces took revenge throughout the country by attacking and killing students and other groups indiscriminately. The novel revolves around three different groups on the eve of such an attack: the Gods Aphrodite, Athena, and Hermes who observe everything from Mt. Olympus; a group of amateur poets; and the police. The chapters alternate in the narration of the events that take place in each group leading up to the police attack. The Gods observe from on high debating whether or not to intervene. They send Hermes to try and warn the members of the poetry group of their impending doom. Although the novel is narrated with a great deal of humor and irony, it constitutes a somber allegory of the repression that gripped Argentina for eight years and of the thousands who fell victim to arbitrary violence. There is no real Jewish presence in the novel save for a few characters who happen to be Jews, representative of a cross section of Argentine society.

Costantini's second novel written in exile, *La larga noche de Francisco Sanctis* (*The Long Night of Francisco Sanctis*; 1984) also gives testimony on the effects of the military dictatorship. Stylistically, the author takes a more direct approach in the novel, as opposed to relying on the distancing technique of satire and/or allegory. Like the "little guys" of *De dioses*, Francisco Sanctis is an antihero who embodies the average Argentine citizen. Sanctis is confronted with a moment of truth in the novel and finds himself at the crossroads of a moral dilemma. He is asked to warn two people, whom he does not know, that they are going to be kidnapped by a death squad that night. He must decide whether or not to warn them, at the same time he must consider the possibility that it could be a trap set for him. The protagonist mulls over his decision in the course of a long night, trying to come to terms with his own moral convictions. Sanctis (and Costantini) turns to the example of Jesus as a man who was also tortured and killed for his convictions, but who was just and fair in his actions. In the end Sanctis appears on a list of *desaparecidos* (those disappeared by the military).

In addition to his extensive narrative and poetry Costantini also wrote several plays and dramatic monologues. His complete dramatic works contained in *¡Chau Pericles! Teatro completo* (Chau Pericles! Complete Theater) were published in 1986. The play *Chau Pericles*, written in 1983 shortly before the return to democracy, consists of a meditation on the state of Argentina after years of military rule. His short monologues are interesting pieces that also provide brief commentaries on a variety of issues. Costantini wrote a play for children while in exile, *Una pipa larga, larga con cabeza de jabalí* (A Long, Long Pipe with a Boar's Head; 1981), which won the National Prize for Theater in Mexico.

Prior to his death Costantini was working on an extensive novel titled *Rapsodia de Raquel Liberman* (Rhapsody of Raquel Liberman) about Jewish immigration to Argentina and the white slave (prostitution) trade operated by the Zwi Migdal. About the novel Costantini said "I work arduously, laboriously, on a novel that I'm sure will 'justify me in the eyes of God,' so to say" (Colby 187).

PRIMARY BIBLIOGRAPHY

Creative Writing

Bandeo. Buenos Aires: Granica, 1975. México, D.F.: Nueva Imagen, 1980.

¡Chau, Pericles! Teatro completo. Buenos Aires: Galerna, 1986.

Cuestiones con la vida. Buenos Aires: Canto y Cuento 1966. Also Buenos Aires, LH, 1970; Buenos Aires: Carlos Hernández, 1975; México, D.F.: Katún, 1982. Buenos Aires: Galerna, 1986.

De dioses, hombrecitos y policías. La Habana: Casa de las Américas, 1979. México, D.F.: Nueva Imagen, 1979. Buenos Aires: Bruguera, 1984. English version as *The Gods, the Little Guys and the Police.* Trans. Toby Talbot. New York: Harper & Row, 1984.

De por aquí no más. Buenos Aires: Stilcograf, 1958; 2nd ed., 1965. Also Buenos Aires: Centro Editor de América Latina, 1969.

En la noche. Buenos Aires: Bruguera, 1985.

Háblenme de Funes. Buenos Aires: Sudamericana, 1970. Also México, D.F.: Nueva Imagen, 1980. Buenos Aires: Centro Editor de América Latina, 1983.

"In the Night." Trans. by Norman Thomas di Giovanni and Susan Ashe. In *Hand in Hand Alongside the Tracks and Other Stories.* Ed. Norman Thomas di Giovanni. London: Constable, 1992. 24-34.

La larga noche de Francisco Sanctis. Buenos Aires: Bruguera, 1984. English version as *The Long Night of Francisco Sanctis*. Trans. Norman Thomas di Giovanni. New York: Harper & Row, 1985.

Más cuestiones con la vida. Buenos Aires: Papeles de Buenos Aires, 1974.

"Rapsodia de Raquel Liberman." [fragment of Costantini's unfinished novel]. *Noaj* 2.2 (1988): 76-81.

Un señor alto, rubio, de bigotes. Buenos Aires: Stilcograf, 1963. Buenos Aires: Centro Editor de América Latina, 1969; 1972.

Tres monólogos. Buenos Aires: Falbo Librero, 1964.

Una vieja historia de caminantes. Buenos Aires: Centro Editor de América Latina, 1967.

Nonfiction

Libro de Trelew. Buenos Aires: Granica, 1973.

SECONDARY BIBLIOGRAPHY

Criticism

Colby, Vineta. "Costantini, Humberto." In *World Authors, 1980-1985*. Ed. Vineta Colby. New York: The H.W. Wilson Company, 1991. 186-88.

Feierstein, Ricardo. "Humberto Costantini: adiós al amigo." *Nueva presencia* 519 (16 Jan., 1987): 12-13.

Flores, Angel. "Humberto Costantini." In his *Spanish American Authors: The Twentieth Century*. New York: The H.W. Wilson Company, 1992. 223-25.

Iegor, Jorge. "Humberto Costantini." *Actitud* (Buenos Aires) 4 (1964): 6-7, 9.

López Mejía, Adelaida. "La visión satírica de Humberto Costantini: *De dioses, hombrecitos y policías*." *Chasqui* 20.2 (1991): 86-97.

Orgambide, Pedro. "Humberto Costantini: heterodoxia y rebeldía." *Noaj* 2.2 (1988): 73-75.

—. "Notas sobre un poema de Humberto Costantini." *Hispamérica* 12.36 (1983): 45-49. Also in *Controversia de ideas sionistas* [Buenos Aires] 2 (1985): 89-93.

Reati, Fernando. *Nombrar lo innombrable: violencia política y novela argentina 1975-1985*. Buenos Aires: Legasa, 1992. 78-83, 146-49.

Stoll, Antonio. "Humberto Costantini y la realidad nacional." *Hoy en la cultura* (Buenos Aires) 16 (1964): 17-18.

Weinstein, Ana E., and Miryam E. Gover de Nasatsky, comps. *Escritores judeo-argentinos: bibliografía 1900-1987*. 2 vols. Buenos Aires: Milá, 1994. I.137-43.

Zavala Alvarado, Lauro. "Tango y polifanía en un relato argentino." *Chasqui* 20.1 (1991): 67-77.

Interviews

"¿En qué están los escritores, Humberto Costantini?" *Crisis* 53 (1987): 79.

Senkman, Leonardo. "De culpas, exilios y milongas." *Nueva Sión* 653 (24 Jan., 1987): 18-19.

Darrell B. Lockhart

COZARINSKY, EDGARDO (Argentina; 1939)

Edgardo Cozarinsky was born in Buenos Aires in 1939. His artistic interests consist of a twofold exploration that encompasses both literature and film. As a literary author, he has published one novel, *Vudú urbano* (*Urban Voodoo*; 1985). As a literary critic Cozarinsky has written on the works of American novelist Henry James (1843-1916), and as a film critic he is the author of *Borges en/y/sobre cine* (*Borges in/and/on Film*; 1981). He has also made three feature length films: . . . *Puntos suspensivos* (Dot Dot Dot), *Les Apprentis-sorcier* (The Sorcerer Apprentices), and *La Guerre d'un seul homme* (One Man's War). Cozarinsky currently resides in Paris, where he has lived since 1974 working as a writer, director, and film critic.

In *Borges en/y/sobre cine* Cozarinsky compiles a series of essays that Jorge Luis Borges (1899-1986) published in the journal *Sur* between 1931 and 1944. Among the essays one finds a sharp analysis of cinematographic language utilized by internationally renown directors. The productions of Josef von Sternberg (1894-1969), Alfred Hitchcock (1899-1980), King Vidor (1895-1984), H.G. Wells (1866-1946), and others, are observed by the clinical eye of the Argentine writer, revealing the artistic quality of the film texts. With *Borges en/y/sobre/cine* Cozarinsky delves deeply into cinematographic theory converting it into the essence of the book. The author presents a large number of films that make their way into Borges's narrative. *Borges en/y/sobre cine* provides a critical approach to as well as a concise and detailed analysis of the films based on the texts of the celebrated Argentine writer. In Cozarinsky's text one observes how the labyrinths and problems of time that comprise the Borgesian universe are transferred to the big screen, where film becomes an amalgamation with the literary production of Borges. As a film critic, he not only studies the technical resources used by directors in order to make a liaison between both branches of art, but at the same time he reevaluates the production of Argentine filmmakers. The principal authorities of the film industry in Argentina, among whom are Leopoldo Torre Nilsson, René Mugica, Hugo Santiago, Ricardo Luna, and Héctor Olivera, are placed under scrutiny in an examination that takes into account the important task of becoming the depository of Borges's work. In addition to providing an objective analysis of cinematographic texts made from the works of Borges, Cozarinsky includes in his book an extensive film bibliography that provides important data concerning the collaborative efforts that went into the filmic recreation of Borges's literary works.

In his novel *Vudú urbano*, Cozarinsky comes face to face with the specter of exile in a dramatic confrontation. The writer penetrates the most intrinsic roots of exile in order to come to terms with internal conflict occasioned by the sensation of foreignness that surrounds the exiled individual. The narrator, displaced from his familiar territory communicates the loss of his cultural identity, in turn exposing a complete disassociation with ethnic constructs. The book is submerged in the sociocultural problematics of Argentina during the 1970s, circumstantially revealing the nefarious happenings that took place during the so-called Dirty War, thereby stressing the separation and fragmentation of the individual. *Vudú urbano*, like its author, presents the fragmentation of the exiled individual as expressed through a loose association of scattered thoughts, memories, and stories.

In the episode titled "Viajero sentimental" ("The Sentimental Journey"), the writer becomes spellbound as he recalls the haunting city of his memory, Buenos Aires. Through the exorcism of memory the narrator finds catharsis. In "El álbum de tarjetas postales del viaje" ("The Postcard Album of the Journey") Cozarinsky assembles thirteen different episodes related to the experience of exile. By sending a fractured message, unraveled by the foreign words of a strange and distant reality, the writer reveals his own burdensome existence. *Vudú urbano* articulates the horrendous reality of the military dictatorship (1976-83) known as the Proceso de Reorganización Nacional (The Process of National Reorganization) in which the military government institutionalized a program of terror and violence and caused thousands of Argentine citizens to leave their country. The sociopsychological conflict of the individual produced by exile emphasizes the difficulty of accepting the alienation that distance, time, and the military dictatorship brought about.

In his book, Cozarinsky delineates the process of cultural uprooting. *Vudú urbano* brings to life dramatic events in one country that led to one man's loss of identity. It is, nonetheless, the story of innumerable exiled Argentines.

Cozarinsky eloquently portrays the condition of the wandering exile for whom memory continues to replay the knowledge and experiences of a past that can never be abandoned.

PRIMARY BIBLIOGRAPHY
Creative Writing
Vudú urbano. Prólogos de Susan Sontag and Guillermo Cabrera Infante. Barcelona: Anagrama, 1985. English version as *Urban Voodoo*. Preface by Susan Sontag. New York: Lumen Books, 1985.
Nonfiction
Borges en/y/sobre cine. Madrid: Fundamentos, 1981. English version as *Borges in/and/on Film*. Trans. by Gloria Waldman and Ronald Christ. New York: Lumen Books, 1988.
El laberinto de la apariencia: estudios sobre Henry James. Buenos Aires: Losada, 1964.

SECONDARY BIBLIOGRAPHY
Cabrera Infante, Guillermo. "Notes inégales." *Vudú urbano*. Barcelona: Anagrama, 1985. 11-17.
Goldberg, Florinda F. Rev. of *Vudú urbano*. *Noaj* 1.2 (1988): 111-14.
Lindstrom, Naomi. *Jewish Issues in Argentine Literature: From Gerchunoff to Szichman*. Columbia: U of Missouri P, 1989. 167-68.
Matamoro, Blas. "Kiosko." *Cuadernos hispanoamericanos* 438 (1986): 166-74.

Marcelo Willcham

DIAMENT, MARIO (Argentina; 1942)

Diament has worked principally as a journalist, having studied literature and philosophy at the Hebrew University in Jerusalem. Diament has won various awards for his dramatic production, and additionally he has published several works of political and cultural analysis. Diament covered the Arab-Israel War for Jacobo Timerman's newspaper *La Opinión* (Opinion), and he has had extensive experience as a foreign correspondent.

Although Diament is not ranked among the most prolific of the younger Argentine dramatists nor is he necessarily the most touted (I know of no interpretive criticism beyond brief journalistic notices of his work), he may be considered one of the most representative figures of the dramatists who emerged after the military coup of 1966 that inaugurated almost fifteen years of authoritarian rule. *Crónica de un secuestro* (Chronicle of a Kidnapping) dates from 1971, the beginning of this period; *El invitado* (The Guest) is from 1979, at the height of the Proceso and the so-called Dirty War against alleged subversives; *Equinoccio* (Equinox) was first performed in 1983, virtually on the eve of the transition to constitutional democracy.

All three of these works center on the discourse of authoritarianism, with special emphasis on its installation in a bourgeois mentality of social existence. Concomitantly, all three works are designed to provoke in the spectator a complex inventory of questions concerning the origins, the maintenance, and the survival of this discourse, the relative weight of its eloquence as it moves along various social axes, and what the possibilities are for one to detect its ideological slippages, its internal coherences so as to begin to deconstruct it. While Diament's characters are as a group incapable of such an undertaking, his theater can only make sense if the dramatist has faith in the ability of the spectators to disengage themselves from any naturalistic identity with the characters and commit themselves to a repudiation of the authoritarian mentality. In a superficial sense, Diament's theater is a theater of despair, and the danger exists that the spectator, even if s/he does not endorse the discourse of fascism and even, in fact, rejects it in an attack of ideological *nausée*, will merely experience angered frustration without being able to contemplate a way out of the labyrinth of authoritarianism. I use "contemplate" here in a metaphorical sense, since Diament's theater does not provide a dramatic universe for literal contemplation in which the ideal spectator I am hypothesizing he envisions is able to mount a counterdiscourse that will deconstruct authoritarian discourse and install in its place an alternative social ideology. The aggressiveness of the kidnappers in *Crónica* is not adequate to this purpose, since their social standing is ambiguous (two possible ways of reading them are as free-floating ideologues engaged in spontaneous acts of guerrilla terror or as misfits converting their resentments into antisocial acts). And the brief appearance of Mariela at the end of *Equinoccio* to challenge the acquiescence of her lover with the system of repression is not enough to more than suggest a counterdiscourse beyond angry negatives. Diament must rely on an audience able from the start to penetrate the dense texture of authoritarianism, understand immediately its perverse and cynical reasoning, and be brave enough to disavow any sympathy either for the victims (because of their acquiescence) or the victimizers, without being offered any representation of social behavior.

Despite its being checked at a point prior to any coherent meditation on alternatives to authoritarianism, Diament's theater demonstrates exceptional dramatic dexterity. Like so many contemporary Argentine dramas executed within severe space constraints and without enough budget for more than a handful of actors and props, these texts rely on the intensity of the dialogue, the inventive use of seemingly innocuous triggers of dramatic confrontation, and abrupt and disconcerting transitions in order to engage the audience with the convoluted nature of the social discourse being configured through the theatrical text.

Conversaciones con un judío (Conversations with a Jew; 1977), which was published by Jacobo Timerman, is a series of interviews with Máximo Yagupsky, a major intellectual and social figure of the Argentine Jewish community whose roots go back to the Jewish agricultural settlements in the Mesopotamian province of Entre Ríos. Yagupsky edited the intellectual review *Judaica* between 1933 and 1946. Organized around twelve themes—e.g., What is a Jew?, Integration and Assimilation, Judaism and Society, Israel and the Diáspora—the conversation between Diament and Yagupsky constitutes an extremely valuable survey of the historical panorama of Judaism in Argentina and the social primes that are so eloquently reflected in Argentine-Jewish cultural production as well as a survey of concerns relating to the Jewish presence in contemporary Argentina. The latter is especially crucial for the time in which *Conversaciones* was published, in the first years following the March 1976 military coup and at the height of the Dirty War against subversion. The Dirty War in particular singled out Jews, and Timerman himself was to fall victim to it (see the entry on him in this dictionary).

Diament is also the author of short fiction. The collection *La pena y la gloria* (The Pain and the Glory) was published in 1970, and most of the texts of that collection were repeated in *El exilio* (Exile; 1975). Many of Diament's stories deal with themes of cultural conflict and manifestations of structural violence in contemporary society, including narratives that specifically refer, like *Crónica de un secuestro*, to recent Argentine social history, often with specific references to the experience of Argentine Jews (cf. "El terrorista" [The Terrorist]) and to the conflicts of daily life in Israel ("Exilio"). An excellent, if somewhat schematic, example of Diament's stories is "Tardío" (Belated), which deals with the experience of a young Argentine Jewish immigrant son who travels to Europe to search for his family's roots, only to end up reenacting the Holocaust in the guise of postwar industrialization and its dependency on migrant workers. The latter and the conditions of their employment are represented as extensions of slave laborers in the concentration camps.

His most recent play, *Interviu* (Interview), about a young journalist's interview with an all-but-forgotten actress of the silver screen premiered in the Teatro Municipal General San Martín (Buenos Aires Municipal Theater) in July 1994.

PRIMARY BIBLIOGRAPHY

Conversaciones con un judío. Buenos Aires: Ediciones Timerman, 1977. Also, Buenos Aires: Fraterna, 1986.

El exilio. Buenos Aires: Conjunta Editores, 1975.

Interviu. Unpublished; Debuted in Buenos Aires, 1994.

La pena y la gloria. Buenos Aires: Hernández Editor, 1970.

Teatro: Crónica de un secuestro; El invitado; Equinoccio. Buenos Aires: Fraterna, 1989.

SECONDARY BIBLIOGRAPHY

Foster, David William. Rev. of *Teatro: Crónica de un secuestro; El invitado; Equinoccio*. *Latin American Theatre Review* 25.1 (1991): 173-74.

David William Foster

DICKMANN, MAX (Argentina; 1902-91)

Max Dickmann was born in Buenos Aires on August 8, 1902 to Alejandro Dickmann and Celina Waismann. He received his education at the Colegio Nacional Mariano Moreno and was married to Ofelia A. Pessina. He served as a literary critic to the journal *Nosotros* (Us) and was a contributor to many newspapers—*La Razón* (Reason), *Noticias Gráficas* (Graphic News), *La Vanguardia* (Vanguard), *The Standard* (Buenos Aires), and *El Día* (The Day [Montevideo]). Dickmann was a member of the Sociedad Argentina de Escritores (S.A.D.E.) and the P.E.N. Club, an organization for poets, playwrights, editors, essayists, and novelists. Dickmann's work was recognized in 1935 when he was awarded the first municipal prize for literature for the novel *Madre América* (Mother America) and in 1953 the Faja de Honor from S.A.D.E. for the novel *Los habitantes de la noche* (Inhabitants of the Night). Dickmann also specialized in translating English-language works (including those from the U.S., which at that time were not very prestigious) by John Dos Passos (1896-1970), William

Faulkner (1897-1962), Percival Christopher Wren (1885-1941), Elmer Rice (1892-1967), and Robert Sherwood (1896-1955). Dickmann's own social realist novels attracted much critical attention in the 1930s, when he made his greatest impact as a writer, reflecting his socialist perspective and concern for immigrants. Dickmann also dealt with general themes of Argentine interest—for example, conflicts like those between city and country and social diversity as exemplified in his wide range of characters, which make Dickmann's novels into a "broad mirror of the psychology of the Argentine" (Hilton v. 2, 72; Herrera 191; Lindstrom, *Jewish Issues* 21, 26).

Some of Dickmann's most significant work was written in the 1930s, also known as the "infamous decade," which was a very difficult time for Argentina as a nation and the Jews of that nation in particular. Dickmann's work (including his novel *Madre América*, for which he is probably best remembered) can be better understood within the larger historical context. In the early 1930s, it became clear that the nationalism of previous decades had replaced its atheism with a devout Catholicism, resulting in the emergence of ultra-rightist Catholic nationalism, which was also rabidly antisemitic. The uncertainty prompted by the political facade of democracy (a favorite theme of Dickmann), a worsening economy, and popular sector protests led these nationalists to seek scapegoats to blame for Argentina's domestic problems. In the infamous decade, irrational anti-Semitism displaced all rational thought via an obsessive quest for the "Jewish conspiracy." Groups as diverse as capitalists, communists, entrepreneurs, workers, liberals, atheists, masons, and intellectuals represented a nefarious threat, which was employed as a means to rationalize the contradictions and inconsistencies of Argentine nationalism and the fanaticism of rightist Catholicism. The antisemitic pretext was still anticommunism, although it became mixed with racism, as reflected in the novels entitled *El Kahal* (The Kahal; 1938) and *Oro* (Gold; 1938) written by Gustavo Adolfo Martínez Zuviría, the director of the National Library and a popular writer who used the pen name of Hugo Wast. Published in the same year as Dickmann's *Madre América*, Wast's novels displayed both anticommunist and antisemitic hatred and exemplified Argentine social and moral decay in the 1930s, a major theme in Dickmann's work.

David William Foster explains the linkage between the "infamous decade" and *Madre América* in the way this novel reflects the "moral and ethical decline of the period as, in the wake of the institutional disruption of the military coup of September 6, 1930, all manner of opportunists struggled to gain a share of power in the new 'nationalist' state" (Foster 91). In contrast to the nationalists' glorified quest for "national destiny," Dickmann in *Madre América* sought to depict the "most unredeemed versions of ignoble human corruption." Consequently, the general tone of the novel is relentlessly sarcastic in its persistent depiction of the social, moral, and political bankruptcy of that period (Foster 93). The fragmentary manner in which Dickmann wrote this novel mirrored the fragmented nature of Argentine society. In this sense, Foster concludes that "*Madre América* remains one of the most eloquent evaluations of the moral and ethical decline of Argentina during the infamous decade of the thirties" (Foster 96).

In light of the above discussion, *Madre América* seeks to address the theme of corruption, which is inherent in the political system. Set in the small imaginary city of San Itatí, the novel explores the nature of politics and politicians of that town, which serves as a metaphor for the bankruptcy of the Argentine body politic in the 1930s. Politicians only sought financial aggrandizement and power. Their pledges of justice to average Argentines were merely empty words to secure their votes. The politician only feigned concern for the public while really being motivated by personal ambition. Dickmann noted that the middle class acquiesced to political corruption so long as it continued being prosperous with the politicians striving to maintain the status quo. One of the main points Dickmann attempted to make was that all politicians, no matter how sincere initially, eventually were corrupted by the political system (Goodman 203).

Based on the corpus of his work, it is clear that Max Dickmann is one of the most significant social critics among Argentine Jewish writers, particularly in the "infamous decade" of the 1930s. Dickmann addressed practically every important social, political, and economic concern faced by Argentina. While his novels range over three decades, they continue to have a lasting impact. He wrote a trilogy on man's struggle against nature and the life of the average people. These three works—*Europa* (Europe; 1930), *Madre América*, and *Gente* (People; 1936)—contain no specific Jewish themes and only sometimes indirectly refer to Jewish characters or themes (Goodman 41). So while Dickmann rarely dealt with Jewish life, he still can be identified as a Jewish writer by reflecting basic Jewish values in his work (Goodman ii). Dickmann's later novels, which also treat wide-ranging social and political topics, reflect the approach of his 1930s trilogy (Goodman 41).

PRIMARY BIBLIOGRAPHY
Creative Writing
Los atrapados. Buenos Aires: Santiago Rueda, 1962.
El dinero no cree en Dios. Buenos Aires: Santiago Rueda, 1958.
Esta generación perdida. Buenos Aires: Santiago Rueda, 1945.

Europa. Buenos Aires: Palacio del Libro, 1930.

Los frutos amargos, novela. Buenos Aires: Claridad, 1941.

Gente (Historia de una generación). Buenos Aires/Montevideo: Sociedad Amigos del Libro Rioplatense, 1936.

Los habitantes de la noche. Buenos Aires: Santiago Rueda, 1952.

Madre América, novela. Buenos Aires: Claridad, 1935.

El motín de los ilusos. Buenos Aires: Santiago Rueda, 1949.

La porteña, crónica de lo ocurrido a la Señorita Amelita Martínez Aules llamada también Melita. Buenos Aires: Santiago Rueda, 1968.

SECONDARY BIBLIOGRAPHY

Agosti, Héctor Pablo. *El hombre prisionero*. Buenos Aires: Claridad, 1938.

—. *Las novelas de Max Dickmann*. Buenos Aires: Claridad, 1939? Also as, "Las novelas de Max Dickmann." In *Un novelista argentino*. Héctor P. Agosti, et al. Buenos Aires: Santiago Rueda, n.d. 5-27.

Besouchet, Lidia. "Max Dickmann: el hombre y el escritor." *Un novelista argentino*. Héctor P. Agosti, et al. Buenos Aires: Santiago Rueda, n.d. 28-31.

Cobo, Armando J. *¿Adónde va la literatura argentina? La novela: redescubrimiento de Max Dickmann*. Buenos Aires: Ediciones de Losange, 1954.

D'Elia, Miguel Alfredo. *La obra de Max Dickmann y la moderna novela argentina*. Buenos Aires: n.p., 1946.

Flores, Angel. "Argentina's Lost Generation." Rev. of *Esta generación perdida*. *Inter-American* 5.5 (May 1946): 35-36.

—. "Two Writers Worth Knowing." Rev. of *Los frutos amargos*. *Inter-American*. 1.6 (1942): 42-43.

Foster, David William. "Max Dickmann's *Madre América*: A Refracted Image of the *Década infame*." In his *Social Realism in the Argentine Novel*. Chapel Hill: University of North Carolina, Department of Romance Languages, 1986. 90-96.

García, Germán. *La novela argentina*. Buenos Aires: Editorial Sudamericana, 1952. 234-35.

González y Contreras, G. *Figuras volcadas*. La Habana, Cuba: 1939.

—. "El sentido americano de Max Dickmann." *Revista de las Indias* (Bogotá) 21 (Sept. 1940): 322-24. Also as "El sentido americano de Max Dickmann." *Un novelista argentino*. Héctor P. Agosti, et al. Buenos Aires: Santiago Rueda, n.d. 32-34.

Goodman, Robert. "The Image of the Jew in Argentine Literature as Seen by Argentine Jewish Writers." Ph.D. dissertation, New York University, 1972

Herrera, Francisco. "Dickmann, Max." In *Enciclopedia de la literatura argentina.* Ed. Pedro Orgambide and Roberto Yahni. Buenos Aires: Sudamericana, 1970. 191.

Hilton, Ronald, ed. *Who's Who in Latin America: A Biographical Dictionary of Notable Living Men and Women of Latin America.* 3rd ed. vol. 2. Detroit: Blaine Ethridge, 1971.

Kurlat, Ethel. "Max Dickmann: el novelista y el hombre." *Revista iberoamericana* 15 (1944): 49-56. Also as "Max Dickmann: el novelista y el hombre." *Un novelista argentino.* Héctor P. Agosti, et al. Buenos Aires: Santiago Rueda, n.d. 35-40.

Lasplaces, Alberto. "*Madre América.*" *Un novelista argentino.* Héctor P. Agosti, et al. Buenos Aires: Santiago Rueda, n.d. 41-48.

—. "La novela en América. A propósito de la novela de Max Dickmann, *Madre América.*" *Nosotros,* 2a. época, 4 (1976): 372-83.

Liacho, Lázaro. "La naturaleza y el espíritu del nuevo mundo: *Madre América* de Max Dickmann." *Dinámica porteña.* Buenos Aires: Editorial Viau y Zona, 1936. 50-64.

Lindstrom, Naomi. *Jewish Issues in Argentine Literature: From Gerchunoff to Szichman.* Columbia: University of Missouri Press, 1989. 21, 26.

Magdaleno, Mauricio. "El sentimiento americano en la obra de Max Dickmann." In *Un novelista argentino.* Héctor P. Agosti, et al. Buenos Aires: Santiago Rueda, n.d. 49-52.

—. "Tres libros de esencia americana." *Revista Iberoamericana* 3 (April 1940): 145-60.

Mallea Abarca, Enrique. "Variaciones sobre una novela de Max Dickmann." *Nosotros* 7.75 (June 1942): 301-12.

Menezes, María Wanderly. *Un novelista argentino.* Buenos Aires: Santiago Rueda, 1942.

Raven, Fritjof. Rev. of *Gente. Revista iberoamericana* 3.6 (1941): 459-60.

Sennett, Maurice R. *Max Dickmann: An Ear to the Argentine Ground.* Chicago: n.p., 1943.

Socas, María Angélica. "Tres mujeres en las novelas de Max Dickmann." *Atenea* (Chile) 37.299 (May 1950): 206-11.

Allan Metz

DINES, ALBERTO (Brazil; 1932)

Alberto Dines was born on February 19, 1932 in Rio de Janeiro. His parents had immigrated to Brazil from the city of Rozno, in Ukraine. A journalist, author, biographer, and script writer, during his formative years Dines was enrolled in elementary and secondary Jewish institutions of learning. As a pupil at the Escola Popular Israelita-Brasileira Scholem Aleichem he was once afforded a glimpse of Stefan Zweig (1881-1942), then a renowned political refugee in Rio de Janeiro, who honored an invitation to visit his school. The Austrian refugee would become, many years later, the main focus of Dines's book *Morte no paraíso: A tragédia de Stefan Zweig* (Death in Paradise: The Tragedy of Stefan Zweig; 1981). As a young adult, Dines studied at the distinguished Colégio Andrews. During these years he was a member of the Dror, a Zionist organization whose chapter in Rio de Janeiro he initiated and organized with the help of some friends. He is currently married to Norma Khouri, also a journalist, and has children and grandchildren from his first marriage.

Since his early teens, he was fascinated by cinema. He produced small documentaries and would get odd jobs with movie crews. In fact, his career in journalism began with the Jewish newspaper *Jornal Israelita* (Jewish Post) of Rio de Janeiro, to which he contributed articles and reviews on current films of the day. A short time later he became a contributor to *A Cena Muda* (The Silent Scene), a publication dedicated to cinema. In 1952 he went to work for *Visão* (Vision), which would turn out to be a very successful weekly magazine at the time. Dines remained there as one of its main editors, in charge of cultural and political affairs. That same year he became a syndicated journalist. He would eventually try his talents as a screen writer and director. In 1956 he went to work at *Manchete* (Headline), a weekly magazine of national prestige where he worked for three years. He was later invited to work for the newspapers *Última Hora* (Latest Hour News), *Diário da Noite* (Nightly News), and *Jornal do Brasil* (The Brazil Post), always in editorial positions. Returning to *Manchete*, he became the main editor of the weekly magazine *Fatos e Fotos* (Facts and Photos), starting with its second issue. Finally, he returned to work for the *Jornal do Brasil* where he stayed for twelve years. At the same time he acquired the part-time position of affiliated professor of Journalism at the Catholic University of Rio de Janeiro.

In 1972 he published *Posso?* (Can I?), a collection of short stories in which the title story "Posso?" deals with the theme of acculturation from the Jewish perspective. A surrealist view of an encounter between a Jew and Catholics on Christmas night, the short story advances a subject that today is rather common: the beginning of a process of mutual acknowledgement between Judaism and Catholicism. The narrative frames an exchange of good will, typical of the season, among the Catholic parishioners and the Jew, in both Italian and Hebrew, creating a surrealistic climate of reciprocal love and brotherhood, thereby dispensing with centuries of misunderstandings and resentment.

Dines accepted an invitation from Columbia University in New York for a visiting professorship position for the academic year 1974-75. While there he conducted seminars and gave lectures at the University's School of Journalism and the School of International Affairs. Once back in Brazil he went to work at Editora Abril (Abril Publishing House) in São Paulo. In 1988, as a recipient of the Brazilian Vitae Foundation Research Scholarship, he traveled to Portugal to carry out research for his book *Vínculos do fogo* (Bonds of Fire; 1992). The book focuses on the history of the Inquisition and on the personal story of oppression of Antonio José da Silva, o Judeo. While in Lisbon he published *O baú de Abravanel* (Abravanel's Trunk; 1990), in which he traces the story of the distinguished Jewish Abravanel family from the thirteenth to the twentieth century. In the book—classified as a chronicle by the author—the presence of Sílvio Santos, a popular Brazilian television personality whose real last name is Abravanel, is a strong leitmotif.

Dines remained in Lisbon at the invitation of Editora Abril as the publisher's representative in Portugal and to launch *Exame* (Exam), a magazine devoted to business affairs. Aside from the latter, three more magazines were introduced by his initiative to the Portuguese readership.

At this writing, Alberto Dines is drafting a second volume of *Vínculos do fogo* which will concentrate on the Inquisition's persecutions in Brazil. He is also preparing a revised edition of *Morte no paraíso*.

PRIMARY BIBLIOGRAPHY
Creative Writing
E por que não eu? Rio de Janeiro: Codecri Editores, 1979.

Posso? Rio de Janeiro: Sabiá, 1972.

Vinte histórias curtas. (Dines, et al.) Rio de Janeiro: Antunes & Cia., 1960.

Nonfiction
O baú de Abravanel: Uma crônica de sete séculos até Sílvio Santos. São Paulo: Companhia das Letras, 1990.

Morte no paraíso: A tragédia de Stefan Zweig. Rio de Janeiro: Nova Fronteira, 1981.

Papel do jornal. São Paulo: Summus, 1986.

*Vínculos do fogo: Antônio José da Silva, o Judeu e outras histórias da Inqui-
sição em Portugal e no Brasil.* São Paulo: Companhia das Letras, 1992.

Regina Igel

DORFMAN, ARIEL (Chile; 1942)

Ariel Dorfman was born in Buenos Aires, Argentina on May 6, 1942
to Adolfo Dorfman and Fanny Zelicovich. His grandparents had come to Argentina after escaping the pogroms in Eastern Europe. His father, an economist,
left Argentina to take a job in New York with the United Nations when Ariel
was only two years old. The family lived in New York for a period of ten years
before taking up permanent residence in Chile in 1954. In 1967 Ariel Dorfman
became a naturalized Chilean citizen. In 1973 he was expelled from Chile for his
outspoken stance against dictator Augusto Pinochet, who had successfully over-
thrown the government of Salvador Allende. Prior to being forced into exile, his
books had been publicly burned in Santiago and he had received numerous death
threats. After his departure from Chile he lived for varying periods of time in
France and Holland until finally settling in the United States where he currently
is (1996) a professor at Duke University. He continues to spend time yearly in
Chile.

As one of the most active intellectuals in Latin America, Ariel Dorfman
is an assiduous participant in public forums concerning literature and human
rights. His articles appear regularly in newspapers such as *The New York Times*
or *El País.* Dorfman is also a well-regarded literary critic, and author of novels,
short stories, plays, and poetry.

Dorfman has never expressed any close ties to a Jewish identity, a fact
that he attributes to a variety of factors: his upbringing by parents who were not
practicing Jews as well as the fact that circumstances have never allowed that he
live in one place long enough to become part of a Jewish community. Dorfman
concedes that he considers himself to be first and foremost a Chilean and/or
Latin American writer (Glickman 13-14).

One must accept Dorfman's premise that he is not a Jewish writer if a
narrow definition of the term is understood. Nonetheless, Dorfman's books and
articles on human rights and the right to national self-determination clearly
address issues that have long formed part of the agenda of Jewish communities.

Moros en la costa (*Hard Rain*; 1973) is the first novel written by Dorfman. It confronts the problem of good versus evil during the period of the Unidad Popular (1970-73) when Salvador Allende was president of Chile. *Moros* is an avant-garde work whose technical innovations parallel the social innovations of the new socialist government. The brutal dictatorship of General Augusto Pinochet forced Dorfman into exile, and caused him to abandon writing novels for years, and instead dedicate his energies to opposing the dictatorship. *Viudas* (*Widows*; 1981) is Dorfman's second novel. Set in Greece during War World II, in a small town about to be invaded by Nazi troops, *Viudas* tells how a group of women resist the military invasion, and continue to fight against fascism once their men have been "disappeared." The relationship of this plot with the Holocaust and Latin American Juntas is obvious, and this reading is plausible when the reader knows that the author was born Jewish and considered himself a socialist. Dorfman also wrote a stage version of this work.

Dorfman's third novel is *La última canción de Manuel Sendero* (*The Last Song of Manuel Sendero*; 1982). While the main character of the novel, David Wiseman, is Jewish, no topics of specific Jewish content or concern are to be found in the text. Dorfman negates that Wiseman is his alter ego, however, he does admit that the character's words contain a "strong autobiographical resonance" (Glickman 14). The novel essentially portrays the experience of exile and one can easily sense Dorfman's own diaspora in *La última canción*. In this book the author realizes the postmodern aphorism that there is no center. It also marks Dorfman's departure from Marxist and dogmatic attitudes in search of a new political and social perspective. He presents himself as "the flying Dutchman," in Spanish "el judío errante" (the wandering Jew), hoping that his literature will redeem him and his class (Latin American intellectuals), because during the Cold War they failed to provide Latin America with viable models of social, political and economic coexistence. *La última canción* also explores issues of deterritorialization as expressed in relation to instances of both interior and exterior exile. Half the book is science fiction, a technique Dorfman repeats in his fourth novel, *Máscaras* (*Mascara*; 1988). With this novel, Dorfman introduces an innovation in his mode of production, to write and publish simultaneously in Spanish and English. This bilingual ability (as a native speaker of both languages) affords him a privileged position as citizen of both worlds, the First World and that of developing nations, thus he serves as a bridge between the two shores of Western civilization. His latest work, *Konfidenz* (1994), is a spy novel that takes place in Paris at the beginning of World War II. It explores the question of the individual at the service of operant ideologies.

As a dramatist Dorfman has written *Death and the Maiden* (1991), a play highly acclaimed by public and critics alike, directed in 1992 on Broadway by Mike Nichols. It is a political and moral thriller about power, torture, and the ongoing, painful healing felt by societies in a process of transition to a democratic regime. *Death* won the 1991 Lawrence Olivier award for best play of the year. The cinematographic version was directed by Roman Polanski and released in 1994.

Ariel Dorfman gained international fame in 1971 when he published with Armand Mattelart *Para leer el pato Donald. Comunicación de masa y colonialismo* (*How to Read Donald Duck*). This is a key text for understanding the colonization of Latin American popular culture by the United States and other First World nations such as France (i.e., the elephant Babar). He studied texts like Donald Duck, the Lone Ranger, Babar, and American magazines with Spanish editions such as *Reader's Digest* in order to examine how these texts were instruments to teach Third World countries how to behave according to the rules of American imperialism (anticommunist policies, consumerism, trivialization of indigenous cultures, etc.). Even though these books contain unnecessary Leninist elements (speaking from a post-Cold War perspective), they helped to teach Latin American readers and educators how to protect themselves from the colonizing process. At the same time, the success of the English translation served to change the attitude of those who produced these texts in First World countries, prompting them to be more sensitive to the needs of the Latin American consumer. *Para leer* was translated into twelve languages and has been an extraordinary success in many countries, ultimately becoming the Hispanic and Thirld World versions of Roland Barthes's *Mythologies* (1957). Dorfman subsequently rewrote some of these texts as his political views changed, shifting from a dogmatic Leninist frame of reference to that of poststructuralism and postmodernism.

As a literary critic Dorfman has critiqued both the important figures of Latin American literature (José María Arguedas [1911-69], Gabriel García Márquez [1928], Alejo Carpentier [1904-82]), and writers in other languages like Anne Frank (1929-44) and her *Diary* (1952). *Imaginación y violencia en América Latina* (Imagination and Violence in Latin America; 1970) was a product of the intellectual convulsions of 1968 and became a starting point in the debate regarding the function of social art in the utopian new society to be created (the inflationary superstructure of the 1960s in the words of Fredric Jameson). His most recent book in literary criticism is *Some Write to the Future: Essays on Contemporary Latin American Fiction* (1991).

PRIMARY BIBLIOGRAPHY
Creative Writing

Cría ojos. México, D.F.: Nueva Imagen, 1979. Buenos Aires: Legasa, 1988.

Cuentos casi completos. Buenos Aires: Ediciones Letra Buena, 1991.

Cuentos para militares ("La batalla de los colores" y otros cuentos). Santiago de Chile: Emisión, 1986.

Death and the Maiden. New York: Penguin, 1991. Spanish version as *Teatro 1. La muerte y la doncella*. Buenos Aires: Ediciones de la Flor, 1992.

Dorando la píldora. Santiago de Chile: Las Ediciones del Ornitorrinco, 1985.

Konfidenz. Buenos Aires: Planeta, 1994. English version as *Konfidenz*. New York: Farrar, Straus and Giroux, 1995.

Máscaras. Buenos Aires: Sudamericana, 1988. English version as *Mascara*. New York: Viking-Penguin, 1988.

Missing. Trans. by Edith Grossman. London: Amnesty International, 1982.

Moros en la costa. Buenos Aires: Sudamericana, 1973. English version as *Hard Rain*. Trans. by George Shivers and Ariel Dorfman. New York: Readers International, 1990.

My House Is on Fire. Trans. by George Shivers and Ariel Dorfman. New York: Viking, 1990.

Pastel de choclo. Santiago de Chile: Sinfronteras, 1986. English version as *Last Waltz in Santiago*. New York: Viking-Penguin, 1988.

Pruebas al canto. México, D.F.: Nueva Imagen, 1980.

La rebelión de los conejos mágicos. Buenos Aires: Ediciones de la Flor, 1987. Barcelona: Ediciones B, 1988. English version as, "The Rebellion of the Magical Rabbits." In *Where Angels Glide at Dawn: New Stories from Latin America*. Ed. Lori M. Carlson and Cynthia L. Ventura. Intro. by Isabel Allende. New York: HarperCollins, 1990. 7-25.

Teatro 2: Viudas; Lector. Buenos Aires: Ediciones de la Flor, 1996.

Travesía. Montevideo: Banda oriental, 1986.

La última canción de Manuel Sendero. México, D.F.: Siglo XXI, 1982. English version as *The Last Song of Manuel Sendero*. Trans. by George R. Shivers and Ariel Dorfman. New York: Viking, 1987.

Viudas. México, D.F.: Siglo XXI, 1981. English version as *Widows*. Trans. by Stephen Kessler. New York: Vintage, 1984.

Nonfiction

El absurdo entre cuatro paredes: el teatro de Harold Pinter. Santiago de Chile: Universitaria, 1968.

Con sangre en el ojo, (with Marcelo Montecino). México, D.F.: Nueva Imagen, 1981. [Texts by Dorfman and photographs by Montecino]

Culture et résistance au Chili. Grand-Saconnex: Institut d'action culturelle, 1978.

De elefantes literatura y miedo: ensayos sobre la comunicación americana. La Habana: Casa de las Américas, 1988.

Ensayos quemados en Chile. (Inocencia y neocolonialismo). Buenos Aires: Ediciones de la Flor, 1974.

Hacia la liberación del lector latinoamericano. Hanover, NH: Ediciones del Norte, 1984.

Imaginación y violencia en América Latina: ensayos. Santiago de Chile: Universitaria, 1970. Barcelona: Anagrama, 1972.

Para leer al pato Donald. Comunicación de masa y colonialismo, (with Armando Mattelart). Buenos Aires: Siglo XXI, 1973. English version as *How to Read Donald Duck: Imperialist Ideology in the Disney Comic*. Trans. by David Kunzle. New York: International General, 1975.

Patos, elefantes y héroes: la infancia como subdesarrollo. Buenos Aires: Ediciones de la Flor, 1985.

Reader's nuestro que estás en la tierra: ensayos sobre el imperialismo cultural. México, D.F.: Nueva Imagen, 1980. English version as *The Empire's Old Clothes: What the Lone Ranger, Babar, and Other Innocent Heroes Do to Our Minds*. Trans. by Clark Hansen. New York: Pantheon, 1983.

Sin ir más lejos. Ensayos y crónicas irreverentes. Santiago de Chile: Pehuén, 1986.

Sobre las artes del espectáculo y fiestas en América Latina: documento de información y trabajo para la reunión de expertos organizada por la Unesco en Bogotá. La Habana: Unesco, 1976.

Some Write to the Future: Essays on Contemporary Latin American Fiction. Trans. by George Shivers and Ariel Dorfman. Durham/London: Duke UP, 1991.

Los sueños nucleares de Reagan. Buenos Aires: Legasa, 1986.

Superman y sus amigos del alma (with Manuel Jofré). Buenos Aires: Galerna, 1974.

La última aventura del Llanero Solitario. San José de Costa Rica: EDUCA, 1979.

SECONDARY BIBLIOGRAPHY
Criticism

Alcides Jofré, Manuel. "*La muerte y la doncella* de Ariel Dorfman: transición democrática y crisis de la memoria." *Atenea* (Chile) 469 (1994): 87-99.

"Ariel Dorfman." In *Contemporary Literary Criticism*. Detroit: Gale Research Company, 1988. Vol. 48, 87-95.

Barr, Lois Baer. "Deconstructing Authoritarian Codes: Ariel Dorfman." In her *Isaac Unbound: Patriarchal Traditions in the Latin American Jewish Novel*. Tempe, AZ: ASU Center for Latin American Studies, 1995. 131-58.

Braun, Lucille V. "Narrative Strategies in *La última canción de Manuel Sendero*." *Revista canadiense de estudios hispánicos* 20.3 (1996): 409-32.

Claro-Mayo, Juan. "Dorfman, cuentista comprometido." *Revista iberoamericana* 47.114-115 (1981): 339-45.

Flora, Cornelia Butler. "Roasting Donald Duck: Alternative Comics and Photonovels in Latin America." *Journal of Popular Culture* 18.1 (1984): 163-83.

Glickman, Nora. "Ariel Dorfman." *Tradition and Innovation: Reflections on Latin American Jewish Writing*. Ed. Robert DiAntonio and Nora Glickman. New York: SUNY Press, 1993. 13-15.

McMurray, Emily J. "Ariel Dorfman." In *Hispanic Writers: A Selection of Sketches from Contemporary Authors*. Ed. Bryan Ryan. Detroit/New York: Gale Research Inc., 1991. 168-71.

Oropesa, Salvador A. *La obra de Ariel Dorfman: ficción y crítica*. Madrid: Pliegos, 1992.

Interviews

Boyers, Peggy, and Juan Carlos Lertora. "Ideology, Exile, Language: An Interview with Ariel Dorfman." *Salmagundi* 82-83 (Spring-Summer 1989): 142-63.

Epple, Juan Armando. "Los trabajos y los días en el exilio: entrevista a Ariel Dorfman." *Plural* 9.104 (1980): 15-22.

Incledon, John. "Liberating the Reader: A Conversation with Ariel Dorfman." *Chasqui* 20.1 (1991): 95-107.

Kafka, Paul. "On Exile & Return. An Interview with Ariel Dorfman." *The Bloomsbury Review* 9.6 (1989): 12-14.

Muñoz, Silverio. "Entrevista a Ariel Dorfman." *Prismal/Cabral* 3-4 (Spring 1979): 60-76.

Wisenberg, S.L. "Ariel Dorfman: A Conversation." *Another Chicago Magazine* 18 (1988): 196-210.

Salvador Oropesa

DRAGÚN, OSVALDO (Argentina; 1929)

Osvaldo Dragún was born into a Jewish family in the province of Entre Ríos on May 7, 1929. He moved to Buenos Aires in 1944, where his contact with texts by Eugene O'Neill (1888-1953) encouraged him to write for the stage and to participate in the Teatro Independiente (Independent Theater) movement, which played a major role in Buenos Aires culture. In 1956, following the fall of Peronism, Oscar Ferrigno, an actor and the director of the Teatro Popular Fray Mocho (Fray Mocho Popular Theater) troupe, staged Dragun's first play, titled *La peste viene de Melos* (The Plague Is Coming from Melos). This work as well as its immediate successor, *Tupac Amarú* (the play takes its name from the last Inca leader; 1957), signal the ideologic concerns central to the dramaturgy of Dragún through the use of historical metaphors (the invasion of Melos by the Athenian empire and the Inca rebellion against the Spanish empire). These consist primarily of the necessity to discover modes of self-determination of the people against imperialism and of Latin American theater against foreign models. Dragún can be grouped together with other young authors of the time such as Ricardo Halac (1935), Germán Rozenmacher (1936-71), Roberto Cossa (1934), and Carlos Somigliana (1932-87), supporters of critical realism. His work is characterized by a search for forms that converge in both technical and aesthetic terms toward popular modes of expression. For this reason his most well-known works are those that utilize a transformation of the space traditionally used by the Circo Criollo (Creole Circus) whose empty stage, free of the alienating impositions of technical development, offers him a more effective freedom of expression. Thus his works such as *Historias para ser contadas* (Stories to Be Told; 1957) and *Los de la mesa 10* (The People at Table 10; 1957) are born. The latter was later made into a film by Simón Feldman in 1960. In these plays the actors, who are called on in the play to assume various characters, work on an empty stage placing their bodies at the service of the dramatic needs. Due to the almost nonexistent scenary and the limited necessity of theatrical props these plays were successfully staged by many groups (both professional and amateur) in Argentina, Chile, Uruguay, Spain, and the rest of Latin America. *Historia del hombre que se convirtió en perro* (*The Story of the Man Who Turned Into a Dog*; 1957) was staged with some modifications by the Teatro Campesino (Farm Workers Theater) directed by Luis Valdez (1940) in his struggle for the rights of the Chicano minority in the United States.

Dragún's work should be studied within the framework of Leftist culture, not only for the influence of Bertolt Brecht (1898-1956) and the definition of a popular and political theater, but also for its decisive participation in the Cuban Revolution. Dragún was the director of the Seminario de Autores Dramáticos de La Habana (Dramatic Author's Forum of Havana) from 1961 to 1963. He also won the Casa de las Américas award (considered to be the Latin American Pulitzer) for theater in 1962 for his play *Milagro en el mercado viejo* (Miracle in the Old Market). Dragún currently (1995) directs the International Institute for Latin American and Caribbean Theater based in Havana. Likewise, his experience as an exile during the Argentine military dictatorship of 1976-83 led him into contact with the leftist culture of Spain, Mexico, and Venezuela, where he not only wrote for the stage but also for film and television.

Nonetheless, Dragún's theater is affiliated with highly developed Latin American theatrical genres (Argentine in particular). The *sainete* (a short humorous play) and the grotesque, including comedy, melodrama and the circus, are of significant importance to his work. For this reason he negates any direct association of his theater with Brechtian models. From these associations arise, among others, works such as *Y nos dijeron que éramos inmortales* (*And They Told Us We Were Immortal*; 1962), one of the dramatist's most intense works, which debuted in the Idische Folks Theater (IFT) of Buenos Aires in 1963. It was followed by *Amoretta* (1964), a comedy; *Heroica de Buenos Aires* (Hero of Buenos Aires; 1966), an epoch play on a grand scale which won Dragún his second Casa de las Américas prize and which has special significance to the author in that it attempts to summarize his social view; *El amasijo* (The Plot, also known as *Dos en la ciudad* [Two in the City] or *¡Un maldito domingo!* [One Damned Sunday!]), staged in 1968 at the Teatro ABC in Buenos Aires; *Hoy se comen al flaco* (Today They Eat Skinny; 1981), which was written as a project for UNESCO, takes up the figure of the gaucho and the Creole circus; *Mi obelisco y yo* (My Obelisk and I; 1981), Dragún's contribution to the inaugural Teatro Abierto (Open Theater), in which his passion for Buenos Aires is again made manifest; and finally, *Al violador* (To the Violator; 1981), and *Al perdedor* (To the Loser), a work of fascinating cruelty, which debuted in 1982 in the IFT theater.

In *¡Arriba, Corazón!* (*Onward, Corazón!* [corazón literally means heart, but it is also the name of the protagonist]; 1987), matters of specific Jewish concern acquire a greater presence and profundity. It is an autobiographical full-length play that debuted in the Teatro Municipal General San Martín (General San Martín Municipal Theater) on April 23, 1987. Like many of the writers of his generation tied to the Marxist left, internationalism and cosmopolitanism, Dragún relegates specific Jewish concerns to the more general problematics of immigration in Argentina.

However, the Jewish question in Dragún's texts seems to be based on egalitarianism promoted from a Marxism that, going beyond questions of race, religion, or sexuality, opens a space in which subaltern groups are not singled out: woman, Jew, and worker together confront the advancing exploitation of capitalism. Beginning with *Tupac Amarú*, the oppressed character, upon realizing his situation, enters into a messianic and contestatory paradigm against the omnipotent Other, thereby fulfilling a sacrificial destiny before a community that does not understand him. The marginated character relies on his rebellion and plans his actions around a liberating mission of salvation in order to come to terms with his guilt and free himself from the progressive "animalization" and conformity of the middle class. "Deep down," states Dragún, referring to *Historias para ser contadas*, "the three stories are the story of my father, whom Argentine society has animalized" (Giella, et al.; "Osvaldo Dragún: teatro, creación y realidad latinoamericana" 16).

This paradigm, whose residual failure is to be found in the character of Juan in *¡Arriba, Corazón!*, goes through various transformations from the heroic gestures of the first works to the brotherly encounter of *Y nos dijeron que éramos inmortales* and the antiheroic renouncement of the mother in *Heroica de Buenos Aires*.

Thus, the Jew becomes a symbol, an imperative superego questions society in a landscape of economic and political oppression. Nonetheless, he does so outside of the specific historical circumstances of the Argentine Jewish community. As much the (few) explicitly Jewish characters as the non-Jewish ones allow themselves to assimilate to a conformity in which, like Samuel of *Y nos dijeron . . .*, Giuliana of *Amoretta*, José and María of *El amasijo*, and even Tupac Amarú, become accustomed to waiting, losing memory, and deferring to submission.

This emblemization of the oppressed through the figure of the Jew emerges again in *¡Arriba, Corazón!*, which brings together the most subtle techniques of Dragunian theater (and even inverts them: one character now requires three actors), but also delves into the theme of the double (Jew/Argentine), within a constant tension between metaphoric generalization and ethnic particularity. Corazón is a victim of the capitalist system which uprooted him from a rural setting and forced his family into the harshness of the city where—reelaborating the tradition of national theater on immigration destiny and breaking the *locus amoenus* of the Jewish gauchos—he becomes aware of the generalized oppression, of war and of freedom. However, as an intellectual and as a Jew he lacks a place with which to identify. Corazón is repeatedly confronted with dichotomous models of identification: soldier/castration; father/conformity; his Uncle Juan/idealism; Mara (half Polish, half French, living in Mexico, and Jewish)/uprootedness; his Uncle Manuel/surrender to assimilation. Corazón is the *moishe* (kike), an identity that comes to him from his friendship with Negro, who himself is the synthesis of the marginated Argentine and the only one who can, in the end, show him the exact place in which to forge his identity. The Jewish and Argentine elements of his identity come closer together as the play progresses: "¿Cuál es la diferencia? Cada vez nos parecemos más. Sin saber si vamos o venimos... si hemos llegado o nos estamos yendo" (What's the difference? We look more and more alike. Not knowing if we're coming or going... if we've arrived or are leaving" [87]). Joined by fear, persecuted, and compulsively led toward treason, they end up fashioning a bond of love by means of a signal of greeting that unites them homosocially and makes them accomplices against oppression.

PRIMARY BIBLIOGRAPHY

El amasijo. Buenos Aires: Calatayud, 1968. Also, in *9 dramaturgos hispano-americanos: antología del teatro hispanoamericano del siglo XX.* 3 vols. Ed. Frank Dauster, Leon Lyday, and George Woodyard. Ottawa: GIROL Books, 1989. I.207-67.

Amoretta. Buenos Aires: Carro de Tespis, 1965. Also, Buenos Aires: Argentores, 1973.

¡Arriba, Corazón!. Buenos Aires: Teatro Municipal General San Martín, 1987. English version as *Onward, Corazón.* Trans. by Nora Glickman and Gloria F. Waldman. In *Argentine Jewish Theatre: A Critical Anthology.* Ed. Nora Glickman and Gloria F. Waldman. Lewisburg: Bucknell UP, 1996. 267-324.

Heroica de Buenos Aires. La Habana: Casa de las Américas, 1966. Also, Buenos Aires: Astral, 1967. Also, *Teatro argentino contemporáneo: antología.* Madrid: Centro de Documentación Teatral, Ministerio de Cultura; Sociedad Estatal Quinto Centenario; Fondo de Cultura Económica, 1992. 353-92.

Los hijos del terremoto. Gestos 2 (1986): 159-213.

Historias con cárcel. In *Camino del teatro latinoamericano.* La Habana: Casa de las Américas, 1973. 11-114.

Historia de mi esquina; Los de la mesa 10; Historias para ser contadas. Buenos Aires: G. Dávalos y G. Hernández, 1965.

Historia del hombre que se convirtió en perro. In *Teatro breve hispanoamericano contemporáneo.* Ed. Carlos Solórzano. Madrid: Aguilar, 1969. 13-24. English version as *The Story of the Man Who Turned into a Dog.*

The Orgy: Modern One-Act Plays from Latin America. Ed. and trans. by Gerardo Luzuriaga and Robert S. Rudder. Los Angeles: UCLA Latin American Center, 1974. 29-40.

Historias para ser contadas. Buenos Aires: Talía, 1957. Also, Ottawa: GIROL Books, 1982.

Historias para ser contadas; Al perdedor. Rosario, Argentina: Ediciones Paralelo 32, 1982.

El jardín del infierno. *Cuadernos de Bellas Artes* 5 (1962): 51-81. Also in *Tres jueces para un largo silencio*. Buenos Aires: Centro Editor de América Latina, 1966. 71-112.

¡Un maldito domingo!; Y nos dijeron que éramos inmortales; Milagro en el mercado viejo. Madrid: Taurus, 1968.

Milagro en el mercado viejo. La Habana: Casa de las Américas, 1963. Also, Buenos Aires: Producciones Norte, 1963.

Mi obelisco y yo. In *7 dramaturgos argentinos: antología del teatro hispano-americano del siglo XX*. Ed. Miguel Angel Giella, Peter Roster, and Leandro Urbina. Ottawa: GIROL Books, 1983. 31-54. Also in *Teatro Abierto 1981: 21 estrenos argentinos*. Buenos Aires: Corregidor, 1992. 61-79.

La peste viene de melos. Buenos Aires: Ariadna, 1956.

The Story of Panchito González. *The Orgy: Modern One-Act Plays from Latin America*. Ed. and trans. by Gerardo Luzuriaga and Robert S. Rudder. Los Angeles: UCLA Latin American Center, 1974. 41-51.

Teatro: Historia de mi esquina; Los de la mesa diez; Historias para ser contadas. Buenos Aires: G. Dávalos, 1965.

Teatro: Hoy se comen al flaco; Al violador. Ottawa: GIROL Books, 1981.

Tupac Amarú. Buenos Aires: Losange, 1957.

Y nos dijeron que éramos inmortales. Xalapa, México: Universidad Veracruzana, 1962. Also, Buenos Aires: Los Monteagudos, 1963. English version as *And They Told Us We Were Immortal*. Trans. by Alden James Green. In *The Modern Stage in Latin America: Six Plays*. Ed. George W. Woodyard. New York: E.P. Dutton, 1971. 119-79.

SECONDARY BIBLIOGRAPHY
Criticism

Alvarez Borland, Isabel. "*Milagro en el mercado viejo*, metadrama y racconto en Osvaldo Dragun." *Alba de América* 7.12-13 (1989): 39-46.

Armando, Rose Marie. "Osvaldo Dragún." *Teatro argentino contemporáneo.* Buenos Aires: Revista Cultura, 1985. 45-51.

Bixler, Jacqueline Eyring. "The Game of Reading and the Creation of Meaning in *El amasijo.*" *Revista canadiense de estudios hispánicos* 12:1 (1987): 1-16.

Bonilla, Maggie, Nathalie Daleau, and Jean Konrad Kasso, Ximena Mandakovic. "Tradition et dictature chez Osvaldo Dragún: *Hoy se comen al flaco.*" *La Licorne* (Poitiers, France) 7 (1983): 99-110.

Dauster, Frank N. "Brecht y Dragún: teoría y práctica." In his *Ensayos sobre teatro hispanoamericano.* México, D.F.: SepSetentas, 1975. 189-97.

—. *Los hijos del terremoto*: imágenes de un recuerdo." *Latin American Theatre Review* 22.1 (1988): 5-11.

Foster, David William. "Estrategias narrativas en *Las historias para ser contadas* de Osvaldo Dragún." *Anales de literatura hispanoamericana* 6.7 (1978): 131-40.

Galich, Manuel. "De *Amoretta* a *Historias con cárcel.*" *Conjunto* 16 (1973): 82-86.

Giella, Miguel Angel. "Osvaldo Dragún: texto dramático y medios de producción." In *Teatro argentino de los '60: polémica, continuidad y ruptura.* Ed. Osvaldo Pellettieri. Buenos Aires: Corregidor, 1989. 99-108.

Gladhart, Amalia. "Narrative Foregrounding in the Plays of Osvaldo Dragun." *Latin American Theatre Review* 26.2 (1993): 93-109.

González Ortega, Nelson. "Teatro y sociedad en Hispanoamérica: *Historias para ser contadas* de Osvaldo Dragún." *Moderna-Sprak* [Sweden] 88.1 (1994): 75-82.

Howell, Susana. "*Historias para ser contadas* y *Dos viejos pánicos*: crítica y espectáculo." *Prismal/Cabral* 1 (1977): 17-24.

Leonard, Candyce Crew. "Dragún's Distancing Techniques in *Historias para ser contadas* and *El amasijo.*" *Latin American Theatre Review* 16.2 (1983): 37-42.

Levinson, Nina. "Una lectura de *Heroica de Buenos Aires.*" *Prismal/Cabral* 1 (1977): 25-34.

Lutz, Robyn R. "The Stylization of Theme in Dragún's *Historias para ser contadas.*" *Latin American Literary Review* 13 (1978): 29-37.

Méndez-Faith, Teresa. "Visión y revisión social en la obra de Osvaldo Dragún." In *Reflexiones sobre teatro latinoamericano del siglo veinte.* IITCTL (Instituto Internacional de Teoría y Crítica del Teatro Latinoamericano). Buenos Aires: Galerna/Lemke Verlag, 1989. 95-108.

Monleón, José. "Un teatro que vive y participa." *Teatro* 29 (1987): 22-26.

Ortega, Julio. "Una nota a las *Historias* de Dragún." *Latin American Theatre Review* 13.2 (1980): 73-75.

Pellettieri, Osvaldo. "El teatro de Osvaldo Dragún y las poéticas teatrales de Buenos Aires en los cincuenta." *Latin American Theatre Review* 29.2 (1996): 5-14.

Reati, Fernando. "*Y nos dijeron que éramos inmortales*: La experiencia iniciática en el texto y en la historia." *Latin American Theatre Review* 22.2 (1989): 37-46.

Reynolds, Bonnie E. "Time and Responsibility in Dragún's *Tupac Amarú*." *Latin American Theatre Review* 13.1 (1979): 47-53.

Rodríguez de Anca, Antonio. "Madre Coraje en la Argentina." *Teatro argentino contemporáneo: antología*. Madrid: Centro de Documentación Teatral, Ministerio de Cultura; Sociedad Estatal Quinto Centenario; Fondo de Cultura Económica, 1992. 347-51.

Romero, Luis A. "La Argentina de Dragún." *Teatro* (Argentina) 29 (1987): 8-12.

Rubio, Isaac. "La Argentina de Osvaldo Dragún: entre Ionesco y Brecht." *NS/N* 3.5-6 (1978): 179-98.

Schmidt, Donald L. "El teatro de Osvaldo Dragún." *Latin American Theatre Review* 2.2 (1969): 3-20. Also as, "The Theatre of Osvaldo Dragún." In *Dramatists in Revolt: The New Latin American Theatre*. Ed. Leon F. Lyday and George W. Woodyard. Austin: U of Texas P, 1976. 77-94.

Weinstein, Ana E., and Miryam Gover de Nasatsky, comps. *Escritores judeo-argentinos: bibliografía 1900-1987*. 2 vols. Buenos Aires: Milá, 1994. I.164-69.

Woodyard, George W. "Imágenes teatrales de Tupac Amarú: génesis de un mito." *Conjunto* 37 (1978): 62-68.

—. "Osvaldo Dragún." *Latin American Writers*. 3 vols. Ed. Carlos A. Solé and María Isabel Abreu. New York: Charles Scribner's Sons, 1989. III.1377-82.

Zalacaín, Daniel. "Proceso de estructuración absurdista en *El amasijo*." *Discurso literario* 5.2 (1988): 495-501.

Zayas de Lima, Perla. *Diccionario de autores teatrales argentinos 1950-1990*. Buenos Aires: Galerna, 1991. 100-3.

—. "El teatro épico en la versión de Osvaldo Dragún." In her *Revelamiento del teatro argentino (1943-1975)*. Buenos Aires: Rodolfo Alonso, 1983. 77-88.

Interviews

Amo, Alvaro del, and Carlos Rodríguez Sanz. "Conversación con Osvaldo Dragún." *Primer acto* 77 (1966): 12-17.

Campa, Román V. de la. "Entrevista con el dramaturgo Osvaldo Dragún." *Latin American Theatre Review* 11.1 (1977): 84-90.

Giella, Miguel Angel, Peter Roster, and Leandro Urbina. "Osvaldo Dragún: la honesta desnudez." *Teatro: Hoy se comen al flaco; Al violador*. Ottawa: GIROL Books, 1981. 39-71.

—. "Osvaldo Dragún: teatro, creación y realidad latinoamericana." *Teatro: Hoy se comen al flaco; Al violador*. Ottawa: GIROL Books, 1981. 7-38.

Morero, Sergio. "Una historia para ser contada. Con Osvaldo Dragún autor de *¡Arriba, Corazón!*." *Teatro* (Argentina) 29 (1987): 15-21.

Naios Najchaus, Teresa. "Osvaldo Dragún." In her *Conversaciones con el teatro argentino de hoy: Nº II (1981-1984)*. Buenos Aires: Agon, 1984. 120-26.

Pérez, Carmen Z. "Entrevista a Osvaldo Dragún." *Exegesis* 2.6 (1989): 27-33.

"Por un teatrista integral: Osvaldo Dragun." *Primer acto: cuadernos de investigación teatral* 240 (1991): 128-31.

Gustavo Geirola

DUJOVNE ORTIZ, ALICIA (Argentina; 1939)

Alicia Dujovne Ortiz was born in Buenos Aires in 1939 and since 1978 she has lived in Paris. She grew up in a non-religious family with a Jewish father and a Catholic mother. In her twenties, however, she became an active Zionist and rediscovered her Russian Jewish origin. She envisioned herself as a centaur or a mermaid, as a double being with a duplicate identity. She has worked as a columnist for *La Nación* and *La Opinión* in Argentina, for *El Excelsior* in Mexico, and for *Le Monde* in France. Her writings are characterized by the presence of parody and humor as a form of escape and by the usage of a feminine language —in her opinion, words are marked by gender—that shapes the imaginary world described by the author.

In her books it is possible to recognize two periods: the first—up to and including *El agujero en la tierra* (The Hole in the Earth; 1983)—is characterized by the close attention paid to language, which is baroque, bright and sensual. In her second period, the main characteristic is the awareness of her exile in France, and her identity as a Jewish woman.

In her collections of poems language becomes a vital component in the creative process. These books—*Orejas invisibles para el rumor de nuestros pasos* (Invisible Ears for the Murmur in Our Steps; 1966), *El mapa del olvidado tesoro* (The Map of the Forgotten Treasure; 1967), and *Recetas, florecillas y otros contentos* (Recipes, Little Flowers and other Joys; 1973)—deal with the ingredients of every day life, simple sensations that tend to escape modern men and women. These books manifest an essential primitivism, dedicated to delicate souls. Throughout the poems of *Orejas invisibles*, Dujovne lays a foundation that she will develop in later books: she poeticizes the small elements that silently enter our spirit. With an earthy language, the author writes poems to the coconut, the eucalyptus tree, a pot, scalded milk, the balcony, old tangos, a bouquet of flowers and, also, to her newborn daughter to whom the book is dedicated. These elements reappear in *Recetas*, but on this occasion the poetic voice has discovered love, sex, and its own erotic dimension. The second book of poems, *El mapa*, possesses autobiographical references and is characterized by oral connections. In this book, the reader faces for the first time a word whose importance will be central throughout Dujovne's work: *mapa* (map). The author shows an authentic fixation with it, with the exact location of places or persons, with the place where it is possible to develop a life, an idea, or a personality. The poems draw a seasonal Latin American map as a triangle with its center in La Paz (Bolivia). Starting from this city, the poetic voice—remembering from time to time its childhood—travels through a mineral and vegetable Latin America, piercing its mountains, lakes, rivers, stones, and fruits, reestablishing an old mythic relation with the natural elements. The poetic voice arrives in Macchu Picchu (Peru) and descends into the Peruvian mines, but it prefers the pampas and the tropical forests it finds in Brazil. It then visits Chile, arriving finally in Argentina; again to the pampas that are compared to a giant lung of endless sighs. The trip doesn't end in Buenos Aires—the inner city of the poetic voice—but continues through the south, San Martín de los Andes, where peace takes human form and it is possible to communicate with nature. After visiting Patagonia, the voice arrives in Mendoza and continues east to San Luis, Rincón del Este (Eastern Corner), where it falls in love. By the time the trip ends, Latin American fecundity has penetratd the five senses of the poetic voice.

In a book published almost twenty years later, *Buenos Aires* (1984)—written originally in French—the author takes another trip, a journey around a complex dilemma: the *porteño* (Buenos Aires native) identity. In this book of essays, Alicia Dujovne contemplates, with plenty of autobiographical details, the metaphysical city problem: an endless and rootless immigrant metropolis. To be *porteño* is to be defined by the gaze of the Other, however, the gaze doesn't mean proximity, but distance. In much the same way that the *porteña* (woman born in Buenos Aires) is defined by the male gaze, Buenos Aires finds its identity in the European stare, ignoring other South American countries. Buenos Aires—far from the world center and a mirror of the pampas—is a borderless city that fills its emptiness with the sadness and anxiety of the immigrants—Italians, Spaniards, Russians, Jews, Turks, Poles—reflecting this relevant melting pot in the tango. Throughout the book, Dujovne explores the different areas of Buenos Aires: while the center is a territory common to every *porteño*, the neighborhoods are his intimate city regions. Dujovne knows her city street by street, because she lived as a child in the west, as an adult in the east. Later, she moved downtown and finally to the north. From here—the richer section of Buenos Aires—her exile was only a natural step forward.

The preoccupation with maps appears early on in her first novel, *El buzón de la esquina* (The Corner Mailbox; 1964). The novel takes place in the neighborhood of Floresta, where Jacinta, the central character, lives with her family. But the narrator wants to be more precise and situates Jacinta's home in the corner of Laguna and Gregorio de Laferrère streets. The narrator provides the reader with a map of the neighborhood. Within its four corners, a micro-space that represents any city in the world, but at the same time symbolizes a private city region, Jacinta develops her unique female personality. With an elaborate language that covers several registers from religious to humorous, the novel narrates Jacinta's inner growth from her adolescent years to the peaceful end of her life together with her lover, the Russian immigrant Jrein. The novel illustrates the female struggle for independence: Jacinta experiences freedom while she was seated in a bench in Olivera park after the birth of her seven angelic daughters. She then leaves her husband and works as a dressmaker. Although the novel is written in a humorous tone—the name Jacinta echoes the onomatopoeic sound for laughter in Spanish—the message is that people are entitled to freedom, because each person is different and it is unfair to apply the same rules to everybody.

Unlike her first novel, which is located in the city, her second, *El agujero en la tierra*, is situated in the countryside. An improvised family—composed of the prostitute Pura (Virginal), the Bulgarian immigrant Stoyán, the prostitute's daughter Amapola (Poppy) and a dog—emigrates from the city in decay and its conservative inhabitants—represented by an old villa in the neighborhood of Palermo and its owner Esperanza (Hope)—to the village of Los Yuyos (The Weeds). In Los Yuyos, the family starts the construction of a new house and a new life surrounded by new friends, which carry a history that is the history of Argentina, a land of immigrants. In the tradition of Pascal, Plato and Jorge Luis Borges (1899-1986), the novel has a circular structure, similar to a tree trunk, which ends with the hole opened by the fall of a eucalyptus tree, the most common tree in Argentina along with the poplar. Contrary to the emptiness left by the disappearance of the Palermo villa, the peculiar community of Los Yuyos found its lost dreams, desires, and happiness on the hole left by the fallen tree. The novel is written with a experimentalist style, paying close attention to the language that reflects the oral discourse and popular registers of its characters.

¡Vamos a Vladivostok! (Let's Go to Vladivostok!; which appeared only in French with the title *L'arbre de la gitane*; 1990) inaugurates the second period in Dujovne's work. It is a testimonial novel, in which Dujovne reinvents the history of her parents' families. Her father's family emigrates from Russia and settles in Entre Ríos, whereas her mother's family is of Spanish origin. In this novel Dujovne presents the problem of identity, of belonging to two worlds and having two faces: Jewish and Christian in equal parts, but not being wholly either.

PRIMARY BIBLIOGRAPHY
Creative Writing

El agujero en la tierra. Caracas: Monte Avila, 1983.

El buzón de la esquina. Buenos Aires: Calicanto, 1977.

"Courage or Cowardice." Trans. by Marcela Kogan. In *You Can't Drown the Fire. Latin American Women Writing in Exile*. Ed. Alicia Partnoy. Pittsburgh: Cleis Press, 1988. 91-102. (From *¡Vamos a Vladivostok!*, unpublished)

Mapa del olvidado tesoro. Buenos Aires: Kraft, 1967.

Orejas invisibles para el rumor de nuestros pasos. Buenos Aires: Omeba, 1966.

Recetas, florecilla y otros contentos. Buenos Aires: Rayuela, 1973.

Wara la petite indienne de l'Altiplano. Christophe Kuhn, phots. Paris: Larousse, 1983.

Nonfiction

Buenos Aires. Seyssel: Champ Vallon, 1984. (In French) Partial English version as "Buenos Aires." Trans. by Caren Kaplan and Aurora Wolfgang. In *Critical Fictions. The Politics of Imaginative Writing*. Ed. Philomena Mariani. Seattle: Bay P, 1991. 115-30.

Eva Perón: la biografía. Buenos Aires: Aguilar, 1995.

Maradona soy yo. Esteban Buch and Alicia Dujovne Ortiz, trads. Buenos Aires: Emecé, 1993. (Translation of *Maradona c'est moi*).

María Elena Walsh. Madrid: Júcar, 1982.
Le Mexique: Le Guatemala. With Nanon Gardin. Paris: Larousse, 1984.
La sourire des dauphins. Paris: Gallimard, 1989.

SECONDARY BIBLIOGRAPHY
Criticism
Bataillon, Laure. "Alicia Dujovne Ortiz." In *Traduire, écrire*. Saint Nazaire:
    Arcane 17, 1991. 107-13.
Kaplan, Caren. "The Poetics of Displacement in Alicia Dujovne Ortiz's *Buenos
    Aires*." *Discourse* 8 (1986-87): 84-100.
Interviews
"Entrevista a Alicia Dujovne Ortiz: las tribulaciones de un centauro argentino
    exiliado en París." *Noaj* 1 (1988): 87-95.
Fingueret, Manuela. "Una porteña en París." *Nueva Sión* 604 (1984): 20-21.

                                                        Carmen de Urioste

DZIALOVSKY, FRANCISCO (Brazil; date unknown)

Francisco Dzialovsky, about whom no biographical information could
be obtained, is the author of *O terceiro testamento* (The Third Testament; 1987),
a novel that recounts the Jewish immigrant experience in Brazil. It is constructed
around the narrative device of a Yiddish radio program, "O Terceiro Testamento," that serves to strengthen the cohesiveness of the Jewish community in Rio
de Janeiro. The format of the weekly program consists of the discussion of a
wide range of topics that cover religion, Jewish history, biblical interpretation,
and famous Jewish personalities.

As is common in narratives of the immigrant experience, assimilation
is a principal theme throughout the novel. The radio show itself becomes an
indicator of the effects of assimilation on the community as Portuguese gradually
takes over as the dominant language, replacing Yiddish and by extension signaling the erosion of the traditional values and customs associated with the culture
of Yiddishkeit (DiAntonio). Dzialovsky populates his novel with a number of
unique characters who all provide a different outlook on the joys and difficulties
of Jewish life in Brazil. There are abundant intertextual and historical references
throughout the text that link Jewish existence in Brazil with the global experience

of life in the Diaspora in general. Likewise, the author details the components of Brazilian culture that both enhance and hinder the expression of Jewishness.

What Dzialovsky depicts in his novel is the difficult process of forging a new identity based on old traditions and new circumstances. The author does not portray this fusion of cultures in dry historical language with lengthy descriptions of hardship and conflict. Rather, he infuses his narrative with a good deal of humor expressed through characters who confront challenges with good-natured aplomb. Furthermore, there is a conscious effort to link Brazilian and Jewish history to a common past. For example, a historian presents the argument that Brazil's indigenous peoples are the descendants of the lost ten tribes of Israel (90). It is also proposed that the name Brazil comes from the Hebrew word *barzel* (iron) dating back to King Solomon's expedition to the continent in search of material to build the temple and his consequent discovery of the metal. It was the Lusitanian accent that later transformed *barzel* into Brazil (149-50). Certainly these are not theories that Dzialovsky himself presents as factual, but as fictional hypotheses they serve the purpose of demonstrating the assimilatory desire to belong.

One of the more interesting characters in the novel is the elderly Ruth, the madam of a brothel. Although, Dzialovsky does not specify one may certainly draw the conclusion that Ruth arrived in Brazil via the white slave (prostitution) trade run by Jewish organized crime groups. The character Rafael also alludes to this practice that flourished in the early part of the century, especially in Argentina, but also in Brazil. The novel ends with the demise of the radio program and the creation of a television program called "O Quarto Testamento" (The Fourth Testament), the product of a new generation now completely Brazilianized.

Although the claim on the book cover that Dzialovsky follows in the tradition of Isaac Bashevis Singer (1904-91), Saul Bellow (1915), and Moacyr Scliar (1937) overstates his position in the global arena, *O terceiro testamento* does make an interesting and entertaining contribution to the growing corpus of Brazilian Jewish literature.

PRIMARY BIBLIOGRAPHY

O terceiro testamento. Rio de Janeiro: Anima, 1987.

SECONDARY BIBLIOGRAPHY

DiAntonio, Robert. "Resonances of the Yiddishkeit Tradition in the Contemporary Brazilian Narrative." In *Tradition and Innovation: Reflections on*

Latin American Jewish Writing. Ed. Robert DiAntonio and Nora Glickman. Albany: SUNY Press, 1993. 45-60.

                                                    Darrell B. Lockhart

EICHELBAUM, SAMUEL (Argentina; 1894-1967)

It is difficult to conceive of a more unlikely marriage of author and
subject than that of the shy, scholarly, introspective, self-analytical Samuel
Eichelbaum, with the quintessential expression of Argentine machismo of the
mean streets (*bajo fondo*) of Buenos Aires at the turn of the century, *el guapo*,
Ecuménico, of *Un guapo del 900* (1940). After a literary career dedicated almost
exclusively to the depiction and definition of the psychological problems of the
Argentine middle class, it is ironic that despite critical acclaim, his sole popular
and commercial success should stem from the antithesis of his normal sphere of
dramatic interest. *Un guapo* received the national drama award for that year and
was later made into a movie by Argentine director Leopoldo Torre Nilsson,
receiving the national award for the best screenplay in 1961. An earlier autobiographical note of 1928, perhaps unconsciously but nonetheless poignantly, may
provide some insight into this general lack of popular success in Eichelbaum's
concluding declaration that he is a Jew and one of the dramatists who earned the
least in the country (Cruz 13). While the question as to whether there is an
implied cause and effect remains open to debate, there is no doubt as to the
validity of Eichelbaum's claim of lack of popular or commercial success. As
early as 1920, in a prologue to an edition of *La mala sed* (The Bad Thirst;
1920), José Pagano noted that Eichelbaum was an artist among literary merchants
who wrote purely for esthetic satisfaction (Pagano i-iv). Edmundo Guibourg later
commented that the dedicated, respected Eichelbaum neither made money for his
producers nor was concerned about doing so (11). More than a decade later,
Theodore Apstein confirmed that Eichelbaum still had not been able to make a
livelihood as a dramatist (while many authors of less serious stature had become
wealthy) and was forced to earn his living by editing the "amusements" section
of a newspaper (237).

While other Argentine writers had tapped the underworld of the *compadrito* or *guapo* (terms which are roughly equivalent to political ward, boss,
bodyguard or henchman) for literary inspiration, their motivation stemmed more

from a fascination with or a deliberate romanticization of an earthier and more colorful Argentine way of life (i.e., Jorge Luis Borges [1899-1986]). In contrast, Eichelbaum's resurrection of Ecuménico and his lowly environment reflected a deeper desire to demonstrate to his critics his unquestioned ability to write so-called authentic Argentine drama. Such dramatic authenticity had been cast in doubt by those noting an undeniably foreign or alien outlook in his work, a criticism which Eichelbaum attributed to his foreign last name, and again by implication, to his Jewish ethnic identity (Introduction to *Un guapo* 10). It would appear that his condition as a Jew, far outweighed the authenticity of his birth as a native (Argentine) son to create equally authentic Argentine drama. One representative criticism cited the intractability of the Jewish religion and customs as factors inhibiting the Jew from blending with the national ethic, and by exten-sion, implying an equivalent inhibition in the capability to produce "authentic" Argentine literature (Casadevall 115-18, 173). It is interesting to note that a foreign or alien vision had not been similarly attributed to the works of the Italo-Argentine dramatists, Francisco Defilippis Novoa (1889-1930) and Armando Discépolo (1887-1971), who with Eichelbaum are credited with reinfusing into Argentine drama the psychological dimension it had woefully lacked since the plays of Florencio Sánchez (1875-1910) at the turn of the century (Castagnino 119-20, 139; Ordaz, *El teatro* 138-49; Godoy Froy 49).

Eichelbaum, born November 14, 1894 in Domínguez, Entre Ríos, shared the memory of an early childhood in the Jewish agricultural colonies (established by Baron Maurice Hirsch at the turn of the century) with other Argentine Jewish writers such as Alberto Gerchunoff (1883-1950) and César Tiempo (1906-80). Contrary to the lyrical, almost biblical provincial experience of Gerchunoff in *Los gauchos judíos* (*The Jewish Gauchos of the Pampas*; 1910), the elder Eichel-baum (a former mechanic in the Russian Navy), found life too restricted in rural Argentina, especially with respect to the formal education of his children. To finance his move to Buenos Aires, he set fire to two of his fields and with the sale of the crop from the third, effected the move (E. Eichelbaum, et al. 3). This event served as the basis for the story, "La buena cosecha" (The Good Harvest; [*Tormenta de Dios*]). In Buenos Aires the younger Eichelbaum became friends with Alberto Gerchunoff and shared with him the nocturnal *academia* (academe or university) of the streets and cafes of Buenos Aires with other budding Argen-tine writers (Gerchunoff iii; Petit de Murat 8-10). Eichelbaum confesses to an early vocation for the theatre when at the age of thirteen he unsuccessfully at-tempted to have a *sainete* (musical skit), *El lobo manso* (The Meek Wolf; be-tween 1901-08), produced in nearby Rosario (E. Eichelbaum, et al 3). Undaunted by this rejection, he returned with *Por el mal camino* (On the Wrong Path), written at seventeen and presented in Yiddish by the Jewish company Guttentag around 1911 (Cruz 14). He was formally initiated into Argentine drama with the production of *La quietud del pueblo* (The Stillness of the People; 1919), by the prestigious Argentine company of Muiño y Alippi. His vocation as dramatist was confirmed with the opening of *La mala sed* to critical acclaim. Hereafter, with the exception of three collections of stories, *Un monstruo en libertad* (A Freed Monster; 1925), *Tormenta de Dios* (Storm from God; 1929), and *El viajero inmóvil* (The Immobile Traveler; 1933), Eichelbaum regularly wrote and produced dramatic works until 1942, when the long silence that enveloped Argentine literature and drama in general during the Perón era was in effect. Collaborating with Ulises Petit de Murat in 1948, he wrote and attempted to have the play *Un patricio del 80* (A Patrician of 1880) produced to open the Buenos Aires fall season. Considered too politically sensitive, the play was rejected, and Eichelbaum and Petit de Murat were dismissed from their administrative posts in *Argentores* (the national writers' organization).

After the silence of the Perón years, Eichelbaum returned to the Argentine stage in 1952 with a number of works in which the exploration of Argentine middle-class psychology alternated with themes more universal in nature, both in location and concept. *Un rostro perdido* (A Lost Face; 1952), followed the traditional Eichelbaum preoccupation with the Argentine bourgeoisie. It was followed by *Dos brasas* (Two Live Coals; 1955), an examination of the uncontrolled avarice of a North American couple that leads to tragedy, and *Las aguas del mundo* (The Waters of the World; 1957), in which Eichelbaum returned his drama to provincial Argentina. His last works, written in 1966 but never produced, were; *Subsuelo* (Basement), a return to the Argentine middle-class; *Un cuervo sobre el imperio* (A Crow over the Empire), a deposed queen's vengeance upon a disloyal lover; and *Gabriel el olvidado* (Gabriel the Forgotten), an unwed mother who elects to rear her child alone and pursue her career as an actress.

Despite his lack of popular or commercial success, Eichelbaum received national acclaim for his work during his long and fruitful career. In 1930 he was awarded the Municipal Prize (Buenos Aires) for the best dramatic work and the Jockey Club Prize for the best original work in prose. In 1952-53, he received the (biennial) Alberto Gerchunoff Award for outstanding dramatist. In 1946, he was the Argentine representative to the International Congress of Writers in Washington, D.C. With his death in 1967, Argentine drama lost its most brilliant and intellectual expression of introspection and self-analysis in the voice of its native Judeo-Argentine son, Samuel Eichelbaum.

No overview of Eichelbaum's work can ignore the question as to what degree his Jewish origin is reflected in his work. While he does assert his complete identification with his Argentine environment, his early native environment was also that of other Argentine Jewish writers, such as Gerchunoff and Tiempo, both of whose works reflect a more obvious and consistent Jewish orientation. Juan Gelman (1930) proposes that all literature written in Spanish should be considered as of Spanish (Hispanic) origin. He is convinced, however, that his Jewish ethnic identity has added a distinct dimension to his work, where the unconscious selection of a word, phrase or sentence may be a subconscious reflection of his Jewish ancestry (84, 89). Applying this guideline, the focus of this discussion will center on the explicit versus the implicit Jewish presence in Eichelbaum's work.

The explicit Jewish presence is easy to identify in his early collections of stories. As previously noted, the protagonist, Bernardo Drugova (modeled on the real-life senior Eichelbaum) burned his fields to effect his removal to the city. The Jewish chacarero (farmer), Don David, whose wheat crop is rotting in the fields (due to non-delivery of harvesting machinery) details the suffering and poverty of his life to the station master in "Lo que la luna vio" (What the Moon Saw [*Tormenta de Dios*]). In "Las ideas del señor Rosoff, el Tolstoiano" (The Ideas of Mr. Rosoff, the Follower of Tolstoy [*Tormenta de Dios*]), the socialist ideal of the brotherhood of man, expounded by the *ruso* or Jew Rosoff, are violently rejected as alien by an assembly of striking taxi drivers. The tragic figure of the impoverished, disillusioned, immigrant who commits suicide in "El senor Lubovitsky, depositario" (Mr. Lubovitsky, Trustee; [*Un monstruo en libertad*, republished in *El viajero inmóvil*]), portrays a more somber vision of the Jewish condition in Argentina during the 1920s, influenced undoubtedly by the events of the Semana Trágica (Tragic Week) in 1919 (when Jews in Buenos Aires were beaten and their homes and businesses burned in the name of Argentine nationalism). The courtship and marriage of Eichelbaum's parents on the ship bringing them to Argentina inspired the story, "En tierra firme" (On firm Ground [*El viajero inmóvil*]). The prize for the wager between two destitute writers is the right to appropriate a dramatic personage endowed with the highest and most enduring characteristics of the Jewish tradition.

Eichelbaum's early drama also reflects an explicit Jewish presence. Sonya and her husband, the Jewish entrepreneurs of the small factory in Buenos Aires in *El dogma* (Dogma; 1922), embody the socialist ideals of Eichelbaum senior. The explicit Jewish presence reappeared in two other Eichelbaum dramas in 1926. *El judío Aarón* (*Aarón the Jew*) returned Eichelbaum to the Jewish agricultural colonies, but his vision is one of conflict; the first, between the elders and the Jewish youth and secondly, between the colonists and their local workers (*peones*). The youth, when not deserting the ancestral farms, spend their time and money aping Argentine bourgeois attitudes and dress. The Sanhedrin quality of the elders' council has dissipated and deteriorated into a generational conflict of language and a more modern agrarian approach. While compromise is ultimately effected between the colonists and the *peones*, the spiritual and actual decline of the colonist movement had begun. The Jewish Doctor Gorovich early introduces the element of Jewish self-hate (later described in greater detail by other Jewish authors, e.g., Senkman) into the Eichelbaum dramatic spectrum, insisting to an Argentine commissioner that he feels different from other Jews, to the extent that he even forgets his Jewish origins and says "no" automatically when queried as to his ethnic background (Senkman 11).

Ivonne, of *Nadie la conoció nunca* (No One Ever Knew Her; 1926), is shamed into confessing her Jewish identity when friends of her lover boast of having publicly mocked and embarrassed an elderly Jew by cutting off his beard and forcing him to shout antisemitic slogans. Her decision to atone for her life of deception by leaving her Gentile lover is nullified by his offer of marriage, effecting an implausible Judeo-Christian resolution of centuries of Jewish rejection and humiliation (53). In the trauma of post-Semana Trágica Argentina, such a patent solution was undoubtedly the most socially acceptable (if unrealistic) at the time.

The last explicit Jewish presence in Eichelbaum's theater is that of Leber in *Divorcio nupcial* (Nuptial Divorce; 1941). Here, the urban Jew uneasily strives for an acceptance within Argentine society. When he is asked at a gathering to tell Jewish jokes and explain their current popularity in Argentine conversation (especially those concerning Hitler), Leber responds that it is the Jews themselves who are the authors, mocking or debasing themselves to deflect or divert the antipathy of antisemites. When it is noted that his words could also be construed as antisemitic, Leber comments that he is not surprised, as he rarely frequents Jewish society (270-72), thereby joining Dr. Gorovich and Ivonne in the Eichelbaum depiction of a subtle Jewish self-hate. Leber's omnipresent social insecurity surfaces again in the perceived snub occasioned by a friend's failure to offer his hand in greeting to Leber in his dressing room, an omission his friend explains is in keeping with etiquette among gentlemen in the intimacy of the bedroom (303).

Returning to Gelman's thesis of the inescapable, if unconscious, Judaic dimension in any Jewish author's work, the implicit Jewish presence in Eichelbaum is evidenced by the form and specific thematic focus of his work. Obviously, introspection, self-analysis and discursiveness are not the exclusive property of the Judaic tradition, in view of the influence of Henrik Ibsen (1828-1906), Henri René Lenormand (1882-1951), August Strindberg (1849-1912), Fyodor

Mikhailovich Dostoyevsky (1821-1881), Luigi Pirandello (1867-1936) and Eugene O'Neill (1888-1953), among others, almost universally cited in his drama by his many critics and biographers (e.g., Alfredo de la Guardia, Bernardo Canal-Feijoo, Luis Ordaz). Conversely, it cannot be denied that the Jewish ethnic tradition is also rich in these dramatic elements, and as such it can be judged to be an implicit influence in the form and content of Eichelbaum's work. The Jewish ethic abounds in the tradition of the discursive, introspective self-analytical approach to human ideas and behavior. From the meticulous, highly-detailed explanations of the ancient texts of the Torah, through the tortured writings of philosophers such as Maimónides (1135-1204) and Baruch Spinoza (1632-77), to the analytical writings of Sigmund Freud (1856-1939), there is obviously sufficient historical precedent to ascribe Eichelbaum's self-confessed "maniacal" interest in introspection and self-analysis to his Jewish heritage. His characters not only seek to find the meaning of their actions through lengthy self-analysis, but must always explain the motives behind their actions (Cruz 22, 24), in long dialogues or monologues, a technique, at the time, unfamiliar to the Argentine theater. Even when he deliberately attempted to rid his drama of this aspect, as applied to the uneducated Ecuménico from the depths of Argentine society, Eichelbaum could not avoid endowing him with the capacity to examine and articulate the complex system of values which impel him to prefer incarceration to a freedom based on dishonesty. As he explains to Navidad (his mother), he could no longer serve a political boss whose manhood was diminished, in his eyes, by his wife's unsuspected infidelity. Ecuménico's killing of the wife's lover, without the merited punishment, would only serve to tarnish his manhood as defined by the *guapo* ethic of courage, loyalty, and honor. By his silence and incarceration, he exults that even the bones of his victim will rise up to applaud the nobility of his actions (73). Other equally unlikely candidates for dramatic introspection and self-analysis are Felipa, the rural serving girl of *Pájaro de barro* (Clay Bird; 1940); Servando, the humble cart-driver of *Un tal Servando Gómez* (A Certain Servando Gómez; 1942) and Laureano, the provincial ex-sailor of *Las aguas del mundo* (1957).

Enhancing the implicit Jewish presence in Eichelbaum's theatre of introspection and self-analysis, is his emphasis upon the strength and determination of the female protagonists of his works. Joining the biblical Esther and her Jewish sisters through the ages, the social workers and labor activists of New York at the turn of the century (Howe), and persisting to our own time in the contemporary figure of Ruth Bader Ginsburg, the U.S. Supreme Court justice, the Jewish woman has been a strong, articulate and determined defender of the dignity and self-worth of the woman in a male-dominated, indifferent or uncomprehending society. Such is the mettle of Eichelbaum's women, whether Argentine middle- or lower-class. While again the claim of Jewish exclusivity cannot ignore the cited influence of Ibsen's Nora nor the equally strong women of Federico García Lorca (1898-1936) as in *Bodas de sangre* (*Blood Wedding*; 1933 [Ordaz, *El teatro* 162]), Eichelbaum's women bear the special stamp of his introspective and analytical vision, and the necessity to explain their actions, whether to sympathic or hostile listeners.

Through the virtue of hindsight and by contemporary standards, Eichelbaum's female protagonists can justly be classified as feminists, since they fight to make their own free choices and to be respected for such decisions, even if they go against prevalent societal mores. P.A. Karavellas has divided the Eichelbaum female protagonists into five categories: the independents, the victims (of men), the mothers, the matriarchs, and the spinster sisters (87). Outstanding among the independents are Felipa of *Pájaro de barro*, who elects to raise her illegitimate child alone rather than marry the father, the spineless son of Doña Pilar (the landowner mistress), an equally strong woman. Alicia of *Soledad es tu nombre* (Solitude Is Your Name; 1924), elects to conserve her self-esteem and dignity by encouraging her lover to return to his wife and family, paying the price with her ensuing solitude. Even women cited as victims of male arrogance display an independence of spirit and action which effectively nullifies their victimization. A representative victim is Blanca in *Divorcio nupcial*, who leaves her husband and child, convinced that she was valued solely for her role as mother, rather than for her intrinsic worth as a human being. Leda of *Gabriel el olvidado*, joins Felipa in rejecting an insincere offer of marriage from a weak, indifferent lover, choosing to raise her child as a single mother and pursue a career as an actress.

Navidad, of *Un guapo*, epitomizes the matriarch among the Eichelbaum women. More father than mother in strength, she lives and inculcates in Ecuménico the *guapo* ethic of the rough streets. It is to her that Ecuménico turns for approval, or at least for an understanding of his actions. Her sole concession to maternal vulnerability is to regret that with his imprisonment, Ecuménico will not be there to cross her hands and close her eyes when she dies (72). And finally the spinster sister, Virginia of *La hermana terca* (The Obstinate Sister; 1924), accepts the stigma of single motherhood (alleged by a former lover) to continue rearing a child who is actually her younger brother. Eichelbaum's women willingly submit to ostracism, loneliness, noncomprehension, and hostility in a male-dominated society to maintain their belief in their ideals and their own self-worth.

While not achieving the popularity nor the commercial success he had sought, Eichelbaum effectively demonstrated to the nation and the world at large, his capability to create high-quality, "authentic" Argentine drama, cited by critics as on a par with that of Strindberg in the Swedish theater, and O'Neill in the American theater (Cruz 73). Even more importantly, it is drama that extends beyond national boundaries to mirror the universal concern of the simple, as well as cultured human being, in maintaining a sense of dignity and self-worth in a sometimes incomprehensible or hostile world. In subjecting the motivation behind seemingly incomprehensible human behavior to his sensitive, compassionate and universal dramatic lens, Samuel Eichelbaum has enriched Argentine literature with a legacy of introspective and self-analytical dramatic works, in which both the Jewish heritage and the Argentine national ethic combine to create a unique and profound expression of the human condition.

PRIMARY BIBLIOGRAPHY

Las aguas del mundo. Buenos Aires: Carro de Tespis, 1959.

La cáscara de nuez. (with Pedro F. Pico) *Teatro popular* 133 (1921).

Cuando tengas un hijo. Buenos Aires: El Inca, 1931.

Doctor. (with Pedro F. Pico) *Bambalinas* 254 (1922): 1-21..

El dogma; El camino de fuego. Buenos Aires: *Bambalinas* 5.236 (14 Oct. 1922): n.p.

Dos brasas. Madrid: Aguilar, 1962.

En tu vida estoy yo. Buenos Aires: M. Gleizer, 1934.

El gato y su selva; Un guapo del 900; Pájaro de barro; Dos brasas. Buenos Aires: Sudamericana, 1952.

Un guapo del 900; Las aguas del mundo. Buenos Aires: Ediciones Culturales Argentinas, 1967.

La hermana terca. Buenos Aires: Claridad, 1924.

Un hogar. Buenos Aires: M. Gleizer, 1923.

La Juana Figueroa. (with Pedro F. Pico) *El teatro argentino* 47 (1921): 1-16.

El judío Aarón. Buenos Aires: Talía, 1926. English version as *Aarón the Jew*. Trans. by Nora Glickman and Gloria F. Waldman. In *Argentine Jewish Theatre: A Critical Anthology*. Ed. Nora Glickman and Gloria F. Waldman. Lewisburg: Bucknell UP, 1996. 24-54.

El lobo manso. Unpublished, variously attributed between 1901 to 1908.

Lotería sin premios. (with Agustín Remón) Unpublished, 1930.

La mala sed. Buenos Aires: Talleres Gráficos, 1920.

Un monstruo en libertad (includes *Instinto [narración escénica]*). Buenos Aires: M. Gleizer, 1925.

N.N. Homicida. Buenos Aires: Carro de Tespis, 1927.

Pájaro de barro. Buenos Aires: Sur, 1940.

Pájaro de barro; Vergüenza de querer. Buenos Aires: EUDEBA, 1965.

Un patricio del 80. (With Ulises Petit de Murat). Buenos Aires: Talía, 1969.

Por el mal camino. Unpublished, 1912.

La quietud del pueblo. Unpublished, 1919.

Ricardo de Gales, príncipe criollo. Buenos Aires/Montevideo: Sociedad Amigos del Libro Rioplatense, 1933.

Un romance turco. (with Pedro F. Pico) *La escena* suppl. 9 (1920): 1-13.

Rostro perdido. Buenos Aires: Departamento de Teatro del Centro Cultural J. N. Bialik, 1986.

Rostro perdido; Subsuelo; Un cuervo sobre el imperio; Gabriel, el olvidado. Buenos Aires: EUDEBA, 1966.

El ruedo de las almas. Buenos Aires: *La escena* 6.259 (1923): 1-24.

Señorita. Buenos Aires: El Inca, 1931.

Soledad es tu nombre; La mala sed. Buenos Aires: M. Gleizer, 1932.

Un tal Servando Gómez. Buenos Aires: Losange, 1954.

Un tal Servando Gómez; Vergüenza de querer; Divorcio nupcial. Buenos Aires: Ediciones Conducta, 1942.

Tejido de madre; Nadie la conoció nunca. Buenos Aires: Carro de Tespis, 1956.

Tormenta de Dios. Buenos Aires: El Inca, 1929.

El viajero inmóvil y otros cuentos. Buenos Aires: Sociedad Amigos del Libro Rioplatense, 1933. Reissued, Buenos Aires: Paidós, 1968.

Vergüenza de querer. Buenos Aires: Talleres Gráficos Celina, 1971.

Viva el padre Krantz. Unpublished, 1928.

SECONDARY BIBLIOGRAPHY

Apstein, Theodore. *Books Abroad* 19 (1945): 237-41.

Berenguer Carisomo, Arturo. *Teatro argentino contemporáneo*. Madrid: Aguilar, 1962. Prologue, xxiii-xxv, li.

Blanco Amores de Pagella, Angela. *Nuevos temas en el teatro argentino*. Buenos Aires: Huemul, 1965. 60-4, 119-29, 132-33.

Canal Feijoo, Bernardo. "Cuatro piezas de Eichelbaum." *El gato y su selva; Un guapo del 900; Pájaro de barro; Dos brasas*. Buenos Aires: Sudamericana, 1952. 7-20.

Casadevall, Domingo. *El teatro nacional: sinópsis y perspectivas*. Buenos Aires: E.C.A., 1961. 111, 172-73.

Castagnino, Raúl Héctor. *Literatura dramática argentina: 1717-1967*. Buenos Aires: Pleamar, 1968. 141-42.

Cerretani, Arturo. "El teatro de Samuel Eichelbaum." *Síntesis* 3.36 (1930): 213-29.

Cruz, Jorge. *Samuel Eichelbaum*. Buenos Aires: Ediciones Culturales Argentinas, 1962.

Eichelbaum, Edmundo, Luis Ordaz, and César Tiempo. "Homenaje a Samuel Eichelbaum." *Clarín* (Buenos Aires) April 28, 1977: 1-3.

Foppa, Tito Livio. *Diccionario teatral del Río de la Plata*. Buenos Aires: Carro de Tespis, 1961. 270-71.

Foster, David William. "Argentine Jewish Dramatists: Aspects of a National Consciousness." In his *Cultural Diversity in Latin American Literature*. Albuquerque: U of New Mexico P, 1994. 95-150. Also in *Folio* 17 (1987): 74-103.

—. "Strategic Defamiliarization in *Un guapo del 900* de Samuel Eichelbaum." In his *The Argentine Teatro Independiente, 1930-1955*. York, SC: Spanish Literature Publishing Company, 1986. 35-50.

Freitas, Newton. "*Pájaro de barro* (de Samuel Eichelbaum)." In *Ensayos americanos*. Buenos Aires: Schapire, 1942. 193-96.

Gardiol, Rita. *Argentina's Jewish Short Story Writers*. Ball State Monograph Number 32. Muncie, IN: Ball State University, 1986. 13-15.

Gerchunoff, Alberto. "Samuel Eichelbaum." *Un tal Servando Gomez; Vergüenza de querer; Divorcio nupcial*. Buenos Aires: Ediciones Conducta, 1942. i-xi.

Gelman, Juan. "Lo judío y la literatura en castellano." *Hispamérica* 21.62 (1992): 85-90.

Giordano, Enrique. "La generación del 27: Samuel Eichelbaum y la composición paratáctica-teatralista." In his *La teatralización de la obra dramática: de Florencio Sánchez a Roberto Arlt*. México, D.F.: Premià, 1982. 111-57.

—. "*Un guapo del 900* de Samuel Eichelbaum." In *Historia y crítica de la literatura hispanoamericana 3. Epoca contemporánea*. Ed. Cedomil Goic. Barcelona: Editorial Crítica, 1988. 557-60.

Godoy Froy, Marta. *Introducción al teatro de Samuel Eichelbaum*. Buenos Aires: Plus Ultra, 1982.

Gordon, Marjorie Salgado. "Alberto Gerchunoff and Samuel Eichelbaum: Two Literary Reflections of Judeo-argentinidad." Ph.D. diss., University of Maryland, College Park, 1982.

Guardia, Alfredo de la. "Raíz y espíritu del teatro de Eichelbaum." *Nosotros* (2nd period) 25 (1938): 385-400.

—. "Homenaje a Eichelbaum." *Comentario* 48 (1966): 33-37.

—. "La honra instintiva en cuatro personajes de Eichelbaum." *Raices* 27 (1971): 40-41. Also in his *Imagen del drama*. Buenos Aires: Schapire, 1954. 131-44.

—. "Samuel Eichelbaum, dos estudios psicológicos [*Vergüenza de querer* y *Divorcio nupcial*]." *Nosotros* (2nd period) 14 (1941): 84-86.

Guibourg, Edmundo. "Una semblanza de Samuel Eichelbaum." Prologue to *El viajero inmóvil*. Buenos Aires: Paidós, 1968. 9-12.

Howe, Irving. *World of Our Fathers*. New York: Harcourt, Brace and Jovanovich, 1976. 297-300.

Jones, Willis Knapp. "Three Great Latin American Dramatists: Eichelbaum, Usigli, and Marqués." *Specialia* 1 (1969): 43-49.

Karavellas, Panos D. *La dramaturgia de Samuel Eichelbaum*. Montevideo: Ediciones Geminis, 1976.

Lange, Norah. "A Samuel Eichelbaum." In her *Dicursos*. Buenos Aires: C.A.Y.D.E., 1942. 145-51.

Lindstrom, Naomi. "Anomalous Eloquence in a Drama by Samuel Eichelbaum." *Chasqui* 11.1 (1981): 3-12.

Morán, Julio César. "Conducta humana y coherencia en *Un guapo del 900* de Samuel Eichelbaum." In *Estudios literarios e interdisciplinarios*. La Plata: Universidad Nacional de La Plata, Facultad de Humanidades y Ciencias de la Educación, Departamento de Letras, 1968. 71-96.

Ordaz, Luis. "Prólogo." In *El teatro argentino 10. Samuel Eichelbaum: Pájaro de barro; Dos brasas*. Buenos Aires: Centro Editor de América Latina, 1980. i-ix.

—. "Samuel Eichelbaum." In *Enciclopedia de la literatura argentina*. Ed. Pedro Orgambide and Roberto Yahni. Buenos Aires: Sudamericana, 1970. 207-9.

—. "Samuel Eichelbaum o la instrospección." *Historia de la literatura argentina*. Vol. III. Buenos Aires: Centro Editor de América Latina, 1981. 505-28.

—. *El teatro en el Río de la Plata*. Buenos Aires: Leviatán, 1946. 160-65.

Pagano, José León. "Prólogo." *La mala sed*. Buenos Aires: Talleres Gráficos, 1920. i-iv.

Pak-Artsi, Diana I. "Aportes de cuatro autores judíos a la literatura argentina: Gerchunoff, Espinoza, Verbitsky y Eichelbaum." Ph.D. diss., Arizona State University, Tempe, 1989.

Palant, Pablo T. "Samuel Eichelbaum." In *Pájaro de barro; Vergüenza de querer*. Buenos Aires: EUDEBA, 1965. 5-11.

Petit de Murat, Ulises. *Samuel Eichelbaum*. Buenos Aires: A-Z Editora, 1986.

Plá, Roger. "El teatro de Eichelbaum." *Contrapunto* 1.1 (1944): 8-9, 15.

Quackenbush, L. Howard. "Samuel Eichelbaum." Ed. Carlos A. Solé and María Isabel Abreu. *Latin American Writers: Volume II*. New York: Charles Scribner's Sons, 1989. 797-801.

Sagaseta, Julia Elena. "Estudio preliminar." In *Un guapo del 900*. Buenos Aires: Kapelusz, 1976. 9-30.

Scarano, Laura Rosana. "Hacia una nueva ética de coraje: *Un guapo del 900* de Samuel Eichelbaum." *Revista letras* 37 (1988): 183-88.

Senkman, Leonardo. *La identidad judía en la literatura argentina*. Buenos Aires: Pardés, 1983.

Soto, Luis Emilio. "Ensayo sobre el teatro de Eichelbaum." In *Cuando tengas un hijo*. Buenos Aires: El Inca, 1931. 5-45.

Vidal, Hernán. "*Dos brasas*: trasfondo de excremento para una sátira social." *Explicación de textos literarios* 4 (1975): 3-9.

Zayas de Lima, Perla. *Diccionario de autores teatrales argentinos, 1950-1990*. Buenos Aires: Galerna, 1991. 104-6.

Maggi Salgado Gordon

ESPINOZA, ENRIQUE (Pseud. of Samuel Glusberg; Argentina; 1898-1987)

Samuel Glusberg was a distinguished twentieth-century Argentine Jewish writer and journalist. A constant through most of his adult professional life was his editorship of a literary journal entitled *Babel*, which therefore will be treated prominently in this essay, and other similar journals. Being Jewish, Glusberg was concerned about Jewish themes such as identity, immigration, anti-Semitism, and the Holocaust as reflected in his short stories and in an opinion survey published in *Babel* by him in 1945, which will be discussed to in this essay as well. In addition to Jewish concerns, Glusberg was associated with a number of major Argentine literary figures of his time, including the poet and essayist Leopoldo Lugones (1874-1938).

Born in Kishinev, Russia in 1898, Samuel Glusberg came to Buenos Aires when he was seven years old. He lived for a considerable length of time in Santiago, Chile, for health (i.e., respiratory problems), personal, and political reasons. He was described as a quiet even-tempered man—influential, simple, productive. Even a cursory overview of Argentine literature would be incomplete without him. He grew up in Buenos Aires and by the Argentine Centenary (1909-1910), he already closely identified with his new land (Díaz Arrieta 256). In 1928, he helped found the Sociedad Argentina de Escritores (S.A.D.E. [The Argentine Writer's Society]), whose first president was Leopoldo Lugones, with Glusberg as secretary (González Vera, *Algunos* 51; *Encyclopedia Judaica*, s.v. "Journalism: Espinoza, Enrique" v.10 column 310, and "Spanish and Portuguese Literature" v.15 column 255). Besides *Babel*, he published in Argentina *Las copas* (The Wineglasses; 1921) by Pedro Prado (1886-1952) and in Chile, among other works, *De un lado y otro* (From One Side and Another; 1956), *Compañeros de viaje* (Travelling Companions; 1937), *El espíritu criollo* (The Creole Spirit; 1951), *Tres clásicos ingleses de la Pampa* (Three English Classics of the Pampa; 1951), and *Conciencia histórica* (Historical Conscience; 1952). Most of his work consisted of small volumes which reflected the profundity and refinement of his culture. Glusberg was often considered to be an exemplary writer (Díaz Arrieta 256-57). His work also demonstrated a constant preoccupation with what is Argentine, but his patriotism never extended to the military and religious aspects of nationalism (González Vera, *Algunos* 51). His constants as a writer are liberty, sympathy for new forms of social understanding, the mission of the writer, the unity of the human race, ethics, and the relation of the individual with society. While such values were not new in themselves, they helped sustain Glusberg during times of military dictatorships, fascism, and persecution that had taken control in other countries (González Vera, *Algunos* 55-56). Notwithstanding some criticism by and lack of support from Jewish newspapers regarding Glusberg's short-lived *Cuadernos de oriente y occidente* (Notebooks from the East and West), this title together with *Babel* and *La vida literaria* (Literary Life) ranged in content from news about Jewish concerns to the most exquisite criticisms of literature and art, reflecting the editorial skills of Glusberg (Pujol 48). Glusberg was a great admirer of Domingo Faustino Sarmiento (1811-88), Martín Fierro (the Argentine literary folk hero created by writer José Hernández [1834-86] in the epic poem *El gaucho Martín Fierro* [1872]), Horacio Quiroga (1878-1937), Guillermo Enrique (William Henry) Hudson (1841-1922), and, especially, Leopoldo Lugones for whom he had a special admiration and whose secretary he was. Glusberg, through his literary and publishing endeavors, also collaborated with and/or was influenced by Ezequiel Martínez Estrada (1895-1964), Arturo

Cancela (1892-1957) and many others, including intellectuals outside of Argentina like North American writer and social critic Waldo Frank (1889-1967) and Peruvian Marxist thinker José Carlos Mariátegui (1894-1930) (González Vera *Algunos*, 35-58 passim.; Liebermann, 126-27).

Babel was originally founded by Samuel Glusberg in Buenos Aires in April 1921, ceasing publication in early 1929. This magazine of art and criticism brought together with absolute eclecticism, but without a polemical and confrontational spirit, the contributions of new and established intellectuals such as Roberto Gache (1891-1966), Horacio Quiroga, Leopoldo Lugones, Pedro Henríquez Ureña (1884-1946), Ezequiel Martínez Estrada, Arturo Cancela, Alfonsina Storni (1892-1938), Enrique Banchs (1888-1968), Hernán Díaz Arrieta (1891-?), Alberto Gerchunoff (1884-1950), Arturo Marasso (1890-1970), Benito Lynch (1880-1951), Luis Franco (1898-?), Mario Bravo (1882-?), and José Ingenieros (1877-1925). In addition, several special issues were devoted to Lugones, Quiroga, and Lynch. Following the demise of *Babel* in 1929, Glusberg then published *La vida literaria* (1928-31) and its successor, *Trapalanda* (1931-33), both of which were widely read and esteemed. Glusberg later moved to Chile in 1935 where *Babel* was reestablished in a second series, beginning with issue number 1 for May 1939, achieving well-deserved continental recognition (Lafleur, et al. 143-44). Critical acclaim was soon forthcoming with the reappearance of *Babel* when a review by the prestigious Chilean newspaper *El Mercurio* (Mercury) was reprinted on the back cover of this first issue. *El Mercurio* reported that Enrique Espinosa was well known among all learned Chileans. He was responsible for a number of publications in Buenos Aires, reflective of an international culture. For example, he published works of the best Latin American writers; was responsible for the best and most exquisite editions of works by Lugones and Quiroga; edited the best Argentine poets and created an unforgettable magazine distinguished by its spirit of selection, *Trapalanda*. *El Mercurio* then likened him to Joaquín García Monge (1881-1958) from Costa Rica as one of the benefactors of American letters. *Babel* retained the warmth and elevating spirit of *Trapalanda*. *El Mercurio* closed with the observation that Samuel Glusberg was certainly capable of achieving what he promised ("Babel." *El Mercurio* [May 11, 1939], 3; "Un juicio de *El Mercurio*," back cover).

In 1941 *Babel* suspended publication but returned as a bi-monthly in 1944, experiencing a period of great success. Glusberg, in addition to being editor, also supervised its printing and mailing and even manufactured paper in order to avoid inflated costs of production. *Babel* catered to a select unorthodox audience, rather than to the general public, due in large part to its price and nature. Indeed, high prices caused its demise in 1951. As a disinterested critic,

Glusberg was unique among his contemporaries. He devoted most of his life to magazines and even sacrificed his future as a writer for them.

Special mention should be made of a unique survey of Latin American intellectual opinion on Jews that appeared in an issue of *Babel* (26.6 [1945]), which was dedicated to the so-called "Jewish question." It opened with a quotation from Friedrich Nietzsche: "The thinker concerned with the future of Europe should, in all his speculations on this future, take into account the Jews and the Russians as the most certain and probable factors in the give and take of [political] forces." An excerpt from a book entitled *The Jew in Our Day* (1944) by the North American Jewish writer Waldo Frank preceded the symposium on the Jewish question, consisting of three questions which Glusberg had sent out to several intellectuals from various Latin American countries and a presentation of the responses received.

Essentially a self-made man, Glusberg was conscious of his modest social origins and was not comfortable in the aristocratic milieu of much of Argentine cultural life, a fact which may, at least in part, explain his increasing alienation from that scene and eventual move to Chile in 1935. He was mildly nationalistic and critical of those who looked to Europe for inspiration. He did not advocate radical social change but rather was idealistically committed to union and harmony within the hemisphere, which should be achieved via spiritual means and not political struggle. In short, he sought a Pan-American, continental perspective (King, 42). This concern is reflected by Glusberg's inclusion in the *Babel* issue on the Jewish theme of North American writer Waldo Frank, who shared Glusberg's vision. Glusberg's fictional work also emphasized Jewish and immigrant life, a theme shared by other Argentine Jewish writers such as Alberto Gerchunoff, César Tiempo (1906-80), Carlos Grünberg (1903-68), and José Rabinovich (1903-79). Thus, Glusberg retained his ethnic concerns while also emphasizing his new Argentine roots (Weisbrot 109). For example, his best-known work, *La levita gris* (The Grey Frockcoat; 1924) is a collection of tales about immigrant Jews coping with life in Buenos Aires. He also wrote a second collection of short stories entitled *Ruth y Noemí* (Ruth and Naomi; 1934). Robert Goodman observes, regarding the contents of Glusberg's stories (and those of other Argentine Jewish writers like Lázaro Liacho [1906-69]), that approximately half deal with philosophical, political, social, or Jewish themes while the other half contain no special message. "They are intended solely as literature—with no effort to convey a message or present a picture of Jewish life" (202).

Glusberg has been described as the "quintessence of the cosmopolitan thinker who still affirms his Judaic heritage" (Weisbrot 186). As symbolized by his pen name of Enrique Espinoza, Glusberg admired Baruch Spinoza (1632-77) and Heinrich Heine (1797-1856), which demonstrated his desire to draw upon both Jewish and non-Jewish traditions. Waldo Frank, whom Glusberg greatly admired, best sums up the man who was Samuel Glusberg. Frank describes him as "the dynamic immigrant Jew with a Prophet's America in his heart. . ." (Frank, *Memoirs* 171).

Glusberg's most important contribution is his literary journal *Babel*. His survey offered a unique insight into a cross section of Latin American intellectual opinion, and therefore the Latin American mentality, regarding matters of Jewish concern at a critical point in world history, made possible by the concerns, talents, and influence of Samuel Glusberg.

PRIMARY BIBLIOGRAPHY
Creative Writing

Gajes del oficio. Santiago de Chile: Ediciones Extremo Sur, 1968. Also, Buenos Aires: Ediciones del Regreso, 1976.

La levita gris: cuentos judíos de ambiente porteño. Buenos Aires: Babel, 1924.

La noria: cien sonetos sumamente prosaicos. Buenos Aires: Losada, 1962.

Quince sonetos conmemorativos. Santiago de Chile: Editorial Universitaria, 1960.

Ruth y Noemí. Buenos Aires: Babel, 1934.

Tres epístolas: a Pablo Neruda, González Vera y Manuel Rojas. Santiago de Chile: Babel, 1969.

Nonfiction

El angel y el león. Santiago de Chile: Babel, [1950-59?].

El castellano y Babel: réplica a Babel y el castellano de Arturo Capdevila. Buenos Aires: Ediciones del Regreso, 1974.

Chicos de España (1935). Buenos Aires: Ediciones Perseo, 1935.

Compañeros de viaje. Santiago: Nascimento, 1937.

Conciencia histórica. Santiago de Chile: Babel, 1952.

El espíritu criollo: Sarmiento, Hernández, Lugones. Santiago de Chile: Babel, 1951.

Heine, el ángel y el león. Buenos Aires: Babel, 1953.

Imágenes de Lugones. Buenos Aires: Babel, 1984.

José Santos González Vera: clásico del humor. Santiago: Andrés Bello, 1982.

Manuel Rojas, narrador, 1895 [i.e. 1896]-1973. Buenos Aires: Babel, 1976.

Spinoza, águila y paloma. Buenos Aires: Babel, 1978.

"Symposium, la cuestión judía." *Babel* 6.26 (March-April 1945): 55-64.

Trayectoria de Horacio Quiroga. Buenos Aires: Babel, 1980.

Trinchera. Buenos Aires: Biblioteca Argentina de Buenas Ediciones Literarias, 1932. Reissued as *De un lado y otro.* Santiago de Chile: Babel, 1956.

Editions

Díaz Arrieta, Hernán. *Leer y escribir.* Santiago de Chile: Zig-Zag, 1962.

Martínez Estrada, Ezequiel. *En torno a Kafka, y otros ensayos.* Barcelona: Seix Barral, 1967.

—. *Para una revisión de las letras argentinas; prolegómenos.* Buenos Aires: Losada, 1967.

Prado, Pedro. *Las copas.* Buenos Aires: S. Glusberg, 1921.

Sarmiento, Domingo Faustino. *Vida de San Martín.* Buenos Aires: Claridad, 1939.

SECONDARY BIBLIOGRAPHY

Babel. (March-April 1945): inside front cover.

"Babel." (Editorial). *El Mercurio* (11 May, 1939): 3.

Díaz Arrieta, Hernán (Alone, pseud.). *Historia personal de la literatura chilena: desde don Alonso de Ercilla hasta Pablo Neruda.* 2nd ed. Santiago de Chile: Nascimiento, 1959.

Encyclopedia Judaica. 1972. S.v. "Journalism: Espinoza, Enrique"; "Spanish and Portuguese Literature."

Frank, Waldo. *The Jew in Our Time.* New York: Duell, Sloan and Pearce, 1944.

—. *Memoirs of Waldo Frank.* Ed. by Alan Trachtenberg. Amherst: University of Massachusetts Press, 1973.

Gardiol, Rita M. *Argentina's Jewish Short Story Writers.* Muncie, IN: Ball State University, 1986. 16-18.

González Vera, José Santos. *Algunos.* Santiago de Chile: Nascimiento, 1959.

—. *Vidas mínimas.* 6th ed. Santiago: Nascimiento, 1962.

Goodman, Robert. "The Image of the Jew in Argentine Literature as Seen by Argentine Jewish Writers." Ph.D. diss., New York University, 1972.

"Un juicio de *El Mercurio.*" *Babel* (May 11, 1939): Back cover.

King, John. *Sur: A Study of the Argentine Literary Journal and Its Role in the Development of a Culture, 1931-1970.* Cambridge: Cambridge University Press, 1986.

Lafleur, Rene, Sergio D. Provenzano, and Fernando P. Alonso. *Las revistas literarias argentinas, 1893-1967.* Buenos Aires: Centro Editor de América Latina, 1968.

Liebermann, José. *Los judíos en la Argentina.* Buenos Aires: Libra, 1966.

Lindstrom, Naomi. *Jewish Issues in Argentine Literature: From Gerchunoff to Szichman.* Columbia: University of Missouri Press, 1989. 18-19.

Méndez, Jesús. "Argentine Intellectuals in the Twentieth Century, 1900-1943." Ph.D. diss., University of Texas, 1980.

Metz, Allan. *Leopoldo Lugones y los judíos: las contradicciones del nacionalismo argentino.* Buenos Aires: Milá, 1992.

Pujol, Sergio Alejandro. "Las revistas culturales de los inmigrantes en Buenos Aires, 1914-1930." *Todo es historia* 17.212 (1984): 46-55.

Weisbrot, Robert. *The Jews of Argentina from the Inquisition to Perón.* Philadelphia: The Jewish Publication Society of America, 1979.

Allan Metz

FEIERSTEIN, RICARDO (Argentina; 1942)

Ricardo Feierstein—Argentine-Jewish architect, journalist, critic, short story writer, novelist, and poet—has taken on the momentous responsibility of speaking for his generation. His credentials: he was born in Buenos Aires in 1942; he was educated there, and along the way became very active in socialist and Zionist movements. He took his family to live on a kibbutz in Israel just before the Yom Kippur war. Later, they returned to live in Buenos Aires. As cultural director for the AMIA (Jewish Mutual Association of Buenos Aires), he directs the Editorial Milá publishing house and *Raíces: Judaísmo contemporáneo* (Roots: Contemporary Judaism), a cultural review.

Since childhood, Feierstein has been very active and highly visible in Jewish cultural affairs. He has written for and edited numerous Jewish-sponsored periodicals, in particular *Nueva presencia* (New Presence) which focuses on human rights issues. His essays on Jewish themes were collected in *Judaísmo 2000* (Judaism 2000; 1988). Feierstein has written in many genres: poetry, short story, novel, journalism, ethnography, and history. His poetry is highly personal. *La balada del sol* (The Song of the Sun; 1969) is a farewell to childhood. *Inventadiario* (Inventadiary; 1972) deals with the poet's sense of self, his home, his family, and his Jewish-Argentine identity. *Letras en equilibrio* (Letters in Balance; 1975) was written after the Yom Kippur War. His poetry is complex yet simple, caustic yet forgiving. Important poems include "Las buenas razones" (Good Reasons), an affectionate love poem dedicated to his wife and "Argentina

1983" which characterizes the hope felt at the time of Argentina's return to democracy.

Feierstein grew up reading works of the two competing, though intertwined groups that dominated the Argentine literary scene in the first half of the twentieth century: the social realist and testimonial literature, "la experiencia vivida," (lived experience) of the Boedo movement (Roberto Arlt [1900-42], Juan Gelman [1930]) and the exaggerated estheticism of the Florida group, (Jorge Luis Borges ([1899-1986], Manuel Mujica Láinez [1910-84]). Much of his work, prose as well as poetry, represents an attempt to synthesize these two diverging tendencies. Social commentary is expressed through explosive images. His poems are characterized by aggressive metaphors and calculated rhythms.

Composed of both realistic and wildly distorted imagery, "Viejos judíos" (Old Jews; published in *Mestizo* 19-21) is charged with emotions that evolve as the poem does. "Viejos judíos" is a harsh poem as well as a hopeful one; it is also an expression of reconciliation. It is Feierstein's most intensely Jewish poem. Buenos Aires's aging immigrant Jewish population, the group that was never able to adapt to Argentine life, is the poem's subject. These Jews yearn for the old country; they are eternally out of place in the new one and often reduced in status and wealth. Late in the poem, the narrator admits to an affection for these lost souls.

In "Nosotros, la generación del desierto" (*We, the Generation in the Wilderness*; 1984), Feierstein turns his attention to those who are about his age and have shared the experience of growing up in a world which did not need them. Self-consciously, these people, born in Argentina in the early forties, feel themselves on the outskirts of history, living in a psychic no-man's land. Great events—the Second World War, the Holocaust, the founding of the State of Israel—took place far away, and besides, they were too young to really know what was happening. They can glimpse the Promised Land, and that is all. This is a poem of alienation and reluctant acceptance. This lengthy poem is told in the first-person plural. From the first word, *Nosotros* (We), the analysis, self-criticism, memories, and hopes are communal rather than personal. The group includes Jews, but is not limited to them; age and a certain life experience are more important for membership than ethnic background. The poet has taken on the role of bard, that is, the voice of his cohort. Not quite a prophet who condemns, rather he makes public his group's shared successes (few) and failures (many). Stanzas describing important moments in the "history" of this generation are set against key moments in twentieth-century history. The focal point moves through space and time: the European ghetto, a kibbutz in the Galilee, a middle-class neighborhood in Buenos Aires are some of the scenes; childhood, young adulthood, impending middle age are the times of life recalled. "Nosotros, la generación del desierto" is about getting older without finding meaning or achieving greatness. It deals with a searching for answers in endless, futile discussion with others equally at sea. One's personal past is not useful as a source of understanding; the future is vague and treacherous with death hovering closer and closer.

After all the criticism and self-doubt, the ending of "Nosotros, la generación del desierto" is uplifting. The poet-preacher-prophet praises his generation for its heroic deeds and protests. Its members have been cleansed and purified by their joint experience, and they will serve as an example to future generations. Memories and concomitant nostalgia are often present in Feierstein's thinking and writing, but he is not bound over to the past. Taken together, the poems are insistently positive, even uplifting in their message. In "Como asesinar la indiferencia," (How to Kill Indifference, in *Letras en equilibrio* [Letters in Balance; 1975]) the reader is told that a proper way to approach one's existence is: "Una cosa tan simple: morder la vida" (Such a simple thing: bite into life). In the "Datos" (Facts) section from *Inventadiario*, a group of poems is organized like an old-fashioned Argentine identity document. They are poems of self-discovery. For example, in "Cédula de identidad Número" (Passbook Number), the poet seeks his most basic identity. In "Nombre y apellido" (Full Name), he relates, in rapid fire, the experiences which have taught him who he is. His "Domicilio" (Place of Residence) is none other than the woman he loves.

The trilogy of novels *Sinfonía inocente* (Innocent Symphony; published collectively in 1984) has a complex structure and an endlessly varied style. As the title suggests, the action is ordered as if it were a symphony in three movements; there are rising and descending sections. Point of view shifts from first to third person and even at times to first person plural. Examining a group of people, the novel has no central protagonist. El Lungo, a character loosely based on Feierstein himself, comes closest to this distinction.

Entre la izquierda y la pared (Between the Left and the Wall; 1983), the first part of the trilogy, presents the shared adolescence and young adulthood of a group of Jews in the Buenos Aires of the 1950s and 60s. Much of the novel is organized as a series of linked but not necessarily consecutive paragraphs. The style is "stream of memory" rather than "stream of consciousness." The effect is that of a snapshot album or perhaps the tapes of an oral historian. The memories recorded are in part those of reactions to events which are taking place far from Buenos Aires: Castro, Lamumba, Algeria, the Red Guards, Prague Spring. The novel's time frame shifts backwards and forwards; the perceptions of children meld with those of adults. An Israel Independence Day party, Hebrew lessons, summer trips are recalled. Slowly but surely, El Lungo and his friend El Barbas grow up.

In *El caramelo descompuesto* (The Spoiled Candy; 1979), the second part, the scene shifts to Israel. El Lungo, El Barbas, and a group of Argentinean acquaintances are newcomers on a kibbutz in the Galilee. Transliterated Hebrew words and phrases are so prevalent that it would be difficult to read the novel without knowing at least some of them. The mode of this novel is mostly talk. There are endless conversations, sometimes presented as quasi-dramatic texts. The history of the kibbutz movement, its intellectual underpinnings, its mores are discussed and rediscussed.

The newcomers and the kibbutznikim must try to live together in this isolated hamlet governed by rules far different from anything known in Argentina. El Lungo, his wife known as Ella (She), and their friends try very hard to adjust. But they find themselves humming "Buenos Aires Querido" (My Dear Buenos Aires, a sentimental tango) and feeling themselves out of place. They cannot quite figure out how things operate on the kibbutz. But far more seriously, the ideal of the kibbutz that they grew up with in their Zionist youth movements simply does not exist any longer; the outsiders could not become insiders because they were looking for an "inside" that had disappeared.

When *Escala uno en cincuenta* (One to Fifty Scale; 1984), the third part, commences, El Lungo and company have returned to Buenos Aires. This novel too is highly discursive as the characters talk rather than act. Revolution old and new is debated. Roundtables on Jewish writing are duly recorded. The experience in Israel is rehashed. Meanwhile, the Argentinean political situation deteriorates. Having been away from Argentina, the returnees feel out of touch; they find it difficult to communicate with former colleagues. Moreover, they struggle to reintegrate themselves into a Buenos Aires Jewish community they view as materialistic and self-centered. Gradually, though, old ties are re-established. Now an architect, El Lungo suffers from flashbacks to life on the kibbutz during the Yom Kippur war. He has written two novels about his generation, entitled *Entre la izquierda y la pared* and *El caramelo descompuesto*, and is working on a third one filled with memories and everyday events. The theme of "la generación del desierto" becomes a refrain. At a meeting of the Jewish establishment leaders, El Lungo decries the lack of intellectual production by his contemporaries. He calls for reform in Jewish institutions, values, and identity, nothing less. He maps a future for his transitional generation which would take it from spiritual exile and a search for a new Latin American Jewish identity. The audience attacks him. Near the trilogy's end, the focus shifts back to the innocence of childhood. El Lungo's children are talking. Games and schools are described;

stories are told. The poem "Nosotros, la generación en el desierto" serves as an epilogue.

In his next novel *Mestizo* (Mixed Blood; 1988), Feierstein explores the generational issue in another way. While the term *mestizo* normally refers to those born with both Spanish and Indigenous ancestry, this title refers to those who have two cultural heritages: Jewish and Latin American. Adapting the techniques of oral history found in *Integración y marginalidad: Historias de vidas de inmigrantes judíos a la Argentina* (Integration and Marginality: Life Stories of Jewish Immigrants to Argentina; 1985) which he co-edited, Feierstein weaves much of *Mestizo* from a series of fictionalized testimonial accounts. Jewish life in Poland and immigrant life in Argentina are recounted by elderly Jews; the immigrant voices create a composite picture of the old country. These speakers are survivors who in spite of harsh, even impossible conditions did not perish. They crossed the ocean, worked for a pittance, opened small businesses, and had large families. This time the prose is sprinkled with Yiddish phrases (here translated); Poland is a setting for a Latin American novel. Though *Mestizo* is ostensibly a murder mystery, it serves as a way to explore the origins of David Schnaiderman, the novel's sometime protagonist. Looking for roots, Schnaiderman finds them in the person of his grandfather, Moishe Búrej, a man who in Europe showed great strength and stubbornness, but who could never quite assimilate into his new country. Búrej is an emblematic figure, combining moral clarity with a resistance to change.

In 1993, Feierstein published *Historia de los judíos argentinos* (History of the Jews of Argentina), a comprehensive work in which he traces the Jewish presence in Argentina from the days of the Inquisition to the present. He tells of the farming collaboratives and the urban ghettos, the artistic triumphs and the business empires established by Argentina's Jews.

Ricardo Feierstein sees himself as a mestizo, a mixture of Jewish and Argentine culture. He perceives such a union as fortunate and productive.

PRIMARY BIBLIOGRAPHY
Creative Writing

"Amigos." In *40 Cuentos Breves Argentinos-Siglo XX*. Ed. Fernando Sorrentino. Buenos Aires: Plus Ultra, 1977, 1981. 89-93.

"Argentina 1983." Trans. by J. Kates and Stephen A. Sadow. *The Minnesota Review* 30/31 (1989): 36.

Bailáte un tango, Ricardo. Buenos Aires: Centro Editor de América Latina, 1973.

La balada del sol. Buenos Aires: Indice, 1969.

"El Camino." In *39 cuentos argentinos de vanguardia.* Ed. Carlos Mastrángelo. Buenos Aires: Plus Ultra, 1985. 172-78.

El caramelo descompuesto. Buenos Aires: Pardés, 1979.

Cuentos con rabia y oficina. Buenos Aires: Stilcograf, 1965.

Cuentos con un gris absurdo. Buenos Aires: Editores Dos, 1970.

Cuentos para hombres solos. Buenos Aires: Instituto Amigos del Libro, 1967.

Entre la izquierda y la pared. Buenos Aires: Pardés, 1983.

Escala uno en cincuenta. Buenos Aires: Pardés, 1984.

Inventadiario. Buenos Aires: Tiempo de Hoy, 1972.

Letras en equilibrio. Caracas: Ediciones Arbol de Fuego, 1975.

Lucy en el cielo con diamantes. Buenos Aires: Ediciones Papiro, 1972.

Mestizo. Buenos Aires: Milá, 1988. Revised and reissued edition, Buenos Aires: Planeta, 1994.

"*Mestizo* de Ricardo Feierstein (selection)." In *Anthologie de la littérature hispano-américaine du XXe siècle.* Ed. Jean Franco and Jean Lemogodeuc. Paris: Presses Universitaires de France, 1993. 371-73.

"Nostalgia." Trans. by J. Kates and Stephen A. Sadow. *Literary Olympians II: A Crosscurrents Anthology.* San Diego: Crosscurrents, 1987. 134.

El pequeño Kleinmentch ilustrado. Buenos Aires: Pardés, 1980.

Sinfonía Inocente. (Re-edition in one volume of the trilogy made up of *El caramelo descompuesto, Entre la izquierda y la pared,* and *Escala uno en cincuenta*). Introductory study by Andrés Avellaneda. Buenos Aires: Pardés, 1984.

La vida no es sueño. Buenos Aires: Ediciones de la Flor, 1987.

"Vital Statistics (selections)." Trans. by J. Kates and Stephen A. Sadow. *International Poetry Review* 17 (1991): 58-69.

We, the Generation of the Wilderness. (A bilingual edition in Spanish and English). Translation and introduction by J. Kates and Stephen A. Sadow. Boston: Ford-Brown, 1989.

"We, the Generation in the Wilderness (selections)." Trans. by J. Kates and Stephen A. Sadow. *Pig Iron Review Anthology of Third World Literature.* Youngstown, Ohio: Pig Iron Press, 1988. 96.

Nonfiction

Historia de los judíos argentinos. Buenos Aires: Planeta, 1993.

Integración y marginalidad: historias de vidas de inmigrantes judíos en Argentina. Edited by Ricardo Feierstein, Sara Itzigshon, Leonardo Senkman, and Isidro Nicorski. Buenos Aires: Editorial Pardés and the American Jewish Committee, 1985.

Judaísmo 2000. Buenos Aires: Lugar Editorial, 1988.

Editions

Cuentos judíos latinoamericanos. Selección y prólogo de Ricardo Feierstein. Buenos Aires: Milá, 1989.

SECONDARY BIBLIOGRAPHY

Aizenberg, Edna. "Identidad judía, pluralidad y sobrevivencia: *Mestizo* de Ricardo Feierstein." *Noaj* 4.5 (1990): 60-63.

—. "Jewish Identity, Pluralism, and Survival: Feierstein's *Mestizo* as Minority Discourse." In *Tradition and Innovation: Reflections on Latin American Jewish Writing.* Ed. Robert DiAntonio and Nora Glickman. Albany, NY: State University of New York Press, 1993. 107-15.

Avellaneda, Andrés. "*Mestizo* de Ricardo Feierstein: la confusa marca en el umbral." Epilogue to *Mestizo.* Buenos Aires: Milá, 1988. 323-31.

—. "Para leer una trilogía." Prologue to *Sinfonía Inocente.* Buenos Aires: Pardés, 1984. i-xvi.

—. Rev. of *Entre la izquierda y la pared. Hispamérica* 14.40 (1985): 123-24.

—. Rev. of *Escala uno en cincuenta. Hispania* 68.4 (1985): 787-88.

Foster, David William. Rev. of *Escala uno en cincuenta. World Literature Today* 58 (1984): 572.

Glickman, Nora. "Introduction II." In *Tradition and Innovation: Reflections on Latin American Jewish Writing.* Ed. Robert DiAntonio and Nora Glickman. Albany: State University of New York Press, 1993. 15-16.

Goldberg, Florinda. "The Complex Roses of Jerusalem: The Theme of Israel in Argentinean Jewish Poetry." In *Tradition and Innovation: Reflections on Latin American Jewish Writing.* Ed. Robert DiAntonio and Nora Glickman. Albany, NY: State University of New York Press, 1993. 82-83.

Lindstrom, Naomi. *Jewish Issues in Argentine Literature.* Columbia: University of Missouri Press, 1989. 165, 167-68.

—Rev. of *Cuentos judíos latinoamericanos. Hispania* 73.4 (1990): 997-98.

—. Rev. of *Mestizo. Hispania* 74.3 (1991): 689-90.

Refour, Cristel. *Una identidad judeoargentina: la narrativa de Ricardo Feierstein.* Buenos Aires: Milá, 1992.

Sadow, Stephen A. "La traducción como puente cultural." *Raíces* 2 (1992): 71-3.

Sadow, Stephen, and J. Kates. Introduction to *We, the Generation in the Wilderness.* Boston: Ford-Brown, 1989. 7-10.

Senkman, Leonardo. *La identidad judía en la literatura argentina*. Buenos Aires: Editorial Pardés, 1983. 408-11.

—. "Jewish Latin American Writers and Collective Memory." In *Tradition and Innovation: Reflections on Latin American Jewish Writing*. Ed. Robert DiAntonio and Nora Glickman. Albany: State University of New York Press, 1993. 35, 38.

Verdevoye, Paul. "Le métissage judéo-argentin dans la trilogie *Sinfonía inocente* de Ricardo Feierstein." Rouen, France: Publications de la Université de Rouen, *C.R.I.A.R.* No. 166 (1990): n.p.

Stephen A. Sadow

FIJMAN, JACOBO (Argentina; 1898-1970)

Jacobo Fijman was born in Bessarabia in 1898, emigrated to Argentina in 1902, and died in 1970. During the 1920s he was associated with the avant-garde *martínfierrista* group of poets. His collection from that period, the 1926 *Molino rojo* (Red Mill), is, of his three books of poetry, the one most clearly in the avant-garde mode. It places striking poetic analogies and symbols at the center of attention, and the obscurity of the referents creates considerable latitude for interpretation. Though the 1926 volume represents Fijman's furthest venture into this particular experimental terrain, all his poetry can be viewed as to some degree avant-garde.

Fijman's characteristic selection of symbolic and metaphorical allusions follows, for the most part, classical and biblical convention. He often makes allegorical reference to stars, doves, deserts, roads, dreams, silence, night, dawn, and the sea. Yet his use of this standard repertory creates an effect of strangeness. For example, he at times refers to *soles* (suns) in the plural, and the sun may appear as a dead, cold mass.

Fijman is known as well for the exceptional path his life took. Though from a Jewish family, he was drawn to the passionately mystical side of Catholicism. He was extremely absorbed in his inner states and sought to express them in art: he was a graphic artist and violinist as well as a poet. Fijman's preoccupation with otherworldly and esthetic concerns at the expense of practicalities, along with his poverty, would make it a continual struggle for him to care for himself. In 1921 he spent six months in a psychiatric asylum after falling into the hands of the police. Fijman was trained as a secondary-level French teacher and held a teaching position for a time, but he often changed employment. Not all of his jobs required an education; over the years, he was increasingly employed well below his capacities.

Despite his occasional difficulty in looking after himself, Fijman became an active participant in the Buenos Aires avant-garde from 1923 on. The poet Leopoldo Marechal (1900-79), who was especially responsible for discovering him and involving him in the avant-garde, used him as the model for a character in a novel. Samuel Tessler appears in Marechal's famous *Adán Buenosayres*, a lengthy allegorical novel that was finally published in 1948. Fijman's fictional transform has a caustic tongue, which he deploys chiefly against the telluric cultural nationalism that characterized one sector of the *martínfierrista* avant-garde.

During his *martínfierrista* period, Fijman composed the poems that in 1926 were collected as *Molino rojo*, which would always be his most important book. This collection includes "Canto del cisne" (Swan Song), the author's most famous individual poem. The poem's frequent citation may owe much to its autobiographical references to Fijman's experiences as a psychiatric patient and as a Jewish practitioner of Christian rituals. Its opening line is the isolated word "Demencia," which appears to have the status of an assertion. In the second line, *dementia* is metaphorically characterized as "el camino más alto y más desierto" (the highest and most deserted road).

Fijman's poetry exhibited a typically twentieth-century trend of poetic innovation but also gave evidence of his fund of knowledge, an unusually historical and classical one. Though he was an avant-gardist as a poet, in his reading he pursued a great-books program. He read Aristotle, scholastic philosophy, patristic writings, and mathematics, and studied Latin and Greek. Fijman took an informed interest in the occult sciences and read astrology and such classics of divination as Nostradamus. His poetry also reveals his reliance on biblical sources. Fijman favored biblical texts composed in an emotionally charged language, often relying on hermetic symbols and metaphors. He drew particularly on Jewish prophetic literature and the Apocalypse. *Molino rojo* follows many stylistic conventions of the books of the prophets, above all in the poetic speaker's outraged condemnation of the corruption, hypocrisy, and mindless revelry he sees around him.

In 1929, seized with religious excitement, Fijman had himself baptized, though his faith was always of an idiosyncratic nature, little resembling doctrinal Catholicism. Fijman's poetry, as well, embodies a variant strain of Christianity. Its deviance is evident in such features as the poetic speaker's tendency to identify himself as a Christ and the allusions to occult arts. The year after his conversion, he published the poetry collection *Hecho de estampas* (Made of Images), the only one of his books to be reissued in its entirety (1981). Though some of its poems express a continuing distrust of and dissatisfaction with the world made by human beings, others are in a jubilant mode. "Poema VII" is representative of Fijman's poems that follow a trajectory typical of the self-accounts of mystics. It employs the symbolic imagery of darkness and light often found in mystical discourse. In the beginning stanza, the poetic *I* is gnawed at by "el lobo de la media noche" (the midnight wolf), but a star comes to offer him comfort and guidance and in the closing stanza he enjoys "todos los soles" (all the suns) and "la luz entera de la mañana" (the complete morning light).

In 1931 Fijman published *Estrella de la mañana* (Morning Star). Of his three collections, this last one contains the greatest proportion of signs of redemption and celebration, such as doves, angels, stars, and light. The lyrical *I* frequently speaks of having glimpsed a plenitude of perfection. While the preponderant allusive debt is to Christian cultural tradition, *Estrella de la mañana* continues to utilize Jewish references and those drawn from magic and the occult arts.

Subsequently, Fijman wrote less but continued to be a great reader. He had been based in Buenos Aires but now moved around the interior of the country, with stays also in Paraguay and Brazil. He lived for a time as a street musician, playing the violin, and took various laborer jobs. During this period he grew increasingly impoverished.

In 1942, the indigent and virtually homeless Fijman was again hospitalized and eventually became a permanent resident of the Hospicio Neuropsiquiátrico Dr. Borda, a large psychiatric facility in Buenos Aires. Fijman remained institutionalized not only for his eccentric behavior but for his inability to provide for himself. During this latter part of his life he published no new collections of poetry, though he did write from time to time and continued to develop his ideas about poetics, religion, and philosophy. The poet and editor Vicente Zito Lema (1939), who was interested in the relation between artistic originality and mental disorders, held lengthy conversations with Fijman in the Borda Asylum in the late 1960s. With collaborators, Zito Lema sparked a revival of interest in Fijman with the May 1969 inaugural issue of the magazine *Talismán*, entitled *Jacobo Fijman, poeta en hospicio* (Jacobo Fijman, Poet in an Asylum). Zito Lema sought to correct the perception that Fijman was an inactive remainder from a bygone era and to show his continuing creativity. *Talismán* published some of the author's more recent poems. The special issue includes reproductions of Fijman's visual work, executed in an understated, personal variant of the surrealist manner. An interview with Zito Lema, appearing in the same issue, revealed Fijman to be an informative and coherent interlocutor. His eccentricity was manifested chiefly in the exceptionally lyrical and abstract mode in which he responded to questions. Among other points touched on, he clarified that his baptism had not replaced or diminished his Jewish identity and he acknowledged his continuing debt to Jewish thought.

Fijman and Zito Lema produced a book based on their sessions, *El pensamiento de Jacobo Fijman; o, el viaje hacia la otra realidad* (The Thought of Jacobo Fijman or the Journey to the Other Reality), published in 1970, the year of Fijman's death. Zito Lema edited Fijman's tape-recorded reflections into a text called "Los fuegos mentales" (Mental Fires). Here Fijman employs an elliptical, aphoristic discourse to give an account of his life, his work, his readings, and his belief system. The volume also includes a lengthy interview, with both parties speaking in the poetic, elevated register that Fijman seems to have found natural.

Interest in Fijman continued to rise during the 1980s. In 1981, Ediciones Mano de Obra of Buenos Aires reissued *Hecho de estampas*. In 1983, La Torre Abolida, a Buenos Aires concern, published Fijman's *Obra poética* (Poetic Work), a selection by E. Vásquez. In 1985, Carlos Vitale's selection of Fijman's *Poemas* appeared in Zaragoza, published by Olifant. These new editions were important in restoring the availability of Fijman's texts, whose small print runs and unsystematic distribution had made them difficult to obtain.

Fijman continues to be rediscovered for various reasons. His anomalous conversion and the heterodoxy of his poetry offer a puzzle in cultural identity, while he is also a fascinating case for those interested in the link between creativity and psychiatric disorders. However, the fundamental appeal of his poetry is in its powerfully innovative character. Perhaps the most distinctively novel factor in his poetic project is his avant-garde treatment of references drawn in great part from the repertory established by literary and biblical tradition.

PRIMARY BIBLIOGRAPHY

Estrella de la mañana. Buenos Aires: Número, 1931.

Hecho de estampas. Buenos Aires: Manuel Gleizer, 1930. Reissued Buenos Aires: Ediciones Mano de Obra, 1981.

Molino rojo. Buenos Aires: El Inca, 1926.

Obra poética. Ed. E. Vásquez. Buenos Aires: La Torre Abolida, 1983.

El pensamiento de Jacobo Fijman; o, el viaje hacia la otra realidad. With Vicente Zito Lema. Buenos Aires: Rodolfo Alonso, 1970.

Poemas. Ed. Carlos Vitale. Zaragoza: Olifant, 1985.

SECONDARY BIBLIOGRAPHY

Bajarlía, Juan Jacobo. *Fijman: poeta entre dos vidas.* Buenos Aires: Ediciones de la Flor, 1992.

Calmels, Daniel. *El Cristo rojo: cuerpo y escritura en la obra de Jacobo Fijman. Apuntes para una biografía.* Buenos Aires: Topía, 1996.

Fernández, Ruth. *Fijman, el poeta celestial y su obra.* Buenos Aires: Tekne, 1985.

Herrera, Francisco. "Jacobo Fijman." *Enciclopedia de la literatura argentina.* Ed. Pedro Orgambide and Roberto Yahni. Buenos Aires: Sudamericana, 1970. 244.

Lindstrom, Naomi. "Jacobo Fijman: Jewish Poet?" In *Tradition and Innovation: Reflections on Latin American Jewish Writing.* Ed. Robert DiAntonio and Nora Glickman. Albany: SUNY Press, 1993. 89-98.

—. *Jewish Issues in Argentine Literature: From Gerchunoff to Szichman.* Columbia: University of Missouri Press, 1989. 19-20.

Masiello, Francine. "Ex-Centric Odyssey: The Poetry of Jacobo Fijman." *Hispanic Review* 6.2 (Spring 1985): 33-44.

Senkman, Leonardo. "Bautismo y locura." In his *La identidad judía en la literatura argentina.* Buenos Aires: Pardés, 1983. 295.

—. "Etnicidad y literatura en los años 20: Jacobo Fijman en las letras argentinas." *Río de la Plata* [Paris] 4-6 (1987): 163-75.

Talismán [Buenos Aires: Ediciones Cero] 1 (May 1969). Special issue *Jacobo Fijman, poeta en hospicio.*

Naomi Lindstrom

FINGUERET, MANUELA (Argentina; 1945)

Manuela Fingueret was born on August 9, 1945. She grew up in the Buenos Aires *barrio* (neighborhood) of La Chacarita, an area of the city that was then heavily populated by immigrants. She was trained as a teacher and journalist and has worked at both; she also is an active member of the Buenos Aires cultural and artistic community. Fingueret has been instrumental in promoting Jewish cultural activity in Buenos Aires through her myriad professional activities. She co-directed the Area de Cultura Judía del Centro Cultural General San Martín (Jewish Culture Division of the General San Martín Cultural Center), the leading cultural and artistic center of Buenos Aires, from 1983 to 1986, and from 1987 to 1989 she was the director. In 1993 she served as the programming and artistic director of FM Jai, a Jewish radio station in Buenos Aires. She has worked for numerous Jewish publications, including *Nueva Sión* [New Zion], and she is currently the editor of *Arca del Sur* (Southern Ark). As a writer, Fingueret has gained a considerable reputation as a poet, having published six collections of poetry to date. Nevertheless, her most recent work is a novel with which she has demonstrated that her talent as a writer crosses the boundaries of literary genres. Fingueret's literature springs from the depths of her identity as a Jewish-Argentine/Argentine-Jew. It is an identity that she embraces and defines as being culturally complex and dually enriching. She views her writing and her Jewishness as an act of resistance against the authoritarianism and antipluralistic ideology that informs much of the sociopolitical history of Argentina (see her essays "¿Ser o no ser?" [To Be or Not to Be] and "Ser judía en mi país" [To Be Jewish in My Country]).

Fingueret's first poetry collection, *Tumultos contenidos* (Contained Tumult) appeared in 1975. The poems seek to examine the inner turmoil of the individual, to exorcise the mystery of death, and to find pleasure in the forbidden, dark corners of the soul. Emotion and physical sensation fill the body in a tumultuous combination of joy, pain, desire, love, fear, and courage in a celebration of life.

In *Heredarás Babel* (You Will Inherit Babel; 1977), the poet focuses intently on language and the creation of a scriptural text. Each poem in the volume is preceded by a scripture taken from the Old Testament. The poems themselves consist of a kind of poetic midrashic exegesis of the scripture that inspired it. Fingueret retells Jewish history and tradition through poems that evoke the flood, the tower of Babel, the covenant of circumcision, the transformation of Lot's wife into a pillar of salt, the delivery of the ten commandments, Job's long-suffering, the prophecies of Isaiah and Ezequiel, the wisdom of Proverbs, and the poetry of Psalms and the Song of Songs. *Heredarás Babel* is significant to Latin American Jewish literature because it is one of a handful of texts in which an author moves away from a superficial thematic approach to a more aesthetically Jewish approach. Put differently, *Heredarás Babel* is a text that interprets Jewishness as essence, as opposed to Jewishness as experience.

La piedra es una llaga en el tiempo (The Stone Is a Sore in Time; 1980) constitutes an elegiac interpretation of Latin American identity. Much like the Biblical passages found in *Heredarás Babel*, the poet incorporates indigenous texts between her own verses to draw upon the ancient past of the South American continent. In many ways the volume elicits a comparison to *Canto general*

(*General Song*; 1950) by Pablo Neruda (1904-73). The past is the foundation for the identity of modern Latin America, and by summoning the grandeur of centuries past one sees a reflection of the present.

The years of violent military repression (1976-83) in Argentina are the subject of Fingueret's next volume of poetry, *Ciudad en fuga y otros infiernos (1976-1983)* (City in Flight and Other Hells; 1984). The city, of course, is Buenos Aires during the most virulent moments of the dictatorship in which the presence of fear and death permeated the streets. The series of what the poet calls open letters to a city in flight are particularly telling testimonies of the paralysis that gripped Argentine society. The poems speak both to and of the thousands of disappeared, the tortured, and the exiled inhabitants of a once vibrant city. In the second half of the volume "Otros infiernos" (Other Hells) the poet returns in part to more specifically Jewish themes. The two poems "Jerusalem" and "Jerusalem dorada" (Golden Jerusalem) are reverent odes to the ancient city that unites the Jewish past and present.

In *Eva y las máscaras* (Eve and the Masks; 1987) Fingueret draws on the figure of Eve for inspiration. The poems in this volume, in contrast to those of the two previous collections, are composed of brief and lexically concise verses that immediately conjure up the desired images. *Eva y las máscaras* comprises the poetic record of an on-going search for the self. It is in these poems that Fingueret achieves a complete view of her identity as an Argentine Jew. She calls on the collective Jewish memory of the past as well as the experience of the present in order to forge an identity from the two central elements of her being. The members of her Jewish family as well as other influences like Dylan Thomas (1914-53) and Julio Cortázar (1914-84) find themselves the subjects of her verses. The poem "¿Pueblo elegido?" (Chosen People?) pays homage to the continuity of Jewish identity through time, while at the same time another untitled poem speaks to the evolutionary aspect of Jewish identity within the space of Buenos Aires: "Barro la vereda una y otra vez en las tardes de verano, / descalza como las shikses del barrio. / Mi madre maldice, porque teme una / asimilación temprana" (I sweep the sidewalk time and again on summer afternoons, / barefoot like the neighborhood shiksas. / My mother curses, because she fears an / early assimilation [56]).

Fingueret's most recent collection of poems, *Los huecos de tu cuerpo* (The Hollows of Your Body; 1992), is dedicated to her deceased mother, who is the subject of the volume. The poems of *Los huecos de tu cuerpo* continues the search for identity; first to recover the identity of the immigrant mother, and then to find the identity of the self refracted in the image of the mother. Fingueret addresses her speech directly to Elohim and to her mother in a supplicatory yet increasingly forceful tone to create a powerfully moving poetic discourse.

Fingueret's latest work, the novel *Blues de la calle Leiva* (Leiva Street Blues; 1995), is a narrative of nostalgic reminiscence based on her own experience of early childhood in the Buenos Aires neighborhood of La Chacarita. As early as her first collection of poetry, Fingueret incorporated both La Chacarita and Leiva street into her work. However, the conventions of narrative allow her to elaborate on the dimensions of this space to which she habitually returns in her work. Set mostly in the 1950s, but ending in 1976, the novel is structured as a series of stories told by the young female narrator who observes with great detail the people and events of the neighborhood from the vantage point of her living room window that overlooks Leiva street. La Chacarita was at the time a neighborhood that was largely inhabited by a mixture of Jewish, Spanish, and Italian immigrants, as well as people who had come to Buenos Aires from the interior of the country. Fingueret populates her narrative with a multiplicity of entertaining characters who often find themselves in ludicrous predicaments. The novel is narrated with a great deal of humor mixed with references to popular culture and political events, especially those associated with Peronism. The end of the novel, however, narrates the "disappearance" of the neighborhood priest by the military in 1976. *Blues de la calle Leiva* is a splendidly fresh addition to the vast number of novels about the Jewish immigrant experience in Argentina. It does not gloss over the difficulty of those early years, and yet it leaves the reader with a yearning for the happier times lived by the protagonist. Nevertheless, Fingueret readily admits that the past is subject to memory as she states in the epilogue: "No siempre el pasado fue mejor. La memoria acusa o embellece" (The past was not always better. Memory accuses or embellishes [234]).

Finally, *Las picardías de Hérshele* (Hershele's Mischief; 1989) is a children's book that Fingueret wrote with friend and fellow Argentine author Eliahu Toker (1934). The two authors explain in their brief introduction to the text that the work is based on the Yiddish tales that they grew up with. The book narrates the picaresque adventures of the protagonist Hérshele Ostropolier, a poor Polish Jew. The stories revolve around Hérshele's experience with Reb Bórejl, a Hasidic teacher. The text combines humor with Jewish culture in the best of the Yiddish story-telling tradition.

PRIMARY BIBLIOGRAPHY
Creative Writing
Blues de la calle Leiva. Buenos Aires: Planeta, 1995.

Ciudad en fuga y otros infiernos, 1976-1983. Buenos Aires: Botella al Mar,
    1984.
Eva y las máscaras. Buenos Aires: Ultimo Reino, 1987.
Herederás Babel. Buenos Aires: Botella al Mar, 1977.
Los huecos de tu cuerpo. Buenos Aires: Grupo Editor Latinoamericano, 1992.
"Jerusalem," "Rug as Lyric." Trans. by Ricardo Pau-Llosa. *Beloit Poetry Journal*
    32.4 (1982): 2-3.
Las picardías de Hérshele. (With Eliahu Toker). Buenos Aires: Colihue, 1989.
La piedra es una llaga en el tiempo. Buenos Aires: Botella al Mar, 1980.
Tumultos contenidos. Buenos Aires: Galerna, 1975.

Nonfiction

"Escritores argentinos y judíos: medio siglo fructífero e indefinible." In *Judíos*
    & argentinos: judíos argentinos. Ed. Martha Wolff, Myrtha Schalom,
    and Manrique Zago. Buenos Aires: Marique Zago Ediciones, 1988. 214-
    17.
Los jóvenes en los 90: la imaginación lejos del poder. (Edited and with a pro-
    logue by Fingueret). Buenos Aires: Almagesto, 1993.
"Lo materno y lo externo." In *Pluralismo e identidad: lo judío en la literatura*
    latinoamericana. Jaime Barylko, Aída Bortnik, et al. Buenos Aires:
    Milá, 1986. 115-21.
"Ser judía en mi país: ese oscuro objeto de deseo." In *El imaginario judío en la*
    literatura de América Latina: visión y realidad. Ed. Patricia Finzi,
    Eliahu Toker and Marcos Faerman. Buenos Aires: Shalom, 1992. 116-
    17.
"¿Ser o no ser?: un conflicto vigente en relación a la cultura judeo-argentina."
    Controversia de ideas sionistas (Buenos Aires) (1989-1990): 88-89.

Darrell B. Lockhart

FREILICH SEGAL, ALICIA (Venezuela; 1939)

   Alicia Freilich Segal was born in 1939 in Caracas, Venezuela. She was
the first child of Máximo Freilich, who left Poland in 1928, and Rebeca War-
szawska for whom he returned in 1937. Her father, who died at the age of
eighty-seven, was a well-known poet, journalist, and correspondent for the New
York periodical *The Forward.* Her mother's warm hospitality made their home

the gathering place of Venezuela's Jewish intelligentsia and an important stop for all Jewish artists and political figures travelling to the country. Freilich Segal has a sister, Miriam, who is also a poet and journalist.

Freilich Segal holds a doctoral degree in Literature from the Universidad Central de Venezuela. Her dissertation, "El niño en la cuentística venezolana" (The Child in the Venezuelan Short Story) was published in 1960. She has been a teacher and professor of literature for over eighteen years.

From 1973 to 1975 she was the Executive Director for the Confederación de Asociaciones Israelitas Venezolanas (Federation of Venezuelan Israelite Associations), a prominent Jewish political organization in Venezuela. In that capacity she appeared before national and international organizations as its official spokesperson and representative on occasions such as the United Nations' resolution condemning Zionism as a form of racism.

In 1960 Freilich Segal traveled to Israel. The emotional and mental impact of the trip was profound, and can be seen in all her writings. Her absolute conviction that a Jewish state must exist as a "nucleus of the Jews, forever" (*Legítima defensa* 79) is one of the explicit and implicit constants in her writings: essay, journalistic pieces, critical notes, and two works of fiction.

In the tradition of the great Latin American thinkers, her articles in such journals as *El Nacional* (The National), *El Universal* (The Universal), and in magazines such as *Imagen* (Image), *Resumen* (Summary), and *Ultimas noticias* (Latest News), are what Alicia calls "periodismo cultural y de opinión" (editorial and cultural journalism. Her major themes are amply displayed in hundreds of intensely critical and controversial essays which are aesthetic creations in their own right, and they present a view of the world seen through the eyes of a Jewish Venezuelan woman. They have been anthologized in the volumes *Triálogo* (Trialogue; 1973), *Cuarta dimensión* (The Fourth Dimension; 1975), *Entrevistados en carne y hueso* (Flesh and Blood Interviews; 1977), *La venedemocracia* (Democracy Venezuelan Style; 1978), and *Legítima defensa* (Legitimate Defense; 1984). In 1974 she was awarded the Francisco de Miranda medal for journalistic excellence by the Venezuelan government.

With a keen journalistic eye, Freilich Segal analyzes universal themes through her very personal vision of the Jewish Venezuelan experience. *Triálogo* and *Legítima defensa* simultaneously display biting humor and poetic language. According to the author, *Triálogo* refers to the relationship among three polarities: a phenomenon, a perceptor, and the public. Both works explore this relationship through historical subjects. For instance, the Jew's history of exile and statelessness; Shylock and the horrific consequences of myth; anti-Semitism, Russian style; fascism and Zionism; the unpardonableness of all ignorance and misinformation concerning the Holocaust; and finally, Neo-nazism or the Fourth Reich. At other times her focus is more biographical. She draws parallels between the lives of writers Isaac Babel (1894-1941) and other Jewish Russians with Aleksandr Solzhenitsyn (1918) and Boris Pasternak (1890-1960); Sholem Aleichem (1859-1916) and Jewish humor; and Italian Jewish writers, specifically Natalia Ginzburg (1916) and Giorgio Bassani (1916).

In *Legítima defensa*, Freilich Segal forces readers to reevaluate their public and private conscience as she accuses all democratic societies of blind and knowing complicity in the triumph of totalitarianism in our century. The first essay, "Los recibidos" (The Welcomed Ones), is an autobiographical piece haunted by what she terms her ethical indignation upon discovering how her aunt and uncle miraculously survived Auschwitz. In an effort to define and understand their persecution and terror she outlines a definition of human suffering in the world. While Freilich Segal dedicates this book to her aunt and uncle in particular, and to the generation of Jews who found peace and freedom in hospitable places such as Venezuela, she characterizes the work as a warning to the generation of the 1960s, for whom "Auschwitz, Treblinka, and Buchenwald are remote and unbelievable legends" (69). Her plea is that in view of its consequences, Nazism must not be seen as just another historical "ism" but as an ultimate force of destruction.

Her perceptive prologue to the volume *Cinco novelas de Guillermo Meneses* (Five Novels of Guillermo Meneses; 1972), marks the beginning of her literary criticism. She is the first critic to point out that in addition to Guillermo Meneses's (1911-77) superb talent as a short story writer, for which he was already famous, he is the founder of the modern Venezuelan novel. Other writers who are subjects of her literary criticism include the Venezuelans Salvador Garmendia (1924), Laura Antillano (1950), Julio Garmendia (1898-1977), David Alizo (1941), Carlos Noguera (1943), Rómulo Gallegos (1884-1969), César Uribe (1897-1951), Miguel Otero Silva (1908), Adriano González León (1931), José Balza (1931), and Elisa Lerner (1934), the Colombian Germán Espinosa (1938), the Peruvian poet Manuel Scorza (1928-84), and the Argentinean Mario Szichman (1946). She has also written on Jean-Paul Sartre (1905-80) and Emir Rodríguez Monegal (1921-85).

Acknowledging Isaac Bashevis Singer (1904-91) and Jorge Luis Borges (1899-1986) as admired influences, Freilich Segal incorporates themes related to Jewish identity and to narrative theory in her fiction and non-fiction alike. One obsessive motive is the transfer of personal and group identities to art forms. Another one is the displacement of characters and the need for readers to engage in a synchronic reading of the text, maintaining a constantly questioning attitude in order to end with an existential narrative of their own creation. She assesses the effect of Jewish history on the quest for familial and cultural belonging.

Charting the spiritual and physical journey of the European Jews to Latin America in this century, Freilich Segal includes the sometimes troubled journey that their children must also travel in search of an identity of their own. At times she projects a cosmic vision of the so-called children of the Holocaust, nostalgically holding on to their neurotic guilt and always envisioning their destiny as lurking persecution. At the same time, she demonstrates a deep appreciation of the contributions of Judaism to world civilization, and pays homage to the Venezuelan culture which was open to her. The fight against anti-Semitism and its long-lasting impact becomes, in her work, part of a deep commitment to human rights for all.

In 1987 Alicia Freilich Segal published her first work of fiction, the beautifully evocative novel *Claper*, which immediately required a second printing. The very week of its publication, the France Presse International News Service referred to her as the third most-read author in Venezuela.

Claper, a term coined by the author and now part of the Venezuelan lexicon, refers to the man who peddles goods (clap, clap) from door to door and on credit. Although he travels on foot bearing a heavy load, he is firmly supported by an inner strength derived from the legacy of Talmudic wisdom. The claper, in turn, will hand down this wisdom as part of that never-changing internal baggage that is the Jewish culture.

The novel is a fictional account based on actual conversations held in Yiddish between one such claper, Freilich Segal's own father Max, and herself. Thanks to the generosity of the land and people who so warmly welcomed these immigrant Jews, Freilich Segal succeeded in becoming an accomplished professional woman able to move through all levels of its society.

Since it is not divided into chapters or sections, the structure of the novel might at first disorient the reader. The author explains that this form more faithfully reproduces the never-ending dialogue that goes on between parent and child, between humans and God, and within humans themselves. The book is not easily defined or categorized. It is fictionalized autobiography, history, and ultimately another moving story of displacement in the long history of the Jewish people. It is narrated by two voices chatting away in the timeless realm of the imagination. Tight, unadorned, and simple, the style ranges from the romantic lyrics of Latin boleros to centuries-tested Yiddish parables that give the work a poetic and spiritual undertow. In both narratives readers hear, taste, and smell local life. Enchanted by the aroma of humble cabbage soup and the juiciness of ripe mangoes, the reader's attention sways between the sinister and ever-present sound of Cossack boots and the hot sensuality of salsa and mambo rhythms; between the moving solemnity of a Shabbath dinner, where there is only water to share with the guest, and the unending display of luscious fruits with unpronounceable names, vegetables, and flowers with which the fertile, colorful Caribbean welcomes the immigrant in black suit and hat.

Max's narrative is steeped in sage Talmudic teachings, Yiddish bittersweet humor, and ancient superstition, full of the life-giving and life-nurturing strength that survived for centuries in the thousands of shtetls that once populated Eastern Europe. It is the idiom of people who hungered for food and desperately needed the most basic human comforts but who were never needy of spiritual connectedness, familial warmth, or faith in a God who, to paraphrase Martin Buber (1878-1965), was not to be talked about, but to be talked to and with. Max the claper always speaks to his particular god (with a g, never G). His narrative is the history of the persecution of the Jew, starting from the Middle Ages and generously sprinkled with moving and humorous tales of the Ashkenazy and Sephardic voyages, up to his arrival in America.

Alicia, this claper's Venezuelan-born, university-educated, strong and independent-minded daughter, writes in a sophisticated and literate Spanish. Her voice is cosmopolitan, elegant, and redolent of the feminist psychoanalytic, Marxist, Zionist, intellectual and political jargon of her milieu. In her narrative one sees the important changes that Jewish immigration brought about, including a new awareness of the outside world. It is a rich source of cultural and political history of Venezuela from the 1940s to the 1970s. Alicia is a woman struggling to find her place, a woman who loves and respects the traditions of her upbringing, even as she struggles to break away from them.

The theme of our immutable bonds to the past is taken up again in Freilich Segal's second work of fiction, *Colombina descubierta* (Discovered Colombine; 1991), for which she received the prestigious Fernando Jeno International Literary Prize in Mexico, selected unanimously from among texts published in Spanish, Yiddish, and Hebrew in 1990-1991. The selecting jury stated:

> [Alicia Segal] reaches the reader, his very fiber, with an innate linguistic clarity, an accurate intuition and an imaginary power capable of suggesting the most unconventional settings and situations, in which as if by magic, clues, enigmas, and mysteries are intertwined much as they were in Columbus himself. *Colombina descubierta* leaves an indelible and very unique imprint of the world of creative Jewish literature of our time. (*Nuevo Mundo Israelita*, Nov. 1992)

The author weaves a labyrinthine tale of Columbus, the expulsion of the Jews from Spain, the terror of the Inquisition, the encounter with the New World, and the complex issue of marranismo from a sensitive feminist perspective creating an enormous physical and emotional tapestry. She thus intertwines past, present, and future.

The narration takes place in both the fifteenth and twentieth century in which the reader is witness to and participant in this compelling story. Here again is Freilich Segal's theme of the search for an individual and a collective Jewish identity accompanied by the inevitable and weary search for a primary space.

In *Colombina descubierta* Freilich Segal explores this theme by means of an elaborately introspective literary process, one which digs deep into our conscious and subconscious memory, and demands a confrontation with what is found. One is forced to confront truth and conjecture, tradition and adventure, the intimate and the public. In essence, one is forced to both discover and conceal. The text is exciting and fast moving. The reader must be willing to be engaged in uncovering the most incredible of all cover-ups: whether Columbus's journeys were wanderings, adventures, or flight. This Columbus who has here been transformed into a woman.

The book is divided into four chapters, or monologues as the author calls them: 1) "En el nombre del Padre" (In the Name of the Father), 2) "Y del Hijo" (And the Son), 3) "Y del Espíritu Santo" (And the Holy Ghost), 4) "Santísima Trinidad" (The Holy Trinity), and "Amén," a prologue. It narrates two very intriguing and long journeys to the unknown; two, that perhaps, were always the same. One is that of a persecuted Jewish Columbus looking for safe lands for himself and his people; the other journey is undertaken five-hundred years later (or is it?) by Biná Colom, who like the claper's daughter, struggles to find her place in the world, and like Columbus, is the subject of many myths. In the course of these monologues Biná Colom takes upon herself many names and splits into several personalities: Cristina, Paloma/Colomba, and Colombina.

The first chapter, "En en nombre del Padre," is the story of Colombina's father who like many Marranos believed that with financial success he could become what he was not, that he could buy a new identity. It is narrated by Biná Colom, a Sephardic Jew who—as her name implies (Biná is Hebrew for discernment, understanding, knowledge)—is thinking and trying to understand her life as a woman. As the novel unfolds, Colombina is a sad old woman talking to the moon on a beach in Barcelona. The time is October 12th, 1992. It is the eve of lavish festivities celebrating the five-hundred-year anniversary of the

Encounter. The moon and the lyrical prose mesmerize the reader into forgetting that the novel was published in 1991, long before the narrated events take place.

The second chapter, "Y del Hijo," is the story of Fernando Colón, who wrote a biography of his father in which he denies Columbus's Jewishness and, therefore, protects himself from being discovered as the son of a Converso. In the novel, this man is Biná Colom's very alienated, manipulating, and dishonest son. A university professor and the only person ever to see her (Colombus's) diary. He and only he knows the truth.

"Y del Espíritu Santo," the third monologue, is narrated by Father Goriccio, Columbus's confidant. He is a model for the author, through whom she pays homage to a wise Franciscan priest, "poeta y traductor de lenguas indígenas" (fine poet and translator of indigenous languages [El Universal, Oct. 13, 1991]), Fray Cesáreo de Armelleda of Caracas. Goriccio is friend and "brother" to Colombina/Cristina, who will not allow herself to be baptized, reminding the father instead of his Jewish roots.

The fourth chapter, "Santísima Trinidad," is the story of Columbus the Converso Jew who leaves Spain, not in search of spices, gold, or souls, but in search of the land of Israel as a haven for his persecuted people. In this section the relationship between Columbus, the subject, and the Spanish Queen, his ruler, takes on a charming and ironic twist as Freilich Segal changes it into the quintessentially modern relationship of patient and therapist. Here Doctora Isabel del Castillo is an ambitious and ruthless professional, indifferent to the real needs of her patient. Colombina as Paloma peacefully accepts the many roles life has forced on her, including that of navigator. Her narrative is as simple and direct as navigational charts, or even a diary.

Colombina is the child of a divided world, the world of being and seeming to be. She is a vital Jewish character pushing to reach the limits of the impossible, and as such personifies the struggle of all who attempt to strive for a better place. She is one and many, and so epitomizes the issue of multiple identities that distinguishes Freilich Segal's work.

Freilich Segal's work deals with the complex issue of historical origin. Her themes are the conflict between old roots, and the culture one belongs to by birth, language, and choice. Her view of the world is one of community, a diverse community where Jews must act accordingly. Essentially, her work is about what it means, and has always meant, to be the exile, the uprooted, the one struggling to come to terms with an identity that is multicultural as well as fully assimilated into the dominant culture. Freilich Segal is currently (1995) working on a third novel.

PRIMARY BIBLIOGRAPHY
Creative Writing
Claper. Caracas: Planeta, 1987.
Colombina descubierta. Caracas: Planeta, 1991.
Nonfiction
Cuarta dimensión. Caracas: Biblioteca Nacional, Síntesis Dosmil, 1975.
Entrevistados en carne y hueso. Caracas: Librería Suma, 1977.
Legítima defensa. Caracas: Seleven, 1984.
"El misiú: Interview with Máximo Freilich, Her Father." In *Echad: an Anthology of Latin American Jewish Writings.* Ed. Robert and Roberta Kalechofsky. Marblehead, MA: Micah Publications, 1980. 274-79.
"Prólogo." *Cinco novelas de Guillermo Meneses.* Caracas: Monte Avila, 1972. 1-9.
Triálogo. Caracas: Tiempo Nuevo, 1973.
La venedemocracia. Caracas: Monte Avila, 1978.

SECONDARY BIBLIOGRAPHY
Aizenberg, Edna. Rev. of *Colombina descubierta. Hispamérica* 22.66 (1993): 120-22.
Cunha-Giabbai, Gloria de. "Literatura e historia en *Colombina descubierta* de Alicia Freilich." *Monographic Review/Revista monográfica* 8 (1992): 273-79.
Goldberg, Florinda F. Rev. of *Colombina descubierta. Noaj* 6.7-8 (1992): 156-58.
Kliksberg, Bernardo. Rev. of *Cláper. Noaj* 2.2 (1988): 118-20.

Joan Friedman

FUTORANSKY, LUISA (Argentina; 1939)

From her first books of poetry, which she published in her early twenties, Luisa Futoransky has remained consistent in her central themes: the voyage, exile, love. These are constellated by the many points on her personal map, and with equal fluency she draws on Jewish tradition—the Bible, tales of the Hasidim (the Baal Shem Tov, Rabbi Nahman of Bratslav), the land of Israel past and present—as well as the cultures where she has lived. However, being Jewish is rarely her subject. Rather it grants a certain historical contact to her experience, helping to illuminate and above all question the world around her.

Born and raised in Buenos Aries, she studied music and literature, and received her law degree from the university there. During the 1960s she travelled extensively throughout Latin America and left Argentina permanently in 1971, when she was a guest at the Iowa Writers Workshop. Subsequently she lived in Spain and Rome, with several visits to Israel, and for a couple of years taught opera in Japan. In the late 1970s, she moved to Peking, working in the Spanish-language bureau of the Chinese state radio. From there, in 1981, she settled in Paris where she has lived ever since.

Futoransky established herself as a poet first and she did not turn to fiction until she was forty. All her writing shows her to be a poet of lived experience, though not limited merely to what she herself has lived; the work is constantly inhabited by other voices, whether of friends, lovers, or companions of the road (be they people she met personally or figures from history and literature). Her fiction thus became an extension of the poetry, employing the same direct language rooted in anecdote and reflection. But what makes her style most attractive is the sharp humor that enables her to swallow the bitter with the sweet, a humor directed above all at herself. Because, in spite of the sufferings that love and also exile may bring, she persists, stubborn as ever, on the path that was always her own.

The course of her first several books of poetry marks a process of opening out towards the world and assuming the full dimensions of her poetic voice. *Trago fuerte* (Strong Drink; 1963) begins with a few lines from the *Song of Songs* as it traces the quest that love implies and the difficulty of learning to love not only another person but also oneself. In *El corazón de los lugares* (The Heart of Places; 1964), the journey describes a wider realm, extending across the A-merican continent and beyond; here the poet seeks to enter something deeper that the self, a mystery which can only be approached through travelling, in this way likening her experience as a Jew to that of gypsies. *Babel, Babel* (1968), by contrast, immerses itself in the specifics of history, achieving a tone of testimony mixed with prophecy. The poet seeks to challenge God, who seems so far away in a world where love is lacking and disasters multiply.

With *Lo regado por lo seco* (The Watered for the Dry; 1972), her first book after leaving Argentina, she begins to explore the condition of exile. She considers the figure of "stupid Ulysses, spouting literature" while his wife enjoys herself at home. But for Ulysses the voyage came to an end, whereas for Futoransky it always starts over again. Perhaps Israel could be her new home, she seems to wonder, and here she devotes many poems to reflecting about that land.

In 1969 she had made her first trip to Israel (the rest of her family eventually moved there), and the visit made a strong impression on her. She recognizes in "Feudo de Lot" (Lot's Feud) that "each land has its favorite fruits and . . . there is no place like this for the clusters of madness" (32). In another poem, after a night spent with a man who may have been an Arab, she reflects on the child she might have had. The land is full of uprooted people from the world over, and she feels a deep tenderness for them all, with the cruel history that has been their destiny. Yet, that is not enough in the end to make it her home: she wants more from the world than to be united in that history.

Partir digo (To Leave, I Say; 1982), her first book from Paris, collects the poems from a decade of her most distant travels. Here she enters fully into the theme of exile, not just to write about it but to embody its effects, in the play of desires and intensities accumulated from such various sojourns. As in the textures of her prose, which she began writing by this time, there is an impatience in the poet's voice where memory and imagination mix continually, where other voices and images recall one another in the spark of a word or a phrase.

Paris, however, seems to have settled her somewhat, for her subsequent books of poems dwell less in the trials of exile than in more personal assessments of what she has gathered from her travels. *El diván de la puerta dorada* (The Couch of the Golden Door; 1984) considers "the passionate shipwreck that is [her] life" at that point, alone and past forty. Her style has grown more economical, yet rich in its narrative implications, while the poems suggest that perhaps one shouldn't go searching for love, but rather learn to receive it on its own terms. Poetry has been her constant companion throughout the world, and in *La sanguina* (Red Pencil Drawing; 1987) what is felt above all are the absences she has accumulated. The places she has known—Jerusalem, Naxos, even Paris—resound with such absences. Yet she still desires to sing of love, whatever its disappointments, because through language she reanimates that presence which was worth knowing in spite of it all. *Fauces* (Jaws; 1994) finds her more tranquil and even wiser, deciphering time's secrets, appreciating the pleasures that remain beyond the loss of love. Here, her travels follow the Mediterranean world, and in part it is a book of self-portraits, but what emerges more than ever in these poems is her playful side, with an incisive humor that cuts to the quick of language.

Futoransky's three novels, like her poetry, followed a mostly autobiographical line. Her prose moves with a tireless energy, full of humor and the constant desire to know the world. Each book, in its way, concerns the uncertain existence of foreigners in general, and Latin Americans in particular, trying to build a life of their own; each constructed like a different mosaic, they offer a multiple vision of places, times, voices. *Son cuentos chinos* (Tall Tales; 1983), written in Paris, is presented in the form of an intimate journal, which allows her to bring up at will memories of her Jewish childhood in Buenos Aires, her tangles with the Chinese bureaucracy in Peking, her amorous adventures with two African diplomats and other themes. Her second novel, *De pe a pa* (A to Z; 1986), follows her experiences after arriving in Paris and is told more or less in the form of an alphabetical primer, reflecting the new language that she had to learn. The freshness and magic of a language that still feels new propels her to experiment in a widely ranging style. In *Urracas* (Magpies; 1992) she explores her pleasure in digressions, as she tells the story of two women friends taking the train from Paris to Switzerland. The window beside them looks out not only upon the passing landscape but into their memories and preoccupations revealing the complexity of their mutual feelings.

With *Urracas* Futoransky reached another level as a writer in exile, for the book first appeared in French translation two years before its publication in Spanish. She has lately written two nonfiction books as well: *Pelos* (Hair; 1990), which studies representation of hair through myth and literature, and *Viajes de bodas* (Honeymoons), a literary tour of honeymoons which is not yet published. In recent years she has also begun to receive recognition for her writing in the form of prestigious awards: in 1990 she was named a Chevalier des Arts et Lettres by the French government, and in 1991 she received a Guggenheim fellowship.

PRIMARY BIBLIOGRAPHY
Creative Writing

Antología (1963-1984). Buenos Aires: Libros de Tierra Firme, 1985.

Babel, Babel. Buenos Aires: La Loca Poesía, 1968.

El corazón de los lugares. Buenos Aires: Perrot, 1964.

De pe a pa: o de Pekín a París. Barcelona: Anagrama, 1986. "Like They Used To Be," excerpt in English translated by E. Bell. *Fiction* 12.2 (1994): 163-65.

"Derrota Tiananmen," "Libro de horas de Colmar." *Noaj* 4.5 (1990): 74.

El diván de la puerta dorada. Madrid: Torremozas, 1984.

Fauces. Unpublished (1994).

"La mala hora/The Wrong Time." Trans. by Jason Weiss. *Sphinx* (Paris) 2 (1985): 45.

El nombre de los vientos. Zaragoza: Litho Arte, 1976.

Lo regado por lo seco. Buenos Aires: Noé, 1972.

La Parca, enfrente. Buenos Aires: Libros de Tierra Firma, 1995.

Partir, digo. Valencia: Prometeo, 1982.

La sanguina. Barcelona: Taifa, 1987.

Son cuentos chinos. Madrid: Albatros Hiperión, 1983. Also, Buenos Aires: Planeta, 1991.

Trago fuerte. Potosí, Bolivia: Potosí, 1963.

Urracas. Buenos Aires: Planeta, 1992.

"Wrinkles," "The Evil Hour," More Chagall than Chagall," "Stormy Weather," "Vinho verde." Poems trans. by Celeste Kostopulos-Cooperman. *The Renewal of the Vision: Voices of Latin American Women Poets 1940-1980.* Ed. Majorie Agosín and Cola Franzen. Peterborough, England. Spectacular Diseases Press, 1987. 52-56.

Nonfiction

Pelos. Madrid: Temas de Hoy, 1990.

"El vértigo de escribir." *Clarín* 29 Oct. 1992: 18.

Viajes de bodas. Forthcoming.

SECONDARY BIBLIOGRAPHY
Criticism

Espinosa, Elia. "Entre albas y crepúsculos." *Plural* (2nd ser.) 161 (1985): 52-53.

Gimbernat González, Ester. "*De pe a pa*: alfabeto de la magia." In her *Aventuras del desacuerdo: novelistas argentinas de los 80.* Buenos Aires: Danilo Albero Vergara, 1992. 117-23.

Goldberg, Florinda F. Rev. of *La Parca, enfrente. Reflejos* (Jerusalem) 4 (December 1995): 131-32.

Leiva, Angel. "Luisa Futoransky: 'Injuriamos porque somos injuriados.'" *ABC domingo* 14 March, 1976: 42.

Modern, Rodolfo. "Temporada en Pekín." *La Gaceta* 17 Nov., 1991: n.p.

Pasquini, Claudia. "Tribulaciones de una argentina en China." *Crisis* 48 (1986): 87-88.

Pezzoni, Enrique. "*El corazón de los lugares.*" *Sur* 294 (1965): 121-25.

Rezzano, Arturo. "*Babel, Babel.*" *Davar* 118 (1968): 152-53.

Scwartz, Marcy E. Rev. of *Urracas. Hispamérica* 23.69 (1994): 114-17.

Interviews

Fondebrider, Jorge. "Luisa Futoransky: el corazón de los lugares." In *Conversaciones con la poesía argentina.* Comp. Jorge Fondebrider. Buenos Aires: Libros de Tierra Firme, 1995. 357-70.

Pfeiffer, Erna. "Mis bienes raíces son mi lengua: Luisa Futoransky." In her *Exiliadas emigrantes viajeras: encuentros con diez escritoras latinoamericanas*. Madrid: Vervuert/Iberoamericana, 1995. 53-69.

Senkman, Leonardo. "El lenguaje de mi judeidad." *Noaj* 3.3-4 (1985): 160-65.

Speranza, Graciela. "Luisa Futoransky." *Primer plano* (Argentina) 31 Jan., 1993: 6-7.

Jason Weiss

GALEMIRE, JULIA (Uruguay; 1923)

Among the writers that emerged during the 1980s in Uruguay, Julia Galemire, an Uruguayan-Sephardic poet stands out. She was born in Montevideo to her parents Menajem Galemire and Matilde Meseri, both originally from Smyrna, Turkey. She also had a brother, now deceased, and a sister. At home there was never a formal literary tradition, however, her father—a small business man fond of even the most minimal manifestation of religiosity and Jewish culture—was a great reader and composer of stories that he transmitted orally to friends and neighbors.

Even though Galemire chose to dedicate herself professionally to a career in nursing, literature in its varied forms has attracted her since adolescence, especially poetry and the critical essay. Consequently, she attended classes given by professor Eugenio Petit Muñoz in 1945 and 1946, a renowned faculty member in the School of Humanities, and she also took classes with professor Roberto Ibañez in 1955 and 1956, another well-respected figure in Uruguayan literature.

In 1987, now retired from nursing and having written various poems, Galemire decided to publish a number of them in the *Semanario Hebreo* (Hebrew Weekly), edited by José Ierosolimski, a prominent journalist within the Jewish community. Following the advice of Daniel Rafael Stawski, an Uruguayan-Israeli poet with whom she had shared her manuscripts, Galemire decided to put together a book. Stawski himself won the V Premio Mundial Fernando Rielo de Poesía Mística de España (V Fernando Rielo World Prize for Spanish Mystic Poetry) with his book *Sacrificio y piedra del silencio* (Sacrifice and Stone of Silence) in 1985.

In 1989 her first published text, *Fabular de la piedra* (Fables of the Stone), appeared. It contains twenty-five poems, and it has been commented that they require numerous readings, not so much for their ambiguity, but for their conceptual profundity. Inherent in the poems is a search for more pure forms of expression, which is made manifest through a poetic discourse that is held together tightly with few metaphors or images. Concerning the content, the reader becomes aware of a combination of a certain magical element with daily experiences. It is interesting to note, likewise, that the last poem of the collection, "Raíces" (Roots), deals with the poet's Jewish identity. The poem includes a quotation from the Talmud Yerushalmi about the destruction of the Second Temple, and it consists of a twilight evocation of the Wailing Wall in Jerusalem.

In 1990 Galemire joined the literary workshop sponsored by professors Silvia Lago and Jorge Arbeleche who later edited a book of poetry and short stories written by the participants of the workshop including one of Galemire's poems, "El color de los seres" (The Color of Beings). Around the same time she also was studying literature and art with various other Uruguayan professors.

The second book, published in 1991 is titled *La escritura o el sueño* (Writing or Sleep/Dream). This volume reflects the evolution of a poet that, in spite of having emerged late on the literary scene, is in full process of perfecting her talents. As in the first collection of poems, the literary discourse of *La escritura o el sueño* is hermetic, and a full assimilation of meaning requires more than one reading. However, the poems in this collection end up being more accessible to the reader: the majority are written in poetic prose form, the language is simpler and there are more visual images. The organization of the book is also more elaborate. The poems presented are divided into three sections: "Diálogos" (Dialogues) either consist of comments on or are dedicated to other writers, "La escritura y el sueño" reflects spiritual preoccupations and, "Transiciones" (Transitions) is gleaned from daily experiences.

Galemire's work has been well received in Uruguay and the author is beginning to be known in other countries as well. Aside from Uruguay, critical attention has been given to her work in Colombia and the United States, and two of her poems have been set to music.

Galemire currently resides in Montevideo and she has recently completed a third volume of poetry titled *Al sur del aire* (South of the Air; 1994). In 1993 an essay written by Galemire about the poetry of Argentine Roberto Juarroz appeared in *Revista Graffitti* (Graffitti Journal).

PRIMARY BIBLIOGRAPHY

Al sur del aire. Montevideo: Graffiti, 1994.
La escritura o el sueño. Montevideo: Signos, 1991.
Fabular de la piedra. Montevideo: Proyección, 1989.

SECONDARY BIBLIOGRAPHY

Berruti de Castro, Fablana. "Reportaje de Julia Galemire: atrapar la belleza del mundo." *Lea* Dec. 2, 1989: 24.

García Brunel, Blanca. "*Fabular de la piedra* de Julia Galemire." *Semanario hebreo* March 22, 1990: 14.

Millan Redin, Hermes. Rev. of *La escritura o el sueño*." *La Juventud* Nov. 1, 1991: 13.

Renée Scott

GELMAN, JUAN (Argentina; 1930)

The life of Argentine poet Juan Gelman parallels in many ways the vicissitudes of contemporary Argentine history. He was thirteen at the time of the 1943 coup d'etat that led to the Peronist government (1946-55), and his formative years were lived under the tumultuous changes brought about by Peronismo; he reached maturity at a time when long-lasting military dictatorships began to alternate with short-term constitutional governments, a situation which prevailed from 1955 until 1983. Argentina had barely twelve years of constitutional governments in the five decades following Gelman's birth. Stated differently: during his first fifty-three years of life there were only eight years of uninterrupted constitutional governments in Argentina; twenty-two years of unsuccessful constitutional governments ended by military coups; and twenty-three years of de facto military governments.

Gelman was born in the city of Buenos Aires in 1930, into a family of Ukrainian immigrants with a progressive and activist past: his father, a carpenter and railroad worker, had participated in the 1905 Russian revolution; his mother, the daughter of a rabbi, had been a medical student in Odessa. He attended a typical, secular public high school in Argentina, and at the age of fifteen he joined the Communist Youth. During the next twenty years his relationship with the Communist Party eroded as he carried out an uncompromising search for intellectual and political independence that, once found, led him to break with the party in 1964. He began working as a journalist in the early 1950s, in party publications such as the newspaper *Our World*, and for the Chinese news agency Xin Hua. Along with other leftist writers and poets he founded the poetry group El Pan Duro (Stale Bread) in 1955, as well as the journal and publishing house

Nueva Expresión (New Expression). Strong internal criticism of local Communist Party politics began to emerge in Argentina in the late 1950s. First, in the wake of the Cuban revolution of 1959, there was internal disagreement over the methods of the revolutionary left and its possibilities for success; later dissent centered around the left's proper position vis-à-vis Peronism in Argentine politics. Like many other intellectuals, artists, and writers committed to the Argentine Communist Party, Gelman ended up breaking his ties to the organization in order to commence a political and ideological quest which would characterize both his generation and the following one.

At the end of the 1960s, many liberal intellectuals associated themselves with the leftist wing of Peronism, or Revolutionary Peronism, as did Gelman. He soon joined one of its factions, the Movimiento Peronista Montonero (Montonero Peronist Movement), an affiliation lasting until 1979, when he broke with the group, publicly censuring their exclusively military objectives. It was also in the 1960s and early 1970s that he established himself as a journalist in the Argentine weekly magazines *Primera Plana* (First Page) and *Panorama*, in the journals *Los libros* (Books) and *Crisis*, and in the daily newspapers *La Opinión* (The Opinion) and *Noticias* (The News).

In 1975, during the worst year of the rightist repression which characterized the short-lived presidency of Perón's widow María Estela Martínez, Gelman left Argentina. He made a brief, clandestine trip back the following year, when the government was already in the hands of the military dictatorship that would be responsible for the disappearance of more than thirty thousand Argentine citizens. Gelman's twenty-year-old son and his son's nineteen-year-old pregnant wife were disappeared in 1976. Gelman lived in exile for thirteen years, residing at different times in Rome, Madrid, Managua, Paris, New York, and Mexico, where he worked as a translator and carried out political actions from abroad against the Argentine dictatorship. In 1988, once the judicial barriers to his return were overcome, he was able to return to Argentina. In 1990 the remains of his disappeared son were found and buried.

Much in the way that Gelman's life exemplifies the tragedies of contemporary Argentine history, so does his poetry serve as a chorus proposing a mode of interpretation of that history and commenting on it in an aesthetic and literary key. Although in many of his texts the connection with immediate reality is clear in such themes as the call for justice, social Utopia, or the impact of persecution and exile, this connection is even more evident in the formal features of these texts. The poetry in Gelman's first four books—*Violín y otras cuestiones* (Violin and Other Issues; 1956); *El juego en que andamos* (The Game We're In; 1961); *Velorio del solo* (Loner's Wake; 1961), and *Gotán* (i.e Tan/go, Go/tan; 1962)—

represents the highest moment of the near-hegemonic poetic school of the 1960s, a movement which aspired to bring the poetic text closer to its social and historical context through the combination of narrative and lyrical languages; the use of unpretentious discourses (colloquial forms of language, social languages unconnected with erudite culture); and through a discussion of daily life and humble events as if they were parts of a popular Epic or of a popular Utopia.

These first four books may be seen as the culmination of that school of poetry precisely because they sustained and rejected its principles at the same time, transcending them through a type of dialectic which has since become a hallmark of Gelman's style. At one end of the spectrum, one finds narrative prose, political themes grounded in specific circumstances, and utopian and optimistic messages in these poems, while at the other there is a brilliant set of short texts written in the tradition of high love and elegiac lyric. In these first four books, an elevated tone and pure poetic diction combine, sometimes uncomfortably, with historical references, political rhetoric, and the pedagogical clarity of ideological slogans. But lyrical subjectivity is not in the end smothered by social protest because Gelman was already conscious that expressing protest in a poem is more the task of language than of content.

By the early 1960s, young Argentine writers had enriched their work by incorporating cultural theory of the left (from Georgy Lukacs and Jean-Paul Sartre to Bertolt Brecht, Walter Benjamin and Antonio Gramsci), and their lives had been impacted by the great political and social events of the time (in the international arena, the Cold War, postwar Imperialism, the Chinese and Cuban revolutions; in the domestic, the constant threat of military dictatorships and the new role of Peronism). Their writing and their theoretical positions on life, politics, and literature, revived the ancient debate between didacticism and aestheticism in art. Many of the committed leftist writers favored "realist" styles and believed in the efficacy of mimetic practices, but another sector of the young generation of writers struggled against the tradition of an authoritarian voice or perspective in the text, as well as against the concept of total and complete meanings in literature (in fiction, this stance is exemplified by the early work of Manuel Puig (1933-89), Luis Gusmán (1944), and Héctor Libertella (1945); in poetry, by Alejandra Pizarnik (1936-72) and Leónidas Lamborghini (1927).

It is precisely at this moment when Gelman's poetry experimented with intersecting the style of pure poetry with that of social poetry, and advanced the prospect of bridging didacticism and aestheticism. If *Gotán*, published in 1962, epitomized the highest standard of committed poetry, then the second edition of his next book, *Cólera buey* (Ox-like Anger)—poems written between 1962 and 1968, published as a volume in 1971—refines the quest for balance and rupture between the distinct poetics which was emerging in his previous work. The eight different collections composing the unitary volume *Cólera buey* show this quest as much in the structuring of the texts as in their rhetorical stock. The two poetics are represented through an internal tripartite arrangement of the collection: first, a set of texts marked by a strong personal tone, by predominant love themes and by a traditional lyric I; then, an elegiac text about the death of Ernesto "Che" Guevara ("Thoughts"); and finally, two sections of "translations" of apocryphal poets and poems. The rhetorical elements of the collection give it a strong Modernist flavor, linking Gelman's poetry to the Spanish American tradition of discursive experimentation of the 1920s and the 1930s, represented above all by the works of Vicente Huidobro (1893-1948) and César Vallejo (1892-1938): elimination of capitalization and punctuation marks; disruption of standard spelling, syntax, and logical word order; liberal use of neologisms and of regular word-formation rules. The discursive transgressions, and the disruptions of meaning thus obtained, return the book to the territory of pure poetry. Even so, between different poems of each book, and sometimes even in the same poem, Gelman's poetry moves from the practice of pure poetry to the practice of social poetry; it experiments with the disruption of meaning, only to return to pedagogical clarity. If one of his poems mentions the Parnassus—"arthur rimbaud dijo que hay que cambiar la vida y dejó de escribir es decir dejó de alucinar la vida y fue a áfrica . . ." (arthur rimbaud said life must be changed and he stopped writing that is to say he stopped hallucinating life and went to africa;)—it still associates it with the political and social issues that so strongly characterized his first book: ". . . y entre tantos ingleses franceses portugueses y demás aves de rapiña rimbaud contrabandeó . . . y cuando por ello fue castigado su culpa verdadera nunca fue mencionada esas bestias cobardes prefieren no meneallo condenan ciertamente las formas de querer intervenir" (. . . and among so many english, french, portuguese, and other birds of prey rimbaud smuggled . . . and when because of that he was punished his true fault was never mentioned those cowardly beasts prefer not to touch it they certainly condemn the forms of interventionalist desire" ("Explicação [Explanation], in *Perros célebres vientos* [Famous Dogs Winds; from *Cólera buey*, in Fondebrider, ed. *Antología poética*, 80]).

The last section of *Cólera buey*'s tripartite arrangement is composed of apocryphal "translations" written at the same time or just before the texts in Gelman's next collection, *Los poemas de Sidney West. Traducciones III* (The Poems of Sidney West. Translations III), published in 1969. The "translations" define Gelman's poetics even more rigorously as a deliberate attempt to establish a poetic style with no focal point of reference (replaced in these poems by alien and distant spaces and times) and depriving the poetic I of its privilege of enunciation. The distancing effect thus obtained helps to objectify sentimental intimacy by diverting it from the scrutiny of readers; it also helps to express—without the disadvantages of didacticism—strong ideological meanings such as the universalization of social injustice and social suffering, or the urgency to demythify the category of petty-bourgeois identity.

These poetic practices point toward Gelman's later work. In the book *Fábulas* (Fables; written in 1971, published in 1973) the technique of "becoming another," first evident in the apocryphal "translations," is now refined by the use of another discursive disguise. This is a factitious moralizing tone that depreciates a prestigious genre and displaces contexts so as to lead one to understand facts in a different way; in effect, de-fabling fables and draining away common sense. In *Relaciones* (Relationships), written between 1971 and 1973, and published in 1973—the last of his texts published in Argentina before his long exile—new techniques are added to intensify the rupture of meaning, such as the constant use of slashes among different lines or in the same line, and the repetition of questions which serve to undermine certainties. In this manner the social criticism of his first poems becomes a social criticism of poetic language which nevertheless does not disregard extraliterary discourses, history, politics, and ideology. In similar fashion, Gelman's later poetry speaks about exile; by doing so, he regained his Jewish heritage. The poems collected in the books *Citas y comentarios* (Quotations and Commentaries), written between 1978 and 1979, published in 1980; *com/posiciones* (com/positions; 1983-1984, published in 1986); and *dibaxu* (beneath; 1983-1985, published in 1994), speak of banishment using the archaic Spanish language of the Jews expelled from Spain in the fifteenth century, the Sephardic Ladino of the sixteenth century, or, in free and modified translation, the voice of Jewish poets of various times and places who sang out about survival and loss, like Salomon Ibn Gabirol, Abba Yose Ben Hanin, Joseph Tsarfati, and Yehuda Halevi.

In *Relaciones* and especially in his next book, published while he was already in exile (*Hechos* [Facts]; written in Buenos Aires between 1974 and 1978, published in Spain in 1980), Gelman perfects the distancing/buffering techniques he had previously used to express intimate emotions, and strives to eliminate the traditional separation between the personal and the political (the private and the public) in order to create a manner of writing where **the personal is political**. This project is patent in the apocryphal "translations" and in the use of archaic Spanish and Ladino, where language, space and time reinstate the impact of tragic contemporary events in ostensibly escapist poetry. In these texts the new poetic project is also evident in the subtle, surreptitious doses of History injected into poems that belong to the tradition of high sentimental poetry. This is the case of text number XXIX in *dibaxu*, a classic example of a love poem: "no stan muridos lus paxarus / di nuestras bezus / stan muridos lus bezus / lus paxarus volan mil verdi sulvidar / *pondrí mi spantu londji* / *dibaxu del pasadu* / *qui arde* / *cayadu com'il sol*" (the birds of our kisses are not dead / the kisses are dead / the birds fly in the green forgetting / *I will put my fear away* / *under the past* / *which burns* / *as silent as the sun* [Fondebrider 213; my emphasis]).

In the exile poems that recall the impotence and pain caused by the genocide carried out by the military dictatorship of 1976-1983 (such as the poems included in *Notas* [Notes], *Carta abierta* [Open Letter], *Si dulcemente* [If Tenderly], all written between 1979-80 and published together in the volume *Si dulcemente* in 1980; and *Hacia el Sur* [To the South], written and published in 1982), Gelman continues to work on this project, creating a true "politics of intimacy" where grief does not indulge itself in solipsism but connects itself with a social and collective experience of pain, stressing the need to keep memory obstinately alive. As a means of manifesting his doleful compassion for the tortured and the assassinated victims of the dictatorship, or his call never to forget the struggle for a better existence in Latin America, Gelman saturates his exile texts with strategies of language such as the use of diminutives, of taxing interrogations, of stutterings and deformations of affective language common to children. He thus moves the high poetic diction down to the level of intimate and familiar language, defamiliarizing political content by drastic leaps from the intimate and confidential to the epic and public, from the high literary style to the "minor" tragedies of history. It is in this way, for example, that the poem "si dulcemente" (if tenderly) was written: "si dulcemente por tu cabeza pasaban las olas / del que se tiró al mar / qué pasa con los hermanitos / que entierraron? [sic] / hojitas les crecen de los dedos? / arbolitos? / otoños / que los deshojan como mudos?" (if tenderly through your head there passed the waves / of the one who was thrown in the sea / what happens to the little brothers / they buried? / do tiny leaves grow from their fingers? / little trees? / do autumns / unleave them as if they were voiceless? [Fondebrider 164]). "Ruiseñores de nuevo" (Nightingales again), from the book *Hacia el Sur*, uses the same strategies and techniques: "los muertos se ponen pálidos como magdalena cuando amasaba / sus panes con más lágrimas que harina? / hasta que venga el día? / día en que toda américa latina subirá lentamente? / . . . / pasa walt whitman con el ruiseñor al hombro cantando / en paumanok / pasa el comandante guevara a hombros del ruiseñor / pasa el ruiseñor que se alejó de la vida callado como / burrito andino / en representación de los que caen por la vida" (do the dead grow as pale as magdalena when she kneaded / her bread with more tears than flour? / until the day comes? / the day in which all latin america will slowly rise? / . . . / walt whitman passes by with the nightingale on his shoulder singing / in paumonok / comandante guevara passes by on the shoulders of the shoulders of the nightingale / the nightingale passes by, the one that took leave from life silent as / an andean burro / representing those fallen for life . . . [Fondebrider 185]. The poetic prose of *Bajo la lluvia ajena. Notas al pie de una derrota* (Under an Alien Rain.

Footnotes to a Defeat; written in 1980, published 1983), as well as an *oratory* celebrating the sacrifice and the courage to the Mothers of Mayo Square (*La junta luz* [The Joined Light; 1985]), can also be included in this same poetic project. But above all, *Carta a mi madre* (Letter to My Mother; 1989), is the text that masterfully unites the marks of recent history with the irruption of intimate personal feelings. Written in the classic tradition of a lament for the death of a loved one, this text questions and rhetorically admonishes the one who passed away: "te llevó el cáncer? / no mi última carta? / la leíste, respondiste, moriste / adivinaste que me preparaba a volver? / . . . / vos / que contuviste tu muerte tanto tiempo / por qué no me esperaste un poco más? / temías por mi vida?" (did cancer take you away? / not my last letter? / you read it, answered it, died / did you guess that I was preparing to return? / . . . / you / who held back your death for so long / why didn't you wait for me a little longer? / did you fear for my life? [Fondebrider 225]). However, the text also introduces gnomic questions and answers whereby laments for an individual death are transformed into a reflection on collective pain and the need to remember: "qué olvido es paz? / . . . / quién podrá desmadrar al desterrado? / tiempo que no volvés / mares que te arrancaste de la espalda / . . . / me buscabas también así? / hermanos en el miedo me quisiste? / en un pañal de espanto? / . . . / ya no nos perdonemos" (which forgetting is peace? / . . . / who could un-mother the exiled? / time you do not return / seas you tore away from your shoulders / . . . / were you also looking for me in this way? / brothers in fear did you love me? / in a diaper of terror? / . . . / let's not forgive ourselves [Fondebrider 231-34]).

PRIMARY BIBLIOGRAPHY

Antología personal. Buenos Aires: Instituto Movilizador de Fondos Cooperativos, 1993.

Antología poética (1956-1989). Introduction, selection, and bibliography by Lilián Uribe. Montevideo: Vintén Editor, 1993.

Antología poética. Introduction, selection, and bibliography by Jorge Fondebrider. Colección Austral. Biblioteca de literatura hispánica. Buenos Aires: Espasa Calpe Argentina, 1994.

Anunciaciones. Madrid: Visor, 1988.

Bajo la lluvia ajena (notas al pie de una derrota). [1980] In Osvaldo Bayer y Juan Gelman, *Exilios*. Buenos Aires: Legasa, 1983.

Carta a mi madre. Buenos Aires: Libros de Tierra Firme, 1989.

Citas y comentarios. [1979 and 1978-79] Madrid: Visor, 1982.

Cólera buey. [1963] Preface by Mario Trejo. La Habana: La Tertulia, 1964.

Cólera buey. Buenos Aires: La Rosa Blindada, 1971. New edition, including the books *El amante mundial, Rostros, Perros célebres vientos, Sefiní, Traducciones I. Los poemas de John Wendell, Traduuciones II. Los poemas de Yamanokuchi Ando*. Also, Buenos Aires: Libros de Tierra Firme, 1984; Buenos Aires: Seix Barral Biblioteca Breve, 1994.

com/posiciones. Barcelona: Llibres del Mall, 1986.

de palabra. Preface by Julio Cortázar. Madrid: Visor, 1994. Includes *Relaciones, Hechos, Notas, Carta abierta, Si dulcemente, Comentarios, Citas, Bajo la lluvia ajena, Hacia el Sur, com/posiciones, eso, Anunciaciones*, and *Carta a mi madre*.

dibaxu. [1983-85] Colección Biblioteca Breve. Buenos Aires: Seix Barral, 1994.

En abierta oscuridad. México, D.F.: Siglo XXI, 1993.

Fábulas. [1971] Buenos Aires: La Rosa Blindada, 1973.

Gotán. Buenos Aires: La Rosa Blindada, 1962.

Hacia el Sur. México, D.F.: Marcha, 1982.

Hacia el Sur y otros poemas. Buenos Aires: Espasa Calpe, 1995.

Hechos y Relaciones. [1974-78 and 1971-73] Preface by Eduardo Galeano. Barcelona: Lumen, 1980. Also includes *Relaciones*.

Interrupciones I. Preface by Julio Cortázar. Buenos Aires: Libros de Tierra Firme, 1988. Includes *Relaciones, Hechos, Notas, Carta abierta, Si dulcemente, Comentarios*, and *Citas*.

Interrupciones II. Buenos Aires: Libros de Tierra Firme, 1986. Includes the new books *com/posiciones* and *eso* [1983-84], and also *Hacia el Sur* and *Bajo la lluvia ajena*.

El juego en que andamos. [1956-58] Buenos Aires: Nueva Expresión, 1959.

La junta luz (oratorio a las Madres de la Plaza de Mayo). Buenos Aires: Libros de Tierra Firme, 1985.

Obra poética. Buenos Aires: Corregidor, 1975. Rpt. 1984. Includes most of the poems published by Gelman until 1975. Both editions are plagued with misprints and they were rejected by the author.

Poemas. La Habana: Casa de las Américas, 1969. Includes poems from *Violín y otras cuestiones, El juego en que andamos, Velorio del solo, Gotán*, and *Cólera buey*.

Los poemas de Sidney West. Barcelona: Llibres de Sinera, 1973. Also, Buenos Aires: Seix Barral Biblioteca Breve, 1994.

Poesía. Preface by Víctor Casaus. La Habana: Casa de las Américas, 1985. A selection of representative poems.

Relaciones. [1971-73] Buenos Aires: La Rosa Blindada, 1973.

Salarios del impío. [1984-92] Buenos Aires: Libros de Tierra Firme, 1992.

Si dulcemente. Poem-preface by José María Valverde. Barcelona: Lumen, 1980. Also includes the books *Notas* [1979] and *Carta abierta* [1980].

Traducciones III. Los poemas de Sidney West. [1968-69] Buenos Aires: Galerna, 1969.

Velorio del solo. Buenos Aires: Nueva Expresión, 1961.

Violín y otras cuestiones. Preface by Raúl González Tuñón. Buenos Aires: M. Gleizer, 1956.

Violín y otras cuestiones. El juego en que andamos. Velorio del sol. Gotán. Buenos Aires: Caldén, 1970.

Violín y otras cuestiones. El juego en que andamos. Velorio del sol. Gotán. Buenos Aires: Libros de Tierra Firme, 1989.

SECONDARY BIBLIOGRAPHY
Criticism

Achúgar, Hugo. "La poesía de Juan Gelman o la ternura desatada." *Hispamérica* 14.41 (1985): 95-101.

Benedetti, Mario. "Gelman hace delirar a las palabras." In his *La realidad y la palabra.* Barcelona: Destino, 1990. 283-97.

Boccanera, Jorge. *Confiar en el misterio. Viaje por la poesía de Juan Gelman.* Buenos Aires: Sudamericana, 1994.

—, comp. *Gelman: testimonio inédito, reportajes, crítica, poemas.* Buenos Aires: Ideas, Letras, Artes en la Crisis, 1988.

Borinsky, Alicia. "Interlocución y aporía. Notas a propósito de Alberto Girri y Juan Gelman." *Revista iberoamericana* 125 (1983): 879-87.

Dalmaroni, Miguel. *Juan Gelman. Contra las fabulaciones del mundo.* Colección Perfiles 5. Buenos Aires: Almagesto, 1993.

Foffani, Enrique. "La lengua salvada: acerca de *dibaxu* de Juan Gelman." In *Culturas del Río de la Plata (1973-1995): transgresión e intercambio.* Ed. Roland Spiller. Frankfurt am Main: Vervuert Verlag, 1995. 183-202.

Giordano, Jaime. "Juan Gelman o el dolor de los otros." *Inti: revista de literatura hispánica* 18-19 (1984): 169-90.

Murray, Frederic W. "A Cultural Poetics of Social Protest: The Poetry of Juan Gelman, Jaime Augusto Shelley, and Juan Pintó." In his *The Aesthetics of Contemporary Spanish American Social Protest Poetry*. New York: The Edwin Mellen Press, 1990. 154-87.

Olivera-Williams, María Rosa. "*Citas y Comentarios* de Juan Gelman o la (re)creación amorosa de la patria en el exilio." *Inti: revista de literatura hispánica* 29-30 (1989): 79-88.

Paris, Diana. "Juan Gelman y el discurso de la ajenidad." In *Literatura e identidad latinoamericana—siglo XX*. IV Simposio Internacional de Literatura. Ed. Juana Alcira Arancibia. Westminster, CA: Instituto Literario y Cultural Hispánico, 1991. 157-70.

Schreibman, Susana. *Selected Poems of Juan Gelman. A Bilingual Edition*. M.A. Thesis in Creative Writing. Department of English, University of Pennsylvania, 1990.

Sillato, María del Carmen. "'com/posiciones' de Juan Gelman o cómo traducir los mil rostros de la realidad." *Hispamérica* 24.72 (1995): 3-14.

—. *Juan Gelman: las estrategias de la otredad. Heteronimia, intertextualidad, traducción*. Buenos Aires: Beatriz Viterbo, 1996.

Uribe, Lilian. "Bibliografía de/sobre Juan Gelman." *Inti: revista de literatura hispánica* 32-33 (1990-91): 275-83.

—, ed. *Como el temblor del aire. La poesía de Juan Gelman. Ensayos críticos*. Montevideo: Vintén, 1995.

Weinstein, Ana E., and Miryam E. Gover de Nasatsky, comps. *Escritores judeoargentinos: bibliografía 1900-1987*. 2 vols. Buenos Aires: Milá, 1994. 1:232-38.

Interviews

Benedetti, Mario. "Juan Gelman y su ardua empresa de matar la melancolía." In his *Los poetas comunicantes*. 2nd ed. México, D.F.: Marcha Editores, 1981. 187-208.

Fondebrider, Jorge. "Juan Gelman: obsesión, ritmo y silencio." In *Conversaciones con la poesía argentina*. Comp. Jorge Fondebrider. Buenos Aires: Libros de Tierra Firme, 1995. 249-64.

Mero, Roberto. *Conversaciones con Juan Gelman*. Buenos Aires: Contrapunto, 1987.

Senkman, Leonardo. "Entrevista a Juan Gelman." *Noaj* 7-8 (1992): 106-13.

Andrés Avellaneda

GERCHUNOFF, ALBERTO (Argentina; 1884-1950)

It in no way diminishes the stature of Alberto Gerchunoff in Argentine literature as an essayist, novelist, journalist, and literary critic to judge his collection of stories, *Los gauchos judíos* (*The Jewish Gauchos of the Pampas*; 1910), as his finest and most enduring contribution to Argentine letters. The hitherto parochial Jew of the agricultural colonies entered upon the Argentine national literary scene and became the focus of a still-continuing debate as to the manner and extent of the Jew's acculturation within the Argentine national identity. Leonardo Senkman calls it a "literary and national baptism" (17). Even as intellectual and cosmopolitan an author as Jorge Luis Borges (1899-1986) considers it the foremost reflection of Gerchunoff's innermost thoughts and emotions and the core from which his literary work emanates. Since its publication, Argentine literature has frequently and exhaustively debated the interaction of the Jewish immigrant with a national culture—a preoccupation not duplicated in any other American literature, with the exception of the United States's literary explosion of the 1950s with writers such as Philip Roth (1933), Saul Bellow (1915), Bernard Malamud (1914-86), et al. *Los gauchos judíos* acquired an international audience when it was translated into English by Prudencio de Pereda in 1955 and became a movie under the aegis of Juan José Jusid in 1975.

While Gerchunoff's avowed intent was to demonstrate the harmonious integration of the Jewish immigrant with the telluric and ideological nature of his Argentine environment, his literary kinship with Sholem Aleichem (1859-1916) is a function of their shared sensitivity in capturing distinctive Jewish communities in a specific time and space through literary vignettes. As Aleichem immortalized life in the Eastern European Jewish *shtetl* of Karisileve through the eyes of Tevye, the milkman, so Alberto Gerchunoff performed the same function for the Jewish Colonization Association (J.C.A.) agricultural colonies of Baron Hirsch on the Argentine plains. It may be argued that the contrast between Aleichem's ironic and melancholy vision of the reality of the Jew's precarious existence in Eastern Europe and Gerchunoff's romanticized remembrance of the colonies as an almost biblical re-creation of an Argentine New Zion is sharp enough to invalidate such an assessment. Both authors did, however, recapture for succeeding generations, an era and a lifestyle which were to disappear; the European through fear and hostility; the Argentine, through abandonment of the rural for the urban environment. In addition, their literary vignettes of different areas and periods of Jewish cultural formation underscore the resistance of the Judaic tradition to assault, whether by a hostile European or a more benign

Argentine environment. And finally, while Aleichem's realism contrasts sharply with Gerchunoff's romanticism, both display a melancholy optimism in a Jewish continuum. Tevye reluctantly abandons the familiar, Judaic routine of the no-longer habitable Karisileve for a freer Jewish life in America, while despite hints of local anti-Semitism, Gerchunoff envisions a future Argentina where complete religious and ethnic harmony will reign.

Gerchunoff's image of an Argentine New Zion is fashioned in the first chapter of *Los gauchos judíos* in the sordid and the eternally snow-covered town of Tulcin in Russia. There, before a small boy, the town elders and the visiting Sephardic rabbi envisage a return to the biblical mission of the Jew as a tiller of the soil, fulfilling his traditional destiny on the plains of Argentina. This chapter also enunciates what were to be Gerchunoff's three main literary themes: the heartland/Judaism, the homeland/Argentina, and the Cervantes *academe*/Don Quijote. The Jewish elders of the heartland hail the Argentine homeland as a New Zion, as the Sephardic rabbi prophesies a new Jewish *Siglo de Oro* (Golden Age) in Argentina as had occurred in Spain until the Diaspora in 1492; whereby Gerchunoff became an inheritor, through the Sephardic Hispanic cultural tradition, of the literary fellowship of Quixotism.

The Argentine New Zion became a reality on his arrival at the age of six at the agricultural colony of Moisés Ville, Province of Santa Fe, where he stayed until the death of his father, when the family moved in the colony of Rajil in Entre Ríos. Finding it difficult to cope alone, the widow Gerchunoff relocated the family to Buenos Aires in 1895, where the twelve-year-old Alberto worked at a variety of menial factory jobs, including weaver and cigarette maker, and also as a street vendor, to accumulate the funds necessary to pursue a secondary education. Unable to finish for lack of money, Gerchunoff continued his informal education in the public libraries of Buenos Aires. In the course of such studies, he met Enrique Dickmann (1874-1955) who introduced him to the Argentine Socialist Party and members of the influential inner literary circle, which included Leopoldo Lugones (1874-1938), Manuel Gálvez (1889-1950), José Ingenieros (1877-1925), Ricardo Rojas (1882-1957), and Roberto Payró (1876-1928). Payró sponsored his entry to the staff of *La Nación* (The Nation, Buenos Aires's most prestigious newspaper) in 1908, where he remained as a writer of obituaries, columnist, reviewer, and commentator, in addition to working independently as a novelist, satirist, and essayist, until his sudden death in 1950.

Los gauchos judíos, a compilation of articles which began appearing in *La Nación* in 1908, was published at the time of the Argentine Centennial in 1910, against a background of hope and optimism for ethnic harmony. It represents Gerchunoff's blueprint for a successful synthesis of the heartland with the homeland. The cowed *shtetl* dweller combines with the Argentine prototype, the gaucho, to produce a bold, compassionate, freedom-loving hybrid who incorporates the best of both cultures. Unfortunately, the synthesis does not withstand close analysis. The Jewish colonist was more accurately a sedentary *chacarero* (farmer) rather than a nomadic, *macho*, solitary rider of the plains of Argentine legend. Yet it does reflect what Gerchunoff assessed to be the Jew's best hope for complete integration into the new Argentina. Beginning with the assimilation of the tortured but noble features of the Jewish immigrant with those of the robust, local Argentines through marriage in his early writings and culminating in *Los gauchos judíos*, Gerchunoff traces a trajectory for Jewish acceptance in the Argentine New Zion, which basically advocates total Jewish assimilation into the Argentine body politic and individual. The Semana Trágica (The Tragic Week) in 1919 in which Jewish inhabitants of Buenos Aires were assaulted and their businesses vandalized by bands of roving youths, however, made the continuance of such ethnic myopia difficult to sustain. A hint of latent anti-Semitism had surfaced to disturb some of the idyllic vignettes of *Los gauchos judíos* as in the death of Rabbi Abraham, Gerchunoff's father, murdered by a drunken gaucho (47-49), who (Gerchunoff neglects to state) was beaten to death on the spot by the enraged colonists; the false accusation of horsetheft against a colonist who was prejudged guilty because he opted to pay an unjust fine rather than lose precious harvesting manhours in a court appearance (78-81); and "La lechuza" (The Owl), where the tragic arrival of a bloodied, riderless horse presages the death of the rider at the hands of local bandits to a fearful mother and sister (49-53).

But Gerchunoff did not deliberately or directly challenge Argentine anti-Semitism in print until a prologue to the Argentine edition of a book on modern Jewish thought, *Renacimiento de Israel* (Rebirth of Israel) by Ludwig Lewisohn in 1942, wherein he passionately decries the political, social, and personal humiliations and restrictions imposed upon the Jew in the name of Argentine nationalism, (*El pino y la palmera* 67-81). Other articles dealing with the precarious Jewish situation globally, as well as in Argentina, appeared in 1944 and 1945 (*El pino y la palmera* 135-69, 170-81). But as he admitted to the pathetic incapacity of the Jewish heartland to be fully assimilated into any national homeland, to the point of de-assimilation (as had occurred in Spain, Germany, Romania, Hungary and Italy (*El pino y la palmera* 165), even when it so desired, Gerchunoff persisted in seeking a viable formula. The revised synthesis, rather than seeking total assimilation, now emphasized multiethnicity or multiculturalism. The Jew retained his ethnic identity within the synthesis, abandoning the concept of a *crisol de razas* (racial fusion) to create a new Argentine national entity. The Jew was no longer simply an Argentine, but now a Judeo-Argentine, primarily, through exclusion and secondarily, by choice.

The Jewish heartland is a continuum in Gerchunoff's work. In *Enrique Heine* (1932), Gerchunoff says Kaddish (a Hebrew prayer for the dead) at Heine's grave in Paris, in response to a Heine lament that no one would say Kaddish for him at his death in a foreign land. Jacopo Botoshansky theorizes that Heine's attraction for Gerchunoff stemmed from his misinterpretation of Heine's statement that he was a German poet, in the same manner as Gerchunoff considered himself an Argentine writer. Botoshansky cites the actual quote reflecting the idea that Heine was actually a poet in Germany, stressing the artist rather than the nationality (150). Baruch Spinoza (1632-77) is remembered in *Los amores de Baruj Spinoza* (The Loves of Baruch Spinoza; 1932), the recounting of an alleged love affair with the daughter of his patron. *El pino y la palmera* (The Pine and the Palm Tree; 1952), a posthumous collection of his writings, chronicles his lifelong preoccupation with the Jewish condition both in Argentina and abroad. Articles abound on specific Jewish figures, such as Maimónides, Rabbi Sem Tob, and others. He evinces surprise that others are amazed at the rapid acculturation of the Jew to Argentina, ignoring the fact that the Jew was simply resuming a language and culture which had been an inheritance from the Sephardic experience in Spain. He further confesses that after a exhausting day in the atmosphere of a totally Christian environment, he draws on the magic of Scholem Aleichem's tales of the Karisileve ghetto to revive his spirits and to gird himself for the next day's battle of survival (31-32, 45-52, 55-66, 103-12).

The cloak of silence which enveloped most Argentine writers during the Perón era also affected Gerchunoff's literary production. With the post-Holocaust years, he became a vociferous supporter of the creation of the State of Israel (a haven he only previously advocated for those orthodox Jews who were unable to adapt to the freedom and openness of a national homeland (cited in *Davar* 31-33 (1951): 77-78), making numerous speeches and appearances on Israel's behalf. His last published discussion of the Jewish heartland appeared in the newspaper, *El Tiempo* (Time) of Bogotá in rebuttal to an anti-Semitic article. Here he expressed his painful solidarity with all Jews who had suffered, simply for being so, and with those who uphold the values of spirituality and truth (*El pino y la palmera* 188-89).

Defense of the Jewish heartland was matched by equal passion for his adopted Argentine homeland. Each discussion of Judaism was echoed by a passionate declaration of the special destiny of the homeland. Argentina was indeed the New Zion despite some defects in her treatment of her Jewish citizens. With assimilation, the Jew would become an Argentine like any other and share in its glorious future. Even in the grim reality of the Semana Trágica and the anti-Semitic nationalistic atmosphere of 1930s and 1940s, Gerchunoff persisted in the hope that this was a temporary phenomena, imported from abroad, which would be finally and decisively rejected by thinking and sensitive Argentines of good will (*El pino y la palmera* 81). While conceding the naivete of such optimism in the face of overwhelming evidence to the contrary, it should be remembered that Gerchunoff had known no other homeland. The nostalgia for the colonies of the J.C.A., where he absorbed the myth of the gaucho; the camaraderie of the early bohemia of the cafes of Buenos Aires with noted Argentine literary and political figures; the national recognition accorded his literary endeavors; his elder statesman status in the Jewish community, all combined to make Argentina his own particular New Zion, despite its deficiencies.

Los gauchos judíos early affirmed Gerchunoff's deep love for his adopted homeland, a New World re-creation of the historic agrarian biblical heartland. *Las imágenes del país* (National Images; 1931); *Entre Ríos, mi país* (Entre Ríos, My Homeland; 1950); and *Argentina, país de advenimiento* (Argentina, Land of the Future; 1952) are paeans of praise for Argentina's capacity to fulfill her glorious destiny. Cognizant of some imperfections in his beloved's image, he focused his satirical wit on the pseudo-intellectualism of the Argentine middle class in *El hombre que habló en la Sorbona* (The Man Who Spoke at the Sorbonne; 1926). *La asamblea de la bohardilla* (The Assembly in the Attic; 1925), *Pequeñas prosas* (Simple Prose; 1926), *Historias y proezas de amor* (Tales and Deeds of Love; 1926), and *El hombre importante* (The Important Man; 1934), discuss universal ideas within the context of any urban, educated society, similar to that of Argentina. Conversely, *Cuentos de ayer* (Tales of Yesteryear; 1919) and *Roberto Payró* (1919) reflect a specific reality of the homeland. The autobiographical story, "El día de las grandes ganancias" (The Day of Great Gain [*Cuentos de ayer*]) describes Gerchunoff's first day as a street peddler, a job which afforded him the greatest suffering and humiliation of his life (*Entre Ríos* 31). *Roberto Payró* was a plea for the release of his friend and mentor, who had been imprisoned by the Germans during World War I. *La clínica del doctor Mefistófeles* (The Clinic of Dr. Mephistopheles; 1937), returns Gerchunoff to the world of intellectual fantasy and irony, as he assembles historic figures from the past (from Helen of Troy to Savaronola) to discuss the deficiencies of mankind in general and political systems in particular, especially communism and dictatorship.

His only foray into Argentine politics, *El nuevo régimen* (The New Regime; 1918), a political tract highly critical of the government of Hipólito Irigoyen, proved disastrous. Shortly after its publication, Gerchunoff lost the only

political appointment he ever held, the Vicerectorship of the Colegio Carlos
Pellegrini de Pilar (Kántor, "Obra y anecdotario de Alberto Gerchunoff" 161).
How much of a role this played in his subsequent silence on specific political
figures and issues can be debated.

There can be no debate, however, on Gerchunoff's sincere and deep
emotional attachment to the Argentine homeland on a par with his love for the
Jewish heartland. The Argentine New Zion of *Los gauchos judíos*, even with her
image slightly tarnished by anti-Semitism, evokes fervent expressions of devotion. As he states in his autobiography, it was under the incomparable sky of the
vast Argentine plains that his existence was marked indelibly by a national fervor
which erased his origins and made him truly an Argentine (*Entre Ríos* 26). He
does not simply wish to exalt Jewish life, because he is also deeply Argentine,
and as such, the homeland has profoundly affected his artistic formation (*Entre
Ríos* 36). But his most fervent declaration of loyalty is reserved for his provincial
homeland, Entre Ríos. He literally exults, "Soy de allá, amigos míos. . . Entre
Ríos, tierra benévola. . . diste fondo a mi alma. . . Amigos míos, soy de allá"
(I'm from there, my friends. . . Entre Ríos, beneficent land. . . you gave depth
to my soul. . . My friends, I'm from there [*Entre Ríos* 58-59]).

Gerchunoff was no stranger to the hallowed tradition of the Hispanic
man of letters to explore the Quijote/Cervantes philosophic legacy. Having established his right to this Quixotic inheritance under the Sephardic umbrella of
Judaic fraternity, Gerchunoff hoped to assume the mantle of an Argentine Quijote of the pen. Introduced to Quijote as a youthful factory worker by a gaunt but
garrulous Asturian companion *(Entre Ríos* 29-30), the adventures of the Knight
of the Sorrowful Countenance, along with the Bible and the tales of Scholem
Aleichem, became a spiritual resource at the day's end for a weary or discouraged Gerchunoff. He early announces his Quixotism in *Los gauchos judíos* in the
vignette, "Las bodas de Camacho" (The Wedding of Camacho [55-61]), where
the "desocupado lector" (idle reader) is reminded of the similarities between Gerchunoff's tale and the Cervantes *bodas*, to underline the bond of a common
humanity linking the people and events of the Argentine pampas with those of
Cervantes's sixteenth-century Spain (61).

La jofaina maravillosa (The Wondrous Wash Basin; 1924), continues
this theme in a series of essays on various facets of the Quijote legend, and
emphasizes the importance that Quijote exercises over Gerchunoff's life and
work. He is the symbol of our desires, inspires us to live heroically, and is our
shield against those whose vision is mired in the dull earth (21). *Retorno a Don
Quijote* (Return to Don Quijote; 1951) is a collection of earlier essays on Quijote, with a prologue by Jorge Luis Borges in which he lauds Gerchunoff's

ability to capture the intimacy and magic of Quijote in both the oral and written word. In addition to general essays on Cervantes and Quijote, Gerchunoff comments upon those writers he also deems to have been followers of the Quixotic ideal, to include Voltaire (1694-1778), Erasmus (1466-1536), and the Argentine, Roberto Payró, whose articles on the atrocities committed by the Germans against the Belgian people during their occupation of Brussels, published in *La Nación* of Buenos Aires, resulted in his imprisonment by the German authorities during World War I. In effect, Gerchunoff gave notice that, as a convert to Quixotism, he too would use his pen to focus attention on issues that government administrators and judges would not normally consider to be the province of the writer (13-19).

The contradictions inherent in Gerchunoff's positive vision of the Jew in Argentine society and its often negative reality have elicited equally controversial commentary on the relevance of his writing to the more serious issues in Jewish Argentine literature. Sharpest division exists between the pre-Holocaust and post-Holocaust generations of Jewish-Argentine writers, the latter almost tacitly accusing him of a conspiracy of silence. Pre-Holocaust writers, including such Gerchunoff contemporaries as César Tiempo (pseud. of Israel Zeitlin [1906-80]), Enrique Espinoza (pseud. of Samuel Glusberg [1897-1987]), Lázaro Liacho (1897-1969), Samuel Eichelbaum (1894-1967), as well as later authors, such as Carlos Grünberg (1903-68) and Bernardo Verbitsky (1907-79), assign him the role of elder brother, one who shared the emotional, psychological, and physical trauma inherent in making the successful transition to the national literary scene from the artistically and culturally limited environment of the JCA colonies. Carlos Grünberg hails him as "nuestro sumo sacerdote" (our high priest [57]). Jacopo Botoshansky underlines the fact that Gerchunoff remained a visible and conscientious Jewish presence, even as he pried open the doors for acceptance of the work of other Argentine writers as national literature (150). Enrique Espinoza also remembers him as a precursor who blazed a trail for other Argentine Jewish writers (68). And as a speaker at numerous events in the Jewish community, there can be no doubt of his visible and emotional identification with the Judaic tradition in Argentina.

Post-Holocaust critics have been less tolerant of the social and political tightrope Gerchunoff walked in recording the Jewish condition in Argentina. There is an implication of consorting with the enemy by selling his (Jewish) birthright for a mess of (Argentine) porridge, and maintaining a deliberate policy of myopia toward Argentine anti-Semitism to protect his special status as the accepted or token Jewish writer of the elite national literary circle. David Viñas (1929) ridicules the intellectually-rebellious, nocturnal bohemia of the early days in Buenos Aires—defined by Gerchunoff as the period in which he and others found themselves as writers (Kántor, "Obra y anecdotario" 152)—as the self-indulgence of a group of young bourgeoisie to sleep late, engage in nightly dilettante political discussions, climaxed by overeating and drinking, and subsequent vomiting in a vestibule the next day. He dismisses Gerchunoff's advocacy of Jewish assimilation as an expedient to avoid the only other options: "irse o el suicidio" (to leave or commit suicide) in order to maintain his elitist literary position. Gerchunoff had willingly become an apologist for the upper-middle class (137, 185, 179). Also criticized has been Gerchunoff's tendency to overstate the compatibility of Christianity and Judaism "to secure for the Jew a firm place in Argentine society" (Lindstrom 11).

Equally skeptical is Saúl Sosnowski's assessment that Gerchunoff's assimilationist attitude stemmed only from a desire to belong to the elitist literary class, and "misdirected sense of gratitude and loyalty to his adopted country prevented him from an accurate reading of the country's ills" (3). Somewhat kinder is Leonardo Senkman, who while agreeing with the negative view of the pastoral, biblical idyll that is *Los gauchos judíos*, does accept as mitigating factors, Gerchunoff's sense of personal loyalty to Leopoldo Lugones (1874-1938; Argentine poet and friend and Director of the 1910 Centennial celebration) and the generally optimistic atmosphere of the Argentine Centennial to harmonious Jewish Argentine interaction. In fairness to Gerchunoff, however, Senkman also cites other Argentine Jewish writers who used literature to legitimize the Jew's status in Argentina, including Nicolás Rapoport (1884-1961) *La querencia* (Home; 1929), Samuel Glusberg, *Ruth y Noemí* (1934), José Chudnovsky (1915-66), *Pueblo pan* (1967), Pablo Schvartzman (1927), *Cuentos criollos con judíos* (Native Tales with Jews; 1967), César Tiempo *Pan criollo*, (Home-baked Bread; 1938), and Samuel Eichelbaum, *El guapo del 900* (The Political Bodyguard of the 1900s; 1940); (Senkman 32, 62, 460). Also singled out for criticism has been Gerchunoff's lukewarm pre-Holocaust support for a national Jewish homeland in Palestine, except for the minority of devout or religious Jews unable or unwilling to adapt to any other land (*El pino y la palmera* 77).

As in the affairs of men, the truth undoubtedly lies somewhere between the polarities. Neither a naive, misguided idealist nor a deceitful, guileful tool of the upper-middle class, Gerchunoff undoubtedly eschewed the only possible alternative of the Jew in the pre-Holocaust world—a delicate balancing act which had historically permitted the Jew to survive in equally uncertain environments. Gerchunoff defined traditional Jewish optimism as simply a somber faith in better times for the Jew (*El pino y la palmera* 18). His faith was only a continuum of the Jewish tradition operative at the Diaspora, as Spanish Jews retained the keys to their homes against their eventual return (a reality achieved only after centuries). The pathetic victims of the Holocaust strain our credulity with their continued faith in deliverance and ultimate survival, even in the despair of the death camps. Yet the State of Israel has become the concrete realization of their hope.

There was no other homeland to which Gerchunoff could escape. Even in the relatively more liberal atmosphere of the United States, the unfortunate Leo Frank was lynched in Georgia in 1915 on a false accusation of rape. As late as 1944, U.S. university professors commenting on anti-Semitism in the United States, advocated assimilation as the sole effective antidote. To counter their perception as a so-called cultural irritant, Jews were counseled against entering over-populated, visible occupations such as public entertainment and to curtail the formation of specific Jewish organizations (cf. Graeber and Britt 98-99, 145-47). Irving Howe's (1920) *World of Our Fathers* (1976), mirrors the daily struggles of the Jewish immigrants from Eastern Europe to integrate into the American mainstream from the ghetto-like slums of New York's Lower East Side. The Dreyfuss case had exposed a sore nerve of anti-Semitism in philosophically ultra-liberal France, which shocked the French Jewish community and the world.

Despite anti-Semitism, its accompanying hostility and humiliations, Argentina had awarded her adopted son a national recognition not previously accorded a Jewish writer in Latin American literature. Gerchunoff's so-called delicate pioneering role as the sole Jewish presence in Argentine literature diminished as other Jewish Argentine authors achieved "national recognition in the arts and humanities" (Lindstrom 11). In effect, Gerchunoff had achieved his personal, if imperfect, New Zion in Argentina. The dilemma of ethnic origin opposed to nationality is still being enacted, as in the example of Jacobo Timerman (1923; editor of the newspaper *La Opinión* [The Opinion] of Buenos Aires), who was imprisoned, tortured, and exiled to Israel by the Argentine authorities in the 1980s (see his *Prisoner Without a Name, Cell Without a Number*; 1981), yet who has returned to live in Argentina after the overthrow of the military Junta.

If a work of art is to be valued solely by its relevance to social realism or political correctness, then Gerchunoff's work may indeed be lacking. If, however, a work of art is also defined as a repository of beauty, uniqueness, expression, thought, and emotion, then Gerchunoff and *Los gauchos judíos* have earned their place in the annals of Jewish Latin American literature. As Scholem Aleichem recreated the Russian Czarist *shtetl* atmosphere in his tales of Karisileve, so Gerchunoff immortalized the adaptation of Jewish immigrants to the joys and hardships of Argentine rural life in Moisés Ville and Rajil. Neil Simon (1927) has done the same for the Jewish community of the 1950s in Brighton Beach while the Lubavitchers of Crown Heights, N.Y., currently await the coming of their Aleichem.

Even with the pompous, somewhat inflated language and character, obvious biblical parallels noted by critics (Botoshansky 149), *Los gauchos judíos* suspends in time a unique moment in Jewish New World history. Favel Daglach, of the scholarly curls and *bombachas* (wide gaucho riding pants), whether as a caricature or an unrealized, romanticized hope, will forever stroll through Moisés Ville as the ultimate incarnation of a nostalgic desire to reconcile Jewish tradition with Argentine culture. The J.C.A. colonies were a fertile breeding ground for a generation of especially-gifted Jewish Argentine writers, but Gerchunoff has so imprinted his special vision of the Jew's relationship to Argentina upon literary consciousness that no serious discussion of Jewish Argentine identity can ignore his unique contribution. He is Scholem Aleichem on the Argentine pampas, the Argentine psalmist, David, singing his Song of Songs to his beloved (Argentina), the Jewish gaucho *cantor* (minstrel) of the colonies. Even the most skeptical critic would not dispute the sincerity of Gerchunoff's affirmation of his *argentinidad* (Argentinism), Soy de allá, amigos míos. . . . Soy de allá.

PRIMARY BIBLIOGRAPHY
Creative Writing

La asamblea de la bohardilla. Buenos Aires: Manuel Gleizer, 1925.

La clínica del Dr. Mefistófeles: moderna milagrería en diez jornadas. Santiago de Chile: Ercilla, 1937.

Comedia de pequeños burgueses. A three act play serialized in *Nosotros* (Buenos Aires) 38 (1912): 193-206; *Nosotros* 39 (1912): 278-95; Act Three was never published.

Cuentos de ayer. Buenos Aires: Ediciones Selectas América, 1919. Also, Buenos Aires: Fraterna, 1985.

Los gauchos judíos. La Plata, Arg.: J. Sesé, 1910; Buenos Aires: Manuel Gleizer, 1936; Santiago de Chile: Ercilla, 1940; Buenos Aires: Sudamericana, 1950; Buenos Aires: Editorial Universitaria de Buenos Aires, 1964. Buenos Aires: Fraterna, 1983. English version as *The Jewish Gauchos of the Pampas.* Trans. Prudencio de Pereda. New York: Abelard-Shulman, 1955.

Historias y proezas de amor. Buenos Aires: Manuel Gleizer, 1926; Buenos Aires: Emecé, 1962.

El hombre importante. Montevideo/Buenos Aires: Sociedad Amigos del Libro Rioplatense, 1934; Buenos Aires: Hachette, 1960.

El hombre que habló en la Sorbona. Buenos Aires: Manuel Gleizer, 1926.

Pequeñas prosas. Buenos Aires: Manuel Gleizer, 1926.

Nonfiction

Los amores de Baruj Spinoza. Buenos Aires: BABEL [Biblioteca de Buenas Ediciones Literarias], 1932.

Argentina, país de advenimiento. Buenos Aires: Losada, 1952.

Autobiografía. Buenos Aires: Libreros y Editores del Polígano, 1983.

Buenos Aires, la metrópoli de mañana. Buenos Aires: Cuadernos de Buenos Aires, 1960.

Enrique Heine, el poeta de nuestra intimidad. Buenos Aires: BABEL, 1927.

Entre Ríos, mi país (Contains autobiography). Buenos Aires: Futuro, 1950; Buenos Aires: Plus Ultra, 1973.

Figuras de nuestro tiempo. Buenos Aires: Vernácula, 1979.

Las imágenes del país. Buenos Aires: Azul, 1931. (Reprint of *Argentina, país de advenimiento*)

La jofaina maravillosa: agenda cervantina. Buenos Aires: BABEL, 1923; Buenos Aires: Manuel Gleizer, 1927; Buenos Aires: Losada, 1938, 1945, 1953.

Nuestro Señor Don Quijote. Buenos Aires: Coni, 1913.

Nuestros escritores: Roberto J. Payró. Buenos Aires: J. Menéndez, 1925.

El pino y la palmera. Buenos Aires: Sociedad Hebraica Argentina, 1952.

El problema judío. Buenos Aires: Macabi, 1945. (Reprinted as *El pino y la palmera*, 1952)

Retorno a Don Quijote. Prologue by Jorge Luis Borges. Buenos Aires: Sudamericana, 1951.

SECONDARY BIBLIOGRAPHY

Aizenberg, Edna. "Alberto Gerchunoff: ¿Gaucho judío o antigaucho europeizante?" *Anuario de letras* (Mexico) 15 (1977): 197-215.

—. "Parricide on the Pampa: Deconstructing Gerchunoff and His Jewish Gauchos." *Folio* 17 (1987): 24-39.

Ayala Gauna, Velmira. "Alberto Gerchunoff y su mensaje." *Cuadernos de la Diligencia* (Rosario, Arg.) 2.4 (1961): 14-23.

Barchilón, José. "Alberto Gerchunoff." In his *Gerchunoff/Bufano*. San Juan, Argentina: Editorial Sanjuanina, 1973. 13-42.

Borges, Jorge Luis, and Manuel Mujica Lainez. *Figuras de nuestro tiempo: Alberto Gerchunoff.* Buenos Aires: Vernácula/Plus Ultra, 1979.

Botoshansky, Jacopo. "Kadisch en memoria de Reb Alberto." *Davar* 31-33 (1951): 144-51.

Davar (Buenos Aires). 31-33 (1951). Special issue on Alberto Gerchunoff.

Eichelbaum, Samuel. "Su memoria es nuestra herencia." *Davar* 31-33 (1951): 107-13.

Espinosa, Enrique. "Alberto Gerchunoff y *Los gauchos judíos.*" *Davar* 31-33 (1951): 61-71.

Gálvez, Manuel. *Amigos y maestros de mi juventud.* Buenos Aires: Hachette, 1961. 38-9, 44-6, 84-5, 101-2, 104-5.

—. *El mal metafísico.* Buenos Aires: Espasa-Calpe, 1943. 2nd ed. 1962. (A novel whose protagonist is based on Alberto Gerchunoff)

—. *En el mundo de los seres ficticios. Recuerdos de la vida literaria.* Vol. II. Buenos Aires: Hachette, 1961. 73-86.

Ghiano, Juan Carlos. "En homenaje a la memoria de Alberto Gerchunoff." *La Nación* (Buenos Aires) 4 Jan. 1976, 3rd Sec., 1.

—. "Gerchunoff cuentista." In *Cuentos de ayer*, by A. Gerchunoff. Buenos Aires: Fraterna, 1985. 9-21.

Giusti, Roberto. "El espíritu y la obra de Alberto Gerchunoff." In his *Poetas de América y otros ensayos.* Buenos Aires: Losada, 1956. 139-49.

—. "Veinte años de vida: recuerdos y divagaciones." *Nosotros* (Buenos Aires) 219-20 (1927): 5-51.

Glickman, Nora. "Biografía como auto-reflexión." *Folio* 17 (1987): 23-41.

Gordon, Marjorie Salgado. "Alberto Gerchunoff and the 'Bridge' on the River Plate." *Hispania* 75.2 (1992): 287-93.

—. "Alberto Gerchunoff and Samuel Eichelbaum: Two Literary Reflections of Judeo-Argentinidad." Ph.D. diss., University of Maryland, College Park, 1982.

Gover de Nasatsky, Miryam Esther. *Bibliografía de Alberto Gerchunoff.* Buenos Aires: Fondo Nacional de las Artes y Sociedad Hebraica Argentina, 1976.

Graeber, Isaque, and Stewart Britt. *Jews in a Gentile World.* New York: Macmillan, 1942.

Grünberg, Carlos. "A Alberto Gerchunoff." *Davar* 31-33 (1951): 57.

Herrera, Francisco. "Alberto Gerchunoff." In *Enciclopedia de la literatura argentina.* Ed. Pedro Orgambide and Roberto Yahni. Buenos Aires: Sudamericana, 1970. 269-70.

Howe, Irving G. *World of our Fathers.* New York: Harcourt, Brace, and Jovanovich, 1976.

Jaroslavsky de Lowy, Sara. *Alberto Gerchunoff: vida y obra: Bibliografía: Antología.* New York: Hispanic Institute, Columbia University, 1957.

Kantor, Manuel. *Alberto Gerchunoff.* Buenos Aires: Ejecutivo Sudamericano del Congreso Judío Mundial, 1969.

—. "Obra y anecdotario de Alberto Gerchunoff." In *El hombre importante,* by A. Gerchunoff. Buenos Aires: Hachette, 1960. 137-69.

Karduner, Luis. "Misión del escritor judío en la literatura argentina." *Judaica* (Buenos Aires) 16 (1934): 145-49.

Koremblit, Bernardo Ezequiel. "Gerchunoff o el vellocinio de la literatura." *Davar* 100 (1964): 242-47.

Leguizamón, Martiniano. "Los gauchos judíos." In his *Páginas argentinas.* Buenos Aires: Librería Nacional, Ed. J. Lajouane y Cía, 1911. 179-87.

Lerner, Isaías. "La obra literaria de Alberto Gerchunoff." *Davar* 63 (1956): 59-66.

Leyes, Elio C. *Voz telúrica en Gerchunoff.* Prólogo de Bernardo Ezequiel Koremblit. Rosario: Ateneo Judeo-Argentino "19 de abril," 1979.

Liacho, Lázaro. *Alberto Gerchunoff.* Buenos Aires: Colombo, 1975.

Lindstrom, Naomi. *Jewish Issues in Argentine Literature: From Gerchunoff to Szichman.* Columbia: U of Missouri P, 1989. 9-11, 51-60.

Longo, Iris Estela. "Presencia de Gerchunoff en la narrativa argentina." In her *Voces de Entre Ríos (Aportes al conocimiento de la literatura regional).* Santa Fe, Argentina: Colmegna, 1986. 130-51.

Martínez Estrada, Ezequiel. "Alberto Gerchunoff: apunte hecho de memoria." In *Para una revisión de las letras argentinas.* Writings by Martínez Estrada compiled by Enrique Espinoza. Buenos Aires: Losada, 1967. 123-25.

Resnick, Rosa Perla. "La obra literaria de Alberto Gerchunoff." *Judaica* (Buenos Aires) 139 (1945): 12-26.

Senkman, Leonardo. *La identidad judía en la literatura argentina.* Buenos Aires: Pardés, 1983. 17-57.

Sosnowski, Saúl. "Contemporary Jewish-Argentine Writers: Tradition and Politics." *Latin American Literary Review* 6.12 (1978): 1-14.

Stambler, Beatriz Marquis. *Vida y obra de Alberto Gerchunoff.* Madrid: Albar, 1985.

Tiempo, César. "Alberto Gerchunoff, manos y vida." *Hispania* 35.1 (1952): 37-41.

—. "Mano de obra." *Davar* 31-33 (1951): 131-39.

Timerman, Jacobo. *Prisoner Without a Name, Cell Without a Number.* Trans. by Toby Talbot. New York: Knopf, 1981. Spanish version, *Preso sin nombre, celda sin número.* Buenos Aires: El Cid, 1982.

Viñas, David. "Gerchunoff: gauchos, judíos y xenofobia." In his *Literatura argentina y realidad política: apogeo de la oligarquía*. Buenos Aires: Siglo XX, 1975. 165-85.

Weinstein, Ana E., and Miryam Gover de Nasatsky, comps. *Escritores judeoargentinos: bibliografía 1900-1987*. 2 vols. Buenos Aires: Milá, 1994. I.239-58.

Winter, Calvert J. "Some Jewish Writers of the Argentine." *Hispania* 19.4 (1936): 431-36.

Maggi Salgado Gordon

GERSON, SARA (Mexico; date unknown)

Sara Gerson—about whom no biographical information could be obtained at the time of this writing—is best known for her vast accomplishments in children's literature. She has published more than thirty books in Mexico directed at young readers, which are educational in focus. Her best known books for children are those of the Pluvio series in which the title character embarks on different adventures around the globe learning about different geographical areas, climes, and ecologies. Other texts focus on teaching children about the indigenous cultures and history of Mexico. Gerson has also written several books aimed at helping children cope with such potentially frightening situations as the first day of school or a visit to the doctor or dentist.

Gerson's first and to date only book written for an adult audience is her novel *Nueva casa* (New Home; 1993). Written as a series of interconnected stories, the novel is a testament to the magnitude of the modern Jewish diaspora. Each chapter narrates the story of Jewish families from different parts of the world who emigrate to Mexico in search of a haven from war and persecution. Jews from Russia, Poland, Syria, Turkey and even Japan make their way to Mexico by way of France, Spain, Holland, Israel, New York, Panama, and Nicaragua. They have survived the pogroms of Russia and Poland, the nazism of war-torn Europe, the conflicts of the Middle East, and the bombing of Japan. Although each episode stands alone as a separate story, some characters do reappear throughout the text and by the end the narrator ties the tales together as a testimony to the diversity and strength of the Jewish community in Mexico. The novel is also an excellent illustration of Jewish polyglotism that results from life in the galut. Gerson has provided a glossary of the Arabic, Hebrew, Ladino, Yiddish, Russian, German, and Japanese terms used in the text in order to aid the task of the reader.

Nueva casa is not a very outstanding text in purely literary terms. Nevertheless, what makes the novel so interesting is the depiction of Jewish immigration to Mexico and the portrayal of the Jewish community in that country. In this sense it is thematically similar to other recent Mexican Jewish novels like *La bobe* (1990) by Sabina Berman (1954) or *Novia que te vea* (1992) by Rosa Nissán (1939), although it not as artistically sound as either. Such common themes as assimilation, intermarriage and the weakening of traditional values are included along with tales of danger and survival. The topic of intermarriage is presented in two different episodes with two distinct outcomes. In the first, Max—whose name was changed from Motke to Maximiliano upon arriving at the port of Vera Cruz from Poland—marries a non-Jewish Mexican woman, Teresita. In a reversal of the common narrative scheme, Teresita converts to Judaism. However, she is not totally accepted by the Jewish community as reflected in the comments of some of the women who declare that she is not "really" Jewish. In the second case the son is banished for having married a non-Jewish woman and the family members mourn his "death."

Ultimately, *Nueva casa* is about finding a place to settle, a new home, to bring an end to the wandering of exile. Mexico, for Gerson's Jews, is that home. Nevertheless, the author is careful not to paint Mexico as a paradisiacal Eden or promised land. The Jewish community faces real threats of anti-Semitism from such nationalist groups as the *Camisas doradas* (Gold Shirts) who adopted many tenets of Nazi ideology. Gerson manages to evoke the grandeur of the Jewish past, the anguish of persecution and loss, and the hope for the future, dealing with issues of Jewish identity within the context of modern Mexico. *Nueva casa*, therefore, makes a significant contribution to the growing body of Mexican Jewish literature.

PRIMARY BIBLIOGRAPHY

Creative Writing

Nueva casa. México, D.F.: Grijalbo, 1993.

Children's Literature

Castillos de arena. Ilustraciones de Alejandra Walls. México, D.F.: Trillas, 1986.
La civilización maya. With Shulamit Goldsmit. Ilustraciones de Bruno López. México, D.F.: Trillas, 1988.
La cometa roja. México, D.F.: Trillas, 1988.

Las culturas prehispánicas: olmecas, zapotecas, mixtecos, teotihuacanos, toltecas. With Shulamit Goldsmit. Ilustraciones de Bruno López. México, D.F.: Trillas, 1987.

El encuentro. México, D.F.: Trillas, 1988.

El escondite. Ilustraciones de Alejandra Walls. México, D.F.: Trillas, 1986.

El hada Dalia. Ilustraciones de Alejandra Walls. México, D.F.: Trillas, 1986.

La hormiga viajera. México, D.F.: Trillas, 1989.

El hospital. México, D.F.: Trillas, 1990.

El huerto de doña Rosa. Ilustraciones de Luisa de Noriega. México, D.F.: Trillas, 1986.

La independencia de México. México, D.F.: Trillas, 1989.

Luisa y el arco iris. Ilustraciones de Luisa de Noriega. México, D.F.: Trillas, 1986.

México colonial. México, D.F.: Trillas, 1989.

La noche más oscura del mundo. Ilustraciones de Luisa de Noriega. México, D.F.: Trillas, 1986.

Una nueva nación. México, D.F.: Trillas, 1991.

La orquesta. Ilustraciones de Luisa de Noriega. México, D.F.: Trillas, 1987.

Pedro aprende a nadar. Ilustraciones de Alejandra Walls. México, D.F.: Trillas, 1986.

Pepe el gorrión. México, D.F.: Trillas, 1988.

Pluvio a la orilla del mar. Ilustraciones de Luisa de Noriega. México, D.F.: Trillas, 1984.

Pluvio aprende ecología. México, D.F.: Trillas, 1988.

Pluvio conoce el desierto. Ilustraciones de Luisa de Noriega. México, D.F.: Trillas, 1984.

Pluvio en el océano. Ilustraciones de Luisa de Noriega. México, D.F.: Trillas, 1984.

Pluvio en los polos. Ilustraciones de Luisa de Noriega. México, D.F.: Trillas, 1986.

Pluvio recorre las Islas Galápagos. Ilustraciones de Luisa de Noriega. México, D.F.: Trillas, 1985.

Pluvio recorre las praderas africanas. México, D.F.: Trillas, 1987.

Pluvio visita la selva. Ilustraciones de Luisa de Noriega. México, D.F.: Trillas, 1985.

El primer día de clases. México, D.F.: Trillas, 1990.

La primera vez que fui al dentista. México, D.F.: Trillas, 1990.

Vamos a tener un bebé. México, D.F.: Trillas, 1990.

Una visita al doctor. México, D.F.: Trillas, 1990.
Ya no me chupo el dedo. México: Trillas, 1990.

SECONDARY BIBLIOGRAPHY

Vogt, Wolfgang. *"Nueva casa."* In his *Latinoamérica, México, Guadalajara: ensayos literarios.* Guadalajara: Agata, 1995. 156-58.

Darrell B. Lockhart

GERVITZ, GLORIA (Mexico; 1943)

Gloria Gervitz was born in Mexico on March 29, 1943. From 1969 to 1973 she studied Art History at the Universidad Iberoamericana. In addition to her native language Spanish, she speaks English and Yiddish. She is the author of several collections of poems, *Shajarit* (Morning Prayer; 1979), *Fragmento de ventana* (Window Fragment; 1986), and *Yiskor* (Remember; 1987). *Migraciones* (Migrations; 1991) is a compilation of new versions of the latter two volumes that also includes a previously unpublished section titled "Leteo." Her latest collection of poetry, *Pythia*, was published in 1993 and was made possible by a grant from the Consejo Nacional para la Cultura y las Artes (National Council for Culture and the Arts).

The author's literary formation is not only broad but highly eclectic as well. She has been an avid reader from a very early age, and she has translated works by Anna Akhmatova (1888-1966), Osip Mandelshtam (1891-1938), Lorine Niedicker (1903-70), Susan Howe (1937), Rita Dove (1952), and Samuel Beckett (1906-89). Likewise, she has published critical essays on the works of Marguerite Yourcenar (1903-87), Clarice Lispector (1925-77), and Nadezhda Mandelshtam (1899-1980).

Since 1981 Gervitz's poetry began to appear in numerous anthologies published in Mexico, Argentina, and Colombia. Gervitz's relationship with Jewish themes became apparent in 1989 when a selection of her poetry appeared in *Panorama de la poesía judía contemporánea* (Panorama of Contemporary Jewish Poetry; 1989), edited by Argentine poet Eliahu Toker (1932). A number of her poems have appeared in English translation in several different volumes: *Mouth to Mouth: Poems by Twelve Contemporary Mexican Women* (1993) and *Ruido de sueños—Noise of Dreams* (1994), a bilingual anthology of Mexican poetry.

Gervitz's works have been translated into English in their entirety (although not completely available in published form yet). The English translation of *Migraciones*, by Mark Schafer, is due to be released in the near future. A variety of her poems have also appeared in French, Russian, and Norwegian translation.

It should be mentioned that Gervitz's poetry has been published in a large number of journals and literary supplements that include, to mention a few of the most significant, *Vuelta, Revista de la Universidad de México, Diálogos,* and *Punto de partida* in Mexico; *Discurso literario, Revista iberoamericana, Hispamérica,* and *Realidad aparte* in the United States; *Golpe de dados, Prometeo,* and *El espectador,* in Colombia; and *Noaj* in Jerusalem.

It may be easily stated that Gloria Gervitz has enjoyed great success as a poet. However, her success is neither based on her compliance with the latest currents in literary fashion nor for having taken advantage of the growing interest in feminine and feminist topics. On the contrary, what has happened is that more and more readers discovered that perfect poetic corpus of exquisitely concentrated and controlled tonality, that, as if by magic, shifts between multiple transcodifications of tone and detail. It may be surprising to speak of great success if one considers that such a judgment is based on a relatively small production. However, one should take into consideration that the author never submits something for publication unless she is absolutely convinced that she has given her best to the text. Therefore, her poems are refined, elaborated and reelaborated, at times for years, until the end result leaves the reader not only with an infinite thirst for more but also with the realization of having caught a glimpse of the very core of it all.

Shajarit, as was mentioned previously, is the first of the poetry collections published. The title means "morning prayer" in Hebrew, and the text offers a vast array of tones and forms of subjectivity. Replete with dazzling images, practically nonexistent in Mexican poetry prior to its publication, the volume insinuates the search for control of the word that will distinguish subsequent works by the author.

In *Shajarit*, Gervitz presents a series of purely sensorial perceptions of Judaism and Christianity, dreams, awakening, death, sensuality and sexuality, colors and sounds, birds and flowers, past and present, grandmothers, mothers, daughters. All elements cross, intertwine, and ultimately come together in a unique voice to offer a polished, faultless text.

Shajarit is the first step toward a much broader vision represented in *Fragmento de ventana*. The latter is a very long text about which the author, in a letter to Mexican poet Ramón Xirau (1924), states that she attempted to create a "poema-río, que se bifurca, que a veces se ensancha. . . hasta llegar al final de sí mismo. . . ¿Al mar quizá?, no lo sé. En todo caso la ventana queda abierta" (river-poem, that forks, and that at times widens. . . until reaching its own end. . . Perhaps, the sea? I don't know. In any case, the window remains open [Gervitz, letter]).

The poem is written in first person by an "I" whose task is to explore what it means to be a conscious human being, at a specific moment in life and History. The "I" serves both as the textual nucleus and as a point of irradiation of elements that are intimately linked by a network of associations. The resulting textual pattern is a wavering that goes from the individual to the universal and from the known to the merely intuited. It should be made clear that all this is made manifest from an aesthetic position that refuses to establish dividing lines among different planes. All melds together: emotions, memories, time, space, pain, happiness, reality lived and reality dreamt.

The intensity of the author's vision, passionately rooted in the past and the present, forces the reader to examine not only his/her life, but also his/her beliefs. There is no doubt, then, that the world that is presented in *Fragmento de ventana* is a kind of sacred space where the reader, who also travels along the poem-river, participates in a continuous exploration of unknown lands and unexpected depths. In that sacred space, the "I" divides and subdivides multiple times in structures of different length, density and theme. However, what is generally understood by sacred space is converted here into subversive space. What thus appears is a world of totally arbitrary rules where everything is complex, multicolored, and multidimensional.

In reference to a Jewish substratum in Gervitz's work, the poem contains, aside from its obvious theme, a large number of paratactic constructions that recall archaic forms of poetry. The result for the reader is the sensation that what one is reading is more similar to biblical verses than to a contemporary text. The biblical reference becomes more extensive when the author takes up man and woman at their original genesis, mentioning apples that rot and a time before the disaster. Hebraic and Christian themes and the interior and the exterior come together in pages of accentuated eroticism on which also appear fauna and flora of eminently surrealist origins.

Toward the end, the poem becomes almost a prayer, and as with the paratactic constructions, the form and rhythm also resemble Bible verses. The intense symbolism of the last part is directed to woman/women. Upon revealing all the restrictions imposed on women by orthodox Judaism and Catholicism alike, it breaks completely with the premises of patriarchal discourse. The series of feminine voices, all of which are searching for their own identity, range from the young to the mature woman, to the very old, who now simply awaits death. The multiplicity of voices form a single chorus, converting *Fragmento de ventana* into an exemplary text of pure poetry.

Yiskor (1987) contains two parts: the first "Fragmento de ventana" and "Del libro de Yiskor" (From the Book of Yiskor). The first is a new version of the previous volume. The second, "Del libro de Yiskor," provides two fundamental themes. First, the reader cannot help but perceive the form and influence of rites and prayers, and second, one cannot ignore that the text refers to an entire collection of documents, also published in volumes called *Yiskor*. In these volumes the world is warned to not forget, to always have in mind that which the survivors of the Holocaust remember and denounce.

The chorus of feminine voices that speak always in first person from an "I" that is at once profound and caustic observes the results of the inexorable passage of time. The poem, elegiac in its tonality, conjoins unusual images with enormous suggestive power. Likewise, there is a very effective system of alternating questions, assertions, and metaphors.

While it is a given that Gloria Gervitz's poetry has deep roots in Jewish tradition, one cannot overlook the fact that the poet is grounded in two worlds: the Jewish world of her parents and the Mexican world of her maternal grandmother. It is precisely in the confluence of these two worlds that the themes central to her poetry reside: life, death, time, exile, memory, forgetting, eroticism, internal and external influences, reality and the real fed by the imagination and memories.

One very important aspect of this volume is the fact that the author adheres to an aesthetic position that translates the dichotomy memory/forgetting into word/silence. Indeed, *Yiskor* is enriched as much by words as by silences. Full of blank spaces, the text opens new horizons and foreshadows what is yet to come. It is important to observe that any consideration of *Yiskor* must make mention of the beauty of the book itself, which includes a series of paintings by Julia Giménez Cacho. It is both amazing and astounding to see the direct relationship that exists between the verbal images of the poet and the drawings of the artist.

Migraciones is composed of the new version of "Fragmento de ventana," the second part of *Yiskor*, and a new text titled "Leteo." Gervitz fulfills a double mission by adding "Leteo." On the one hand, she widens and divides the river/poem that she has been creating, while at the same time "Fragmento de ventana" and "Del libro de Yiskor" go through a process of refinement that sharpens them.

In "Leteo" one notices a radical change with respect to the versification of the first versions of "Fragmento de ventana" and "Del libro de Yiskor." The ample verses, the uninterrupted rhythm and the long stretches of before, are now contrasted to a tendency to achieve greater balance in the text. The verses and stanzas have become shorter, more concise, and the theme has become practically ethereal. Recovery, testimony, and recuperation constitute the central core of "Leteo." The greater part of the themes considered previously are recovered, and testimony is revealed by means of a variety of voices that penetrate the poetic corpus, at times simultaneously, at times alternating. These voices belong to women that recover all that memory had left to be forgotten. If superficially *Migraciones* seems to attempt to recover the past, on a much more profound level, where the poet delves, she achieves a new way of seeing and understanding the present. The converse dichotomy of past/present ceases to be such and becomes a whole with few or no limitations. All that was believed to be forgotten, plus what is feared forgotten, bursts forth like a volcano in eruption, filling holes and gaps and transforming the subjective yesterday and today into a totalizing reality that encompasses everything.

The themes of exile, the mother, and death appear in "Leteo" with a tone of great urgency. The voices of that generation of Jewish grandmothers, mothers, and daughters that at one time or another escaped the catastrophes that threatened them in their countries of origin are the same that tell of yearnings, losses and, lastly, about the pain caused from having to live on a different continent, with a different language and different customs. The topic of the mother that emerges and reemerges throughout "Leteo" functions as a leitmotif to which is joined the theme of death. At times the figures of the mother and grandmother are confused, while at others there is a complete metamorphosis that transforms both the mother and grandmother into the daughter.

The theme of death, that in normal circumstances tends to be associated with the grandmother or the mother, emerges in "Leteo" as the juxtaposition of elements that are either dissimilar or unexpected. Thus the author joins infancy with death: Infancy is only the first step, a simple preamble to death. Repeated again and again, the cases of juxtaposition enrich a constant state of tension in which what was believed to be, in reality is not. Infancy and death, which have always been seen as distant, are no more than a manifestation of a beguiling illusion.

By means of shrewdly utilized resources, with a great command of the word and with a unique and personal voice, Gloria Gervitz manages to make *Migraciones* into a true triumph.

Pythia is Gervitz's latest collection of poetry. Textually it is very concentrated, and it can be said that the text was torn from silence. Aesthetically,
Pythia continues the poet's concentrated zeal to find just the right word, the
purest expression, a process that—as mentioned earlier—had begun with the first
publication. Likewise, thematically one can identify a progression that has its
origin in *Shajarit*, the "morning prayer," which symbolically becomes just that:
a prayer and a beginning. *Shajarit* is followed by *Fragmento de ventana*, whose
mission within the progression is to make it perfectly clear that women and men,
as imperfect beings, can only manage to glimpse tiny fragments of their own life
and the reality that surrounds them. *Fragmento de ventana* was followed by
Yiskor, signalling the imperative, "remember." Later, as a third part to *Migraciones*, came "Leteo," that is "forgetting," followed by *Pythia* which is "revelation" and/or "oracle." Prayer and beginnings, fragments, memory and forgetting
precede, then, the oracle and revelation, that constitute the central axis of *Pythia*.
Undoubtedly, this work presents the author's most daring production. She constructs her poem on the foundation of fragments, enormously laden and dense,
that resist any attempt at synthesis. Here, little is remembered and little is forgotten, because the priority is the almost frenetic search for absolute dominion over
the word.

Pythia is divided into five parts, none of which has its own title. Essential to the first four parts is the problem of language. The reader not only feels
but sees and even, one could say, touches directly, the anxiety-ridden search for
the "revelation" that will allow the author to find the exact word, which is not
only simple, but multiple and pluridimensional.

The fifth part presents three *colotipias* (examples of nineteenth-century
literary printing technique) by the photographer Luz María Mejía. As with the
relation between the verbal text of Gervitz and the pictorial texts of Julia Giménez Cacho in *Yiskor*, in *Pythia*, word and *colotipia* unite and communicate.

The theme of exile, which carried such weight in "Leteo," appears again,
although transformed, in *Pythia*. What was before the yearnings, loss, and pain
of the immigrants is converted into the exile of the word, which must find its
own place on the blank pages of the text. The arrangement of the verses on the
pages, some of which only contain two to four verses, and the empty spaces
constitute another gainful aspect in the totality of the work. From the blank
spaces, which represent silence, spring those few words that manage to express
everything.

The sacred space that was seen in *Fragmento de ventana* reappears in
Pythia transformed into erotic space. It is evident that the common denominator

in the works remains the same. There are many changes and many modifications, but the effort is always fruitful in the new texts, which both absorb and enchant.

PRIMARY BIBLIOGRAPHY

Fragmento de ventana. México, D.F.: Villicaña, 1986. Fragments in *República de poetas.* Ed. Sergio Mondragón. México, D.F.: Martín Casillas, 1985: 123-35; Also, *La sirena en el espejo: antología de nueva poesía mexicana 1972-1989.* Ed. Manuel Ulacia, et al. México, D.F.: Edicones el Tucán de Virginia, 1990: 107-14.

"La llave del jardín." *Noaj* 7-8 (1992): 20-21.

Migraciones. México, D.F.: Fondo de Cultura Económica, 1991.

Poems from *Shajarit* and *Yiskor.* Translated by Stephen Tapscott. In *Mouth to Mouth: Poems by Twelve Contemporary Mexican Women.* Ed. Forrest Gander. Intro. by Julio Ortega. Minneapolis: Milkweed Editions, 1993. 101-17.

Pythia. México, D.F.: Mario del Valle, 1993. English version as *Pythia.* Trans. by Deborah Owen and Burton Raffel. *The Literary Review* [Fairleigh Dickinson University] 38.3 (1995): 388-416. Fragments of *Pythia* in English translation by Brandel France de Bravo with the author in *Ruido de sueños/Noise of Dreams.* Ed. El Grupo Tramontano-The Tramontane Group. México, D.F.: El Tucán de Virginia, 1994. 96-99.

Shajarit. México, D.F.: Madero, 1979. Fragments in *Palabra nueva: dos décadas de poesía en México.* Ed. Sandro Cohen. México, D.F.: Premià, 1981: 68-73. Fragments also in *Poesía erótica mexicana 1889-1980.* 2 vols. Ed. Enrique Jaramillo Levi. México, D.F.: Domés, 1982. I.227-29.

Yiskor. México, D.F.: Esnard, 1987.

SECONDARY BIBLIOGRAPHY
Criticism

Cross, Elsa. Rev. of *Fragmento de ventana. Revista de la Universidad de México* 42.434 (1987): 51-52.

Díaz Enciso, Adriana. Rev. of *Migraciones. Vuelta* 16.186 (1992): 53.

Dorra, Raúl. Rev. of *Migraciones. Noaj* 7-8 (1992): 158-61.

Goldberg, Florinda F. Rev. of *Yiskor. Noaj* 2.2 (1988): 116-18.

Minc, Rose S. "*Fragmento de ventana*: hacia una hagiografía de las olvidadas." *Folio* 17 (1987): 119-27.

Schafer, Mark. "Toward the Light: The Poetry of Gloria Gervitz." *The Literary Review* [Fairleigh Dickinson University] 38.3 (1995): 385-87.

Interviews

Pollack, Beth, and Ricardo Aguilar Melantzón. "Entrevista con Gloria Gervitz."
Noaj 10 (1995): 93-97.

Rose S. Minc

GHIVELDER, ZEVI (Brazil; 1934)

Brazilian Zevi Ghivelder is both a literary author and a well-known journalist. His most recent book, *Missões em Israel* (Missions in Israel; 1993), is a compilation of his most outstanding journalistic pieces written over a period of thirty-four years. As a journalist, Ghivelder covered many assignments in Israel and the Middle East. The volume is divided into several sections that contain articles on key events in the history of Israel. The trial of Adolf Eichmann in 1961, which he covered for the Brazilian publication *Manchete*, the Six Day War of 1967, the Yom Kippur War of 1973, and most recently the Gulf War figure prominently in the book. Ghivelder's reporting is characterized by his attention to detail and his insightful observations that make *Missões em Israel* a valuable record of the sociopolitical events that have shaped the modern State of Israel. The book is enhanced by a section of photographs that provides a visual record of the topics covered.

In 1969, Ghivelder published his only novel, *As seis puntas da estrela* (The Six Points of the Star), which received a special mention of the national Walmap Prize for literature. The novel remains one of the most direct treatments of the Jewish experience in Brazil. One of the text's most outstanding features is its depiction of a wide range of Jewish topics which include immigration, assimilation, the Holocaust, religious orthodoxy, secularism, as well both the Ashkenazic and Sephardic communities. Robert DiAntonio has identified the novel as being steeped in the Yiddishkeit tradition. The plot revolves around the central character, Favel Alterman, a poor immigrant to Brazil from Bessarabia. It is in certain terms an immigrant success story as Alterman climbs the social ladder from peddler, to small businessman, to entrepreneur. He also plays an important role in providing relief to Holocaust survivors who arrive in Brazil. Ghivelder's treatment of the Holocaust as one of the overriding themes of the book makes it unique among the works of Brazilian Jewish authors.

Jewish themes are also prevalent in Ghivelder's collection of poetry, *Sonetos atentos* (Attentive Sonnets; 1990). The sonnets are grouped under subheadings according to subject. The poems of the "Diário de guerra" (War Diary) are inspired by Ghivelder's first-hand experience with the Yom Kippur War. In "Êxodo" (Exodus), the poems constitute a celebration of Pessach, and in "Fecundo de iras" (Fecund with Rage) they are emotive reactions to the Holocaust. The last two sections of poems, "Temente" (Fearful), and "Livro de orações" (Prayer Book) express a relationship to Jewish religiosity and devotion to tradition.

PRIMARY BIBLIOGRAPHY
Creative Writing
As seis pontas da estrela. Rio de Janeiro: Bloch, 1969.
Sonetos atentos. Rio de Janeiro: Rocco, 1990.
Nonfiction
Missões em Israel: as jornadas de um repórter brasileiro no Oriente Médio. Rio de Janeiro: Imago, 1993.

SECONDARY BIBLIOGRAPHY
DiAntonio, Robert. "The Brazilianization of the Yiddishkeit Tradition." *Latin American Literary Review* 17.34 (1989): 40-51.
Igel, Regina. Rev. of *Sonetos atentos. Noaj* 6 (1991): 72-74.

Darrell B. Lockhart

GLANTZ, MARGO (Mexico; 1930)

An active writer and researcher, Margo Glantz has been professor of literature at the Universidad Nacional Autónoma de México and Director of Literature of the National Institute of Arts. She has also been the cultural attaché at the Mexican embassy in London and a visiting professor of literature at Yale University. Her first novel, *Las mil y una calorías (novela dietética)* (One Thousand and One Calories [A Dietetic Novel]; 1978), is an avant-garde collection of *greguerías* (puns and humorous quotes). *Doscientas ballenas azules* (Two Hundred Blue Whales; 1979) is also an avant-garde work which exploits the trends of the nouveau roman. Her third work, *No pronunciarás* (Thou Shall Not Say; 1980) follows the line of literary exploration started with *Las mil*; *No pronunciarás* declares: "sabemos que la Biblia es un plagio" (we all know that the Bible is plagiarism [24]). According to Naomi Lindstrom "[this text] contains a coherent analysis of what is the act of naming according to the naming community" (286). Glantz takes the title of her following text from Jewish tradition concerning a woman's hair. The author explains that according to religious Jews, the hair of a woman must remain hidden, and only the husband may see it. Only the husband can touch it: the hair of a Jewish woman is like the Arab veil (35). *De la amorosa inclinación a enredarse en cabellos* (The Loving Tendency To Entangle Oneself in Tresses; 1984) is a postmodern pastiche in which the author attempts to subvert Jewish and patriarchal orthodoxy. She shows the paradox of things that have been created for the purpose of remaining hidden. The rewriting of Mary as a Jewish character is a provocative aspect of the text. *Síndrome de naufragios* [Syndrome of Shipwrecks; 1984), in which Noah is assimilated into popular culture continues in the same vein as previous works. According to Glantz "it is a novel without characters. The characters are big natural catastrophes, from the Flood to hurricanes. At the same time it is autobiographical because it is the story of a divorce" (Gliemmo 36). These so-called novels challenge the traditional concept of their genre by virtue of the lack of a defined plot, the impossibility of memory to retain past information and the absence of recurrent characters.

Las genealogías (*The Family Tree*; 1981) collects memories of Glantz's Jewish family. She writes: "Perhaps what attracts me about my Jewish past and present is an awareness of its vividness, its colour and its grotesqueness, the same awareness that makes real Jews a minor race with a major sense of humour, with their ordinary cruelty, their unfortunate tenderness and their occasional shamelessness" (*The Family Tree* 1). In this autobiographical pseudonovel Glantz recounts the immigration of her Ukrainian parents to Mexico after the Soviet Revolution. Jacobo Glantz, Margo's father, became a well-known Yiddish poet. This interesting account captures the life and culture of the Jewish community in Mexico City from the 1920s to the present. It chronicles the process of acculturation suffered by the Mexican Jewish community, how they ended up being assimilated in the Mexican melting pot, the mestizaje preached by the Mexican Revolution. It also describes Jewish customs, having in mind a gentile reader.

Another of Glantz's texts, *El día de tu boda* (Your Wedding Day; 1982), is a collection of love postcards with brief commentaries dating from the postrevolutionary period. Glantz explores nostalgia, the aesthetics of the *cursi* (kitsch) and the European origin of the Mexican middle-class concept of family.

As a literary critic Glantz has published *Repeticiones* (Repetitions; 1979), a compilation of articles about Mexican literature from Martín Luis Guzmán (1887-1976) to *la Onda* (the Mexican "New Wave"). *Intervención y pretexto* (Intervention and Excuse; 1980) is a second compilation of essays. A key article in this latter volume is "Kafka y Job: los dos hermanos" (Kafka and Job: The Two Brothers), in which Glantz explains her position about God and The Bible. Magdalena García Pinto considers that Glantz's feminine discourse, like that of other female writers, perceives the relationship between objects and (Wo)man as one of coexistence, not of ownership as can be inferred of the invention from God's words by Men (33). One additional selection of essays is *La lengua en la mano* (With Tongue in Hand; 1983), which includes the riveting piece "Húmeda identidad: *María* de Jorge Isaacs" (Humid Identity: Jorge Isaacs's *María*) where Glantz tries to explain the ideology of the tear. *Erosiones* (Erosions; 1984) is a compilation of articles published previously in such popular magazines as *Vogue*, *UnomásUno*, *Sábado* or *Escénica*. It includes "Las tiendas de color canela" [The Cinnamon Colored Stores), an article about the Polish Jewish writer Bruno Schulz (1892-1942) who was murdered by the Gestapo in 1942.

Glantz edited *Onda y escritura en México (jóvenes de 20 a 33)* (New Wave and Writing in Mexico [Young Writers from 20 to 33]; 1971). This book gave name to the Mexican literary movement born after the massacre of Tlatelolco in 1968, although some writers such as José Agustín (1944) have disagreed. Glantz has also edited and translated texts about Mexico written by foreign intellectuals: *Viajes en México: crónicas extranjeras* (Travels in Mexico: Foreign Chronicles; 1982).

Glantz has expressed that her identity as a Mexican Jew is natural to her, although in great part folkloric, and that a certain sense of exile, in many aspects, defines her Jewishness (Glickman 19). She also adds that she has "become territorialized" by belonging to Mexican literature, because Mexican literature is a minority member within the context of Hispanic writing in general.

PRIMARY BIBLIOGRAPHY
Creative Writing
De la amorosa inclinación a enredarse en cabellos. México, D.F.: Océano, 1984.
Doscientas ballenas azules. México, D.F.: La Máquina de Escribir, 1979.
Las genealogías. México, D.F.: Martín Casillas, 1981. English version as *The Family Tree: an Illustrated Novel.* Trans. by Susan Bassnett. London: Serpent's Tail, 1991.
Las mil y una calorías (novela dietética). México, D.F.: Premià,1978.
No pronunciarás. México, D.F.: Premiá, 1980.
Síndrome de naufragios. México, D.F.: Joaquín Mortiz, 1984.
Nonfiction
Borrones y borradores. México, D.F.: Universidad Autónoma Nacional de México/El Equilibrista, 1992.

El día de tu boda. México, D.F.: SEP, 1982.

Erosiones. México, D.F.: Universidad Autónoma del Estado de México, 1984.

Esquince de cintura: ensayos sobre narrativa mexicana del siglo XX. México, D.F.: Consejo Nacional para la Cultura y las Artes 1994.

Intervención y pretexto. México, D.F.: Universidad Nacional Autónoma de México, 1980.

La lengua en la mano. México, D.F.: Premià, 1983.

Repeticiones. Ensayos sobre literatura mexicana. Xalapa: Universidad Veracruzana, 1979.

Sor Juana Inés de la Cruz: ¿hagiografía o autobiografía? México, D.F.: Grijalbo, 1995.

Editions

Un folletín realizado; la aventura del conde de Raousset-Boulbon en Sonora. México, D.F.: Sep/Setentas, 1973.

La Malinche, sus padres y sus hijos. México, D.F.: UNAM, 1994.

Notas y comentarios sobre Alvar Núñez Cabeza de Vaca. México, D.F.: Grijalbo, 1993.

Onda y escritura en México (jóvenes de 20 a 33). México, D.F.: Siglo Veintiuno, 1971.

Viajes en México. Crónicas extranjeras. 2 vols. México, D.F.: Fondo de Cultura Económica, 1982.

SECONDARY BIBLIOGRAPHY
Criticism

García Pinto, Magdalena. "La problemática de la sexualidad en la escritura de Margo Glantz." In *Coloquio internacional. Escritura y sexualidad en la literatura hispanoamericana.* Ed. Alain Sicard and Fernando Moreno. Madrid: Espiral Hispanoamericana, 1990. 31-47.

Glickman, Nora. "Margo Glantz." In *Tradition and Innovation. Reflections on Latin American Jewish Writing.* Ed. Robert DiAntonio and Nora Glickman. Albany: SUNY Press, 1993. 18-20.

Jörgensen, Beth E. "Margo Glantz, Tongue in Hand." In *Reinterpreting the Spanish American Essay: Women Writers of the 19th and 20th Centuries.* Ed. Doris Meyer. Austin: U of Texas P, 1995. 188-96.

Lindstrom, Naomi. "*No pronunciarás* de Margo Glantz: los nombres como señas de la imaginación cultural." *Revista iberoamericana* 56 (1990): 275-87.

Otero-Krauthammer, Elizabeth. "Integración de la identidad judía en *Las genealogías* de Margo Glantz." *Revista iberoamericana* 51 (1985): 867-73.

Pasternac, Nora. "La escritura fragmentaria." In *Sin imágenes falsas, sin falsos espejos: narradoras mexicanas del siglo XX.* Ed. Aralia López González. México, D.F.: El Colegio de México, 1995. 339-66.

Senkman, Leonardo. "Jewish Latin American Writers and Collective Memory." In *Tradition and Innovation: Reflections on Latin American Jewish Writing.* Ed. Robert DiAntonio and Nora Glickman. Albany: SUNY Press, 1993. 33-43.

Valenzuela, Luisa. "Mis brujas favoritas." In *Theory and Practice of Feminist Literary Criticism.* Ed. Gabriela Mora and Karen S. Van Hooft. Ypsilanti, Michigan: Bilingual Press/Editorial Bilingüe, 1982. 88-95.

Interviews

García Pinto, Magdalena. "Margo Glantz." In her *Historias íntimas: conversaciones con diez escritoras latinoamericanas.* Hanover, NH: Ediciones del Norte, 1988. 97-121. English version in her *Women writers of Latin America: Intimate Histories.* Trans. by Trudy Blach and Magdalena García Pinto. Austin: U of Texas P, 1991. 105-22.

Gliemmo, Graciela. "Margo Glantz." In her *Las huellas de la memoria: entrevistas a escritores latinoamericanos.* Buenos Aires: Beas Ediciones, 1994. 41-55.

—. "La transgresión que no cesa. Charla con la escritora mexicana Margo Glantz." *Feminaria* 3.6 (1990): 36-37.

Miller, Beth. "Margo Glantz." In her *A la sombra del volcán: conversaciones sobre la narrativa mexicana actual.* México, D.F.: Universidad de Guadalajara-Xalli/Universidad Veracruzana/ Consejo Nacional para la Cultura y las Artes/Instituto Nacional de Bellas Artes, 1990. 69-85.

Pfeiffer, Erna. "Tenemos que reescribir el mundo: Margo Glantz." In her *EntreVistas: diez escritoras mexicanas desde bastidores.* Frankfurt am Main: Vervuert Verlag, 1992. 91-111.

Valdivieso, Mercedes. "Conversación con Margo Glantz." *Literatura chilena: creación y crítica* 9.1 (Jan.-Mar. 1985): 32-34.

                                                        Salvador Oropesa

GLICKMAN, NORA (Argentina; 1944)

Nora Glickman was born in La Pampa, Argentina, and studied in Israel, England, and in the United States. She is the author of two books of short stories: *Uno de sus Juanes* (One of Her Johns; 1983) and *Mujeres, memorias, malogros* (Women, Memories, Failures; 1991), as well as other fictional pieces which have appeared in many journals and anthologies and have been translated into English, Hebrew, and Portuguese. Several of her plays have been presented on the stage in the United States, and dramatic readings have been held in several countries. She is a professor of Spanish at Queens College of New York and lives in the suburban neighborhood of Scarsdale.

Glickman is also a prolific critic and has written extensively on contemporary Latin American literature, with special emphasis on Argentine theatre and narrative. Her doctoral dissertation research on "The Jewish Image in Brazilian and Argentine Literature" (1972) led to further critical studies, including her book *La trata de blancas* (The White Slave Trade; 1984) that includes a translation from Yiddish of Leib Malach's play *Regeneración* (Regeneration). Glickman edited two volumes of *Modern Jewish Studies* devoted to Argentine fiction and criticism (1993), co-edited with Robert DiAntonio a volume of critical essays entitled *Tradition and Innovation: Reflections on Latin American Jewish Writing* (1993), and she co-edited with Gloria Waldman the volume, *Argentine Jewish Theatre: A Critical Anthology* (1996). Her third collection of short stories entitled *Clavel tempranero* (Early Carnation) is scheduled for publication in the near future.

Uno de sus Juanes is a collection of eighteen short stories that recreate the Argentinian and New York worlds experienced by the author. Glickman tries to achieve an integration of different modes of perception. Rather than imposing lengthy explanations of people and events, these short stories express memory and referential reality in brief flashes, mixing autobiography and fiction, reconstructing the complexity of experience. Her short stories here cover a variety of subjects and themes, they deal with women's issues and a palimpsest of cultural scenarios and worlds. Different events and scenes overlap; they reproduce pictures of the past where several cultural attitudes prevail. The settings are Argentina and the United States, where the author resides. The Argentinean tales are written from the perspective of the Jewish immigration. Through the representation of rural life the author examines psychological traits of the farmers, their lives and problems. There is a clear distinction between male and female roles. Women from different social classes are presented as mothers and daughters, and there is a definite feminist perspective: women are strong and capable of having erotic fantasies within their assigned spaces, men have more access to public spaces and are more free to come and go as they please. The tales create a documentary of life in the country and of the protagonists' revelations of experience. Children, adolescents and adults expose a world of warmth, laughter and carefree games, their adult realities are woven by fantasies of acculturation, love and gender identification. The short stories that take place in United States deal with the professional academic experiences of women. These short stories project a parodic stance; life and the world are full of absurdity and misunderstandings. The academic code and the rituals associated with it, like looking or advertising for a job match the absurdity of the society at large. Irony is directed towards a criticism of human behavior and certain constants of female knowledge and attitudes. Other tales analyze family dynamics, particularly male-female tensions, from a woman's point of view. They present mother and daughter conflicts, married and single women; in each tale a woman struggles to control her environment and to assert her rights as she perceives them. Women are trapped in their social roles and learn to survive their marginal roles. The author has said that the concept of voyeurism has always fascinated her and that several of the stories in *Uno de sus Juanes* partake of that fantasy. If Don Juan was a man of many women, the protagonist of the collection is a woman of many Juanes, thus reversing the familiar roles.

In *Mujeres, memorias, malogros*, her second book of short stories, Glickman has kept her intimate and confidential tone. The book is divided into three parts and is reminiscent of her first collection. The stories evoke Jewish-Argentine life in the Pampas showing the rural immigrant population. These stories are like a family album, very lyrical at times, full of sensations and emotions that represent the hidden world of the author. The Pampa landscape brings together beings and objects, they are nostalgic souvenirs of times past. Glickman's original voice discovers once more the time of childhood and adolescence, confronts the present of maturity and implied roles. Another group of stories features a more satirical rendering of daily existence: urban, suburban, and campus varieties. Contemporary living produces a contrast to the idyllic past, life in the cities is more frenetic and almost unworkable. To combat the absurdities of modern life the protagonists establish solidarity with other women. *Mujeres, memorias, malogros* ends with some self-reflective texts about the nature of writing and the conflictive relationship experienced by the author. These stories, some of them very brief, are filled with humor.

Glickman's narrative anticipates her inclinations as a playwright: her prose reflects a direct and oral language that we usually associate with the theater. Glickman's love for the theater was awakened in childhood when her parents took her periodically to Buenos Aires to see plays, including Yiddish theatre. She has written several plays. The first one, *Noticias de suburbio* (Suburban News; 1993) is about the experience of being Hispanic and living in a suburb of New York, of surviving in two cultures, and of coming to terms with a white,

Anglo-Saxon culture. The main character Alicia, is a young Argentine divorcee, mother of two children, who after fifteen years in the United States is not sure anymore in what language she dreams. Her language has become a hybrid "Spanglish." Karen, Alicia's American neighbor, is aggressive, ambitious, and determined to protect and guide her friend. Alicia wants to start a new life and is looking for someone that will help her with the house and children. Alicia combines characteristics of a suburbanite American lifestyle with a Latino temperament: she is disorganized, unpunctual, easily distracted, always overwhelmed. After a long search, she finds the person she needs, an illegal immigrant named Magdalena. At first, Alicia tries to teach Magdalena, the maid, how to take her place as a housekeeper and mother. But it is only thanks to Magdalena that Alicia can become a "liberated" woman and rediscover cultural affinities with her neglected Latin American roots. Magdalena brings along with her what she calls a "survival kit" for her life in exile. While Alicia is addicted to soap operas out of boredom, Magda's real life stories surpass the melodrama presented on the screen. When both women create a company called "ALIMAGDA," Magdalena turns out to be the more enterprising of the two and has to deal with modern technology (the computer).

In *Noticias de suburbio*, Glickman presents once more her feminist views and perspectives. She brings to the play a real sisterhood, a community of women that crosses the boundaries of class. The harmonious society projected may be utopian, but it is essentially a realistic play, closer to the way people try to succeed in United States. What is interesting is the way in which Glickman combines the exploration of women's subjetivity with a group solidarity that inspires resistence and activism. It is a project that brings hope of change in the future while revealing the traditional roles assigned to women in the family.

A Day in New York is a play based in one of Glickman's short stories. A Hispanic college lecturer spends her day commuting between various colleges, while she listens to books on tape in her car, Voltaire's *Candide* in particular. The plot is mixed with the lives of Holocaust survivors living in New York. One of them, a woman named Golda, interrupts lectures with paranoid mind lapses from the past and present, from concrete memories of the white slave trade to chaotic recollections. The main character of the play is trying to make some sense of her life but the day is long and full of experiences. At two o'clock in the morning she goes to a large supermarket that is open twenty-four hours and finds some comfort from the tumultuous day of surviving in New York.

Una tal Raquel Liberman (A Certain Raquel Liberman; 1994), is a play based on the life of the Polish immigrant who denounced the white slave trade in Argentina in the 1930s. The author based her drama in authentic documents:

letters and other testimonies found in Buenos Aires. It is a play that condemns the slave trade and exploitation of women. Inspired by a real-life story, it engages the reader's participation in uncovering the parts of this historical puzzle.

In her works, Glickman creates a mixture of several cultures and identities. She translates her experience as a Latin American Jewish woman into a personal and distinctive mode of expression. She combines in her writings different attitudes and feelings mixed with her own spaces and desires, overflowing with hidden mysteries.

PRIMARY BIBLIOGRAPHY
Creative Writing

"Los años de varón." *Discurso literario* 2.2 (1985): 403-11.

"Autopistas," "Mis otras hijas." *Confluencia* 4.1 (1988): 173.

"Los Bécquer." *Linden Lane Magazine* 2 (April, 1982): 10-12.

"A Day in New York." In *In Other Words: Literature by Latinas of the United States*. Ed. Roberta Fernández. Houston: Arte Público Press, 1994. 424-32.

A Day in New York. Unpublished play, 1994.

"The Last Emigrant." Trans. by John Benson. *Short Stories by Latin American Women: The Magic and the Real*. Ed. Celia Correas de Zapata. Houston: Arte Público Press, 1990. 89-93. Also in *Tropical Synagogues: Short Stories by Jewish-Latin American Writers*. Ed. with introduction by Ilán Stavans. New York: Holmes & Meier, 1994. 90-94.

"Juan manso y salvaje." *Alba de América* 2 (1985): 257-59.

"Mi niño y tú." *Puro cuento* (Argentina) 31 (1994): 5.

Mujeres, memorias, malogros. Buenos Aires: Milá, 1991.

Noticias de suburbio. In *En un acto: antología de teatro femenino latinoamericano*. Medellín, Colombia: University of Antioquia Press, 1995. 152-70.

"Puesto vacante." *The Bilingual Review/La revista bilingüe* 9 (1973): 27-31.

"El renguito de Hamelín." *Chasqui* 17.1 (1988): 148-51.

"Sonrisa musical." *Abigarrada* 3.6 (1985): 7.

"Tag-sale." *Rocky Mountain Review of Language and Literature* 41.1-2 (1987): 73-75.

"El último de los colonos." In *Cien años de narrativa judeoargentina 1889-1989*. Comp. Ricardo Feierstein. Buenos Aires: Milá, 1990. 368-73.

"El último de los colonos," "Tag-sale," "Dios salve América." *Hispanic Immigrant Writers and the Family*. Ed. Silvio Torres Baillant. New York: Ollantay Press, 1992. 40-56.

Una tal Raquel Liberman. Unpublished play, 1994.

Uno de sus Juanes. Buenos Aires: Ediciones de la Flor, 1983.

Nonfiction

La trata de blancas. Regeneración: drama en cuatro actos de Leib Malaj. Trans. of *Regeneración* from Yiddish by Nora Glickman and Rosalía Rosembuj. Buenos Aires: Pardés, 1984.

Editions

Argentine Jewish Theatre: A Critical Anthology. (Ed. with Gloria Waldman) Lewisburg: Bucknell UP, 1996.

Tradition and Innovation: Reflections on Latin American Jewish Writing, (Ed. with Robert DiAntonio). New York: SUNY Press, 1993.

SECONDARY BIBLIOGRAPHY

Baumgarten, Murray. "Urban Life and Jewish Memory in the Tales of Moacyr Scliar and Nora Glickman." *Tradition and Innovation: Reflections on Latin American Jewish Writing*. Ed. Robert DiAntonio and Nora Glickman. New York: SUNY Press, 1993. 61-72.

Barr, Lois Baer. Rev. of *Uno de sus Juanes*. *Chasqui* 20.2 (1991): 138-39.

Cox, Victoria. "Nora Glickman: Between Several Cultures." *The Buenos Aires Herald* 4 June, 1995: 8.

Lindstrom, Naomi. *Jewish Issues in Argentine Literature: From Gerchunoff to Szichman*. Columbia: U of Missouri P, 1989. 41, 46, 79-80.

—. Rev. of *Mujeres, memorias, malogros. World Literature Today* 65.4 (1991): 675.

Lockhart, Darrell B. Rev. of *Mujeres, memorias, malogros. Chasqui* 21.1 (1992): 123.

Martínez, Elena. "La problemática de la mujer en los textos de Julia Ortiz Griffin, Mireya Robles y Nora Glickman." In *New Voices in Latin American Literature*. Ed. Miguel Falquez-Certain. New York: Ollantay Press, 1993. 186-205.

—. Rev. of *Mujeres, memorias, malogros. Letras femeninas* 18.1-2 (1992): 169-72.

Schiminovich, Flora. "*Noticias de suburbio*: una visión utópica de relación entre mujeres." In *En un acto: antología de teatro femenino latinoamericano*. Medellín, Colombia: University of Antioquia Press, 1995. 146-52.

Torres-Baillant, Silvio. *Hispanic Immigrant Writers and the Family*. New York: Ollantay Press, 1994. 40-42, 87-93.

Flora Schiminovich

GOLDEMBERG, ISAAC (Peru; 1945)

Isaac Goldemberg, a noted poet and novelist, was born in Chepén, a small town in northern Peru, on November 15, 1945. Having lived with his mother's family and Catholic tradition for eight years, he left for Lima, his father, and a newly acquired Jewish identity at the age of eight. To say that Goldemberg's life is the stuff of fiction is doubly true, for not only is it richly complex and exceptional in its diversity but it also becomes the basis for his poetic and narrative endeavors. The journeys and the tales of adaptation that he recounts are brilliant re-creations of his personal history, which he calls on at least one occasion a fragmented life. After graduating from high school, Goldemberg spent two years in Israel, and following a brief return to Peru, he traveled to New York City, where he has lived since 1964. He studied at the University of Madrid, City College of New York, and New York University. He taught for a number of years at NYU, and he frequently gives lectures and readings of his works. Goldemberg is the author of two novels, *La vida a plazos de don Jacobo Lerner* (1978; first published in English translation as *The Fragmented Life of Don Jacobo Lerner*; 1976) and *Tiempo al tiempo* (*Play by Play*; 1984). His poetic works include *Tiempo de silencio* (Time of Silence; 1969), *De Chepén a La Habana* (From Chepén to Havana; 1973), the bilingual *Hombre de paso / Just Passing Through* (1981), and *La vida al contado* (Life in Cash; 1992). His dramatization of the poetry of César Vallejo (1892-1938), entitled *To Express My Life I Have Only My Death*, premiered Off-Off Broadway in 1968.

While Goldemberg is an assimilated Jew living in one of the multicultural capitals of the world, his writings show a strong interest in the role of the outsider in search of identity. His characters are often intensely marginalized, fighting for legitimacy against the odds. The protagonists of his novels—on radically different versions of life's journey—can never break the ties that bind them to a distant and tortured past. *La vida a plazos de don Jacobo Lerner* and *Tiempo al tiempo* are bittersweet chronicles of the margins of society and thus of events that rarely make their way into history. The poetic speakers, in contrast, use their medium not as message but as a means of self-discovery, of self-validation. The very expression of alterity, in essence the positing of a voice, acts as an instrument for defining and legitimizing the self.

From a structural perspective, *La vida a plazos de don Jacobo Lerner* is arguably Goldemberg's most ambitious work. The narrative focuses on the experiences of a Russian Jewish immigrant in Lima during the 1920s and 1930s. The novelist gives his protagonist a precarious centrality, however, by presenting

Don Jacobo Lerner's self and circumstance through the perspectives of other characters and through the chronicles of his time, including the *Alma Hebrea*, the newspaper of the Jewish community in Lima. Jacobo Lerner has no voice in the text; his status as outsider extends to the literary work into which he is inscribed. Even his thoughts are rendered diegetically, that is, mediated through a narrative persona. The immigrant seeks to confirm, or to reinvent, his identity in a hostile environment, and the search is recorded in a document that approaches its subject indirectly. In poststructuralist parlance, the novel offers a deferred look at Don Jacobo, through the commentaries of his illegitimate son, a close friend and fellow merchant, his sister-in-law, his one-time mistress, and indeed more opaquely, through chronicles of events and clippings from the *Alma Hebrea*.

Here, as in Goldemberg's work in general, the major theme is dislocation, the plight of the Jew in the Diaspora. Leaving a homeland that was never really home, Jacobo Lerner finds himself in a strange land, at loose ends in social, religious, economic, and linguistic terms, increasingly relegated to the margins. His story is significant and symbolic. While some of his fellow Jews may achieve greater success in the New World, the novel points in poignant fashion to the ironies of assimilation. Jacobo Lerner and his landsmen reveal that it is undeniably difficult to be true to oneself and to keep the faith while endeavoring to demonstrate patriotism toward a new country and a new way of life. The Jewish community is defined, after all, by difference, and these particular wandering Jews remain in a state of eternal transition. Some may come closer than others to the elusive center that is mainstream society, but there is always a distance between emulation and acceptance. By emphasizing varieties of discourse, Goldemberg makes language an analogue of the transitional process, whereby the individual is neither the former self nor the (paradoxically phrased) desired other. The discursive fragments, like the fragmented life, bespeak an inescapable foreignness. At the same time, the New World encounters of the homeless Jews establish a link with a peripatetic tradition, to suggest a type of patriotism without *patria*. Within this scheme, Jacobo Lerner functions as an unlikely father figure, yet the incongruity of this emblematic role is hardly inappropriate.

Tiempo al tiempo is a rewriting of sorts of the earlier novel. The focal figure is, like Jacobo Lerner, an outcast, but Marquitos Karushansky Avila is in a different stage of his life, more reminiscent perhaps of Lerner's son Efraín (and thus of Goldemberg himself). Raised by his Peruvian mother to the age of twelve, Marquitos discovers his Jewish identity as he leaves the provinces to live in the city with his father. The guiding motif of *Tiempo al tiempo* is soccer, in which Marquitos excels. In two parts or "halves," a narrator elaborates the stages of the protagonist's life as if he were announcing a game in the National Stadium in Lima. The reader suffers with Marquitos as he endures the trials of isolation, both in a Jewish school for boys and in a Catholic military academy (León Pinelo and Leoncio Prado, respectively, the two schools attended by Goldemberg himself). A colleague from each of the schools describes Marquitos's ordeals, and once again Goldemberg creates a narrative correlative of social marginalization by excluding the protagonist from the narration proper. After his expulsion from the academy, Marquitos disappears, showing up later in Israel during the conflict of 1967, only to die tragically.

As in the case of Jacobo Lerner, Marquitos Karushansky Avila is depicted as both individualized and representative. His position represents an especially awkward middle ground between Old World Judaism and provincial Peruvian Catholicism. This makes his predicament unique, but only in degree, for he symbolizes those deemed inferior by blood or by racial (or ethnic) mix. Goldemberg chooses to convert the rite of circumcision and the phallic intensity of Marquitos's conflicts in the two schools—together with the sexual connotations of the ballgame that serves as frame—into signs of difference, of public scrutiny, and ultimately of oppression. It is not easy to be a Jew and a Peruvian, to bear slings and arrows from two genealogical directions. Goldemberg foregrounds the historical destiny of Marquitos Karushansky by placing data from biblical, local, national, and international sources at the bottom of many pages, as if to intimate that over five thousand years and innumerable encounters with fate were the tie that binds the Jewish people.

Of the four poetry collections, *Hombre de paso / Just Passing Through*, with English translations by Goldemberg and David Unger, is by virtue of its bilingualism an obvious vehicle through which to capture the varied traditions that inform the lyric persona. Yiddish, Quechua, Castilian, and points in between provide linguistic options, just as rabbis, Inca chieftains, Spanish conquistadors, and grey-bearded peddlers, like fish out of water, commingle. The prayers of Bar Mitzvah and Yom Kippur burst forth in the land of Wiracocha. Goldemberg's is a private voice made public, and, with Unger's, a collaborative voice. There seems to be, in poetic composition, a recognition of shared experience, of something akin to intertextuality on an existential plane. The poet shares his search for the self with numerous predecessors, thereby marking the ironies of solitude and of difference. *Hombre de paso*, like *La vida al contado*, repeats a number of poems from the earlier collections. The poet demonstrates a strong technique, a succinct and cryptic form of expression, a secure sense of self, and as would follow, a pronounced sense of humor. The examination of his roots and of his identity is necessarily self-directed but never egotistical, energized as it is by inward and outward movement, from his soul to the spirit of this people, a term that has a comprehensive and deep meaning.

La vida al contado opens with a brief autobiographical sketch in which Goldemberg charts his literary trajectory. He notes that from 1985 to 1988 he made four trips to Peru, where he renewed ties with family and friends, where he fell in love with a childhood friend, and where, for the first time, he began to write love poetry. Among the writers who have most inspired his own works, he cites César Vallejo, Ciro Alegría (1909-67), and José María Arguedas (1911-69), together with Jorge Luis Borges (1899-1986) and Franz Kafka (1883-1924).

PRIMARY BIBLIOGRAPHY
Creative Writing

De Chepén a La Habana. New York: Editorial Bayú-Menoráh, 1973.

Hombre de paso / Just Passing Through. Trans. by David Unger and Isaac Goldemberg. Hanover, NH: Ediciones del Norte, 1981.

Tiempo al tiempo. Hanover, NH: Ediciones del Norte, 1984. English version as *Play by Play.* Trans. by Hardie St. Martin. New York: Persea Books, 1984.

Tiempo de silencio. Colección de Poesía Hispanoamericana. Palencia, Spain: Colón, 1969.

La vida al contado. Hanover, NH: Ediciones del Norte, 1992. Also, Lima: Lluvia Editores, 1992.

La vida a plazos de don Jacobo Lerner. Lima: Libre 1, 1978. Also, Hanover, NH: Ediciones del Norte, 1980. English version as *The Fragmented Life of Don Jacobo Lerner.* Trans. by Robert S. Picciotto. New York: Persea Books, 1976.

Nonfiction

"Crónicas/genealogías/cronologías." *Hispamérica* 14.42 (1985): 73-78. English version as "On Being a Writer in Peru and Other Places." Trans. by David Unger. In *Lives on the Line: The Testimony of Contemporary Latin American Authors.* Ed. with introduction by Doris Meyer. Berkeley/Los Angeles: U of California P, 1988. 300-5.

SECONDARY BIBLIOGRAPHY
Criticism

Barr, Lois Baer. "Unbinding the Ties: Isaac Goldemberg." In her *Isaac Unbound: Patriarchal Traditions in the Latin American Jewish Novel.* Tempe, AZ: ASU Center for Latin American Studies, 1995. 11-31.

Friedman, Edward H. "Marginal Narrative: Levels of Discourse in Isaac Goldemberg's *La vida a plazos de don Jacobo Lerner.*" *Chasqui* 11.1 (1981): 13-20. Reprinted in *Modern Jewish Studies* Annual V [*Yiddish* 5.4] (1984): 72-81.

—. "The Novel as Revisionist History: Art as Process in Mario Szichman's *A las 20:25 la señora entró en la inmortalidad* and Isaac Goldemberg's *Tiempo al tiempo.*" *Modern Jewish Studies* 8.2 (1993): 24-33.

Mirkin, Zulema. "Polifonía narrativa y visión del mundo en *La vida a plazos de don Jacobo Lerner.*" *Alba de América* 3.4-5 (1985): 71-79.

Nouhaud, Dorita. "Notre Père si êtes aux cieux." *Cahiers du Centre d'Etudes et du Recherches sur les Littéraires de l'Imaginaire* 9 (1984): 43-52. [on *Jacobo Lerner*]

Roses, Lorraine E. "Isaac Goldemberg." In *Spanish American Authors: The Twentieth Century.* Ed. Angel Flores. New York: The H. W. Wilson Company, 1992. 374-77.

—. "El lector como jurado: el monólogo interior en *La vida a plazos de don Jacobo Lerner.*" *Dispositio: revista hispánica de semiótica literaria* 2.1 (1984): 225-32.

Rosser, Harry L. "Being and Time in *La vida a plazos de don Jacobo Lerner.*" *Chasqui* 17.1 (1988): 43-49.

Schneider, Judith Morganroth. "Cultural Meanings in Isaac Goldemberg's Fiction." *Folio* 17 (1987): 43-49.

Tittler, Jonathan. "*The Fragmented Life of Don Jacobo Lerner*: The Esthetics of Fragmentation." In his *Narrative Irony in the Contemporary Spanish-American Novel.* Ithaca: Cornell UP, 1984. 172-85.

Interviews

Gazarian Gautier, Marie-Lise. "Isaac Goldemberg." In her *Interviews with Latin American Writers.* Normal, IL: Dalkey Archive Press, 1989. 131-54.

Stavans, Ilán. "Judaísmo y letras latinoamericanas: entrevista a Isaac Goldemberg." *Folio* 17 (1987): 141-50.

Edward H. Friedman

GOLDENBERG, JORGE (Argentina; 1941)

Goldenberg came to prominence when he won the 1975 Cuban Casa de las Américas Prize (the Latin American Pulizter) in theater for *Relevo 1923*

(Changing of the Guard 1923). Goldenberg, in the documentary theatrical tradition of Helmut Hochhuth (1931) and Peter Weiss (1916-82) in Germany and Vicente Leñero (1932) in Mexico, deals in *Relevo 1923* with the assassination of a military leader by a foreign radical anarchist during the labor uprisings in Argentina's Patagonia in the 1920s. For Goldenberg the "drama" is the historical event itself, an event that the "play" both represents and interprets. Beginning with several Brechtian procedures to call attention to the theatricalness of the play, actors who appear as actors (rather than as dramatis personae) undertake first to reenact in a documentary fashion the events of the 1921 assassination and the 1923 killing of the original assassin, and then to enact in nondocumentary fashion several hypothetical confrontations between the protagonists of the historical events and an *inquiridor* (inquiror), who is, in a sense, the devil's advocate of history, intent upon laying bare the human and social meanings of the events in question. The result is several levels of documentariness: the dramatic event, the reenactment of the event as part of the play, the hypothetical confrontations from the perspective of historical inquisitiion, and, finally, the structure of the play itself as a coordination of the preceding elements into a text of broader sociohistorical value as literary commentary. In this play and others, Goldenberg established himself as a pivotal figure in Argentine theater in the utilization of archival material and its presentation as such in a documentary format. Of particular note is the earlier *Argentine Quebracho Company* (1972) and the later *Cartas de Moreno* (Letters from Moreno; 1987), the latter dealing with one of the Argentine founding fathers, who died mysteriously at sea.

Goldenberg's most notable other play, however, is *Knepp* (1983), one of the major plays of the return to democracy in Argentina; it was performed during the first year of the new democratic government in the country's major state theater, Buenos Aires's Teatro Municipal General San Martín. Knepp is the embodiment of the impersonal apparatus of state terror, and Goldenberg uses him to weave a complex pattern of how terror, dictatorship, torture, disappearances, and the collaboration of victims with their own oppression is possible in a presumedly modern, sophisticated, and progressive society. In this sense, it is an important document in what has come to be viewed as the imperative to question the ideology of modernism in Latin America, which brings with it both the need for and the legitimation of the police state whose existence is beyond the realm of the knowledge and the control of even a putatively informed citizenry.

Goldenberg's most specifically Jewish work is *Krinsky* (1986). The play is the evocation of the figure of Adolfo Krinsky, an eccentric Russian immigrant who worked as a librarian in a Jewish center in San Martín, the author's birthplace and a suburb northwest of Buenos Aires. A loner and a bachelor, Krinsky's body was discovered several days after his death in his shabby apartment; he was wearing his everyday raggedy overcoat, but it was discovered that the coat was lined with banknotes. Goldenberg uses these evocative facts, virtual commonplaces of the lives of unassimilated immigrants, to dramatize both the question of cultural and ethnic clash and the inevitable dissolution of Jewish immigrant folk society in the hegemonic context of modern Argentina. The text is organized around a series of vignettes, and Krinsky is, without his intending to be such, made into a spokesperson of cultural memory, cultural conflict, and cultural disappearance. Written at a time in which Jewish cultural and intellectual figures felt especially constrained to account for anti-Semitism in Argentina (both as part of the specific texture of neofascist military dictatorships and as an integral part of Argentine modernity), *Krinsky* turns on the principal issue of what value remembering the past might have, a proposition that has broad implications when we recall that the report of the official government commission on the disappeared has the Holocaust-evoking title of *Nunca más* (Never More; 1984 [published in English in 1986 with the Spanish title]) and the imperatives to remember that such an allusion implies.

Although Goldenberg's theater does not as a whole deal with Jewish themes, where his production does overlap significantly with Argentine Jewish culture is in the interpretation of sociohistorical events and the establishment of resonances between recent occurrences and those of the past. Goldenberg has also worked extensively with another dramatist, Oscar Viale (1932), on film scripts, one of the most notable being Juan José Jusid's *Los gauchos judíos* (The Jewish Gauchos; 1975), based on Alberto Gerchunoff's 1910 romantic and assimilationist narrative of Jewish immigrants in the nineteenth century in Argentina's Mesopotamia region. Unfortunately, despite the high profile of major figures from the Argentine Jewish creative community, Jusid's film lacks precisely the hard documentary dimension that characterizes Goldenberg's major dramatic works. Goldenberg also worked with María Luisa Bemberg on the script for *De eso no se habla* (I Don't Want to Talk about It; 1993), a film starring Marcelo Mastroiani.

PRIMARY BIBLIOGRAPHY

Cartas a Moreno. Buenos Aires: Teatro Municipal General San Martín, 1987.
  Bound with Marisel Lloberas Chavalier, *Acordate de la Francisca*.
Fifty-fifty. *Tramoya* (1ra época) 12 (Jul-Sep, 1978): 91-128.
Knepp. In *Teatro argentino contemporáneo: antología*. Madrid: Centro de Documentación Teatral, Ministerio de Cultura; Sociedad Estatal Quinto Centenario; Fondo de Cultura Económica, 1992. 951-1011.

Krinsky. Buenos Aires: Ediciones de Arte Gaglianone, 1984. Also Buenos Aires: Teatro Municipal General San Martín, 1986. English version as *Krinsky.* Trans. Nora Glickman and Gloria F. Waldman. In *Argentine Jewish Theatre: A Critical Anthology.* Ed. Nora Glickman and Gloria F. Waldman. Lewisburg: Bucknell UP, 1996. 158-95.

Poniendo la casa en orden. Hispamérica 16.42 (1985): 99-121.

Rajemos, marqués, rajemos. In *El arca de Noé: antología de teatro para niños.* Ed. Emilio Carballido. México, D.F.: Editores Mexicanos Unidos, 1979. 15-54.

Relevo 1923. La Habana: Casa de las Américas, 1975.

SECONDARY BIBLIOGRAPHY
Criticism

Feierstein, Ricardo. "Sonata de espectros." *Nueva presencia* 469 (May 27, 1986): 25-26.

Foster, David William. "*Krinsky* de Jorge Goldenberg y la identidad étnica argentina." *Noaj* 4.5 (1990): 51-54. Also *Latin American Theatre Review* 24.2 (1991): 101-105.

Hacker, Jorge. "El *Krinsky* de Jorge Goldenberg: teatro judío bien escrito." *Nueva Sión* 607 (Dec. 12, 1984): 27.

Ishmael-Bissett, Judith. *The Function of Documentation in Two Latin American Plays:* El juicio *and* Relevo 1923. Tempe: Center for Latin American Studies, Arizona State University, 1976.

Minster, Dina. "Goldenberg y la imagen de la historia." *Nueva Sión* 668 (Nov. 10, 1987): 23.

Monteaguado, Luciano. "El valor de una decisión." *Knepp,* q.v., pp. 953-58.

Østergaard, Ane-Grethe. "*Relevo 1923*: discurso metateatral. Análisis de la enunciación." *Cahiers du Monde Hispanique et Luso-Brésilien/Caravelle* 41 (1983): 63-80.

Pianca, Marina. "Jorge Goldenberg." In her *Testimonios de teatro latinoamericano.* Buenos Aires: Grupo Editor Latinoamericano, 1991. 85-103.

Toro, Fernando de. *Brecht en el teatro hispanoamericano contemporáneo: acercamiento semiótico al teatro épico en Hispanoamérica.* Ottawa: Girol Books, 1984. 208-20.

Weinstein, Ana E., and Miryam E. Gover de Nasatsky, comps. *Escritores judeo-argentinos: bibliografía 1900-1987.* 2 vols. Buenos Aires: Milá, 1994. I.272-74.

Wolf, Sergio. "*Krinsky*, los fantasmas de un judío errante." *Nueva Sión* 641 (July 26, 1986): 25.

Interviews

Morero, Sergio. "Entre el amor y la utopía." *Teatro* (Argentina) 6.26 (1986): 46-55.

Troncone, Carlos. "Fidelidad a los sueños, batalla contra el tiempo." Discussion of *Krinsky* with Jaime Kogan, director. *Teatro* 6.26 (1986): 56-60.

David William Foster

GOLOBOFF, GERARDO MARIO (Argentina; 1939)

Gerardo Mario Goloboff was born in 1939 in Carlos Casares, one of the original agricultural colonies established by the Jewish Colonization Association in the late nineteenth century. Trained as a lawyer, he devoted himself to literature, founding the literary journal *Nuevos Aires* (New Breezes) and writing critical essays on Roberto Arlt (1900-42) and Jorge Luis Borges (1899-1986). In 1993 he attempted to establish his residence in Argentina after twenty years in exile during which he lived and taught literary theory and Latin American Literature at the Universities of Toulouse and Paris-Nanterre.

If Goloboff's collection of poetry, *Entre la diáspora y octubre* (Between the Diaspora and October; 1966), reveals a certain optimism for realizing justice through socialism, the novel, *Caballos por el fondo de los ojos* (Horses in the Depths of Our Eyes; 1976), announces a futility and an obsessive paranoia which refute any possibility of dwelling any place comfortably except perhaps in language. Yet language is also elusive because one cannot capture reality through words. Herman, the protagonist, is caught between the generation who came to Argentina to farm and to prosper and the generation of his son Roberto which so deeply feels Argentine that he joins a terrorist group. He is also torn between his gentile wife and his onetime lover Nora who has made aliyah to Israel. The novel opens with his identification of the son's corpse and ends with Nora's letter of condolence. Goloboff also places Herman in limbo between literary forms—verse, theatrical dialogue, stream of consciousness prose, and third-person omniscient narration.

Goloboff's sense of exile informs all of his work (Senkman 329). His trilogy set in the Pampas town of Algarrobos—an amalgam of fact and fiction surrounding the towns founded by the Jewish agricultural colonists in the late nineteenth century—continues his preoccupation with language, literary form, and with justice. In the first novel, *Criador de palomas* (Dove Breeder; 1988), Algarrobos is at once a primordial Garden of Eden and a mysterious inferno in which evil and mysterious events happen in a random manner and against which there is no protection. Told in the first person by an orphaned Jewish boy, called only El Pibe (the Kid), the novel relates the mysterious deaths of his beloved uncle Negro and his beautiful doves. Imagery of the biblical story of the flood adds an ironic touch as there seems to be no covenant with God, nor any justice for random evil acts. The mutilated doves allude to the systematic violence of Argentina in the turbulent fifties and during the military juntas of the so-called Proceso de Reorganización Nacional (Process of National Reorganization [1976-83]).

In the next novel, *La luna que cae* (The Falling Moon; 1989), Goloboff experiments with second-person narration: a strangely omniscient narrator addresses El Pibe, now a twenty-three-year-old, and Rosa, the former lover of one of Tío Negro's friends. This novel marks the young man's return to Algarrobos after an unexplained absence to learn more about his past and about his uncle's mysterious death. Rosa and El Pibe share a brief liaison which serves as a refuge from the violent society in which they live. El Pibe turns to a psychic and oral historian from a closeby town, the Dream Man from Smith, in order to find some answers, but the enigmatic man does not reveal very much. A poetic novel, this work explores the feminine aspects of life unlike the first one which emphasized male-bonding.

In the final novel, *El soñador de Smith* (The Dream Man from Smith; 1990), the narration is told in the third person allowing the Dream Man's words to be told directly in first person. The rhythm of the story is purposely plodding, and the atmosphere has the torpor of a humid summer afternoon after a heavy meal. The psychic's obesity renders him immobile, but the world comes to him for advice and information. Gatina comes because she wants to bury the bodies of the dead found in Sigal's well. She is thwarted by the rest of the community which views her as a crazy woman. As Nora Glickman points out, her name, a rough anagram of Antigone, links her to the moral necessity to honor the dead. El Pibe leaves the Soñador's farm as floodwaters surround the house. He has learned a great deal about his uncle's past, but he still has no conclusive information about Tío Negro's death.

In his latest novel, *Comuna Verdad* (Truth Commune; 1995), Goloboff returns to the same town, although it is not part of the Algarrobos trilogy. The novel is based on historical fact and in an epilogue to the text Goloboff reveals the sources for the information and characters it presents. The plot revolves around a group of Italian and Jewish immigrants who form an anarchist commune on the outskirts of town where their mainstay is the production of salt. Their utopia comes to a quick and violent end with the military coup d'etat of 1943. The novel presents an interesting and rather obsure episode in the nation's history. Like his previous works, this is a higly lyrical novel.

Goloboff's carefully crafted fiction deals with the identity crisis of the Jewish intellectual. Taking refuge in the hermetically sealed world of language ("Restos de Bitácora" [Remains of the Binnacle; 1986]), the author realizes how fragile and defenseless that world is. Over and over in Goloboff's fiction, the issues of good and evil, of violence and injustice are addressed. His Algarrobos trilogy, particularly *El criador de palomas*, contributes mightily to the literature of the so-called Dirty War. His subtle, economical, and poetic prose integrate European (with particular resonances from the Spanish Generations of 1898 and 1927), Yiddish, and Gaucho influences to form a fascinating hybrid.

PRIMARY BIBLIOGRAPHY
Creative Writing
Caballos por el fondo de los ojos. Barcelona: Planeta, 1976. Excerpt in English
    translation by David Pritchard. In *Echad: An Anthology of Latin American Jewish Writings.* Ed. Robert and Roberta Kalechofsky. Marblehead, MA: Micah Publications, 1980. 13-15.
Criador de palomas. Buenos Aires: Bruguera, 1984. Barcelona: Muchnik, 1989.
Comuna Verdad. Madrid: Anaya & Mario Muchnik, 1995.
Entre la diáspora y octubre. Buenos Aires: Stilcograf, 1966.
La luna que cae. Barcelona: Muchnik, 1989.
"La pasión según San Martín." *Caravelle* 33 (1979): 187-92. Also in *Cuentos judíos latinoamericanos.* Ed. Ricardo Feierstein. Buenos Aires: Milá, 1989. 168-74. English version as "The Passion According to San Martín." Trans. by Ilán Stavans. In *Tropical Synagogues: Short Stories by Jewish-Latin American Writers.* Ed. Ilán Stavans. New York: Holmes & Meier, 1994. 83-89.
El Soñador de Smith. Barcelona: Muchnik, 1990.
Nonfiction
"Una experiencia literaria de la identidad judía." *Insula: revista de letras y ciencias humanas* 47.549-550 (1992): 9-11.
Genio y figura de Roberto Arlt. Buenos Aires: Editorial Universitaria de Buenos Aires (EUDEBA), 1988.
Leer Borges. Buenos Aires: Huemul, 1978.

"Las lenguas del exilio." In *Literatura argentina hoy: de la dictadura a la democracia.* Ed. Karl Kohut and Andrea Pagni. Frankfurt am Main: Vervuert Verlag, 1989. 135-40.

"Nuestra Babel." *Noaj* 1.1 (1987): 72-75.

"Restos de Bitácora." *Teoría del discurso poético.* Travaux de l'Université de Toulouse-Le Mirail. (Série A 37) (1986): 87-89.

SECONDARY BIBLIOGRAPHY

Criticism

Aizenberg, Edna. "Parricide in the Pampa: Deconstructing Gerchunoff and his Jewish Gauchos." *Folio* 17 (1987): 24-39.

—. "The Writing of the disaster: Gerardo Mario Goloboff's *Criador de palomas.*" *Inti* 28 (1988): 67-73.

Barr, Lois Baer. "Noah in the Pampas: A Trilogy. Gerardo Mario Goloboff." In her *Isaac Unbound: Patriarchal Traditions in the Latin American Jewish Novel.* Tempe, AZ: ASU Center for Latin American Studies, 1995. 107-30.

—. "Noah in the Pampas: Syncretism in Goloboff's *Criador de palomas.*" In *Tradition and Innovation: Reflections on Latin American Jewish Writing.* Ed. Robert DiAntonio and Nora Glickman. Albany: SUNY Press, 1993. 125-34.

—. Rev. of *La luna que cae. Noaj* 4.5 (1990): 113-15.

Gilberto de León, Olver. "Un mítico viaje hacia la infancia." *La Prensa* 8 Dec. 1985; Suplemento dominical: 3.

Glickman, Nora. "Discovering Self in History: Aída Bortnik and Gerardo Mario Goloboff." In *The Jewish Diaspora in Latin America: New Studies on History and Literature.* Ed. David Sheinin and Lois Baer Barr. New York: Garland, 1996. 61-73.

—. Rev. of *El Soñador de Smith. World Literature Today* 66.1 (Winter 1992): 96-97.

Gutiérrez Girardot, Rafael. "La tierra prometida: la trilogía novelística de Gerardo Mario Goloboff." *Hispamérica* 21.62 (1992): 111-26.

Renard, María Adela. Rev. of *Criador de palomas. La Prensa* 3 Feb. 1985: Sec. 1, 11.

Senkman, Leonardo. "Goloboff: The Creation of a Mythical Town." *Yiddish* 9.1 (1993): 105-10.

—. *La identidad judía en la literatura argentina.* Buenos Aires: Pardés, 1983. 329-37.

Sosnowski, Saúl. "Gerardo Mario Goloboff: hacia el décimo mes en la diáspora."
La orilla inminente: escritores judíos argentinos. Buenos Aires: Legasa,
1987. 69-111.

Taffetani, Oscar. "El poder de la ficción." *La Razón* 13 Oct., 1985; Cultura:
10-11.

Weinstein, Ana E., and Miryam E. Gover de Nasatsky, comps. *Escritores judeo-
argentinos: bibliografía 1900-1987*. 2 vols. Buenos Aires: Milá, 1994.
I.275-79.

Interviews

"Entrevista a Gerardo Mario Goloboff." *Noaj* 2.2 (1988): 96-100.

Isod, Liliana. "No sería quien soy y no escribiría como escribo si no fuese judío." *Mundo israelita* 3311 (May 22, 1987): 6.

Senkman, Leonardo. "Escribir para buscar los orígenes de los enigmas que nos
acosan." *Nueva Sión* 598 (July 20, 1984): 23-24.

Lois Baer Barr

GRAIVER, BERNARDO (Argentina; 1902-83)

Graiver was active during the years of the Teatro Independiente (Independent Theater) in the period 1930-1940 as an actor, director, and dramatist; he
also wrote poetry and fiction.

Graiver's *El hijo del rabino* (The Rabbi's Son; 1932) is a paradigmatic
text of the cultural conflicts in Argentina during the first half of this century
when the Jewish community began to participate more fully in Argentine public
life and to mingle with the dominant non-Jewish society. These conflicts were
exacerbated by the economic crisis of the 1930s and the attendant breakdown in
institutional life, which led to an emphasis on Catholic nationalism with strong
and evident ties to German fascism and its anti-Semitism. Graiver's work joins
texts by César Tiempo (pseud. of Israel Zeitlin [1906-80]) and Samuel Eichelbaum (1894-1967) in making use of the very public space of theater to explore
Jewish/gentile conflicts and to defend Jewish cultural identity; this practice will
be continued in subsequent decades by José Rabinovich (1903-79), Germán
Rozenmacher (1936-71), and Osvaldo Dragún (1929).

Graiver's play is notably strident, and it essentially uses its characters
as antagonists in a religious debate in which the respective families of the new

parents David (Jewish) and Luisa (Catholic) argue over religious rights to their newborn son. David and Luisa are bystanders in the debate between the former's father, a rabbi, and the latter's uncle, a bishop, with each adducing reasons of spiritual sovereignty. The Rabbi scores the best points, which, however, certainly must have served to alienate touchy spectators and a conservative press. Moreover, the decision by the protagonist and his wife to remain nonreligious and to raise their son as neither a Catholic nor a Jew, but to allow him to choose his own religion cannot have been to the liking of either traditional Catholics or traditional Jews in the Argentina of the 1930s. Graiver has his characters speak primarily in verbal formulas that promote conventional or folk wisdom as though it were absolute truth. It is against this verbal backdrop of conventional wisdom that David's and Luisa's interpretation of their personal and social imperative with respect to their newborn son becomes compelling as an appeal to the audience to accept a new shared wisdom of religious ecumenicalism. As David says at the end of the play, "Here we respect all beliefs" (35), an assertion that, to a great extent, is true in contemporary Argentina. Judaism remains essentially conservative and the Catholic Church continues to be committedly pre-Vatican II, with the result that religious cultural identity is weaker in that country than probably any other nation of Latin America.

PRIMARY BIBLIOGRAPHY
Creative Writing
Ene está desnuda. Buenos Aires: Nueva Realidad, 1958.

El hijo del rabino. Buenos Aires: Metrópolis, 1930. Also *Argentores; revista teatral* 3.125 (1936): 1-35.

De errores vivimos. Buenos Aires: Voz Viva, 1955.

Magdalena. Buenos Aires: Láinez, 1936.

Las memorias de Juan Gordoni: suicida 901. Buenos Aires: n.p., 1932.

Mensajes de amor y de paz. Buenos Aires: Voz Viva, 1957.

"Minoría selecta." *Claridad* 262 (1933): n.p.

Mujer en la tercera sangre. Buenos Aires: n.p., 1968.

Poemas en serie. 1ra. parte. La Plata, Argentina: n.p., 1926.

Poemas en serie. 2da. parte. La Plata, Argentina: n.p., 1927.

Semsíramis. Buenos Aires: Argonauta, 1949.

Tío Trapo. Buenos Aires: Colombo, 1961.

El último de los profetas. Buenos Aires: n.p., 1928.
Nonfiction
Argentina bíblica y biblónica: historia de la humanidad en la Argentina bíblica y biblónica. Buenos Aires: Albatros, 1980.

El libro de los negativos. Buenos Aires: Anaconda, 1934.

Partida de nacimiento de Cristóbal Colón: español, gallego, sefaradí. With Fernán Mira. Buenos Aires: Meridiano Hispánico, 1976.

SECONDARY BIBLIOGRAPHY

Foster, David William. "Argentine Jewish Dramatists: Aspects of a National Consciousness." *Folio* 17 (1987): 74-103.

—. "Four Argentine-Jewish Dramas of Cultural Conflict." *Modern Jewish Studies* 7.4 (1990): 99-119.

—. "Matrimony and Religious Conflict: Bernardo Graiver's *El hijo del rabino.*" In *Tradition and Innovation: Reflections on Latin American Jewish Writing.* Ed. Robert DiAntonio, and Nora Glickman. Albany: SUNY Press, 1993. 99-106.

Weinstein, Ana E., and Miryam E. Gover de Nasatsky, comps. *Escritores judeo-argentinos: bibliografía 1900-1987.* 2 vols. Buenos Aires: Milá, 1994. I.284-87.

Zayas de Lima, Perla. *Diccionario de autores teatrales argentinos, 1950-1990.* Buenos Aires: Galerna, 1991. 135-36.

David William Foster

GRIMANI, SANTIAGO (Pseud. of Santiago Oscar Grunbaum; Argentina; 1925-88)

Santiago Grimani was born in Trieste, Italy on January 28, 1925. He received his early schooling in Italy before coming to Argentina where he continued his education at the university level in Buenos Aires. He was active in the literary community as both a writer and a critic. Grimani published six works of fiction and one volume of literary criticism. His last work, *Grimanescas* (Grimanesques; 1988), was published in March 1988, the same month he passed away. Grimani twice received the Faja de Honor (Sash of Honor) from the Sociedad Argentina de Escritores (Argentine Writers' Society). As an Italian Jewish immigrant he formed part of a small group of other writers like Humberto Costantini (1924-87) and Clara Weil (1924-85) who shared the same background.

Grimani's early works are all short-story collections which were published within a three-year period: *El fiat verde* (The Green Fiat; 1976), *Un pro-*

blemita color naranja (A Little Orange-Colored Problem; 1976), *Desde Delos en frecuencia modulada* (From Delos in FM; 1978), *Reina negra a rey blanco. ¡Jaque!* (Black Queen to White King. Check!; 1979). The author utilizes a wide array of places, characters, and time periods in his stories which all contribute the creation of highly original, well-developed narratives. One of the principal motifs throughout Grimani's stories is his preoccupation with the common person, especially the marginalized individual. Moreover, his stories are often thought-provoking pieces that entertain while requiring the reader to actively engage in a dialogue with the author through the text. *Reina negra a rey blanco* is clearly one of the best examples of the breadth of Grimani's creative range. The title story opens the volume and in the space of just two pages it presents the issue of race relations as an adult narrator observes the interaction between a white boy (presumable the narrator's son) and a black girl. The second story, "La montaña sin nombre" (The Mountain with No Name) takes the reader to Africa and presents the encounter between the Zulu and Swazi peoples. In "¡Viva Villa!" (Long Live Pancho Villa!) the reader is transported to the heart of the Mexican Revolution. As in his previous volumes, *Reina negra a rey blanco* contains a significant number of stories that present Jewish themes. The story "Golem" takes place in the Prague ghetto with an old rabbi who teaches the secrets of the golem and Jewish mysticism to a high-ranking official. The short parable-like stories grouped under the heading "Mis mejores jasídicos apócrifos" (My Best Apocryphal Hasidic Tales) are humourous pieces in which a lesson is presented in a short tale involving a rabbi. In "La última cruz" (The Last Cross) Grimani depicts Jewish survival in a way that is both moving and horrific. It takes place in the rubble of a Jewish settlement that the Romans have razed to the ground, killing the inhabitants, crucifying many of them and enslaving the survivors. The protagonist, Ruth, crawls from the rubble to view the devastation and discovers a man dying on a cross. She takes pity on him by climbing up to thrust a knife into his throat, but first she impregnates herself before he dies in order to bring new life and ensure survival. *Grimanescas* is a compilation of stories from the previous volumes, together with new material, that are of specifically Jewish content. The brief story "Cuaranta cartonios" (Forty Post Cards) is not only interesting for its content, but also because it is written in Ladino. The volume also contains a short dramatic text titled "Intelectuales judíos, ¡Uníos! (Jewish Intellectuals, Unite!). In the play, subtitled "Un juguete teatral en dos escenas" (A Theatrical Toy in Two Scenes), a group of Jewish intellectuals and writers in Buenos Aires invite the American rabbi of the community to a meeting in the hope of obtaining funds to subvent their publications. When Rabbi Richardson learns of their intent at the meeting he becomes indignant and states "los

[218]), they in turn become angry and throw him out. While it is not a particularly advanced work in terms of dramatic style, in is still quite interesting for the topic it presents.

Los pasillos de la memoria (The Halls of Memory; 1982) is Grimani's lenghty autobiographical novel. It narrates the story of a young boy growing up Jewish in Italy in the 1930s, the rise of fascism, Mussolini, and the Second World War. The novel is tinged with the author's characteristic humor, but it also gives serious treatment to the tragic events that unfold. Grimani's second novel, *La guerilla del cuarto mundo* (The War of the Fourth World; 1983) is more politically satirical and ideologically motivated than *Los pasillos*. Although it is also narrated with humor, it is a darker irony that manifests itself in this novel about a group of guerilla rabbis who plan to overthrow the Israeli government. The novel lends itself to debate and openly challenges many conventional conceptions and ideologies with a wry smile. Grimani leaves few issues untouched by his radical rabbis whose raucous views, opinions, and politics are meant to stimulate a reaction in the reader. In the prologue Ricardo Feierstein warns that many readers will be outraged before reaching the last page (7).

In spite of his numerous works of high artistic quality and his literary awards, Santiago Grimani has not left a lasting imprint on Argentine literature, and even as a Jewish writer he is not well known. Not surprisingly then, there is virtually no critical evaluation of his works to date. Nevertheless, his writing does merit future consideration by readers and critics for his insightful contributions to Argentine literature in general, and for the way in which he portrays aspects of Jewish identity on a global level.

PRIMARY BIBLIOGRAPHY
Creative Writing
Desde Delos en frecuencia modulada. Buenos Aires: Intersea, 1978.

El fiat verde. Buenos Aires: Intersea, 1976.

Grimanescas. Prólogo de Bernardo E. Koremblit. Buenos Aires: Milá, 1988.

La guerilla del cuarto mundo. Prólogo de Ricardo Feierstein. Buenos Aires: Pardés, 1983.

Los pasillos de la memoria. Santiago del Estero, Argentina: Enrique Rueda, 1982.

Un problemita color naranja. Buenos Aires: Intersea, 1976.

Reina negra a rey blanco. ¡Jaque!. Buenos Aires: Macondo, 1979.

Nonfiction

Los atípicos: Balzac, Chejov, O'Henry, Schwab. Prólogo de Susana Marchese.
Buenos Aires: Intersea, 1978.

Darrell B. Lockhart

GROSSMANN, JUDITH (Brazil; 1931)

Judith Grossmann is the daughter of Rumanian immigrants to Brazil.
She received a degree in Anglo-Germanic letters from the Universidade Federal
do Rio de Janeiro (The Federal University of Rio de Janeiro) in 1954. In 1963
she was awarded a Fulbright fellowship and studied at the University of Chicago.
When she returned to Brazil, she taught literary theory at the Universidade Esta-
dual do Rio de Janeiro (The State University of Rio de Janeiro). In 1966, she
moved to Bahia and became a professor of literary theory at the Universidade
Federal da Bahia (The Federal University of Bahia). She has formally held that
post since 1974.

Grossmann collaborated in the Sunday literary supplement of the *Jornal
do Brasil*, a journal which had a tremendous impact on Brazilian letters in the
late 1950s. Her first short story was published in 1964, and since that time her
work has been anthologized in numerous collections of Brazilian short stories.
In 1959 she published her first collection of poems, *Linhagem do Rocinante: 35
poemas* (Heritage of Rocinante: 35 Poems). The book contained many of the
concretist tendencies that would become characteristic of her poetry. In 1970 she
published a volume of short stories entitled *O meio da pedra* (The Middle of the
Stone) a tome which gained significant critical acclaim for demonstrating the
author's unique way of utilizing language. In 1976, Grossmann was awarded the
"Prêmio Brasília" (Brasilia Award) from the Cultural Foundation of the Federal
District. In 1977 she published *A noite estrelada: estórias do ínterim*, (The Starry
Night: Stories of the Interim) a series of short stories that distinguished her as
one of Brazil's most expressive short-story writers. *Outros trópicos* (Other Trop-
ics; 1980), and *Cantos delituosos* (Punishable Songs; 1985) are Grossmann's two
novels.

Much of Grossmann's writing is characterized by an erotic aesthetic—common among contemporary Brazilian women writers—and several of her
stories have appeared in anthologies of Brazilian erotic narrative, most notably

in the popular *Muito prazer: contos eróticos femininos* (A Pleasure: Feminine Erotic Short Stories; 1982) and in the follow-up anthology—published in response to the overwhelming popularity of the first text—*O prazer é todo meu: contos eróticos femininos* (The Pleasure Is All Mine: Feminine Erotic Short Stories; 1985). Grossmann's writing is considered to present a dense and profound optic on particular psychological states of being. The focus of her writing is often on childhood, primarily presented in dream-like images. Another recurring theme is that of being the perpetual foreigner, unable to fit into the dominant culture. Many of Grossmann's texts have been determined to be semi-autobiographical with a preponderance of introspective feminine protagonists (the exception being her novel, *Outros trópicos*, told from the vantage point of a male protagonist). Her works have been analyzed primarily from the psychoanalytic viewpoint and many comparisons have been made between her style of writing and that of Brazil's most famous woman writer, Clarice Lispector (1920-77).

Jewish themes in Grossmann's writing are not readily apparent, even in stories that she specifically designates as being related to Judaica. The rootlessness that has been determined to be characteristic of her work may be one of the ways in which Jewishness takes form in her writing, as connected to the concept of the eternal wanderer associated with Jewish history.

In her collection of short stories entitled *A noite estrelada* she includes an entire section of what she terms her "Livro hebraico" (Hebraic Book), comprised of twenty-two short narratives. In the majority of the stories there is little that may be seen as directly connected to Jewish themes, and even in those in which the link may be established, what the reader finds are often fleeting images, descriptions, themes, or names that may be connected to Judaism. For example, "Ultima Alvanira e primeira" (Last Alvanira and First) entails the protagonist's return to her childhood home, long since abandoned for her new unnamed country across the ocean. While the details of her departure and of the whereabouts of her family members are never made clear, the issue of memory, a common motif in Jewish writing, is highlighted in the story.

In other stories, the question of memory surfaces again, such as in "Regiões insondáveis"(Impenetrable Regions), in which a German couple living in the United States has a disagreement over the husband's predilection to pass time in the bath tub. When asked what he is doing, his reply is that he must forget—forget what he is doing to himself (144). His wife, feeling abandoned, loses herself in her studies, among them contemporary Hebrew.

While the theme of memory is a recurrent throughout the stories, there are other more fleeting images that may be seen as connected to Jewish imagery.

For example, in the story "Interlope" Grossmann mentions a trip to the movies. The protagonist becomes fixated on the movie star on the screen and on his delicate nose: "Podia ser que por isso as coisas terminassem assim tão perfeitamente. . ." (It must be for that reason that things always turn out so perfect [190]). The topic of a so-called Jewish appearance is also apparent in "Judicante," in which the protagonist discusses how his Jewishness has always been apparent to others, without him ever having to declare it.

"A Sra. Büchern em Lebenwald" (Mrs. Büchern in Lebenwald) tells the story of a woman with a mysterious past who comes to live in a small town. She explains her past to one young man, a story that at times is almost unbearable for him to hear and the reader is led to believe that Sra. Büchern is a Holocaust survivor. When she befriends another young man, the theme of survivor guilt is touched upon as he explains to her how uncomfortable he is with his Judaism. He tells her of all of the things that shame him, among them "E de como se envergonhava de que estivessem todos vivos, e de que também ele, [. . .], estivesse também, vivo, sendo esta a maior de suas vergonhas" (And of how he was shamed by the fact that they were all alive, and that he was also, and this was what caused him the greatest shame [236]).

The final story of the "Livro hebraico," "Gerardo, o Belga" (Gerardo, the Belgium) encapsulates the concept of perpetual wandering and extends it to refer not only to Jews, but to everyone. In the narrative the reader learns of the friends and travels of Gerardo and of his life as the son of Belgium immigrants in Brazil, always referred to as "the Belgium" and of how, upon moving to Belgium, he was always referred to as "the Brazilian." The crux of the story, and that which makes it of particular interest at present, is the nature of living on the hyphen, never wholly one thing or the other, never belonging.

Although Judith Grossmann's writing is not defined by the incorporation of themes and imagery related to Jewish identity, she does nonetheless contribute in a small way to the development of that particular literary discourse in Brazil.

PRIMARY BIBLIOGRAPHY

Creative Writing

Cantos delituosos: romance. Rio de Janeiro: Nova Fronteira, 1985.

Linhagem de Rocinante: 35 poemas. Rio de Janeiro: Livraria São José, 1959.

O meio da pedra: nonas estórias genéticas. Rio de Janeiro: José Alvaro, 1970.

"O mistério das cartas assassinadas." *Histórias de amor infeliz.* 2nd ed. Ed. Esdras do Nascimento. Rio de Janeiro: Nórdica, 1985. 294-303.

"O mundo de Ana Marland." *O prazer é todo meu: contos eróticos femininos.* Ed. Márcia Denser. Rio de Janeiro: Record, 1985. 25-32.

A noite estrelada. Rio de Janeiro: Francisco Alves, 1977.

Outros trópicos. Rio de Janeiro: José Olympio, 1980.

"Tanganica." *Muito prazer: contos eróticos femeninos.* Ed. Márcia Denser. Rio de Janeiro: Record, 1982. 28-36.

Nonfiction

(Ed.) *Herberto Sales: os melhores contos.* São Paulo: Global, 1993.

Temas de teoria da literatura. São Paulo: Atica, 1982.

SECONDARY BIBLIOGRAPHY

Farias, José Niraldo de. "A tensão entre a intimidade e a imensidão en *Outros trópicos* de Judith Grossman." *Minas Gerais: Suplemento literário* 15.832 (11 Sept., 1982): 6-7.

Quinlan, Susan Canty. "The Mysterious Space of Exile: *Punishable Songs* by Judith Grossmann." In *International Women's Writing: New Landscapes of Identity.* Ed. Anne L. Brown and Marjanne E. Goozé. Westport, CT: Greenwood, 1995. 115-25.

Simões, Heliana. "A literatura de Judith Grossman." *Tempo brasileiro* 42-43 (1975): 37-42.

Melissa Fitch Lockhart

GRÜNBERG, CARLOS M. (Argentina; 1903-68)

Carlos Mardoqueo Grünberg was born on August 29, 1903 in Buenos Aires. He belonged to the post-immigrant generation of Argentine Jews who were able to obtain a university education and establish a certain degree of upward social mobility within Argentine society. In fact, he earned two advanced degrees from the University of Buenos Aires; one in philosophy (1926) and another in law (1930). As a poet, Grünberg was associated with other avant-garde writers of the 1920s known as the *martínfierristas* for their association with the highly influential literary journal *Martín Fierro*, founded in 1924. His early collections of poetry, *Las cámaras del rey* (The King's Chambers; 1922) and *El libro del tiempo* (The Book of Time; 1924), represent this phase of the poet's early career.

In addition to writing his own poetry, Grünberg also taught Spanish literature, and he translated the works of other Jewish poets into Spanish, including those of Heinrich Heine (1797-1856), and H. N. Bialik (1873-1934). He was a regular contributor to the Spanish-language literary and cultural journal *Judaica*, and he carried out a number of other cultural projects such as a translation of the *Haggadah* in 1946. His rendering of the Passover text into the ornate and eloquent lexicon of old Spanish earned him considerable recognition. Grünberg was also active in the Zionist movement and his friend Moshe Tov appointed him as a liaison between the State of Israel and the Argentine government in 1948. A year later, the Chancellor of Israel, D. Moshe Sharet commissioned him to be a special representative of the State of Israel before the government of Argentina. Grünberg details these experiences in a note at the end of *Junto a un río de Babel* (261).

Together with César Tiempo (1906-80) and Lázaro Liacho (1898-1969), Grünberg was instrumental in establishing a strong Argentine Jewish poetic tradition. Outspoken about their Jewishness, they eagerly sought to incorporate Jewish issues into their work and to forge a poetic expression of identity informed by their unique dual cultural heritage. It is in his later volumes that Grünberg focuses solely on Jewish matters, most specifically Jewish-Argentine relations and Zionism. There is also a marked difference in the poet's style and tone from verses of experimental lyricism to a poetry characterized by decidedly bleak lamentations on the Jewish situation in Argentina and abroad.

The 1940 collection of poems *Mester de judería* (Minstrelsy of the Jews) consecrated Grünberg as a poet. Jorge Luis Borges (1899-1986) wrote a laudatory prologue to the volume in which he praised Grünberg's poetic depth. More significantly, Borges emphasizes the point that in spite of the Jewish themes Grünberg is "inconfundiblemente argentino" (unmistakably Argentine [xiii]), and he likens the poet's work to that of the canonical writers Leopoldo Lugones (1874-1938) and Ezequiel Martínez Estrada (1895-1964). The title of the collection is a play on words that recalls the medieval Spanish tradition of the *mester de juglaría*, a type of poetry, mostly in the form of ballads and epics that was recited and sung by the *juglares*, roving public entertainers of the Middle Ages who entertained audiences with their poetry and comic antics. The title, then, is the first sign of one of the main ideological undercurrents that runs throughout the collection; the effort to legitimate the Jewish presence in Argentina through the poetic representation of a Hispano-Jewish connection. This is accomplished by incorporating archaic Spanish lexicon and syntax that conjures up the Sephardic tradition of the Iberian peninsula, a practice common among the early Jewish Argentine writers of Ashkenazic origin (Senkman 46-47). Nevertheless, in many poems Grünberg is more overt in his effort to establish compatibility between both sides of his identity. In "Mestizo" (Mixed Breed), for example, he juxtaposes Jewish and Argentine historical and geographical references to create a single, new identity. Grünberg's conceptualization of the Jewish Argentine *mestizo* subverts a familiar term in Latin American culture in order to introduce the Jewish component in a less threatening manner. *Mestizo* is the term used to identify Latin Americans of mixed Hispanic and indigenous ethnicity. Used metaphorically, the term connotes the meaning that the poet wishes to convey. Grünberg does not refer to literal ethnic *mestizaje*, rather he proposes a cultural *mestizaje* between the codes of signification intrinsic to Hispanic (Argentine) and Jewish sociocultural identities. The poet and novelist Ricardo Feierstein (1942) carries on where Grünberg left off and more fully develops this ideological posture in his novel *Mestizo* (1988).

In other poems, Grünberg openly extols the virtues of Argentina as home for the Jews and forthrightly declares his unwavering patriotism for the nation. While many poems speak directly to the often precarious situation of the Jews in Argentina with regard to anti-Semitism, these do not detract from the overall tribute to the country as the new *patria* or homeland of the Jews. Grünberg does dedicate a significant portion of the collection to expressing his anger, frustration, and dismay at the injustice and prevalence of anti-Semitism, especially in light of the horrific events taking place in Europe. Argentina's neutral position during World War II further complicated matters for Jews and provided fertile ground for the planting of Nazi ideology on Argentine soil.

Mester de judería is presented as a representation of Jewish life in the Diaspora from birth to death. It opens with the poem "Circuncisión" (Circumcision), in which the poet carefully explains to the eight-day-old child that the blood spilled at his bris is the first lesson at being Jewish, primarily that it costs blood to be a Jew. The collection closes with the poem "Cementerio" (Cemetery), a rather somber look at the end to which we all succumb. The poems in between, in addition to the themes already presented, touch on Jewish exile, displacement, and the search for a place to call home, which Grünberg has found in Argentina. While he strongly adheres to a culturally-defined Jewish identity, the poet makes it quite clear throughout the volume that he has no religious affiliation to Judaism. In fact, he brazenly declares his atheism in several poems and he expresses the disdain directed at him by other Jews for his areligious stance. In the poem "Sinagoga" (Synagogue), written in response to anti-Semitic attacks against two of the principal synagogues of Buenos Aires, Grünberg wanders through the temple, pondering the meaning and history of the objects inside and concludes with a questioning of his own relationship with such a place.

Grünberg's next volume of poetry did not appear until 1965. *Junto a un río de Babel* (By a River of Babel) reveals a much different tone in the poet's voice. Similarly, it reflects the many political changes in Argentina and in Palestine over the course of the twenty-five years since the publication of *Mester*. *Junto a un río* focuses on the creation of the State of Israel, or better stated, on the postnational reality of Israel. The poems alternate between praising the new Jewish homeland and questioning the consequences of Israel as a political nation as it effects the position of Argentine Jews. The decade of the 1960s was one of extreme anti-Semitic sentiment in which Jews finally were convinced to relinquish hopes of full integration into Argentine society. One of the major accusations raised against the Jews was that of dual loyalty. The majority of poems underscore the irresoluble problematics for diaspora Jews, like Grünberg, who feel a spiritual or emotional commitment to Israel, but who do not share the Zionist fervor to make aliyah to the new nation. In several poems, "Desclasado" (Declassed), "Segunda" (Second [-Class Citizen]), "Sub" (Sub), the poet bewails the fact that in Argentina he is a second-class citizen for being a Jew and in Israel he is a second-class Jew for being an Argentine. The majority of the Zion-theme poems are grouped under the headings "Promisión" (Promise) and "Siónidas" (Songs of Zion), but the theme is recurrent throughout the volume. *Junto a un río* opens with the section "Hitlermedio" (Hitlerintermission), the poems in which express the need for the State of Israel. In the following sections the theme gradually changes to address the numerous and complicated problematics, especially for Diaspora Jews, that accompany Israel as a Jewish state. Finally, while he still faithfully supports Argentina as his home, Grünberg does not convey the patriotic zeal found in the previous volume. The overriding emotional impression that permeates *Junto a un río* is one of discontent and sadness over the way that history ultimately unfolded.

Carlos M. Grünberg's poetry continues to provide ample ground for the reevaluation of the Argentine Jewish experience. As one of the founders of a still flourishing literary tradition his works have made a lasting impact on subsequent generations of writers who carry on the task of portraying Jewish identity in Argentina through the optic of literature.

PRIMARY BIBLIOGRAPHY

Las cámaras del rey. Buenos Aires: Del Autor, 1922.

El libro del tiempo. Buenos Aires: Manuel Gleizer, 1924.

Junto al río de Babel. Buenos Aires: Acervo Cultural, 1965.

Mester de judería. Prologue by Jorge Luis Borges. Buenos Aires: Argirópolis, 1940.

SECONDARY BIBLIOGRAPHY

Borges, Jorge Luis. "Prólogo." *Mester de judería*. Buenos Aires: Argirópolis, 1940. xi-xvi.

Ceselli, Juan J. Rev. of *Junto a un río de Babel*. *Davar* 109 (1966): 122-25.

Espinoza, Enrique. *De un lado al otro*. Buenos Aires: Del Regreso, 1975. 90-94.

Goldberg, Florinda. "The Complex Roses of Jerusalem: The Theme of Israel in Argentinian Jewish Poetry." *Tradition and Innovation: Reflections on Latin American Jewish Writing*. Ed. Robert DiAntonio And Nora Glickman. Albany: SUNY Press, 1993. 73-87.

Guillot Muñoz, Alvaro. "Carlos M. Grünberg, poeta laico." *Judaica* 96 (1941): 261-67.

Koremblit, Bernardo E. "*Junto a un río de babel*, de Carlos M. Grünberg." *Davar* 110 (1966): 49-55.

Kovadloff, Jacobo, et al. "Homenaje a Carlos M. Grünberg." *Davar* 119 (1968): 26-40.

Lindstrom, Naomi. "Zionist Thought and Songs of Zion: Two Jewish Argentine Poets." *Judaica latinoamericana: estudios histórico-sociales II*. Jerusalem: Asociación Israelí de Investigadores del Judaísmo Latinoamericano; Editorial Universitaria Magnes, Universidad Hebrea, 1993. 275-87.

Noé, Julio. "La poesía." In *Historia de la literatura argentina*. Vol. 4. Ed. Rafael Alberto Arrieta. Buenos Aires: Peuser, 1959. 122-24.

Portnoy, Antonio. "Un intérprete del alma judía." *Judaica* 91 (1941): 25-29.

Senkman, Leonardo. *La identidad judía en la literatura argentina*. Buenos Aires: Pardés, 1983. 46-48, 323-27.

Tiempo, César. "El mejor y el mayor de todos nosotros." *Mundo israelita* 2819 (3 Dec., 1977): 4, 13.

Victorero, Miguel M. "*Mester de judería*, por Carlos M. Grünberg." *Claridad* 346 (1941): 135-36.

Weinstein, Ana E., and Miryam Gover de Nasatsky, comps. *Escritores judeoargentinos: bibliografía 1900-1987*. 2 vols. Buenos Aires: Milá, 1994. I.295-301.

Darrell B. Lockhart

GURALNIK, SONIA (Chile; 1925)

Born in Russia in 1925, Sonia Guralnik lived the first 10 years of her life in a small province near Kiev in the Ukraine. As a child she emigrated to

Chile with her family where she currently resides. Guralnik discovered her writing ability late in life but has since become quite prolific with three collections of short stories: *El samovar* (The Samovar; 1984), *Relatos en sepia* (Tales in Sepia; 1987), and *Recuento de la mujer gusano* (Recount of the Catepillar Woman; 1991). Several of the stories from these volumes have appeared separately in national magazines. Also, some of her work is currently being translated for publication in English. Her latest project, a book focusing on Jewish immigration to Chile and the theme of exile in general, is soon to be published under the title of *Dirección particular* (Home Address), and she is currently writing her memories of life during the Pinochet dictatorship.

For Guralnik, who describes herself as a Russian Jewish Chilean who is also many other things, writing is like a war, a theme that she knows all too well. In all of Guralnik's writing, there is a struggle to remember, to witness, to never forget the many wars in the world, both personal and sociopolitical. However, she has stated that it was the war after the *coup d'état* in Chile in 1973 that gave her cause to begin what she calls her own war of words. Her writing is a battlefield against forgetting the stories of her youth, the trials of living in exile, the hope and nostalgia associated with emigration, and love of family, community, and God. In this remembering, Guralnik's Jewish identity is central to her fight, and as such, is visible in a variety of themes that permeate her quite autobiographical writing with a great sense of inspiration mixed with nostalgia.

The theme of emigration is essential in all of Guralnik's short-story collections. In *El samovar*, many of the sixteen stories either take place in Russia or between that time and space and Latin America. As the title indicates, the few chosen possessions that the family carries with them often have a symbolic importance in the memory for generations to come. One story in particular, "Los cordeles" (The Cords), tells of a family's emigration from Russia to Chile from the point of view of the naïve young daughter who doesn't understand the danger involved and the need to disguise their identity. She explains the importance of the few items they could take with them and remarks that her mother could not abandon her silver menorah, the clock, or the samovar. Even though she left many other objects of greater material value, she took with her these three items pertaining to her Jewish and Russian identity and her history. During the description of the long voyage of the family by train to the sea, then to Buenos Aires on a ship symbolically christened *The Liberty*, and finally across the Andes again by train to Chile where the father awaits his wife and children. The child's perspective expresses the fears, hopes, and confusion of emigration felt by people of all ages. At the end, the secret meaning of the cords becomes clear when reader and narrator alike realize that entwined and hidden in them was the family's entire savings to be used for a new beginning in Chile.

The idea of a new beginning, filled with both remembrance and hope for the future appears often in Guralnik's writing where family and community play such an important role in fighting the solitude or even a possible loss of identity caused by life in exile. As already noted, this theme is central to Guralnik's forthcoming book, but it is quite apparent in her prior works as well. Often, the father represents the Jewish heritage with strict observance of Shabbat, prayers, and all other rites and traditions. This is the case in stories such as "Sobre el riel de las normas" (On the Standard Track [*Relatos en Sepia*]). In relation to Israel, there are direct references to feeling alienated both by language and traditions during her visits as in "En una plaza de Natanya" (In a Park in Natanya [*Recuento de la mujer gusano*]), and "La torre shalom" (The Synagogue Tower; [*El samovar*]). In these stories and others, the confusion and nostalgia of life in exile are articulated as rejection, suffocation, and the anxiety of being lost in Israel where the Jewish protagonist should feel most welcomed by family and history.

However, tradition itself is a very positive element in Guralnik's works, and it is frequently used as an arm to fight division of the family for political reasons as in the story "Los sábados gigantes" (The Giant Saturdays [*Recuento de la mujer gusano*]), where a wife and mother denied the possibility of becoming involved in politics attempts to bring her politically divided family together each Saturday to share a meal, a tradition, which she offers in the hope of at least a temporary peace and reconciliation.

In the sequence of Guralnik's collections of stories, there is a notable increase in a political awareness and with this a maturity in the voices of the narrators emerges that contrasts with the naïve perspective found mostly in *El samovar*, but also apparent in some stories of the other two works. Whereas in the first book there are only allusions to the pogroms and persecution in several historical moments, in *Relatos en sepia* Guralnik begins to witness more directly the Holocaust, specifically in "Bajando el Rhin," and "Es la humedad" (It's the Humidity). In the first story, several elderly women travelling down the Rhine recognize a torturer and remember their experiences in the concentration camps. In the second, a young couple is about to move into a new apartment. Their Uncle Manuel showing it to them remembers the couple that used to live there. He explains how they arrived terrified in exile without knowing anyone and with what he calls tattoos of horror on their arms. The young generation, unconcerned with these memories asks practical questions, admires the view and speaks of the future while Uncle Manuel disappears only after noticing how the waves of the sea wash away everything. In the Chilean context of what has been referred to as another holocaust under the Pinochet dictatorship, Guralnik inscribes the theme of absence and the feeling of being abandoned by the disappearance, torture, and death of family and community members in "El chaquetón vacío" (The Empty Overcoat [*Recuento de la mujer gusano*]). In telling this story and (re)constructing this history, the narrator is able to (re)create a new discursive world and fight time that seems to have stopped. Even in what she refers to as the exile of her own home with the empty jacket of her absent daughter, a reminder of the emptiness she feels without her, the narrator concludes her memory with brilliant eyes, possibly from tears, but more likely from the hope that her daughter will encounter a greater freedom in exile.

The direct references to remembering the Holocaust and the dictatorship in these stories narrated from an adult perspective contrast with the innocent remarks of goyim ignorance and childhood experiences of anti-Semitism and even of a naïve hope for mutual enlightenment between Catholic and Jewish traditions in Chile that appear in many stories, such as "La casa de los leones" (The Lion House), "El vendedor de cuadros" (The Painting Vendor), and "Que mi cuerpo repose" (That My Body May Rest) included in *El samovar*, and "Con flores amarillas" (With Yellow Flowers), and "Por los milagros" (For Miracles) from *Relatos en sepia*.

Guralnik's works are profoundly autobiographical to the extent that it is very easy to confuse the narrators with the author and these short stories with personal memoirs. In fact, in the final paragraph of "Nunca tuve una profesión" (I Never Had a Profession), the last story from *Recuento de la mujer gusano*, the narrator explains that she has converted her life into a novel and her thoughts into writing. In this way, she has become a professional and a person. It is next to impossible not to hear the voice of Sonia Guralnik through these words and in many other passages as well. Thus, although the aforementioned themes and Jewish concerns are abundant in these works, there are many other personal elements which relate to Guralnik's individual experiences and struggles as a Chilean and as a woman who is also a widow. This is especially evident in *Recuento de la mujer gusano* where in a series of stories time and memory are problematized with the death of the narrator's husband, who after marriage had assumed the role of family patriarch to symbolize tradition and stability. The narrator discovers her own time through memory in "Rosas color té" (Tea Colored Roses) stating that she can only constitute the future by scrutinizing the past.

Sonia Guralnik's writing, besides being extraordinarily personal, is a fascinating remembrance and recording of these memories, many of which are related to emigration, exile, assimilation, tradition, history, identity and other Jewish concerns. Her simplicity of style and warmth describe very complex and often painful topics in an incredibly inspirational light. It is most likely for this reason that she has received various literary awards in Latin America and is deservedly beginning to be recognized internationally as well. Still residing in Chile and a member of literary organizations such as the Society of Chilean Writers and the Soffia Group, Sonia Guralnik, a Jewish Russian Chilean who is first and foremost a human being, continues to remember past and present battles in order to inspire a more peaceful future.

PRIMARY BIBLIOGRAPHY

"La bailarina en el bar." *La Nación* (Santiago) Sept. 19, 1993: n.p.

"De boina roja." *La Nación* (Santiago) March 11, 1994): n.p.

Dirección particular. Forthcoming.

Recuento de la mujer gusano. Santiago: Sudamericana, 1991.

Relatos en sepia. Santiago: Ergo Sum, 1987.

El samovar. Santiago: Carlos Ruiz-Tagle, 1984.

"Veraneos," "Giselle." In *El cuento feminista latinoamericano.* Ed. Adriana Santa Cruz and Viviana Erazo. Santiago: Fempress, 1988. 35-41.

SECONDARY BIBLIOGRAPHY

Guerrero, Pedro Pablo. "El hallazgo de la escritura." *La Nación* (Santiago) March 27, 1994: 6.

Iturra, Carlos. "Buscando la metamorfosis." *El País* (Ed. Internacional-Madrid) June 11-17, 1992: 11.

Ortúzar, Carmen. "Una forma de existir." *El Mercurio* (Santiago) Dec. 11, 1987: 4.

Ruiz-Tagle, Carlos. "Prólogo." *El samovar.* Santiago: Carlos Ruiz-Tagle, 1984. 5-9.

Vargas Saavedra, Luis. *"Recuento de la mujer gusano."* *La Nación* (Santiago) March 27, 1994: 6.

Stacey D. Skar

GUTMAN, DANIEL (Argentina; 1954)

Daniel Gutman, born in Buenos Aires on May 29, 1954, has worked as a journalist and as a scriptwriter. He established himself early in his literary career as a poet, although his two most recent works are novels. In response to a question regarding the way in which Jewishness has shaped his literature, Gutman replies that it has been minimal. He states, "I lack a Jewish education; I did not come from a home that kept the traditions and rituals of the Jewish calendar. Nor did I, as a child, hear my elders speak Yiddish or Hebrew" (Glickman 21). Nonetheless, his works do reflect to one degree or another his connection with Jewish heritage on both a thematic and philosophical level.

Gutman's first collection of poetry, *Culpas y culpables* (Guilt and the Guilty) was published in 1974. In 1975 he won the Primer Premio Fondo Nacional de las Artes (National Foundation for the Arts First Prize) for his *Piedra de toque* (Touchstone), which was not actually published until 1980. *Piedra de toque* is a complex poetic gesture that operates on the trope of the touchstone as a measure of poetic and philosophical integrity. The poems, which in reality are poetico-narrative meditations, are divided into sections that are inspired by a wide range of other writers whom one can assume are the major influences on Gutman's own thinking. Each section is likewise divided into five parts, "Agua" (Water), "Tierra" (Earth), "Aire" (Air), "Fuego" (Fire), and "Quintaesencia" (Quintessence), which consist of brief philosophical postulations. *Plenitud del vacío* (Plenitude of Emptyness; 1986) continues in the same philosophical vein as the previous volume, but it also reveals the poet's effort to create a poetic text that relies more on the aesthetic effect of poetry as art, as opposed to the previous focus on logic and cognitive science. Thematically, Gutman turns to God, the poet as creator, and the word as creative power, as well as eroticism and orientalism. *Erosión* (Erosion; 1989) is Gutman's final collection of poetry published to date. The title not only refers to the literal act of cultural and linguistic erosion, but more importantly it is derived from the combination of *Eros* and *Sión* (Zion). This same kind of word play occurs throughout the volume as in the combination of *mi Sión/misión* (my Zion/mission). Gutman achieves a poetic fusion of Greek and Hebrew traditions that finds its point of union in the Spanish language. The volume may be seen as a poetic summation of the erotically charged ethos that informs Zionism as an ideology and as a political movement.

The novel *Contra tiempo* (Against Time; 1990) is Gutman's contribution to the large body of quincentenary literature that surfaced in Latin America as a reaction to the five-hundred year anniversary of Columbus's encounter with the

New World, as well as the enormous world market for such literature. Many Latin American writers sought to rehistoricize the encounter, conquest, and colonization of the Americas through often long, neobaroque narrations tinged with elements of magic realism and preternatural occurrences. Gutman's novel both conforms to and undermines this continental narrative project of historical revisionism. The teaser on the back cover seems to cater to market expectations of the "marvelous real" with talk of mysterious happenings, unexplained events, temporal Borgesian labyrinths, and mythology. The novel is based on the premise that a sixteenth-century caravel suddenly arrives one night at the port of Buenos Aires. The only two crew members on board, Salomón de Echizo and Alvaro de Aquino, purport to have set sail from Spain in 1506. The mariners' archaic manner of speech and dress, coupled with their knowledge of history convince the authorities that they are indeed witness to a most uncanny phenomenon. As the novel progresses it begins to take on the characteristics of a detective novel as the protagonist, Jaime Vitale, a journalist for the military seeks to uncover and explain the mystery of the anachronistic ship and its two-man crew. After a trip to Spain and a visit to the Archive of the Indies in Seville, Vitale is able to verify that the two men are in fact who they claim to be. However, much to the chagrin of the military, it turns out that the officials have fallen victim to the most elaborate scam in national history, the result of which is the heist of the Spanish crown jewels. The remainder of the novel revolves around the recovery of the stolen treasure and the unravelling of the thieves' trickery. Structurally, the novel is an intricate combination of alternating narrative personae and styles that weave the mystery. The author also plays with the idea of literary creation and textual authority. For instance, in the epilogue Jaime Vitale ponders the idea of writing a novel about his experience, which is in fact the novel that the reader has just completed, but isn't sure how to structure it. What is perhaps most clever about Gutman's text is how he manages to subvert the overused technique of magical realism, giving a logical explanation for all the events, much like a skeptic exposes a magician's sleight of hand. While references to Jewish identity in the novel are few they do add another thematically interesting dimension to this complex text.

Gutman's subsequent novel, *Control remoto* (Remote Control; 1992), is a science-fiction work of dystopian nature. It constitutes a disturbing look into the not so distant future. Although the novel begins in 1995, it takes place mostly in the year 2035, by which time society has changed dramatically for the worse. The protagonist, Gabriel B, is a news reporter who suffers an accident that results in a comatose state of forty years. He awakens to find a world ruled by television and a global society willingly subjected to the power of the electronic image. The majority of the world population had been decimated by *El Síndrome* (the Sindrome), defined as a complete shut-down of the body's immune system due to the intense proliferation of television wave emission. Once the cause was discovered it led to the creation of one central world television station located beneath the ancient city of Persepolis, Iran in a new underground metropolis known as the *Centro* (Center). Gabriel B manages to gain entrance into the central city and to pursue the continuance of his television career. An intercalated subtext to the novel is to be found in the chapters titled "Del memorial de H" (From H's Report), which constitute a type of diary that traces the rise of Hitler and the Third Reich in the twentieth century and links television to a Nazi plot for world domination. What Gabriel B discovers is that the television of the future is in fact the continuation of Nazi ideology in an evolved and even more frightening manifestation, the purpose of which is to create a technological master race. Gutman intertwines the history of Nazism with a futuristic narrative that portrays television as the great evil of the twenty-first century in which human existence has been reduced to the consumption of contrived, mind-numbing images that slowly deprive the individual of any sense of reality. The author presents a frightening future where plants and animals, after having been driven to extinction, are replaced by robotic replicas, the so-called leader of the world is nothing more than an artificial image, and people have reached such a level of complicity with violence on television that they watch bizarre programs that end in the actual death of the participants. The Hitlerian figure in the novel is the deformed HoraCulo (a play on words that is derived from the words "hour" and "ass," but which also it is revealed later refers to *oráculo* (oracle). HoraCulo is the host of the most popular show on television on which he divines the future of the participants by examining their excrement. He his also the director of the Zyklon B Project, which takes its name from the toxic gas used by the Nazis to exterminate the Jews in the gas chambers. In addition, it is revealed toward the end of the novel that he is the H of the "Del memorial de H" chapters. Gabriel B manages to put a stop to HoraCulo's insidious plan by destroying the main television antenna bringing a halt to the constant emission of programs and consequently breaking the mesmerizing spell on the people. Gutman's novel stands as a strong indictment of the state of the mass media and its power to manipulate societal behavior.

PRIMARY BIBLIOGRAPHY

Contra tiempo. Buenos Aires: Emecé, 1990.
Control remoto. Buenos Aires: Planeta, 1992.
Culpas y culpables. Buenos Aires: Omphalos, 1974.

Erosión. Buenos Aires: Ultimo Reino, 1989.
Piedra de toque. Buenos Aires: Corregidor, 1980.
Plenitud del vacío. Buenos Aires: Grupo Editor Latinoamericano, 1985.

SECONDARY BIBLIOGRAPHY
Criticism
Goldberg, Florinda F. "Rev. of *Erosión. Noaj* 4.5 (1990): 109-10.
Kanalenstein, Rubén. "Daniel Gutman: entre la plenitud y el vacío." *Nueva Sión*
634 (22 March, 1986): 25.
Pérez Martín, N. Rev. of *Plenitud del vacío. Señales* 187 (1986): 28.
Tapia, Atols. Rev. of *Piedra de toque. Pájaro de fuego* 25 (1980): 27.
Interviews
Glickman, Nora. "Daniel Gutman." In *Tradition and Innovation: Reflections on
Latin American Jewish Writing.* Ed. Robert DiAntonio and Nora Glick-
man. Albany: SUNY Press, 1993. 21-23.

Darrell B. Lockhart

HALAC, RICARDO (Argentina; 1935)

Ricardo Halac was born in Buenos Aires to Jewish parents who emigrated from Syria. He grew up not only with Spanish, but also surrounded by the
native Arabic and French of his parents. Halac's works—which have received
various national and international awards—would seem to belong to that group
of "Argentine Jews [who have] pursued various strategies of assimilation into the
dominant Hispanic and Catholic culture of Argentina" (Foster 97). Indeed, in his
now abundant theatrical production consisting of some thirteen works, and his
novel *El soltero* (The Bachelor; 1976), made into a movie in 1977, Halac is concerned, even in his latest play, *Mil años, un día* (*A Thousand Years, One Day*;
1993), with the inhuman determination of "social causality that can do more than
individual responsibility" (Pellettieri, "El teatro de Ricardo Halac" 39).

Influenced in his youth by Bertolt Brecht (1898-1956), who nevertheless
left no lasting impression on his work, Halac decided to learn German. He received a scholarship which allowed him to study in Germany, where he came
into direct contact with Brecht's theater. Lacking the scenic technology required
by a Brechtian theatrical production, and like other leftist authors of the 1960s,

his formal theatrical style was marked by Arthur Miller (1915) and Tennessee Williams (1911-81), and by the revalorization of the tradition of realism and the grotesque. For this reason, critics have defined a series of phases in his works that allow one to see the transformation of his writing from reflexive realism to critical realism (cf. Pellettieri).

What concerns Halac are not so much questions of ethnic identity, but rather of social class. However, his focus does not tend to lead to an epic or historical theater that allows the visualization of exploitative conditions and the imperialist advancement of successive capitalist reaccommodations. Rather, Halac focuses his dramatic inquiries on the progressive deterioration of the Argentine middle class. Like most of the theater of his generation, this process is accompanied by a change of discursive strategies that, one after another, incorporate certain absurdist tactics, vaudeville, and farce, while never providing a structural redefinition of bourgeois theatricality (Italian-style theater, stage vs. audience, character-spectator identification). Nevertheless, there are timid attempts in more recent works to achieve a larger participation from the audience, and there are even elements of rupture with regard to some conventions (the fourth wall in *Segundo tiempo* [Second Half]; 1976). Therefore, from a position of questioning that begins with realist works like *Soledad para cuatro* (Solitude for Four; 1961), and *Fin de diciembre* (End of December; 1965), the dramatic process follows a path of introspection (*Estela de madrugada* [Estela at Dawn; 1968]), and then begins to ponder the idea of enclosure and the limits or illusions of a possible freedom (*El soltero, Tentempié I,* and *Tentempié II* [Midday Snack I and II; 1968], and *Segundo tiempo*). While the sense of disillusionment becomes sharper, Halac's writing—moving from the reflection of youthful illusions to the cross-roads of maturity—continues to incorporate elements of humor, the stage gag, and even stereotypes, for the purpose of making the mirror image of the public's downfall bearable. If *El destete* (The Weaning; 1978) successfully brings an end to this process, *Un trabajo fabuloso* (A Fabulous Job; 1988) clearly shows its limitations and even its exhaustion. It then became necessary to find a different mode of expression, and as was the case with almost all theater during the military dictatorship (1976-83) and the unstable democracy that followed, the use of metaphor and its universalist projection formed a major part of Halac's dramatic production. Halac's last stage of writing includes the works *Lejana tierra prometida* (Far Off Promised Land; 1981), *Ruido de rotas cadenas* (Clatter of Broken Chains; 1983), both written for the Teatro Abierto (Open Theater) cycles of those years, and *El dúo Sosa-Echagüe* (The Sosa-Echagüe Duo; 1984), written for a new cycle that never materialized. Halac's most recent work is *Mil años, un día,* a play that portrays the persecution and expulsion of the Jews from Spain in 1492.

The inventory of metaphors of desperation that Nora Glickman makes in her study of Halac's latest work does not convincingly manage to tie it to a questioning of Jewish identity, neither in essentialist terms, nor through connections with a specific ethnicity with historical insertion into the national panorama of Argentina. *Mil años, un día*, as the author indicates, is not a historical drama but rather annuls any temporal dimension whatsoever. The play represents the identification of the intellectual at the crossroads of a history of powers that push him to make decisions more than produce articulate speeches of collective demands. The character Isaac Levy, the attending physician of Queen Isabella, describes the stages of a process that goes from euphoria for science to the desperate acceptance of the mysteries of the Kabbalah and magic. The Jew here is the exiled individual, the persecuted, the martyred, the porter of the remains of an ethic, and discoverer of a collective dignity that is impossible to contain within scientific orthodoxy. *Mil años, un día* may also be read as a metaphor for the desperate history of Argentine intellectuals of the decades following the fall of Perón in 1955, their call to consciousness about the relationship between Peronism and the working class, their struggles and resistances, victories and betrayals, and the indelible yet tenacious corrosion of the enthusiasm and confusion with the outdated liberal proposals of the democracy of president Raúl Alfonsín (1983-89).

Any study of Jewish writing in Argentina must discuss not only its representation but also its lack of representation. If in Halac's work there is no mention of his Jewish ancestry, no principal or secondary characters that portray it, then *Mil años, un día* achieves nothing more than a utilization of the figure of Jew as a metaphor to "speak of the tragedy of modern man with his confusion, searching, and disorientation at a time when in the entire world discrimination, racism, and persecution of all that is different, is undergoing a resurgence" (Boero 9).

Thought of in more grandiose scenic terms, Halac develops the same theme as in *El dúo Sosa-Echagüe*: the difference that separates the intellectual or the artist as much from the hegemonic powers, which he both flirts with and aspires to, as from the masses, which he wants to represent.

However, there is one point that should be kept in mind that forms part of the structural questioning of his generation: all his theater, his novel, and some of his scripts for television can be read as an investigation into the fundamental Judeo-Christian phantasm: the limits of manhood and the determinations of paternity. His writing delves into the implacable symbolic inscriptions that determine youthful rebellion (of son against father), the imaginary challenges that women pose, and the unforgivable status of bachelorhood. These issues, that at first glance admit a certain realistic quality, will later be used to employ other discourses that bring into account social violence and dramatically process it. For that reason, *Un trabajo fabuloso* is the key work that closes one stage of searching and opens another: the movement of the demands of the father on the Father. It is no longer about interpersonal relationships, precarious identities, or inconsequential individuality but about the demands of a system that, moved by a suffocating monotheism, liquidates all difference, and that in its fervor for homogeneity and unity, ends up rebelling against its own productive structure of the patriarchal family. Raúl of *El soltero* is sacrificed at a party in which his office mates do not forgive him his resistance to marriage, and thereby his difference. Nevertheless, he still conforms to the patriarchal paradigm by deciding to get married to Cecilia and be the adoptive father of her children. The social imperatives of be successful, be happy, be a good son, and be a good father become almost impossible to fulfill. The figure of the Jew portrayed in Isaac does not go beyond these desperations: the unity of his people is forced by the fatality of the fact that it is not dialectic; his adhesion to the cause of his people is, as his acceptance of the nonexistence of God, compulsively emotional and irrational, and the love to which he appeals in the end creates his identity and his consolation for the downfall with the typical messianic leftovers of the intellectual of the sixties.

PRIMARY BIBLIOGRAPHY
Creative Writing
El destete; Un trabajo fabuloso. Rosario, Argentina: Ediciones Paralelo 32, 1984.

Fin de diciembre; Estela de madrugada. Buenos Aires: The Angel Press Editora, 1965.

Lejana tierra prometida. In *7 dramaturgos argentinos.* Ottawa, Canada: GIROL, 1983. 103-36. Also in *Teatro Abierto 1981: 21 estrenos argentinos.* Vol II. Buenos Aires: Corregidor, 1992. 181-205.

Soledad para cuatro. Buenos Aires: Talía, 1962.

El soltero. Buenos Aires: Galerna, 1977.

Teatro: Soledad para cuatro; Segundo tiempo; Ruido de rotas cadenas; El dúo Sosa-Echagüe. Vol. I. Buenos Aires: Corregidor, 1987.

Teatro: Estela de madrugada; Tentempié I; Tentempié II. Vol. II. Buenos Aires: Corregidor, 1990.

Teatro: Mil años, un día. Vol. III. Buenos Aires: Corregidor, 1993. English version as *A Thousand Years, One Day*. Trans. by Nora Glickman and Gloria F. Waldman. In *Argentine Jewish Theatre: A Critical Anthology*. Ed. Nora Glickman and Gloria F. Waldman. Lewisburg: Bucknell UP, 1996. 203-62.

¡Viva la anarquía! Hispamérica 24.70 (1995): 61-94.

Nonfiction

"La obsesión de partir." In *Pluralismo e identidad: lo judío en la literatura latinoamericana*. Buenos Aires: Milá, 1986. 195-97.

Yo fui testigo. Buenos Aires: Perfil, 1986.

SECONDARY BIBLIOGRAPHY

Criticism

Armando, Rose Marie. *Teatro argentino contemporáneo*. Buenos Aires: Revista Cultura/Colección Union Carbide, 1985. 85-90.

Berruti, Rómulo. "*Fin de diciembre* de Ricardo Halac." *Talía* 5.27 (1955): 15.

Boero, Alejandra. "A propósito de *Mil años, un día*." In *Teatro: Mil años, un día*. Vol. III. Buenos Aires: Corregidor, 1993. 9-10.

Dabbah, Clara. "Dos estrenos, un autor." *Eco contemporáneo* 8.9 (1965): 112-13.

Espinosa, Pedro. "Un jalón más: *Fin de diciembre*." *Teatro XX* 14 (1965): 8.

—. "Versión imprecisa." *Teatro XX* 15 (1965): 7.

Foster, David William. "Argentine Jewish Dramatists: Aspects of a National Consciousness." *Cultural Diversity in Latin American Literature*. Albuquerque: U of New Mexico P, 1994. 95-150.

Giella, Miguel Angel. "Ricardo Halac: *Lejana tierra prometida*." In his *Teatro Abierto 1981: teatro argentino bajo vigilancia*. Vol. I. Buenos Aires: Corregidor, 1992. 163-75.

Glickman, Nora. "Metáforas de desesperación en *Mil años, un día*." In *Teatro: Mil años, un día*. Vol. III. Buenos Aires: Corregidor, 1993. 11-26. Also as "Metaphors of Disorder and Displacement in *Mil años, un día*, by Ricardo Halac." In *Tradition and Innovation: Reflections on Latin American Jewish Writing*. Ed. Robert DiAntonio and Nora Glickman. Albany, NY: SUNY Press, 1993. 115-23.

Malinow, Inés. "4 espectáculos." *Lyra* 186.8 (1962): 192-93.

Mazza Leiva, Francisco. "El caso Halac." *Hoy en la cultura* 22 (1965): 20.

N.E. "¿Judío o inocente?" *La luz* 1058 (1972): 20-21.

Orgambide, Pedro. "Realismo y vanguardia." *Lyra* 201.3 (1967): 112-13.

Pellettieri, Osvaldo. *"El destete* o la simulación en la lucha por la vida."* In *Teatro Argentino durante el Proceso: 1976-1983.* Ed. Juana Arancibia and Zulema Mirkin. Buenos Aires: Vinciguerra, 1992. 123-29.

—. "Ricardo Halac y sus veinticinco años de realismo." *Latin American Theatre Review* 20.2 (1987): 85-89.

—. "El teatro de Ricardo Halac (I)." In *Teatro.* Vol. I. Buenos Aires: Corregidor, 1987. 15-39.

—. "El teatro de Ricardo Halac (II)." In *Teatro.* Vol. II. Buenos Aires: Corregidor, 1990. 9-25.

Rozitchner, León. *Ser judío.* Buenos Aires: Ediciones de la Flor, 1967.

Tirri, Néstor. *Realismo y teatro argentino.* Buenos Aires: La Bastilla, 1973. 113-21.

Weinstein, Ana E., and Miryam E. Gover de Nasatsky, comps. *Escritores judeoargentinos: bibliografía 1900-1987.* 2 vols. Buenos Aires: Milá, 1994. I.311-15.

Zayas de Lima, Perla. *Diccionario de autores teatrales argentinos 1950-1990.* Buenos Aires: Galerna, 1991. 144-46.

Interviews

Espinosa, Pedro. "Interrogatorio al teatro argentino." *El escarabajo de oro* 20 (1963): 13.

Glickman, Nora. "Entrevista con Ricardo Halac." *Latin American Theatre Review* 23.2 (1990): 55-61.

"¿Imprudencia, impericia o valentía?" *Raíces* 37 (1972): 47-49.

Naios Najchaus, Teresa. "Halac con *Tiempo*: La tierra prometida hay que buscarla aquí." *Tiempo* 151 (1981): 19-20.

"Ricardo Halac." In *Encuesta a la literatura argentina contemporánea.* Buenos Aires: Centro Editor de América Latina, 1982. 157-63.

Gustavo Geirola

HEKER, LILIANA (Argentina; 1943)

Born in Buenos Aires in 1943 to a Jewish family of the *pequeña burguesía* (petit bourgeois), this novelist, short story writer, and essayist belongs both ideologically and chronologically to the group of Argentine writers known as the Generation of the 1960s. She recalls that from the time she was four years old she would invent stories, on the patio of her grandmother's house, that were much more interesting than her childhood reality. She also recognizes that she owes her avid love of reading to her older sister who influenced her affinity for literature. However, it was her own decision that led Heker to follow a literary career at age twenty-one, abandoning her scientific studies.

At age seventeen she began to study physics at the Facultad de Ciencias Exactas at the Universidad de Buenos Aires, and at the same time, to work for the literary journal *El grillo de papel* (The Paper Cricket). She became the editing secretary and soon began to publish her first short stories. It was during this time that her association and friendship with Abelardo Castillo (1935) and his group began, with whom she founded two literary journals of undeniable artistic resonance: the first, *El escarabajo de oro* (The Golden Scarab; 1961-74), Heker subdirected, and the second, *El ornitorrinco* (The Platypus; 1977-86), she co-directed with Castillo. She interviewed such writers as Jorge Luis Borges (1899-1986), Severino Croato (1930) and Abelardo Castillo, among others (*Diálogos sobre la vida y la muerte* [Dialogues on Life and Death]). The essays, criticism, and ideological debates that Heker published in these journals consolidate characteristics of her own writing and likewise established her responsibility with respect to the Argentine reader. One example that stands out in this regard is the polemic that she maintained with Julio Cortázar (1914-84), published in *El ornitorrinco*, on the role of writers and artists that remained in Argentina under the military dictatorship of the 1970s, a very risky situation of which she was a part. Cortázar defended the perspective of the exiled or self-exiled writer who could expose the reality of what was happening in Argentina outside of the country. For Heker this writing did not count since the "right receptor" wasn't reading it and since "it should be immersed in the situation that it pretends to act upon" (*El Ornitorrinco* 10 [Oct.-Nov. 1983]: 4-5).

The narrative of Liliana Heker includes the collections of short stories *Los que vieron la zarza* (Those Who Beheld the Burning Bush; 1966), that won the Mención Unica (Honorable Mention) from the Cuban Concurso Hispano-americano de Literatura de Casa de las Américas (Casa de las Américas Hispanic American Literature Competition), and the Faja de Honor literary award from the Sociedad Argentina de Escritores (The Argentine Writers Society) in 1967; *Acuario* (Aquarius; 1972); *Las peras del mal* (The Pears of Evil; 1982); *Un resplandor que se apagó en el mundo* (A Brilliant Light That Was Extinguished from the World; 1977), a tryptic of nouvelles; the novel *Zona de clivaje* (The Cleavage Zone; 1987), which was awarded the biennial Primer Premio Municipal (First Municipal Prize) for novel 1986-87; and *Los bordes de lo real* (The Borders of What Is Real; 1991), which is a complete collection of her short stories.

Alberto Manguel (1948) has translated into English all of Heker's short fiction. There are also translations of her works in numerous anthologies in German, Dutch, Russian, Polish, and Turkish.

Heker has worked as a professor of mathematics, chemistry, and physics, as a translator, and a computer programmer. She currently resides in Buenos Aires with her husband and coordinates workshops on narrative technique.

Although she began to write what she calls "espantosos poemas" (dreadful poems) at age thirteen and continued with enormous unfinished novels, her years of literary apprenticeship took place during her time with *El grillo de papel* (Frouman-Smith, "Entrevista" 108-9). She considers as fundamental to her development the reading of Jean-Paul Sartre (1905-80), Thomas Mann (1875-1955), and Henrik Ibsen (1828-1906), which provided her with a proper view of the world. By the same token such North American writers as Ernest Hemingway (1899-1961), William Saroyan (1908-81), Flannery O'Connor (1925-64), Raymond Carter (1938-88), and Katherine Anne Porter (1890-1980) influenced her style of writing.

The primary theme of her collection of stories *Los que vieron la zarza*, published at age twenty-three, is rooted in the period and language of childhood, a stage of life that Heker considers to be of great significance due to the intensity of feelings, "el egoísmo, la especulación, el amor, la perversidad, los celos, el altruísmo, son en esa época sentimientos que avasallan y que impulsan conductas en apariencia inexplicables. . ." (egotism, speculation, love, perversity, jealousy, altruism, are during that time feelings that subdue and that impel apparently inexplicable behaviour [Frouman-Smith, "Entrevista" 109-10]).

Her preoccupation with childhood reappears in the short story collections that follow. Behaviour and the apparent games of children often reveal conflictive relationships on the domestic stage and/or the failure(s) of adults. Heker recognizes that part of her narrative is autobiographical, for example, "Vida de familia" (Family Life), "Retrato de un genio" (Potrait of a Genius), "La sinfonía pastoral" (The Pastoral Symphony), "Georgina Requeni o la elegida" (Georgina Requeni or the Chosen Girl), and "Los primeros principios o arte poética" ("Early Beginnings or Ars Poetica"). Likewise, in her first novel, *Zona de clivaje*, certain biographical aspects such as the protagonist's interests, the age at which she starts to study physics, to write, and search for self- awareness are reiterated.

In each new volume Heker amplifies her manner of portraying reality. She explores the insanity and the absurdity that change and define the existence of some of her characters. However, she makes clear that it is not dementia but rather language that has been expanded (Frouman-Smith, "Entrevista" 108). Writing is always a quest for Heker for whom specifically feminine writing creates a reality that responds to the desire to develop an expression that is the prolongation of the body, the constant immersion in an environment of the presumably day-to-day routine, the familiar, the natural, which suddenly becomes unfamiliar or unnatural thereby introducing the unexpected, as is suggested by the title of the collection of her complete short stories *Los bordes de lo real*. In this zone the rise and fall of human experiences come into contact revealing an introverted view (relationship with the inner world) that upon articulation externalizes bordering zones between the rational and the irrational, the conscious and the unconscious.

Heker approaches reality in slow motion, reaching both lunacy and the absurd. Critical analises of the work point out that all the characters in *Los bordes de lo real* are confronted with loneliness, incommunication, incomprehension, and desertion as attributes of daily life. Some forge ahead after struggling but many remain defeated. In "Berkeley o Mariana del Universo" ("Berkeley or Mariana of the Universe") loneliness is necessary for activating the imagination since this is not a collective act. Likewise, in "Un secreto para vos" (A Secret for You), creation is a solitary act. The father in "Casi un melodrama" (Almost a Melodrama) has to leave his family in order to follow his dream of writing. In "Don Juan de la Casa Blanca" (Don Juan of the White House), love, for fear of alcohol, saves the protagonists from loneliness. For Heker, Néstor Parini in "Los que vieron la zarza" meant "un salto cuántico, como si se [le] hubiese concedido ver[se]. . . atravesando [su] propio límite" (a quantum leap, as if she had been allowed to see herself crossing her own border ["Prólogo" to *Los Bordes* 15]).

In *Zona de clivaje*, some biographical facts in the story reiterate her purpose of focusing on the conflict of woman as a profound and thinking being. The protagonist Irene Lauson emancipates herself on various levels upon examining the problematic of artistic expression while meditating about her own identity, converting the creative process into her own self-analysis. The critics consider that in this novel of apprenticeship or education (Bildungsroman) Irene goes through a process of self discovery (Frouman-Smith; Da-Re). It is also a self-reflective novel or metaliterary and metacritical with intertextual references that expand the possibilities of interpretation. The narration occurs in the present with flashbacks, alternating personal experiences and sensorial perceptions with reflection about what is apprehended. At thirty years of age Irene recalls when she was seventeen, was studying physics and initiating her relationship with Alfredo, whose ideology would mark her. She also learned about the ups and downs of life, love, and the masculine double standard. He has love affairs while she remains faithful to him. He dominates the relationship, he tells her of his amorous adventures which she seems to accept coldly, but which deep down bother

her. Upon confronting the last conquest of the forty-three-year-old professor—a seventeen-year-old that reflects/resembles her old self—she refuses to continue playing the game. She establishes her independence by betraying him with a stranger, thus terminating an unequal relationship. Having proven to herself, as she will write years later, that the descent to her lowest possible condition and the constant humiliation turned out to be her pathway to freedom as she was driven to obtain her own independence. In the novel Heker searches for freedom of expression and free articulation, while she interweaves personal experiences that imply suffering—without vain sentimentalism—and a tremendous but necessary sacrifice in the final rite of passage. The subjective feminine perspective of the narrator, the characterization of the protagonists, the articulation of the Buenos Aires ideolect tinged with diverse registers configure a polyphonic structure that does not hide the illogical borderline that guides the characters, subverting the appearance of rationality and daily reality.

Judaic elements are manifested through the author's invention of her own reality: in the tenacious struggle for self-expression, in the internal effort to create and recreate new situations, and in the game played as a girl in her grandmother's home, an environment in which she assimilates the oral tradition that transforms the facts kaleidoscopically. From another perspective, in *Zona de clivaje*, the portrayal and discourse of Guirnalda, Irene's mother, show more concretely the continuity of the Jewish tradition in the face of a world in a constant state of change. Dialogue between mother and daughter incorporates both *lunfardo* (Buenos Aires slang) and Hebrew. Guirnalda sings sad songs that fuel Irene's imagination. In the first collection of stories, *Los que vieron la zarza*, the title is suggestive of the story of Moses to whom God manifested himself in the form of a burning bush and was instructed to lead the Jews out of Egypt. In a certain sense this is an analogous circumstance to that of the characters who must overcome tremendous difficulties in order to obtain what is inwardly desired but is not always achieved.

Heker's most recent novel, *El fin de la historia* (The End of the Story; 1996), is based on the circumstances of the military dictatorship of 1976-1983. It is the story of the protagonist Leonora Ordaz, a leftist revolutionary who becomes involved with the guerilla group known as the Montoneros. She is kidnapped and tortured by the military. When her name turns up on a list of disappeared persons, her longtime friend Diana Glass decides to write a novel based on Leonora's experience. While there is a certain Jewish element to the novel, the primary focus is on articulating the violent past of the dictatorship and the subsequent psychological ramifications for the generation of Argentines who were witness to the period.

PRIMARY BIBLIOGRAPHY
Creative Writing
Acuario. Buenos Aires: Centro Editor de América Latina, 1972.

"Berkeley or Mariana of the Universe." Trans. by Alberto Manguel. In *Short Stories by Latin American Women: The Magic and the Real.* Ed. by Celia Correas de Zapata. Houston: Arte Público Press, 1990. 101-6.

Los bordes de lo real. Buenos Aires: Alfaguara, 1991

"Early Beginnings, or Ars Poetica." Trans. by Alberto Manguel. *The Literary Review* (Special issue "Argentine Writing in the Eighties," ed. by William Katra) 32.4 (1989): 504-07.

El fin de la historia. Buenos Aires: Alfaguara, 1996.

"Jocasta." Trans. by Alberto Manguel. In *Evening Games: Tales of Parents and Children.* Ed. Alberto Manguel. New York: Clarkson N. Potter, 1986. 161-68.

Los que vieron la zarza. Buenos Aires: Jorge Alvarez, 1966.

Las peras del mal. Buenos Aires: Belgrano, 1982.

Un resplandor que se apagó en el mundo. Buenos Aires: Sudamericana, 1977.

The Stolen Party. Trans. by Alberto Manguel. Toronto: Coach House Press, 1994.

"The Stolen Party." Trans. by Alberto Manguel. In *Other Fires: Short Fiction by Latin American Women.* Ed. Alberto Manguel. New York: Clarkson N. Potter, 1986. 151-58.

"When Everything Shines." Trans. by Celeste Kostopulos-Cooperman. In *Secret Weavers: Stories of the Fantastic by Women of Argentina and Chile.* Ed. Marjorie Agosín. Fredonia, NY: White Pine Press, 1992. 287-95.

Zona de clivaje. Buenos Aires: Legasa, 1987.

Nonfiction
Diálogos sobre la vida y la muerte. Compiled and coordinated by Liliana Heker. Buenos Aires: Grupo Editor de Buenos Aires, 1980.

"Exilio y literatura: polémica con Julio Cortázar." Parts 1 and 2. *El ornitorrinco* 4.7 (1980): 3-5; 5.10 (1981): 3-7. Reprinted in *Cuadernos hispanoamericanos* 517-519 (1993): 590-604.

SECONDARY BIBLIOGRAPHY
Criticism
Agosín, Marjorie. "Ana María Shua, Marisa Di Giorgio y Liliana Heker." In her *Literatura fantástica del Cono Sur: las mujeres.* San José: Editorial Universitaria Centroamericana, 1992. 55-66.

Antogno, Carlos O. "Un libro necesario." *El Litoral* (Buenos Aires) 5 Oct., 1991: n.p.

Barbieri, Enrique. "El culto de la desdicha." *Clarín* (Buenos Aires) 9 Feb., 1978: n.p.

Bajarlía, Juan Jacobo. "Alegorías reales." *Clarín* (Buenos Aires) 18 Feb., 1982: 6.

Battista, Vicente. "Los cuentos de Liliana Heker y una escritura persuasiva. La realidad se esconde en los bordes." *Clarín* (Buenos Aires) 26 Sept., 1991: 7.

Caporale, Lisandro. "Encuentro de lo visible y lo invisible." *El francotirador literario* (Buenos Aires) Marzo, 1992: 3.

Da-Re, María Viviana, and Gabriela Fernández. "*Zona de clivaje* de Liliana Heker y la tradición de la novela de educación." In *VI Congreso Nacional de Literatura Argentina: Actas*. Córdoba: Universidad Nacional de Córdoba, 1993. 155-64.

—. "*Zona de clivaje*: la necesidad de la traición." In *La novela argentina de los 80*. Ed. Roland Spiller. Frankfurt am Main, Germany: Vervuert Verlag, 1991. 229-38.

Dio Bleichmar, Emilce. Rev. of *Zona de clivaje*. *Cuadernos hispanoamericanos* 464 (1989): 157-61.

Frouman-Smith, Erica. Rev. of *Zona de clivaje*. *Letras femeninas* 17.1-2 (1991): 143-45.

—. "Woman on the verge of a breakthrough: Liliana Heker's *Zona de clivaje* as a female bildungsroman." *Letras femeninas* 19.1-2 (1993): 100-12.

Gimbernat González, Ester. "Clivaje de espejos, ecos de la escritura: *Zona de clivaje*." In her *Aventuras del desacuerdo: novelistas argentinas de los 80*. Buenos Aires: Danilo Albero Vergara, 1992. 294-99.

Lagunas, Alberto. "El mejor libro argentino de 1977 se llama *Un resplandor que se apagó en el mundo*." *Claudia* (Buenos Aires) 247 (1978): n.p.

Mantaras Loedel, Graciela. "Liliana Heker o el dolor de la magia." *Marcha* (Buenos Aires) 4 Nov., 1966: 31.

—. "La pasión de los fuertes." *Primera plana* (Buenos Aires) 26 July, 1966: 80.

Pérez, Zelaschi, Adolfo L. "*Las peras del mal*." *La prensa* (Buenos Aires) 28 March, 1982: 7.

Piña, Cristina. "Una novela necesaria." *Clarín* (Buenos Aires) 7 Jan., 1988: 6.

Weinstein, Ana E., and Miryam E. Gover de Nasatsky, comps. *Escritores judeo-argentinos: bibliografía 1900-1987*. 2 vols. Buenos Aires: Milá, 1994. I.316-20

Interviews

Agosín, Marjorie. "Entrevista a Liliana Heker." In her *Literatura fantástica del Cono Sur: las mujeres*. San José: Editorial Universitaria Centroamericana, 1992. 121-29.

Fingueret, Manuela. "Articular una literatura para la próxima década." *Nueva presencia* 154 (June 13, 1980): 10-15.

Flores Correa, Mónica. "¿Tiene sexo la literatura?" *Pájaro de fuego*. 36 (1981): 41-42.

Frouman-Smith, Erica. "Entrevista con Liliana Heker." *Chasqui* 21.1 (1992): 106-16.

"Liliana Heker." In *Encuesta a la literatura argentina contemporánea*. Buenos Aires: Centro Editor de América Latina, 1982. 108-15.

Vázquez Santamaría, Jorge. "Cazando grillos con Liliana Heker." *El escarabajo de oro* 28 (1965): 21-22.

Silvia Sauter
Mariana Petrea

IOLOVITCH, MARCOS (Brazil; date unknown)

Almost nothing is known about Marcos Iolovitch, author of a thin book on the hardships and ordeals experienced by himself and his family upon their immigration to Brazil titled *Numa clara manhã de abril* (On a Clear April Morning; 1940). Writing a preface for the book's second edition (1987), author Moacyr Scliar (1937) discloses that he has personally met Iolovitch and describes him as "a delicate person, a small framed man, elegant and of an enchanting kindness" (8). Scliar, himself a very renowned Brazilian author, reveals that Iolovitch has published a collection of poetry, *Preces profanas* (Profane Prayers; publication information unattainable), as a "proclamation against injustice and oppression", since he was "like many intellectuals of his times, a politically committed man" (8).

Numa clara manhã de abril can be seen as a book engaged in the criticism of ways and means used by the Jewish Colonization Association when controlling the flow of immigrants to Rio Grande do Sul. Moreover, it is also an argument for a nihilistic approach to life conceived by Iolovitch from his readings of Arthur Schopenhauer (1788-1860). The novel, which contains autobiographical characteristics, tells of the hard times endured by his family starting with the time they left Russia to settle in the Quatro Irmãos farm. Fleeing there, they moved to Porto Alegre and the young Marcos (with a different name in the novel) sampled the bitter taste of solitude, poverty, hunger, and a variety of personal frustrations. The novel is an unredeemingly personal description of family situations, social pressures, and eventually, of a few moments of respite in an otherwise rough life experience partially endured in the country, but mostly in the city.

Moacyr Scliar refers to the novel as a text that should not be praised by a high standard of literary values, but rather as a documentary narrative, and as such, its importance should be estimated as "invaluable" (7).

PRIMARY BIBLIOGRAPHY

Numa clara manhã de abril. Prefácio de Moacyr Scliar. Porto Alegre: Oficina da Livraria do Globo, 1940. 2nd ed. Editora Movimento/Instituto Cultural Judaico Marc Chagall, 1987.

Regina Igel

ISAACS, JORGE (Colombia; 1837-95)

While Jorge Isaacs was dying in Ibagué, Colombia, the central interior of the country, he told his wife Felisa and their seven surviving children to bury him in Medellín, the capital of Antioquia. He wasn't born there, nor did he spend much time there, compared to the years in Bogotá, and the time he spent wandering around the country and the continent. But the State of Antioquia had supposedly been settled by Jews and is still known for its fiscal and physical Jewish characteristics. From his deathbed, Isaacs looked up at the priest who was ritually asking the dying man if he believed in Jesus Christ. "He's one of our race," was the affirmation (Eduardo Zuleta, "El semitismo de Antioquia," 1926; Mesa Bernal 222). Shortly before, Isaacs had been celebrating his racial roots as a distant son of Spain who had found his way back, through Inquisitions and exile, to the extension of the mother country (see, for example, his poem "Tierra de Córdoba" [Land of Córdoba; 1892). But the celebration sounds like the kind of defensive, or equivocal, affirmation that he would make to the priest. The truth was that neither his identity as a Christian, nor the putative Jewish origins of Antioquia were to be taken for granted; his pronouncements are practically provocations.

As the son of a *converso*, Isaacs would gradually assume and then embrace his Jewish identity, almost as a rebellious response to those who called him Jew as an intended offense. And the province traditionally associated with Jewishness, Antioquia, has had its own history of simultaneously accepting and denying the connection (cf. Mesa Bernal). Isaacs's own doubled or indefinite identity, in other words, is rehearsed against a background of debated doublings of the local homeland he chose at the end of his peregrinations.

Where he began, however, was not the coffee culture of smart (Jewish?) businessmen in Medellín, but in the conservative center of sugar plantations and slavery, Cali in the southern Cauca valley. Cali is, at least, where his family had established a plantation and thrived, for awhile. But some would say that this origin is a fiction, a pretension towards centrality, because his real birthplace was in the jungle region of Chocó. It was there where his English-Sephardic father emigrated from Jamaica in search of gold (cf. Caicedo Licona). What Jorge Senior found instead was a wife of Catalán and Italian background who required her husband to convert to Catholicism. Of their dozen children, Jorge was born in 1837. That is, just before the ruling sectors definitively split into the Liberals and Conservatives who would engage in apparently endless civil wars. These gave Colombia the unenviable distinction of being practically the only Latin American country that did not achieve some kind of national consolidation in the nineteenth century.

Isaacs lived on the comfortable family plantation until he was sent to school in Bogotá, just as Efraín was sent in the semiautobiographical *María* (1867). In the capital, he studied with Liberals when President López's Radical Liberal government responded to a decade of slave uprisings by abolishing slavery in 1851. Fifteen years later Isaacs's nostalgic novel tells us that nothing was gained. Instead of new national projects that might have reconciled Conservatives and Liberals, abolition precipitated a Civil War in Antioquia, Isaacs's Cauca, and other slaveholding southern provinces.

After coming home to find his father's health and fortune waning, Isaacs joined the fight to protect his family's privilege. First in 1854, and again in 1860, he enlisted in the government's forces to put down left-wing liberal rebellions. In the meantime, Isaacs met and soon married Felisa Gonzales, a mere girl whom he describes in the ideal terms he will use of María. By 1863, his patrimony in ruins, Isaacs went to Bogotá to defend himself, unsuccessfully, against creditors. He lost in business but won constant recognition as a poet by the members of "el Mosaico" (Mosaic), the literary circle that published his book of poems that same year. Running out of money, Isaacs finally accepted a job in 1865 as inspector of the road being built along the jungle of the Pacific Coast.

There he started to write *María*, the only nineteenth-century Spanish American novel that became a continental classic printed in pirated editions from Mexico to Argentina. But by 1905, the novel was added to the Vatican's index of prohibited books. Why?, asks an incredulous Ecuadorian newspaper. "Because it's about a Jewess, and that smells of infernal brimstone" (*El telégrafo*, July 29, 1905).

Still a Conservative in 1866, Isaacs was a congressional deputy for his region and director of a Conservative newspaper when he suddenly announced his new sympathies with the Radical wing of the Liberal Party. Apparently dramatic shifts of allegiance like this one were not terribly surprising, though, especially since the laissez-faire Radicals favored a monoculture for export and gain from the foreign exchange. Both, however, were opposed to the left, "Draconian" wing of the Liberal Party, made up of the artisans, manufacturers, and small farmers who fought for protectionism and against free trade. Isaacs liked to attribute his political change of heart to intellectual progress, as when he quipped to a Conservative critic, "I have come out of the darkness into the light." But given the political alliances of that period between the so-called Radicals and Conservatives and given his family ties to English-Jamaican commerce, that early conversion was hardly spectacular.

His real break with conservatism and Catholicism (Isaacs became a Free Mason) would come in 1868. For the next two years, he served as Secretary in the House of Representatives and then became Consul in Chile. In Chile Isaacs created a literary stir, publishing frequently in local newspapers. Back in Colombia in 1873, he began to make bold but bad business decisions, speculating in one promising venture after another. By the "Holy War" of 1875, when the church itself recruited armies, the theocratic Conservatives finally split from the Radicals who insisted on the separation of church and state. Isaacs defended the central government; but this time it was anti-oligarchic and anti-ecclesiastical. The year 1887 saw him intensely busy with reform of both primary and secondary education in the Cauca region, as well as his growing defense of Indigenous peoples' rights. "If the African race has been protected in the Cauca by the wise law that liberated it entirely from slavery, the indigenous people, who even now live in a feudal system in the south of the state, demand the same protection. It is only just, and legal, and humanitarian, that they obtain it" (Arciniegas, *Genio y figura de Jorge Isaacs* 8). After barely three months he had to surrender, hoping to regain his seat in Congress. But his optimism evidently seemed misplaced in a national government from which he had tried to secede.

Isaacs lost his seat, and lost his faith in belonging to Colombia. That same year, General Julio A. Roca became president of the now finally consolidated country of Argentina, and a year later, Isaacs was dedicating a long poem to

Roca, hoping in advance that he might be buried under the same soil that covered the glorious remains of Manuel Belgrano and Bernardino Rivadavia, in case his own bones would be refused burial in Colombia. The 1881 poem is entitled "Saulo" (Saul), full of Old Testament allusions. Isaacs's sentimental attachments to Colombia continued to be a source of insecurity, and in another, far shorter poem written a decade later, he traces his origins back to England, "La patria de Shakespeare" (Land of Shakespeare; 1892) "¡Patria de mis mayores!. . . Noble madre,/ de Israel desvalido, protectora/ llevo en el alma numen de tus bardos,/ mi corazón es templo de tus glorias" (Homeland of my fathers!. . . Noble mother,/ of homeless Israel the protectress/ In me survives the spirit of your bards,/ my heart is the temple of your glory [*Poesías. La luna en la velada; Saulo; Traducciones* 275). But Isaacs stayed in Colombia (except for a visit to Argentina at President Roca's invitation), and was reintegrated into the government; that is at a benign distance from the capital. President Rafael Núñez named him secretary of a scientific mission to discover natural resources in the country. This led to an intensified interest in Colombia's human profile, specifically in Indigenous life. His first ethnographic studies date from 1884, and appeared in the *Anales de instrucción pública*.

More than a progression, Isaacs's life seemed to be a stalemate between conservative privilege, based on the apparent homogeneity of the ruling class, and enlightened liberalism, which promised equal rights and opportunities to the now impoverished writer. He also seemed poised between repeated and failed attempts to recover the patriarchal order of his childhood and the struggle to establish himself in a new commercial economy. This indecision may have been a certain kind of position that cannot take sides, because partiality would make little sense after history has apparently passed one by. Yet Isaacs persisted in participating, and Jaime Mejía Duque concludes that it was with a chronic case of bad faith; whatever the failed business venture or the frustrated political campaign at hand, the fault always lay with others. This political and economic (im)posture, claiming to want improvement and continually enjoying the privilege of displacing responsibility, may have spilled over from what Mejía describes as Isaacs's writerly petulance. Although he laments his frustrated potential as a writer of an original creative spirit, the repeated frustration of that potential is what motivates his very poignant novel about impossible and unproductive love. How could it be otherwise, when the protagonists are themselves divided, racially Jewish and culturally Caucasian (Catholic and ultimately theocratic) planters? María, the narrator would lament as he thought about ending his own life, of course I believed in her, she belonged to my race.

Isaacs finally was buried in Medellín, ten years after his death. And in 1962, he was commemorated by the Colombian government with a bronze bust presented to the Hebrew University of Jerusalem. The Hebrew inscription simply calls him "poet," but in Spanish the plaque reads "Llevó al romanticismo de la lengua española el espíritu lírico de su estirpe hebrea" (He brought to Spanish language romanticism the lyrical spirit of his Hebrew roots/race).

PRIMARY BIBLIOGRAPHY
Creative Writing

"Camilo." *Boletín de la Academia Colombiana* (Bogotá) 2.9-11 (1937): 270-99. Six chapters of an unfinished novel.

Canciones y coplas populares. Bogotá: Procultura, 1985.

"La luna en la velada." *La Fe* (Bogotá) 2 (May 19, 1868): 13-14.

María. Bogotá: Imprenta Gaitán, 1867; Imprenta M. Rivas, 1869. Modern critical editions of *María*: Ed. with prologue by Gustavo Mejía. Caracas: Ayacucho, 1978. Ed. with prologue by Roberto F. Giusti. Buenos Aires: Losada, novena ed., 1982. Ed. with introduction by Donald Mcgrady. Madrid: Cátedra, 1986, 2nd. ed, 1991. English version as, *María: A South American Romance.* Trans. by Rollo Ogden. New York: Harper & Brothers, 1890.

Obras completas. Medellín: R. Montoya y Montoya, 1966.

Paulina Lamberti. Bolívar (Bogotá) 12 (1952): 245-80. Drama.

Poesías. Bogotá: Imprenta el Mosaico, 1864.

Poesías completas de Jorge Isaacs. Preliminary study by Baldomero Sanín Cano. Barcelona: Maucci, 1920.

Poesías. La luna en la velada; Saulo; Traducciones. Ed. Armando Romero Lozano. Cali: Biblioteca de la Universidad del Valle, 1967.

Saulo (Canto I). Bogotá: Imprenta de Echeverri, 1881.

Nonfiction

A mis amigos y a los comerciantes del Cauca. Cali: Imprenta de Hurtado, 1875.

Estudio sobre las tribus indígenas del Magdalena. In *Anales de instrucción pública de los Estados Unidos de Colombia.* (Bogot), 7.45 (1884): 177-354. Also as vol. 133 of the Biblioteca Popular de Cultura Colombiana, Bogotá: Ministerio de Educación Nacional, 1951.

"Leyendo a *María.*" *El Pasatiempo* (Bogotá) 3.42 (August 14, 1880): 336.

Los motilones. Cali?, 1875?

La revolución radical en Antioquia. Bogotá: Imprenta de Gaitán, 1880.

SECONDARY BIBLIOGRAPHY

Anderson Imbert, Enrique. "*María* de Jorge Isaacs." In *Historia y crítica de la literatura hispanoamericana 2: del romanticismo al modernismo*. Ed. Cedomil Goic. Barcelona: Editorial Crítica, 1991. 295-302.

Arciniegas, Germán. "150 años del natalicio de Jorge Isaacs: el paisaje como protagonista en *María*." *Correo de los Andes* 47-48 (1987): 28-37.

—. *Genio y figura de Jorge Isaacs*. Buenos Aires: Editorial Universitaria de Buenos Aires, 1967.

Borges, Jorge Luis. "Vindicación de la María de Jorge Isaacs." *Correo de los Andes* 44 (1987): 30-32.

Brushwood, John S. "Codes of Character Definition: Jorge Isaacs's *María*." In his *Genteel Barbarism: Experiments in Analysis of Nineteenth-Century Spanish-American Novels*. Lincoln/London: U of Nebraska P, 1981. 81-106.

Caicedo Licona, Carlos Arturo. *Jorge Isaacs, su María, sus luchas*. Medellín: Lealón, 1989.

Caro, Miguel Angel. *Estudio sobre las tribus indígenas del Magdalena*. Bogotá: Ministerio de Educación Nacional, 1951.

Carvajal, Mario. *Jorge Isaacs, hijo de Cali*. Cali: Carvajal y Cía, 1943.

—. *Vida y pasión de Jorge Issacs*. Manizales, Colombia: A. Zapata, 1937.

Cristina Z., María Teresa. "Jorge Isaacs." In *Gran Enciclopedia de Colombia*. Tomo 4, Literatura. Bogotá: Círculo de Lectores, 1992. 89-100.

Gay, Erica. "Storia di un idillio fra amore e morte: a proposito di *María* di Jorge Isaacs." *Letterature d'America: Revista Trimestrale* 4.16 (1983): 71-87.

Gómez Valderrama, Pedro. *Jorge Isaacs*. Bogotá: Procultura, 1989.

Góngora, Leonel. *Soñé vagar: la poética correspondencia inédita de un Jorge Isaacs*. Bogotá: Puntos Gráficos, 1991.

Lagos-Pope, María Inés. "Estructura dual y sociedad patriarcal en *María*. *Revista de estudios colombianos* 8 (1990): 12-20.

Laguado, Arturo. "Jorge Isaacs en su tiempo." *Boletín cultural y bibliográfico* 20.2 (1983): 107-11.

López Michelson, Alfonso. "Ensayo sobre la influencia semítica en *María*." *Revista de las Indias* (2da época) 62 (1944): 5-10.

Magnarelli, Sharon. "The Love Story: Reading and Writing in Jorge Isaacs's *María*." *The Lost Rib: Female Characters in the Spanish-American Novel*. Lewisburg, PA: Bucknell UP, 1985. 19-37.

McGrady, Donald. *Bibliografía sobre Jorge Isaacs*. Bogotá: Caro y Cuervo, 1971.

—. *Jorge Isaacs*. New York: Twayne Publishers, 1972.

Mejía, Gustavo. "Prólogo." *María* de Jorge Isaacs. Caracas: Ayacucho, 1978. ix-xxxii.

Mejía Duque, Jaime. *Isaacs y "María": el hombre y su novela*. Bogotá: La Carreta, 1979.

Mejía Vallejo, Manuel, ed. *María más allá de Paraíso*. Cali: Editorial Alonso Quijada, 1984.

Mesa Bernal, Daniel. *Polémica sobre el origen del pueblo antioqueño*. Bogotá: Fondo Cultural Cafetero, 1988.

Molloy, Sylvia. "Paraíso perdido y economía terrenal en *María*." *Sin nombre* 14.3 (1984): 36-55.

Perus Coinet, Francoise. "*María* de Jorge Isaacs o la negación del espacio novelesco." *Nueva revista de filología hispánica* 35.2 (1987): 721-51.

Promis, José. "Las tres caras de *María*: lectura de las lecturas de la novela de Jorge Isaacs." *Revista signos: estudios de lengua y literatura* 24.29 (1991): 67-75.

Rodríguez Guerrero, Ignacio. *Ediciones de la novela "María" de Jorge Isaacs (1867-1967)*. Pasto: Imprenta del Departamento, 1967.

Sklodowska, Elzbieta. "*María* de Jorge Isaacs, ante la crítica." *Thesaurus: boletín del Instituto Caro y Cuervo* 38.3 (1983): 617-24.

Sommer, Doris. "El mal de *María*: (Con)fusión en un romance nacional." *MLN* 104.2 (1989): 429-74.

—. "*María*'s Disease: A National Romance (Con)founded." In her *Foundational Fictions: The National Romances of Latin America*. Berkeley/Los Angeles: U of California P, 1991. 172-203.

El telégrafo (Quito, Ecuador). July 29, 1905: pag. unknown.

Tittler, Jonathan. "Tropos tropicales: paisajes figurados en *María*, *La vorágine* y *El otoño del patriarca*." *Discurso literario* 2.2 (1985): 507-18.

Velasco Madriñán, Luis Carlos. *El explorador Jorge Isaacs*. Cali: Imprenta Deptal, 1967.

—. *Jorge Isaacs: el caballero e las lágrimas*. Cali: Editorial América, 1942.

Velasco Madriñán, Luis Eduardo. "Isaacs en la Guajira." *Correo de los Andes* 18 (1982): 88-89.

Williams, Raymond L. "The Problem of Unity in Fiction: Narrator and Self in *María*." *MLN* 101.2 (1986): 342-53.

Zanetti, Susana. *Jorge Isaacs*. Buenos Aires: Centro Editorial de América Latina, 1967.

Doris Sommer

ISAACSON, JOSÉ (Argentina; 1922)

José Isaacson was born on August 14, 1922 in Buenos Aires. He is an active member of the Buenos Aires literary community, both as a literary critic and a creative author. He has served in a variety of administrative capacities in national and international literary organizations, he is the recipient of numerous awards, and his works have been widely anthologized and published in journals (see Weinstein and Gover de Nasatsky). His endeavors as a critic include works on Franz Kafka (1883-1924), Jorge Luis Borges (1899-1986), José Hernández (1834-86), and Macedonio Fernández (1874-1952).

Isaacson is above all a poet, to which his numerous collections of verse attest. His early works such as *Las canciones de Ele-í* (The Songs of Ele-í; 1952), *Amor y amar* (Love and To Love; 1960), *Elogio de la poesía* (Praise of Poetry; 1963), and *Oda a la alegría* (Ode to Happiness; 1965), all share a celebratory poetic mood and a carefree lyricism. Thematically, the poems of these volumes focus on love and the joy of life. The collection *Oda a Buenos Aires* (Ode to Buenos Aires; 1966) is an elegiac homage to the poet's native city. It constitutes a poetic tour through the streets and neighborhoods of Buenos Aires. Isaacson's verse is accompanied by numerous illustrative sketches of the city by Rodrigo Bonomé.

Isaacson's most accomplished volume of poetry is his lengthy (almost three-hundred pages), philosophical, and highly emotive *Cuaderno Spinoza* (Spinoza Notebook; 1977). It is composed in the form of an open letter to and dialogue with Baruch Spinoza (1632-1677), the seventeenth-century Sephardic philosopher. Written in the year that marked the three-hundredth anniversary of the death of Spinoza, it is not merely a celebration in his honor. Leonardo Senkman points out that Isaacson exhumes the figure of Spinoza as an ideological gesture in reaction to the changing sociopolitical atmosphere of Argentina, but he criticizes the poet for his doing so as an act of self-legitimation. Isaacson makes a connection between his own Sephardic heritage and that of Spinoza and then enters into a dialogue with him, establishing a number of commonalities between them. Both Senkman and Naomi Lindstrom have examined the complexities of this poetic act of communication that invites the reader's active participation, as well as the motivating factors behind its creation. Regardless of the multiple critical assessments that can be drawn from the work, there can be no debate as to its significant contribution to the relatively small body of works by Sephardic authors in Latin America.

PRIMARY BIBLIOGRAPHY
Creative Writing
Amor y amar. Buenos Aires: Américalee, 1960.

Amor y amar (Includes *Amor y amar*, *Elogio de la poesía*, *Oda a la alegría*). Buenos Aires: Américalee, 1968.

Las canciones de Ele-í. Buenos Aires: Lautaro, 1975.

Cuaderno Spinoza. Buenos Aires: Marymar, 1977.

Elogio de la poesía. Buenos Aires: Hachette, 1963.

El metal y la voz. Buenos Aires: Américalee, 1956.

Oda a Buenos Aires. Buenos Aires: Américalee, 1966.

Oda a la alegría. Buenos Aires: Américalee, 1965.

El pasajero. Buenos Aires: Américalee, 1969.

Poemas del conocer. Buenos Aires: Marymar, 1984.

Nonfiction
La Argentina como pensamiento. Buenos Aires: Marymar, 1983.

Antropología literaria: una estética de la persona. Buenos Aires: Marymar, 1982.

Borges entre los nombres y el Nombre. Buenos Aires: Fundación del Libro, 1987.

Encuentro político con José Hernández. Notas y digresiones. Buenos Aires: Marymar, 1986.

Introducción a los diarios de Kafka, la escritura como dialéctica de los límites. Buenos Aires: Marymar, 1977.

Kafka: la imposibilidad como proyecto. Buenos Aires: Plus Ultra, 1974.

Macedonio Fernández, sus ideas políticas y estéticas. Buenos Aires: Belgrano, 1981.

El neohumanismo de la actual poesía argentina: elementos para una antropología literaria. Buenos Aires: Comentario, 1968.

Pensar la Argentina. Buenos Aires: Plus Ultra, 1986.

El poeta en la sociedad de masas: elementos para una antropología literaria. Buenos Aires: Américalee, 1969.

La revolución de la persona. Buenos Aires: Marymar, 1980.

Editions
Comunidades judías de Latinoamérica. 5th ed. Buenos Aires: Candelabro, 1971-1972.

Cuarenta años de poesía argentina: 1920-1960. (With Enrique Urquía) 3 vols. Buenos Aires: Albada, 1962-1964.

Martín Fierro centenario: testimonios. Buenos Aires: Ministerio de Cultura y Educación, Subsecretaría de Cultura, 1972. Reissued as *Martín Fierro: cien años de crítica.* Buenos Aires: Plus Ultra, 1986.

Poesía de la Argentina, de Tejeda a Lugones. Buenos Aires: Editorial Universitaria de Buenos Aires, 1965.

El populismo en la Argentina. Buenos Aires: Plus Ultra, 1974.

SECONDARY BIBLIOGRAPHY

Criticism

Ara, Guillermo. *Suma de la poesía argentina, 1538-1968. Parte I: Crítica.* Buenos Aires: Guadalupe, 1970. 164-65.

Guardia, Alfredo. "Certidumbre de la poesía." Prologue to *El pasajero.* Buenos Aires: Américalee, 1969. 11-19.

Lindstrom, Naomi. "José Isaacson: An Open Letter to Spinoza." In her *Jewish Issues in Argentine Literature: From Gerchunoff to Szichman.* Columbia: U of Missouri P, 1989. 113-29.

Mastronardi, Carlos. "Isaacson y la esperanza." *Comentario* 25 (1960): 25-32.

—. "*El metal y la voz.*" *Sur* 264 (1960): 78-81.

Mendía, José A. "*Cuaderno Spinoza*, de José Isaacson: un diálogo entre dos siglos." *Pájaro de fuego* 1 (1977): 24-25.

Senkman, Leonardo. "Nobleza y precariedad de la condición judía." In his *La identidad judía en la literatura argentina.* Buenos Aires: Pardés, 1983. 351-63.

Urquía, Carlos E. "*El metal y la voz.*" *Comentario* 18 (1958): 89-91.

Weinberg, Gregorio. "El poeta de la sociedad de masas." *Sur* 324 (1970): 83-86.

Weinstein, Ana E., and Miryam E. Gover de Nasatsky, comps. *Escritores judeo-argentinos: bibliografía 1900-1987.* 2 vols. Buenos Aires: Milá, 1994. I.324-33.

Yagupsky, Máximo G. "José Isaacson, premio municipal de poesía." *Comentario* 27 (1961): 101-2.

Interviews

Ploschuk, Ariel. "Dialogando con José Isaacson: Negar el componente judío en la civilización occidental es una absurda amputación." *Mundo Israelita* 2994 (4 April, 1981): 6, 15.

—. "Mi condición judía es inseparable de mi evaluación de la realidad argentina, afirma José Isaacson." *Mundo Israelita* 3106 (28 May, 1983): 8.

Darrell B. Lockhart

JACOBS, BÁRBARA (Mexico; 1947)

Bárbara Jacobs was born in Mexico City in 1947. She attended preparatory school in Montreal, Canada, and she completed her bachelors degree at the National Autonomous University (UNAM) in Mexico City. She gained additional academic background from 1974 to 1977 as a researcher and professor at the College of Mexico. Her novel *Las hojas muertas* (*The Dead Leaves*; 1987) earned her the Xavier Villaurrutia literary prize in Mexico and six years later was translated into English and published in the United States. The novel was later selected by the Secretary of Public Education to be placed in the libraries of secondary schools in Mexico. Her books and articles have been published in Argentina, Spain, the United States, and Mexico, and some of her stories have appeared in anthologies and various journals in English, Italian, and German. She has lectured at numerous universities in Mexico, the United States, Canada, Spain, and Argentina. Jacobs has received the prestigious scholarship of the National Foundation for Culture and Arts (Mexico) in 1992-93 and was an AT&T Fellow for a residency at the International Writing Program at the University of Iowa in 1993. Jacobs compiled a book of short stories in collaboration with Augusto Monterroso (1921) titled *Antología del cuento triste* (An Anthology of Sad Short Stories; 1993). Other published texts include the short story collections *Un justo acuerdo* (A Fair Deal; 1979), *Doce cuentos en contra* (Twelve Stories Against; 1982), the novel *Las siete vidas de Saab, alias el Rizos* (The Seven Escapes of Saab, Alias Curly Locks; 1992), and a book of essays, *Escrito en el tiempo* (Written in Time; 1990). Her most recent book bears the title *Vida con mi amigo* (Life with My Friend; 1994). Many of her essays and short stories have been published, but not in book form. Every two weeks she writes essays in the Mexican daily *La Jornada*.

The works of Bárbara Jacobs are strongly influenced by her childhood. She was educated in a family in which five languages were spoken, as her grandparents were from Lebanon and she identifies them as being of Jewish and Maronite descent; her father was Lebanese-North American, and her nanny an indigenous Meso-American. All of these elements have made her creative spirit somewhat restless and the themes of her novels very diverse, multicultural, and colorful. For example, the book *Antología del cuento triste* provides the reader with one hundred years of short stories from the Western literary tradition, in six languages, and includes fourteen different nationalities.

In the novel *Las hojas muertas*, Jacobs affords the reader a perspective of herself as a young girl, and later as a woman. She records and reflects on the most memorable sayings and memories of her family. While she does not develop a thematic of the problems of Jewish immigrants directly, Jacobs vividly paints the experience of a Lebanese Maronite family that arrived in the United States at the end of the nineteenth century. The novel discusses the problems of social and religious acculturation the Lebanese immigrants suffer in the United States and Mexico. Jacobs also utilizes the experience of her grandparents to give insight into the problems that the children of immigrants have, being both Lebanese and North American. This is interesting because it shows how traditions and the mother language, Arabic, are passed on to the second generation, and how in this manner cultural heritage and roots are preserved. This also illustrates how her grandmother adapts to a different religious environment. With no practicing Maronite group accessible in the area where she lives, she begins to practice Catholicism.

Jacobs relates the adventures of her father when he studied journalism in Moscow and his participation in the Lincoln Brigade during the Spanish Civil War. His participation resulted in his being placed under surveillance by the United States military. Later, he secretly married his second cousin (also Lebanese) in Mexico, and dropped out of the military, due to the way that he had been treated. From this point on, he lived permanently in Mexico City, where Bárbara and her siblings were born.

Jacobs imparts to the reader the problems that confront her family, especially the experiences of her father. The author succeeds in transmitting in detail the joys, frustrations, fears, and heartaches with such sensitivity that the reader both suffers from and enjoys the work. Within the context of Lebanese families, she portrays the strong kinship of her parents' matrimony, while at the same time the intense grudge that her father's brother and sister hold against him for abandoning them in the United States.

Doce cuentos en contra is divided into a number of stories that are realistic, interesting, and that consistently catch the reader's attention. The stories are narrated with incredible freshness, allowing the reader to enjoy the book. Jacobs's narrations deal with topics such as life, family, professional frustrations, and mystery. In the stories "Carol dice" (Carol Says) and "Notas y clave" (Notes with a Key), Jacobs treats the problems of adaptation, depression, and the struggles of young Latins in religious schools in Canada. They adjust and learn to live in a culture that is totally different from their own and encounter the typical assortment of adolescent Latin identity problems in foreign lands. The description of the life of the characters is clear and precise, and Jacobs is careful to control the direction of each story. She does not treat the theme of Judaism directly, but rather weaves her tales around the problematic condition of minorities in general.

The book *Escrito en el tiempo* is a collection of fifty-three letters that was inspired by themes dealt with in *Time* magazine in 1984. Jacobs sent two letters to *Time*, but they were not accepted for publication. Nonetheless, she continued writing as if it were part of a literary exercise that forced her to write on a particular theme within a predetermined time period. This helped her to develop her abilities as a writer. She wrote the letters in the form of short essays, which should not be classified as polemics but rather as a way to express her ideas about diverse themes covered in *Time*.

The novel *Las siete fugas de Saab, alias el Rizos* is derived from the stories that the protagonist, Saab, writes to his sister, and from a diary that she writes when she was in the process of changing physically from a girl to a woman. Jacobs presents the problems that confront Saab and his sister as they go through adolescence, such as anxieties, fears, and doubts. Their problems illustrate how this is a time of physical, emotional, and familial conflicts for young people. Their problems arise because they do not know what they want. Likewise, they feel confused by all that surrounds them, due to the fact that they are mature physically but not emotionally. The inexperience and poor judgement of youth makes them vulnerable to fall into vices such as drugs, in the hope that they can find an easy escape from their problems. Jacobs paints the lives of the characters in her work with a mesh of words, legends, and traditions from the Middle East.

In her most recent work, *Vida con mi amigo*, Jacobs provides a view of her intimate life by way of dialogues that she had with her husband. Through the narrative presentation of different landscapes of geography and literature, the reader becomes acquainted with the author's spirituality and married life. Jacobs demonstrates the richness of her knowledge of world literature through her conversations with her husband and her skillful writing.

PRIMARY BIBLIOGRAPHY
Creative Writing

"Apuntes contra un marido juicioso: el de Virginia Woolf." *Revista de la Universidad de México* 32.12 (1978): 13-14.

Doce cuentos en contra. México, D.F.: Martín Casillas, 1982.

Las hojas muertas. México, D.F.: Ediciones Era, 1987; Barcelona: Muchnik, 1988; México, D.F.: Secretaría de Educación Pública/Ediciones Era, 1994. English version as *The Dead Leaves*. Trans. by David Unger. Willimantic, CT: Curbstone Press, 1993.

Un justo acuerdo. México, D.F.: La Máquina de Escribir, 1979.

"Motivaciones." *Hispamérica* 19.56-57 (1990): 115-20.

"Retrato conjetural." *Revista de bellas artes* 131.2 (1974): 20-21.

Las siete fugas de Saab, alias el Rizos. México, D.F.: Alfaguara/Consejo Nacional para la Cultura y las Artes, 1992.

"The Time I Got Drunk." Trans. by Cynthia Steele. In *TriQuarterly* 85 (1992): 292-99. Special issue, *New Writing from Mexico*, Ed. Reginald Gibbons.

Nonfiction

Escrito en el tiempo. México, D.F.: Ediciones Era, 1985.

Vida con mi amigo. Madrid: Alfaguara, 1994.

Editions

Antología del cuento triste. With Augusto Monterroso. Barcelona: Edhasa, 1992; Benos Aires: Sudamericana, 1993; México, D.F.: Hermes, 1993.

SECONDARY BIBLIOGRAPHY

Anaya, Marina. "La resurrección de las hojas." (*Las hojas muertas*) *Plural* 18.205 (1988): 70-71.

Bradu, Fabienne. "Crónica de narrativa: hacer de la infancia una literatura." [*Las hojas muertas*]. *Vuelta* 12.140 (1988): 42-45.

—. Rev. of *Doce cuentos en contra. Vuelta* 6.71 (1982): 37-38.

—. Rev. of *Escrito en el tiempo. Araucaria de Chile* 33 (1986): 173-78.

—. Rev. of *Escrito en el tiempo. Vuelta* 10.113 (1986): 54-55.

Jiménez de Baez, Yvette. "Marginalidad e historia o tiempo de mujer en los relatos de Bárbara Jacobs; Programa Interdisciplinario de Estudios de la Mujer." In *Mujer y literatura mexicana y chicana: Culturas en contacto, II.* Ed. Aralia López González. México, D.F.: Colegio de México, 1990; Tijuana: Colegio de la Frontera Norte, 1990. 127-37.

Marquet, Antonio. "El ocaso de Emile Jacobs." (*Las hojas muertas*) *Plural* 18.205 (1988): 69-70.

Molina, Silvia. Rev. of *Las siete fugas de Saab, alias el Rizos. Nexos* 15.178 (1992): 88-89.

Rojas-Trempe, Lady. "La iniciación y el discurso de dos adolescentes en 'Carol dice' de Bárbara Jacobs." In *Cuento contigo: la ficción en México.* Ed. Alfredo Pavón. Tlaxcala: Universidad Autónoma de Tlaxcala, 1993. 117-27.

Estela Zamora McGlade

KALINA, ROSA (Costa Rica; 1934)

Rosa (Rosita) Kalina de Piszk is one of Costa Rica's foremost poets and social critics. She was born October 3, 1934, in San José. Her educational background is varied, having studied in many areas from oncology to theater. Kalina received a degree in English literature from the University of Costa Rica with a thesis on Bernard Malamud's (1914-86) *The Assistant* (1957). She worked for a time as a high school English teacher, helping to found the Santa Ana High School. From 1965 to 1970 she was employed as an executive secretary for the Johnson County Health Department in Iowa City, Iowa. At the University of Costa Rica she taught English and worked on *Kanina*, a literary magazine from the University of Costa Rica.

Kalina has published much short fiction in the literary supplement of *La Nación* (The Nation), Costa Rica's foremost newspaper, to which she continues to contribute fiction and essays. Much of her work has appeared in *Herencia judía* (Jewish Heritage), a journal of Jewish interests from Bogotá, Colombia. She has long been, and continues to be, an essayist and social critic on the pages of her country's newspaper, writing on a wide variety of themes from a recent article on the perceptions of a travelling exhibit on Anne Frank's (1929-44) life brought to Costa Rica by the Dutch government, to her several interviews with Isaac Bashevis Singer (1904-91).

In 1988 she was awarded the "Premio Nacional de Poesía" (National Poetry Prize) for her book *Los signos y el tiempo* (The Signs and Time; 1987).

Her work underscores deeply existential, religious, and esoteric themes which can best be explored in *Cruce de niebla* (Foggy Crossing; 1987), and *Detrás de las palabras* (Behind the Words; 1983). The use of Judaic symbology and motifs is strongly evident in all of her works. While she prefers to be considered a Costa Rican, Jewish aspects are integral components of her world view. She has been characterized as a Jewish poet par excellance in her melding of Jewish tradition with a steadfast humanistic vision. The dean of Costa Rican critics, María Salvadora Ortiz of the Center for Latin American Cultural Identity has said the following about Kalina's work: "The poetic production of Rosita Kalina is made outstanding by the fact that it incorporates into our poetry a vision of the Judeo-Christian world. In many of her poems she deconstructs old images as she creates new biblical myths around the women of our times. This allows the reader to reflect upon a new historical vision that is woven into feminine images in distinct epochs" (15).

In Costa Rica where the three-thousand member Jewish community is only a fraction of the nation's population, the poetry of Rosita Kalina is recognized by critics and scholars as an integral component of mainstream Costa Rican literature and culture.

PRIMARY BIBLIOGRAPHY
Creative Writing
"Alba." *La Nación* 11 Nov., 1967: 33.
"La carta." *Herencia judía* (2da serie) 13 (1977): 44.
"Cinco poesías." *Revenar* 2.5 (1982): 33.
Cruce de niebla. San José: Costa Rica, 1981.
"Dayeinu (Enough Already)," "Testimonies." Trans. by Celeste Kostopulos-
    Cooperman. In *These Are Not Sweet Girls: Poetry by Latin American
    Women.* Ed. Marjorie Agosín. Fredonia, NY: White Pine Press, 1994.
    284-86.
"El despertar," "Desenlace." *Herencia judía* (2da serie) 9 (1976): 29.
Detrás de las palabras. San José: Costa Rica, 1983.
"Dos poesías." *Revista cúpula* 5 (1981): 28.
"La escultura." *La Nación* 9 Sept., 1967: 51.
"Eterna fe." *Nuevo ideal* [Bogotá] 3.3 (1965): 10-11.
"In memoriam." *La Nación* 23 Dec., 1967: 51.
"Poesías." *Análisis* [Dominican Republic] 63-64 (1981): 35-37.
Nonfiction
"Judíos sefarditas en Costa Rica, antes y después del siglo XIX." Parts 1 and 2.
    Maguen (Caracas) 42 (1982): 36-38; 43 (1983): 36-47.

SECONDARY BIBLIOGRAPHY
Baeza Flores, Alberto. "Poesía costarricense: acentos de tres mundos." *La Nación*
    8 July, 1980: 15-A.
—. "El universo femenino que hay en *Detrás de las palabras.*" *La Nación* (Lit-
    erary supplement *Ancora*) 18 Sept., 1983: 1.
Bustos A., Myriam. "Rosa miedosa y evasiva." *La Nación* 4 June, 1983: 15-A.
Chase, Alfonso. "*Cruce de niebla,* nuevo libro de Rosita Kalina." *La Nación* 19
    April, 1980: 5-B.
—. "Destino y fe en la poesía de Rosa Kalina." *La prensa libre* 16 Sept., 1983:
    10.
Ortiz, María Salvadora. *La República* 19 July, 1987: 15.

Porras, José. "*Cruce de niebla*, de Rosita Kalina." *La República* 11 Oct, 1980: n.p.

Zipfel y García, Carlos. "La poesía de Rosa Kalina." *La prensa libre* 13 June, 1983: 7.

Robert DiAntonio

KAMENSZAIN, TAMARA (Argentina; 1947)

Born in Buenos Aires on February 9, 1947, Kamenszain spent her childhood close to and protected by Jewish tradition which she, in turn, transmits to her writing. In her memories as well as throughout her literary development the figure of her grandfather stands out. He was a "fabulador nato" (born storyteller) of tales loosely inspired by the Bible and the Talmud, stories from which a large part of Kamenszain's own artistic production emanates. She confesses that her literary vocation began to develop as a result of this narrative relationship with her grandfather ("Toda escritura es femenina y judía" 130).

She finished her secondary education in Buenos Aires (1960-64) and later graduated from the Facultad de Filosofía y Letras (School of Philosophy and Letters) of the Universidad de Buenos Aires (1965-70). She has had a very active career in the field of journalism and publishing, having worked as editor and correspondent for a number of newspapers and publishing houses. Some of the more important include the journals and newspapers *Revista 2001, La Opinión, Plural, UnoMásUno*, and the publishing houses of Granica and Aguilar-Altea-Taurus-Alfaguara. Her teaching activities include coordinating workshops on essay, poetry, and theoretical writing at the Universidad Nacional Autónoma de México in Mexico City and the Centro Cultural San Martín as well as the Colegio Argentino de Filosofía (1979-91) in Argentina. She was invited to Johns Hopkins University as a visiting professor for the Spring 1994 semester. She has won a variety of awards for her work, the most outstanding being the John Simon Guggenheim Memorial Foundation Fellowship in Poetry (1988-89). She has participated in numerous (some twenty-four between 1979-94) conferences, colloquiums, and seminars. Kamenszain currently resides in Buenos Aires.

Her publications include four books of poetry and one volume of essays: *De este lado del Mediterráneo* (From This Side of the Mediterranean; 1973) which won the Premio de Apoyo a la Producción Poética del Fondo Nacional de las Artes (The National Foundation for the Arts Support Award for Poetic Production); *Los no* (The Noh; 1977); *La casa grande* (The Large House; 1986); *Vida de living* (Life in the Living Room; 1991); the essayistic text is entitled *El texto silencioso: tradición y vanguardia en la poesía sudamericana* (The Silent Text: Tradition and Vanguard in South American Poetry; 1983), and won the Tercer Premio Nacional de Ensayo (National Award for Essay) of the Secretaría de Cultura de la Nación Argentina (1987) awarded for the best work produced during the three-year period 1983-1986.

Tamara Kamenszain emerges chronologically from the well-known Generation of the 1960s as one of the literary voices that integrates a feminine dimension into her writing. She also offers a perspective that alters Jewish tradition, resemantisizing this heritage with both inter- and extratextual contemporary elements (references to the Bible, to philosophers, writers, singers) as well as metaliterary elements (reflection on the creative process itself), adding to this the sociopolitical and cultural past and present of both sides of the Mediterranean.

De este lado del Mediterráneo is directly based on the books of the Sacred Scriptures. Kamenszain herself recounts her beginnings: "supone necesariamente apelar a la lengua materna, al origen, al grado cero de la letra, allí donde habita la Torá o, para decirlo en plural, allí donde habitan *Las Escrituras* (it necessarily assumes an appeal to the mother tongue, to the origin, to the grade zero of the letter, there where the Torah dwells, or to say it in plural terms, there where the Scriptures dwell. "*Toda . . .*" 132). Upon verbalizing oral tradition, reinterpreting scripture, and entering into contact with ancestral roots while retaining values from the millennial past, her writing becomes enriched, freely accommodating itself to the demands of a new existencial situation. Her family serves as a model, in particular her grandfather, which reinforces her sense of self-acceptance, granting both a fondness for and a meaning to life.

Among the current vital themes that Kamenszain's writing proposes some of the most outstanding include the search for a feminine identity, self-awareness and self-definition, human existence in terms of the anguish, solitude, and destiny of the human condition on the one hand, while on the other the author is preoccupied with the function of language as an indispensable epistemilogical instrument for the acquisition and transmission of knowledge, and likewise, as an indispensable instrument for poetry. *De este lado del Mediterráneo* explores "el camino inverso" (the inverse path [9]) of the past. Frequently, the speaker reflects on circular time, cyclical reiterations, the very memory of her grandparents' experiences—that she listened to in her childhood and which, consequently, she has made her own (14, 19). The cycle of birth and death converted into a Paradise Lost for a wise Eve who is capable of communicating with the natural world, especially the serpent, while Adam is excluded from this space due to his inability to communicate with the natural world (cf. Lindstrom). Each circle of birth and death is completed, but it remains open to other renovations. This, in turn, implies a process of development in which suffering, sacrifice or death, and birth revolve. This is likened to language that when joined to life is "un círculo, una flecha que vuelve sobre sí misma" (a circle, an arrow that returns to itself [28]). There is continuous movement (an allusion to Heraclitus, the philosopher of the future), in which all that is new is but an amalgam of the past. The reference to time (chronological and eternal) becomes a metaliterary reflection of the creative act itself (34). Humanity is immersed in the temporal future both here and there, on this side of the Mediterranean and on the other.

For critic Naomi Lindstrom, *De este lado* "reveals its female perspective, not because it manifests some stylistic or linguistic qualities peculiar to women, but, more demonstrably, by virtue of its thematic emphasis on female entities . . . women characters in well-known narratives and to female divinities and forces" (7). An example being the archetypical configuration of femininity, the dichotomy of moon-woman ("La luna y yo" [The Moon and I] 22) that confers on the work a symbolic dimension thereby opening it up to innumerable interpretive possibilities. The figure of the Moabite visionary Ruth, mythified to the archetypical dimension of the Great Mother, in communion with Nature "en cuyo vientre se genera el complicado tejido de palabras" (in whose womb is generated the complicated weave of words [40]) symbolizes the maternal (magical) space of poetic genesis. At present, the magical element of a purer and more innocent age has disappeared and is being replaced with the sophistication and technology that traps the individual in his/her solitude (mirrors, walls, electricity). The senses atrophy, "el tacto está enfundado en bloques de cemento y nadie más llevará a los pájaros a los pájaros en un arco porque Noé murió con el nacimiento de los paraguas" (touch is encased in blocks of cement and no one else will carry birds on an ark because Noah died with the birth of the umbrella [22]).

The kaleidoscopic vision that Kamenszain creates extends and disseminates between the traditional and the new, the past and the future, the text and the context (17-18). It evokes the idea of Jorge Luis Borges (1899-1986) that only poetic vision, for one instant, can catch a glimpse of the Aleph.

The second book, *Los no*, contains poems that Kamenszain herself sees as a different kind of writing which is in her words "más objetiva" (more objective ["Toda . . ." 131]). There is a constant interrelation between reality, representation, and symbol. The poet differentiates herself from the speaker in the poem but at the same time she diversifies, expands, and multiplies herself, and converted into a spectator and actress, she becomes conscious of human existence because of it. In this collection of poems theatrical, carnavalesque, and circus terminology reoccurs from the first verse on.

La casa grande continues in the same direction taken in Los no coupling "lo enunciativo y lo irracional, lo intimista y lo objetivado" (what is enunciated and what is irrational, what is intimate and what is objective; "Toda . . ." 132). Its end result is the hermetic creation that Kamenszain associates with a Judaic heritage. In the Kabbalah as in hermetic poetry, everything is written in code (132). With this text she returns to poetry, to a feminine tradition and its corresponding language, the word that is continually invented and that generates more ample forms of sealing the union or the circle that Kamenszain weaves as a reflection of life. Critic Jorge Panesi observes that the author "prefiere tener una máscara" (prefers to have a mask [169]), and that "Casa y Living son ahora escenarios tramposamente vitales" (Casa grande and Vida de living are now unreliably vital stages [169]). In Vida de living the speaker observes and listens using the senses in order to apprehend the collective environment that the living room connotes, a stage or space which is traditionally feminine. It is a homey space of family events and portraits, Buenos Aires voices with borrowed expressions, melodies, and tango verses. The poem is written in such a way that it communicates the nature of feminine intimacy, as well as the memory that revives the dead and the past bringing them back with nostalgia, with the flavor of a tango. As Panesi points out, the poet mends the forgotten fabric to make it new again (175). With Vida de living this creative trajectory is closed by means of a present consciousness that revives the past to establish the basis for a creative future.

In the essays contained in El texto silencioso, Kamenszain penetrates the works of vanguard authors to whom she is attracted due to the spiritual renovation and technical changes they propose. With ease, fondness, and a broad base of theoretical knowledge she achieves a brilliant and meticulous study of the poetry of Macedonio Fernández (1874-1952), Oliverio Girondo (1891-1967), Juan L. Ortiz (1896-1978), Enrique Lihn (1929), and Francisco Madariaga (1927). The volume is concluded by two appendices. In the first, "Bordado y costura del texto" (Embroidery and Stitching of the Text) which is always feminine as long as it is carefully sewn, be it by a man or woman artist, she examines the nature of the poetic text. In the second appendix, "El círculo de tiza del Talmud" (The Chalk Circle of the Talmud) she explores the task of the biblical exegetes and the writings of Jacques Lacan (1901-81), both "daughters" of the Torah and the unconscious, respectively.

Kamenszain discovers nature and the power of the word through Jewish tradition and expands the role of woman, "la sujeta" (the subject/ed), as she calls her, that cultivates and manipulates the word with skill. Her Jewish identity, a predominant element in her writing which overflows with vitality, offers the kaleidoscopic image of mirrors that reflect a variety of scenes and stages of feminine life with its rituals, myths, magic, and simple reality without exageration. This writing questions the very integration into the world as a writer, an experience in which life and self-identity are united with the Sacred Scriptures. This careful searching of tradition brings to the surface the marked tendency of a continous renovation that emerges from the confluence of the past and present in her poetic production.

PRIMARY BIBLIOGRAPHY
Creative Writing

La casa grande. Buenos Aires: Sudamericana, 1986. Eleven poems from *La casa grande* in English: *Argentine Writing in the Eighties*. Selection by William Katra. Trans. by Carlos and Monique Altschul. Special edition of *The Literary Review* (Fairleigh Dickinson University) 32.4 (1989): 512-17. Also, "The Big House." Trans. by Oscar Montero. In *Women's Writing in Latin America: An Anthology*. Ed. Sara Castro-Klarén, Sylvia Molloy and Beatriz Sarlo. Boulder, CO: Westview Press, 1991. 217-21.

De este lado del Mediterráneo. Buenos Aires: Ediciones Noé, 1973.

"Eliahu," "Como pez en el agua," "Todo nuevo bajo el sol," "De este lado del Mediterráneo," "Intento de inventar una historia." In *Prosa junta*. Prólogo de Mario Tobelem. Buenos Aires: Ediciones Megápolis, 1972. 33-45.

Los no. Buenos Aires: Sudamericana, 1977. Two poems from *Los no* in English: *Ten Latin American Women Poets*. Selection by Mary Crow. Trans. by Carlos and Monique Altschul. Special edition of *Colorado State Review* 7.1 (1979): 16.

"Los No," "Hoyo," "Vitral es el ojo dibujado," "Se interna sigilosa," "Por el hilo de saliva," "Burbuja, pez o mariposa." In *Antología de la poesía hispanoamericana actual*. Selección de Julio Ortega. México, D.F.: Siglo XXI, 1987. 468-71

"Todo es un viaje en tren," "Como el bailarín de teatro No," "Como el público de teatro No," "Los músicos de teatro No," "Quien ve," "El paisaje ya estela en el cuadro," "En una pequeña tarima," "Semidios de la tragedia." In *Antología de la poesía argentina*. Tomo III. Selección de Raúl Gustavo Aguirre. Buenos Aires: Ediciones Fausto, 1979. 1582-86.

"Venere manda Cupido sulla tierra," "Destino," "Al estampado de la infancia," "Si de fotos recorrida la memoria," "El ropero caja negra." In *Voces y fragmentos: poesía argentina hoy*. Selección de Jorge Boccanera. Morelia, Michoacán: Editorial de la Universidad Michoacana, 1981. 151-57.

Vida de living. Buenos Aires: Sudamericana, 1991.

Nonfiction

El texto silencioso: tradición y vanguardia en la poesía sudamericana. México, D.F.: Universidad Nacional Autónoma de México, Coordinación de Humanidades, 1983.

"Toda escritura es femenina y judía." In *Pluralismo e identidad: lo judío en la literatura latinoamericana*. Jaime Barylko, et al. Buenos Aires: Milá, 1986. 129-32.

SECONDARY BIBLIOGRAPHY
Criticism

Alonso, Rodolfo. "Inteligente mirada crítica sobre nuestra poesía" (*El texto silencioso*). *La Gaceta* 24 April, 1983): 2da sección, 3.

Antunez, Rocío. "Los riesgos de producir" (*El texto silencioso*). *Casa del tiempo: revista de la Universidad Autónoma Metropolitana* 3.36 (Dec. 1983-Jan. 1984): 83.

Avellaneda, Andrés. "La experiencia del lenguaje" (*Los no*). *La Opinión* (31 Aug., 1977): 20.

Bellesi, Diana. "La casa de un lenguaje" (*La casa grande*). *Diario de poesía* 3 (1986): 32.

Carrera, Arturo. "Un libro planeado como un hogar" (*La casa grande*). *La Razón* (28 Sept., 1986): 7.

Chitarroni, Luis. "*La casa grande*." *Vuelta sudamericana* 5 (1986): 45.

Gramuglio, María Teresa. Rev. of *El texto silencioso*." *Punto de vista* 21 (1984): 43.

Kirkpatrick, Gwen. "La poesía de las argentinas frente al patriarcado." *Nuevo texto crítico* 2.4 (1989): 129-35.

Libertella, Héctor. "Algo sobre la novísima literatura argentina" (*De este lado del Mediterráneo*). *Hispamérica* 2.6 (1974): 13-19.

Lindstrom, Naomi. "Female Divinities and Story-telling in the Work of Tamara Kamenszain." *Studies in 20th Century Literature* 20.1 (1996): 221-33.

Miguel, María Esther de. "El teatro y la escritura" (*Los no*). *El cronista comercial* (10 Aug., 1977): 19.

——. "Tradición y vanguardia en la poesía" (*El texto silencioso*). *El cronista comercial* (4 May, 1983): 23.

Milán, Eduardo. "El admirable decoro textual" (*El texto silencioso*). *Revista de la Universidad de México* 39.24 (1983): 52.

Moreno, María. "Retrato de una joven poetiza argentina" (*Los no*). *La Opinión* (24 Jan., 1978): 11.

Negroni, María. "Rev. of *El texto silencioso* and *La casa grande*." *Hispamérica* 16.48 (1987): 143-46.

Panesi, Jorge. "Banquetes en el living: Tamara Kamenszain" (*La casa grande* y *Vida de living*). *Hispamérica* 22.64-65 (1993): 167-75.

Petit de Murat, Ulises. "Macedonio comparece" (*El texto silencioso*). *Revista la semana* 330 (7 de abril, 1983): 37.

Pezzoni, Enrique. "TK, escribir sobre el desamparo" (*La casa grande*). *El Clarín* (*Suplemento de Cultura y Nación*) (2 Oct., 1986): 8.

—. "*La casa grande*, convergencia simbólica de una vida: Tamara Kamenszain, cuerpo, deseo, poesía." *Clarín* 2 Oct., 1986: 8.

Saavedra, Guillermo. "Cantar y recantar aquellos viejos tangos" (*Vida de living*). *Clarín* (Suplemento *Cultura y Nación*) 29 Aug., 1991): 6.

Sefamí, Jacobo. "Tamara Kamenszain." *Contemporary Spanish American Poets: A Bibliography of Primary and Secondary Sources*. Comp. Jacobo Sefami. Westport, CT: Greenwood Press, 1992. 103.

Stephens, Doris. "Argentine Literature 1973." *Hispania* 57.2 (1974): 357.

Toledo, Alejandro. "*El texto silencioso*." *UnoMásUno* (Suplemento *Sábado*) 16 July, 1983: 10.

Interviews

Faimberg, Graciela. "De profesión literatas." (Interview with Tamara Kamenszain and Alicia Dujovne Ortiz). *Plural* (Buenos Aires) 35 (1984): 10-16.

Fingueret, Manuela. "La triple diáspora de los judíos argentinos exiliados." *Nueva Sión* (Buenos Aires) 600 (18 Aug., 1984): 28-29.

Silvia Sauter
Mariana Petrea

KARTUN, MAURICIO (Argentina; 1946)

Argentine dramatist Mauricio Kartun was born in the Buenos Aires suburb of San Martín, a place to which he often returns in his works. His father was born in one of the Jewish colonies in the province of Santa Fe, and his mother was a Spanish immigrant. Kartun's early interest in literature led him to write a series of short stories, for which he earned a small local award. However, he found his true vocation in the theater arts. Not only is he a dramatist but he is also a director and an actor, having appeared in numerous stage, television, and feature film roles. Likewise, he is an active participant in theater seminars and conferences in Argentina and abroad, and he teaches courses and conducts workshops on theater.

Kartun belongs to a generation of Argentine dramatists that began to write in the early 1970s. He names Augusto Boal (1931) and Ricardo Monti (1944) as being the principal influences on his formation as playwright (Roffo 11). Two of Kartun's first works, *Gente muy así* (People Like That; 1976) and *El hambre da para todo* (Hunger's Good for Everything; 1978) were written and performed for a popular subgenre of theater at the time known as "café-concert." *Gente*, the story of a pair of overbearing parents who attempt to turn their son into an intellectual, has been described as prototypical of Jewish humor (Guinzburg).

In spite of his relative success during the 1970s, his first work to attract a large public audience was *Chau Misterix* (Goodbye Misterix) which debuted in 1980. The play established Kartun as one of the leading new Argentine dramatists. It relies heavily on popular culture for its theatrical referents and on a great deal of humor, mixed with nostalgia and irony. The play takes its title from the popular comic book superhero, Misterix, who derived his power from an atomic suit. *Misterix* was a comic book of Italian origin that gained wide diffusion in Argentina in the late 1940s and 1950s. The use of Misterix in the play situates the action temporally in the late 1950s, as do several other political referents. The play takes on the attributes of a comic book both in set design and through the characters who undergo numerous transformations from a group of neighborhood children into comic-book personalities. The protagonist, Rubén, imagines himself to be Misterix, and his friends take on a variety of roles from helpless heroine to villain. In his imagination Rubén becomes the superhero to compensate for his feelings of inadequacy. As the play advances, Misterix appears less frequently, signaling Rubén's loss of childhood. Likewise, the dramatic tension builds to a crescendo that ultimately explodes in violence. The presentation of a seemingly benign situation that turns violent is common to many of Kartun's plays. *Chau Misterix* is a play steeped in the popular culture of Argentina, especially that of preceeding generations or periods, and it also presents several interesting parallels with the rise and fall of Peronism.

Kartun participated in two consecutive cycles of the Teatro Abierto (Open Theater) movement. It began in 1981 as an artistic response against the political and cultural repression of the military dictatorship (1976-83). The theatrical community came together to produce twenty-one short plays that indirectly addressed the repression through the use of metaphor. The movement was such a success that it was repeated in 1982 and 1983, and it also inspired the parallel movements of Danza Abierta (Open Dance) and Cine Abierto (Open Film). In 1982 Kartun presented his *La casita de los viejos* (The Folk's House), recognized as one of the best plays of the season. For Teatro Abierto 83, he offered *Cumbia, morena, cumbia* (Dancing the Cumbia), which received the Argentores prize for best short play of 1983. Both plays, in keeping with the underlying ideology of Teatro Abierto, are contestatory works that present the effects of the dictatorship on the common citizen.

Pericones (the Pericón is a traditional dance) is Kartun's most elaborate play. It was staged in April 1987 at the Teatro Municipal General San Martín (General San Martín Municipal Theater), Argentina's most technically advanced theatrical complex. *Pericones* is a parodic farce of Argentine history that calls into question many of the nation's myths. Like in *Chau Misterix*, Kartun makes ample use of popular culture and the comic book motif as semiotic encodements in *Pericones*. The play is styled after the adventure novels of Emilio Salgari (1862-1911), an Italian novelist whose stories of the American Old West and pirates were widely consumed by adolescent readers in Argentina, and they were also produced in comic book form. Kartun declares this influence in his interview with Analía Roffo (13). The play essentially questions the concept of national identity through an irreverent demythification—accomplished via the melding of *historia* (history) with *historieta* (comic book)—of what being Argentine means. There is no one central character in the play, rather the multiple characters together form the image of Argentina, the real protagonist of the work. Each one represents a different social class or sector (the military, the oligarchy, the intellectual, the masses), or ideological posture (liberalism, nationalism, utopic socialism, imperialism). It is not difficult to perceive the presence of Kartun himself in the play through the young, idealistic Lucio Kuhn. Spatially, the play takes place on board a refrigerated ship loaded with frozen beef, the obvious sign of Argentina's major industry. Temporally, it is situated in 1889 and the dramatic action unfolds on three national dates; May 25 (the anniversary of the May Revolution and the creation of the government); June 20, (Flag Day); and July 9 (Independence Day). Each of the three acts is loosely associated with a period in Argentine history. The first is identified with the Generation of 1880, general Julio A. Roca, the *Conquista del desierto* (Conquest of the Desert), and the country depends economically on England and culturally on France. The second act alludes to the *década infame* (infamous decade) of 1930, a period of virulent fascism. The final act recalls the period just prior to the most recent military coup d'etat in 1976. *Pericones* continues the dramatist's practice of creating works that have a "clara intención de agitación y propaganda" (clear intention of agitation and propaganda [Roffo 11]). Although the play cannot be considered as an agit-prop work, it is both political and didactic in its parodic representation of the historical past that connects with the context of the contemporary reader/spectator Kartun utilizes the past to allegorize the present and to create a view of modern Argentine reality. This reality is manifest through the multiple and constant bombardment of theatrical codes, both visual and discursive, in which national myths and symbols are used to create a charicaturesque portrait of the country. This use of parody with comic book features creates a distancing effect between the real world of the reader/spectator and the dramatic world. This distance provides for the possibility of social critique behind the disguise of humor and it questions the relevancy of a system of values and norms that constitute the sociocultural reality of contemporary Argentina.

In the 1989 play, *El partener* (The Partner), Kartun returns to a more realist style of theater, though he continues to incorporate popular culture references. Osvaldo Pellettieri has called the play a tragicomedy and defines its style as a *neosainete* (the *sainete* is a traditional style of drama ["Mauricio Kartun: entre el realismo y el neosainete"]). The play revolves around the troubled relationship of a father and son. The father is a washed-up, small-time entertainer who still dreams of success. The play brings to the stage the many social issues relevant to the past and present history of Argentina.

Kartun's next play, *Salto al cielo* (Jump to the Sky; 1991 [published 1993]), represents a break in style from his earlier works, although he remains close to the realism of previous plays. The piece is loosely based on *The Birds*, by Aristophanes (445-380? c.e.). The central theme is that of the creation of a utopia, which it shares with *Pericones*. In the play, various "birds" dialogue on the nature and possibility of a utopic space. They decide to leave the city in search of a new land, where they will be free to design their own type of freedom and lifestyle. The play, again, makes obvious political references to recent Argentine history.

Most recently, Kartun wrote a play based on the case of the American anarchists Nicola Sacco and Bartolomeo Vanzetti. *Sacco y Vanzetti* premiered in the Metropolitan Theater of Buenos Aires in October 1992. He wrote another play, *Lejos de aquí* (Far from Here; 1994), in collaboration with Roberto Cossa (1934), which recently debuted in Buenos Aires, and a play for childrens' theater, *La leyenda de Robin Hood* (The Legend of Robin Hood; 1994) in collaboration with Tito Lorefice. Kartun also wrote the songs for the play *Aquellos gau-*

chos judíos (Those Jewish Gauchos; 1995), by Cossa and Ricardo Halac (1935). His latest play, *Como un puñal en las carnes* (Like a Knife in the Flesh; 1996), consists of three monologues. He is currently (1996) working on a play based on the anarchist movement in Argentina.

References specific to Jewish identity are virtually absent from Kartun's work, but other aspects of Jewishness are revealed, perhaps most prevalent is his humor. Kartun came to be one of the most important playwrights in Argentina in the 1980s and his works had a great impact on the nature of theater in the country. His recent productions promise that his role as a leading dramatist will continue well into the future.

PRIMARY BIBLIOGRAPHY

La casita de los viejos. In *Teatro Abierto 1982.* Ed. Nora Mazziotti. Buenos Aires: Puntosur, 1989. 47-62. Also in *Teatro: 8 autores.* Buenos Aires: Argentores, 1985. 138-60.

Chau Misterix. Buenos Aires: Torres Agüero, 1989. Also in *Teatro: 4 autores.* Buenos Aires: Argentores, 1982. 34-81.

Civilización . . . ¿o barbarie?. (With Humberto Riva) 1973, unpublished.

Como un puñal en las carnes. Teatro XXI: Revista del GETEA (Buenos Aires) 2.2 (1996): 103-13.

Cumbia morena cumbia. In *Teatro: 8 autores.* Buenos Aires: Argentores, 1985. 149-93.

Gente muy así. 1976, unpublished.

El hambre da para todo. 1978, unpublished.

Lejos de aquí. (With Roberto Cossa) 1994, unpublished.

La leyenda de Robin Hood. (With Tito Lorefice) 1994, unpublished.

El partener. In *Compañía; El partener,* by Eduardo Rovner and Mauricio Kartun. Ottawa: GIROL, 1993. 35-64. Also in *El clásico binomio; El partener,* by Rafael Bruza, Jorge Ricci, and Mauricio Kartun. Santa Fe, Argentina: Universidad Nacional del Litoral, 1989. 69-106.

Pericones. Buenos Aires: Teatro Municipal General San Martín, 1987. Also in *Teatro argentino contemporáneo: antología.* Madrid: Centro de Documentación Teatral, Ministerio de Cultura; Sociedad Estatal Quinto Centenario; Fondo de Cultura Económica, 1992. 1107-95.

Sacco y Vanzetti. 1992, unpublished.

Salto al cielo. In *Del parricidio a la utopía: el teatro argentino en 4 claves mayores.* Ottawa: GIROL, 1993.

Teatro. (Contains *Chau Misterix*, *La casita de los viejos*, *Cumbia morena cumbia*, *Pericones*, *El partener*, *Salto al cielo*). Buenos Aires: Corregidor, 1993.

SECONDARY BIBLIOGRAPHY
Criticism

Berman, Mónica, et al. "Apuntes y reflexiones sobre una obra argentina: *El partener*." *Revista espacio* 5 (1989): 95-103.

Cosentino, Olga. "Una epopeya para la historieta." *Teatro* 7.29 (1987): 50-55.

Dubatti, Jorge. A. "Identidad y utopía." *Teatro argentino contemporáneo: antología*. Madrid: Centro de Documentación Teatral, Ministerio de Cultura; Sociedad Estatal Quinto Centenario; Fondo de Cultura Económica, 1992. 1101-5.

Feierstein, Ricardo. "Saludable irreverencia." [*Pericones*] *Nueva presencia* 513 (8 May, 1987): 32.

Gómez, Rubén Darío. "Los Pericones de Mauricio Kartun." *El despertador* 12 (1987): n.p.

Guinzburg, Mirta, and Jorge Guinzburg. "El humor judío llegó a la Argentina." In *Judíos y argentinos: judíos argentinos*. Ed. Martha Wolff and Myrtha Schalom. Buenos Aires: Manrique Zago, 1988. 206-9.

Lockhart, Darrell B. "Pasos para negar la realidad: *Cumbia morena cumbia* de Mauricio Kartun." In *Teatro argentino durante el Proceso (1976-1983): ensayos críticos - entrevistas*. Ed. Juana A. Arancibia and Zulema Mirkin. Buenos Aires: Vinciguerra, 1992. 75-90.

Mogliani, Laura. "*Salto al cielo*: el desarrollo de una utopía." In *Teatro argentino de los '90*. Ed. Osvaldo Pellettieri. Buenos Aires: Galerna/Revista Espacio, 1992. 79-83.

Pellettieri, Osvaldo. "Mauricio Kartun: entre el realismo y el neosainete." In *Teatro*, by M. Kartun. Buenos Aires: Corregidor, 1993. 9-33.

—. *El partener*, la tragicomedia de la impostura y el desamparo." In *El clásico binomio; El partener*, by Rafael Bruza, Jorge Ricci, and Mauricio Kartun. Santa Fe, Argentina: Universidad Nacional del Litoral, 1989. 49-67.

—. *El partener*: un texto cuestionador de la modernidad." In *Compañía; El partener*, by Rovner and Kartun. Ottawa: GIROL, 1993. xvii-xxiv.

—. "El texto espectacular de *El partener* de Mauricio Kartun." In his *Cien años de teatro argentino: del Moreira a Teatro Abierto*. Buenos Aires: Galerna, 1990. 153-73. An earlier version of this article appeared *La escena latinoamericana* 1 (1989): 11-19.

Quiroga, Osvaldo. "Poética reflexión sobre la soledad." [*El partener*] *La Nación* 16 Sept., 1988: n.p.

Troncone, Carlos. "Cuando el teatro es una fiesta." [Interview with director Jaime Kogan on the production of *Pericones*]. *Teatro* 7.29 (1987): 56-58.

Weinstein, Ana E., and Miryam E. Gover de Nasatsky, comps. "Mauricio Kartun." *Escritores judeo-argentinos: bibliografía 1900-1987.* 2 vols. Buenos Aires: Milá, 1994. I.367-68.

Zayas de Lima, Perla. "Mauricio Kartun." In *Diccionario de autores teatrales argentinos (1950-1990).* Buenos Aires: Galerna, 1991. 155-56.

Interviews

Dubatti, Jorge. "El teatro de M. Kartun: identidad y utopía." In *Teatro*, by M. Kartun. Buenos Aires: Corregidor, 1993. 279-86.

Massa, Cristina. "Entrevista a Mauricio Kartun." *Teatro XXI: Revista del GETEA* (Buenos Aires) 2.2 (1996): 101-2.

Roffo, Analía. "El autor." In *Pericones*, by M. Kartun. Buenos Aires: Teatro Municipal General San Martín, 1987. 9-15. Also as "La utopía de organizar el caos." *Teatro* 7.29 (1987): 42-48.

Darrell B. Lockhart

KORDON, BERNARDO (Argentina; 1915)

Although few details are available about this author's personal life we know that he was born in Buenos Aires in 1915, the son of Russian immigrants. His father, a socialist and free thinker, brought with him not only a family but also a printing press, a factor which quite likely influenced the author's early interest in publishing. Kordon also claims to have been strongly influenced by having frequented the movies as a child, a habit he believes influenced his somewhat cinematic manner of seeing and describing things. A radical youth and inveterate wanderer, this author never completed his formal education but claims that his universities were the streets, first in Buenos Aires then in Brazil and Chile, Europe, and the Far East (personal letter from Kordon, July 4, 1985).

His first publications appeared in *Capricornio* (Capricorn), a magazine he founded as a youthful member of the Asociación de Jóvenes Literarios (Association of Young Literary Men) a group of anarquists, activists and communists who tended to mix politics and literature. His first book, *La vuelta de Rocha* (The Rocha Loop; 1936) was also under the auspices of this group although its actual printing costs were funded by his mother as a gift.

Although Kordon has written several novels and four books of journalistic essays (most of which relate to his numerous travels and observations in China), he is best known for his short stories. These stories, repeatedly recombined in new collections under a variety of titles are more easily considered by topic, content, or tone than by volume or chronology. The title of one of his collections, *Manía ambulatoria* (Wanderlust; 1978) expresses a fundamental self-concept of the author's—that he is a wayfarer traveling through life on foot, by taxi, train, or plane who first as an adolescent outside his *barrio* (neighborhood), then as an adult to near and faraway lands merely describes the persons, places, and things he encounters along life's way. Many of his tales are partially autobiographic in the sense that they record, in a blend of fantasy and verisimilitude, people he has seen, stories he has lived, heard, intuited, or invented in his travels through life. Some of Kordon's stories actually are written in first person, reinforcing the author's identification with his protagonists. Kordon's most frequent themes are death, solitude, and poverty. He presents them in moving stories whose protagonists are always antiheroes, the poor, the marginal, the rootless, the solitary: contraband runners, street vendors, opportunists, prostitutes, petty criminals, blacks, Indians, even the popular idols of the day, all are presented with quiet, telling understatement in a conversational voice redolent with authentic *lunfardo porteño* (Buenos Aires slang). Sometimes with humor or irony, always with compassion, Kordon manages to convey both the humanity and the existential loneliness of his characters as he describes their doomed efforts to escape their fate as born losers. He shows their strengths and weaknesses, poverty and helplessness, despair, and resignation, along with the apparently trivial happenings that lead them to failure or tragedy.

Kordon is at his best when describing people in moments of quiet desperation—the lonely man who travels to a distant hotel where he quietly commits suicide, the grieving spouse whose wife is buried alive in an earthquake; the stoic Chilean peasant woman whose infant is battered to death as she carries him in a shawl on her back together with her contraband whiskey bottles; the heartbroken husband who quietly goes on eating, unable to verbalize his grief when his wife tells him she has been diagnosed as dying of cancer; the abandoned husband who punishes his estranged wife by dragging his children with him when he throws himself beneath the wheels of an on-coming train; the unemployed laborer who philosophically accepts the fact that he may have eaten a worker's severed fingers during the lunch barbecue at the saw mill; the weary prostitute murdered when she refuses to surrender her purse to thieves—all are moving tales authentically chronicling the tragedies of hundreds of so-called little people the author has met or heard of in his journey through life.

Some of Kordon's stories present mysterious tales of death or fatal forces with a starkness that makes them plausible. In "Un día menos" (One Day Less; 1966) a youth dreams of walking along the beach with his brother who had died the year before—and later finds in his pocket the I.D. his brother gave him in the dream. "Estero" (a place name first spelled "Estero," 1978, then spelled "Esteco" in a later publication; 1986) tells of a strange curse compelling generations of men in a family to return home to the death awaiting them in their native village. "Domingo en el río" (Sunday at the River; 1960) describes a jealous child who comes to believe that she has magical powers when her wish that her mother's admirer would die in an accident is realized. "Un hombre en la casa" (A Man in the House; 1966) describes the relief a battered woman's children experience when their brutal stepfather chokes to death on a fish bone. "Hotel comercio" (Commercial Hotel; 1956) relates how a traveling salesman, lodged in a hotel room whose previous occupant had committed suicide, yields to the power of suggestion and does the same. "Función de cine en Auschwitz" (Movie in Auschwitz; 1978) describes the eerie sensation the writer experienced when viewing a movie of the Holocaust in Auschwitz. Because Kordon had lived some years in Chile, the sight of some Chilean coins among the victims' remains made him feel that he himself had been one of the victims, such was his overwhelming sense of identification with them.

Several stories stress varying aspects of human compassion. "Nuestra señora de los gatos" (Our Lady of the Cats; 1960) tells of a poor woman living in the town dump who begs food to feed the city's stray cats. "Adiós pampa mía (Good-bye My Pampa; 1978) shows how a young prostitute foils the scam of two male companions when their victim arouses her sympathy. The fickleness of human nature is reflected in "La conquista" (The Conquest; 1960), the age-old story of a young man who, after promising discretion to a young woman he seduces, promptly goes off bragging about his conquest.

Real violence appears in several stories. "Sábado inglés" (Free Saturday; 1936) describes how a youth loitering outside a restaurant looking for adventure on his day off from work is beaten mercilessly by police while a crowd of non-intervening passersby looks on. "Los ojos de Celina" (Celina's Eyes; 1966) chronicles a woman's calculating murder of her daughter-in-law. "El sordomudo" (The Deaf Mute; 1966) describes a truck driver's revenge on the hitchhiker who senselessly murdered his partner, a bright young deaf-mute.

The stoicism so often shown by ordinary people is portrayed in stories like "Soy la Rosa Loyola, Señor," (I'm Rosa Loyola, Sir; 1968), which describes the sacrifices a young woman makes in her determination to raise her illegitimate son decently. In "La desconocida" (The Stranger; 1960), a husband, after learning that his wife has cancer, weeps in private, realizing that after all their years of marriage she is basically a stranger to him, and then, unable to express his anguish, simply goes on quietly eating his dinner.

Despite the authenticity and realism which characterize most of his work, Kordon also had an abiding interest in the ambiguous and fatalistic which he sometimes combines with a kind of black or grotesque humor. In "La última huelga de los basureros (The Garbage Collectors' Last Strike; 1968) he uses macabre humor to describe how a garbage collector's work crew avenges his death at the hands of an impatient motorist by crushing that motorist in their garbage compactor. The ensuing furor results in a strike so long that all the inhabitants eventually have to abandon the garbage-heaped city.

"Buenos Ayres año 3536" (Buenos Aires in the Year 3536; 1968) is a whimsically futuristic tale about an anthropologist in the year 3536 who writes home describing the savages he has found in his exploration of an apparently abandoned land. He relates that they seem to have worshipped a killing God called the "car" and reports legends of another God called "Perón" whom they seem to have worshipped in the past.

Some of Kordon's longer stories (which might be considered short novels) are truly memorable. "Toribio Torres, alias Gardelito" (1956) begins with a humorous description of a street-wise youth living by his wits who develops into a con artist. Gradually the story becomes more somber as he outsmarts himself by trying to con some crooks, is betrayed, and finally shot. "Kid Ñandubay" (1971), one of Kordon's few stories with a specifically Jewish theme, tells the story of Jacobo Berstein, a Polish immigrant who learned to fight at school when his classmates ridiculed his Yiddish/Polish accent, became the best fighter in his *barrio* and went on to become "Kid Ñandubay," a professional boxer. The story builds to a climatic bout in which fans shout that his opponent should kill the Jew. Hearing that cry, The Kid recovers his control, and punishes his opponent so thoroughly that the public, forgetting its earlier bias, begins to cheer for him. Although he loses the fight on points, the Kid nevertheless comes away feeling that he has finally vindicated his Jewishness.

"Andate paraguayo" (Beat It, Paraguayan; 1972) is based on a true story. Had he written nothing else, this story alone would make Bernardo Kordon memorable. Written with an interesting point and counterpoint technique, its theme is a protest that simultaneously inveighs against both government persecution and public indifference to that persecution. The story, which at first seems amusing, gradually shocks and then horrifies the reader as its implications become clear. Fabiana López, an Argentine woman from a *villa miseria* or city slum, abandoned by her Paraguayan lover when he wins the lottery's grand prize, becomes a national cause célebre, appearing on television and in newspapers as the abandoned woman. The entire nation rallies to Fabiana's cause and the courtroom overflows with public supporters anxious to see that justice is done and the Paraguayan made to share his riches with her. Then the story abruptly splits into two parallel narrations, alternating between scenes of the outraged populous outside the courtroom demanding justice for Fabiana and scenes, in italics, that describe another trial underway in a more obscure courtroom attracting no public notice, but having much deeper significance—the trial of a rural school teacher who had been arrested, questioned, and tortured as a suspected political activist. After describing the teacher's unwarranted torture, the narrative continuing Fabiana's story ironically begins with someone protesting that they have no right to do that to an Argentine woman. Kordon interposes no personal comments or judgments in this story but merely allows the concurrently presented trials to speak for themselves, juxtaposing the segments so that the incongruity of the public's reaction gradually becomes shockingly clear.

In *Candombé* (the title is the name of an African dance and percussion instrument; 1938), a long essay rather than a novel, Kordon briefly reviews the history of the slave trade in South America and notes that the forcible conversion of the slaves never entirely eradicated their African beliefs in witchcraft and fetishism. He discusses the importance of dance and music (principally the drums and castanets) in African rituals, gives the words of some songs and concludes that the milonga rhythm so popular in Argentina derives from Candombé music.

Un horizonte de cemento (Cement Horizon; 1940) is a short novel depicting twenty-four hours in the life of an aging panhandler. We witness his rage and frustration when he is picked up by the police and harassed by street urchins who try to steal the fish he has caught. When he sells his fish for a few coins, we witness his indecision about how to use the money (should he use it for food or a night's sleep in a warm bed?), then sadly see him opt for a drink at the nearest bar. Kordon shows the loneliness and abject poverty of his subject as he makes the reader share his illusion, frustration, and ultimate resignation.

Muerte en el Valle (Death in the Valley; 1943) a testimonial novel, was written as Juan De Luigi explains in the preface, to document the tragic death of the author's Chilean journalist friend, Raul Dell' Sendero. Here Kordon both attempts to vindicate his friend and expose the abuse of power to which he was subjected by politicians. Kordon describes how they used his credulous friend for their own ends both during his mortal illness and even after his death. In life they promised him positions which never materialized; in death they vied for public approval by their attention to his corpse. In this testimonial novel, Kordon's final disillusionment with his liberal causes and with communism itself is evident.

Perhaps because of the attempt to sustain length, Kordon's novels are not as compelling as his stories. *Reina del Plata* (Queen of La Plata; 1946) is a somewhat biographical novel about three young men from different social backgrounds who meet and share their dreams and aspirations of making a life for themselves in the city during the Yrigoyen years after the great "crash" of world markets. One aspires to be a movie star, one a student, the third to "really live." After they are arrested for hopping a boxcar everything starts to go downhill. Occasionally thereafter, as each tries to grub out a living, they meet over the years. Much later, one of them helps out a youth who, reminiscent of himself, arrives from the provinces idealistic and defenseless, to make his way in the city.

In *De ahora en adelante* (From Now On; 1952) the reader is introduced to Rafael, who long after he left for Paris as a youthful adventurer, returns, lonely, chastened, and unsuccessful, to visit the old friend who has married the woman he could have had, and attained the success he'd hoped for. He promises himself, yet again, that from now on things will be different. The reader, of course, realizes that nothing will change.

Lampeão (1953), narrates in novelistic form the real life story of Virgolino Ferreira da Silva and his band of famous Brazilian outlaws. After avenging their father's death by killing the avaricious landowner who'd shot him without provocation, Virgolino escaped with his younger brother and joined a band of renegades. Because of his lightning quick eyes and sharp shooting he soon earned the name of Lampeão (Lightning Flash), and became almost a legendary folk hero, feared, admired, and sung of by peasants but hunted for years by police, the military, and professional tracers. Inevitably, he was eventually tracked down and killed—outgunned only when his pursuers came through jungle and mountain terrain armed with machine guns.

A punto de reventar (At the Bursting Point; 1971) narrated in first person, describes a wanderer who lived by his wits in Brazil, Chile, and Paris, but ended up, literally, "a punto de reventar." It also contains an interjected story about a Chilean woman whose family died in an earthquake. Essentially, the point of the novel seems to be to portray yet other characters who, browbeaten by life, struggle on.

Los navegantes (The Navigators; 1972) is a collection of stories which might be considered a novel because several of its tales are linked with a connected theme. The narrator, a machinist in the merchant marine, describes his life aboard ship. Using first person, Kordon ably captures the long periods of loneliness and boredom that lead to excessive drinking and whoring when seamen come ashore. He laments the commercialization that has overtaken seafaring and reduced the captain's legendary power to that of a mere company agent.

Based on the theory expressed in its title that in life some people are born losers while fate destines others for success, *Vencedores y vencidos* (Winners and Losers; 1985) describes how an artistic and talented but drug-addicted journalist sinks into misery, degradation, and a lonely death, while others, through industry or quirks of fate, rise to positions of wealth or power. Awkwardly interspersed but unrelated chapters describe another set of losers: a young woman who throws herself under the wheels of an on-coming train, her desconsolate, uncomprehending mother and the mother's cheeky young relative who bullies her into handouts while refusing to work and hanging out with the neighborhood toughs.

Several of Kordon's short stories have been made into movies: *Alias Gardelito* (which won an international award in Italy; [based on the story by the same name]), *El ayudante* (The Assistant), *El grito de Celina* (Celina's Cry), and *Fuimos a la ciudad* (We Went to the City). Several have also won awards: the *Faja de Honor* (Sash of Honor) of the Argentine Writers Society for "Domingo en el Río," a second place Municipality of Buenos Aires Award for "Adios pampa mía," a first place Municipal Award for "Historia de sobrevivientes" (A Story of Survivors; 1982) and a national first prize for a children's story "La laucha Napoleón" (Napoleon, the Mouse).

In addition to fiction Kordon has also written several books of essays resulting from his more than eight trips to China. As is usual in Kordon's works, much of the material in his first work on China, *Reportaje a China*, (Report on China; 1964) is repeated in subsequent volumes: *China o la revolución para siempre*, (China or the Everlasting Revolution; 1969, *Viaje nada secreto al país misterioso: China extraña y clara,* (Non-secret Journey to the Land of Mystery: Limpid and Exotic China; 1984). Although the writer never clarifies the auspices under which he traveled in China, given the timing of his visits (during the period of the "Hundred Flowers," the Cultural Revolution, the Fall of the Band of Four) when China was essentially closed to foreigners, his astonishing access to highly placed officials and normally proscribed places (army installations, prisons, hospitals), it is clear that Kordon was no ordinary tourist. His use of the plural throughout ("We were invited," "we were told") fails to reveal whether he was a member of a visiting cultural delegation or traveling alone with his wife Marina.

Apparently, Kordon's fascination with Chinese culture began when the Beijing Opera visited Buenos Aires in 1957 and continued with his first visit to that country the following year. So taken was he with Chinese theater, its use of music, mime, acrobatics, color, and symbolic substitutions for reality, that he considered a knowledge of Chinese theater and theatrics essential to the understanding of China and the Chinese. In his somewhat naive enthusiasm, he even described Mao as the "directorial genius" of China's psychodrama (*Viaje* 12). In these essays Kordon describes his personal interviews with members of the red guard, military and civilian officials, the Minister of Culture and Mao Tse-tung himself. He appears eager to display the extent of his study of Chinese history and literature, his familiarity with Mao's little red book (which he terms "poetic" (*Viaje* 135), and his admiration for the works of past and present revolutionary poets and writers like Lu Sin (1881-1936) and Chen Yi (1901-72).

In communist China as elsewhere, Kordon remained essentially an observer of the human condition, recording and writing what he saw and felt in his travels. Although this admiration for Communism diminished with his subsequent disillusionment with politics and politicians, Kordon's fascination with China seems to have endured.

Overall, it is Kordon's gift for story telling, for distilling the essence of observed reality through the filter of his own sensitivities and perceptions that make his narratives memorable. Kordon is at his best in short stories, where his apparent artlessness resonates with cultural authenticity as he describes the minutiae of everyday lives, echoes the authentic *lunfardo* of Buenos Aires against the authentic backdrop of its streets, painting the milieu of his anti-heroic protagonists, or describes the countless people and places he has seen.

Just as Bernardo Verbitsky (1907-79) is considered the chronicler of the city (specifically, of Buenos Aires) with its immigrants, its hard-working poor and middle class, Kordon is likewise considered a chronicler of social realism and the city milieu—with the difference that his tales chronicle the lives of the city's poor and marginal substrata. In both authors, the authentic backdrop of a minutely described milieu presents a telling view of people, places, and culture.

Though Kordon rejects any comparisons between his work and that of other Argentine authors, one may find in his works echoes of two authors whose authenticity he greatly admired: the Mexican, Juan Rulfo (1918-86), and the Brazilian, Graciliano Ramos (1892-1953).

PRIMARY BIBLIOGRAPHY
Creative Writing
A punto de reventar seguido de Kid Ñandubay. Buenos Aires: Losada, 1971.

Adiós pampa mía. Caracas: Monte Avila, 1978.

Alias Gardelito. Un horizonte de cemento. Kid Ñandubay. Buenos Aires: Galerna, 1981.

Alias Gardelito y otros cuentos. La Habana: Casa de las Américas, 1974.

Bairestop. Buenos Aires: Losada, 1975.

Cuentos de Bernardo Kordón. Buenos Aires: Tiempo Contemporáneo, 1969.

De ahora en adelante. Buenos Aires: Siglo Veinte, 1952. Also, Buenos Aires: Sudestada, 1968.

Un día menos. Buenos Aires: Sudamericana, 1966.

Domingo en el río. Buenos Aires: Palestra, 1960. Also, Buenos Aires: Jorge Alvarez, 1967.

Hacele bien a la gente, cuentos porteños. Buenos Aires: Jorge Alvarez, 1968.

Historias de sobrevivientes. Buenos Aires. Bruguera, 1982.

Un horizonte de cemento. Buenos Aires: AIAPE, 1940. Also, Buenos Aires: Siglo Veinte, 1940; 1963.

La isla. Buenos Aires: Problemas, 1940.

Lampeao, novela de los desiertos brasileiros. Buenos Aires: Ediciones del Pórtico, 1953.

Los que se fueron. Buenos Aires: Torres Agüero, 1984.

Macumbá: relatos de la tierra verde. Ilustraciones de Caribé. Buenos Aires: Tiempo Nuestro, 1939.

Manía ambulatoria. Prólogo de Ulyses Petit de Murat. Buenos Aires: El Ateneo, 1978.

El misterioso cocinero volador y otros relatos. Selección, presentación y noticia bibliográfica por Jorge B. Rivera. Buenos Aires: Centro Editor de América Latina, 1982.

Muerte en el valle. Presentación de Juan de Luigi. Santiago de Chile: Cultura, 1943.

Los navegantes. Buenos Aires: Losada, 1972.

Una región perdida. Buenos Aires: Siglo Veinte, 1951.

Reina del Plata. Novela. Buenos Aires: Cronos, 1946. Also, Buenos Aires: Jorge Alvarez, 1966; Buenos Aires: Centro Editor de América Latina, 1973; Buenos Aires: Milton, 1983.

Relatos porteños. Buenos Aires: Editorial de Belgrano, 1982.

Sus mejores cuentos porteños. Buenos Aires: Siglo Veinte, 1972.

Tambores en la selva (Stanley). Buenos Aires: Abril, 1946.

Un taxi amarillo y negro en Pakistán y otros relatos kordonianos. Estudio preliminar de Juan José Sebreli. Prólogo de Pablo Neruda. Buenos Aires:
Sudamericana, 1986.

Todos los cuentos. Buenos Aires: Corregidor, 1975.

Tormenta en otoño. Buenos Aires: Siglo Veinte, 1943.

Vagabundo en Tombuctú. Buenos Aires: Cauce, 1956.

Vagabundo en Tombuctú, Alias Gardelito y otros relatos. Buenos Aires: Losada,
1961.

Vencedores y vencidos. Buenos Aires: Capricornio, 1965. Also, Buenos Aires:
Centro Editor de América Latina, 1968.

La vuelta de Rocha: brochazos y relatos porteños. Ilustraciones de Arrigo To-
desca. Buenos Aires: Ediciones A.J.E., 1936.

Nonfiction

Candombé; contribución al estudio de la raza negra en el Río de la Plata. Buenos Aires: Continente, 1938.

China o la revolución para siempre. Buenos Aires: Jorge Alvarez, 1969.

Reportaje a China: una visión personal del país que conmueve al mundo. Buenos Aires: Treinta Días, 1964.

600 millones y uno (China vista con ojos argentinos). Buenos Aires: Leviatán,
1958.

El teatro tradicional chino. Buenos Aires: Siglo Veinte, 1959.

Viaje nada secreto al país de los misterios: China extraña y clara. Buenos Aires:
Leonardo Buschi, 1984.

Editions

Así escriben los chinos: desde la tradición oral hasta nuestros días. Buenos
Aires: Orión, 1976.

SECONDARY BIBLIOGRAPHY
Criticism

Foster, David William. "Defining the Context, Bernardo Kordon's *Reina del
Plata*: Spatialization of the City in the Narrative of Social Realism." In
his *Social Realism in the Argentine Narrative.* Chapel Hill: North Carolina Studies in the Romance Languages and Literatures, 1986. 31-42.

Gardiol, Rita. "Bernardo Kordon." *Argentina's Jewish Short Story Writers.* Indiana: Ball State University Monograph Series, No. 32, 1986. 23-27.

Herrera, Francisco. "Kordon, Bernardo." *Enciclopedia de la literatura argentina.*
Ed. Pedro Orgambide y Roberto Yahni. Buenos Aires: Sudamericana,
1970. 349-50.

Lafforgue, Jorge. "Kordon: vagabundo porteño." *Davar* 119 (1968): 142-46.

La Hoz de Klinsky, Magda, Mariela Herrera de Gómez, and Alicia Beatriz Castañeda. "Recreación de un orden matriarcal castrador en 'Los ojos de Celina' de Bernardo Kordon." In *Crítica literaria de la literatura latinoamericana del siglo XX. III Simposio Internacional de Literatura*, Universidad Nacional de Salta (August 4-9, 1986). Ed. Juana Alcira Arancibia. Westminster, CA: Instituto Literario y Cultural Hispánico, 1990. 253-64.

Matamoro, Blas. "Bernardo Kordon: *Relatos porteños.*" *Cuadernos hispanoamericanos* 389 (1982): 494-96.

Petit de Murat, Ulyses. "El barco ebrio de Bernardo Kordon." *Manía ambulatoria*. Buenos Aires: El Ateneo, 1978. xi-xvi.

Rivera, Jorge, "Bernardo Kordon: escorzo de un narrador argentino." *Cuadernos hispanomericanos* 398 (1983): 372-85.

—. "Estudio preliminar." *El misterioso cocinero volador y otros relatos*. Buenos Aires: Centro Editor de América Latina, 1982. i-x.

—. Prólogo: Bernardo Kordon y la aventura de la existencia." *Alias Gardelito. Un horizonte de cemento. Kid Ñandubay*. Buenos Aires: Galerna, 1981. 9-12.

Romano, Eduardo. "Reedición de una novela implacable." *Tiempo Argentino* May 19, 1985: 6.

Rosemberg, Fernando. *Los cuentos y relatos de Bernardo Kordon*. Buenos Aires: Dirección General de Cultura, 1980.

Sebreli, Juan José. "Prólogo." *Un taxi amarillo y negro en Pakistán*. Buenos Aires: Sudamericana, 1986. 7-18.

—. "Toribio Torres: un hombre argentino." *Centro* (Buenos Aires) 14 (1959): 163-69.

Senkman, Leonardo. "'Función de cine en Auschwitz' de Bernardo Kordon." In his *La identidad judía en la literatura argentina*. Buenos Aires: Pardés, 1983. 382-84.

—. "'Kid Ñandubay,' o el aprendizaje a golpes de ser judío." *La identidad judía en la literatura argentina*. Buenos Aires: Pardés, 1983. 135-37.

Weinstein, Ana E., and Miryam E. Gover de Nasatsky, comps. *Escritores judeoargentinos: bibliografía 1900-1987*. 2 vols. Buenos Aires: Milá, 1994. I.381-88.

Interviews

"Bernardo Kordon." *Encuesta a la literatura argentina contemporánea*. Buenos Aires: Centro Editor de América Latina, 1982. 241-45.

Giardinelli, Mempo. "Bernardo Kordon: escribir es un ejercicio dudoso porque es un ejercicio solitario." *Así se escribe un cuento*. Buenos Aires: Beas Ediciones, 1992. 265-71. Also in *Puro cuento* 4.21 (1990): 2-5.

Ploshchuk, Ariel. "Dialogando con Bernardo Kordon: tendría que ser ciego para no percibir mi condición judía." *Mundo israelita* 2999 (May 9, 1981): 17, 33-34.

Rita Gardiol

KOVADLOFF, SANTIAGO (Argentina; 1942)

Santiago Kovadloff was born December 14, 1942 in Buenos Aires. He received a degree in philosophy from the Universidad de Buenos Aires, where he now holds a teaching position. In addition, he contributes regularly to a number of journals and newspapers in Argentina and abroad. He has lived in Brazil and he has worked as the cultural liaison to the Brazilian and Portuguese embassies in Buenos Aires. His contact and involvement with the Lusophone world has led him to be an active promoter of Portuguese and Brazilian literature. He has translated the works of such world-renown authors as Joaquim Maria Machado de Assis (1839-1908), Fernando Pessoa (1888-1935), João Guimarães Rosa (1908-67), and Mário de Andrade (1893-1945) into Spanish. Likewise, he has compiled many anthologies of Brazilian and Portuguese fiction and poetry (see Weinstein and Gover de Nasatsky). Kovadloff has been awarded various literary prizes over the course of his career for his poetry and essays. In addition, he has published children's literature.

Kovadloff has penned six poetry collections that stand out for their lexical precision, poetic imagery, and wide universe of thematic representations. María Rosa Lojo very concisely traces Kovadloff's progression as a poet in his first four published volumes starting with *Zonas e indagaciones* (Zones and Inquiries; 1978), followed by *Canto abierto* (Open Song; 1979), *Ciertos hechos* (Certain Facts; 1985), and finally *Ben David* (1988). Of these four volumes *Ben David* is the most closely tied to a poetic discourse of identity. The very title seems to intimate the search for identity contained in the poems, linking the poet to father, family, and history. The poet's quest leads him to a desacralization of Jewish tradition, a loss that is both lamented and understood. This is made apparent in the poem that closes the volume, "Iom Kippur": Mi hija, Señor, no es como yo la quise / ni yo, Señor, como ella me soñó. / Aún así, / sentados y en ayunas, / los cuatro juntos / miramos televisión. (Mi daughter, Lord, is not as I wanted her / nor am I, Lord, how she dreamt me. / Even so, / seated and in fast / the four of us together / watch television [91]). His most recent collections of poetry are *El fondo de los días* (The Depth of the Days; 1992), characterized by a melancholic undertone, and *La vida es siempre más o menos* (Life Is Always More or Less; 1994). The latter consists of a collection of ingenuously wise remarks and observations made by his three young children and which Kovadloff has rendered into poetic format.

Kovadloff has published one volume of short stories, *Mundo menor* (Lesser World; 1986), although one hesitates to call it a volume since it contains only two. "La vida ausente" (The Absent Life) is a well-developed story that operates on at least two separate narrative levels. It begins with the descriptive scene of soldiers in the heat of battle, but the reader soon realizes that what is taking place is merely a child playing with toy soldiers. The recurrent violent "war scenes," however, serve to prepare the reader for the eventual outcome of the story. On an emotional level the tale revolves around the relationship between the young boy and his father, who is dangerously involved in anti-government activity. When faced with the choice of fleeing for his life at a moment's notice or taking his son owl hunting at night he opts for the second. After having shot an owl and sharing a moment of father/son bonding they are confronted by a group of officials. They tell the boy to run home and the last thing he hears is the sound of his father being shot. Kovadloff's story is a telling metaphor for the violence-torn social reality brought on by the military dictatorship of 1976-83, known as the Proceso de Reorganización Nacional (Process of National Reorganization).

While Kovadloff is well respected as a poet and short story writer he is best known for being one of Argentina's most insightful and outspoken cultural critics and for his essays that display his talent for sharp intellectual acuity. Kovadloff wrote consistently during the military dictatorship, publishing in Buenos Aires newspapers and journals in a relentless effort to appraise the socio-cultural demise of Argentine society during that period. He was even more prolific, and more severely critical, after the return to democracy in 1983. His essays have been collectively published in a number of volumes: *Una cultura de cata-cumbas* (A Culture of Catacombs; 1982), *Argentina, oscuro país. Ensayos sobre un tiempo de quebranto* (Argentina, Dark Country. Essays about a Time of Upheaval; 1983), the essays in which comprise a brilliant analysis of the ideological and social forces that governed the country, *Males antiguos* (Ancient Evils; 1985), and *Por un futuro imperfecto* (For an Imperfect Future; 1987). In 1992

Kovadloff published an anthology of essays gathered from the previous volumes titled *La nueva ignorancia: ensayos reunidos* (The New Ignorance: Collected Essays). The volume represents almost ten years of Kovadloff's intellectual activism. The title is indicative of the project Kovadloff undertakes: to expose the damage caused by the military government, explicate the problems intrinsic to the process of redemocratization, and (re)construct the foundation for a national social and cultural identity. As in his previous volumes, Kovadloff has divided *La nueva ignorancia* into thematically organized sections that deal with such issues as the period of the Proceso, the past and the future, marginalized sectors of society, Jewish issues, and even his own thoughts on a theory of poetics. Nevertheless, in the preface he advises the reader not to approach the book from a thematic stand point, but to consider each essay as a product of the instance that inspired it. Santiago Kovadloff was, and continues to be, in no uncertain terms the most outspoken essayist of the Proceso and post-Proceso period. His style as an essayist is very traditional in that he writes short, concise, expository essays that speak immediately and directly to the heart of a given topic. He seldom utilizes rhetorical devices or tropes in his writing, but instead composes logically ordered, persuasive arguments with great conviction. Kovadloff's dissent as a writer is strictly contestatory in nature, and even goes beyond mere protest to be used as a weapon in the fight against authoritarianism.

Kovadloff, like other contemporary Jewish intellectuals—Jacobo Timerman (1923), Marcos Aguinis (1935), and Ricardo Feierstein (1942) immediately come to mind—shows a profound concern for articulating the Jewish experience in Argentina. His "Un lugar en el tiempo: la Argentina como vivencia de los judíos" (A Place in Time: Argentina as the Lived Experience of the Jews [originally published in *Por un futuro imperfecto* and included in *La nueva ignorancia*) is not only one of his best essays on a Jewish topic, but it is perhaps the most cogent essay written by any author on the problematics of Jewish-Argentine identity. Kovadloff presumes that the reader—the average, educated, culturally cognizant Argentine citizen—is aware of at least the basic facts surrounding the history of Jewish immigration to Argentina. What he proposes as the thesis of the essay is that the Jewish presence in Argentina "merece renovada atención filosófica" (deserves renewed philosophic attention [*La nueva ignorancia* 191]). Kovadloff defines the Jews' migration from Europe to Argentina as a transition from Jewish existence in space to one in time. He ascribes to the notion of Jewish identity as a fluid process of transformation once, that is, the Jews left the restrictive space that confined identity to a static state of reality. He goes on to explain that Jewish identity passed from an infinitive state (*ser*/to be), to a progressive state (*siendo*/being) that made possible the transformation of Jewish identity into an ongoing process of self-identification in relation to new environments and attitudes; a positive advance in the conceptualization of a pluralistic Jewish identity (193). With the fall of Hipólito Yrigoyen in 1930 and the subsequent rise of General Uriburu that marked the beginning of the *década infame* (infamous decade), Argentine Jews were forced to abandon hopes of a pluralistic society. The anti-Semitic repression of the Uriburu regime dashed all hopes of Argentina being "concebida como dimensión de futuro para el judaísmo" (conceived of as a future dimension for Judaism [194]).

Kovadloff unequivocally places the blame for the impediment of Jewish integration into Argentine society on two fundamentally hegemonic forces in Argentina: the Catholic church and the Armed Forces. The ideology of Catholicism—as it is conceived in Argentina—inhibits full participation in society by anyone who is not Catholic. The Jew, by the very nature of his being, can only hope for second-class citizenship, at the very best. He can never attain full citizenship, because true Argentine identity—as defined by the Catholic church—is determined first and foremost by its innate Catholicism on which *argentinidad* is based. The Armed Forces proscribe Jewishness as part of Argentine identity, Kovadloff asserts, by means of two norms of nationalistic ideology established in 1930. These are the "authoritarian conception of political power and the essentialist vision of national identity" (196). The Armed Forces operate in conjunction with the church as the moral reserve of the nation, conserving the religious and moral principles of society as established by the church with authoritarian zeal. The principal point made by Kovadloff in his essay is that the Jew in Argentina, as perceived by official religious and governmental hegemonic powers, embodies the enemy, the outsider, the threat to all that is good and decent. The very nature of the Jew is subversive. He is, in Kovadloff's words, an ontological out-law (198).

It should be made clear that Kovadloff does not attack Catholics, but rather the institution of the Catholic church that wields such unforgiving power over Argentine society. He does not suggest that Catholics were safe from the war waged by the military. There were many priests and nuns who disappeared or were forced to flee the country, not to mention the thousands of Catholic citizens who fell prey to military repression. Such individuals, however, had surely gone against, or were judged to have gone against, the official stance of the Church and the military.

Kovadloff includes six other essays on specifically Jewish topics in *La nueva ignorancia*. His "Antisemitas: la lógica del odio" (Anti-Semites: The Logic of Hatred) is a particularly perceptive look at the ideological underpinnings of anti-Semitism. It was reprinted in *La maga: noticias de cultura* (The Magician:

Cultural News; a leading source of cultural criticism and news in Buenos Aires) following the July 1994 terrorist attack on the AMIA (The Jewish Mutual Aid Society) building in Buenos Aires that killed close to one-hundred people and almost completely destroyed the largest Jewish archive in Latin America. Other essays center on topics like Israel, the Bible, Yiddish, and Martin Buber.

It is not surprising that Kovadloff, like Marcos Aguinis, turns time and again to the theme of cultural pluralism, and the lack thereof in Argentina, as one of the most significant factors impeding a complete transformation of Argentine society that would break free from the authoritarian regimes that began in the mid-nineteenth century with Juan Manuel de Rosas and that have resurfaced over the last century on numerous occasions. As an intellectual who finds himself in a position of the minority Other, the ideal of pluralism and the incorporation of alterity within Argentine society appeals to his own self-identification. However, he perceives it on a grander scale as being the element that could most benefit the society in which he lives. This viewpoint is in direct conflict with the military conception in which a prescribed ideal of identity is forced upon the individual. In fact, one of the most damaging effects of the dictatorship was the proscription of almost all cultural expression. In the essay "Un concepto decisivo: el de cultura nacional" (A Decisive Concept: That of National Culture), which first appeared in 1982, the author differentiates between these two conceptions of identity that he calls *cultura nacional* and *cultura imperial* (imperial culture [*La nueva ignorancia* 17-19]). Kovadloff perceives national culture as consisting of a process whereby identity is formed by means of continual (re)transformation. Imperial culture, on the other hand, is a permanent fixture that is indisputable and should be adhered to unquestioningly. It is a matter of time and space in which change affords stability.

Kovadloff asserts that the boundaries that define and inform national culture/identity should be kept open to constant reformulations in order to avoid becoming obsolete with the passage of time. The constant renovation of self-definition—individually and collectively—conforms to what Kovadloff calls the imperative to win permanent validity (18). He laments that during the Proceso, national identity was dictated and paralyzed by fear. He states that it is not just the fear induced by tyranny, but also the fear of discovering what oneself has become. He characterizes national identity as embodying what remained hidden rather than what was readily apparent.

In Kovadloff's earlier essays—those written during the end of the Proceso or shortly thereafter—the most immediately recognizable element is the contestatory nature of the discourse. Likewise, the author looks to the future with hope, ready to rebuild after the disaster. In contrast, in the later essays—written four to almost ten years after the return to democracy—Kovadloff reveals a much more meditative, reflective tone. Many of the essays deal with his concern that the desired change has been slow to come, and that while the government has changed, many of the same societal attitudes persist. In the essay "Por un futuro imperfecto" (1987) Kovadloff examines the future of Argentina with decidedly less hope than the return to democracy had seemed to promise. He finds that what is needed in Argentina is a complete renovation of the internal conflicts that impede the progress of the country as a truly democratic society. He points out the difference between enduring—what Argentines are currently doing—and being.

Kovadloff sees Argentines as being constantly polarized between opposing ideologies. Everything is seen in black and white, good and bad, wrong and right. There is no room for a multiplicity of ideas. If Argentina cannot overcome its extreme intolerance to pluralism, Kovadloff warns that Argentines are doomed to repeat their past.

In his 1991 essay "El mal nuestro de cada día" (Our Daily Illness) Kovadloff portrays an even bleaker picture of Argentina's future that he sees in rapid decay. He emphatically declares in his opening statement: "Hace ya mucho que la decadencia argentina resulta inocultable. Fuimos una nación que supo atraer a los hijos de otros pueblos. Somos una nación que repudia y expulsa a sus propios hijos" (It's been a long time since Argentine decadence is indisguisable. We were a nation that knew how to attract the children of other countries. We are a nation that repudiates and expels its own children [56]). He maintains that Argentina does not change and that successive generations of Argentines merely replace one another without transforming the nature of the nation's identity. He describes Argentina as being trapped in time. Whereas in "Un concepto decisivo" he viewed time as a vehicle for the transformation of identity within the space of Argentina, he now sees time as having come to a standstill. Kovadloff describes a completely decadent Argentina in which primitivism is the most outstanding characteristic of society. By primitivism he means to signify the insistence on living for the moment and the stagnation of a culture that is unwilling to undertake a project of transformation. The decadent Argentine, Kovadloff explains, is the person who is void of principles, beliefs, and interests, one who does not seek change, but who is more interested in enduring in the present. The author remonstrates that decadence in Argentine society is fast annihilating any semblance of national identity.

Kovadloff's perceptions of the problematics of Argentine identity, and its survival, call attention to the devastating effects not only of the Proceso, but of a variety of societal mores than have contributed to the decay of a meaningful identity, one that is based on the ideals of pluralism, change, and the constant reevaluation of the cultural codes operant in the concept of *argentinidad*.

His recent essay *El silencio primordial* (1993) is a philosophical text in which he takes up the theme of silence as a presence in a variety of disciplines, ranging from mathematics to poetry. Kovadloff's latest essayistic undertaking is titled *Lo irremediable: Moisés y el espíritu trágico del judaísmo* (That Which Is Irremediable: Moses and the Tragic Spirit of Judaism; 1996).

PRIMARY BIBLIOGRAPHY
Creative Writing

Ben David. Buenos Aires: Torres Agüero, 1988.

Canto abierto. Buenos Aires: Botella al Mar, 1979.

Ciertos hechos. Rosario: El Lagrimal Trifurca, 1985.

El fondo de los días. Buenos Aires: Torres Agüero, 1992.

Lugar común. (With Daniel Freidemberg). Buenos Aires: El Escarabajo de Oro, 1981.

Mundo menor. Buenos Aires: Torres Agüero, 1986.

La vida es siempre más o menos. Buenos Aires: Sudamericana, 1994.

"Which Is To Say," "Country." Trans. by Ricardo Pau-Llosa. *Beloit Poetry Journal* 32.4 (1982): 8-9.

Zonas e indagaciones. Buenos Aires: Botella al Mar, 1978.

Children's Literature

Agustina y cada cosa. Buenos Aires: Colihue, 1989.

República de evidencia. Buenos Aires: Lugar, 1993.

Nonfiction

"Antisemitas: la lógica del odio." *La maga: noticias de cultura* 3.131 (1994): 48.

Argentina, oscuro país: ensayos sobre un tiempo de quebranto. Buenos Aires: Torres Agüero, 1983.

Las ceremonias de la destrucción. Un estudio sobre el suicidio como comportamiento colectivo. (With Eduardo Kalina). Buenos Aires: Ediciones de la Flor, 1981.

Una cultura de catacumbas y otros ensayos. Buenos Aires: Botella al Mar, 1982.

"Dos conductas dominantes en el judaísmo argentino contemporáneo." *Controversia de ideas sionistas* (Buenos Aires) (1985): 33-54.

La droga, máscara del miedo. Estudio sobre una expresión del conformismo social. (With Eduardo Kalina). Caracas: Monte Avila, 1978.

"El ejercicio judío de la literatura." In *El imaginario judío en la literatura de América Latina: visión y realidad*. Ed. Patricia Finzi, Eliahu Toker, and Marcos Faerman. Buenos Aires: Editorial Shalom, 1992. 100-2.

Lo irremediable: Moisés y el espíritu trágico del judaísmo. Buenos Aires: Emecé, 1996.

Males antiguos. Buenos Aires: Botella al Mar, 1985.

La nueva ignorancia: ensayos reunidos. Buenos Aires: REI Argentina, 1992.

Los poderes del poeta: poesía y conocimiento en el Brasil del siglo XX. Madrid: Instituto de Cooperación Iberoamericana, Ediciones de Cultura Hispánica, 1991.

Por un futuro imperfecto: ensayos. Buenos Aires: Botella al Mar, 1987.

Producción poética. Producción psicoanalítica. Buenos Aires: Mayéutica, 1985.

"Las sendas de lo judío." In *El imaginario judío en la literatura de América Latina: visión y realidad*. Ed. Patricia Finzi, Eliahu Toker, and Marcos Faerman. Buenos Aires: Grupo Editorial Shalom, 1992. 204-5.

El silencio primordial. Buenos Aires: Emecé, 1993.

SECONDARY BIBLIOGRAPHY
Criticism

Fingueret, Manuela. "Acerca de *Una cultura de catacumbas*, de Santiago Kovadloff." *Nueva Sión* 594 (1984): 23.

—. "La aldea para describir el mundo" (*Mundo menor*). *Nueva Sión* 663 (22 Aug., 1987): 23.

—. "Poeta entre el amor y la muerte" (*Ciertos hechos*). *Nueva Sión* 620 (8 Oct., 1985): 21.

Foster, David William. *Violence in Argentine Literature: Cultural Responses to Tyranny*. Columbia and London: U of Missouri P, 1995. 49-55.

Klein, Laura. "*Zonas e indagaciones*, de Santiago Kovadloff." *Nova arte* 5 (1980): 29.

Lojo, María Rosa. "Santiago Kovadloff: profundidad de lo sencillo." *Cultura de la Argentina contemporánea* 6.31 (1989): 20-22.

Senkman, Leonardo. Rev. of *Ben David. Noaj* 4.5 (1990): 110-12.

Weinstein, Ana E., and Miryam E. Gover de Nasatsky, comps. *Escritores judeoargentinos: bibliografía 1900-1987*. 2 vols. Buenos Aires: Milá, 1994. I.405-11.

Interviews

Fingueret, Manuela. "Argentinidad y judaísmo son instancias complementarias. Diálogo con Santiago Kovadloff, un lúcido intelectual argentino." *Nueva presencia* 484 (10 Oct., 1986): 6-9.

Gallone, Osvaldo. "Los silencios de Kovadloff." *Primer Plano* (Suplemento de Cultura de *Página/12*) 11 July, 1993: 6.

"Respuesta a la encuesta sobre literatura argentina de la década 1970-1980." *Torre de papel* 1 (1980): 180-81.

Sabato, Ernesto. "Precipitarse en la literatura, precipitarse en la vida. Diálogo con Ernesto Sabato." *Nueva Sión* 664 (22 Aug., 1987): 20-21.

"Santiago Kovadloff." In *Encuesta a la literatura argentina contemporánea.* Buenos Aires: Centro Editor de América Latina, 1982. 116-20.

Darrell B. Lockhart

KOZAMEH, ALICIA (Argentina; 1953)

Alicia Kozameh was born in Rosario, Argentina, in 1953. She moved to Los Angeles, California in 1980, lived one year in Mexico in 1983, returned to Buenos Aires in 1984, and in 1988 returned once again to Los Angeles, where she currently resides. She has produced four novels, published numerous short stories and articles, written a screenplay, founded and directed a literary magazine, and been imprisoned.

Kozameh was baptized a Catholic, even though her mother is Jewish and the family of her father belonged to the Greek Orthodox Church. The swell of anti-Semitism in Argentina had forced her parents to marry in the Catholic Church, the result of which produced a rift in the relations between the families of both parents. It was the effects of this rift which would strain Kozameh's own relationship with her parents, along with a series of physical uprootings.

Because Kozameh's father was a commercial banker, the family was forced to move from city to city when Alicia was young. After having lived in six cities in eight years, Kozameh's parents sent her to Catholic boarding school, the rigid and authoritarian nature of which served only to foment her political activism. At sixteen, she was expelled from Catholic school for organizing a stoppage, causing the school to shut down for a time during the *Rosariazo*, a series of explosive protests by workers and students in the streets of Rosario. Graduating from *colegio* two years behind her class, Kozameh entered the Universidad Nacional de Rosario at the age of twenty, where she studied literature and philosophy, while becoming more politically involved. But at the age of twenty-two, before having completed her studies, she was jailed by the military regime for possession of subversive literature.

Two events occurred in Kozameh's early life that would impact her greatly: the death of her older sister and the murder of her uncle. It was the death of her sister, when Alicia was seventeen, which would form the subject matter of her novel *Patas de avestruz* (Ostrich Legs; 1988). And it was the assassination of her uncle, a highly respected physician in Rosario, which would increase the chain of threats and persecution against Kozameh herself, culminating in her imprisonment one year later in 1975. In her novel *Pasos bajo el agua* (*Steps Under Water*; 1987) she details those three years and three months during which she was incarcerated in the basement of Police Headquarters in Rosario and Villa Devoto in Buenos Aires, as well as her "probation" and exile in California that followed.

For Kozameh, the act of writing a novel is like any of the manifold forms of suffering. And though the end product offers very little in the way of happiness, save a brief, tepid moment of satisfaction in a well-turned phrase, it is the laboriously painful process which aids survival. This process, as she has described it, becomes a kind of extirpation, a rooting out of accumulated pain and anguish. As such, the act is wholly physiological, consisting of a wrenching set of bodily processes and reactions.

But writing for Kozameh is not catharsis, a cleaning, a purging of her obsessions. In fact, for her there is nothing clean and final about the process of writing. As Kozameh describes it, the novel is not written, but rather expelled, even spilled; it is suffered, bled. Pain, anguish and confusion, visceral or lodged in the throat like a rat, heave forth in throes, and at the cost of losing vital fluids. For Kozameh, then, writing is emetic. It is not only leakage, drainage, but also synthesis and transformation, a pressing of vomit, tears, sweat, lymph and plasma, of pain, suffering and anguish into words and phrases, into text, ultimately into novels. Indeed, a whole tissue of notions connected to the physiological processes unfolds through the corpus of Kozameh's work, notably in her two most recent novels. While the subject matter in both *Patas de avestruz* and *Pasos bajo el agua* is ostensibly unconnected, at the marrow of her fiction is the very notion of articulation; that is, articulation in a corporeal sense of physical movement broken down into joints and segments as well as the more linguistic notion of verbal expression.

Pasos bajo el agua might be called a testimonial, given the very real historical subject matter it treats, as well as the author's partial intention in the foreword of the novel to make publicly known those events which she, along with the others who shared the same ward, underwent during the military dictatorship in the 1970s. While the primordial objective of the testimonial form is to make public, to express, to articulate the unspeakable pain and horror suffered by those whose voices cannot be accounted for, *Pasos bajo el agua* is not truly a testimonial in the strictest generic sense. First and foremost the novel is, as the author herself has maintained, a literary creation. Her aim was to convert the years spent in prison and the time on probation and in exile into breathing fiction (*ficción viva*), to pierce every minute of those years, to relive every shiver of sensation of that reality indelibly tinctured with death and life and with the same intensity with which it was passed.

What is most notable about *Pasos bajo el agua*, then, is just how agitated the text is. Formally, the novel defamiliarizes itself as fiction, laying bare the whole problematic of literary expression during a period marked by rupture and silence. To this end the novel is disembodied, stitched together of different textual forms and voices. Letters, diary entries, notes surreptitiously passed from one to another facilitate a communication that has effectively been cauterized by imprisonment and exile. Similarly, the narration is not monologic: the narration of Sara, the protagonist of the novel, twins with third-person omniscient narration and indirect free style, as well as the narration and thoughts of other characters. Bursts of voices from the authoritarian figures in the novel (Sara's mother, the physicians in the ward, the *milicos*) intrude on thought and conversation. The tone of the text is similarly shaded; it is ironic, humorous, even ludic, at times fretful, but never desperate or mournful. Likewise, the narration is at once colloquial and concrete, as well as slippery and sensorial, reflecting her own inability to make tangible the ineffable feeling of being swallowed up in the maw of that terror.

Pasos bajo el agua is political, though one might say in the most private of senses; it is interpersonal. Relationships, effectively severed by the military dictatorship's campaign of disappearance, incarceration and death, hang like thrum on a loom: connections between companions, between friends, between mother and child must be reestablished, woven anew. In a very palpable sense, then, the novel is about the rediscovery, and the rearticulation of the protagonist's own body, her own words and thoughts while in prison, in freedom, and in exile in California.

Throughout the course of the novel, Sara is engaged in continual physical and mental activity, always working to force open her pores and follicles occluded by unfamiliar airs, agitating her limbs to pump the blood that has settled in fear of the unknown. What movement or expression once functioned in those zones of freedom can no longer be articulated, verbally or physically, in incarceration. It is the gradual rediscovery of her own body which produces a vital lubrication for the various defense mechanisms which have been desiccated by a continual gnashing of fear, horror, pain, and oblivion. It is the rearticulation of her body that creates new survival mechanisms as well as acting as a stimulation of those neurons deadened of feeling for friends and family members on the outside.

The idea of recuperation, of maintaining and reenforcing the plexus of personal relations is also at the center of her short story "El encuentro. Pájaros" ("The Reunion. Birds"; 1994), which is set in the early eighties during the most fragile moment in Argentina's transition toward democracy. The story concerns four friends and their attempts to organize a reunion for all the women, some thirty of them, who shared the same prison ward. The four inseparable women, all of whose voices weave through the main narration, continually push forward, run into and become entangled in each other's gestures and words while on the way to put in a telephone call to the other ex-prisoners in order to confirm their arrival. Their attempts, however, are frustrated, first by an overwhelming sense of alienation and even hostility the women feel from the city that contains them, a city that drones away while its inhabitants suffer in silence (as one character puts it, everyone in the city must have at least one person dead, disappeared, or imprisoned in their family), and the inability to recover the rhythm of their daily lives.

With the disruptive presence of the *milicos*, the members of the secret police who trail and harass the women, the story suggests just how tenuous and constructed the notion of freedom in democratic Argentina truly is. Threats and intimidation, suspicion, fear and uncertainty still exist, and the story proper ends with the reunion never becoming realized, though the ending is left open. The force of the women's conviction, as well as their physical movements through the city, leads the reader to believe that despite the threats, the reunion will be held. "El encuentro. Pájaros" makes manifest just how necessary the women's defense and survival mechanisms that were developed and used in prison are in the space of so-called freedom. That the friends argue, insult each other, compliment each other, support each other, that they laugh at and with each other, as well as suffer and grow sad together, only affirms the idea that as a group, rolling along in one single wave of overwhelming, tonic force can they resist and crack up the deafening silence that has enveloped others.

Kozameh's third novel, *Patas de avestruz*, is based on Kozameh's own relationship with her older sister Liliana, who was born with her umbilical cord wrapped around her neck; the massive loss of oxygen to the brain left her physically and mentally retarded and contributed ultimately to her death at the age of twenty-one. The novel emerged as the product of a long series of difficult hypnosis sessions which Kozameh underwent in order to be able to write about her dead sister.

In contrast to the frenetic movement in "El encuentro. Pájaros," and the beginning of *Pasos bajo el agua*, which opens with the protagonist Sara, just released from prison, running up the stairs to the outdoor terrace in order to experience anew the once-familiar view overlooking the family patio, *Patas de avestruz* lingers over the image of a dying organism. In this first scene, the physically and mentally arrested form being scrutinized by Alcira, the young narrator of the novel, is her older sister, Mariana. As Alcira describes her, Mariana's contorted figure is shadowed by her own thick, dark, curly hair, and she sits sprawled on the filthy ground, grunting for food. The scene is significant in that it fixes the contrast between the two sisters that will be explored throughout the novel. Mariana is inert, frail, wholly dependant, and her needs devour the attention of the family. Alcira is the vibrant, strong, and creative one who is, in effect, neglected by her parents. If in this opening scene Alcira, who chronologically is four years old, considers her own body useless—as she reasons, it came from the same hips that produced her sister—it is over the course of the novel where, in fact, she develops apart from her dormant sister, physically, sexually, and verbally.

It is not until the end of the novel, when Alcira submits her own literary creation for a high school literary competition that she comes to terms with her ambiguous relationship with her sister, one fraught with extremes of love and hate, need, and rejection. Only by effectively confronting Mariana, by finally accepting her and her death through the distance established by the text can Alcira herself gain and advance her own consciousness, one which is fully displayed by the thirty-five-year-old Alcira who is the principal narrative voice of the novel. It is significant, then, that the teenage Alcira entitles her composition "I am not a murderer," as the elder Alcira's ultimate narration and, in fact, Kozameh's novel is, in effect, a sororicide. But it is through the very process of writing, of pounding out sentence after sentence, kneading out images of her dead sister in all of her defects that Alcira imbues her with a vibrant quality which she never really possessed. In contrast with the opening scene of the novel, *Patas de avestruz* ends with Alcira figuratively and literally embracing her sister, mentally holding her up in a celebratory dance overflowing with emotion and laughter.

Writing for both Kozameh as well as for her characters, whether in the form of Alcira's short story in *Patas de avestruz*, Sara's "freedom notebook" that she smuggles out of prison in *Pasos bajo el agua*, or the written notes passed during break time in "El encuentro. Pájaros," is indispensable and vital in the most literal sense of the word; that is, as a function writing becomes a part and an organ necessary to life. For Kozameh, the act is a means through which to express those phantasms and specters manifested in the form of her obsessions. In effect, it is the process of textually reliving, of suffering, and even of enjoying these most emboweled of ghosts and demons that makes them incarnate, which conjures them up. As Kozameh describes it, every word she puts down on paper is wrought from the hate, love, confusion, and, in effect, all the visceral anguish that has accumulated from the past. And at the same time, every word set forth establishes a distance which allows her to bear their full emotional weight. The process of writing, with its physiological and mental wear, becomes for her a necessary elaboration of ills as well as a therapy. The end result, as all of her characters display at the end of their own experiences, is an individual fortification as well as a look to the future.

Kozameh's fiction is just now beginning to receive critical articulation within the rather heterogeneous landscape of post-dictatorship Argentine literature. Because of her lamentably unique situation as one of the very few women imprisoned by the regime who are currently writing fiction, Kozameh is continually searching for new modes of linguistic and formal expression that reflect Argentina's concrete political situation as well as her own private obsessions. Kozameh's writing, even from the relatively fluid zone of exile, still invokes and provokes those intimate phantasms and demons of her own past, both as a child and from the years of living and suffering under the repression of the military dictatorship. In effect, Kozameh's fiction accepts the painful burden of not only conjuring up her own personal ghosts but perhaps more impossibly, those of her country as well.

PRIMARY BIBLIOGRAPHY
Creative Writing

"Bosquejo de alturas." *Hispamérica* 23.67 (1994): 81-93.

"Dos días en la relación de mi cuñada Inés con este mundo perentorio." *Confluencia* 11.1 (1995): 230-40.

"El encuentro. Pájaros"/"The Reunion. Birds." Trans. by David E. Davis. In *Memoria colectiva y política de olvido: Argentina y Uruguay. 1970-1990.* Ed. Adriana Bergero and Fernando Reati. Publication forthcoming.

Pasos bajo el agua. Buenos Aires: Contrapunto, 1987. English version as *Steps Under Water.* Trans. by David E. Davis. Los Angeles/Berkeley: U of California P, 1996. (Contains additional chapters not found in the original Spanish edition.)

Patas de avestruz. Unpublished Manuscript. Chapters of the novel have appeared in *Fin de siglo* 12 (June 1988): 35-37.

Nonfiction

"Debes saberlo todo. . ." Parts 1-6. *Nueva Sión.* 7 (1984): 12-13; 8 (1984): 16-17; 9 (1984): 16-17; 10 (1984): 14-15; 11 (1984): 1-11; 12 (1984): 10-11.

SECONDARY BIBLIOGRAPHY

Criticism

Pfeiffer, Erna. "La mujer ante el espejo: autorretratos literarios de mujeres latino-americanas." In *La nueva mujer en la escritura de autoras hispánicas: ensayos críticos.* Ed. Juana Arancibia and Yolanda Rosas. Montevideo: Graffiti, 1995. 101-23.

Interviews

López-Cabrales, María del Mar. "El compromiso de la escritura: Alicia Koza-meh." *Confluencia* 11.1 (1995): 187-96.

Pfeiffer, Erna. "Escribir es un drenaje doloroso: Alicia Kozameh." In her *Exiliadas, emigrantes, viajeras: encuentros con diez escritoras latinoamericanas.* Madrid: Vervuert/Iberoamericana, 1994. 89-108.

David E. Davis

KOZER, JOSÉ (Cuba; 1940)

José Kozer was born in Havana, Cuba in 1940. He lived on the island until 1960, when he moved to the United States. Since 1965 he has been teaching Latin American literature at Queens College, the City University of New York.

Even though he has published in other literary genres such as essay and translation, José Kozer is in essence a poet. Up to the present he has written over three thousand poems that have been published in book form in Argentina, the United States, Mexico, the Dominican Republic, and Spain. Also, some of his work has been translated into English, Hebrew, Greek, and Portuguese.

Kozer, as is the case with other Latin American writers who began publishing after the triumph of the Cuban revolution—and therefore belong to that historically torn generation—undertakes a quest of existential questioning in his works through the careful use of direct and sometimes colloquial language.

One important characteristic of this prolific poet is the frequent incorporation of his family and diverse heritage into his poetry. A genealogical tracing of Kozer's family tree helps to explain the at times mundane mentions of different geographical areas in his poetry. Having been born and lived in Cuba for the first twenty years of his life gave Kozer the Spanish language in which he writes. His maternal grandparents and his mother emigrated to Cuba from Czechoslovakia. His father emigrated to the island from Poland, and Kozer's own daughters were born in the United States. In essence, Kozer is the first and only Cuban-born member in his family, but he possesses an Eastern European Jewish tradition that is reflected throughout his poetry. In other words, it can be stated that Kozer's bipolar marginalization—that of being Jewish and living in exile—is almost shown obsessively in his poetry. In spite of his condition as exile, it is difficult to identify Kozer as a Cuban-American writer from New York. His poetry does not reveal the customary pain of a Cuban exile writer driven from his homeland. Instead, Kozer constantly returns to the past, either to the pre-revolutionary Cuba in which he lived or to the land and experiences of his Jewish ancestors. It is almost as if the poet has not had a presence in the United States. For Kozer, Cuba is not a springboard, a point of departure. Rather, like for many other first generation Cuban-Americans, Kozer's constant frame of reference is the island that he knew, that is, the recollection of a world that he inhabited at one point.

The cultural syncretism that forms his being obliges the poet to define himself as hybrid: he is a mixture of languages, cultures, ethnicities. This is at its best portrayed in the poem "Gaudemus" (in Latin, Let's Enjoy Ourselves) found in *Bajo este cien* (Under This One Hundred; 1983) where Kozer declares that his identity is a combination of varied elements. For example, the poet begins by expressing that his Spanish diction is a blend of Mexicanisms, Peruvianisms, and Cubanisms. Also, he acknowledges that religious syncretisms—Jewish, Catholic, Buddhist—are present in his spiritual journey. In sum, there is a clear message in Kozer's poetry to encourage the physical and spiritual diversity and unity of all mankind.

His use of religious themes is not limited to Jewish tradition as he ingresses into Christian imagery and Oriental philosophy as well. For example, in the book *Y así tomaron posesión en las ciudades* (And They Took Possession of the Cities; 1978) there is a section entitled "Interludio" (Interlude) the poet includes four poems that explore the mystic Oriental world for the first time in his writing. Kozer will explore Oriental philosophy as a recurring theme in his later books, *Jarrón de abreviaturas* (Pot of Abbreviations; 1980) and *La garza sin sombras* (Heron Without Shadows; 1985). On the other hand, a later book, *Carece de causa* (Lacks Cause; 1988), follows the parts of the Catholic mass:

Introitus, Dies Irae, Offertorium, Miserere, Graduale, and Communio. To this effect Jacobo Sefamí explains that "Perhaps this perfect religious order counterpoises the chaotic implications of exile, extermination, war, and death" (204). Some of the most frequent protagonists of Kozer's poetry are the members of his family and Jewish ancestors: his father, grandmother, wife, and daughters are carefully presented throughout his poems. For example, in *Bajo este cien*, his wife Guadalupe is mentioned in eight different poems and is presented as the source and purpose of life. During the difficult times that the poet experiences she is the source of peace and joy. On another occasion the father and the grandmother are the protagonists of other poems. In the particular case of "Evocación de la abuela" (Evocation of Grandmother at Home) and "Requiem del sastre" (Requiem of the Tailor) intertwines domestic work or a trade with some type of sacred spiritual splendor.

As stated earlier, Kozer's poetry is in a constant search for wholeness. It is difficult to categorize this poet as pertaining to a particular school of thought, philosophical tendency, or geographic area as his works can be classified as encyclopedic. Without doubt, José Kozer is not only a prolific writer but one of the first major Cuban poets to have emerged from the contemporary diaspora.

PRIMARY BIBLIOGRAPHY
Creative Writing

Antología breve. Santo Domingo, Dominican Republic: Luna Cabeza Caliente, 1981.

The Ark Upon the Number. Trans. Ammiel Alcalay. Merrick, NY: Cross-Cultural Communications, 1982.

Bajo este cien. México: Fondo de Cultura Económica, 1983.

Carece de causa. Buenos Aires: Ultimo Reino, 1988.

El carillón de los muertos. Buenos Aires: Ultimo Reino, 1987.

De Chepén a La Habana. In collaboration with Isaac Goldemberg. New York: Bayú Menoráh, 1973.

De donde oscilan los seres en sus proporciones. La Laguna, Tenerife, Canary Islands: H.A. Editor, 1990.

Díptico de la restitución. Madrid: Ediciones del Tapir, 1986.

Este judío de números y letras. Tenerife, Canary Islands: Nuestro Arte, 1975.

La garza sin sombras. Barcelona: Ediciones Libres del Mall, 1985.

Una índole. Caracas: Pequeña Venecia, 1991, 1994.

Jarrón de abreviaturas. México, D.F.: Premiá, 1980.

Nueve láminas (glorieta) y otros poemas. Iztapalapa, Mexico: Universidad Autónoma Metropolitana, 1984.

Padres y otras profesiones. New York: Antiediciones Villa Miseria, 1972.

Las plagas. New York: Exilio, 1971.

Poemas de Guadalupe. Buenos Aires: Ediciones por la Poesía, 1973.

La rueca de los semblantes. León, Spain: Instituto Fray Bernardino de Sahagún, 1980.

Trazas del lirondo. Iztapalapa, Mexico: Universidad Autónoma Metropolitana, 1993.

Y así tomaron posesión en las ciudades. Barcelona: Ambito Literario, 1978. Also, México, D.F.: Universidad Nacional Autónoma de México, 1979.

Nonfiction

Nueva poesía hispanoamericana en Estados Unidos. San Salvador: Nueva Cultura, 1971.

SECONDARY BIBLIOGRAPHY
Criticism

Alvarez Cáccamo, José María. "*Este judío de números y letras*: palabra familiar y mitológica." *Peñalabra* 17 (1975): 36-37.

Aranguren, José G. "La poesía como cauterio." *Kurpil* 5 (1975): 35-37.

Borgeson, Paul W., Jr. "La persona y la poesía de José Kozer." *Plural* 166 (1985): 59-60.

Heredia, Aída. "El discurso de lo cotidiano y lo espiritual en dos poemas de José Kozer." *Lucero* 3 (1992): 45-52.

López Adorno, Pedro. "Teoría y práctica de la arquitectura poética kozeriana: apuntes para *Bajo este cien* y *La garza sin sombras.*" *Revista iberoamericana* 135-136 (1986): 605-11.

Martín, Sabas. "José Kozer: pasión y transfiguración de la palabra." *Cuadernos americanos* 258 (1985): 141-47. Also in *Hora de poesía* 36 (1984): 74-83; and *Chasqui* 14.2-3 (1984): 60-66.

Minc, Rosa. "Convergencias judeo-cubanas en la poesía de José Kozer." *Cuadernos americanos* 240.5 (1980): 111-17.

—. "Revelación y consecración de lo hebraico en la poesía de José Kozer." *Chasqui* 10.1 (1980): 26-35.

O'Hara, Edgar. "Danza en la noria de José Kozer." *La palabra y el hombre: revista de la Universidad Veracruzana* 77 (1991): 189-94.

Padrón, Jorge. "La poesía de José Kozer." *Revista de cultura* 71 (1981): 39-43.

—. "El texto como teoría y como experiencia." *Cuadernos hispanoamericanos* 399 (1983): 162-69.

Pérez Firmat, Gustavo. "No Man's Language." In his *Life on the Hyphen: The Cuban-American Way*. Austin: U of Texas P, 1994. 156-207.

—. "Noción de José Kozer." *La palabra y el hombre: revista de la Universidad Veracruzana* 77 (1991): 151-60. Also in *Revista iberoamericana* 56.152-53 (1990): 1247-56.

Rodríguez Padrón, Jorge. "Cauce de comunión: *Carece de causa* de José Kozer." *Inti* 29-30 (1989): 89-99.

—. "José Kozer: el texto como teoría y como experiencia." *Cuadernos hispano-americanos* 399 (1983): 162-66.

—. "La poesía de José Kozer." *Eco* 223 (1980): 83-87.

—. "*La rueca de los semblantes* de José Kozer." *Hora de poesía* 13 (1980): 31-36.

Romero, Alberto. "Padres y otras profesiones." *Envíos* 5 (1973): 40.

Savariego, Berta. "Kozer, José." *Dictionary of Twentieth-Century Cuban Literature*. Ed. Julio Martínez. Westport, CT: Greenwood Press, 1990. 233-36.

Sefamí, Jacobo. "The Family, the World: The Poetry of José Kozer." *Tradition and Innovation: Reflections on Latin American Jewish Writing*. Ed. Robert DiAntonio and Nora Glickman. New York: SUNY Press, 1993. 201-9.

Zapata, Miguel Angel. "José Kozer y la poesía como testimonio de la cotidianeidad." *Inti* 26-27 (1987-88): 171-86.

Interviews

Heredia, Aída. "Una conversación con José Kozer." *Periódico de poesía* 14 (1990): 8-13.

Reis, Roberto. "Entrevista: José Kozer." *Chasqui* 6.1 (1976): 95-99.

José B. Alvarez IV

KRAUZE, ETHEL (Mexico; 1954)

Ethel Krauze graduated from the Universidad Nacional Autónoma de México with an advanced degree in Hispanic language and literature and also received a degree in French letters from the Alianza Francesa in Paris. She is an author, script writer, and producer of several cultural programs for televison as well as a journalist and editor for the news periodicals *Excélsior* and *Unomásuno*. In 1987 she received a literary award from the Instituto Nacional de Bellas Artes

(National Institute of Fine Arts) for narrative. Krauze has published novels, short stories, poetry, and theater. In her autobiography, *Entre la cruz y la estrella* (Between the Cross and the Star; 1990), the author relates the story of her family that arrived in Mexico from the Ukraine together with the story of double identity, an inherent part of being Jewish in a largely Catholic Mexico. As she confesses in her work, Krauze was raised among the Yiddish of her grandparents, the Spanish of her generation and the Nahuatl of her indigenous *nana*, María. The books deals with Judeo-Mexican tradition and the process of acculturation that is so common among the newer generations. *Entre la cruz y la estrella* together with two short stories, "Isaías VII" (Isaiah VII), and "Niñas de cuento" (Storybook Girls), are Krauze's works that deal more directly with Jewish themes. Both short stories, included in the volume *El lunes te amaré* (I'll Love You on Monday; 1987), contain an autobiographical background and narrate the experience of adolescent boys or girls that live in a dual world: a world in which many times the Jew celebrates Christmas and prays the rosary.

It should be made clear that in spite of the aforementioned texts which adhere to Jewish themes, throughout her main body of literature Krauze tends to relate the experience of women, be they Jewish or not. Indeed, in *El lunes te amaré* and *Intermedio para mujeres* (Intermission for Women; 1982), both short story collections, the author delves into the experiences of Woman. Among the principal themes in this category the following can be mentioned: marriage, generation gaps between women, being a lover, and adolescent love. It should be emphasized that, as the author herself has stated in a partial reprinting of an interview which appeared in the journal *FEM* (Hernández Carballido, 42), Krauze does not write pamphletary feminist literature, but rather writes about authentic experiences. Without a doubt, the experience of Ethel Krauze is that of being a woman. In her three novels, *Donde las cosas vuelan* (Where Things Fly; 1985), *Infinita* (Infinite; 1992), and *Mujeres en Nueva York* (Women in New York; 1993), the situation of contemporary Mexican women is portrayed in detail, perhaps with greater emphasis than in previous texts. In the first of the above mentioned novels two lovers travel to the Northern border of Mexico. It is precisely there where the author finds the perfect parallel between the distant, poor, Americanized geographical border and the often times unobtainable borders of love. In her second novel, *Infinita*, the author undertakes a profound study of women's feelings and emotions, and of lesbianism in a society that in many cases does not comprehend the emotional needs of women and in which all sexual activity that does not follow traditional social canons is rejected. In *Mujeres en Nueva York*, her latest novel, Krauze seems capable of penetrating women's souls with particular expertise. This is a work filled with grace and at the same time with desperation. The text tells the story of four Mexican women who arrive in New York on a pleasure trip and find themselves confronted with old apprehensions, fears, and tragic internal worlds.

Krauze's poetic works are extensive and through her use of themes dealing with amorous relationships and eroticism the poet's great sensibility to human nature is made evident. Much of her poetry is found in anthologies such as *El cuerpo del deseo: poesía erótica femenina en el México actual* (The Body of Desire: Feminine Erotic Poetry in Contemporary Mexico; 1989) or her "Poema" (Poem) found in the bilingual volume of poetry *Fertile Rhythms: Contemporary Women Poets of Mexico* (1989). Undoubtedly, Ethel Krauze is an author within Mexican literature who has gone practically unstudied. Her themes vary from the specifically Jewish to the more broad feminine experience, both within and outside of Judaism. As a writer she is an excellent example of what a female Jewish author has to offer the literature of Mexico; a literature that finally has begun to open its doors to previously unstudied, not to mention unthought of, literary material.

PRIMARY BIBLIOGRAPHY
Creative Writing

Canciones de amor antiguo. Azcapotzalco, México: UAM, 1988.

"Canciones para cantarle al amante," "Diálogo," "Intermedio dos," "Tres poemas," "Instantáneas." In *El Cuerpo del deseo: poesía erótica en el México actual*. Ed. Valeria Manca. Xalapa, México: UNAM, 1989. 157-70.

Entre la cruz y la estrella. Colección De cuerpo entero. México, D.F.: UNAM/ Corunda, 1990.

De mugir a mujer. México, D.F.: INBA/UNAM, 1983.

Donde las cosas vuelan. México, D.F: Oceáno, 1985.

El lunes te amaré. México, D.F.: Océano, 1987.

Fuegos y juegos. México, D.F.: Universidad Autónoma Metropolitana, 1985.

Ha venido a buscarte. México, D.F.: Plaza y Valdés, 1989.

Infinita. México, D.F.: Joaquín Mortiz, 1992.

Intermedio para mujeres. México, D.F.: Océano, 1982.

Juan. México, D.F.: Aldus, 1994.

Mujeres en Nueva York. México D.F.: Grijalbo, 1993.

Nana María. México, D.F.: CIDCLI/Limusa, 1987.

Niñas. México, D.F.: Colección Práctica de Vuelo, 1982.

Para cantar. México D.F.: Oasis, 1984.

"Poema." *The Fertile Rhythms: Contemporary Women Poets of Mexico*. Ed. Thomas Hoeksema. Pittsburgh, PA: Latin American Literary Review Press, 1989. 80-81.

Poemas de mar y amor. México, D.F.: UNAM, 1982.

"The Mule Going Round the Well". *New Writing From Mexico*. Ed. by Reginald Gibbons. Special issue of *TriQuarterly* 85 (1992): 106-12.

Relámpagos. Saltillo, México: Instituto Coahuilense de Cultura, 1995.

Nonfiction

Como acercarse a la poesía. México, D.F.: Limusa, 1992.

"Los escritores mexicanos judíos." *Noaj* 3.3-4 (1989): 96-100.

SECONDARY BIBLIOGRAPHY

Criticism

Demaree, Kristyna P. "*Donde las cosas vuelan* y los múltiples espacios fronterizos." In *Mujer y literatura mexicana y chicana: culturas en contacto*. Tijuana, México: El Colegio de México, Programa Interdisciplinario de Estudios de la Mujer, El Colegio de la Frontera Norte, 1987. 259-64.

Domecq, Brianda. "Desde los ojos de ella: la narrativa de Ethel Krauze." In her *Mujer que publica . . . mujer pública: Ensayos sobre literatura femenina*. México, D.F.: Diana, 1994. 211-39.

—. "La mirada desnuda, visión de mujer." In *Sin imágenes falsas, sin falsos espejos: narradoras mexicanas del siglo XX*. Ed. Aralia López González. México, D.F.: El Colegio de México, 1995. 579-604.

Interviews

Hernández Carballido, Elvira. "Ethel Krauze." *Fem* 86 (1990): 42.

Miller, Beth. "Ethel Krauze." *A la sombra del volcán: conversaciones sobre la narrativa mexicana actual*. Guadalajara: Universidad de Guadalajara-Xalli/Universidad Veracruzana/Consejo Nacional para la Cultura y las Artes/Instituto Nacional de Bellas Artes, 1990. 173-92.

Daniela Schuvaks

LAITER, SALOMÓN (Mexico; 1937)

Salomón Laiter was born in Mexico City in 1937. Aside from being a literary author, Laiter is also an artist whose paintings have merited considerable attention as well as a film director. He participated in the V Festival de Cine Latinoamericano (Fifth Latin American Film Festival) in Havana with the film *Genocidio en Guatemala* (Genocide in Guatemala [1983]). Laiter may be included in the same generation of Jewish Mexican writers as Margo Glantz (1930), Angelina Muñiz-Huberman (1936), and Esther Seligson (1941), however, he has not enjoyed the same national recognition as his contemporaries. As a writer he is far less productive and considerably less talented than the aforementioned authors.

Nevertheless, Laiter's first text, a novel entitled *David*, was published in 1976 by Joaquín Mortiz, one of Mexico's leading publishing houses. The novel may be loosely defined as a narrative of social protest, roughly comparable to the proletarian novels of the 1930s in the United States such as *Jews without Money* (1930) by Michael Gold (1894-1967), or *Bottom Dogs* (1930) by Edward Dahlberg (1900-77). Laiter's text is not only similar to these American novels in its ideological stance, but also in the fact that it takes place mainly in the United States, specifically New York. The protagonist (David) is a young boy born in Mexico to Jewish refugees from Lithuania and Germany just prior to the outbreak of World War II. As the result of a fall, David seriously injures his hand impaling it on an iron bar. In order to receive better medical treatment his mother takes the boy to New York, where they have relatives living, for an operation. This event takes place following the war and in the midst of American right-wing anticommunist fervor in which leftist intellectuals and communist sympathizers were subject to an unrelenting witch hunt. Laiter uses the protagonist's stay in New York as an opportunity to witness, through the eyes of the child, the evils of American capitalism which has brought about a complete disintegration of society. Dr. Pearson, the boy's surgeon, is portrayed as a cliché of a doctor who keeps the innocent patient waiting mercilessly while he's out playing golf, interrupts treatment for private telephone calls, generally treats the patient with cold scientific demeanor, and who makes sure the payment has cleared before letting the patient go. David is witness to the outcasts and downtrodden on the streets of New York ghettos. He describes in length how the streets are occupied by alcoholics and drug addicts who seem to announce the extinction of the human race, pimps who ruthlessly beat their prostitutes, and newborn babies who must compete with rats for food. In essence he feels that he has discovered the truth behind the false image of the United States. He declares proudly that the people in Mexico are better, that life in Mexico is better. The streets are safe there, one can live and breath, run through the fields and climb palm trees to pick the dates (94). The people in Mexico don't bask in the glory of having killed two hundred thousand innocent people with the atomic bomb.

The text is often confusing, lacking any semblance of narrative coherence, and the plot is quite uncompelling. The structure of the novel seems to reflect the author's vision of social chaos and upheaval. This is also made evident in David's prophetic visions of apocalyptic destruction and impending doom. A countdown (associated with nuclear warfare) is repeated throughout the novel, seemingly signaling the arrival of Armageddon, and a continuation of human holocausts. The novel purports to be a testimony of Jewish immigration to Mexico, however, this theme is never really developed. There is some brief discussion of Nazi Germany, of concentration camps and persecution of the Jews. David's uncle Grisha and a cousin arrive in Mexico after having survived Dachau. The novel treats their experiences as contributing elements of global human suffering. Although the narrator states that David, since the age of eleven, has carried on his shoulders two thousand years of Jewish exile (153), there is in reality little evidence of such a burden. The characters are never truly developed in the novel. They serve, rather, as mouthpieces to convey the author's political and ideological views, mainly through often lengthy diatribes directed against the United States, which the reader is supposed to believe are the views of a ten-year-old boy. Laiter's insistence on thematizing postwar United States society through discussing Roosevelt, Hoover, anticommunist frenzy, the atomic scientists, the Rosenberg trials, the bombing of Hiroshima, and even the Vietnam war, while minimizing the Jewish experience in Mexico or the Mexican response to and involvement in World War II, makes it difficult to consider the novel as anything but a lengthy anti-American narrative. Unfortunately, the author's viewpoint is hampered by the minimal artistic value that can be attributed to the text as a literary work.

La mujer de Lot (Lot's Wife; 1986), a collection of short stories, is Laiter's second work. The reader who may be expecting a collection of stories of specific Jewish content or themes may be disappointed since Jewish identity is not the central focus of Laiter's stories, as was the case with *David*. Even the title story does not deal in any way with the biblical Lot's wife. She is only mentioned as a synecdoche for all women. Much like *David*, Laiter's stories are centered around topics of death, social and moral decay, desperation, and persecution. A general pessimistic view of the human condition pervades the volume. He continues his portrayal of American society in stories such as "La pasión según Johnny Hamburger" (Passion According to Johnny Hamburger), which describes the seedy underside of society with its prostitution, pornography, drug abuse, and rampant violence. "Old Emmy" is a short portrayal of a black prostitute addicted to drugs and scraping by on the margins of a society that rejects and scorns her because of her race. "La última finalidad de la pandilla" (The Gang's Last Purpose) takes place during the 1960s and deals with minority organizations such as the Black Panthers and the Young Lords who fight for justice in an unjust society. The author's portrayal of youth in Mexico is equally lacking in any kind of hope or optimistic outlook for the future. The characters go from one meaningless relationship to the next, dealing with drugs, suicide, and a general hopelessness. The best stories of the collection are the more developed ones such as "Breve memoria de un atentado" (Brief Memory of a Assassination Attempt), which narrates an attempt on the life of Russian revolutionary Leon Trotsky and, of course, the United States's involvement in that attempt. Specific Jewish themes surface in the stories "El rabino de Praga" (The Rabbi of Prague), a brief story in which the narrator observes Franz Kafka and compares himself to the writer; both have the need to escape the confines of Prague, and obliquely, Jewish life there. Perhaps the most intimately telling story of the collection is "Atentado" (Terrorist Attack), which takes place during the Olympic games in Munich. The narrator relates the events of the Olympic games, the souvenirs, the inflated prices, the redemption of Germany as a civilized country, and the technology of modern sports all in juxtaposition to the ironic location of the stadium just meters from the concentration camp of Dachau. The games are disrupted by the assassination of nine athletes, and the event ends up being described as an occasion for First World nations to reaffirm their dominance over the Third World. While the volume was published in 1986, some of the stories actually were written as early as 1963.

Salomón Laiter may not be one of the most prolific of Mexican authors, even within the category of Jewish Mexican writers, but his works do merit consideration for their unique outlook on modern society. Jewish themes are generally more ancillary than central to his narrative, nevertheless, the author does employ frequent biblical, historical, and cultural references which lend to his writing a particularly Jewish perspective.

PRIMARY BIBLIOGRAPHY

David. México, D.F.: Joaquín Mortiz, 1976.
La mujer de Lot. México: D.F.: Claves Latinoamericanas, 1986.

SECONDARY BIBLIOGRAPHY

McMurray, George R. Rev. of *David*. *Chasqui* 6.2 (1977): 96-97.

Plaza, Galvarino. Rev. of *David. Cuadernos hispanoamericanos* 316 (1976): 243-
44.

Darrell B. Lockhart

LAN MISCHNE, SERGIO (Mexico; Date unknown)

Sergio Lan Mischne is the author of one relatively unknown, yet quite interesting text. His collection of short stories titled *Historia de la humanidad, abreviada . . . y otros cuentos* (Brief History of Humanity, and Other Stories; 1988) makes a valuable contribution to Mexican literature for its imaginative and philosophical qualities as well as for its unique Jewish perspective. The overall facile nature of the stories—the language employed, the simple narrative/anecdotal structure, the straightforward dialogues—give the reader the impression that they are directed toward an adolescent audience. The stories could be defined best as tales, parables, or fables in which moral dilemmas are resolved, life's enigmas are elucidated, good triumphs over evil, and love conquers all. Lan Mischne's stories rely heavily on elements of the fantastic and/or supernatural: life after death experiences in "La historia de Alejandro y Dorotea" (The Story of Alejandro and Dorotea), and "Debe haber un error" (There Must Be a Mistake), or revelatory dreams as in "Espejismo" (Illusion), and even a story narrated by a child in the process of being born, "La respuesta" (The Answer). These stories, together with several others from the collection, all address issues concerning the purpose of life.

The volume contains a glossary of Yiddish and Hebrew words to aid the unfamiliarized reader with the variety of terms used throughout the text. However, of the eleven stories included in the volume only two are of specific Jewish content. "La epidemia" (The Epidemic) is a moving epistolary narration set in fourteenth-century Europe at the height of the Bubonic Plague. A dying man writes a letter to his love in which he describes the death of the village tzaddik and the horrors lived by all. He also describes how the Jews are being blamed for starting the epidemic by allegedly killing people, rats, and pigs and then contaminating the water by dumping the corpses in the wells. The narrator further questions how God could allow such horrors to befall his Chosen People. The story "Nostalgia" is perhaps the best developed of the collection. It is a didactic tale dealing with the problematics of Jewish identity, particularly in the diaspora. The narrator, Arele, tells the story of his upbringing in Lithuania and his brother's emigration to Mexico. While still a young man in Lithuania, Arele is one day visited by God who tells him that he should join his brother in Mexico, that he is needed there. Due to the rising anti-Semitism of Stalin's Russia and Hitler's Germany he is convinced and emigrates to Mexico, although he maintained reservations about imminent assimilation and loss of Jewish tradition. He worries about the possibility of children attending cheder or of Jews being able to keep the laws of kashrut. Once in the New World, Arele is befriended by Kubyd who takes him under his wing, and under whose tutelage he soon becomes a very wealthy and very assimilated Jew. It is revealed that Kubyd was a dybbuk who was trying to deceive Arele into renouncing his Jewishness altogether. In the end Arele asserts his Jewishness, however, he does not reembrace his Judaism. He nostalgically reminisces about the days of his youth in Lithuania when Judaism completely enveloped their lives, and yet he has eagerly incorporated his new country and new customs into his life. The tale may seem a bit simplistic at first, but it does succeed in raising some interesting questions regarding contemporary Jewish identity.

All the stories are written in such a way as to teach the young reader ethical values, choices, and guidelines to follow consistent with Judeo-Christian tradition. The characters seek inner peace and spiritual redemption of some sort as they go through life, or death, as the case may be and learn important lessons along the way.

PRIMARY BIBLIOGRAPHY

Historia de la humanidad, abreviada . . . y otros cuentos. México, D.F.: Alpa Corral, 1988.

Darrell B. Lockhart

LAVENTMAN G., JAIME (Mexico; Date unknown)

Jaime Laventman G.—about whom biographical information is unavailable at the time of this writing—is the author of one volume of short stories. His *El espectro* (The Specter) appeared in 1983 and it remains his only published work to date. While Laventman cannot be considered as a writer who has made a significant contribution to Mexican literary production, his book nevertheless does provide the reader with a uniquely Jewish perspective seldom found in

Mexican fiction. One could argue that it is difficult to place Laventman's stories within the context of Mexican literature at all, since they contain little if any relation to Mexican culture and society. Indeed, Laventman's tales seem to have much more in common with the Yiddish story-telling tradition of Eastern Europe than with Mexican literature. All twenty-one stories included in *El espectro* are of specifically Jewish content and take place, for the most part, in Eastern Europe and Israel.

The most prominent theme throughout the volume is the Holocaust. The horrors of the Nazi persecution of Jews are told through the eyes of concentration camp prisoners, some of whom are survivors while others perish. In the stories "El mesías" (The Messiah), "Leib," and "Deborah," the author paints a horrifically graphic picture of life in such infamous concentration camps as Auschwitz and Dachau. But, Laventman also achieves a poignant portrayal of survival, faith, and human endurance through the characters.

Victims are not the only protagonists in Laventman's stories. He also narrates a number of tales in which Nazi criminals are the central characters. In the story "El espectro," for instance, Adolf Hitler is the protagonist. The author recreates Hitler's last moments of life in which he is haunted by the ghastly specter of a murdered Jew who fills Hitler's mind with the horrifying vision of all the Jews he has killed. Hitler is overcome by the vision and dies, unable to carry out the escape he was planning when the specter appeared. In "El gran dictador" (The Great Dictator), a concentration camp assassin dies as a victim of his own conscience while in hiding in Paraguay.

Laventman utilizes a number of different narrative strategies in his stories, including epistolary writing. His stories also vary from realistic portrayals of human suffering to more fantastic depictions, some taken from Jewish mythology, that include dibbuks, fantastic voyages, dead persons who attend their own funerals, and communication with God. A secondary leitmotif in Laventman's stories is that of separation and reunion of family members or long-lost friends. Desperation and loss are almost always overcome by hope and restoration.

In spite of remaining on the margins of mainstream Mexican literature, *El espectro* does constitute an important contribution to the growing body of literature written by Jewish Mexican authors.

PRIMARY BIBLIOGRAPHY
El espectro: cuentos. México, D.F.: Miguel Angel Porrúa, 1983.

Darrell B. Lockhart

LERNER, ELISA (Venezuela; 1932)

Elisa Lerner, born in Caracas, is probably the only female Jewish playwright in the history of the Venezuelan stage. By profession she is an attorney but has also distinguished herself as a writer in the areas of essay and drama. She began her career writing for the Venezuelan magazines *Elite, CAL,* and the humorous *El sádico ilustrado* (The Illustrated Sadist). Lerner's writings tend to be about women and the passing of time as the two relate to the broader subject of the search for men who they believe will bring meaning to their lives. Her essays demonstrate a sensitivity to Jewish material which is rarely evident in her theatre.

Una sonrisa detrás de la metáfora: crónicas (A Smile Behind the Metaphor; 1969) is a collection of essays united by the common thread of interest in North American popular culture, particularly the movies and women associated with them. There are entries on Katharine Hepburn, "Mrs. Miniver," and Blanche du Bois; there are also pieces on writers Susan Sontag (1933) and Mary McCarthy (1912). In a similar vein, Lerner published *Yo amo a Columbo o la pasión dispersa: ensayos 1958-1978* (I Love Columbo or Dispersed Passion: Essays 1958-1978; 1979), which contains reprints of articles that she wrote for newspapers and magazines. The collection, whose title derives from the name of the detective on television, includes reviews of books and movies. *Carriel número cinco (un homenaje al costumbrismo* (Suitcase Number Five [a Homage to Literature of Local Customs; 1983) contains a variety of monologues, dialogues, and remembrances. It has Lerner's favorite topics of womanhood (single, divorced, and even married); Caracas in a state of change, Hollywood movie stars, and a respectable amount of attention to Jewish women, including her mother. One of the memories from her childhood is on how she became a fat girl. *Crónicas ginecológicas* (Gynecological Chronicles; 1984) is a collection of short essays on women as diverse as Barbara Hutton, Shirley Temple, Gloria Swanson, and Eva Perón. Other pieces on women's lives deal with Miss Venezuela, Singer sewing machines, a "crónica femenina del franquismo" (female chronicle of Franquist policies), the women's liberation movement, and William Styron's (1925) novel *Sophie's Choice* (1979). There is also a selection on her Yiddish-speaking mother.

Lerner has written both one-act and full-length plays. Her short pieces include *Una entrevista de prensa o la Bella de inteligencia* (A Newspaper Interview or The Intelligent Beauty; 1976), *El país odontológico* (The Odontological Land; 1976), *La mujer del periódico de la tarde* (The Woman Reporter of the

Afternoon Newspaper; 1976), and *Conversaciones de café en torno a la envidia
. . . o casí* (Café Conversations; 1974). She has offered quite a bit of background information on her first play, *Bella de inteligencia*, which made its debut at La Quimera theatre on 12 October, 1960. She explains in *13 autores del Nuevo Teatro venezolano* (13 Authors of the New Venezuelan Theatre; 1971) that the play is the product of "mi júbilo al sentirme liberada de la pesada carga de la carrera universitaria y al instaurarse la democracia en Venezuela después de la larga dictadura de Pérez Jiménez (my joy at feeling myself free of the heavy burden of my university career and on the restauration of democracy in Venezuela after the long dictatorship of Pérez Jiménez [295]).

Lerner originally published *El país odontológico* in the magazine *Zona franca* (Free Zone) in 1966. The setting is "El Vasto Diente" (The Vast Tooth), a café for writers and artists. The two characters are Mujer and Muchacha; the former (about thirty years old) is a writer, and the latter (about twenty years) aspires to become one. The format of *La mujer del periódico de la tarde* is again a monologue; and the character is another female writer, this time about fifty years old. Her pet peeves are magazines whose audience is fat women and old maids. The language is quite explicit in references to the female sexual and reproductive organs. The subject of loneliness permeates the works and occupies the thoughts of the woman, who can be considered a sort of forerunner of the protagonists of Lerner's full-length plays who think that men are the answer to their problems.

Lerner wrote *Conversaciones de café en torno a la envidia. . . o casi* as her contribution to a collection of plays on the seven deadly sins; her subject is envy. The characters are Hombre and Mujer, and the real themes are nostalgia and loneliness: loneliness equals desperation. Since the life of Mujer is devoid of any substance—at least as she sees it—she oocupies her thoughts with the lives of Hollywood stars; Shelley Winters is "una buena muchacha judía con magnífico apetito" (a good Jewish girl with a magnificent appetite [80]); and Zsa Zsa Gabor makes her think of weddings. She laments the fact that a woman who attains position for herself in the professional world is regarded as a prostitute and that the only contribution women have made to the world is that of envy. The subject of lonely women in search of husbands is the subject of Lerner's two major plays, which for thematic reasons are treated here out of chronological order.

Vida con mamá (Life with Mother) was presented by El Nuevo Grupo in May 1975 and filled the Juana Sujo theatre for three months. It won the Premio del Concejo Municipal del Distrito Federal (Municipal Prize) the first time it was presented. The edition's prologue by Isaac Chocrón calls the play "una averiguación basada en juegos surgidos de recuerdos" and "el éxito más rotundo" (an ascertainment based on games of spurts of memories and the fullest success [9]) of the season. The format of the play is that of a conversation, or fragments of conversations, between a forty-year-old daughter and her elderly mother, with whom she lives. Mother and daughter have conversations on the subjects of marriage and of time, of the latter of which single women are victims. The daughter lives in a continuous present and has no expectations for the future, while the mother's life exists in terms of the past (i.e., before menopause) and the future, about which she is hopeful. She reduces the present to three short phrases: "Los judíos mueren en Europa. La bomba atómica. La violencia" (Jews dying in Europe. The Atomic bomb. Violence [57]). They also talk about menstruation, as a way of pessimistically measuring the passage of time: it is the biological clock ticking away the daughter's reproductive years. The mother's recurrent dream is of her daughter in a wedding dress and of a voice saying, "Su hija debe viajar a Nueva York para casarse" (Your daughter must travel to New York in order to get married [22]). And so she does, in *En el vasto silencio de Manhattan* (In the Vast Silence of Manhattan; 1971).

En el vasto silencio de Manhattan, the winner of the Concurso de Teatro del Ateneo de Caracas (theatrical competition in Caracas) in 1964, has Rosie as its protagonist. She is a more fully developed character than Hija. She also lives with her mother, this time in New Rochelle, outside of New York City. Once again the mother is trying to get her daughter married. Another similarity between the daughters in the two plays is their pessimism; Rosie's is the result of a lifetime of rejection by men. In her conversations with her mother and friends, Rosie speaks almost exclusively and obsessively about men. She is sensitive about the accusatory remark that she hasn't yet married. Rosie's obsession unfairly ascribes to men an image which is impossible to fulfill; had she ever had a man she would have been disappointed, if he were anything less than Promethean. Rosie's unfulfilled life ends, and since she has no family, she has to greet the mourners at her own funeral. The silence in the play's title is a reflexion of the sterility of Rosie's life. Unfortunately, a woman as talented and successful as Elisa Lerner leaves her readers wondering why women have to believe that without men their lives are unfulfilled.

PRIMARY BIBLIOGRAPHY
Creative Writing

Conversaciones de café en torno a la envidia. . . o casi. In *Los siete pecados capitales.* Manuel Trujillo, et al. Colección Teatro. Caracas: Monte Avila, 1974. 75-90.

En el vasto silencio de Manhattan. In *13 autores del Nuevo Teatro venezolano.* Ed. Carlos Miguel Suárez Radillo. Caracas: Monte Avila, 1971. 297-344.

Vida con mamá. Teatro venezolano contemporáneo: antología. Madrid: Centro de Documentación Teatral, Ministerio de Cultura; Sociedad Estatal Quinto Centenario; Fondo de Cultura Económica, 1991. 775-819.

Vida con mamá y tres piezas breves. Includes, *Una entrevista de prensa o la Bella de inteligencia, El país odontológico,* and *La mujer del periódico de la tarde.* Prologue by Isaac Chocrón. Caracas: Monte Avila, 1976.

Nonfiction

Carriel número cinco (un homenaje al costumbrismo). Caracas: El Libro Menor, 1983.

Crónicas ginecológicas. Caracas: Línea, 1984.

Una sonrisa detrás de la metáfora: crónicas, 1968. Caracas: Monte Avila, 1969.

Yo amo a Columbo o la pasión dispersa: ensayos 1958-1978. Caracas: Monte Avila, 1979.

SECONDARY BIBLIOGRAPHY

Azparren Giménez, Leonardo. "Elisa Lerner: la nostalgia como patrimonio personal." *El teatro venezolano y otros teatros.* Caracas: Monte Avila, 1978. 99-106.

Cordoliani, Silda. "Dos mujeres, un país." *Teatro venezolano contemporáneo: antología.* Madrid: Centro de Documentación Teatral, Ministerio de Cultura; Sociedad Estatal Quinto Centenario; Fondo de Cultura Económica, 1991. 769-73.

Klein, Dennis A. "The Theme of Alienation in the Theatre of Elisa Lerner and Isaac Chocrón." *Folio* 17 (1987): 151-66.

Rotker, Susana. *Isaac Chocrón y Elisa Lerner: los transgresores de la literatura venezolana.* Caracas: Fundarte, 1991.

Dennis A. Klein

LEVI CALDERÓN, SARA (Mexico; 1942)

Levi Calderón was born in Mexico City, the daughter of a wealthy Jewish immigrant family; her real name is Sylvia Feldman. She and her partner,

Gina Kaufer, currently reside in San Francisco, where Levi Calderón is completing a collection of erotic stories.

Her only published work is *Dos mujeres* (*The Two Mujeres*; 1990), which has the honor of being the second lesbian novel published in Mexico (the first was Rosamaría Roffiel's [1945] *Amora* [1989]). *Dos mujeres* describes the odyssey of a respectable middle-class urban woman to free herself from the confines of compulsory heterosexuality and, against the opposition of her husband, her sons, her family, and many of her friends, to assert the validity of lesbian desire. The forces of compulsory heterosexuality are overdetermined in the novel, as they are in society, and there are multiple overlapping structures which she must successfully challenge in order to construct for herself a new life based on a transgressive erotic relationship. One of these structures involves Judaism, both as a set of religious principles that condemn homosexual relations and as an ethos that circumscribes the behavior of the Jew in an alien society. Jews may not be a persecuted minority in Mexico, but they unquestionably constitute virtually an undetected minority, and their invisibility may be viewed as necessary in order for them to avoid conflict in a society marked both by its strong nationalism that questions the "Mexicanness" of any immigrant group and its descendants and by a complex folk Catholicism that is suspicious of other religions or religiously-based cultural identities.

Although the protagonist, Valeria, is undoubtedly able to make skillful use of her advanced education to negotiate the difficult passage from hegemonic patriarchy to the fluidity of lesbian erotics but it is precisely her social privilege that leaves her more exposed to the processes of social technology: the demands of class, the conformist urgencies of immigrant subcultures, and the overcompensation of especially marginalized subcultures like the Jews in Latin America, often so concerned not to do anything that would lend credence to anti-Semitic stereotypes: one must not give *shande far di goyim* (shame in front of non-Jews). Such multiple enmeshings can almost make living on the socioeconomic margins look utopian. Needless to say, the fact that Valeria is a Jew is a far from subtle play on questions of fascistic authoritarianism and the persecutions of the detested Other: the victims of persecution (Valeria's parents) become themselves in turn the victimizers of the despised alien, their lesbian daughter (thereby violating the daughter's obligation to subject herself to the father).

PRIMARY BIBLIOGRAPHY

Dos mujeres. México, D.F.: Diana, 1990. English version as *The Two Mujeres*. Trans. by Gina Kaufer. San Francisco: Aunt Lute Books, 1991.

SECONDARY BIBLIOGRAPHY
Criticism
Anhalt, Nedda G. de. "Caleidoscopio erótico." *Sábado*, suplemento de *Unomás-uno* 683 (3 noviembre, 1990): 12-13.

Foster, David William. *Cultural Diversity in Latin American Literature.* Albu-querque: U of New Mexico P, 1994. 50-57.

Martínez, Elena M. Review of *Dos mujeres* (Sara Levi Calderón) and *Amora* (Rosamaría Roffiel). *Letras femeninas* 18.1-2 (1992): 175-79.

Schaefer-Rodríguez, Claudia. "Sara Levi Calderón." In *Latin American Writers on Gay and Lesbian Themes: A Bio-Critical Sourcebook.* Ed. David William Foster. Westport, CT: Greenwood Press, 1994. 199-202.

Interviews
Geduldig, Lisa. "An Interview with Sara Levi Calderón." *OUT/LOOK* (Winter 1991): 37-41.

David William Foster

LEVIN, ELIEZER (Brazil; date unknown)

Brazilian author and businessman Eliezer Levin was born in the Jewish neighborhood of São Paulo known as Bom Retiro. Much like Bom Fim, the Porto Alegre neighborhood depicted in many of the works by fellow Brazilian Moacyr Scliar (1937), or the Barrio Once of Buenos Aires that figures promi-nently in many of the works by Argentine Jewish authors, Levin's childhood environs are central to his fiction. Bom Retiro provides the backdrop for the author's portrayal of the urban Jewish experience in Brazil. Levin has written two novels, *Bom retiro: o bairro da infância* (Bom Retiro: The Childhood Neighborhood; 1972), and *Sessão corrida: que me dizes avozinho?* (Run-on Session: What Do You Have to Say Grandpa?; 1982), and two short-story collec-tions, *Crônicas de meu bairro* (Chronicles of My Neighborhood; 1987), and *Nossas outras vidas* (Our Other Lives; 1989).

The novel *Bom Retiro* is narrated in the voice of the adolescent protago-nist growing up in the close-knit Jewish community in the 1930s and early 1940s. The young boy struggles with his identity as an outsider in relation to mainstream Brazilian society, which at the same time leads to his self-identifica-tion as a Jew. The chapters alternate between those that narrate the main story line and those that consist of short news briefs from other parts of the world of specific Jewish interest. The majority of the news releases deal with the encroaching Nazi menace in Europe, which provide a parallel narrative vein to the novel. The relatively comfortable existence enjoyed by the Jews of Bom Retiro is placed in direct contrast to the impending annihilation of European Jewry. Levin's novel constitutes a solemn treatment of the effects of the Holocaust on the Brazilian Jewish community. In this respect, it is comparable to *As seis pontas da estrela* (1969) by Zevi Ghivelder (1934), which likewise offers a historico-literary rendering of the response of the Brazilian Jewish community to the Holocaust.

Levin's collections of short stories could all be classified as anecdotal in their portrayal of the Jewish experience in Brazil. All of his books contain glossaries with Hebrew and Yiddish words and phrases found sprinkled throughout the body of the text. The extensive incorporation of these languages into his works is more than merely folkloristic in purpose. Foreign words and phrases stand in stark contrast to the dominant Portuguese, and they directly challenge the hegemonic Luso-Catholic discourse of Brazilian society. The underlying ideology of textual polylingualism asserts the alterity of Brazilian Jewish identity. Perhaps most exemplary of this practice is to be found in Levin's most recent work, *Nossas outras vidas*. The title itself indicates otherness, as do the almost forty ministories that comprise the volume. They are a series of vignettes replete with Yiddish and Hebrew expressions and are all thematically specific to Jewish culture, more precisely to the values and traditions of Yiddishkeit. There are four separate sections in the collection titled "Ditos que ouvi no *pletzl*" (Sayings I Heard at the *pletzl* [defined in the glossary as a popular meeting place for conversation and gossip]). They consist of lists of Yiddish proverbs that range from the philosophical, to the didactic, to the humorous.

Levin is without a doubt one of the most assertive of Jewish voices in Brazilian literature. Consequently, his works offer a valuable contribution to the forging of a Jewish discourse in Brazil.

PRIMARY BIBLIOGRAPHY

Bom retiro: o bairro da infância. São Paulo: Martins, 1972. 2nd ed. São Paulo: Perspectiva, 1987.
Crônicas de meu bairro. São Paulo: Perspectiva, 1987.
Nossas outras vidas. São Paulo: Perspectiva, 1989.
Sessão corrida: que me dizes avozinho? São Paulo: Perspectiva, 1982.

SECONDARY BIBLIOGRAPHY
DiAntonio, Robert. "Redemption and Rebirth on a Safe Shore: The Holocaust in Contemporary Brazilian Fiction." *Hispania* 74.4 (1991): 876-80.

Darrell B. Lockhart

LIACHO, LÁZARO (Pseud. of Lázaro Liachovitzky; Argentina; 1906-69)

The son of Polish immigrant Jacob Liachovitzsky, Lázaro Liacho wrote for and edited Yiddish journals and newspapers in Argentina. For convenience's sake, he abbreviated his surname to Liacho (Gardiol 11). Liacho's work reflected a solidary sense of existence with an emphasis on the autobiographical, testimonial, and ethical. From this perspective, Jewish themes were a consistent aspect of his work as was the urban motif as reflected in the title of his posthumous work, *Cantos de tango y vida* (Songs from the Tango and Life; 1970). In addition to his creative efforts, Liacho was active in the Sociedad Argentina de Escritores (S.A.D.E.), the Argentine Society of Writers (Herrera 380).

In his capacity as poet and writer, Liacho treated to a considerable extent the situation of Jewish immigrants in the austere interior agricultural settlements of Argentina. Since Liacho generally was optimistic about Argentina, he frequently portrayed it as the "new Zion." The author's short stories, though, dealt with various themes such as the oppression from which immigrants had escaped while others were set in more contemporary locations from Buenos Aires to Israel. More specifically, some of the subjects and genres treated by Liacho in these stories included the Holocaust, Nazi oppression, Auschwitz, Israel, travelers' tales, mysteries, personal relationships, and symbolism. However, while his writing has been characterized as undeveloped and of little literary value, at the same time he was viewed as providing an impetus to young Jewish writers in Argentina (Gardiol 11-12).

Other comments on Liacho's work have been more favorable. For example, Robert Goodman noted that some of Liacho's poetry and stories are secular in nature while others clearly reflect Jewish themes resulting in a blend of both Jewish and Argentine cultures. Nonetheless, while Liacho demonstrates an honest lyricism and a genuine concern for Jewish suffering, he still is basically an Argentine writer who occasionally treats Jewish themes (Boleslavsky 141-42, as cited by Goodman 41, n. 67). Three volumes of Liacho's poetry were published in 1940 and two volumes of poetry appeared in 1966 and 1969, respectively, containing a mix of Jewish and general subjects (Goodman 41).

The romanticist aspect of Liacho is reflected in his poetry and stories on Israel, all of which were published in 1938 in the journal *Judaica*. They are best understood within an historical context since Liacho produced them a decade before the creation of the state of Israel. It is probable that his generous praise of Israel represented a reaction to increased anti-Semitism in Argentina aided by Nazi propaganda. Following the war and the creation of Israel, however, Liacho ceased writing about Israel, although in his poetry he referred to the possibility of moving there. In his poems to Israel, Liacho professed his love for and loyalty to it but lamented the fact that Israel was so far and remote and thus an unattainable destination. He also described Israel as an eternal spiritual reality, which persevered despite a history of persecution and hatred of the Jews. Liacho further described Israel as a seed blown in the wind, which is firmly established in a persecuted people. Despite Israel's difficult history, Jews refused to relinquish their birthright and heritage. The Jewish people endure just as Jerusalem and the Wailing Wall do, serving as a beckoning symbol of permanence to Jews scattered throughout the world. Liacho also described Israel as the real home for the Jews. Only there could Jews live in peace since it is the land of their ancestors. Throughout several poems, Liacho proclaimed his enduring love of Israel and his willingness to die for it. The fact that Liacho never acted on these sentiments by settling in Israel once it became a reality reflected the prevalent sense of Argentine Jews in relation to Israel. They felt a spiritual tie to Israel and were very cognizant of its significance to Judaism, yet retained a strong affinity for Argentina (Goodman 82-84).

Naomi Lindstrom observed that Liacho was more associated with Jewish themes than, for example, Samuel Eichelbaum (1894-1967). As a poet and essayist, Liacho offered a "classically bucolic treatment to the idea of the Argentine interior as the site of the new Zion" in a collection entitled *Siónidas desde la pampa* (Odes of Zion from the Pampa; 1969), which also included his *Sonata judía de Nueva York* (Jewish Sonata of New York; 1969). While Liacho presented a rural view of Jewish immigrants as a significant underlying theme of his poetry, he also treated the historical Buenos Aires *criollo* (Creole) tradition, reflecting a biculturalism which marked his life (Lindstrom 20). Robert Weisbrot described Liacho as a "famed Jewish writer and the child of colonists" (50), who, while sharing the "ethnic concerns" of his contemporaries who wrote in Yiddish, placed more emphasis on life in Argentina (56). Weisbrot also viewed him as one of the better-known Argentine poets, who later in his career attained national recognition for collections of poetry like *Bocado de pan* (Morsel of Bread; 1931) and *Pan de Buenos Aires* (Bread of Buenos Aires; 1940). Liacho was particularly interested in depicting Jewish-Christian relations in Argentina. Toward the end of his career, Liacho dealt with such subjects as the Bible, religion, and metaphysics as exemplified by works like *Entre Dios y Satán* (Between God and Satan; 1966 [Weisbrot 187]).

Since Liacho was noted for his short stories, it would be worthwhile to consider a collection entitled *Sobre el filo de la vida* (Life's Cutting Edge; 1969). This work consists of twenty-five stories, the highlights of which follow. Several stories have a Holocaust theme. "Ayuda de Cristo (Help from Christ) describes how Jews were marched through a town by Nazi soldiers and eventually executed by their oppressors. "Dios en Auschwitz" (God in Auschwitz), as indicated by the title, tells of the murder of Jews in that concentration camp. "La bestia" (The Beast) is a tale which, in symbolic terms, depicts Jews as collectively being treated as a beast. Violence pervades in many of Liacho's stories as demonstrated in the case of "El asesino y la venganza" (Revenge and the Assassin), the tale of a Jewish refugee from Poland who kills the soldier who had murdered his family in a pogrom years earlier. "El hombre justo" (The Just Man) exceeds the violence of "El asesino. . ." by portraying Nazi atrocities committed agianst Jews.

More indirect symbolism is utilized in the rather fanciful tale entitled "La muerte" (Death). Insects were able to claim the house of a fastidious Jewish widow by purposely bringing on the plague only later, ironically, to fall to exterminators. In a contrasting story, a rabbi's devotion to his son is tested and met in "El héroe y Dios" (God and the Hero).

A number of stories have in common the theme of Israel. For example, "Padre e hijo" (Father and Son) is about a father writing home to his parents in Argentina describing his young son's experiences in an Israeli kibbutz. In "El marrocano" (The Moroccan), a Moroccan-Israeli tries to persuade a visitor from Argentina to remain in Israel to marry her.

Liacho employed other themes and literary styles in this short story collection as reflected in several tales about travelers. One story tells of the revelations of a traveler concerning the unexpected death of his unfaithful wife while another depicts a traveler's short-lived romance with an attractive widow. Liacho utilizes fantasy and surrealism in yet other stories. In "El traje" (The Suit), a used clothes dealer suffers an ill fate after buying a suit which formerly belonged to a suicide victim. In a humorous vein, in "Expendedora de esperanzas" (Dealer in Hopes), a young man unlucky in romance is unsuccessful in repeated attempts to hang himself because a sorceress sold him a rope which broke at each attempt.

Liacho also delved into mystery. "La revelación" (The Revelation) is about the murder of a rich older woman by her younger husband. Other stories involve more realism by relating stories of daily life, some of which are quite tragic. "Clavado a la tierra" (Nailed to the Ground) is the story of a young man who wants to leave his surroundings but cannot due to his job. "La amada judía" (The Jewish Girlfriend) tells of a Christian man spurned due to his Jewish girl-friend's preference for a Jewish husband.

Published in the year he died (at age sixty-three), this short story collection marked and summarized Liacho's many themes and literary styles. *Sobre el filo de la vida* revealed the varying concerns and styles spanning his literary life. As suggested in the title, the stories were gleaned from the "edge of life" and developed throughout his professional career. Some stories recall Old World ghettos while others are set in more contemporary times, reflecting Liacho's changing interests, experiences, and writing styles (Gardiol 11-12).

In addition to his poetry and stories, Liacho also should be remembered for his emotional personal account of and moving tribute to the great Argentine literary figure, Leopoldo Lugones (1874-1930). This tribute, "Glosario del ayer y del mañana: Israel y Leopoldo Lugones" (Glossary of Yesterday and Tomor-row: Israel and Leopoldo Lugones), was written on the third anniversary of Lugones's death and so may be viewed as a symbolic yahrzeit (or death anniver-sary) for Lugones. Liacho begins by relating that on the day of Lugones's death almost three years earlier (February 18, 1938), he was enjoying a vacation with his family on the island of Tigre. He ends his tribute by relating the significant role that Lugones played in his life as well as influential works such as *Las montañas de oro* (The Mountains of Gold; 1897), and *Filosofícula* (1924) that had great impact on him. Liacho also presented in this tribute a chronological account documenting the many instances in which Lugones had befriended and supported Jews both in Argentina and throughout the world.

PRIMARY BIBLIOGRAPHY
Creative Writing

Bocado de pan. Buenos Aires: Editorial INTI, 1931.
Cantos de tango y vida. Posthumous ed. Buenos Aires: Anaconda, 1970.
Dinámica porteña. Buenos Aires: Viau & Zona, 1936.
Entre Dios y Satán; versos. Buenos Aires: Losada, 1966.
El hombre y sus moradas. Buenos Aires: Losada, 1961.
Palabra de hombre. Buenos Aires: Talleres Gráficos Porter, 1934.
Pan de Buenos Aires. Buenos Aires: Librerías Anaconda, 1940.

Siónidas desde la pampa y Sonata judía de Nueva York. Buenos Aires: Candelabro, 1969.

Sobre el filo de la vida; cuentos. Buenos Aires: Candelabro, 1969.

Nonfiction

Alberto Gerchunoff. Buenos Aires: F.A. Colombo, 1975.

Anecdotario judío (folklore, humorismo y chistes). Buenos Aires: M. Gleizer, 1939.

Cinco encuentros con Poemas de integración de Arturo Marasso. Buenos Aires: Claudia, 1966.

Editions

Nordau, Max Simón. *Judaismo y humanismo.* Buenos Aires: M. Gleizer, 1943. Lázaro Liacho, comp.

Tres novelas picarescas. La vida de Lazarillo de Tormes y sus fortunas y adversidades. Buenos Aires: Anaconda, 1937. Prologue by Lázaro Liacho.

SECONDARY BIBLIOGRAPHY

Boleslavsky, L. "Los judíos en la literatura argentina." *Judaica* 9.93 (1941): 141-42.

Gardiol, Rita M. *Argentina's Jewish Short Story Writers.* Muncie, Indiana: Ball State University, 1986. 11-12.

Goodman, Robert. "The Image of the Jew in Argentine Literature as Seen by Argentine Jewish Writers." Ph.D. diss., New York University, 1972. 41, 82-84.

Herrera, Francisco. "Liacho, Lázaro." In *Enciclopedia de la literatura argentina.* Ed. Pedro Orgambide and Roberto Yahni. Buenos Aires: Sudamerica, 1970. 380

Lindstrom, Naomi. *Jewish Issues in Argentine Literature: From Gerchunoff to Szichman.* Columbia: University of Missouri Press. 1989. 8, 18, 20, 61.

—. "Zionist Thought and Songs of Zion: Two Jewish Argentine Poets." In *Judaica latinoamericana: estudios histórico-sociales II.* Asociación Israelí de Investigadores del Judaísmo Latinoamericano. Jerusalem: Editorial Universitaria Magnes, Universidad Hebrea, 1993. 275-87.

Senkman, Leonardo. *La identidad judía en la literatura argentina.* Buenos Aires: Pardés, 1983. 194, 195, 326, 373.

Tiempo, César. "Lázaro Liacho, premio y despedida." *Davar* 121-22 (1969): 57-65.

Weinstein, Ana E., and Miryam Gover de Nasatsky, comps. *Escritores judeoargentinos: biblografía 1900-1987.* 2 vols. Buenos Aires: Milá, 1994. I.418-36.

Weisbrot, Robert. *The Jews of Argentina From the Inquisition to Perón.* Philadelphia: Jewish Publication Society of America, 1979. 50, 56, 187.

Allan Metz

LISPECTOR, CLARICE (Brazil; 1925-77)

Clarice Lispector was born in Techetchelnik, Ukraine, in 1925. Her family emigrated to Brazil where she grew up and studied, having graduated from Law School in 1944. She worked as a journalist, married a Brazilian diplomat, lived in Europe and in the United States with her husband and two sons. After her divorce in 1959, she resided and worked in Rio de Janeiro.

Lispector started to write when she was seven years old. In 1944, the same year she graduated from Law School, she published her first novel: *Perto do coração selvagem* (*Near to the Wild Heart*; 1944). This work already anticipates the dazzling poetic imagination she will display in *Água viva* (*The Stream of Life*; 1973). Lispector's singular world view and unique narrative techniques, which she constantly strove to perfect, are the coordinates of a coherent, ontologically ordered body of work. She focused on the interior life of her characters in order to dynamically portray their private universes.

In 1946 she published *O lustre* (The Chandelier), a novel in which the big city is the context of solitude or confrontation between the fleeting present and an irretrievable past, the contrast between life and death, life in the farm country and the city. In her 1949 novel *A cidade sitiada* (The Besieged City), she attempted to translate a search for an elusive reality scarcely visible to the naked eye. In *Laços de família* (*Family Ties*), a collection of short stories published in 1960, the author portrays middle-class women characters, ranging in age from fifteeen to eighty-nine, in an urban setting. Problems of existence irrespective of class, sex, or age are explored in contrasting situations. Through the plots and internal monologues of her characters, the author questions the conventional roles she assigns to her protagonists. As they move from situation to situation, the characters find themselves in metaphoric prisons, confined by their social roles. The dramatic unity of the stories of *Laços de família* is achieved by internal action, in which a society and its means of coercion are exposed. The characters discover that they are free to conform or rebel, but the options are difficult or problematic. In these stories Lispector challenges conventional roles. The characters' search for an identity is in conflict with the surrounding environment and brings about rage or even madness. The short stories present the dark side of family ties, where bonds of affection become cages or jails. The women characters in "Preciosidade" ("Preciousness"), "Devaneio e embriaguez duma rapariga" ("The Daydreams of a Drunk Woman"), or in the short story that gives title to the collection, "Os laços de família" ("Family Ties"), and in "Feliz aniversário" ("Happy Birthday") discover that they are free to conform or rebel, even when they know that their options are risky or hazardous.

In 1961 *A maçã no escuro* (*The Apple in the Dark*; 1961) appeared. The novel is divided into three parts, each dealing with the forging and development of a character/hero. Martim, the protagonist of this novel, wants to discover himself and others. He initiates his own life practicing a liberating act: a crime. Through his crime, he liberates himself from family and social ties and begins to conquer the language of his being and to reinvent himself as a man, acquiring an awareness of reality. Martim's experience teaches him his own limits. While fleeing justice he learns the meaning of suffering, his path becomes a symbolic search for language. In this novel, earth, water, and fire reflect an epiphanic writing that questions while revealing inner mysteries of being.

The fifth novel by Lispector, *A paixão segundo G. H.* (*The Passion According to G. H.*; 1964) was successful in blending poetic imagination with subtle and metaphysical experiences. In this novel, the author embarks upon a first-person narrative. The epistemological questions repeatedly suggested in the earlier works are here explicated, though the crystal-clear syntax often has the deceptive simplicity of a Blake lyric. A tightly articulated network of images become the symbol of a woman's confrontation with an ultimate reality. A seemingly trivial incident forms the basis of the plot of *A paixão*. The narrator and central character, named simply G. H., decides to clean up the room formerly occupied by her maid, a girl called Janair, who had quit the previous day. G.H. has hardly entered the room when a cockroach emerges from a closet. She tries to kill it but only manages to mangle it with the closet door. The cockroach, still alive, hangs there, legs and antennae turning while a white mass oozes from its body. Hypnotized by the repulsive sight, G. H. falls into a kind of trance. A set of interlocked images, which have in common the suggestion of a many-layered object (the layers of an onion, the geological layers of the earth, the several floors of the building), points to G. H.'s gradual plunge into her inner self. From the recapitulation of her relationship with the former maid, with her lover, and with an aborted child, the narrator moves on to confront her own self and her own existential anguish. The reader discovers that G. H.'s whole life has been a constant effort to arrange things around her, to frame reality according to traditional systems. She is also a sculptor, always trying to impose a shape on the material of life. She is reminiscent of Clarissa Dalloway, Virginia Woolf's (1882-1941) character who is also troubled by the compromises she has made in her life and is able to retain the treasure of a private self. Like Clarissa Dalloway, G. H. has almost become the social mask she has created for herself. Her full name is not known, only her initials are printed on elegant suitcases.

The narrative axis of *A paixão* is that of a quest: writing is experienced as an initiatory route across the topography of living, the path taken by the character G. H. in the light of questions. Her relation with the world is made evident by the writing of this book. Like in many of Lispector's other texts one finds in *A paixão* several lessons of wisdom. This novel is a fictional work, a philosophical inquiry, and a mystical experience.

A collection of stories and chronicles *A legião estrangeira* (*The Foreign Legion*), appeared in 1964. This collection offers some illuminating concepts of Lispector's approach to writing. Here she attempts to explain the intuitive threads that weave the texture of her prose style. She discovers the mystical and poetic nature of her work. The first-person narrator and the surrounding universe encounter each other in a suddenly revealed dimension. The quest of writing and living is related to the notion of time and the consciousness of existential anguish and deceptive contradictions. Lispector reveals in *A legião estrangeira* how solitude and silence played an important part in the creation of her narratives.

One of Clarice Lispector's finest novels, *Água viva*, was published in 1973. It is a significant work in which the question of the relationship between modernity and feminism also encompasses questions of the relationship between life and creation, a recurrent theme in Lispector's writings. A flowing verbal monologue, in which discourse on the creative process is closely intertwined with the unfolding of the first-person subjectivity, constitutes the narrative of *Água viva*. It is a novel made of fragments, of impulses, a series of displacements and disseminations that reflect life as a dynamic and constant process. The narrative form of the novel undoes itself in the form of moments, of the division and fragmentation of the instant, a time that resists a linear and orderly chronology.

Água viva proposes a reflection on the construction of a female self and a critical exploration of the relationship between living and writing. Lispector wants her writing to remain in close contact with life but is aware of the difficult task this project entails. French feminist critics like Hélène Cixous and Luce Irigaray have greatly contributed to our approaching *Água viva* as a specifically identifiable feminine form of experimentation. The novel presents a narrative erotics—a *jouissance*—that replicates the nature of experience in a nonlinear, nonhierarchical, and decentering form associated with the writing of the feminine.

In *Água viva* the question constantly raised is "Who lives? Who lives there?" The novel textualizes this conflict between living and writing. The narrator affirms life by putting herself into the text, by writing herself. *Água viva* tries to recreate a woman's inner life, her inner rhythms, in the very moment and movement of the urge to write. The presence of writing becomes a process of inscription in the novel, one of female self-assertion and self-celebration. *Água viva* presents a particular challenge to accepted conceptual dualisms. The novel explores contradictory relations with so-called traditional patriarchal structures of meaning while exposing an unceasing exploration of its own writerly project.

In Lispector's last novel *A hora da estrela* (*The Hour of the Star*; 1977) the author once more reflects on her role as writer. The questioning takes a more complex turn with the character of Macabea, a pitiable young woman. The novel centers on the story of Macabea, an unskilled office worker who, like many women from the North of Brazil, moves to the big city only to be exploited and victimized. The heroine's name can be associated with the Old Testament. The narrator mentions that the girl Macabea is so ancient that she could be described as biblical. But the relationship with the Bible has only an ironic connotation since Lispector's Macabea is a passive and innocent creature who is deceived by everyone including the fortune teller Madame Carlota. The young woman Macabea seems resigned to her fate, even though she would like to look like Marilyn Monroe. Macabea lives on the margins of society, unaware for the most part of her rights as a human being. She is largely unable to express her own feelings but loves to hear Caruso sing "Una furtiva lácrima." She listens attentively to the talk of a radio announcer and loves the way her boyfriend Olímpico plays with words. The biblical correspondence points to an ironic juxtaposition of weakness and strength. Macabea's misfortunes are painfully moving, her encounter with the fortune teller Madame Carlota will lead the young woman to a tragic end. And yet, when Macabea leaves Madame Carlota she feels transformed hoping to find happiness, but she only meets her death.

A hora da estrela exemplifies most of Lispector's writings, her consistant existential search for self-knowledge and self-expression, her quest of freedom, language, and reality, her interest in the individual and the world. Her plots are usually subordinated to psychological narratives where she transcends the limits of individual experiences into a more complex adventure of being. The poetic force of her prose, the uniqueness of her character's experiences, her new and original way of rethinking tradition, her singular worldview and narrative techniques place her in the mainstream of Latin American writers of the twentieth century. Her originality and strength lie mostly in the way she deconstructs traditional concepts through metaphorical or poetic thinking. The depth and subtlety of her female characters have placed Lispector as an avant-garde writer and also as one of the most representative practitioners of women's writing in Latin America.

Clarice Lispector died in 1977, the same year that *A hora da estrela* was published. After a long battle with cancer she encountered her physical end and was buried at the Cemeterio Israelita do Caju, in Rio de Janeiro.

PRIMARY BIBLIOGRAPHY
Creative Writing

Água viva. Rio de Janeiro: Artenova, 1973. English version as *The Stream of Life*. Trans. by Elizabeth Lowe and Earl Fitz. Minneapolis: U of Minnesota P, 1989.

Alguns contos. Rio de Janeiro: Ministério de Educação e Saúde, 1952.

Uma aprendizagem ou o livro dos prazeres. Rio de Janeiro: Sabiá, 1969. English version as *An Apprenticeship or The Book of Delights*. Trans. by Richard A. Mazzara and Lorri A. Parris. Austin: U of Texas P, 1986.

A bela e a fera. Rio de Janeiro: Nova Fronteira, 1979. English version as "Beauty and the Beast, or the Wound too Great." Trans. by Earl E. Fitz. In *Scents of Wood and Silence: Short Stories by Latin American Women Writers*. Ed. Kathleen Ross and Yvette E. Miller. Pittsburgh: Latin American Literary Review Press, 1991. 113-20.

A cidade sitiada. Rio de Janeiro: A Noite, 1949.

Clarice Lispector. Ed. Samira Youseff Campedelli and Benjamin Abdalla Jr. São Paulo: Abril Educação, 1981.

A descoberta do mundo. Rio de Janeiro: Nova Fronteira, 1984. English version as *Discovering the World*. Trans. by Giovanni Pontiero. Manchester: Carcanet, 1992.

Felicidade clandestina. Rio de Janeiro: Sabiá, 1971.

A hora da estrela. Rio de Janeiro: José Olympio, 1977. English version as *The Hour of the Star*. Trans. by Giovanni Pontiero. Manchester: Carcanet, 1986. Also, New York: New Directions, 1992.

A imitação da rosa. Rio de Janeiro: Artenova, 1973.

Laços de família. Rio de Janeiro: Francisco Alves, 1960. English version as *Family Ties*. Trans. by Giovanni Pontiero. Austin: U of Texas P, 1972; 1987.

A legião estrangeira. Rio de Janeiro: Editora do Autor, 1964. English version as *The Foreign Legion: Chronicles and Stories*. Trans. by Giovanni Pontiero. Manchester: Carcanet, 1986. Also, New York: New Directions, 1992.

O lustre. Rio de Janeiro: Agir, 1946.

A maçã no escuro. Rio de Janeiro: Francisco Alves, 1961. English version as *The Apple in the Dark*. Trans. by Gregory Rabassa. New York: Alfred A. Knopf, 1967. Also, London: Virago Press, 1985; Austin: U of Texas P, 1986.

Onde estivestes de noite. Rio de Janeiro: Artenova, 1974.

A paixão segundo G. H. Rio de Janeiro: Editora do Autor, 1964. English version as *The Passion According to G. H.* Trans. by Ronald A. Sousa. Minneapolis: U of Minnesota P, 1988.

Perto do coração selvagem. Rio de Janeiro: A Noite, 1944. English version as *Near to the Wild Heart*. Trans. by Giovanni Pontiero. New York: New Directions, 1990.

Seleta de Clarice Lispector. Ed. R. C. Gomes and A. G. Hill. Brasília: Instituto Nacional do Livro, 1975.

Um sopro de vida: pulsações. Rio de Janeiro: Nova Fronteira, 1978.

Soulstorm: Stories by Clarice Lispector. (Contains the English translations of *A via crucis do corpo* and *Onde estivestes de noite*). Trans. by Alexis Levitin. Intro. by Grace Paley. New York: New Directions, 1989.

A via crucis do corpo. Rio de Janeiro: Artenova, 1974.

Visão do esplendor: impressões leves. Rio de Janeiro: Francisco Alves, 1975.

Children's Literature

O mistério do coelho pensante. Rio de Janeiro: José Álvaro, 1967.

A mulher que matou os peixes. Rio de Janeiro: Sabiá, 1968. English version as "The Woman Who Killed the Fish." Trans. by Earl E. Fitz. *Latin American Literary Review* 11.21 (1982): 89-101.

Quase de verdade. Rio de Janeiro: Editora Rocco, 1978.

A vida íntima de Laura. Rio de Janeiro: José Olympio, 1974.

Nonfiction

Para não esquecer. São Paulo: Atica, 1978.

De corpo inteiro. (A series of interviews conducted by Lispector) Rio de Janeiro: Artenova, 1975.

SECONDARY BIBLIOGRAPHY
Criticism

Areias, Vilma. "Introducción a Clarice." In *El imaginario judío en la literatura de América Latina: visión y realidad*. Ed. Patricia Finzi, Eliahu Toker and Marcos Faerman. Buenos Aires: Grupo Editorial Shalom, 1992. 140-42.

Borelli, Olga. *Clarice Lispector: esboço para um possível retrato*. Rio de Janeiro: Nova Fronteira, 1981.

Brasil, Assis. *Clarice Lispector*. Rio de Janeiro: Organização Somões, 1969.

Campedelli, S. Y. and B. Abdala Jr. *Clarice Lispector*. São Paulo: Literatura Comentada, 1981.

Castillo, Debra. "Negation: Clarice Lispector." In her *Talking Back: Toward a Latin American Feminist Literary Criticism*. Ithaca/London: Cornell UP, 1992. 185-215.

Cixous, Hélène. *Reading with Clarice Lispector*. Edited, translation and introduction by Verena Andermatt Conley. Minneapolis: U of Minnesota P, 1990.

Coelho, Nelly Novaes. "A escritura existencialista de Clarice Lispector." In her *A literatura feminina no Brasil contemporâneo*. São Paulo: Siciliano, 1993. 173-88.

DiAntonio, Robert E. "Clarice Lispector's *A hora da estrela*: The Actualization of Existential, Religious, and Sociopolitical Paradoxes." In his *Brazilian Fiction: Aspects and Evolution of the Contemporary Narrative*. Fayetteville/London: U of Arkansas P, 1989. 162-74.

Espejo Beshers, Olga. "Clarice Lispector: A Bibliography." *Revista interamericana de bibliografía/Inter-American Review of Bibliography*. 34.3-4 (1984): 385-402.

Fitz, Earl E. "Uma bibliografia de e sôbre Clarice Lispector." *Revista iberoamericana* 50.126 (1984): 293-304.

—. *Clarice Lispector*. Boston: Twayne Publishers, 1985.

—. "Clarice Lispector and the Lyrical Novel: A Re-examination of *A maçã no escuro*." *Luso-Brazilian Review* 14.2 (1971): 153-60.

—. "Freedom and Self-Realization: Feminist Characterization in the Fiction of Clarice Lispector." *Modern Language Studies* 10.3 (1980): 51-56.

—. "The Leitmotif of Darkness in Seven Novels by Clarice Lispector." *Chasqui* 7.2 (1978): 18-28.

—. "Point of View in Clarice Lispector's *A hora da estrela*." *Luso-Brazilian Review* 19.2 (1982): 195-208.

Foster, David William, and Walter Rela. "Clarice Lispector." *Brazilian Literature: A Research Bibliography*. New York: Garland, 1990. 243-48.

Gálvez-Breton, Mara. "Post-Feminist Discourse in Clarice Lispector's *A hora da estrela* [*The Hour of the Star*]." In *Splintering Darkness: Latin Ameri-

can Women Writers in Search of Themselves. Ed. with introduction by Lucía Guerra Cunningham. Pittsburgh: Latin American Literary Review Press, 1990. 63-78.

Hanson, Clare. "Clarice Lispector: A New Eve?" *PN Review* 13.2 (1986): 43-45.

Jozef, Bella. "Clarice Lispector: la recuperación de la palabra poética." *Revista iberoamericana* 50.126 (1984): 239-57.

Lindstrom, Naomi. "Clarice Lispector: Articulating Women's Experience." *Chasqui* 8.1 (1978): 43-52.

—. "A Discourse Analysis of 'Preciosidade' by Clarice Lispector." *Luso-Brazilian Review* 19.2 (1982): 187-94.

—. "A Feminist Discourse Analysis of Clarice Lispector's 'Daydreams of a Drunken Housewife'." *Latin American Literary Review* 19 (1981): 7-16.

Lowe, Elizabeth. *The City in Brazilian Literature.* Rutherford: Fairleigh Dickinson UP, 1982.

—. "Liberating the Rose: Clarice Lispector's *Água viva* [*The Stream of Life*] as a Political Statement." In *Splintering Darkness: Latin American Women Writers in Search of Themselves.* Ed. with introduction by Lucía Guerra Cunningham. Pittsburgh: Latin American Literary Review Press, 1990. 79-84.

Marting, Diane, ed. *Clarice Lispector: A Bio-Bibliography.* Westport, CT: Greenwood Press, 1993.

Moisés, Massaud. "Clarice Lispector: Fiction and Cosmic Vision." *Studies in Short Fiction* 8.1 (1971): 268-81.

Novello, Nicolino. *O ato criador de Clarice Lispector.* Rio de Janeiro: Presença, 1987.

Nunes, Benedito. "Clarice Lispector: artista adrógina ou escritora?" *Revista iberoamericana* 50.126 (1984): 281-89.

—. "Clarice Lispector ou o naufrágio da introspecção." *Colóquio/Letras* 70 (1982): 13-22.

—. *O drama da linguagem: uma leitura de Clarice Lispector.* São Paulo: Atica, 1989.

—. *O mundo de Clarice Lispector.* Manaus: Edições Quirón, 1973.

Oswaldo Cruz, Gilda. "Clarice Lispector cerca de su corazón salvaje." *Quimera* 80 (1988): 12-18.

Patai, Daphne. "Clarice Lispector and the Clamour of the Ineffable." *Kentucky Romance Quarterly* 27 (1980): 133-49.

—. "Clarice Lispector: Myth and Mystification." In her *Myth and Ideology in Contemporary Brazilian Fiction*. Rutherford, NJ: Fairleigh Dickinson UP, 1983. 76-110.

Peixoto, Marta. *Passionate Fictions: Gender, Narrative, and Violence in Clarice Lispector*. Minneapolis: U of Minnesota P, 1994.

Pereira, Teresinha Alves. *Estudo sôbre Clarice Lispector*. Coimbra: Edições Nova Era, 1975.

Pontiero, Giovanni. "Clarice Lispector: An Intuitive Approach to the Fiction." In *Knives and Angels: Women Writers in Latin America*. Ed. Susan Bassnett. London/New Jersey: Zed Books, 1990. 74-85.

—. Testament of Experience: Some Reflections on Clarice Lispector's Last Narrative, *A hora da estrela*." *Ibero-Amerikanisches Archiv* 10.1 (1984): 13-22.

Rodríguez Monegal, Emir. "Clarice Lispector en sus libros y en mi recuerdo." *Revista iberoamericana* 50.126 (1984): 231-38.

Rosenstein, Roy. "Lispector's Children's Literature." *Clarice Lispector: A Bio-Bibliography*. Ed. Diane E. Marting. Westport, CT: Greenwood Press, 1993. 159-67.

Sá, Olga de. *A escritura de Clarice Lispector*. Petrópolis: Vozes, 1979.

—. "Clarice Lispector: processos criativos." *Revista iberoamericana* 50.126 (1984): 259-80.

Schiminovich, Flora. "Lispector's Rethinking of Biblical and Mystical Discourse." In *Tradition and Innovation: Reflections on Latin American Jewish Writing*. Ed. Robert DiAntonio and Nora Glickman. Albany: SUNY Press, 1993. 147-55.

—. "Two Modes of Writing the Female Self: Isabel Allende's *The House of Spirits* and Clarice Lispector's *The Stream of Life*." In *Redefining Autobiography in Twentieth-Century Women's Fiction*. Ed. Colette Hall and Janice Morgan. New York: Garland, 1991. 103-16.

Silverman, Malcolm. *Moderna ficção brasileira*. Trans. by João Guilherme Linke. Brasília: Civilização Brasileira, 1978. 70-84.

Szklo, Gilda Salem. "'O Búfalo': Clarice Lispector e a herança da mística judaica." *Remate de Males* 9 (1989): 107-13.

Vieira, Nelson. "Clarice Lispector: A Jewish Impulse and a Prophecy of Difference." In his *Jewish Voices in Brazilian Literature: A Prophetic Discourse of Alterity*. Gainesville: UP of Florida, 1996. 100-50.

—. "O 'linguagem espiritual' de Clarice Lispector." *Noah* 1.1 (1987): 47-56.

—. *Ser judeu e escritor: três casos brasileiros (Samuel Rawet, Clarice Lispector, Moacyr Scliar*. Rio de Janeiro: CIEC [Centro Interdisciplinar de Estudos Contemporâneos, Escola de Comunicação/Universidade Federal do Rio de Janeiro, 1990.

Waldman, Berta. *Clarice Lispector*. São Paulo: Brasiliense, 1983.

Wengrover, Esther. "La ética cabalística de Clarice Lispector." In *El imaginario judío en la literatura de América Latina: visión y realidad*. Ed. Patricia Finzi, Eliahu Toker and Marcos Faerman. Buenos Aires: Grupo Editorial Shalom, 1992. 143-47.

Interviews

Bloch, Pedro. "Pedro Bloch entrevista Clarice." *Manchete* 637 (4 July 1964): 98-101.

Filho, Remy Gorga. "Clarice Lispector: eu não sou um monstro sagrado." *Revista do livro* (Rio de Janeiro) 13.41 (1970): 112-15.

Gilio, María Esther. "Tristes trópicos." *Crisis* (Buenos Aires) 39 (1976): 43-45.

Lowe, Elizabeth. "The Passion According to Clarice Lispector." *Review* 24 (1979): 34-37.

Zagury, Eliane. "O que Clarice diz de Clarice." *Cadernos brasileiros* 50 (1968): 69-79.

Flora H. Schiminovich

LISPECTOR, ELISA (Brazil; 1911-89)

Elisa Lispector was born in the Ukraine in 1911 and died on January 6, 1989, in Rio de Janeiro. In 1925 her family immigrated to Brazil and settled in Recife, where the author earned her degree as an elementary school teacher from the local Escola Normal (Normal School). A few years later, upon the death of her mother, the family moved to Rio de Janeiro where Lispector, after having passed a highly selective examination process, obtained a job in a branch of the federal government. She soon became known for her interest in labor laws and in women's working conditions and rights. She was selected to represent the Brazilian government on two occasions at international symposia on labor that took place in Geneva. In the same capacity, she traveled to Buenos Aires, Madrid, and Lima to attend and participate in meetings related to Latin American women's working conditions.

Her first book, *Além da fronteira* (Beyond the Frontier), was published in 1945. By then she had already published short stories in several newspapers and magazines.

Her next book was *No exílio* (In Exile; 1948), the only one in Lispector's corpus that addresses her Jewish roots, and her European experiences as a Jew as well as topics related to the creation of the State of Israel, anti-Semitism, and Zion. Autobiographical in nature, the novel contains characters who scarcely veil the identities of members of her family or herself. The protagonist's name Lizza is a slightly altered form of Elisa; Pinkhas is the Yiddish name for Pedro, her father, and Marim, the mother in the novel, is a transmuted form of Marian, the real name of Lispector's mother. They all go through periods of varying degrees of tension related to their displacement to Brazil. The narrative recalls the intimate feelings of solitude and despair as well as solidarity and hope that emerge and fade in the characters through the period of adjustment to the new country. Some traits pertaining to individual characters closely adhere to the real person on whom they were based. For example, Lizza is always concerned about her sick mother, while her father compounds the same apprehension with his anxieties concerning the family's economic survival. A secondary element which heightens the characters' afflictions are the disturbing events against the Jews in Europe, intensified between 1939 and 1945, that reached them through letters, newspapers, and first-hand accounts. The novel remains as an important contribution to Brazilian literature by a Jewish writer in Brazil, as she was a naturalized citizen, on a topic of universal dimension. Moreover, although she cannot be compared to her renowned sister Clarice Lispector (1925-77) in terms of language usage, Elisa's controlled use of literary tropes and devices intimately reflects her characters' intense passions and self reflections, within the nuances and richness of the Portuguese language.

Lispector gradually proceeded to publish fiction, amassing an impressive list of texts which includes short stories, novels, and journalism pieces. Many of the latter were related to her government job in labor.

Lispector earned a Bachelor of Arts degree in Sociology from the Faculdade Nacional de Filosofia (National School of Philosophy) in Rio de Janeiro, and also took art criticism courses at the Fundação Brasileira de Teatro (Brazilian Theater Foundation). In 1962 a third book was published, *O muro de pedras* (The Stone Wall), with which she received the coveted José Lins do Rego Prize, awarded in recognition of promising young authors. The same book also received the Coelho Neto Prize of the Brazilian Academy of Letters.

The essence of Lispector's fictional work addresses human solitude. This condition is presented in her writings not as a predicament, but as a nurturing circumstance that leads her characters to search for a deeper understanding of acts and moods within life's limitations. Lispector's stories emphasize the brevity of human life, the anguished perception that attempts at communication are futile, and the sense that we are all very much alone in this world.

PRIMARY BIBLIOGRAPHY

Além da fronteira. Rio de Janeiro: Leitora, 1945. 2nd ed. Rio de Janeiro: José Olympio, 1988.

Corpo a corpo. Rio de Janeiro: Antares, 1983.

O dia mais longo de Thereza. Rio de Janeiro: Record, 1965. 2nd ed. Rio de Janeiro: Rocco, 1978.

"The Fragile Balance." In *One Hundred Years After Tomorrow: Brazilian Women's Fiction in the 20th Century.* Edited, translated and with an introduction by Darlene Sadlier. Bloomington & Indianapolis: U of Indiana P, 1992. 174-79.

Inventário. Rio de Janeiro: Rocco, 1977.

O muro de pedras. Rio de Janeiro: José Olympio, 1963. 2nd ed. Rio de Janeiro: Rocco, 1976.

No exílio. Rio de Janeiro: Pongetti, 1948. 2nd ed. Brasília: Editora Ebrasa, 1971.

Ronda solitária. Rio de Janeiro: A Noite, 1954.

Sangue no sol. Brasília: Ebrasa, 1970.

O tigre de Bengala. Rio de Janeiro: José Olympio, 1985.

A última porta. Rio de Janeiro: Documentário, 1975.

SECONDARY BIBLIOGRAPHY

Igel, Regina. "Os polos da solidão humana: Elisa Lispector." *O Estado de São Paulo,* "Cultura" July 7, 1985: 7.

Josef, Bella. "Prefácio." *O tigre de Bengala.* Rio de Janeiro: Editora José Olympio, 1985. ix-xi.

Regina Igel

MACTAS, REBECA (Argentina; 1914)

Rebeca Mactas Alperson de Polak was born June 26, 1914 in Carlos Casares, Argentina, one of the farming communities established by the Jewish

Colonization Association. She is the granddaughter of the legendary Mordejai Alperson (1860-1947), who wrote extensively of the Jewish colonization in Yiddish, and who is often considered to be the dean of Yiddish literature in Argentina. Mactas made her living as a journalist and also worked as an editor for the Yiddish periodical *Morgen Zaitung* (Morning Paper).

Mactas was actively engaged in bringing Yiddish and Hebrew literature to a Spanish speaking public through translation. She translated into Spanish two works by José Rabinovich (1903-78), one of the most prolific Jewish writers in Argentina who originally wrote in Yiddish but later switched to Spanish: *Tercera clase* (Third Class; 1944), and *Cabizbajos* (Crestfallen; 1943). She also translated and edited a volume of poetry by Hebrew writer Hayyim Nahman Bialik (1873-1934) and Yehuda Halevi (1085-1140).

Nevertheless, Mactas is best known for her 1936 collection of short stories *Los judíos de Las Acacias* (The Jews of Las Acacias). The collection contains seven stories which all take place on the homesteads of Jewish colonists. While they have a certain telluric commonality with Alberto Gerchunoff's (1884-1950) earlier text, *Los gaucho judíos* (1910), they do not portray the same bucolic view of life in the rural farming colonies. A dominant presence throughout the volume is that of Nature. As the farmers struggle to eke out a living from the land they are at constant odds with and subject to the whims of Nature. The characters do, nonetheless, display a reverent attitude of respect for the land. The text describes the colonies in their post hey-day period. The characters who have remained are the original settlers, now old, who stubbornly cling to their property. In all the stories, city and country are placed in conflict with one another. The children, and in some cases siblings, of the main characters have all gone to the city in order to study, work, and take advantage of business opportunities. In the first story, "La casa" (The House), all of Jaim Kahn's children left the country to make it in Buenos Aires. The eldest son manages to acquire a small fortune and wishing to share his wealth with his parents he builds them a new chalet to take the place of the decrepit mud dwelling that was their home. The parents are grateful but do not wish to have a new home, nonetheless, the old one is destroyed and the modern new house takes its place. Shortly after moving into the new home Jaim Kahn falls ill, having been cut off from his close ties to the earth by the sterile new walls and floors. As his last dying effort he manages to dig a hole in the earth into to which he throws himself. In "Corazón sencillo" (Simple Heart) a cousin, David, who is studying in the city comes to visit Eva and her widowed father on the farm. Eva's father is supporting David's education which makes the young student appreciative, yet ill at ease. In "Fuego" (Fire) it is the estranged brother who returns to the farm in order to ask for money from his only relative. Simón made a fortune in Buenos Aires and didn't speak to his brother for twenty years until he went bankrupt and was forced to humbly return to the country to ask for help. At first Marcos refuses the request, being both financially unable to help as well as indignant at his brother's chutzpah, sending Simón away. He is later repentant of his coldness toward his brother and in a guilt-ridden rage prays that his property be destroyed by fire as punishment. Simón is awakened by the smell and sound of his fields being burned and runs out praising God for answering his prayers. As he runs across one of the burnt fields he trips over the charred body of his brother who is holding a matchbox in his hand. The theme of destructive fires which threaten the lives and liveli-hood of colonists is recurrent in the literature of the rural settlements and can be found in the stories of writers as diverse as Samuel Eichelbaum (1894-1967) and Nora Glickman (1944). "La vuelta del hijo" (The Return of the Son), following the biblical prodigal son motif, describes Natán's return to the country after having lived unfulfilled for a period of time in Buenos Aires. "La vuelta" is the story which least realistically portrays Jewish Argentine life in the colonies. Perhaps in an effort to give the story a more scriptural, parable-like tone Mactas employs the second person singular (tú) and plural (vosotros) voices as opposed to the Argentine *vos*. The story is one of both spiritual and familial redemption as the wayward son returns to the bosom of rural family life and values. At the close of the narration Natán hears a voice proclaim "¡Hijo mío! Haz [sic] vuelto, hijo mío" (My son! You have returned, my son [114]). He is unable to discern the source of the voice pondering whether it came from the nearby cow, the earth itself, or his mother. The famous Argentine dichotomy of civilization versus barbarism is inverted: the country is superior to the problem ridden city. The author's romantic tendencies are apparent throughout the text as Nature is repeatedly portrayed as a redeeming force. In all of these stories it is the rural life that makes possible the upward mobility of those who leave to pursue other dreams in the city, and who often return to the country disillusioned. This is not to say that the rural existence is described in paradisiacal terms or as being economically fruitful. Quite to the contrary, the story "Los judíos de Las Aca-cias" depicts the colony as a dreary abandoned village of dilapidated buildings and old, infirm, even mentally deranged inhabitants. The narrator likens Las Acacias to a blind old hen that lost in the field crouches to the earth in fear, ex-isting by miracle alone (74). Poverty is the narrative force of the story as the narrator describes the desperate situation of the few remaining townspeople. Likewise, in the last story, "Primaveras" (Springs), a youth who prefers to live in the country and make his living from the land must twice return to the city in search of employment leaving behind his bride to be. The hunger suffered during the winter months is described in great detail.

One peculiarity of these stories is that they all take place within the Jewish collectivity. There are very few even secondary non-Jewish characters. The stories do not directly reveal a move away from Jewish tradition or assimilation, though a scant reference to intermarriage is made. Indeed, of those characters who move to the city mention is made of their involvement and prominence of the Buenos Aires Jewish community. Both the positive and the negative characteristics of the colonies are represented in the stories. Jealousy often plays a part among neighbors as they are wont to compare wealth, status, and success. The unforgiving nature of the administrators of the Jewish Colonization Administration is often made evident as mortgages are put at risk and properties are repossessed due to failed crops and bad planning. Another interesting aspect of these stories is that they are often portrayed from a woman's perspective and are sympathetic to the plight of the pioneering women who suffered great hardships and who dutifully took on insurmountable workloads either as wife or daughter of the family patriarch.

Mactas's stories are not only a valuable contribution to the body of Argentine Jewish literature—and Argentine literature in general—for their content, but for their literary quality. The author gives psychological depth to her characters in a discursive style that is both eloquent in its use of lyrical imagery and structurally sound. Her narrations can be characterized by the elements of surprise, irony, spirituality, and sophistication with which they are composed.

PRIMARY BIBLIOGRAPHY

Creative Writing

"Asilo de ancianos." *Judaica* 4 (1933): 162-66.
Los judíos de Las Acacias (cuentos de la vida campesina). Buenos Aires: n.p., 1936.
Leyendas y parábolas judías según la Agadá. Buenos Aires: Israel, 1950.
Primera juventud. Buenos Aires: n.p., 1930.

Editions

Cantos de Jehuda Ha-Levy. Buenos Aires: M. Gleizer, 1932.
Jaim Najman Bialik: Poemas. 2nd. ed. Buenos Aires: Pardés, 49.

SECONDARY BIBLIOGRAPHY

Senkman, Leonardo. *La identidad judía en la literatura argentina*. Buenos Aires: Pardés, 1983. 65-68.

Weinstein, Ana E., and Miryam E. Gover de Nasatsky, comps. *Escritores judeo-argentinos: bibliografía 1900-1987*. 2 vols. Buenos Aires: Milá, 1994. II.5-7.

Darrell B. Lockhart

MOSCONA, MYRIAM (Mexico; 1955)

Myriam Moscona was born in Mexico in 1955. Her parents had emigrated to Mexico from Bulgaria after World War II. She studied journalism and writes for some of the leading cultural journals in Mexico. She has written and produced a radio program for the Instituto Nacional de Bellas Artes (National Institute of Fine Arts), and she has adapted for radio the works of Mexican writer Juan Rulfo (1918-86). Moscona is known in literary circles as a poet, and her works have earned her the reputation of being one of the foremost contemporary women poets in Mexico.

Moscona's first collection of poetry, *Ultimo jardín* (Last Garden), was published in 1983. The volume is organized around a series of different clusters of poems, or poetic gardens, that the poet cultivates with great insistence on verbal precision. The reader enters through the "Puerta de entrada" (Front Gate) and from there encounters the different gardens in which poetic images blossom from the verses: "Jardín en trance" (Garden in Trance), "Jardín de primogénitos" (Garden of the Firstborn), "Jardín de ausentes" (Garden of the Absent), "Jardín de nadie" (No One's Garden), and "Ultimo jardín" (Last Garden). The three poems of "Puerta de entrada" are replete with erotically charged images of the female body that, contrary to what one might expect, convey a sort of tragic sense of female identity in the bleak portrayal of the poet's experience as a woman. Each garden of poems revolves around a different aspect or perspective of identity, but all are written from a very specifically female point of view. In the poems of "Jardín en trance," the poet contemplates her origins in relation to her family lineage. "Jardín de primogénitos" consists of a number of poems that draw heavily on the history and tradition of Jewish women. Moscona utilizes the biblical figures of Eve and Lot's wife to portray not only the dismal situation of women, but more importantly to exalt them as models of rebellion, in spite of the fact that both were severely punished for having committed transgressions against established law. Significantly, Moscona names Lot's wife Goral (destiny).

The poem "Jardín de Auschwitz" ("Auschwitz Garden"), part of the "Ultimo jardín," is written as a dreamscape of nightmarish images wherein death reigns. Finally, the last poem of the collection, "Ultimo jardín," gives a cyclical closure to the volume by proposing the return from the "Jardín de Auschwitz" to a new Garden of Eden.

Las visitantes (The [Women] Visitors; 1989) may be considered a continuation of *Ultimo jardín* and, in fact, several of the poems which first appeared in the latter are repeated in the former. The leitmotif of the collection, which appears in a variety of circumstances, places, and situations, is the position of women as visitors. That is to say that women are never really able to establish roots, to find a place of permanence in society. This predicament is explicitly expressed in the image of immigrant women who find themselves doubly marginalized as female outsiders in a new societal circumstance. Likewise, the dynamics of power struggles between men and women are reiterated throughout the collection. Moscona utilizes the trope of pictorial art in order to create a variety of "Lienzos" (Canvases), "Retratos" (Portraits), "Daguerrotipos" (Daguerreotypes), and "Estampas" (Sketches) that depict women, and women's reality. *Las visitantes* earned Moscona the Premio de Poesía Aguascalientes (Aguascalientes Poetry Prize) in 1988.

El árbol de los nombres (The Tree of Names; 1992) is Moscona's third volume of poetry. It is essentially a collection of interconnecting love poems that are, like her previous works, erotic in nature. In contrast to the two previous volumes, however, *El árbol de los nombres* does not contain the same conflict between men and women, rather the lovers are united. The poems are almost liturgical in nature, and the poet employs a variety of Jewish images and icons in their composition. Nevertheless, the central theme of *El árbol de los nombres* is the act of naming, ultimately as a means of empowerment.

Moscona is also the author of a collection of poems for children titled *Las preguntas de Natalia* (Natalia's Questions; 1991). The poems, which really are a series of questions, are to some degree also about the act of naming and they are somewhat didactic in their questioning. They are accompanied by the vibrant illustrations of Fernando Medina.

Finally, while Moscona's poetry reveals her Jewish heritage in an allusive or less direct manner, in the brief essay "La paradoja de promesas y exilios" (The Paradox of Promises and Exiles; 1992), she writes of her Sephardic heritage, the condition of exile, and the nature of language as a component of identity openly and frankly.

PRIMARY BIBLIOGRAPHY
Creative Writing

El árbol de los nombres. Guadalajara: Secretaría de Cultura, Gobierno de Jalisco, 1992.

"Entre las ramas del olivo. . . / Among the Olive Branches." Trans. by C. M. Mayo. In *Ruido de sueños, Noise of Dreams*. Selection and Translation by El Grupo Tramontano/The Tramontane Group. México, D.F.: El Tucán de Virginia, 1994. 156-59.

"Garden in Peril," Lot's Wife Is Nameless," "Lot's Wife Takes a Name," "Auschwitz Garden," "Lost Garden," "Garden of Beasts," "Last Garden." Trans. by C. D. Wright, Lida Aronne-Amestoy, and Forrest Gander. In *Mouth to Mouth: Poems by Twelve Contemporary Mexican Women*. Ed. Forrest Gander. Intro. by Julio Ortega. Minneapolis: Milkweed Editions, 1993. 191-211.

"Naturalization Papers." Trans. by Cynthia Steele. *TriQuarterly* [Special issue: *New Writing from Mexico*, Ed. Reginald Gibbons] 85 (1992): 347.

Las preguntas de Natalia. Ilustraciones de Fernando Medina. México, D.F.: Dirección General de Publicaciones del Consejo Nacional para la Cultura y las Artes, 1991.

Selection of poems from *Ultimo jardín* and "Matusalenismo." In *El cuerpo del deseo: poesía erótica femenina en el México actual*. Ed. Valeria Manca. Xalapa, México: Universidad Autónoma Metropolitana/Universidad Veracruzana, 1989. 141-46.

"Tres poemas." In *Poesía erótica mexicana 1889-1980*. 2 vols. Ed. Enrique Jaramillo Levi. México, D.F.: Domés, 1982. I.496-98.

Ultimo jardín. México, D.F.: El Tucán de Virginia, 1983.

Las visitantes. México, D.F.: Joaquín Mortiz, 1989.

Nonfiction

De frente y de perfil: semblanzas de poetas. Fotografías de Rogelio Cuéllar. México, D.F.: 1993.

"La paradoja de promesas y exilios." *Noaj* 6.7-8 (1992): 31-33.

SECONDARY BIBLIOGRAPHY

Goldberg, Florinda F. Rev. of *Las visitantes*. *Noaj* 4.5 (1990): 112-13.
Jiménez, Lilian. Rev. of *Las visitantes*. *Plural* 18.216 (1989): 83-84.

Darrell B. Lockhart

MUÑIZ-HUBERMAN, ANGELINA (Mexico; 1936)

A writer and professor of comparative literature at the Universidad Nacional Autónoma de México, Angelina Muñiz-Huberman was born in France in 1936, the child of Republican refugees of the Spanish Civil War. From her Castilian heritage she still retains the pronunciation and the second-person plural pronoun (used only when she is with Spaniards) and her love for Spanish medieval and Golden Age literature. She traces her roots on her mother's side back to converso Jews who never left the peninsula but who throughout the centuries secretly retained vestiges of Judaism. Steeped in the lore of the Bible, the Talmud, and, particularly the Kabbalah, Muñiz-Huberman decided to reclaim her spiritual past by undergoing a formal conversion to Judaism. She has lived in Mexico since she was six years old and her ties to the Mexican intellectual and literary tradition as well as to the tutelage of exiled Republican professors and writers resident in Mexico are apparent. Yet she is always a voracious reader of world literature and she speaks of the influence of writers as diverse as Louisa May Alcott (1832-88), Marcel Proust (1871-1922), Franz Kafka (1883-1924), and Jorge Luis Borges (1899-1986)—a kindred spirit with whom she shares a tendency to create a paradoxical and conflictive interior doubling of personality. Her years as a reviewer of literature for *Excelsior*, *Proceso*, and *Unomásuno* (1963-1976) put her in contact with contemporary Mexican and international writers. She pays little attention to conventional genres and great attention to word choice in her poetry, short stories, novels, and essays. Although she has not written theatre, she has translated plays by Harold Pinter (1930) and William Shakespeare (1564-1616).

All of her work is intertextual and reveals her own personal re-reading and recreation of important works and genres. Her first novel, *Morada interior* (Internal Abode; 1972), which won the Premio Magda Donato, deals with Santa Teresa de Jesús (1515-82) as a modern woman with a spiritual crisis. Her second novel, *Tierra adentro* (Inland; 1977) retells the perilous life of a Jew in Spain at the time of the Expulsion. Many elements of this novel contrast with Muñiz-Huberman's other work: the language in this novel, while characteristically poetic, is simple, the narration is by a single voice, and the ending is happy (Menton 159-162). Although, the form and adventures follow the picaresque tradition, the ideals of the central character do not conform to those of the rogue. "She takes a genre that, as a rule, undermines the aspirations of its protagonists, and, in the process, performs an undermining of her own, by presenting a heroic portrait and a discourse that is ironic only it its deviation from the norm" (Friedman 185). *La guerra del unicornio* (The War of the Unicorn; 1983) is written in the language of epic poetry but deals with the Spanish Civil War.

In yet another re-vision of a well-known source, her novel *Dulcinea encantada* (Enchanted Dulcinea; 1992), winner of the Sor Juana Inés de la Cruz Prize, returns to the subject of the Spanish Civil War, this time from the point of view of a child whose seminal crisis and rupture with Spain and her parents occurs when she and her brother are put on a boat along with other orphans and children of Republicans bound for refuge at the International Children's House in Odessa. This separation and the subsequent death of her brother, with whom she professes to have had an intimate experience, cause her to become mute and dialogue only with herself in her mind. The novel presents her fractured and torturous memories as she traverses Mexico City on its beltway, El Periférico, accompanied by her parents (with whom she was reunited some time after the Civil War) and an unknown driver. If Cervantes's Dulcinea is a projection of Don Quixote, Muñiz-Huberman's Dulcinea lives in her own fantasy world cut off from everyone else. Her statement on the opening page that she has no language and cannot remember her past is soon belied by a vivid and rich retelling of key events in her life in Spain, Odessa, and Mexico.

Muñiz-Huberman's poetry is represented by *El ojo de la creación* (The Eye of Creation; 1992) in which she explores her favorite themes: life and death, creation and destruction, the center of existence, the union of opposites, mystical knowledge, and philosophical postulates. Despite the free verse form, her poetry has a lyrical quality achieved through repetition of sounds, symmetrical verses, and some measure of assonantal and consonantal rhyme. She often borrows the discipline of the sonnet by ending her poems with four concepts which contain the germ of her entire poem and indeed, the germ of her entire collection. Just such a summation occurs in her first poem "El ojo de la creación"—"Corre, se dobla, se afana y suena/ el escondido río de las aguas plácidas/ del ojo de la creación" (It runs, doubles back, toils and babbles/ the hidden river of placid waters/ of the eye of creation [8]). Her poetry—sparse and controlled—contains both the cold, still life vision of the end of life on earth as well as the moment of creation. Her images are as economical and allusive as a haiku or a medieval tapestry. Her poems are carefully crafted to suggest the ecstasy of moments of union with the center of existence and the desolation of the brevity of those unions. Despite the medieval tone of her elemental contemplations of earth, wind, fire and, water or memory, understanding, and will, there is a sharply urban and distinctly contemporary tone to the middle section of poems of the volume. In those poems the egoism of the children of the twentieth century and the horrors of urban rubble and pollution are poetically but bleakly rendered. The third and last set of poems returns to medieval themes, to love as a mystical union and to the strange coitus of lovers amidst the headstones of a cemetery.

Muñiz-Huberman elaborates on the same alchemical, philosophical, and mystical themes in her short stories which are contained in five collections: *Huerto cerrado, huerto sellado* (*Enclosed Garden*; 1985), *El libro de Miriam y Primicias* (The Book of Miriam and Primicias; 1990), *De magias y prodigios* (Of Magic and Prodigies; 1987), *Serpientes y escaleras* (Serpents and Stairways; 1991), and *Narrativa relativa* (Relative Narrative; 1992). In *El libro de Miriam y Primicias*, which contains some of her earliest work, one of the most interesting stories is the vision of the Virgin Mary as a new mother suffering from postpartum depression. The language in most of these stories is much less erudite than in her more recent work. In *Huerto cerrado* she elaborates on a different myth or legend in each story, and in each one there is a transformation of the central character just as in *De magias* each tale tells of a magical transformation or event. The title of her penultimate collection of short stories, *Serpientes y escaleras*, refers to a children's board game played like Chutes and Ladders by going up and down according to the roll of the dice. Unlike Chutes and Ladders, the figures upon which the playing piece descends are not beneficent, but rather they are terrifying—hideous reptiles. Like the snake which inspires terror and fascination, the stories are about those frightening things which control our obsessions. Some of the stories are nightmares. The stories of Part II are children's memories but not stories for children. Here Muñiz-Huberman explores the seriousness of juvenile games and the incestuous sensuality of childhood. Both parents and children are unfaithful in the story which gives the volume its title. Down the serpent's slithery tail they fall from innocence in a story of doubling reminiscent of a Borges tale.

Although Huberman uses fantasy, memory, and the memories of Spanish Civil War survivors, her literature is also a very conscious working of her *Somniario*, a diary of her dreams. She can be very detached and is capable of appreciating her own place within her generation of Mexican writers and, without modesty, her considerable achievements in literature. *El juego de escribir* (The Game of Writing; 1991) reveals the circumstances around the genesis of most of her work. She discusses her early life, the trauma of the death of her older brother, the influences of her aristocratic, literate, and demanding father and the supportive encouragement of her mother, an early feminist by Mexican standards and one of the first women in Mexico to wear pants.

The disciplined rational side of Huberman's thought processes is displayed in her essays on literature and mysticism: *La lengua florida: antología sefardí* (The Blossoming Language: Sephardic Anthology; 1989) and *Las raíces y las ramas: fuentes y derivaciones de la Cábala hispanohebrea* (The Roots and the Branches: Sources and Derivations of the Hispanohebraic Kabbalah; 1993). The anthology of Sephardic literature offers historical background, glossaries of Hebrew and Ladino terms, ample selections of early Hebrew poems, the well-studied *Romancero sefardí* (Sephardi ballad), wedding and funeral songs, proverbs, short stories, as well as selections from a modern novel and a play. The final section contains brief selections from the *Zohar*, from a treatise on angels, and an essay on morality. Muñiz-Huberman provides excellent linguistic descriptions of Ladino as it was spoken at the time of the expulsion as well as the varieties spoken throughout the world in the twentieth century. In *Las raíces y las ramas* the author explains the origins and theory of Spanish Judaic mysticism. Here again, she provides detailed explanations of the literature and an outstanding point of departure for the uninitiated reader interested in learning about Kabbalah.

Angelina Muñiz-Huberman combines many talents and an encyclopedic knowledge of literature and religion in her writing. There is humor and whimsy in *Serpientes y escaleras* but more often her work is serious. Repeatedly, the themes of exile and death lead her to an interior search for more lasting and supportive sources. Suffering leads her to a sense of common experience with other periods of persecution and hatred: the Inquisition, the Spanish Civil War, and the Holocaust. Her position as a seeker makes her curious about other seekers: alchemists, mystics, heretics, knights of chivalry, troubadors, and explorers.

PRIMARY BIBLIOGRAPHY

Creative Writing

"El campanero de Stepenholmer." *Hispamérica* 22.66 (1993): 63-68.

Castillos en la tierra (seudomemorias). México, D.F.: Hora Actual, 1995.

"Ciudad de oro amurallado." *Noaj* 3.3-4 (1989): 43-46.

El juego de escribir. Colección De cuerpo entero. México, D.F.: UNAM/Corunda, 1991.

De magias y prodigios: transmutaciones. México, D.F.: Fondo de Cultura Económica, 1987.

Dulcinea encantada. México, D.F.: Joaquín Mortiz, 1992.

La guerra del unicornio. México, D.F.: Artífice Ediciones, 1983.

Huerto cerrado, huerto sellado. México, D.F.: Editorial Oasis, 1985. English version as *Enclosed garden*. Trans. by Lois Parkinson Zamora. Pittsburgh: Latin American Literary Review Press, 1988.

"Inland." Trans. by Terry Seymour. *Icarus* 6 (Spring 1992): 107-15.

"In the Name of His Name." Trans. by Lois Parkinson Zamora. In *Tropical Synagogues: Short Stories by Jewish-Latin American Authors*. Ed. Ilán Stavans. New York: Holmes & Meier, 1994. 189-92.

El libro de Miriam y Primicias. México, D.F.: Universidad Autónoma Metropolitana, 1990.

La memoria del aire. México, D.F.: Universidad Nacional Autónoma de México, 1995.

Morada interior. México, D.F.: Joaquín Mortiz, 1972.

Narrativa relativa. México, D.F.: Universidad Autónoma de México, 1992.

El ojo de la creación. México, D.F.: Universidad Nacional Autónoma de México, 1992.

"Rising Mournful from the Earth." Trans. by Lois Parkinson Zamora. In *Contemporary Women Authors of Latin America*. 2 vols. Ed. Doris Meyer and Margarite Olmos. Brooklyn: Brooklyn College Press, 1983. II.212-14.

Serpientes y escaleras. México, D.F.: Difusión Cultural UNAM, 1991.

Tierra adentro. México, D.F.: Joaquín Mortiz, 1977.

Vilano al viento. México, D.F.: Universidad Autónoma de México, 1982.

Nonfiction

La lengua florida: antología sefardí. México, D.F.: Fondo de Cultura Económica, 1989.

Las raíces y las ramas: fuentes y derivaciones de la Cábala hispanohebrea. México, D.F.: Fondo de Cultura Económica, 1993.

"Testimonio de una obra en torno al exilio y promisión." *Noaj* 6.7-8 (1992): 25-28.

Las voces de la mística en Ramón Xirau. México, D.F.: Universidad Nacional Autónoma de México, 1995.

SECONDARY BIBLIOGRAPHY

Criticism

Bearse, Grace. "More Mexican Writers to the Fore." *Américas* 34.4 (1982): 59.

Duncan, Ann. "Angelina Muñiz." *The Blackwell Companion to Jewish Culture: From the Eighteenth Century to the Present*. Ed. Glenda Abramson. Cambridge, MA: Basil Blackwell, 1989. 529-30.

Friedman, Edward. "Angelina Muñiz's *Tierra Adentro*: (Re)creating the Subject." In *Tradition and Innovation: Reflections on Latin American Jewish Writing*. Ed. Robert DiAntonio and Nora Glickman. Albany: SUNY Press, 1993. 179-192.

López González, Aralia. "La otra ética: reinterpretación femenina de mujeres míticas." In *Sin imágenes falsas, sin falsos espejos: narradoras mexicanas del siglo XX*. Ed. Aralia López González. México, D.F.: El Colegio de México, 1995. 465-75.

Menton, Seymour. *Latin America's New Historical Novel*. Austin: U of Texas P, 1993. 158-162.

Najenson, José Luis. "*La lengua florida* de Angelina Muñiz: entre el olvido y la vida eterna." *Noaj* 5.6 (1991): 10-11.

Poniatowska, Elena. "Afterword" to *Enclosed Garden*. Trans. by Lois Parkinson Zamora. Pittsburgh: Latin American Literary Review Press, 1988. 97-103.

Prado G., Gloria. "Exilio y extrañamiento: dos perspectivas de una realidad." In *Sin imágenes falsas, sin falsos espejos: narradoras mexicanas del siglo XX*. Ed. Aralia López González. México, D.F.: El Colegio de México, 1995. 415-34.

Schuvaks, Daniela. "Esther Seligson and Angelina Muñiz-Huberman: Jewish Mexican Memory and the Exile to the Darkest Tunnels of the Past." In *The Jewish Diaspora in Latin America: New Studies on History and Literature*. Ed. David Sheinin and Lois Baer Barr. New York: Garland, 1996. 75-88.

Interviews

Interview. *Gaceta UNAM*. 2.28 (April 5, 1984): 18, 25.

Lois Baer Barr

NAJENSON, JOSÉ LUIS (Argentina; 1938)

José Luis Najenson was born in Córdoba, Argentina in 1938. He studied history, anthropology, and political sciences, receiving a Ph.D. in History from Cambridge University in 1982. He won several literary awards for his works that cover essay, poetry, short story, short novel, and literary criticism—among them the Alfonsina Storni Poetry Prize (1982), the La Valdeira Poetry Prize (1986), First Place in the Arturo Capdevila Prize for Fiction (1988), and the First Prize in the Bustarviejo Literary Contest (1988). Following his Zionist ideals, Najenson has lived in Israel since 1983, where he is currently the director of the Central

Institute of Cultural Relations between Israel, Iberoamerica, Spain, and Portugal. He is co-founder of *Aleph, Noaj,* and *Nombre* (Name). He is also the editor of the magazine *Carta de Jerusalem* (Letter from Jerusalem).

Najenson claims the idea that writers who compose their books in Spanish in Israel are not Latin American exile writers but Israeli writers. He considers the works produced by these writers as captive literature, captive of a country—Israel—and its people. It is a literature that doesn't fight for its freedom because it wants to be captive, keeping parts of both worlds.

Najenson's books reveal the influences of Jorge Luis Borges (1899-1986), Horacio Quiroga (1878-1937), and to a lesser degree Roberto Arlt (1900-1942), and the Kabbalah. Dominant themes include eroticism, homesickness, time, and Jewish history. His first collection of short stories is *Tiempo de arrojar piedras* (Time for Throwing Stones; 1981), subtitled *Cuentos de ficción política y religiosa* (Political and Religious Short Stories). Politics provides a framework for this collection's fiction in which historical Jewish personalities participate in fictional situations. "Canonización en Puebla" (Canonization in Puebla), for example, deals with the canonization of Rosa Luxemburg in the year 2179. The devil visits Karl Marx and Frederick Lassalle in "El diablo va de visita a casa del Dr. Marx" (The Devil Pays a Visit to Dr. Marx at Home). However, far from a seemingly political matter, the main theme of this book is time: time of hope, a prophetic, messianic time. To express this time, the author situates the narrative action in the future—three or four centuries beyond present time—and grants the characters the possibility of traveling back to the present. This technique—prominent in science fiction—offers the reader a new perspective of historical events. In addition, time travel can be seen as a play or a dream that provides a forum for the reconsideration of radical opinions. Intertextuality is present throughout the book: biblical ("Sesquicentenario en verde" [Sesquicentennial in Green]); detective fiction ("El filósofo que odiaba a Sherlock Holmes" [The Philosopher Who Hated Sherlock Holmes]); history ("Tiempo de arrojar piedras" [Time for Throwing Stones]); or the chronicle of discovery ("El retorno de la Serpiente Emplumada" [The Return of the Plumed Serpent]).

Memorias de un erotómano y otros cuentos (Memoirs of a Sex Maniac and Other Stories; 1991) includes three separate collections of tales: the first provides the title for the book; the second is "Agencia 2000 y otros cuentos ero-utópicos" (Agency 2000 and Other Ero-Utopian Tales); the third, "Más allá del río Sambatión" (Beyond the Sambatyon River), includes short stories that are also included in a separate book by the same title. Jewish themes or characters are absent from "Memorias," but they are introduced in the second part, and are the keynote in the last part, "Más allá." "Memorias de un erotómano" consists of eight short stories in which the author explores new dimensions of human eroticism in relation to mystery and panic. Each story relates an erotic encounter in which an element of the couple may be inhuman—a computer in "La malinche electrónica" (The Electronic Malinche), a wolfwoman in "De lobizonas y tisis" (About Wolfwomen and Phthisis), a mermaid in "Las falsas sirenas de Disneylandia" (Fake Disneyland Mermaids), the relationship between Cheetah and Jane in "La infidelidad de Tarzán" (Tarzan's Infidelity). In others, the traditional prostitute shows up as part of the love/death initiatory rite ("Iniciación forzada" [Compulsory Initiation]). Irony, levity, and exactness are present in the short stories of "Memorias," characterized as a collection of postmodern fables. The Sambatyon—the river in "Más allá del río Sambatión"—is a mythical Jewish river with stones rather than water that quits flowing on the Sabbath. Also, it was the shelter of the ten lost tribes of Israel. All the tales in "Más allá" are in relation to time—real or mythological—since the Sambatyon is its metaphor and, at the same time, its frontier: the time of the Diaspora in "La estirpe de Core" (The Core Stock), time halting in "Y la luna en el Valle de Ayalón" (And the Moon on the Ayalon Valley), homesickness for Argentina —time slipping through one's fingers—in "Completo con medias lunas" (Full Service with Croissants), and homesickness for Toledo after the Expulsion in "Como candelas" (As candlelight). The short stories of "Más allá" are linked to the Kabbalah, to the power of words, and to hidden wisdom.

In collaboration with Ismael Silva Fuenzalida, Najenson developed a cultural typology of childhood and youth in Latin American, *La infancia y juventud urbanas en Latinoamérica: Elementos para una tipología cultural preliminar* (The Urban Childhood and Youth in Latin American: Factors for a Preliminary Cultural Typology; 1969). It is a modification of the fundamental work by Charles Wagley and M. Harris, "A Tipology [sic] of Latin American Subcultures" in *American Anthropologist*, 57 (1955): 428-51. The investigation presents a sociocultural typology with an anthropological perspective founded on contextual factors as well as social stratification. The study defines terms such as subculture and marginality, within Latin America, explaining the factors that produce their emergence. It identifies eleven different subcultures for the Latin American macro-area, eight of them relating to children and adolescents. The book ends with a comparison between three different subculture types: Subculture of Archaic Category, Marginal Subculture of the Urban Periphery and Deteriorated Downtown, and Discarded Subculture.

PRIMARY BIBLIOGRAPHY
Creative Writing

Más allá del río Sambatión. 1991. (Without the complete bibliographical reference).

Memorias de un erotómano y otros cuentos. Caracas: Monte Avila, 1991.

Nocturnas. Rosario, Argentina: n.p., 1959.

Tiempo de arrojar piedras: cuentos de ficción política y religiosa. Toluca: Universidad Autónoma del Estado de México, 1981.

Nonfiction

A propósito de un análisis neo-marxista del cambio político. Santiago de Chile: Escuela Latinoamericana de Ciencia Política y Administración Pública, 1971.

Cultura nacional y cultura subalterna. Toluca: Universidad Autónoma del Estado de México, 1979.

"La edificante fábula del ornitorrinco y la equidna: ¿Los escritores israelíes en castellano, una generación de tránsito?" *Diálogo* 18 (1987): 45-49.

"Entre la vida y la nostalgia." *Noaj* 7-8 (1992): 90-94.

"La escritura 'cautiva': El dilema de los escritores israelíes en español." *Nuez* 1:1 (1988): 21-23.

La infancia y la juventud urbanas en Latinoamérica: elementos para una tipología cultural preliminar. With Ismael Silva Fuenzalida. Santiago de Chile: Centro para el Desarrollo Económico y Social de América Latina, 1969.

Lenin, la cuestión judía y el Bund. Toluca: Universidad Autónoma del Estado de México, 1981.

Nacionalismo y lucha de clases (1905-1917). México, D.F.: Siglo XXI, 1979.

SECONDARY BIBLIOGRAPHY
Interviews

Senkman, Leonardo. "Cuatro preguntas a José Luis Najenson." *Diálogo* 19 (1989): 23-28.

Zlotchew, Clark M. "Una literatura hispana cautiva: entrevista con José Luis Najenson." *Inti* 34-35 (1991-92): 207-22. English version as "José Luis Najenson." In his *Voices of the River Plate. Interviews with Writers of Argentina and Uruguay.* San Bernardino, CA: The Borgo Press, 1992. 167-82.

Carmen de Urioste

NISSÁN, ROSA (Mexico; 1939)

Mexican novelist Rosa Nissán was born into a Sephardic family in 1939. Her parents were immigrants who arrived in Mexico as children: her mother from Turkey and her father from Jerusalem. Nissan grew up in the home of simple people who were unfamiliar with the arts, good conversation, or communication. What her father earned as the owner of a small business went to buy food and clothing and very rarely toward such extravagances as books or entertainment. The author was the oldest of six children. Her mother was sixteen years old at the time of Rosa's birth and in a period of eight years her five brothers and sisters were born.

Without being religious, Nissan's parents did follow Jewish tradition, and her childhood almost entirely took place within the confines of the Jewish community of Mexico City. She attended a Jewish school and participated in the activities of the Club Deportivo Israelita (Jewish Sports Club). Later, and only reluctantly, did her parents allow her to take journalism courses at the Universidad Femenina. Much like her mother, Nissán started a family very young: she married at the age of seventeen and when she was eighteen the first of her four children was born. However, in contrast to her mother, Nissan felt an artistic void that life at home could not fill.

In 1977 she started to participate in the literary workshops of the famous Mexican writer Elena Poniatowska (1933), and in 1979 she began to dedicate herself professionally to photography and producing audiovisuals, a job she continues to this day. Nissán has commented that her attendance at the workshops had a profound effect on her life thanks to the uplifting attitude of Poniatowska and the stimulating environment of the workshop. She learned to say many things that she never believed could be said.

In 1983 her short stories began to be published, the majority of them inspired from personal experiences. Since the appearance of "La epístola de ese señor" (That Man's Epistle; 1983) in *Polanco*, sixteen of her narrations were published in rapid succession in various Mexican journals.

Her first and only novel, *Novia que te vea* (May You Make a Good Bride), was published in 1993. An autobiographical work, *Novia que te vea*, is narrated in first person by the protagonist, Oshinica, and it presents her childhood and adolescence in a traditional Sephardic family in Mexico City during the 1960s and 1970s. Through the actions and reflections of the narrator-protagonist the reader participates in her search for identity as a Mexican-Sephardic woman. Ending the description of this beautiful novel here would not do it justice. An integral part of the text is the careful and loving recreation of the Sephardic world that is disappearing and that is evoked by means of anecdotes, reconstruction of dialogues, and verses in Judeo-Spanish. *Novia que te vea* was very well received by the Mexican public, and in 1993 a film based on the book was released. Nissán wrote the script together with Hugo Hiriart (1942), and the film was directed by Guita Shyfter. The story of Oshinica continues in the recently published sequel titled *Hisho que te nazca* (May a Son Be Born to You; 1996). The novel is considerably more extensive than its predecessor and it continues in the same vein with the now older and married protagonist learning to cope with a family of her own. Like *Novia*, *Hisho* is replete with Ladino vocabulary and even contains a glossary of words to aid the reader.

Nissán currently lives in Mexico City where she continues her literary activities. She is working on a third novel which she tentatively plans to title *Los viajes de mi cuerpo* (My Body's Journeys). She is also preparing a film script and a dramatic text.

PRIMARY BIBLIOGRAPHY

Novia que te vea. México, D.F.: Planeta, 1992.
Hisho que te nazca. México, D.F.: Plaza & Janés, 1996.

SECONDARY BIBLIOGRAPHY

Lockhart, Darrell B. "Growing Up Jewish in Mexico: Sabina Berman's *La bobe* and Rosa Nissán's *Novia que te vea.*" In *The Other Mirror: Women's Narrative in Mexico, 1980-1995.* Ed. Kristine L. Ibsen. Westport, CT: Greenwood, 1997. 159-74.

Renée Scott

ORGAMBIDE, PEDRO (Argentina; 1929)

Pedro Orgambide was born in Buenos Aires on August 9, 1929. His literary career began in that city during the 1940s and 1950s. In his 1985 autobiography *Todos teníamos veinte años* (We Were All Twenty Years Old), he mentions the poet Raúl González Tuñón (1905-74) and the prose author Álvaro Yunque (1889-1982) as his role models. Both were members of the Communist party and they belonged to the so-called Boedo group, along with Elías Castelnuovo (1893-?), Leónidas Barletta (1902-75), José Portogallo (1904-73), and Enrique Wernicke (1915-68). The Boedo writers focused on a literature of proletarian realism which attracted Orgambide.

An intimist tone, a preoccupation of the hero with the working and lower-middle class, and political commitment characterize this type of writing. Added to this realism around 1940 are writers such as Bernardo Verbitsky (1907-79), Bernardo Kordon (1915), and Alfredo Varela (1914). This social realism includes such themes as economic crisis and the political process of Argentina during the decade of the 1930s, known as the *década infame* (infamous decade), and the backdrop of the European war and genocide. Also added to this spectrum is the disquieting and atypical presence of Roberto Arlt (1900-42) and the revisionist essayists Ezequiel Martínez Estrada (1895-64) with his liberal idealism in *Radiografía de la pampa* (*X-ray of the Pampa*; 1933), and Raúl Scalabrini Ortiz (1898-59) with his populist *El hombre que está solo y espera* (The Man Who Is Alone and Waits; 1931). These essays are fundamental texts that reflect on the identity of the Argentine.

Such is the sociohistoric context under which Orgambide began to publish his first works: *Mitología de la adolescencia* (The Mythology of Adolescence; 1948), a collection of poems, and *Horacio Quiroga, el hombre y su obra* (Horacio Quiroga, the Man and His Work; 1954), an essay on the famous Uruguayan author. During this same time period writers like Humberto Costantini (1924-87), David Viñas (1929), Antonio Di Benedetto (1929-86), and Abelardo Castillo (1935), among others, were initiating their careers. They had in common a proletarian point of view, a critique of capitalism, and the simple technique of realist narration. The later development of Orgambide's work follows a logical evolution with the passage of time, since it will include new techniques and narrative tendencies, influenced by the appearance of the new novel of the sixties and the boom in magical realism in Argentina and Latin America.

However, Orgambide does not entirely abandon the initial realism that appears in *Hotel familias* (Family Hotel; 1972), *Hacer la América* (Make It in America; 1984), and in various short stories from *La mulata y el guerrero* (The Mulata and the Warrior; 1986), for example. In the novel *El páramo* (The Plateau; 1967) and in the stories from *Historias cotidianas y fantásticas* (Fantastic and Daily Stories; 1965), collage as a narrative technique is utilized. The resources of magical realism and the ludic novel clearly surface in *Aventuras de Edmund Ziller en tierras del Nuevo Mundo* (The Adventures of Edmund Ziller in the New World; 1977), written in Mexico, in *El arrabal del mundo* (The World's Slum; 1983), and in *Historias imaginarias de la Argentina* (Imaginary Stories of Argentina; 1986). In these last novels the technique has consisted of the development of a real historical nucleus that can become fantastic under any circumstance.

On the other hand, it is not easy to establish a simple demarcation among the diverse tendencies that Orgambide follows in his work, since aside from prolific, it covers a wide variety of genres. The theater, for example, is where he has ultimately obtained his most resounding successes: *Juan Moreira Supershow* debuted in Buenos Aires in 1972 with elements revived from the Creole Circus of the past century, updated with the special political charge of the 1970s, it was an immense success with the public and a renovating cultural proposal. His more recent theatrical production, *Eva* (1986) was equally successful. It is a political musical written during the author's exile in Mexico in collaboration with the actress Nacha Guevara and the musician Alberto Favero, also exiled from Argentina. *Eva* is written as a response to the Anglo musical by Andrew Lloyd Weber, *Evita*. Orgambide's Eva is a feminine leader of the Third World, in accordance with the Revolutionary Peronism point of view that utilized the figure of Eva Perón as one of the symbols of Latin American liberation. In fact, it is in the theater where Orgambide has managed to reach the greatest possibilities of artistic expression from a line of thought that has always been among his priorities, that of political commitment with its consequent concept of literature as militant activity.

The interest in the political framework of Argentina appears in one of his first novels, *Memorias de un hombre de bien* (Memories of a Well-To-Do Man; 1964), in which he parodies the Buenos Aires bourgeoisie that suffered during the years of Peronism the ascent of the lower classes. His interest in the struggle of the classes and political reality leads Orgambide to incorporate a historical setting into his fiction. In his most complete novel, *Hacer la América*, he uses the period of time at the beginning of the century, when the large numbers of European immigrants into Buenos Aires reached their peak. Various types, therefore, appear in the novel: the Italian, the Turk, the Galician, the Jew, the Pole, and the Englishman. These characters are stereotypes of the waves of emigrants that were escaping poverty and war in Europe. Their destiny in America is risky, their fortune is uncertain, and the promised land is illusory. Nonetheless, these immigrants share the inevitable destiny of mixing with the Creoles and natives, if only on a cultural level. The creation of the Argentine melting pot is the great theme of Orgambide's novel. Therefore, from a classist perspective he also involves the native internal migrants: the gaucho, the Creole, the *compadrito* (a tough, usually of immigrant stock) as other recent arrivals to the Buenos Aires megalopolis. These latter types join the Europeans in the formation of an uprooted new population. *Hacer la América* develops around a real event that consisted of a workers' insurrection headed by the Vassena metallurgic factories in which anarchists and Communist party militants partipated in January of 1919, known as the Semana Trágica or Tragic Week of 1919. Within this framework Orgambide includes Jewish immigration as one more protagonist in the process of the formation of the Argentine population and identity. What stands out in the novel is the role that immigration plays as the bearer of both technology and a conscience that operate on the foundation of what later will become the powerful Argentine middle class. In *Hacer la América* Buenos Aires is the result of different migrations that in turn create the various fascinating, almost mythic, elements of the city: the tango, the *malambo* (a popular and typical Gaucho dance), the poor neighborhoods, the *sainete* (popular short dramatic pieces), the circus, the *milonga* (a popular song and dance), the *murga* (street musicians), and the *candombé* (a popular African dance) make up a Babylon that synthesizes the syncretism by which Latin America is defined. The vision of a continent of racial and cultural mixture as a constant throughout his work causes one to go back to the genesis of Orgambide's own identity which springs from two sources: his paternal grandparents Gdansky, from Russia, and his maternal grandparents Orgambide, Creoles. In *Todos teníamos veinte años*, Orgambide outlines his family history by presenting typical situations of family life and the characteristics or habits of certain members of the family.

Orgambide has touched upon almost all aspects of Jewish history in the Americas in his works. He reflects upon the Jewish presence, always latent, in the historical development of America by writing about the diverse groups of Jews who have settled in Latin America over the centuries: those Jews who came at the time of the conquest, expelled from Spain by the Catholic monarchs, the marranos, dreamers and adventurers, errant wanderers, and mystics, as well as those who came fleeing persecution in Russia and the terrors of European nazism in the twentieth century.

One of Orgambide's most accomplished novels is *Aventuras de Edmund Ziller en tierras del Nuevo Mundo*. The novel is structurally complex and problematic in that it consists of an amalgamation of diverse generic forms and temporal disjunctions. It is essentially the fantastic tale, within a historical framework, of a wandering Jew by the name of Edmund Ziller, who embodies all the characters of the novel. The novel, which depicts a clearly Marxist agenda, progresses by means of the narration of Ziller's adventures. The novel can be read as the representation of the spiritual *mestizaje* (cultural and ethnic mixing) that is produced in Latin America throughout history and the Jewish role in each stage of that development.

Orgambide's preoccupation with issues of social justice is made very apparent in his short novel *Los inquisidores* (The Inquisitors; 1967). The author utilizes alternating thematic threads to weave a text that speaks out against discrimination and acts of violence against minority populations. The inquisitors in the book include the colonial Inquisition in Peru, the nineteenth-century Argentine dictator Rosas, the Tacuaras (a fascist group in Argentina in the 1960s), as well as white supremacist groups in Alabama, New York, and Los Angeles, Nazis, Stalinists, and even Joseph McCarthy. The victims in the novel are largely Jews and African-Americans.

Orgambide's works, in their totality, may be summarized as representing the author's commitment to social justice, his support of Latin American freedom movements in particular, and his belief that freedom must be placed above all other issues. This freedom is generally symbolized by Orgambide in the form of books, reading and writing. Libraries and bookstores, depicted as sacred spaces, are frequently present in Orgambide's works, and they are always looked after by Jewish bibliophiles in almost all his stories and novels.

PRIMARY BIBLIOGRAPHY
Creative Writing

Un amor imprudente. Buenos Aires: Norma, 1995.

El arrabal del mundo. Buenos Aires: Bruguera, 1983. México: Katún, 1984. La Habana: Casa de las Américas, 1987.

Aventuras de Edmund Ziller en tierras del Nuevo Mundo. México: Grijalbo, 1977. Buenos Aires: Abril, 1984.

Las botas de Anselmo Soria. Buenos Aires: Colihue, 1992.

La buena gente. Buenos Aires: Sudamericana, 1970.

Cantares de las Madres de Plaza de Mayo. México: Tierra del Fuego, 1983.

Concierto para caballero solo. Buenos Aires: Stilcograf, 1963.

La convaleciente. Buenos Aires: Legasa, 1987.

Discepolín. Unpublished play, debuted in Buenos Aires, 1989.

El encuentro. Buenos Aires: Stilcograf, 1957.

El escriba. Bogotá: Norma, 1996.

Eva. Unpublished play, debuted in Buenos Aires, 1986.

Hacer la América. Buenos Aires: Bruguera, 1984.

Las hermanas. Buenos Aires: Goyanarte, 1959.

Historias con tangos y corridos. La Habana: Casa de las Américas, 1976. Mexico: Extemporáneos, 1979. Buenos Aires: Abril, 1984.

Historias cotidianas y fantásticas. Buenos Aires: J. Alvarez, 1965.

Historias imaginarias de la Argentina. Buenos Aires: Legasa, 1986.

Hotel familias; Confesiones de un poeta de provincia. Buenos Aires: Ediciones de la Flor, 1972.

Los inquisidores. Buenos Aires: Sudamericana, 1967.

Juan Moreira Supershow. Unpublished play, debuted in Buenos Aires, 1972.

Memorias de un hombre de bien. Buenos Aires: Falbo, 1964. Buenos Aires: Centro Editor de América Latina, 1967. Mexico: Bogavante, 1969.

Mitología de la adolescencia. Buenos Aires: Monteagudo, 1948.

Mujer con violoncello. Buenos Aires: Beas Ediciones, 1993.

La mulata y el guerrero. Buenos Aires: Ediciones del Sol, 1986.

El páramo. Buenos Aires: G. Dávalos y D.C. Hernández, 1965. Buenos Aires: Centro Editor de América Latina, 1967.

Prohibido Gardel. Unpublished play, debuted in Buenos Aires, 1978.

Pura memoria. Buenos Aires: Bruguera, 1985.

Se armó la murga. Unpublished play, debuted in Buenos Aires, 1974.

Un tren o cualquier otra cosa. Unpublished play, debuted in Buenos Aires, 1967.

La vida gris. Unpublished play, debuted in Buenos Aires, 1959.

Nonfiction

Crónicas para las fiestas. Buenos Aires: Jorge Alvarez, 1965.

Enclopedia de la literatura argentina. [Ed. with Roberto Yahni]. Buenos Aires: Sudamericana, 1970.

Horacio Quiroga: el hombre y su obra. Buenos Aires: Stilcograf, 1954.

Horacio Quiroga: una biografía. Buenos Aires: Planeta, 1994.

Gardel y la patria del mito. Buenos Aires: Legasa, 1985.

Genio y figura de Ezequiel Martínez Estrada. Buenos Aires: EUDEBA, 1985.

Radiografía de Martínez Estrada. Buenos Aires: Centro Editor de América Latina, 1970.

Todos teníamos veinte años. Buenos Aires: Pomaire, 1985.

Yo, argentino. Buenos Aires: J. Alvarez, 1968.

SECONDARY BIBLIOGRAPHY
Criticism

Bayer, Oswald. "*El encuentro, por Pedro Orgambide.*" *Comentario* 16 (1957): 89-91.

Brushwood, John. *Cinco novelas de Pedro Orgambide: las dimensiones de la realidad. Revista de Bellas Artes* (Mexico) 16 (1976): 19-25.

Chibán, Alicia. "Lo ficcional como problematización de la historia latinoamericana en Pedro Orgambide." In *VI Congreso Nacional de Literatura*

Argentina: Actas. Córdoba: Universidad Nacional de Córdoba, 1993. 147-54.

Lichtblau, Myron. "Irony and Remembrance in Pedro Orgambide's *Memorias de un hombre de bien.*" In *Homenaje a Luis Leal: estudios sobre literatura hispanoamericana.* Ed. Donald W. Bleznick and Juan O. Valencia. Madrid: Insula, 1978. 51-61.

Lindstrom, Naomi. *Jewish Issues in Argentine Literature: From Gerchunoff to Szichman.* Columbia: U of Missouri P, 1989. 159-60.

Menton, Seymour. *Latin America's New Historical Novel.* Austin: U of Texas P, 1993. 138-49.

Rodríguez Michemberg, Susana Mónica. "'Los otros' o el tercer hombre." *Alba de América* 11.20-21 (1993): 189-98.

Sosnowski, Saúl. "Contemporary Jewish-Argentine Writers: Tradition and Politics." *Latin American Literary Review* 6.12 (1978): 1-14.

—. "¿Quién es Edmund Ziller?" *La semana de Bellas Artes* 8 (1978): 8-11.

Valero Covarrubias, Alicia. "*Memorias de un hombre de bien*: un novela picaresca de Pedro Orgambide." In *Literatura e identidad latinoamericana: siglo XX.* IV Simposio Internacional de Literatura. Ed. Juana Alcira Arancibia. Westminster, CA: Instituto Literario y Cultural Hispánico, 1991. 105-10.

Weinstein, Ana E., and Miryam E. Gover de Nasatsky, comps. *Escritores judeoargentinos: bibliografía 1900-1987.* 2 vols. Buenos Aires: Milá, 1994. II.34-42.

Interviews

Giardinelli, Mempo. "Quiero tres, cuatro páginas, y que en ellas haya un mundo." Interview with P. Orgambide. In his *Así se escribe un cuento.* Buenos Aires: Beas Ediciones, 1992. 233-41.

Cristina Guzzo

PIZARNIK, ALEJANDRA (Argentina; 1936-72)

Alejandra Pizarnik was born in Buenos Aires, the daughter of Jewish Russian immigrants whose original surname was Pozharnik. She attended philosophy and literature courses at the National University and studied journalism and painting as well. Between 1960 and 1964 she lived a more or less bohemian life in Paris.

Her first book of poems, *La tierra más ajena* (The Most Alien Land) appeared in 1955, followed by *La última inocencia* (The Last Innocence; 1956) and *Las aventuras perdidas* (The Lost Adventures; 1958). The fourth book, *Árbol de Diana* (Diana's Tree), was published in 1962 by the prestigious Sur publishing house, with an introduction by Octavio Paz (1914); both facts indicate that she was already recognized as one of the outstanding young poets of Latin America. *Árbol* was followed by *Los trabajos y las noches* (The Labors and the Nights; 1965), *Extracción de la piedra de locura* (Extraction of the Stone of Madness; 1968), and *El infierno musical* (The Musical Hell; 1971). In 1971 she published *La condesa sangrienta* ("The Bloody Countess"), a narration-essay based on the criminal exploits of the psychopathic Hungarian Countess Erzébet Báthory (born ca. 1560). Pizarnik also collaborated in the preparation of an overall anthology of her writings, including her critical essays, that was published in Spain posthumously under the title *El deseo de la palabra* (The Desire of the Word; 1975).

She was awarded a Guggenheim fellowship in 1969, and a Fulbright scholarship in 1971. Her last years were marked by psychological distress, and her untimely death at the age of 36, a probable but not certain suicide, occurred during a short home vacation from a psychiatric institution.

Anthologies of her poetry have continued to be published to the present day, proof of her increasing recognition among the literary public and especially young Latin American poets, on several of whom her influence is very apparent. The most noteworthy of posthumous anthologies include *Textos de Sombra y últimos poemas* (Shadow Texts and Last Poems; 1982), edited by her friends Olga Orozco (1920) and Ana Becciú, which includes unpublished materials; *Alejandra Pizarnik: A Profile* (1987) edited by Frank Graziano, an anthology in English which has been retranslated to Spanish under the title *Semblanza* (Profile; 1992) and which includes selections from her diaries. A number of her texts have been translated into French in their entirety, and many of her poems and narrations have been included in anthologies of Latin American, Jewish, and women's literature in several languages, including English.

Pizarnik was also a gifted translator of French poetry (Yves Bonnefoy [1923], Antonin Artaud [1896-1948], Henri Michaux [1899-1984], Aimé Césaire [1913], Michel Leiris [1901-90]), as well as an insightful literary critic. She wrote essays and reviews on Julio Cortázar (1914-84), Silvina Ocampo (1906), Alberto Girri (1919), Ricardo Molinari (1898-?), Octavio Paz (1914), André Breton (1896-1966), André Pieyre de Mandiargues (1909), Héctor A. Murena

(1923-75), among others, and interviews with writers such as Jorge Luis Borges (1899-1986), Roberto Juarroz (1925), Victoria Ocampo (1891-1979), and Juan José Hernández (1931). These pieces, as well as her own poems, appeared in prestigious literary reviews such as *Sur* (South), *Zona Franca* (Candid Zone), *Cuadernos* (Notebooks), *Mundo Nuevo* (New World), *Papeles de Son Armadans* (Papers of Son Armadans), *Poesía Buenos Aires* (Buenos Aires Poetry), *Testigo* (Witness), *La estafeta literaria* (The Literary Post), *Imagen* (Image), among others, and the literary sections of newspapers such as *La Nación* (The Nation; Buenos Aires) and *La Gaceta* (The Gazette; Tucumán). Though a considerable part of her poetry (especially after *Los trabajos*) consists of prose poems, and some of them assume narrative form, she did not write any conventional fiction. The only exceptions are a short story, "El viento feroz" (The Ferocious Wind; *La Gaceta* (1958) which she never included in a book; "El hombre del antifaz azul" (The Blue Masked Man, *Papeles de Son Armadans* (1969), and *El deseo de la palabra*), a personal rewriting of an episode from *Alice's Adventures in Wonderland* (1865), and the previously mentioned *La condesa sangrienta*. *Textos de sombra* and *El deseo* include a group of prose texts in pseudodramatic or pseudonarrative form characterized by an aggressive comic-anguished vein in which obscenity goes hand in hand with abrupt intertextuality and a violent linguistic creativity which owes much to surrealist experiments with language (cf. Piña, "La palabra obscena").

As a whole, her corpus is relatively small, the result of three different factors: 1) her short life, 2) her rigorous selection of materials when composing each of her books (significantly, the longest of her unitary volumes is the posthumous *Textos de sombra*), and 3) the brevity of the majority of her poems, which only in some of her later books such as *Extracción* and *El infierno* cover more than a portion of a single page. In her diary, interviews, and correspondence she often refers to these brief texts as "fragments." The impression of brevity also consists in the intensity and compression of her style, which led Octavio Paz to compare her poems to a piece of glass that "reflects the sun-rays and concentrates them in a central focus [. . .] the luminous heat of which can burn, melt and even volatilize the unbelievers" (Paz, "*Árbol de Diana*" 9; my translation). The empty space of the page on which her brief texts are inscribed becomes a part of the poems as signifier of a void in which the word struggles to create a haven of sense (cf. Pezzoni 102). Her central themes revolve around existential limits and trials—love, death, loneliness, anguish, the precarious wholeness of self—and poetic creation. Facts of her own biography or environment only enter her poetry transmuted into textual mediations and symbols: absolute beauty, and not direct expression of feeling or anecdote, is her declared goal. And for that goal, she meticulously elaborated all potentialities of language: phonic, semantic, syntactic, symbolic and intertextual. At the same time, her relationship with language was painfully ambivalent, for she was acutely conscious of its limitations and impossibilities, which made her turn to music as an ideal form never to be attained, therefore, just a "musical hell," as expressed by the title of one of her last books.

The question of whether Pizarnik should be considered a Jewish poet or not has become quite an issue for some critics. Cristina Piña, her principal biographer, gives due attention to her growing up in the midst of an immigrant Jewish family that suffered heavy losses during the Holocaust. Piña also mentions her nicknames Blímele (little Flower) and Buma (both derived from *blume*, flower in Yiddish; Flora was her original and legal first name) which were still used by the family and some friends long after she decided to call herself Alejandra. Other interesting facts mentioned by Piña include Pizarnik's attendance at Jewish complementary school during her childhood and a revival of her interest in her own Jewishness towards the end of her life. Additional testimonies inform of her irregular participation in a Zionist youth movement in her late teens and early twenties (though the family, especially the father, was more inclined to universal socialism than to Zionism), and that before she decided to go to Paris in 1960, she was considering Israel as an alternative. Likewise, she felt a special commonality or bond with acquaintances that happened to be Jewish. In her literature Pizarnik never wrote about Jewish themes as such, a fact that some critics interpret as a complete rejection of her Jewish identity. Interestingly enough, the few texts in which she touches upon Jewish subjects share two characteristics: first they are directly or indirectly related to her father, and second most of them were not included in her books and appeared for the first time in the Orozco-Becciú posthumous compilation. One of these texts is "Los muertos y la lluvia" (The Dead and the Rain; *Textos* 31-32), a prose piece in which she evokes her father's burial. Indeed, the text ends with a quotation from the Talmud relating the dead to the rain, but the cemetery is referred to as "extraño y judío," "strange or alien and Jewish"; this irregular construction (instead of "strange Jewish cemetery") suggests that strangeness is in fact a quality of Jewishness itself. Another poem dealing with her deceased father mentions that in his youth (i.e., in Russia) he was not allowed to sing the songs he wanted ("Poema para el padre" [Poem for the Father]; *Textos* 52). In "La muerte y la muchacha (Schubert)" (Death and the Maiden [Schubert]; *Textos* 72), a description which immediately recalls a typical scene by Marc Chagall (whom she admired) is abruptly and negatively interrupted by a distressed question about the "concept of space" involved in such a world. In "Las uniones posibles" (The Possible Unions; *Textos* 16-17) she mentions the option of uniting with the past of a people she does not recognize as her own (Goldberg, "Alejandra Pizarnik: pala-bra y sombra" 58-60; *Alejandra Pizarnik: "Este espacio que somos"* 77-85).

A possible conclusion to be drawn is that the absence of focus on Jewish themes was not the result of lack of acquaintance or of ignorance but rather the deliberate exclusion of a part of herself which did not offer an answer to her existential plight and about which she therefore decided not to write. For Leonar-do Senkman, all her metaphors of herself as an exiled being inserted into an alien, hostile world are backgrounded in the Jewish/immigrant condition. Howev-er, she chose not to transmute that condition aesthetically, through direct themati-zation, but to depict it in all its cruel, unsolvable bereavement. The question that remains open is whether some traits of what can broadly be called her style (as opposed to explicit themes) can be related to Jewishness.

PRIMARY BIBLIOGRAPHY

Alejandra Pizarnik: A Profile. Ed. with introduction by Frank Graziano. Trans. by María Rosa Fort, Frank Graziano, and Suzanne Jill Levine. Durango: Logbridge-Rhodes, 1987. Spanish version as, *Semblanza.* Ed. with intro-duction by Frank Graziano. México: Fondo de Cultura Económica, 1992.

Árbol de Diana. Preface by Octavio Paz. Buenos Aires: Sur, 1962. Also, Buenos Aires: Botella al Mar, 1988.

Las aventuras perdidas. Buenos Aires: Altamar, 1958.

Canto de extramuros. Buenos Aires: Americalee, 1963.

La condesa sangrienta. Buenos Aires: Acuarius, 1971. Also, Buenos Aires: López Crespo, 1976. English Version as "The Bloody Countess." Trans. by Alberto Manguel. In *Other Fires: Short Fiction by Latin American Women.* Ed. Alberto Manguel. New York: Clarkson N. Potter, 1986. 70-87. Also in *Pleasure in the Word: Erotic Writings by Latin American Women.* Ed. Margarite Fernández Olmos and Lizabeth Paravisini-Ge-bert. Fredonia, NY: White Pine Press, 1993. 99-113.

El deseo de la palabra. Ed. with afterword by Antonio Beneyto. Barcelona: Barral, 1975.

Diario, 1960-1961. Bogotá: Talleres Editoriales del Mueseo Rayol/Ediciones Embalaje, 1988.

Entrevistas. Caracas: Endymión, 1978.

Extracción de la piedra de locura. Buenos Aires: Sudamericana, 1968.

Extracción de la piedra de locura. Otros poemas. Madrid: Visor, 1993.

"From Diana's Tree," "Vertigo or Contemplation of Something About to End," Figures and Silences," "Continuity." Trans. by Sylvia Molloy. *Women's*

Writing in Latin America: An Anthology. Ed. Sara Castro-Klarén, et al. Boulder/Oxford: Westview Press, 1991. 204-6.

"From Tree of Diana," "Recognition," "Shadow of Days to Come," "Foundation Stone," Fragments to Overcome Silence," "Suspicion," "Poem for My Father," "Speaking Your Name." Trans. by Susan Bassnett. In *These Are Not Sweet Girls: Poetry by Latin American Women.* Ed. Marjorie Agosín. Fredonia, NY: White Pine Press, 1994. 290-96.

El infierno musical. Buenos Aires: Siglo XXI Argentina, 1971.

"The Mirror of Melancholy," Blood Baths," "Severe Measures." Trans. by Suzanne Jill Levine. In *Secret Weavers: Stories of the Fantastic by Women of Argentina and Chile.* Ed. Marjorie Agosín. Fredonia, NY: White Pine Press, 1992. 133-40.

Nombres y figuras. Barcelona: La Esquina, 1969.

Obras completas: poesía y prosa. Preface by Silvia Baron Supervielle. Buenos Aires: Corregidor, 1990. 2nd ed., rev. Buenos Aires: Corregidor, 1994.

Los pequeños cantos. Caracas: Árbol de Fuego, 1971. 2nd ed. 1987.

Poemas. Preface by Inés Malinow. Medellín: Endymion, 1986.

Poemas. Ed. with preface by Cristina Piña. Buenos Aires: Centro Editor de América Latina, 1988.

Poemas: antología. Ed. with preface by Alejandro Fontenla. Buenos Aires: Centro Editor de América Latina, 1982. 2nd ed. 1987.

Prosa poética. Medellín: Endymion, 1987.

Textos de Sombra y últimos poemas. Ed. Olga Orozco and Ana Becciú. Buenos Aires: Sudamericana, 1982. 2nd. ed. 1985.

La tierra más ajena. Buenos Aires: Botella al Mar, 1955.

Los trabajos y las noches. Buenos Aires: Sudamericana, 1965.

La última inocencia. Buenos Aires: Poesía Buenos Aires, 1956.

La última inocencia y Las aventuras perdidas. Preface by Enrique Molina. Buenos Aires: Botella al Mar, 1976.

"Words," "The Lady Buccaneer of Pernambuco or Hilda the Polygraph," "The Bloody Countess," "In this Night in this World," "Death and the Young Woman (Schubert)." Trans. by Suzanne Jill Levine, Alberto Manguel, María Rosa Fort and Frank Graziano, and Daisy C. de Filippis, respectively. In *Pleasure in the Word: Erotic Writings by Latin American Women.* Ed. Margarite Fernández Olmos and Lizabeth Paravisini-Gebert. Fredonia, NY: White Pine Press, 1993. 93-117.

Zona prohibida. Veracruz: Papel de Envolver, 1982.

SECONDARY BIBLIOGRAPHY
Criticism

Altamiranda, Daniel. "Alejandra Pizarnik." In *Latin American Writers on Gay and Lesbian Themes: A Bio-Critical Sourcebook*. Ed. David William Foster. Westport, CT: Greenwood Press, 1994. 326-36.

Bassnett, Susan. "Speaking with Many Voices: The Poems of Alejandra Pizarnik." In *Knives and Angels: Women Writers in Latin America*. Ed. Susan Bassnett. London/New Jersey: Zed Books, 1990. 36-51. [book title & epigraph taken from a poem by A.P.].

Beneyto, Antonio. "Alejandra Pizarnik: ocultándose en el lenguaje." *Quimera* 34 (1983): 23-27.

Borinsky, Alicia. "Alejandra Pizarnik: The Self and Its Impossible Landscapes." In *A Dream of Light and Shadow: Portraits of Latin American Women Writers*. Ed. Marjorie Agosín. Albuquerque: U of New Mexico P, 1995. 291-302.

—. "Muñecas reemplazables." *Río de la Plata: Culturas* (Paris) 7 (1988): 41-48.

Cámara, Isabel. "Literatura o la política del juego en Alejandra Pizarnik." *Revista iberoamericana* 51.132-133 (1985): 581-89.

Campanella, Hebe N. "La voz de la mujer en la joven poesía argentina: Cuatro registros." *Cuadernos hispanoamericanos* 300 (1975): 543-64.

Caulfield, Carlota. "Entre la poesía y la pintura: elementos surrealistas en *Extracción de la piedra de locura* y *El infierno musical*." *Chasqui* 21.1 (1992): 3-10.

Chávez Silverman, Suzanne. "The Discourse of Madness in the Poetry of Alejandra Pizarnik." *Monographic Review/Revista monográfica* 6 (1990): 274-81.

—. "The Ex-Centric Self: The Poetry of Alejandra Pizarnik." Ph.D. diss., Univ. of California-Davis, 1991.

—. "The Look that Kills: The 'Unacceptable Beauty' of Alejandra Pizarnik's *La condesa sangrienta*." In *¿Entiendes? Queer Readings, Hispanic Writings*. Ed. Emilie L. Bergmann and Paul Julian Smith. Durham/London: Duke UP, 1995. 281-305.

Cobo Borda, Juan Gustavo. "Alejandra Pizarnik, la pequeña sonámbula." *Eco* 151 (1972): 40-64. Also as "Alejandra Pizarnik (1936-1972)." In *Eco, 1960-1975. Ensayistas colombianos*. Ed. A. Rodríguez. Bogotá: Biblioteca Colombiana de Cultura, n.d. 199-217.

DiAntonio, Robert E. "On Seeing Things Darkly in the Poetry of Alejandra Pizarnik: Confessional Poetics or Aesthetic Metaphor?" *Confluencia* 2.2 (1987): 47-52.

Fagundo, Ana María. "Alejandra Pizarnik (1936-1972)." In *Spanish American Women Writers: A Bio-Bibliographical Source Book*. Ed. Diane E. Marting. Westport, CT: Greenwood Press, 1990. 446-52.

Foster, David William. *Gay and Lesbian Themes in Latin American Writing*. Austin: U of Texas P, 1991. 97-102.

—. "Of Power and Virgins: Alejandra Pizarnik's *La condesa sangrienta*." In his *Violence in Argentine Literature: Cultural Responses to Tyranny*. Columbia/London: U of Missouri P, 1995. 98-114.

—. "The Representation of the Body in the Poetry of Alejandra Pizarnik." *Hispanic Review* 62.3 (1994): 319-47.

Gai, Michal Heidi. "Alejandra Pizarnik: *Árbol de Diana*." *Romanic Review* 83.2 (1992): 245-60.

Goldberg, Florinda F. *Alejandra Pizarnik: "Este espacio que somos."* Gaithersburg, MD: Hispamérica, 1994.

—. "Alejandra Pizarnik: palabra y sombra." *Noah* 1 (1987): 58-62.

Gómez Paz, Julieta. "La tierra prometida: Alejandra Pizarnik." In her *Cuatro actitudes poéticas*. Buenos Aires: Conjunta, 1977. 9-47.

Graziano, Frank. "A Death in Which to Live." In *Alejandra Pizarnik: A Profile*. Ed. Frank Graziano. Durango, CO: Logbridge-Rhodes, 1987. 9-17.

Haydu, Susana. "Alejandra Pizarnik: evolución de su lenguaje poético." Ph.D. diss., Yale University, 1991.

Koremblit, Bernardo Ezequiel. *Todas las que ella era: ensayo sobre Alejandra Pizarnik*. Buenos Aires: Corregidor, 1991.

Kuhnheim, Jill S. "Unsettling Silence in the Poetry of Olga Orozco and Alejandra Pizarnik." *Monographic Review/Revista Monográfica* 6 (1990): 258-73.

Lagmanovich, David. "La poesía de Alejandra Pizarnik." In *XVII Congreso del Instituto Internacional de Literatura Iberoamericana*. Madrid: Cultura Hispánica del Centro Iberoamericano de Cooperación, Universidad Complutense de Madrid, 1978. vol. II, 885-95.

La Razón/Cultura. "Suplemento especial: el medio siglo de Alejandra Pizarnik." Buenos Aires, Dec. 28, 1986: 1-5.

Lasarte, Francisco. "Más allá del surrealismo: la poesía de Alejandra Pizarnik." *Revista iberoamericana* 49.125 (1983): 867-77.

Malinow, Inés. "Juicios críticos." *Poesía argentina contemporánea* 1.6 (1980): 2833-40. Also as "Introducción." *Poemas* by Alejandra Pizarnik. Medellín: Endymion, 1986. 7-11.

Malpartida, Juan. "Alejandra Pizarnik." *Cuadernos hispanoamericanos* 479 (1990): 39-41.

Moia, Martha I. "Some Keys to Alejandra Pizarnik." Trans. by Susan Pensak. *Sulfur* 8 (1983): 97-101.

Molina, Enrique. "La hija de insomnio." *Cuadernos hispanoamericanos* 479 (1990): 5-6.

Molinaro, Nina L. "Resistance, Gender, and the Mediation of History in Pizarnik's *La condesa sangrienta* and Ortiz's *Urraca.*" *Letras femeninas* 19.1-2 (1993): 45-54.

Muschietti, Delfina. "Alejandra Pizarnik: la niña asesinada." *Filología* 24 (1989): 231-41.

Orozco, Olga. "Viajera en la noche." *Testigo* 2 (abril-junio, 1966): 71-73.

Paz, Octavio. "*Árbol de Diana.*" In A. Pizarnik, *Árbol de Diana.* Buenos Aires: Sur, 1962. 7-9. Also as O. Paz, *Puertas al campo.* Barcelona: Seix Barral, 1972. 112-13; A.Pizarnik, *Poèmes.* Paris: Nadir, 1984. 12-15.

Pensak, Susan. "Alejandra Pizarnik (Argentina, 1936-1972)." *13th Moon* 5 (1980): 55-74.

Peri Rossi, Cristina. "Alejandra Pizarnik o la tentación de la muerte." *Cuadernos hispanoamericanos* 173 (1973): 584-88.

Pezzoni, Enrique. "Alejandra Pizarnik: la poesía como destino." *Sur* 297 (1965): 101-4. Also in his *El texto y sus voces.* Buenos Aires: Sudamericana, 1986. 156-61.

Piña, Cristina. *Alejandra Pizarnik.* Buenos Aires: Planeta, 1991. The publisher's "Mujeres Argentinas" series.

—. "Alejandra Pizarnik: la construcción/destrucción del sujeto en la escritura." In *Autobiografía y escritura.* Ed. Juan Orbe. Buenos Aires: Corregidor, 1994. 185-96.

—. *La palabra como destino: un acercamiento a la poesía de Alejandra Pizarnik.* Buenos Aires: Botella al Mar, 1981.

—. "La palabra obscena." *Cuadernos hispanoamericanos* 479 (1990): 17-38.

Riker, Katharine. *Feminist Linguistic Theory in the Poetry of Alejandra Pizarnik.* Ph.D. diss., Univ. of New Mexico, 1992.

Rossler, Osvaldo. "Alejandra Pizarnik o la materia verbal que no encuentra salida." In his *Cantores y trágicos de Buenos Aires.* Buenos Aires: Ediciones Tres Tiempos, 1981. 115-77.

Running, Thorpe. "The Poetry of Alejandra Pizarnik." *Chasqui* 14.2-3 (1985): 45-55.

Senkman, Leonardo. "Alejandra Pizarnik: de la morada de las palabras a la intemperie de la muerte." In his *La identidad judía en la literatura argentina*. Buenos Aires: Pardés, 1983. 337-40.

Soncini, Ana. "Itinerario de la palabra en el silencio." *Cuadernos hispanoamericanos* 479 (1990): 7-15.

Sucre, Guillermo. "La metáfora del silencio." In his *La máscara, la transparencia*. Caracas: Monte Avila, 1975. 316-19.

Weinstein, Ana E., and Miryam E. Gover de Nasatsky, comps. "Alejandra Pizarnik." *Escritores judeo-argentinos: bibliografía 1900-1987*. 2 vols. Buenos Aires: Milá, 1994. II.76-84.

Zona Franca 2.16 (1972). Special Issue in honor of Alejandra Pizarnik.

Interviews

Moia, Martha Isabel. "Con Alejandra Pizarnik: algunas claves." *La Nación* Feb. 11, 1973: 5. Also as *Plural* 18 (1973): 8-9.

Florinda F. Goldberg

PLAGER, SILVIA (Argentina; 1942)

Silvia Plager was born in Buenos Aires in 1942 and has published seven books: *Amigas* (Girlfriends; 1982), *Prohibido despertar* (Forbidden Awakening; 1983), *Boca de tormenta* (Mouth of Torment; 1984), a collection of short stories, *A las escondidas* (In Secret; 1986), *Alguien está mirando* (Some One Is Watching; 1991), *Mujeres pudorosas* (Modest Women; 1993), and *Como papas para varenikes* (Like Potatoes for Dumplings; 1994). She has also been active in other parts of the literary community, writing for the Buenos Aires newspapers *Clarín* (The Clarion) and *La prensa* (The Press). Plager was awarded the Premio Corregidor in 1982 and el Tercer Premio Municipal (Third Municipal Prize) in 1983. Various texts have also been included in anthologies and translated into both English and French.

At the core of Plager's work is the confusion associated with the ideology of culture and gender. Although all of her books do not directly focus on Jewish concerns, the usual multiplicities of daily life are augmented for Plager, who as a Jew, a woman, and a writer, embodies the many concerns of race and gender which affect subaltern groups. She addresses these complications in *Mujeres pudorosas*. The provocative nature of her works illustrates her refusal to collaborate with the dominant authority. Her first novel, *Amigas*, deals with the complex relationships of four Argentine women struggling to find their own identities. The protagonists, who are all approaching forty years of age, have lived amid the personal and social upheavals of their time. Martha, Delia, and Susana are childhood friends residing in Buenos Aires who become reunited while anticipating the arrival of Mónica, a fourth schoolmate who has been an expatriate since high school. Martha and Delia, extremely close since their early years, are the main characters not only of this novel, but also of her subsequent book, *Prohibido despertar*. In *Amigas*, Martha's husband and son have left her, yet she is portrayed as the most accomplished of all her friends. Delia believes that Martha's family will return because no one can escape Martha's influence. What we learn in the second book is the relative insignificance of this assessment to Martha's personal happiness. Delia's mother idolized Martha and made every effort to ascertain a continuing friendship between the two girls. Delia's confusion arises not only from her resentful feelings toward a friend whom her mother places on a pedestal above her, but also from her parents' unwillingness to participate in or recognize their own heritage as Jews, and the importance that Argentine politics plays in their lives. Delia herself has also carried on this tradition of non-participation by recommending to her own daughters that they do not become activists of any sort. Thus, although at one time Delia felt a need to rebel, she has preferred to position herself in a more comfortable role and hopes to persuade her daughters to take the easy way out and to do the same. Delia avoids the fear and alienation of the so-called feminists by taking her uncontested place in the system.

Martha, however, implores Delia to write. Delia believes Martha has forced her into writing in order to invent a life for herself where neither her husband nor her daughters are participants. What she discovers is that her repression is like that of all women, something which began before her birth, and continues in those who her own womb has brought forth.

Susana appears as the perfect housewife, proud of her shiny floors, yet afraid of her husband's negative reaction were he to find out about Martha's separation. Susana is also intimidated by her old friends' mode of dress and higher education. Delia and Martha realize that Susana doesn't conform to their world, but nonetheless Delia foresees that the reunion with Mónica will be a success.

Delia suspects that her own husband is having an affair, but she hides her suspicions from Martha. Telling Martha would be a confirmation of this harmful reality. Delia rejects any truth which might cause her problems. Her refusal to finish her book is a retreat from the confrontations which her conventional life has tempered. As the novel ends, Martha decides that it is best not to argue with Delia about things they cannot change. The last two paragraphs show each woman returning to their former roles without modifications. Delia goes into the kitchen to begin preparing dinner while Martha shakes her head and gets up to look out the window. As with all indecisive actions which leave no lasting impressions, the chair cushions where they had sat for hours reinflate, leaving no trace of the women's space there.

In *Prohibido despertar*, we find Martha has left Argentina to visit her son and husband who has taken a temporary position in New York for two years. This text explores Martha's relationship to her son, her husband, Delia and her daughters, and to her place in the masculine world. We discover that Martha often lives vicariously through Delia, and even tells her new lover Javier that Delia's daughters are her own. Often times, unfortunately, it seems easier for women either as writers or liars to pretend to live someone else's life rather than their own.

Her journey becomes a sojourn to break away from all that seemed the most valid in her life: religion, home, and social status. She learns that she has been hiding her existence beneath her dowdy school marm clothes and her roles as wife and mother. This time it is Delia who implores her to stop feeling sorry for herself, to go and establish a new life.

En route to New York, Martha stops in Mexico to vacation and see old friends. Here with her itinerary in limbo, her physical space echoes her condition. She is not at home, nor has she arrived at her destination. She is not divorced, yet not quite married anymore. Though she is still a mother, her role as such is one of diminished importance. The only ties to her previous existence are tenuous. She does not write to Delia and even decides not to call her on her birthday, something that she has always done in the past. Within this newfound space, she is able to begin to reinvent herself as a mother, a friend, and a lover.

Javier, her lover, is an expatriate. It is significant that her reinterpretation involves someone who can relate to her previous life in Argentina. His being Argentine helps her to retrace the past more effectively. Her refusal to call Delia allows her to more freely superimpose her own identity while she attempts to break through her past. Martha rejects writing Delia, as this act would be "el testimonio de su metamorfosis" (testimony of her metamorphosis [97]). Once again we see the important connection between the written word and its sustentative value to real life. Nevertheless, it is Delia who says that Martha needs to take this trip and that "no se vive de acuerdo a un programa" (one doesn't live according to a program [178]). These two women have an unmistakably deep bond that has yet to permit them to affirm their individual freedoms.

Martha has found happiness with this new liberty but regains her old role upon her reunion with her husband and son. It becomes more difficult for her to remain liberated when faced with her former reality. She has learned however, that her previous life was created for her by the roles ascribed to her, and that she accepted these functions in a complicitous manner. Even in self imposed exile it is difficult not to perpetuate the repressions of the past.

Boca de tormenta is a collection of 26 hauntingly tragic short stories. Clearly the unifying theme here is the dramatic struggle of the female characters against their stereotyped traits. The protagonists battle their restricted choices, their passive and sedentary existence, while grappling with a tenacious devotion to family, and the compelling and destructive power of love. The title story conveys these conflicts through Ana, a junior high student, whose body belies her age. Although Ana does not have an idealized view of love and marriage because she has watched her cousin become fat and unhappy since her wedding, she still longs for the sensations that her first kiss will bring her. Her desirous hunger is more fully awakened by Sebastian, the seventeen-year-old brother of her best friend. Against the advice of her mother, aunts, cousin, sister, and friend, she decides to explore this feeling and seeks to expand the attention that she has recently received from Sebastian. Expecting to find him in the dark passage between their houses, she is instead confronted by the neighborhood idiot who pronounces judgment upon her by calling her "Mala" (the Bad One). It is a sad comment on how society's values are passed on to all members, even those unable to determine a responsible opinion. Two other stories that strongly present the battle between a woman's self realization and society's expectations are "Nadie ocupará su lugar" (No One Will Take Her Place) and "Flores de azúcar" (Candy Flowers). The first narrative relates the woes of Nora who is overcome by responsibility after her mother's death. Nora gives up her own life to assume the matron role which includes a refusal to confront her father or believe her sister about his incestuous conduct. She kills herself, unable to cope with her hopeless future. In "Flores de azucar," we find Mariel who at close to 40 years of age has finally realized that she has had no life of her own. Time has played a rude game on her. It has given her the same body as her twin sister who she advised against marriage saying it would turn her into a fat cow. When Norma, her twin dies, she is even more tormented by a life that might have been. The death of her father brings Mariel's mother to live with her, furthering her necessity to live another's life in order to make her life seem worthy. Unhappily her body and her life are ruinous, and she agonizes over a love that never materialized to make her feel whole on her own. Evidently her mistake has been not seeking her own successes.

"El silbato" (The Whistle) deals more directly with Jewish themes. It demonstrates the great space that has occurred between the generations, leaving the immigrant's children with an alienation that is twofold. These descendants lack the understanding of their cultural roots and do not fully integrate into the dominant society. "La vereda de enfrente" (The Sidewalk Out Front) is one of the few narratives to directly treat the topic of the Holocaust. A young girl confined to her room by hepatitis interprets the lives of those viewed from her balcony, according to what she thinks she has learned from books, the radio, and movies. The unsightly appearances of her neighbors "la Gringa" (The immigrant woman) and "el Borracho" (the drunkard) and their sons earn her disdain. Upon her recovery she is allowed to do an errand where she is confronted by the realization that this is a family of Holocaust survivors who had lost previous spouses and children to the gas chambers. Although she is somewhat enlightened by this experience, her whispers as the story closes demonstrate the difficulty that she will have incorporating this knowledge into her own existence. The ending is yet another device for the portrayal of the relatively static effect these profound impressions produce in our daily lives.

In *A las escondidas* Plager returns to the theme of women in search of themselves. Within the masculine world, these women are but pieces of the spectrum by which we are all identified: married, separated, attached, or single. Their link is personified in the character of Don Salvatore, the incarnation of various patriarchal stereotypes. The protagonists, Cecilia, Ana, and Nora, begin to question all that Don Salvatore represents. The problematics of the story are characteristic of the battles facing middle-class Argentine women. In spite of their unhappiness all the women, to a certain extent, resist the ultimate confrontations that would rock their safe world. Instead, they prefer to enclose themselves in the little worlds which their comfortable lives afford them. Recognizing how the past has shaped their present causes them to reject or ignore the circumstances which brought them to their current state.

The protagonist in *Alguien está mirando* is a man, Julián. The importance of the prodigal son in Jewish culture is shown early on in the text by the statement, "Ahora el futuro era yo, ese muchacho flaco, único hijo de un matrimonio de inmigrantes" (Now I was the future, that skinny boy, the only child of an immigrant couple [12]). Although the main character in the novel is a man, much of the story's emphasis is placed on the different female characters and their relation to him. His wife's life is constructed from the utopian view of perfect behavior in a perfect world. The object of his obsessive voyeurism, Marina, is a cripple who faces the world as do most women with little hope for recovery from their condition. Julián, however, knows that although he may feel like a failure today, something tomorrow may likely change his luck in the future. He has attempted to break free from his robotic existence but finds himself in a web of lies, trying to live two lives instead of choosing one. The duplicitous nature of Jewish life in Argentina is evident not only in Julián but also in his Polish parents who still cling to the past unable to fully embrace Argentine culture. As the book closes Julián's father tears up some old photographs while whispering a Hebrew prayer. He holds hope that this new country will evolve into the promised land. Julián is still somewhat confused even though he has analyzed the cause of his dilemma. He is an incomplete man. Marina, in the physical sense, is the incomplete woman. His relationship with her as well as his relationship with his wife remain unresolved. Julian, like his father before him has accepted his position for now, as do most women and Jews because "así es" (that's the way it is [190]).

In *Mujeres pudorosas* there is a culmination of style and Jewish themes that reaches beyond all previous works by Plager. The book focuses upon two female characters Graciela, a writer, and Clara, the protagonist of Graciela's novel. Clara's trip to Israel to reunite with a former lover, Eleazar, after the death of her husband, is a pilgrimage for Graciela as well. Graciela explores her own Jewish roots vicariously through the experiences of Clara. Their parallels are many as Graciela begins to shape Clara's life in ways which she cannot yet apply to her own situation. There are also some interesting twists and interpretations in Graciela's novel. Graciela is divorced from her husband Gustavo, but she makes Clara a widow, who after her Gustavo's death, more quickly breaks free. Eleazar is of Arab descent and her reunion with him in Israel helps Clara to reclaim her past which like The Wall "es una enorme cicatriz" (is an enormous scar [65]).

For Clara and Graciela this return to memories of family and religion is an attempt to overcome their pains of the past both religious and personal. "Recordar es un modo de hacer justicia, dice Eleazar" (Remembering is a way of making justice, Eleazar says [68]). Clara's grandfather taught her Jewish history. He explained to her that for Jews injustice is a constant. These two recurring ideas reflect the essential need to redress the study of Jewish literature. As Graciela's novel progresses, the informed reader must extend the semblance of characters to their creator, Plager the original author.

Graciela's sister comments on the rarity of the novel's plot and the fact that it takes place in Israel instead of Argentina. Nevertheless, she recognizes this dual location is in reality part of being Jewish which to her seems easier than "ser algo determinado" (being something determinate [83]). The tempo of the book that Graciela writes is similarly ambiguous. Clara and Eleazar are not following any particular path, nor are they tied to any destiny. What unites these lovers is a common history of misery, injustice, desolation, and fear. To them the flesh is the route to the Promised Land. Graciela's sister has a friend, Norma, who in some aspects resembles Clara. These similarities quickly fade when Graciela meets Norma. She tells Norma how she had begun to write a novel that would have been a replica of an old movie but decided to write something different. Norma is a typical progeny of antiquated ideas and reminds her of most of her own relatives. It is obvious that female writers, both Plager, the author, and Graciela, her character, find it easier to create a truly liberated woman with their pens, rather than to personally be one.

As Plager's novel develops, Graciela finds certain analogies between her female characters, her friends, and her own life. She is introduced to Simon, who like herself, also has enjoyed investigating books, leaving him little thought for analyzing his own existence. Graciela asks herself if she doesn't look to fiction to provide what real life has not been able to. The novel which Graciela is writing hampers her own personal progression. Is Clara's mechanical existence in Buenos Aires a reflection of her state of being? Why does a Jew always need to be in a state of transition? Graciela decides it is time to separate herself from her past and from her characters in order to create a new life. In the second to the last chapter, we find that Graciela is determined to live in the moment, not in the past or the future. The final chapter ends as Clara also opts to enjoy the present.

Jewish women carry a burden of the past unique from all other cultures. Their cultural history exacerbates the need for a future with a happy ending. What Silvia Plager, and her character Graciela, have demonstrated is the necessity to take pleasure in the present. Graciela doesn't know where her romance with Simon will lead her. Clara returns to Buenos Aires without Eleazar, satisfied with her indefinite plans. For these characters there is no definitive end.

Como papas para varenikes is Plager's contribution to the genre of culinary novels that has developed into a worldwide phenomenon following the success of *Como agua para chocolate* (*Like Water for Chocolate*; 1989) by Mexican writer Laura Esquivel (1950). Plager's titillating style progresses through recipes which the male protagonist, Saúl, hopes will lead to "el Kama Sutra Judío" (the Jewish Kama Sutra). Saúl believes sex will not reduce the importance of the meal but rather add to it with active enjoyment. The story centers on the courtship of two main characters, Cathy and Saúl. Their romantic involvement goes from simmering to sizzling paralleled by culinary counterparts for all seduction sequences.

The book begins with a recipe followed by a chapter where the reader is introduced to a youthful Cathy who years later becomes a caterer. Food becomes the metaphor for the indissoluble bonds of Russian cuisine, Judaism, family, and love. Cathy's vocation demonstrates the loss of tradition in modern life as families turn to outsiders for their typically Jewish fare which can be emotionally and chronologically all consuming.

Saúl's wish is fulfilled in the final chapters when he consummates his relationship with Cathy. The book's title alludes to the first time they make love; he is the *papa* and she is the *varenike* earnestly compressing and urging him on. In the end the Jewish Kama Sutra does appear. Here cooking utensils and ingredients join with bodies to enhance the sexual act. The Jewish theme even arises in body positions where couples are to emulate symbolic forms such as the Star of David and the menorah. Clearly this Jewish feast is designed to arouse not only the tastebuds, but to stimulate sexual passion and humor as well.

Silvia Plager deserves consideration because her themes can appeal to a wide spectrum of readers. The complexities of her characters' existences provide a range of interest not only to feminist and Jewish scholars, but also to lay readers who must contend with the normal complications of modern existence.

PRIMARY BIBLIOGRAPHY

A las escondidas. Buenos Aires: Galerna, 1986.

Alguien está mirando. Buenos Aires: Planeta, 1991.

Amigas. Buenos Aires: Galerna, 1982.

Boca de tormenta. Buenos Aires: Galerna, 1984.

Como papas para varenikes. Buenos Aires: Beas Ediciones, 1994.

Mujeres pudorosas. Buenos Aires: Atlántida, 1993.

Prohibido despertar. Buenos Aires: Galerna, 1983.

SECONDARY BIBLIOGRAPHY

Bilbija, Ksenija. "Spanish American Women Writers: Simmering Over a Low Fire." *Studies in 20th Century Literature* 20.1 (1996): 147-65.

Gimbernat González, Ester. "*A las escondidas*: jugando a las casitas." In her *Aventuras del desacuerdo: novelistas argentinas de los 80*. Buenos Aires: Danilo Albero Vergara, 1992. 255-57.

—. "El subversivo territorio del deseo: *Prohibido despertar*." In her *Aventuras del desacuerdo: novelistas argentinas de los 80*. Buenos Aires: Danilo Albero Vergara, 1992. 99-103.

Grosgold, Judith. Rev. of *Mujeres pudorosas*. *Noaj* 10 (1995): 123-24.

Susan Romain Speirs

PORZECANSKI, TERESA (Uruguay; 1945)

Teresa Porzecanski was born in Montevideo May 5, 1945, the descendant of immigrants from Libau in the Baltics on her father's side and Syria on her mother's. Porzecanski has advanced degrees in social work and anthropology which she teaches at the University of the Republic. Her field work in oral history deals with texts about the immigrant experience in Uruguay and about ethnic relations. *Historias de vida de inmigrantes judíos al Uruguay* (Life Stories of Jewish Immigrants to Uruguay; 2nd ed. 1986) provides a model for an anthropological study of the immigrant experience with a detailed history which sets the context for the life stories. She has published a book about the rituals of the Guaraní and Charrúa Indians, and her most recent research deals with aging black workers whose social ascent was impeded by subtle racism in her country.

Porzecanski's fiction has been translated into English, French, Dutch, and German. Her background in anthropology shapes her approach to creative writing which explores hidden recesses of human existence. In her collection of short stories *Construcciones* (Constructions; 1979) the settings are prosaic—the room in a second-class hotel, the laboratory, a muddy village, a kitchen filled with cobwebs—but strange transformations can take place there. The carpenter constructs a totem and gives renewed life to planks of wood. In a more recent work, *La respiración es una fragua* (Breath is a Forge; 1989) she offers minute stories—tiny illuminated images of reality as fragile as bubbles. Once again the settings are lonely and ordinary but the prose is carefully crafted. Porzecanski's intent is serious, to procreate with words.

The novels, just as slender and controlled as her volumes of short stories, take an anthropological approach to her subjects. In Porzecanski's fiction there is a sense of mythic time and experiences which frees the characters from the constrictions of linear time. Crevices, cracks, cemeteries, unoccupied buildings, courtyard apartments, basements, and garbage dumps are some of the hidden areas Porzecanski explores. Her language breaks patterns of syntax and she often breaks the normal rhythm of Spanish by choosing proparoxytonic words (words stressed on the antepenultimate syllable). Her characters are deliberately understated and unremarkable, but she charges the most common elements with magical qualities.

In *La invención de los soles* (Sun Inventions; 1982) the protagonist is revealed in brief vignettes about her various roles as the daughter of immigrants, the proprietor of a notions shop, a researcher, and a writer; however, the mannequin in the shop acquires mystical powers in the eyes of the patrons. Ironically, although the protagonist searches for universal truth and knowledge, it is the mannequin which can predict the future.

In Porzecanski's next work, *Una novela erótica* (An Erotic Novel; 1986), she redefines the parameters of erotic fiction. Just as in Mario Vargas Llosa's (1936) *La tía Julia y el escribidor* (*Aunt Julia and the Scriptwriter*; 1977), the protagonist is a fledgling newswriter for a radio station, but rather than exalt the physical attributes and exploits of the characters, she eschews explicit descriptions of their sexual encounters. There is, however, a description of the relationship of an affluent and jaded sperm with an indulged and bored ova. Porzecanski links novel with eros, that is words with procreation and creation. She deals with many stories of beginnings from Adam and Eve to the Cro-Magnon man, in her search for a literature which will connect with her readers in challenging and new ways. Her work seeks to forge a new solidarity to counteract the solitude and alienation of the hibernal Uruguayans.

As in the first two novels, Porzecanski's most recent novels, *Mesías en Montevideo* (Messiah in Montevideo; 1989) and *Perfumes de Cartago* (Perfumes of Carthage; 1994), present fragments of plot with only a vague linear chronology. In *Mesías in Montevideo*, she links two messianic figures—the underground guerrilla leader and the false Messiah Shabbtai Tzevi—in a story which strips the heroic and romantic qualities from the protagonist. The self-sacrificing prostitute and the Marxist revolutionary, stock characters in Latin American fiction, are portrayed in a very different vein. Once again the setting is the rubble and ruins of a bleak urban landscape. Here tales of torture and subversive activities, are told with ironic distance and ambiguity. The Sephardic ancestor in *Mesías* allowed the reader only a brief vision into the world of the Jews who wandered and finally left the Middle Eastern communities. Porzecanski's return to this world in *Perfumes de Cartago*, after extensive research into the Sephardim and rabbinic lore, funded by a Guggenheim Fellowship, provides rich sensorial vignettes of immgrant life in Uruguay in the turbulent thirties and the communities of Syria and the crises which compelled the Jews to leave. The grandmother and her nursemaid, a descendant of African slaves, carry the prophetic voice in this novel.

If heroic tales of charismatic male leaders are deconstructed, the sense that the community needs liberating myths persists. Porzecanski extends to the fiction reader a subtle and unusual vision of Latin America, and, as a historian and anthropologist, she provides a link with the Jewish past. Her protagonist in *Perfumes de Cartago*, Lunita Mualdab, bears the large iron key to her family's apartment in Montevideo just like those marranos who proudly passed on the key to the homes they left in Spain. Yet Lunita returns to her home after thirty years to find the squalor and decay of a way of life which has all but disappeared. Despair is the staple of Porzecanski's characters and narrators who exhaust themselves in attempts at alchemy and transcendence. Although their transformations lead them to death more often than to a mystical experience of the universe, a certain hope for the future remains because reading and writing can lead them to a collective experience with others. Her characters mirror Porzecanski's desire to achieve an intense form of communication between herself and the reader and between both and the universe.

PRIMARY BIBLIOGRAPHY
Creative Writing

El acertijo y otros cuentos. Montevideo: Editorial Arca, 1967.

Ciudad impune. Montevideo: Monte Sexto, 1986.

"Clashes Down Below" and "Family's End." Trans. by Johnny Payne. *Paper Air* 4.3 (Summer 1990): 79-82.

Construcciones. Montevideo: Arca, 1979.

Esta manzana roja. Montevideo: Letras, 1972. Excerpt in English translation by David Pritchard in *Echad: An Anthology of Latin American Jewish Writings.* Ed. Robert Kalechofsky and Roberta Kalechofsky. Marblehead: Micah Publications, 1980. 124-27.

Intacto el corazón. Montevideo: Banda Oriental, 1976.

Historias para mi abuela. Montevideo: Letras, 1970.

"Implacable Ancestors." Trans. by Johnny Payne. *Stanford Humanities Review* 1.1 (Spring 1989): 25-32.

La invención de los soles. Stockholm: Nordan, 1979.

Mesías en Montevideo. Montevideo: Signos, 1989.

Una novela erótica. Montevideo: Margen, 1986.

"Parricide." Trans. by David Pritchard. In *Echad: An Anthology of Latin American Jewish Writings.* Ed. Robert Kalechofsky and Roberta Kalechofsky. Marblehead: Micah Publications, 1980. 122-23.

Perfumes de Cartago. Montevideo: Trilce, 1994.

La respiración es una fragua. Montevideo: Trilce, 1989.

"Rojl Eisips." In *Cuentos judíos latinoamericanos.* Ed. Ricardo Feierstein. Buenos Aires: Milá, 1989. 225-28.

"The Story of a Cat." Trans. by Roland Hamilton. In *Short Stories by Latin American Women: The Magic and the Real.* Ed. Celia Correas de Zapata. Houston: Arte Público Press, 1990. 176-80.

"Tercera apología." In *Antología del cuento hispanoamericano*. Ed. Fernando Burgos. México, D.F.: Porrúa, 1991. 789-94. Also in *Mujeres en espejo 2: narradoras latinoamericanas, siglo XX*. Ed. Sara Sefchovich. México, D.F.: Folios Ediciones, 1985. 110-13.

"Witchcraft of the Tribe." Trans. by Johnny Payne. *Black Warrior Review* 18.2 (Spring 1992): 126-34.

Nonfiction

Curanderos y caníbales: ensayos antropológicos sobre Guaraníes, Charrúas, Bororos, Terenas y adivinos. Montevideo: Luis A. Retta, 1989; 2da ed. corregida y aumentada, 1993.

Historias de vida de inmigrantes judíos al Uruguay. Editor and preliminary study. 2nd ed. Montevideo: Comunidad Israelita de Montevideo, 1988.

El universo cultural del idisch. Montevideo: Comunidad Israelita, 1992.

SECONDARY BIBLIOGRAPHY
Criticism

Barr, Lois Baer. "Recreating the Code: Teresa Porzecanski." In her *Isaac Unbound: Patriarchal Traditions in the Latin American Jewish Novel*. Tempe, AZ: ASU Center for Latin American Studies, 1995. 159-82.

—. Rev. *La respiración es una fragua*. *Hispamérica* 18.53-54 (1989): 213-15.

Cosse, Rómulo. "Teresa Porzecanski: cuentos en luz." *El Día* 31 Oct., 1980: 5.

Payne, Johnny. "Cutting Up History: The Uses of Aleatory Fiction in Teresa Porzecanski and Harry Matthews." In his *Conquest of the New Word: Experimental Fiction and Translation in the Americas*. Austin: U of Texas P, 1993. 76-98.

—. "Recovering the Body, or Translation in the Panopticon." *ellipsis* 1.1 (1990): 71-83.

Interviews

Kirkpatrick, Gwen. "Entrevista con Teresa Porzecanski." *Discurso Literario* 5.2 (1988): 305-10.

Lois Baer Barr

RABINOVICH, JOSÉ (Argentina; 1903-78)

The hardships of José Rabinovich's early years form a substantial subtext that informs much of his prolific literary production. Born in Bialystok,

Russia (now Poland), he emigrated to Argentina as a young man in 1924, motivated by the desire to escape a grim landscape defined by war, fear, starvation, and cold. Establishing himself in Buenos Aires, Rabinovich worked first as a typesetter before eventually making his living as the owner of a printing press. According to the autobiographical information in the prologue to his novel *El perro de Maidanek* (The Dog from Maidanek; 1968), Rabinovich began to write as an adolescent in a small Russian town in an attempt to overcome the feelings of shame caused by his poverty. Critic Naomi Lindstrom notes that Rabinovich's early Yiddish-language literary production is not readily available ("José Rabinovich: A Poetics of Disputation" 193); an additional bibliographical complication is the difficulty in determining the exact titles of earlier works, the 1928 *Entre el agua y el fuego* (Between Water and Fire) or *Entre el fuego y el agua* (Between Fire and Water) is a case in point.

A considerable number of Rabinovich's hundreds of early short stories, which first appeared in Argentine Jewish newspapers and magazines in Yiddish, were republished in Spanish translation in several collections, including *Cabizbajos* (Heads Bowed; 1943), *Tercera clase* (Third Class; 1944) and *Pan duro* (Hard Bread; 1953). In these short pieces of fiction as well as in the later stories included in *Cuentos de pico y pala* (Stories of the Pick and Shovel; 1971), Rabinovich explores the stark themes of persecution and Jewish suffering. In the opening work of *Cuentos de pico y pala*, "Un año muy, muy fecundo" (A Very, Very Fecund Year), Rabinovich presents the incongruous contrast between nature—neutral, thriving, unaware of human-inflicted brutality—and the war-time degradation experienced by the young Jewish woman Libe, who witnesses the grotesque death of her husband and subsequently is forced to take flight, seeking protection in a heartless world. She takes refuge in the stable of a Christian family, and finds compassion in the life-saving milk of one of the stable's other occupants, a sow. Rabinovich's stories are populated by the most wretched of the poor, the dysentery-plagued, the lice-ridden, the physically impaired: the Jew as "other," inhabiting a society removed to a great degree from the comfort and safety denied to them by a hostile world. In "Piojos" (Lice [*Pan duro*]), war-time refugees attempting to flee Poland are caught in a downward spiral of misery, reaching such abject depths of human debasement that the simple act of delousing brings a heavenly peace and sense of well-being otherwise unattainable in a world gone mad. The hostility and violence which marks the lives of many of Rabinovich's characters turns into cold-blooded cruelty in another story, "Intacto" (Intact [*Cuentos de pico y pala*]), set now in German-occupied Ukraine. In the protagonist, a sadistic yet pathetic German soldier named Lübke, Rabinovich portrays an embodiment of the banality of evil—a Jew-hunting killer and torturer simultaneously brutal and unremarkable, less capable of feeling than a cow. Even without the horrors of persecution, Rabinovich's protagonists confront other difficulties, perhaps the most wrenching being the eternally problematic dialogue between man and his Creator. Jews, pious and not, try to comprehend the often incomprehensible designs of their God—an effort which frecuently is made all the more challenging in the face of apparently meaningless or undeserved hardships. The main character of the short story "Motel el Tiñoso" (Motel the Wretched [*Tercera clase*]) takes refuge in the synagogue to ask God why justice cannot be done, railing against what he perceives to be God's indifference to His people's plight, and when this crisis of faith extends to his relations with the rabbi, the ensuing conflict cleaves the village population. In another piece from the same collection, "Cirios sabáticos" (Sabbath Candles), Míndele is a rabbi's daughter who marries a village miller. When her husband goes off to war, she is left alone, struggling to preserve her faith in both God and the man to whom God has joined her. The unblessed Sabbath candles that she lights each Friday night are her protection from the intrusion of an endlessly complicated external world, yet they are caught in a type of religious cross-fire with the clanging of the church bells. The inescapable sound of the bells magnifies Míndele's feelings of isolation and loss, calling into question the quietly symbolic power of the flame that must compete with the bewildering voice of incessantly pealing bells.

Coexisting with the images of the disenfranchised Jews who struggle to eke out mere subsistence against all odds in the small towns of Russia and Poland, Rabinovich's fiction and drama also turns its eye to the resettled Jews in Argentina. Life in South America's temperate climes, while less harsh, sees few dreams fulfilled, few expectations satisfied. Economic and social problems, the struggle to maintain cultural and religious identity, the impossibility of exorcising the ghosts and demons of the past—and the occasional small personal triumph: these emigrated Jews continue to confront the somber realities of a world little-inclined to allowing them safe and untroubled passage in their day-to-day lives. In "El baterista" (The Drummer [*Cuentos de pico y pala*]), the protagonist, Jacob, is a concentration camp survivor so scarred by his experience that it seems as though he might have at least partially lost his mind. Although many years have passed since the war, Jacob is incapable of comprehending the scope and ultimate significance of the industry of death spawned by so many killers. The faces of his dead wife and daughter haunt him as he plays—images which bring him even closer to insanity. Rabinovich quietly builds on the hallucinatory torments of the drummer whose only solace is to purchase his own cemetery plot in preparation for the death that now defines his life. The situation presented in "Un ilustre vecino" (An Illustrious Neighbor), from the same collection, highlights the problems of assimilation and the conflict between finding community and preserving culture. A lawyer's son courts the daughter of his working-class Jewish neighbors. The lawyer, Mr. Campos, is not pleased at the prospect of such an unequal union: his neighbor is a tailor, the family does not enjoy economically privileged status, and the parents' imperfect, immigrant Spanish is yet another reason for the well-heeled to recoil. Nevertheless, Campos is a good socialist, and as a good socialist who publicly has upheld the ideal of the brotherhood of man, he understands that to recriminate his son's choice would be an uncomfortably reactionary response. It is the inexplicable, ungrateful rejection of the apparently sincere would-be suitor by the Jew that shocks the Campos family as it introduces a destabilizing element into the Argentine social fabric. In the person of Bernardo the tailor, Rabinovich presents an example of oddly haughty humility: the workworn, coarse hand of Bernardo was not meant to shake the elegantly pampered hand of the lawyer. The daughter of the Jew was not meant to marry the son of the gentile; the preservation of Jewish identity is linked to the memory of culture. When the indignant young man decides to convert in order to be able to marry the woman he desires, he is stunned even more to discover that his overture is rejected out of hand: an irresponsible youth seeking meaningless conversion as a mechanism to achieve the object of romantic desire is not what the Jewish community needs. The strength of Jewish culture does not derive from empty gestures made by people who think that their mere presence legitimizes the beliefs of the "other" among them. The themes that Rabinovich treats in many of these short stories reveal a "proletarian" focus that is an essential component of the "social-realist project" in Argentine art (Foster 67); the plight of impoverished Jewish families—in both the old and new worlds—is the touchstone in Rabinovich's fiction and these same conflicts, struggles and anguished crises of faith also define his drama and poetry.

In the opening scene of the four-act piece *Con pecado concebida* (Conceived in Sin; 1975), Rabinovich juxtaposes Christian and Judaic imagery—the cross and priest forming a tableau framed against the barely visible violinist who plays the Kol Nidre. The dying woman receiving Extreme Unction is María, who confesses that her greatest sin was having fallen in love with a Jew. The retrospective presentation of María's unhappy married life; her encounter with the Jewish taxi driver and holocaust survivor, David; and the ensuing difficulties that their mixed-religion relationship entails are the elements which provide Rabinovich with the opportunity to explore the motif of "mixed marriages and the inevitable trials and tribulations arising" (Foster 132) from the problematic union between these different religious groups seemingly divided by overwhelming psychological barriers. María's attempts to bridge the gap that separates her from her lover cannot erase the incomprehension that defines Christian reaction to Jewish culture. María is no more able to adopt Jewish customs superficially than David is capable of escaping his religious heritage or the voices of the past, and their relationship is destined to fail miserably. Rabinovich's presentation of the action in *Con pecado concebida* is marked by "skillful use of conventions of the modern theater that we generally associate with the theater of the absurd" (Foster 133) and the image of the mistreated violinist who reappears throughout the work, threading the haunting melody of the music of the holiest day of the Jewish year, Yom Kippur, provokes a disturbing uncomfortableness intended to question the nature of cultural identity.

El gran castigo (The Great Punishment; 1976) a dramatic work in three acts (and a prologue meant to be read by the author) presents a similarly perturbing depiction in a very different setting. Rabinovich's play is set in a convent located in a small unidentified fishing village during wartime. The mother superior finds herself at wit's end trying to cope with the constant small tragedies that must be confronted: in particular, the arrival of desperate Jewish mothers who are forced by circumstances to bring their young daughters to the convent as a refuge of last resort. Rabinovich's portrayal of the plight of these abandoned daughters cared for by a woman who vacillates between strained kindness and psychological cruelty forms the center of the work. The young Jewish girls, kept in the convent's dark basement and unable to move about in the light of day, are in turn disposed to abandoning their heritage—a pathetic cultural betrayal that brings tragic consequences even as it opens the door to the possibility of redemption of the characters who do maintain their Jewish identity.

Rabinovich's considerable poetic production reconsiders many of the themes found in his prose and theater, in a style generally devoid of sentimentality while simultaneously charged with anguish. Avant-garde tendencies combine with a frank and unambiguous presentation of troubling doubts and a search for answers. *El violinista bajo el tejado* (The Fiddler Under the Roof; 1970) is an example of the poet's desire to infuse his work with reminiscences of "Jewish, especially biblical, stylistic tradition" while at the same time distancing it "from high art" (JR: A Poetics of Disputation" 102). Glimpses of working class life, of simple pleasures, of heart-felt solidarity with one's fellow human beings alternate with pain-filled declamations that starkly outline the worst of the human condition. In numerous long poems structured as monologues, Rabinovich attempts to establish communication with God: does He remember the poet? "Quién será" (Who Can it Be) from the volume *Dios mediante* (With the Help of God; 1976) contrasts the anxiety of the poet with the peace that he seeks in God's remembrance. A similiar type of frustrated dialogue is found in "Larga distancia" (Long

Distance) from the 1969 collection *Rapsodía judía* (Jewish Rhapsody): can God hear the poet's voice? Is He listening? Even as he prays at the Wailing Wall, can a man be sure that his prayers reach God? In another instance of the poet's voice addressing his Creator directly ("Tal vez" [Perhaps] from *Misa de un play boy* [Playboy Mass; 1972]) Rabinovich questions the power of God to console and comfort his creation—perhaps that is not even His intention.

The apocalyptic visions of *Hombre escatimado* (Grudging Man; 1969) bring forth a world populated by tormentors and victims. The horrors of war, in all of its countless manifestations, demand a righteous voice whose clarity sweeps the evil from its hiding. The mother who sinks into insanity after the brutal murder of her young son; the elderly rabbi whose wise, kindly eyes are plucked out by the German soldier—share Rabinovich's universe with grandfathers whose quiet lives are framed by their grandchildrens' concern. Racial, religious, cultural tensions, and Nazi atrocities are all part of Rabinovich's presentation: the poems in this collection sound an alarm which cannot be ignored and Rabinovich squarely places himself with the forces who confront the hatred and the killing. The tranquility enjoyed by fortunate grandparents is a worthy aspiration that perhaps may be made possible through the clamor of enough voices raised against mindless violence.

In an existence marked by youthful suffering, the difficulties of the immigrant experience, a life-long committment to work, and the expression of cultural and religious identity in his literary production, José Rabinovich demonstrates his understanding of the human condition. In his varied and extensive writings, he casts his lot with those most in need of an advocate's voice, adding to the polyphony of Argentine artistic creativity.

PRIMARY BIBLIOGRAPHY

Los acusados. Trans. by Adela Shliapochnik. Buenos Aires: Editorial Israel, 1947; Buenos Aires: Biblioteca Humanitas, 1974.

Alas desplumadas. Buenos Aires: El Hombre, 1972.

El arquero de estrellas. Buenos Aires: El Hombre, 1972.

Cabizbajos. Preface by Elías Castelnuovo. Trans. by Rebeca Mactas de Polak. Buenos Aires: n.p., 1943.

Campanas a media asta. Buenos Aires: Fabril, 1969; Buenos Aires: Candelabro, 1976.

Una cana negra. Buenos Aires: El Hombre, 1972.

Canción sin cuna. Buenos Aires: El Hombre, 1972.

Cazador de luciérnagas. Buenos Aires: El Hombre, 1972.

Cena para un ayuno. Buenos Aires: El Hombre, 1972.

Con pecado concebida. Buenos Aires: Ediciones del Carro de Tespis, 1975.

Cuentos de pico y pala. Buenos Aires: Platense, 1971.

Dios mediante. Buenos Aires: Nuevas Ediciones Argentinas, 1976.

El gran castigo: Obra en tres actos y un prólogo. Buenos Aires: Nuevas Ediciones Argentinas, 1976.

Hombre escatimado. Buenos Aires: Ediciones Dead Weight, 1969.

Luz de eclipse. Buenos Aires: El Hombre, 1972.

Misa de un play boy. Buenos Aires: El Hombre, 1972.

Lo que no se dijo, 1943-1956. Buenos Aires: Gure, 1956.

Los muertos no quieren creerlo. Buenos Aires: Platense, 1969.

Pan duro. Trans. by Adela Shliapochnik. Buenos Aires: Siglo Veinte, 1952.

El perro de Maidanek. Buenos Aires: Platense, 1968.

Rapsodía judía. Buenos Aires: Candelabro, 1969.

Rapsodía negra. Barcelona: Lagis, 1971.

Rapsodía rusa. Barcelona: Lagis, 1971.

Sobras de una juventud. Preface by Ulises Petit de Murat. Buenos Aires: Crisol, 1976. Preface by Enrique de Gandia; Buenos Aires: Crisol, 1977. (Autobiography).

Tercera clase. Preface by Elías Castelnuovo. Trans. by Rebeca Mactas de Polak. Buenos Aires: Sophos, 1944; Barcelona: Linosa, 1969 (without the Castelnuovo preface, but including a prologue by Ricardo Baeza).

Trinos y truenos. Buenos Aires: El Hombre, 1972.

El violinista bajo el tejado. Buenos Aires: Platense, 1970.

Yo soy Cristo. Buenos Aires: El Hombre, 1972.

Yo soy Judas. Barcelona: Linosa, 1971.

SECONDARY BIBLIOGRAPHY
Criticism

Baeza, Ricardo. "Prólogo" to Rabinovich's *Tercera clase.* Barcelona: Editorial Linosa, 1969. Reprinted from Rabinovich, *Los acusados.* Buenos Aires: Editorial Israel, 1947. 2-11.

Dejemos que hablen los críticos. Buenos Aires: Artes Gráficas Cañuelas (printer), 1972. No publisher or editor given. (A collection of brief "clipping"-style comments on Rabinovich's writing).

Foster, David William. "Argentine Jewish Dramatists: Aspects of a National Consciousness." In his *Cultural Diversity in Latin American Literature.* Albuquerque: U of New Mexico P, 1994. 95-150 (specifically on Rabinovich 132-38).

—. "José Rabinovich's Jewish Immigrants." In his *Social Realism in the Argentine Narrative*. North Carolina Studies in the Romance Languages and Literatures. Chapel Hill: University of North Carolina Department of Romance Languages, 1986. 66-71.

Gandia, Enrique de. "Prólogo" to Rabinovich's *Sobras de una juventud*. Buenos Aires: Crisol, 1977. 5-11.

Glickman, Nora. "Tipología del judío moderno en *Con pecado concebida* de José Rabinovich. *Alba de América* 7.12-13 (1989): 61-73.

Lahitte, Ana E. "La poesía de José Rabinovich." *Testigo* (Buenos Aires) 7 (1972): 144-45.

Liacho, Lázaro. "Apuntes sobre la vida y la obra de José Rabinovich." In Rabinovich's *Campanas a media asta*. Buenos Aires: Candelabro, 1976. i-v.

Lindstrom, Naomi. "José Rabinovich: A Poetics of Disputation." In her *Jewish Issues in Argentine Literature: Fron Gerchunoff to Szichman*. Columbia: U of Missouri P, 1989. 102-12.

—. "José Rabinovich: A Poetry of Overt Social Statement." *Yiddish* 9.1 (1993): 72-81.

Melo, Juan Vicente. "En el banquillo de *Los acusados*." *Texto Crítico* 10.29 (1984): 5-19.

Petit de Murat, Ulises. "José Rabinovich, sobreviviente." In Rabinovich's *Sobras de una juventud*. Buenos Aires: Crisol, 1976. 3-7.

Senkman, Leonardo. "Conflictos de aculturación en los relatos de José Rabinovich." In his *La identidad judía en la literatura argentina*. Buenos Aires: Pardés, 1983. 106-52.

Soto, Luis Emilio. "José Rabinovich." In *Historia de la literatura argentina*. 6 vols. Ed. Rafael Alberto Arrieta. Buenos Aires: Peuser, 1959. IV.359-60.

Weinstein, Ana E., and Miryam E. Gover de Nasatsky, comps. *Escritores judeo-argentinos: bibliografía 1900-1987*. 2 vols. Buenos Aires: Milá, 1994. II.91-95.

Interviews

Tiempo, César. "A manera de prólogo. Un diálogo con José Rabinovich". In Rabinovich's *El perro de Maidanek*. Buenos Aires/La Plata: Platense, 1968. 9-49.

—. "30 preguntas a José Rabinovich, un narrador de la estirpe de Agnón." *Davar* (Buenos Aires) 115 (1967): 61-78.

Nancy Posner

RAWET, SAMUEL (Brazil; 1929-84)

Samuel Rawet was born on July 23, 1929, in the little Polish town, Klimontow, and in 1936 he came to Brazil. His parents were small tradespeople ("luftmenshen") and, according to him very poor. Rawet kept in his mind the picture of a world now no longer in existence, that of the shtetl in its medieval form, which lasted in Eastern Europe through the eighteenth and nineteenth centuries, and came to an end with the Second World War.

His childhood and youth were spent in the suburbs of Rio de Janeiro, the setting, later on, of many of his tales. He helped his father and his brothers in their work as Jewish hire-purchase hucksters and later as furniture dealers. At the age of twenty-four he completed his engineering degree, while he was already taking part in literary groups, having done so since 1942. His first published book appeared in 1956 with *Contos do imigrante* (The Immigrant Tales). One aspect pointed out among others by literary critics is that Samuel Rawet was the first to give the theme of immigration and the immigrant the amplitude and standing required for it to be included in Brazilian literature.

Rawet's works comprise short stories, novellas, short essays and plays, these last rejected by him, though they revealed the dramatic vein found in his other writings. Besides the *Contos do imigrante*, he published *Diálogo* (Dialogue; 1963); *Abama* (1964), a novella; *Os sete sonhos* (The Seven Dreams) in 1967 which won the literary prize Prêmio Guimarães Rosa of the Fundação Educacional do Paraná; *O terreno de uma polegada quadrada* (The One Square Inch Lot; 1970); *Viagens de Ahasverus à terra alheia em busca de um passado que não existe porque futuro, e de um futuro que já passou porque sonhado* (The Voyages of Ahasverus to a Foreign Land in Search of a Past that Does Not Exist Because of the Future, and of a Future that has Already Passed because It Was Dreamt; 1970), a novella; *Que os mortos enterrem seus mortos* (Let the Dead Bury Their Dead; 1981), a collection of short stories that was published posthumously.

Also to be mentioned are two plays that were never published. The first was *Os amantes* (The Lovers; 1957), based on a story by Dinah Silveira de Queiroz (1917-1982) was staged in the Municipal Theater of Rio de Janeiro by Nicette Bruno and Paulo Goulart's company. The second play, *A noite que volta* (The Returning Night), about a Jew who collaborated with the Nazis in the concentration camps during the Second World War was produced for television in Rio de Janeiro and São Paulo. *A noite* was later rewritten with its title altered to *O lance de dados* (The Throw of the Dice). Of related interest are the 1970 essays *Consciência e valor* (Conscience and Valor), *Homossexualismo, sexualidade e valor* (Homosexuality, Sexuality, and Valor), *Alienação e realidade* (Alienation and Reality); *Eu-Tu-Ele* (I-Thou-He), in 1972, and *Angústia e conhecimento* (Anguish and Knowledge; 1978). In September 1977, in the periodical *Escrita*, he finally breaks with the Jews in an article entitled "Kafka e a mineralidade judaica ou a tonga da mironga do kabuletê" (Kafka and Judaic Minerality [the remainder is a nonsensical line from a song by Vinícius de Moraes]).

Samuel Rawet entered Brazilian history as one of the engineers who helped to build Brasília. A pioneer, he became disenchanted with the direction the capital was taking. His last years were marked by his isolation and his denial of the values of the Jewish tradition.

In Rawet's literary work there is an ample spiritual and cultural quality, akin to that of a universe of writers and works of the same kind: Martin Buber (1878-1965), Franz Kafka (1883-1924), Maksim Gorky (1868-1936), Fyodor M. Dostoyevsky (1821-81), Jorge Luis Borges (1899-1986), Thomas Mann (1875-1955), Joaquim Maria Machado de Assis (1839-1908) are some of the names that make up this universe of correspondences, of affinities with the writings of Rawet.

Hassidism studied by the Austrian Martin Buber at the beginning of the century would leave a profound impression on the life and ideas of Rawet. He referred to Kafka as that man of Prague who almost hid his wretchedness behind a serene and well-balanced prose. In Borges he extolled the erudition and creation. With Machado de Assis he identified himself by the tragic irony. Many times he showed his admiration for the Brazilian northeastern writers of the 1930s, Graciliano Ramos (1892-1953), José Lins do Rego (1901-57) and Jorge Amado (1912). Other Brazilian writers, his contemporary, Cornélio Penna (1896-1968), and of the present generation, Autran Dourado (1926) were important to his literary universe.

Besides these writers, Rawet has his name associated with that of other writers of Jewish origin such as Saul Bellow (1915) and Philip Roth (1933) in the United States who, given their fundamental differences, consider their Jewishness in existential terms. They question themselves about their condition as Jews in its dynamic relationship with literary writing.

The central themes in Rawet's works are the questioning of the solidarity ties that link men together: the disappointments, the frustrations; the underprivileged, the loneliness; the estrangement from and/or the seeking of the Jewish tradition.

The theme of the immigrant, the dramatic misunderstandings, basic in his writings, appear in greater and more tragic dimensions because that is man's plight, detached from circumstantial elements. It is the weariness produced by the unechoed cry in *Diálogo*. The Holocaust is transmuted into a spiritual reality, into the inner hell of the materiality of fears.

In fact, in Rawet's books not all the tales deal specifically with the Jewish theme. Many deal with conflicting family relationships in which lying and dissembling, insolence and submission prevail. In *Contos do imigrante* not all the stories tell us of the Jewish immigrant or of the problems of adaptation. But in all of them we see a tragic vision of the world reflected in the form of the incommunicability of relationships. This in turn brings out the memory of the suffering and exclusion of the Jewish people.

The main point in Rawet's fiction is the character, on whom the writer focuses his world view. He sees man's situation before the world as double-sided: on one side is man absorbed by reality, on the other man trying to force upon circumstances his own ways, his conception of others and of life.

His characters live through strong opposing feelings, that range from love to hate, expressing the violence, the suppressed fight against the world around them. They are almost always the victims of a world of appearances, of lies. Purity of intent butts against an impassable barrier as concerns other beings. Hence the conflict: incomprehension and a kind of bitter suffering, of life wasting itself away in the lack of understanding and fidelity. Spiritual resistance is the sentiment that reverberates from the attempt at assimilation by those characters, from the ineffectual struggle for their identity.

The developing of anguish in Rawet's protagonist results from his position as a foreigner, from his posture, from a particular way of viewing the world and men. He feels removed from them. The realization of this sentiment may come little by little, taking time to shape itself, or it may happen immediately on first contact with the new country. This feeling of separateness generates two situations, both the cause of the conflicts: insecurity, which brings with it a certain disquiet, and fear. These two elements lead to anguish, in its most extreme sense as an emotional state.

Memory brings to the present the events that shape the life of such a character. Time is superseded by experience, and everything is transformed in accordance with the moment that moves the person to the discovery of a new world, unthought of and obscure, which he could not have foreseen.

Rawet's immigrant is a rover, restless, with no definite aim. Two novellas, *Abama* and *Viagens de Ahasverus. . .* illustrate this. Ahasverus, a metaphor of the Wandering Jew, is someone who roams simultaneously about Brasília, Belém, and Rio de Janeiro in search of himself. Like the protagonist in *Abama*, he lives through the experience of embitterment, exile, and the yearning for redemption. Solitude is a constant in the lives of the people in Rawet's world. His characters never mix with their surroundings. Their lives are in a continous state of fluctuation. Placed among other people, they detach themselves, they hold themselves apart. Isolation is their main characteristic. The gap between individuals is not only a matter of language, but of institutions, customs, habits, and cultural background.

The attempt of Rawet's creatures to come into contact with their fellow beings is always ineffectual, fleeting. Language no longer serves to nourish the meeting between individuals. The short story "O profeta" (The Prophet; *Contos do imigrante*) is one of the best examples of such a condition. The prophet is a negative Messiah, stigmatized, the ineffectual prophet, who reveals a world's inner and absurd disorder, but cannot envision the Promised Land.

PRIMARY BIBLIOGRAPHY
Creative Writing

Abama. Rio de Janeiro: Edições G.R.D., 1964.

Contos do imigrante. Rio de Janeiro: Livraria José Olympio, 1956; 2nd ed. 1972.

10 contos escolhidos. Brasília: Horizonte, Instituto Nacional do Livro, 1982.

Diálogo. Rio de Janeiro: Edições G.R.D., 1963. (2nd ed. Vertente, 1976).

Que os mortos enterrem seus mortos. São Paulo: Vertente, 1981.

Os sete sonhos. Rio de Janeiro: Orfeu, 1967. (2nd edition, Arquivo/MEC, 1971).

O terreno de uma polegada quadrada. Rio de Janeiro: Orfeu, 1969.

Viagens de Ahasverus à terra alheia em busca de um passado que não existe porque futuro, e de um futuro que já passou porque sonhado. Rio de Janeiro: Olivé, 1970.

"Viagens de Ahasverus." Trans. by Elizabeth Lowe. *Fiction* 4.3 (1976): 5-6.

Nonfiction

Angustia e conhecimento. São Paulo: Vertente, 1978.

Alienação e realidade. Rio de Janeiro: Olivé, 1970.

Consciência e valor. Rio de Janeiro: Orfeu, 1970.

Eu-Tu-Ele. Rio de Janeiro: Livraria José Olympio, 1972.

Homossexualismo, sexualidade e valor. Rio de Janeiro: Olivé, 1970.

"Kafka e a mineralidade judaica ou a tonga da mironga do kabuletê." *Escrita* 24 (1977): 22-23.

SECONDARY BIBLIOGRAPHY
Criticism

Ataíde, Vicente de Paula. *A narrativa de ficção*. São Paulo: McGraw-Hill do Brasil, 1974. 131-69.

Berezin, Rifka. "Sobre Samuel Rawet." In *El imaginario judío en la literatura de América Latina: visión y realidad*. Ed. Patricia Finzi, Eliahu Toker, and Marcos Faerman. Buenos Aires: Grupo Editorial Shalom, 1990. 148-50.

Brasil, Assis. *A nova literatura III: O conto*. Rio de Janeiro/Brasília: Companhia Editora Americana/MEC, 1975. 67-72.

Gorga Filho, Remy. "Samuel Rawet, engenheiro-experimentador que construiu os *Contos do imigrante*." *Correio do povo* (Caderno de sábado) 73 (March 22, 1969): 5.

Guinsburg, Jacob. "Os imigrantes." *Shalom* (September 1984): 8-10.

Helena, Lúcia. "Rawet em questão: tentativa de uma análise estrutural." *Jornal de letras* (1969): 7-9.

Parker, John M. "Samuel Rawet." In *A Dictionary of Contemporary Brazilian Authors*. Comp. David William Foster and Roberto Reis. Tempe, Arizona: Center for Latin American Studies/ASU, 1981. 122-23.

Santos, Wendel. "A questão do conto. A forma do conto em Samuel Rawet." *Os três reais da ficção*. Rio de Janeiro: Vozes, 1978. 118-26.

Secco, Carmen Lúcia Tindó. "A alquimiada linguagem em Samuel Rawet." *Correio do povo* (Caderno de sábado) 583 (9 Sept. 1979): 13.

—. "A metáfora do jogo em Samuel Rawet (uma leitura do conto 'O jogo de damas'." *Correio do povo* (Caderno de Sábado) 599 (19 Jan. 1980): 7.

Szklo, Gilda Salem. "A experiência do trágico (recordando Rawet)." *Minas* (Suplemento literário) Dec. 15, 1984: 2-4.

Vieira, Nelson H. "Samuel Rawet: Ethnic Differences from *Shtetl* to *Subúrbio*." In his *Jewish Voices in Brazil: A Prophetic Discourse of Alterity*. Gainesville: UP of Florida, 1996. 51-99.

—. "Samuel Rawet, o judeu errante no Brasil: desordem e diferença." In *Ensayos sobre judaismo latinoamericano*. Proceedings of the V Congreso Internacional de Investigadores sobre Judaísmo Latinoamericano, Buenos Aires, 14-19 August, 1989. Buenos Aires: Milá, 1990. 425-40.

—. "Ser judeu e escritor: três casos brasileiros—Samuel Rawet, Clarice Lispector, Moacyr Scliar." *Papéis Avulsos* 25 (1990): 3-7.

Xavier, Elódia. "Samuel Rawet: o conto interrogativo." In her *O conto brasileiro e sua trajetória: a modalidade urbana dos anos 20 aos anos 70*. Rio de Janeiro: Livraria Padrão, 1987. 109-19.

Interviews

Gomes, Danilo. "Na toca de Samuel Rawet, o solitário caminhante do mundo." *Escritores Brasileiros ao vivo*. Belo Horizonte: Editora Comunicação/Instituto Nacional do Livro, 1979. 159-68.

Gilda Salem Szklo

RAZNOVICH, DIANA (Argentina; 1943)

Currently residing in Buenos Aires after long intervals in Spain (1974-81 and 1989-91) the Argentinean Diana Raznovich is highly acclaimed and best known as a dramatist. Her work has been translated into various languages. Although she writes in Spanish, her emotional and intellectual ties are with the native lands of her grandparents: Russia, Germany, and Austria.

Characteristic of the influence on Raznovich of Central European Jewish thinking is her capacity for abstraction. While Eastern Jewish thinking tends to be anecdotal, Central European Jewish thinking has more to do with science and philosophy, with Sigmund Freud (1856-1939) and Albert Einstein (1879-1955). Instead of illustrating her anecdotes, Raznovich searches for universal metaphors.

Raznovich's Jewish spirit prevails in her language, her way of thinking, and her resorting to humor as a dramatic solution to sad and grave issues. She reproduces childhood experiences that had a strong impact on her and transforms them, in search of the essence of those dreams. Deep down in all her writing one finds a Jewish tale. This feature is instinctive and spontaneous, since it comes from the unconscious.

In her first novel *Para que se cumplan todos tus deseos* (May All Your Wishes Come True; 1990), a magician who is capable of multiplying his money awakens the voracity of those who envy his gift until he is kidnapped, whereupon he loses his gift. The novel is a reflection on the natural talents people have, which they cannot control, and which evaporate when exploited.

Raznovich breaks new ground with her second novel, *Mater erótica* (1991), which takes place in Germany after the fall of the Berlin Wall. This novel, like the rest of her work, questions a woman's sexual liberation, here accompanied by the shaking off of other taboos and symbolized by the fall of communism in Europe.

Throughout her prolific career as a dramatist, Raznovich explores the female role in its multiple manifestations, from the anguish felt by two spinsters who kidnap a T.V. star in the play *Jardín de otoño* (Autumn Garden; 1983), to the multiple possibilities offered by their services at the *Casa matriz* (Matrix House; 1988), where each daughter may rent the kind of mother she wishes. Her *Casa matriz* is a criticism of a consumer society, but it also refers to consuming feelings, rather than to purchasing material objects. Raznovich's female characters need to escape the confinement that suffocates them. Their imprisonment may be metaphorical, as in *Desconcierto* (Disconcert; 1981) a monologue in which a pianist chooses to tell the public her life story rather than perform her concert. In the play *La madre judía postmoderna* (The Postmodern Jewish Mother; 1993) a feminist scholarly woman has to attend psychoanalytic sessions with her forty-year-old son, who refuses to let go of her assumed motherly duties. *De atrás para adelante* (From Back to Front; 1994), her latest comedy, about a Jewish family with a transsexual son, is a reflection on the prejudices of a traditional family toward a child who is different.

Typically Jewish in Raznovich's writing is her search for metaphysical ideas and for universal metaphors. Her Jewish world is not so evident in the situations she creates nor in the anecdotes she tells as in the moments of anguish, laughter, and humor that envelop her characters. Behind the abundance of clichés, Raznovich poses grave philosophical questions and sets her plays in surrealistic, absurd milieus that recreate some of the memorable images of Franz Kafka (1883-1924) and Samuel Beckett (1906-89).

Jardín de otoño is about two spinsters who naively devise a pathetic plot to attract a soap-opera star, whose performance they follow devotedly: they kidnap him at the moment they believe he is going through a dangerous situation, hoping to save him with their love. When they find out their lover is far from being the hero of their dreams, they dismiss him and return to their lost paradise behind the television screen.

Although the characters Raznovich creates are not always Jewish, it is possible to see manifestations of Jewish consciousness in the shift between the life not lived and the myth. From the historical and thematic perspective, *Jardín de otoño* is not a Jewish play. It could be regarded as a criticism of mass culture projected through the communication media. For the playwright, however, it represents a Jewish way of observing reality: The two female characters are bound to the life they would have liked to live but could not. From Raznovich's Jewish perspective, the question that springs up is: "What would have become of the Jews if it had not been for the expulsions, imprisonments and extermina-tions?" Far from mocking her two lonely female protagonists, Raznovich treats them with tenderness and sympathy.

The myth of a lost paradise is another aspect of the play, since it refers to a longing for something marvelous that the Jew misses. The T.V. star is a hero as long as he is acting his role, which permits the women to imagine what ideal love could be like. Through the women's identification with the impossible, through their nostalgia for the unreachable, the spectator confronts his own myths.

The paradox of waiting—symbolized in the loss of hope in the coming of the Messiah—also implies a hopelessness about something better taking place. For a Jew, the physical presence of the Messiah would mean the end of waiting. The Jewish paradox is in the relentless will to wait for his coming and in the hope for a better world, while being fully aware that the world is going from bad to worse. The arrival of the Messiah remains mythical while it is postponed. That is why, by the end of the play, the women prefer to keep waiting for their hero, their Messiah: even when he has surrendered to their demands and promises them to fulfill their expectations of love, they dismiss him and return to their televised myth.

Raznovich chooses *Jardín de otoño* as a metaphor of Jewish culture. Her characters struggle with the relationship between the everyday and mythologized events. In this play the religious rite is consecrated in a ritual space created by the soap opera. Each day, at the same time, the same themes are reproduced obsessively. Through a theatrical act, Raznovich proposes an alchemy created out of two absolutely different worlds. As transplanted beings, however, as much as Jews try to mingle in the world, they fail in their attempt. They are moved by external circumstances that have to do with the need to bear trials such as adapta-tion, or resisting anti-Semitism.

The image of return is best illustrated in the luggage that crowds her protagonist of *Objetos perdidos* (*Lost Belongings*; 1988). The act of having one's suitcases ready for any eventuality, which may be a common image to every wanderer, is particularly appropriate to the Jews. Being surrounded by suitcases conveys the idea that they will have to move on, and that they will never fully belong to any one country. Raznovich also alludes to the experience of repeated warnings that passengers hear when getting off an airplane, not to forget their personal belongings. In her urgent search for her past, Casalia Belprop—whose name is a symbolic weave of multiple migrations—may leave behind items that later become essential, while taking along others that are useless to her.

Certain images ingrained in Casalia generally prevail among Jews: they have to be always prepared to move from place to place without knowing if it is for good, or for a limited period of time. This translates into Raznovich's compulsive literature with a sense of urgency: *Objetos perdidos* was written in just three days.

The monologue is a metaphor of the *desaparecidos* (disappeared) in Argentina, and of the murder and exile of people who escaped the military dictatorship (1976-83). A woman totally lost amidst her luggage, opens it and finds remnants of her past life and fragments of her memory. *Objetos perdidos* could also be associated with an expression used by the Nazis to refer to the belongings that Jews left behind upon their arrival at concentration camps. In another context, the phrase is used in the announcements heard from loudspeakers at stations and airports. The confusion that Raznovich found when she had to leave her country and decide what was important to take and what to leave behind is similar to the one she imagines her ancestors must have suffered before each exile. Raznovich describes the process of transplantation from one country to another with great anguish, since she carries it in her blood.

The protagonist is a woman whose identity is never openly disclosed. From the Jewish perspective, *Objetos perdidos* represents the history of names that have suffered changes through endless migrations. The crowded landscape of luggage that fills the stage stands for the home of the Jew, surrounded by the perpetual presence of suitcases. The summary of her losses makes Casalia want to open some cases to find out what can be salvaged. The human bones she discovers are a prevalent Jewish metaphor for centuries of ancestors transplanted from one place to another. That is why when Casalia recognizes her dead grandmother's coccyx, or her lover's scaffoid bones, her memories become unbearably real.

Raznovich places Casalia in an anonymous place. There is no one to welcome her, except for a voice that warns her to be careful, as there is always the last hope that death can be avoided. The space in *Objetos perdidos* is subjective, yet it has the strength of a nightmare that really takes place, even after Casalia awakens from it. Like Sisyphus, Casalia is condemned to live surrounded by cases which she will open only to close again for the rest of her days.

From her Jewish experience, Raznovich feels best qualified to describe feelings of uncertainty and confusion. Enveloped by suitcases, Casalia's last recourse is to become transformative, to get into a suitcase and become that suitcase herself. These images of *Objetos perdidos* embody the destiny of the Jewish people, always forced to learn new codes, but they also relate to the metaphysical movement of all human beings.

Objetos perdidos shows the individual in an ironic relation to the political system. Casalia tries to decide what to wear and what not to wear, in order to be accepted in that society. But no matter what she does, she concludes that "siempre van a sospechar de mí" (they'll always suspect me), a key phrase because any person who insists on being an individual will always seem suspicious in any system.

Raznovich's plays invite a kaleidoscopic reading. Her writing is poetic and metaphysical rather than ideological, or anecdotal. Influenced by family history and metaphysics, she inserts herself fully as a writer bred in the Jewish tradition.

PRIMARY BIBLIOGRAPHY
Creative Writing

Autógrafos. Unpublished, debuted Teatro Lorange, Buenos Aires, 1983.

Cables pelados. Buenos Aires: Lúdicas, 1987.

Caminata en tu sombra. Buenos Aires: Stilcograf, 1964.

Buscapies. Unpublished, debuted Teatro Sarmiento, Buenos Aires, 1968.

Casa matriz. In *Salirse de madre*. Ed. Hilda Rais. Buenos Aires: Croquiñol, 1989. 163-86.

El contratiempo. Debuted Teatro Payró, Buenos Aires, 1972.

De atrás para adelante. Unpublished, 1994

Desconcierto. In *Teatro Abierto*. Buenos Aires: Ediciones de Teatro Abierto, 1981. 241-46. Also in *Teatro Abierto: 21 estrenos argentinos*. Buenos Aires: Corregidor, 1992. 315-22. English version as *Disconcerted*. Trans. Victoria Martínez. *The Literary Review* 32.4 (1989): 568-72.

El guardagente. Unpublished play, debuted at Sociedad Hebraica Argentina, Buenos Aires, 1971.

Jardín de otoño. Buenos Aires: Subsecretaría de Cultura, Dirección de Bibliotecas, Provincia de Buenos Aires, 1985.

"La liberación de la señora Sara." In *Las ídishe mames son un pueblo aparte*. Buenos Aires: Shalom, 1993. 25-38.

La madre judía post-moderna. Unpublished, 1993.

Máquinas divinas. Unpublished, debuted Centro Cultural San Martín, 1996.

Mater erótica. Barcelona: Robin Book, 1992.

Para que se cumplan todos tus deseos. Madrid: Exadra de Ediciones, 1988.

Paradise y otros monólogos. Buenos Aires: Nuevo Teatro, 1994.

Plaza hay una sola. Unpublished, debuted Plaza Arlt, Buenos Aires, 1969.

Plumas blancas. Buenos Aires: Ediciones Dédalos, 1974.

Objetos perdidos. Unpublished, 1988. English version as *Lost Belongings*. Trans. Nora Glickman and Gloria F. Waldman. In *Argentine Jewish Theatre: A Critical Anthology*. Ed. Nora Glickman and Gloria F. Waldman. Lewisburg: Bucknell UP, 1996. 329-38.

Teatro completo de Diana Raznovich. Buenos Aires: Ediciones Dédalos, 1994.

Tiempo de amar y otros poemas. Buenos Aires: Nuevo Día, 1963.

Nonfiction

Indira Gandhi, el imposible término medio. Madrid: Exadra de Ediciones, 1989.

SECONDARY BIBLIOGRAPHY

Castillejos, Manuel. "El valor del sonido en *Buscapies* de Diana Raznovich." In *Mujer y sociedad en América: IV Simposio Internacional*. Vol. I. Ed. Juana Alcira Arancibia. Westminster, CA; Mexicali: Instituto Literario y Cultural Hispánico; Universidad Autónoma de Baja California, 1988. 233-40.

Foster, David William. Rev. of *Mater erótica*. *World Literature Today* 67.3 (1993): 590.

Glickman, Nora. "Parodia y desmitificación del rol femenino en el teatro de Diana Raznovich." *Latin American Theatre Review* 28.1 (1994): 89-100.

—. "Paradojas y mitos judaicos en dos obras de Diana Raznovich." *Noaj* 9 (1993): 83-87.

Graham-Jones, Jean. "Decir 'no': el aporte de Bortnik, Gambaro y Raznovich al Teatro Abierto '81." In *Teatro argentino durante el Proceso: 1976-1983*. Ed. Juana A. Arancibia and Zulema Mirkin. Buenos Aires: Vinci-guerra, 1992. 181-97.

Martínez, Martha. "Tres nuevas dramaturgas argentinas: Roma Mahieu, Hebe Uhart y Diana Raznovich." *Latin American Theatre Review* 13.2 (1980: 39-45.

Weinstein, Ana E., and Miryam E. Gover de Nasatsky, comps. "Diana Razno-vich." *Escritores judeo-argentinos: bibliografía 1900-1987*. Buenos Aires: Milá, 1994. 103-5.

Zayas de Lima, Perla. *Diccionario de autores teatrales argentinos 1950-1990*. Buenos Aires: Galerna, 1991. 232-33.

Nora Glickman

RIVERA, ANDRÉS (Pseud. of Marcos Ribak; Argentina; 1928)

Andrés Rivera was born on December 12, 1928 in Buenos Aires into a working-class immigrant family. His father was a garment workers union leader who supplied Rivera with pamphlets and texts on workers' rights from an early age. Rivera's proletarian upbringing led to his political activism as an adult in the Communist Party. Likewise, it is the ideological foundation that informs the vast majority of his works. In addition to his literary activities, Rivera works as a journalist. His works, which consist of short story collections and novels, can be divided into two different periods: 1957-72 and 1982-present, having published nothing between 1972 and 1982.

His first work, the extensive proletarian novel *El precio* (The Price), was published in 1957. It provoked somewhat of an uproar upon publication from the conservative middle-class sector of Argentine society who saw in Rivera a threat to the recent progress made following the demise of Juan Perón in 1955. The novel is a typical example of proletarian literature in which characters are presented as a microcosm of representative types found in society, essentially divided between the proletariat and the bourgeoisie (and one need add the traditional oligarchy in the case of Argentina). An interesting aspect of the novel is Rivera's inclusion of Nazis who found their way to Argentina—with Perón's help—after the fall of the Third Reich, typified in the Nazi character Adolfo. If the novel suffers from any one fault it is the oversimplification of the ideological struggle between good (the workers) and evil (the bourgeois factory owners and oligarchs). Leonardo Senkman finds Rivera's stereotypical portrayal of Lev (Wolf) to be a cliché of the avaricious dehumanized industrialist Jewish exploiter, which in turn may be indicative of feelings of self-hatred (69).

In his second novel, *Los que no mueren* (Those Who Don't Die; 1959), as well the short story collections *Sol de sábado* (Saturday Sun; 1962), *Cita* (Appointment; 1965), *El yugo y la marcha* (The Yoke and the March; 1968), and *Ajuste de cuentas* (Settling the Score; 1972), Rivera continues along essentially the same narrative vein. Themes of class struggle, social injustice, ideological conflict, and societal revolution dominate the texts. To a lesser degree the author explores issues of solitude and lack of communication. There is also an ongoing dialogue between these many stories as characters and events resurface from one to the next.

Rivera initiated a new period of writing in 1982 with the publication of a collection of short stories, *Una lectura de la historia* (A Reading of History), in addition to a novel, *Nada que perder* (Nothing to Lose). Almost all critics point to the influence of Jorge Luis Borges (1899-1986) on Rivera's writing, particularly after 1982. *Una lectura de historia*, for instance, readily elicits the reader to compare the stories both thematically and stylistically to Borges's *Historia universal de la infamia* (*A Universal History of Infamy*; 1935). Rivera's stories no longer focus principally on class struggle, but on the struggle against authoritarianism, political corruption, and violence that relate directly to the military dictatorship of 1976-83.

In *Nada que perder* Rivera creates a narrative of identity construction that deals specifically, although not exclusively, with issues of Jewish identity. The novel is predicated on the narrator's need to uncover his father's past in order to verify his legal identity. So that his mother may receive her deceased husband's benefits the narrator must prove that Mauricio and Moisés Reedson are in fact one and the same. His father was an immigrant who arrived in Buenos Aires in 1924 from Russia and who quickly became a garment workers union leader. He must find three witnesses who are willing to attest to his father's identity. For that purpose he turns to three of his father's old friends: Salomón Weld, his father's *shif-brider* (ship-brother), Max Gryn who was also on the same ship, and Rebeca Milner a militant communist who worked with Reedson in the factory. An additional character, the actress Raquel Ellendorf, adds yet another dimension to the plot and also aids in reconstructing the identity of Mauricio/Moisés Reedson. It is significant that the younger Reedson learns that his father rejected what was to be his destiny, becoming the best rabbi of Lomza, by defiantly eating pork in the synagogue in front of everyone. As Leonardo Senkman points out, one of the most important aspects of *Nada que perder* is the author's own reappraisal of his ties to a Jewish identity (69). The novel provides a very interesting look into the labor struggles of the 1930s and for its portrayal of the essentially nonreligious Jewish sector of Argentina that defined Jewishness in terms of social justice.

The 1994 novel *El verdugo en el umbral* (The Executioner in the Threshold) sketchily traces the history of a Jewish family's hardships in a small Russian village, their involvement in the Russian Revolution and eventual emigration to Argentina. Once in Argentina, the family history becomes entwined with national history and politics. The character Reedson also appears in the novel which is governed by an overriding concern to portray the plight of immigrant (largely Italian and Jewish) laborers struggling for better working conditions, wages, and rights.

Rivera's recent works, *En esta dulce tierra* (In This Sweet Land; 1984) *La revolución es un sueño eterno* (The Revolution Is an Eternal Dream; 1987), *El amigo de Baudelaire* (The Friend of Baudelaire; 1991), and *La sierva* (The

Slave Woman; 1992) are historical novels. Both *En esta dulce tierra* and *La revolución* are set in the nineteenth century during the dictatorship of Juan Manuel de Rosas. In fact, his latest novel, *El farmer* (The Farmer; 1996), is narrated from the perspective of the aging dictator, languishing in exile in England. Over the course of one day, huddled next to a fire and with only a dog for company, he recalls his former glory in Argentina. There is a significant deal of intertextuality at play between Rivera's texts and such nineteenth-century Argentine classics as *Amalia* (1855) by José Mármol (1817-71) and *Facundo* (1845) by Domingo Faustino Sarmiento (1811-88 [Morello-Frosch; Perilli]). Furthermore, the novels provide ample opportunity for the reader to draw conclusions regarding the contemporary sociopolitical reality of Argentina, in keeping with the author's own ideological commitment to writing as a tool for social change.

PRIMARY BIBLIOGRAPHY

Ajuste de cuentas. Buenos Aires: Centro Editor de América Latina, 1972.

El amigo de Baudelaire. Buenos Aires: Alfaguara, 1991.

Apuestas. Buenos Aires: Per Abbat, 1986.

Cita. Buenos Aires: La Rosa Blindada, 1965.

En esta dulce tierra. Buenos Aires: Folios, 1984.

El farmer. Buenos Aires: Alfaguara, 1996.

Una lectura de la historia. Buenos Aires: Libros de Tierra Firme, 1982.

Los que no se mueren. Buenos Aires: Nueva Expresión, 1959.

Mitteleuropa. Buenos Aires: Alfguara, 1993.

Nada que perder. Buenos Aires: Centro Editor de América Latina, 1982.

El precio. Buenos Aires: Platina, 1957.

La revolución es un sueño eterno. Buenos Aires: Grupo Editor Latinoamericano, 1987.

La sierva. Buenos Aires: Alfaguara, 1992.

Sol de sábado. Buenos Aires: Platina, 1962.

Los vencedores no dudan. Buenos Aires: Grupo Editor Latinoamericano, 1989.

El verdugo en el umbral. Buenos Aires: Alfaguara, 1994.

El yugo y la marcha. Buenos Aires: Merlín, 1968.

SECONDARY BIBLIOGRAPHY
Criticism

Berg, Edgardo H. "Las relaciones de poder penetran los cuerpos" (*La sierva*). *Confluencia* 9.2 (1994): 150.

Borello, Rodolfo A. *El peronismo (1943-1955) en la narrativa argentina*. Ottawa: Dovehouse Editions, 1991. 117-31.

Gilman, Claudia. "Historia, poder y poética del padecimiento en las novelas de Andrés Rivera." In *La novela argentina de los años 80*. Ed. Roland Spiller. Frankfurt am Main: Vervuert Verlag, 1991. 47-64.

Gramuglio, María Teresa. "Escritura política y política de la escritura: *Una lectura de la historia*." *Punto de vista* 16 (1982): 28-29.

Martínez, Carlos Dámaso. "Historia entre la razón y el delirio: *En esta dulce tierra*. *Punto de vista* 24 (1985): 37-38.

Morello-Frosch, Marta. "Borges and Contemporary Argentine Writers: Continuity and Change." In *Borges and His Successors: The Borgesian Impact on Literature and the Arts*. Ed. Edna Aizenberg. U of Missouri P, 1990. 26-43.

—. "The Opulent *Facundo*: Sarmiento and Modern Argentine Fiction." *Sarmiento: Author of a Nation*. Ed. Tulio Halperín Donghi, Iván Jaksić, Gwen Kirkpatrick, and Francine Masiello. Berkeley/Los Angeles: U of California P, 1994. 347-57.

Perilli, Carmen. "Andrés Rivera. De los poderes de la Letra." In her *Las ratas en la Torre de Babel: la novela argentina entre 1982 y 1992*. Buenos Aires: Letra Buena, 1994. 111-63.

Sarlo, Beatriz. "El riesgo de la literatura: *Apuestas*." *Punto de vista* 27 (1986): 23-24.

Senkman, Leonardo. "De la legitimación del israelita argentino a la asunción de la identidad en algunos escritores judeoargentinos." In *El Cono Sur: dinámica y dimensiones de su literatura. A Symposium*. Ed. Rose S. Minc. Upper Montclair, NJ: Montclair State College, 1985. 56-71.

Waldegaray, Marta Inés. "*La sierva* de Andrés Rivera. . . o cómo narrar la voz del otro." *Confluencia* 8-9.2-1 (1993): 243-48.

Interviews

"Andrés Rivera." *Encuesta a la literatura argentina contemporánea*. Buenos Aires: Centro Editor de América Latina, 1982. 80-84.

Gliemmo, Graciela. "Andrés Rivera." In her *Las huellas de la memoria: entrevistas a escritores latinoamericanos*. Buenos Aires: Beas Ediciones, 1994. 145-57.

Saavedra, Guillermo. "Andrés Rivera: las lecturas de la historia." *La curiosidad impertinente: entrevistas con narradores argentinos*. Buenos Aires: Beatriz Viterbo, 1993. 53-64.

Speranza, Graciela. "Andrés Rivera." In her *Primera persona: conversaciones con quince narradores argentinos.* Buenos Aires: Norma, 1995. 179-94.

Darrell B. Lockhart

ROFFÉ, REINA (Argentina; 1951)

Reina Roffé was born on November 4, 1951, in Buenos Aires. She began writing literature in her youth, studying journalism and literature. She has worked as a journalist in Argentina, the United States, and Spain. In 1979 Roffé won the Borges prize given by the Givre Foundation in Buenos Aires for her short story "Profanación," and in 1981 she was granted a Fulbright scholarship to study in the United States at the University of Iowa as part of their prestigious International Writing Program. She lived in the United States for four years where she gave numerous lectures and symposiums on literature at a variety of universities including The University of Iowa, Vassar College, The University of Chicago, Arizona State University, Columbia University, and Montclair State College. Roffé has lived in Madrid since 1988 where she conducts literary workshops and continues to work as a journalist, writing for a number of cultural journals and newspapers such as *Cambio 16, Marie Claire, Guía del niño,* and *Quimera.*

As a literary critic, Roffé has written a book on Mexican writer Juan Rulfo (1918-86), and she has edited a volume of interviews with important Latin American and Spanish authors that includes Jorge Luis Borges (1899-1986) and Manuel Puig (1932-90), whom Roffé interviewed herself.

As a writer, Roffé has authored novels that call into question traditional assumptions of gender, sexuality, identity, and oppression. Though the theme of Jewish identity is not one of central concern to the author, her novels do occasionally contain elements associated with Jewish history and/or cultural identity and in a new book, tentatively titled *Mis tías, los domingos* (My Aunts, Sundays), Jewish identity takes on a central role (personal letter).

In 1969, at the age of seventeen, she wrote her first novel, *Llamado al puf* (Call to the Ottoman), which met with immediate critical acclaim and won the Pondal Ríos prize in Buenos Aires in 1975 awarded for the best novel by a young writer. *Llamado al puf* chronicles many of the events in the author's own life. She has termed it an "análisis casero de mi infancia" (a homegrown analysis of my childhood). The novel recounts the suffocating and repressive atmosphere of life within a typical middle-class Buenos Aires family. It ends, nonetheless, on an optimistic note with the departure of the protagonist from her dismal home life to enter the world.

In spite of the novel's success, Roffé received much criticism from literary specialists. She was told that her writing had too many feminine registers and that it was necessary to present greater social conscience (*La rompiente* 9). Roffé took the comments into consideration and in the process she betrayed "el mensaje individual, subjetivo, femenino" (the individual, subjective, and feminine message [*La rompiente* 10]) in writing her next novel, *Monte de Venus* (Mons Veneris), which she completed at an inauspicious time: early 1976.

On March 24, 1976 the neofascist military government was installed and the Proceso de Reorganización Nacional (Process of National Reorganization) was implemented. Roffé's novel was immediately censured by military officials. Her narrative represented a fundamental challenge to patriarchy (as represented in the form of authoritarianism), and it was a deconstruction of gender representation and female sexuality. As a consequence, the author was silenced and eventually forced to go into exile. The experience was devastating for Roffé. She moved to Madrid and wrote little in the way of fiction in the years that followed, conserving her attachment with the literary field by working as a journalist, editor, and book reviewer for such Argentine newspapers as *Clarín*, *Convicción*, and *La Opinión*.

Monte de Venus has received little critical attention, perhaps because of the novel's linear nature and realism, which provide little intrigue for the contemporary critic. In spite of the fact that it was written prior to the onset of the dictatorship, the novel foreshadows the events to come. A secondary school serves as a microcosm of Argentina. The text is also a radical critique of Argentine society and underscores the need to foment social change. Thus, it was deemed contrary to public morality and banned. When asked about the censorship of the novel, the author has said: "Creo que la prohibieron porque era una cosa molesta. También había una crítica al sistema educativo y la situación de la mujer" (I believe that they prohibited it because it was bothersome. Also, it contained a critique of the educational system and the predicament of women [Domínguez 6]).

In *Monte de Venus*, all of the characters in one way or another are subalterns in a world that does not recognize that they have a voice or control over their own lives. Their attempts to exert some sort of control over their destinies are greeted with failure and humiliation, presenting a pathetic if not grotesque image to the reader. The hegemonic cultural prohibitions (and in the case of lesbian identity these would include those presented by mainstream feminists) deny the women any opportunity to define an identity that does not fall within prescribed parameters of society. In *Monte de Venus*, Roffé deconstructs the mechanisms and myths of patriarchy that serve to subject the individual to phallocentric tyranny and exposes the few options that exist for self-fulfillment within this system. She presents the reader with an inflammatory text, feminist and radical because it signals that change within the system is impossible.

La rompiente (The Breaking Surf) appeared in 1987, eleven years after her last novel. In contrast to *Monte de Venus*, *La rompiente*, may be considered an academic critic's ideal for its structural and thematic complexity, lending itself to multiple interpretations. It is interesting to note that the novel contains a critical analysis at the end which serves as a veritable instruction booklet on how to read the novel for those who have become perplexed and/or discouraged during the rather arduous task of completing it. *La rompiente* received immediate critical acclaim upon publication, and it won the International Prize for Short Novel in 1986. The novel is in many ways autobiographical, chronicling the displacement of exile, although the author was initially afraid of presenting any sort of text that could be construed to contain any particular flaw of feminine writing.

The text is divided into three parts. The first part is the story of a trip to an unnamed foreign city taken by a young woman. The second part, entitled "la novela" (The Novel), revolves around a group of people that gathers in a café to play cards. It also carries many separate stories, in part read, spoken, interrupted, and commented by this group of friends. The third part of the novel revolves around a "tiempo de silencio" (time of silence) and isolation preceding the trip, in which assorted memories also play a paramount role. Among them are the memories of the death of the protagonist's grandmother, born in Morocco, and its devastating effect on her. Roffé's connection with her Jewish identity also ties in with the central theme of the novel (exile), and the concept of the rootlessness of the wandering Jew, the classic outsider, searching throughout the world for a place in which s/he will be accepted. The grandmother's birthplace (and the fact that she carries the same name as the protagonist, one that remains unknown to the reader) is significant because it harkens back to the Spanish Inquisition and the exile of the Jewish and Arab populations, emphasizing the protagonist's own family history of displacement as well as the double marginalization of being a Jew and a woman.

La rompiente has been the subject of numerous critical articles since its publication. Critics have focused on issues of feminist criticism and writing the female body (Masiello; Martínez de Richter; Tierney-Tello), the symbolism of the journey (Fares and Hermann) and the narrative structure of the text (Gramuglio; Szurmuk). Nonetheless, the feminist critics who have approached the text often discount (as the author herself does) the importance of *Monte de Venus* in setting up the dominant themes which would evolve in *La rompiente*. Beyond this, there has been a tendency among feminist critics to whitewash Roffé's ability to "write the female body," in which they have chosen to overlook inconsistencies in the author's depiction of the female body and feminine space that occasionally work against the text's overt feminist themes.

The destabilization and defamiliarization of gender identity so prevalent in *Monte de Venus* establishes what will become the dominant theme of *La rompiente*, although the novel in its scope and form was a radical break from the realism of the former. The text contains many overlapping voices that at times contradict each other to confuse the reader. The narratives are filled with anecdotes that appear unrelated to the story line and the narrators diverge on tangents that also seem to offer little relation both to one another and to the story. In this sense, the novel most closely approximates the art form of the collage, with assorted, scattered stories pasted together, sometimes complementing one another, other times providing jarring contrasts and clashes.

By utilizing collage, *La rompiente* places itself in opposition to the master narrative and allows for a multiplicity of stories, some inconsequential, to be a part of the schema. Another dimension to this lack of narrative fixation involves the lack of any demarcation of particular cities and the changing names of the characters involved. Even the protagonist, whose name the reader never learns, has an pseudonym, Rahab, the name of a ten-year old prostitute from Morrocco.

The novelty of *La rompiente* is that it converts the reader into an active and agile participant in the process of decoding meaning. Throughout the novel, the reader is often forced to reread extensive passages in order to find out precisely who the narrator is. The text requires an attentive reader, a detective who is flexible and able to read between the lines.

Authoritarian regimes are characterized by their univocality and effort to serve as the sole basis of understanding and, as a result, the literature both during and immediately following the period of authoritarianism in Argentina sought to free up signification and to foster multiple points of meaning and ways of perceiving reality that did not adhere to the hegemonic model. *La rompiente* may be considered an exemplary representative of this tendency. In the novel, the author actively seeks to break the silence that authoritarianism and patriarchy impose and to reevaluate the social and literary structures that have devalued women's presence and manipulated their representation.

Roffé structures her latest novel, *El cielo dividido* (The Divided Sky; 1996), around the literary device of the voyage. Situated in the post-dictatorship era of the late 1980s, the novel revolves around the main character's return trip to Buenos Aires following a long period of exile. She is forced to come to terms with the changes that have transformed not only the country but herself as well. Her voice is joined by six other women, former acquaintances and friends, undergoing the same process. The result is a polyphonic narrative which seeks to articulate the past with the present.

PRIMARY BIBLIOGRAPHY
Creative Writing
El cielo dividido. Buenos Aires: Sudamericana, 1996.
"Una ciudad gris y beige." *Hispamérica* 22.66 (1993): 71-78.
"Fuera de foco." In *Ultimos relatos*. Ed. Nelly Pretel. Buenos Aires: Nemont, 1978. 183-90.
"Let's Hear What He Has to Say." Trans. by H. Ernest Lewald. *The Web: Stories by Argentine Women*. Ed. and Trans. by H. Ernest Lewald. Washington, D.C.: Three Continents Press, 1983. 165-70.
Llamado al puf. Buenos Aires: Pleamar, 1972.
"Llena de mundo." In *Historias del peronismo*. Ed. and intro. by María Angélica Scotti. Buenos Aires: Corregidor, 1973. 21-31.
Monte de Venus. Buenos Aires: Corregidor, 1976.
La rompiente. Buenos Aires: Puntosur, 1987. Also, México, D.F.: Editorial Universitaria de Veracruz, 1987.
Nonfiction
(Ed.) *Espejo de escritores*. Hanover, NH: Ediciones del Norte, 1985.
Juan Rulfo: autobiografía armada. Buenos Aires: Corregidor, 1973. Also, Barcelona: Montesinos, 1992.

SECONDARY BIBLIOGRAPHY
Criticism
Avellaneda, Andrés. "Canon y escritura de mujer: un viaje al centro de la periferia." *Revista espacios* 10 (1991): 87-90.
Fares, Gustavo, and Eliana Hermann. "Reina Roffé." *Escritoras argentinas contemporáneas*. New York: Peter Lang, 1993. 191-216.
Flori, Mónica R. "Reina Roffé." In her *Streams of Silver: Six Contemporary Women Writers from Argentina*. Lewisburg: Bucknell UP, 1995. 215-45. (Critical essay followed by interview with Roffé).

Foster, David William. *Alternate Voices in the Contemporary Latin American Narrative*. Columbia: U of Missouri P, 1985. 76-81.

Gimbernat González, Ester. *"La rompiente o la integración en la escritura."* In her *Aventuras del desacuerdo: novelistas argentinas de los 80*. Buenos Aires: Danilo Albero Vergara, 1992. 186-90.

Gramuglio, María Teresa. "Aproximaciones a *La rompiente*." In *La rompiente*. Buenos Aires: Puntosur, 1987. 127-35.

Kantaris, Elia Geoffrey. "Writing the Same (with a Difference): Sylvia Molloy and Reina Roffé." In his *The subversive Psyche: Contemporary Women's Narrative from Argentina and Uruguay*. Oxford: Clarendon Press/Oxford, 1995. 133-93.

Lockhart, Melissa A. "Reina Roffé." In *Latin American Writers on Gay and Lesbian Themes: A Bio-Critical Sourcebook*. Ed. David William Foster. Westport, CT: Greenwood Press, 1994. 378-82.

Martínez de Richter, Marily. "Textualizaciones de la violencia: *Informe bajo llave* de Marta Lynch y *La rompiente* de Reina Roffé." *Siglo XX/20th Century* 11.1-2 (1993): 89-117.

Masiello, Francine. "Contemporary Argentine Fiction: Liberal (Pre-)texts in the Reign of Terror." *Latin American Research Review* 16.2 (1981): 218-24.

—. "Cuerpo/presencia: mujer y estado social en la narrativa argentina durante el proceso militar." *Nuevo texto crítico* 2.4 (1989): 155-78.

Szurmuk, Mónica. "La textualización de la represión en *La rompiente* de Reina Roffé." *Nuevo texto crítico* 3.5 (1990): 123-31.

Tierney-Tello, Marybeth. "From Silence to Subjectivity: Reading and Writing in Reina Roffé's *La rompiente*. *Latin American Literary Review* 21.42 (1993): 34-56.

Interviews

Domínguez, Nora. "Entrevista con Reina Roffé." *Primer Plano*. Suplemento cultural de *Página 12* [Argentina] (26 June, 1994): 5-6.

Flori, Mónica R. "Entrevista con Reina Roffé: sobre escritura femenina y su última novela *La rompiente*." *Alba de América* 6 (1988): 423-28.

París, Diana. "'Encontrar la propia voz, como en un cofre antiguo': Entrevista a Reina Roffé." *Confluencia* 10.2 (1995): 205-7.

Melissa Fitch Lockhart

ROSENCOF, MAURICIO (Uruguay; 1933)

Perhaps one of the best ways of characterizing Rosencof's writing is to point to some important dates in his life. *Las crónicas del Tuleque* (Tuleque's Chronicles; 1986) includes the sketches on local customs and social types he wrote in the late 1960s for the famous Montevideo intellectual review *Marcha*. It also includes his subsequent production of chronicles for publications in the mid-1980s: the period between these two dates is unrepresented. This is because by the end of the 1960s Rosencof had become deeply involved with the Tupamaros, an urban guerrilla movement of which Rosencof was a leader. (There is an extensive bibliography on the Tupamaros, but perhaps one of the best documents is Costa Gavras's 1973 film, *State of Siege*.) When the movement was obliterated in the early 1970s by the Uruguayan military, with extensive technical assistance from the United States, Rosencof was imprisoned, and his release came only with the amnesty that accompanied Uruguay's return to institutional democracy in the mid-1980s. Rosencof became a symbol of a generation of silenced Uruguayan intellectuals (fortunately, few were permanently silenced as was the case in the parallel Argentine neofascist dictatorship), and his 1988 play *El retorno del Gran Tuleque* (The Great Tuleque's Return) is one of the most important theatrical works in his country during the transition from military rule to democracy.

Because of Rosencof's commitment to the dominant revolutionary ideology of the 1960s, his writing is a combination of a fervent commitment to the notion of the people as defined almost in folkloristic terms and to the concept of continental (i.e., Latin America as a whole) liberation through the promotion of a unifying cultural identity. This is particularly evident in his early ethnographic, testimonial book of twelve narrative sketches published under the title of *La rebelión de los cañeros* (The Rebellion of the Canefield Workers; 1969).

Concomitantly, there is an intense repudiation of elements viewed as impeding this commitment, specifically institutional nationalism (the concept of the privileged Fatherland) and bourgeois social identities. The latter would necessarily include ethnicity, particularly when that ethnicity is derived from European roots and viewed as allied with conservative and reactionary forces. Many Latin American intellectuals in the 1960s viewed Judaism in these terms. As a consequence, there is virtually no reference to Jewish cultural elements in Rosencof's writing. There is an abundance of reference to local details: streets, neighborhood characters, customs and practices, foods, and household beliefs. But despite the first-person voice in many of Rosencof's chronicles, to whatever extent he may have been raised in a Jewish-marked environment, one seeks in vain any interpretation in his writing of such experiences. Whatever references there are are as circumstantial as they might be in a non-Jewish writer.

Thus, Rosencof's principal interest here is the way in which he exemplifies a particular stance of repudiation characteristic of a specific moment of Latin American cultural history. Such a repudiation is to be found among revolutionary intellectuals of other similar immigrant derivation, such as the many writers in Argentina of Italian, Spanish, or Arabic descent; cf. the similar case of Osvaldo Dragún (1929) in Argentina, who only in his most recent theater has made allusion to Jewish themes. Rosencof, however, must be reckoned with as a major figure in contemporary Uruguayan culture. His chronicles are complemented by a significant interest in children's literature (out of an intertwined belief in the "natural" libertarian sentiments of the young and in the need to address a specific cultural production to them as part of the formation of their social consciousness), and he continues to be an important force in the theater. *La calesita rebelde* (The Rebellious Merry-Go-Round; 1967), *Canciones para alegrar a una niña* (Songs to Make a [Girl] Child Happy; 1985), *Vincha Brava* (1987; the title is the name of a bird, but its metonymical meaning is "pugnacious headband"), and *Leyendas del abuelo de la tarde* (Grandfather's Afternoon Tales; 1990) are examples of the former (theater, poetry, novel, and short stories, respectively). Many of the tales in *Leyendas* have a general origin in the Jewish Bible and in Jewish folk narrative. Works on national themes include *". . . y nuestros caballos serán blancos"* (Moreover, Our Horses Will Be White; 1986) and *El vendedor de reliquias* (The Relic Vendor; 1992). However, Rosencof's most original work is perhaps *Memorias del calabozo* (Jail Memories; 1987), a series of conversations with Eleuterio Fernández Huidobro in three volumes that provide a sweeping personal and collective portrayal of the prison culture utilized by the Uruguayan military as a program of social oppression and ideological reform(ul)ation. Unlike the primitive dungeon practices of other Latin American dictatorships, in the case of Uruguay imprisonment was underlain by a specific social program whose dimensions emerge in this memoir. Rosencof also presents his prison experiences in the autobiographical narrative *El bataraz* (The Speckled Rooster; 1992).

PRIMARY BIBLIOGRAPHY
Creative Writing

El bataraz. Montevideo: Arca, 1992.

Los caballos. Montevideo: Sandino, 1967. Also in *Teatro uruguayo contemporáneo: antología.* Madrid: Centro de Documentación Teatral, Ministerio de Cultura; Sociedad Estatal Quinto Centenario; Fondo de Cultura Económica, 1992. 631-88.

La calesita rebelde. Montevideo: Ejido, 1967.

Canciones para alegrar a una niña. Montevideo: Imprenta C.B.A., 1985.

Conversaciones con la alpargata. Montevideo: Arca, 1985.

Los corderitos de Dios y otros cuentos. Montevideo: Cal y Canto, 1995.

Las crónicas del Tuleque. Montevideo: Arca, 1986.

"The Horses." Trans. by Malcolm Coad. *Index on Censorship* 11.3 (June 1982): 35-36.

"Legends of the Afternoon Grandfather." Trans. by Nick Caistor. *Index on Censorship* 14.5 (October 1985): 50-51.

Leyendas del abuelo de la tarde. Ilustraciones, Elbio Ferrario. Montevideo: Arca/TAE [Túpac Amaru Editores], 1990.

La margarita: historia de amor en 25 sonetos. Buenos Aires: Ediciones Colihue, 1995.

Pensión familiar. Montevideo: Sandino, 1963.

Las ranas. Montevideo: Siglo Ilustrado, 1961.

La rebelión de los cañeros. Montevideo: Cuadernos de Información Política y Económica, 1969. Reissued with *Los hombres de arroz.* Montevideo: TAE [Túpac Amaru Editores], 1987.

Teatro escogido (I): Las ranas. Los caballos. El combate en el establo. El hijo que espera. Montevideo: Túpac Amaru Editorial, 1988.

Teatro escogido (II): La valija. El saco de Antonio. . . . y nuestros caballos serán blancos. El regreso del Gran Tuleque. Montevideo: Túpac Amaru Editorial, 1990.

La valija. Montevideo: Aquí, Poesía, 1964.

El vendedor de reliquias: sobre Memoria del fuego de Eduardo Galeano. Montevideo: Arca, 1992.

Vincha brava. Montevideo: Arca, 1987.

. . . y nuestros caballos serán blancos. Montevideo: Arca, 1986.

Nonfiction

"Literatura del calabozo." In *Represión, exilio, y democracia: la cultura uruguaya.* Ed. Saúl Sosnowski. College Park: Universidad de Maryland; Montevideo: Ediciones de la Banda Oriental, 1987.

Memorias del calabozo. 3 vols. Montevideo: TAE [Túpac Amaru Editores], 1987-88.

SECONDARY BIBLIOGRAPHY

Cantillana, Igor. *"Los caballos* de Rosencof y el Teatro Sandino." *Teatro escogido (I)*. Montevideo: Túpac Amaru Editorial, 1988. 111-18.

Castro Vega, Jorge. "Una convocatoria que es un desafío." *Teatro uruguayo contemporáneo: antología*. Madrid: Centro de Documentación Teatral, Ministerio de Cultura; Sociedad Estatal Quinto Centenario; Fondo de Cultura Económica, 1992. 625-28.

—. "Mauricio Rosencof: denuncia, ruptura y construcción de un mundo." *Teatro escogido (I)*. Montevideo: Túpac Amaru Editorial, 1988. 9-29.

—. "La obra dramática de Mauricio Rosencof: apuntes rutinos." *Revista iberoamericana* 58.160-161 (1992): 1193-96.

Freire, Silka. *Mauricio Rosencof: el delirio imaginante*. Montevideo: Arca, 1994.

Maggi, Carlos. "Prólogo." Mauricio Rosencof, . . . *y nuestros caballos serán blancos*. Montevideo: Arca, 1986. 5-9.

Marauda, Lauro. "Rosencof: la crisis de los sueños." Mauricio Rosencof, *Teatro escogido (II)*. Montevideo: Túpac Amaru Editorial, 1988-90. 9-16.

Rama, Angel. *La generación crítica, 1939-1969*. Montevideo: Arca, 1972. passim.

Ulive, Ugo. "Profile: Mauricio Rosencof." *Index on Censorship* 11.3 (June 1982): 36-38.

Interviews

"Freedom Returns." *Index on Censorship* 14.5 (October 1985): 48-50.

David William Foster

ROVINSKI, SAMUEL (Costa Rica; 1932)

Samuel Rovinski was born in Costa Rica in 1932. Although he has written both essays and narrative texts, he is principally known as a playwright. Indeed, together with his compatriots Alberto Cañas (1920) and Daniel Gallegos (1930), Rovinski is considered to be one of the founders of contemporary Costa Rican theater. The best way to characterize the author as well as give a panoramic overview of his most important works is to begin with his play *La víspera del Sábado* (Sabbath Eve; 1985), which contains many autobiographical elements. Rovinski is the son of Jewish parents who emigrated from Poland to Costa Rica following World War I. Although the author was born in the Central American country and grew up completely tied to its culture, the European Jewish tradition of his parents affords him a cultural and spiritual richness that only the children of the diaspora enjoy.

La víspera del Sábado deals with the vicissitudes of the Berlinski family, fighting to overcome the shock of exile, while at the same time striving to integrate into the country that has taken them in. The serene and balanced figure of the mother is placed in contrast to the unstable and adventurous father who, unaware of the environment in which they have settled, embarks on a risky business venture that alters the life of the family and ends up destroying his health. The disastrous consequences of the father's commercial incompetence becomes the central conflict of the drama, and although there is no final denouement, it is inferred that, with the mother's support, care, and control, all will turn out for the best. The symptoms of uprootedness and uncertainty of the older characters are contrasted with the confidence, balance, and vitality of Moisés, the youngest son, who symbolizes the subsequent establishment of the family in the country. Likewise, in La víspera del Sábado, family conflicts are presented that are derived from the events in Poland as a consequence of the Nazi invasion and its indirect repercussions in Costa Rica.

In the short story collection Cuentos judíos de mi tierra (Jewish Tales from My Homeland; 1982), the theme of the diaspora is more fully developed. In one of the best written stories of the collection, "El fantasma pardo" (The Dark Ghost), the protagonist, a Jewish immigrant who has lost his memory as a consequence of a traumatic experience during the Nazi invasion of Poland, recovers it suddenly while sitting in a synagogue in San José. He hears insults shouted against the polacos (Poles; the appellation given to Jews in Costa Rica) that would appear to be the ominous sign that the scene that had induced his amnesia was to be repeated once again. In other stories in the volume, while Rovinski exalts the inherent values of Jewish culture, he also strives to show how the rigid attachment to Jewish values can be an obstacle in the process of adaptation to the new country. In this volume of stories, the author shows the same depth in the treatment of philosophical themes and the command of prose technique that he had already fully made manifest in his novel Ceremonia de Casta (Caste Ceremony; 1976), and which reappear in the collection of stories El embudo de Pandora (Pandora's Snare; 1991).

Ceremonia de Casta is a complex novel. Although it deals with a recurrent literary motif in Latin American narrative—the decadence of the land owning patriarch whose spiritual and physical decay is reflected in the deterioration of the mansion that has been a faithful icon of his power and opulence—it possesses qualities that distinguish it from its counterpart narratives. With the Oedipus complex as its central theme, the novel explores the psychological, social, and philosophical implications in the family of the land owner and by extension in Costa Rican and Latin American society (cf. Carballo). Rovinski more closely follows the style of Thomas Mann (1875-1955) and Marcel Proust (1871-1922) than that of his Latin American contemporaries.

All the stories in *El embudo de Pandora*, the majority of which are suggestively erotic, revolve around a rich conglomeration of characters driven by amorous passion or by the desire to liberate themselves from the spiritual or material binds that keep them from achieving an eternally unattainable happiness. Two stories stand out in this collection: "La pagoda" (The Pagoda), for its formal perfection and poetic language, and the title story "El embudo de Pandora," for its thematic originality.

Rovinski has defined his theater as a theater of the immediate. With few exceptions (*El laberinto* [The Labyrinth; 1985], for example) his works are centered in Costa Rican and Central American reality. In his careful observance of daily life, both political and social, from a humorous, parodic, or ironic perspective, the author goes about dismantling the structures on which cultural discourses are built. The playfulness of the situations is always accompanied by the seriousness of the critical stance. While laughter from the spectator is sought, at the same time he is always expected to recognize a problem and the causes from which it originated. The play that has made Rovinski famous nationally is *Las fisgonas de Paso Ancho* (The Busybodies of Paso Ancho; 1971). In this farce, the playwright satirizes with a fine tuned humor and irony the local authorities, the police, the church, and the media. Through the figures of three of the town's busybodies, the typical local types are caricaturized, while at the same time current issues such as drugs and violence in marginal neighborhoods are presented. The understated satiric tone, which stimulates in the spectator a smile similar to that provoked by circus clowns, has made this work one of the most popular in Costa Rica. The festive tone of playful innocence becomes more serious as well as sharper and more penetrating in the play *Gulliver dormido* (Slumbering Gulliver; 1985). In this work the political system and its agents are the direct target of implacable satire. Inspired by Jonathan Swift's (1667-1745) novel, the giant appears as an unusual, disconcerting, and powerful presence that stirs up, on a magnified scale, all the mechanisms operative in the political machinery. Thus, the ineffectiveness of a variety of political practices, caused by the passiveness of politicians as well as voters, is called into question. The play parodies the manipulation of national political discourse coming from the government and from the parties that support or oppose it, as well as the discourse of the international powers that with their distant rhetoric protect their investments with the pretext of a utopic international stability. In this play Rovinski makes clear how the individual and collective interests of the representatives of the people rarely exercise a policy that benefits those who have elected them.

In *El martirio del pastor* (The Martyrdom of the Pastor; 1983), the local situation is carried beyond national boundaries. The action takes place in El Salvador, and the central character is archbishop Arnulfo Romero. Although this work was published in 1983, due to reasons as much political as economic it could not be staged until 1987. The play was put on by the Compañía Nacional de Teatro (National Theater Company) with great success. The play earned Rovinski international fame as a playwright. It was performed in Mexico, New York, and in 1994 it was staged again by the group Teatro de la Luna (Theater of the Moon), of Arlington, Virginia. The success of this play was due not only to the fact that it is perhaps the author's best work, but also to its topic. Following his assassination, Archbishop Romero became a symbol of resistance against the repression of military dictatorships that in the decade of the 1980s governed many Latin American countries. The play is not, however, a historical work. Rather, it is a drama centered on Romero in which the entire exterior world is configured according to his interior tensions. The play records the step-by-step evolution of Romero who, deeply moved by the death of a Jesuit friend, is transformed from a priest indifferent to the repression suffered by his parishioners into the most vigorous of their defenders. Through the internal drama of the character, all the events during that time in El Salvador are captured in documentary detail.

Although in all of Rovinski's works one sees a polished writer conscious of the written text, one also notes the special attention given to the text's performative potential. Rovinski always seeks an innovative theatrical space beyond the conventional. For instance, in *El martirio del pastor*, the whole theater is converted into a church in which the spectators themselves play the role of the parishioners. In his latest work, *Los pregoneros* (The Town Criers; 1990), which the author characterizes as a comical piece for opera, the stage makes up the center ring of a circus. As in *El martirio del pastor*, in this work there is a double focus that is directed inward to the main character, but also to the outward facts that link him to the Costa Rican context of the moment.

The protagonist of *Los pregoneros* is, like Romero, a dynamic character. The play deals with a journalist who strives at the beginning of his career to portray the news with honesty and professionalism, but who very soon and in spite of his struggle to avoid it, gives in to the interests of the powerbrokers, the businessmen that manipulate the mass media in order to control the country politically and economically. However, the story line is not the most important aspect of the work. The originality of the play lies in its postmodern style in which contemporary theatrical signs (a narrator and Brechtian chorus, for example) are mixed with signs from other theatrical genres such as the opera and the circus tradition.

In *Un modelo para Rosaura* (A Model for Rosaura; 1974) Rovinski continues his social satire, this time focusing on a typical bourgeoisie family. If the reader/spectator of the text is entertained only by the ambiguity of the family conflicts, similar to the case of *Ceremonia de Casta* in which the Oedipal complex is the driving force of interior motivations, he could be disappointed. One of the specifically original aspects of the play is a sustained ambiguity, and what is most innovating about this play in relation to his others is its dual level of fiction, its metatheatricality. The playwright simultaneously thematizes the very process of theatrical production and also invites the receptor to experience intratextual games that add new semantic dimensions to the first level of fiction.

In the essay "Dramatización de lo inmediato" (Dramatization of the Immediate; 1982), Rovinski reflects on his role as playwright. His theater invites the reader/spectator to deconstruct the signs of his time. If theater, like all works of art, should show its formal virtues, it should not, however, become a mere game of signifiers that self-reflectively cause the literary/theatrical text to stand out. For Rovinski the theatrical work should be transcendent, connecting with signs and cultural codes of his time. It should invite the receptor to relate the fictitious world with historical/social referents of his own immediate reality. The playwright calls on his audience to be aware of the abuses of national and international power and to discover the mechanisms by which one is manipulated into serving the interests of power wielding groups; to deconstruct the cultural myths that are obstacles to social dynamism and individual liberty. Rovinski's theatrical works maintain a didactic-moralizing purpose inherited from the Greco-Roman theatrical tradition, but this purpose is always accompanied by contemporary modalities of theatrical discourse and current theatrical conventions. His theater both teaches and entertains. It is a parody that makes us laugh, yet at the same time worry when we discover that the figure we contemplate in the mirror of the stage is our own.

PRIMARY BIBLIOGRAPHY
Creative Writing

Ceremonia de Casta. San José: Editorial Costa Rica, 1979.

Cuentos judíos de mi tierra. San José: Editorial Costa Rica, 1982.

"El dulce sabor de la venganza." *Hispamérica* 24.71 (1995): 73-80.

El embudo de Pandora. San José: Editorial Costa Rica, 1991.

Las fisgonas de Paso Ancho. San José: Editorial Costa Rica, 1971.

Gobierno de alcoba. Madrid: Escelicer, 1964.

"The Grey Phantom." Trans. by Dan Bellm. In *Clamor of Innocence: Stories from Central America.* Ed. Barbara Paschke and David Volpendista. San Francisco: City Lights Books, 1988. 13-19.

Gulliver dormido. San José: Talleres de Litografía Cosmos, 1985.

Herencia de sombras. San José: REI (Red Editorial Iberoamericana)Centroamericana, 1993.

La hora de los vencidos. San José: Editorial Costa Rica, 1963.

Los intereses compuestos. San José: Compañía Nacional de Teatro, 1981.

El laberinto. San José: Editorial Costa Rica, 1969.

El martirio del Pastor. San José: EDUCA, 1983.

"Metaphors." Trans. by Charles Philip Thomas. In *Contemporary Short Stories from Central America.* Ed. Enrique Jaramillo Levi and Leland Chambers. Austin: U of Texas P, 1994. 192-96.

Un modelo para Rosaura. San José: Editorial Costa Rica, 1974.

La pagoda. San José: Prometeo, 1968.

Los pregoneros. San José: Teatro Nacional, 1990.

"Sodom." Trans. by Edith Grossman. In *And We Sold the Rain: Contemporary Fiction from Central America.* Ed. Rosario Santos. New York: Four Walls Eight Windows, 1988. 143-48.

Tres obras de teatro: Gobierno de alcoba; La víspera del Sábado; El laberinto. San José: Editorial Costa Rica, 1985.

Nonfiction

"Ciencia y poesía." *Confluencia* 8.9 (1993): 3-6.

"El cine y el teatro contemporáneo en Costa Rica." *Confluencia* 1.1 (1985): 56-64.

Cuarto creciente. San José: L'Atelier, 1974.

Cultural Policy in Costa Rica. Paris: UNESCO, 1977.

"Dramatización de lo inmediato." *Escena* 7 (1982): 24-25.

"Dramatización de lo inmediato: el sentido de lo trágico." *Escena* 10.19-20 (1988): 111-18.

"En busca del público perdido." *Conjunto* 77 (1988): 44-51.

"León Pacheco: mentor de hombres libres." *Kanina* 5.2 (1981): 11-13.

"Literatura y ética." *Confluencia* 5.1 (1989): 3-8.

SECONDARY BIBLIOGRAPHY
Criticism

Carballo, María Elena. "Padre e hijo en *Ceremonia de Casta*: el mundo de la bastardía." *Revista iberoamericana* 53.138-39 (1987): 56-64.

Pailler, Clara. "Le cafe et l'imaginaire costaricien." *Caravelle* 61 (1983): 93-101.

Rojas, Mario A. "*Gulliver dormido* de Samuel Rovinski: una parodia del discurso del poder." *Latin American Theatre Review* 24.1 (1990): 51-63.

—. "*El martirio del Pastor* de Samuel Rovinski: la dramatización de lo inmediato." In *Reflexiones sobre teatro latinoamericano del siglo XX*. Ed. Miguel Angel Giella and Peter Roster. Buenos Aires: Galerna/Lemcke Verlag, 1989. 153-60.

—. "*El martirio del Pastor*: el texto espectacular y su proceso de producción." *La escena latinoamericana* 1 (1989): 32-35.

—. "*El martirio del Pastor* y su referente." *Alba de América* 7.12-13 (1989): 117-29.

—. Samuel Rovinski and the Dual Identity." In *Tradition and Innovation: Reflections on Latin American Jewish Writing*. Ed. Robert DiAntonio and Nora Glickman. Albany: SUNY Press, 1993. 211-20.

Interviews

Bolet Rodríguez, Teresa. "Entrevista con Samuel Rovinski." *Confluencia* 3.2 (1988): 111-16.

Mario A. Rojas

ROVNER, EDUARDO (Argentina; 1942)

Born in Buenos Aires to a Jewish family originating in Russia, Eduardo Rovner was educated as an electrical engineer at the University of Buenos Aires (1967). An early talent for music led to studies in violin at the Municipal Conservatory of Music; he later played in various orchestras and classical music groups, sometimes on trumpet and flute as well. His humanistic interests led to studies in social psychology in which he also earned a degree (1977). After serving a term as Director of the Teatro Municipal General San Martín (the Buenos Aires Municipal Theater) from 1991-94, Rovner returned to the family business (plumbing supplies and equipment) while continuing to exercise his love for the theatre.

Rovner began his career in 1976 with *Una pareja* (A Couple) at a time when political and theatrical conditions were becoming increasingly difficult in Argentina. A relative late-comer to the theatre, he wrote at first a neo-realistic theatre within the framework of an Argentine legacy of Armando Discépolo (1887-1971) and members of his own, slightly older, generation, many of whom were inspired by Arthur Miller (1915). His later works reveal a willingness to experiment with expressionistic and absurdist techniques. Rovner's technique is to capture a dramatic image, or a theatrical situation, and then to develop it in ways that will surprise and delight the reader/public, as well as himself. Rovner himself insists that the dramatist is not an essayist, and he does not write the story before writing the play. His objective is to discover what is most surprising, most fascinating, most entertaining and most emotionally moving. For the most part his plays deal with ordinary, middle-class people in family situations but with anything other than ordinary results. A gentle man with a quick smile, Rovner has an extraordinary sense of humor, sometimes light, sometimes black, that suffuses virtually all of his plays.

Una pareja was staged in the Payró Theatre with Manuel Lillo as director with an intriguing subtitle "Que es mío y que es tuyo" (What's mine and what's yours), resonant of Edward Albee's (1928) *Who's Afraid of Virginia Woolf?* (1962). The maladjusted couple is involved in a burned-out relationship. When their friends come for a late evening visit, the dialogue ranges through multiple game-playing possibilities including group sex. At the end their differences are unresolved, pointing to sagas of miscommunication and frustration marked by the general insensitivity of both partners. If the husband is guilty of machismo, the wife is equally incapable of understanding personal needs. The net effect is a bleak picture of modern relationships in which the participants fail to make the necessary effort to understand each other's needs and anxieties.

¿Una foto. . .? (A Photo. . . ?), directed by Mirta Santos in 1977, continued in a similar psychological, neo-realistic vein. While taking the baby's photo is the basic premise of this short play, the dramatic action focuses on the parents who manifest signals of distress in their fractured relationship. With a keen sense of the psychological disruptions within modern marriages, Rovner captures the stresses and strains through the microcosmic function of such a simple exercise as taking a photo.

Although *La máscara* (The Mask) was chronologically Rovner's next play, staged by Alberto Ure in 1978, it has disappeared from view because of Rovner's disappointment with its structural and aesthetic unity. *Ultimo premio* (Last Prize) followed in 1981, directed by Néstor Romero in the Payró Theatre. Rovner continued his exploration of deep psychological relationships through two men, Abelardo (age 60) and Daniel (age 25), who live together in a strange symbiosis as a surrogate father-son team. The frictions that exist between them are exacerbated when Abelardo wins a coveted scientific prize for his university work. Through various roles as housekeeper, confessor, friend, and poet, Daniel assuages Abelardo's anxieties. After discoveries on both sides about their respective identities, tempered by darkness, guilt, and blame, the two reconcile their differences. Along with music ranging from the BeeGees to Bach, Rovner sprinkles the play with poetry to enhance the artistic and psychological interaction.

In 1983 Rovner participated in the third cycle of Teatro Abierto (Open Theatre) with *Concierto de aniversario* (Anniversary Concert), directed by Sergio Renán, a play that went on to represent Teatro Abierto in the International Theatre Festival of Havana in 1984 with subsequent performances in Lima and Arizona. In the tradition of the Argentine grotesque, emulating the models of Armando Discépolo and others, Rovner deploys four musicians who come to represent the worst aspects of a society with aggressive behaviors, slavish dedication to useless and repetitive activities, and gross insensitivity to the needs of others. The fascist attitudes of the members of the quartet reach their most aggressive point when one member denies medical attention to his dying wife in order to continue rehearsals. The rhythm of activity among the four is reflected in the music that inspired Rovner, that is, the second movement in pizzicato of Beethoven' Third Quartet ("Rasoumovsky") that provided the fundamental image of the play. Avoiding an intellectual discourse about the evils of totalitarianism and the virtues of love and solidarity, the play achieves its objectives implicitly rather than explicitly around the musical imagery.

The 1985 premiere of *Sueños de náufrago* (Shipwreck Dreams), also directed by Sergio Renán, plumbed the philosophical depths of the essence of life. Rovner's first play written in two acts, with its analepsis from 1940 to the present (1985), it provides an opportunity to pursue the implications of responsibility during the difficult years when humanity reached its lowest levels. The play takes a metatheatrical spin through the character of the playwright, Eugenio, who creates the setting for Arístides alone on an ocean raft, a metaphorical image of man bereft during a time of unspeakable horrors. The second act emphasizes the failures of mankind to find solutions to world problems, at the same time exploring the relationships between the creator and the created. Rovner completes the metatheatrical fantasy by dedicating the play in part to Arístides who has shared in the creative process. Rovner admits that he often fantasizes about meeting with his characters, over a cup of coffee, for example, to discuss their fates and fortunes.

Four years later Osvaldo Pellettieri staged *Y el mundo vendrá* (And the World Will Come; 1989), a play that won Rovner the María Guerrero nomination for best author of the year. Steeped in the grotesque traditions of Discépolo, the play presents a humorous, although pathetic, interpretation of the fantasy-laden, work-resistant Argentinian. While the central character exercises his dream of transforming himself into Zorba the Greek in order to attract tourism to El Tigre, the delta zone of Buenos Aires, the play reflects Rovner's contention that everybody wants to be special and nobody wants to work. With grand projections predicated on a minuscule percentage of huge numbers of world tourists, Zorba with a great deal of fantasy and very little reality spins out a get-rich-quick scheme that will ensure him a comfortable life. The absurdist convention of parlaying an essentially rational premise little by little into a grotesque extrapolation is indicative of the process by which members of the society victimize themselves with unrealistic expectations. The play also reflects a political attitude of expecting that an external solution will solve Argentina's problems by some sort of magic; the notion of working in order to achieve or to make progress is not endemic in the national character. Foreign companies clearly do not locate in Argentina in order to solve Argentina's problems but rather to make money.

Rovner's major successes in the theatre came in 1991 when he was awarded the Casa de las Américas Prize for *Volvió una noche* (She Returned One Night) and also the Argentores Prize for the best theatre work of the 1991 season, *Cuarteto* (Quartet). The staging of *Cuarteto* by Sergio Renán in the Sala Casacuberta of the General San Martín Municipal Theatre gave him an opportunity to develop more fully the premise of *Concierto de aniversario*, a play that had had only eight performances under the auspices of Teatro Abierto. The new play, dedicated, "nuevamente, a quienes sufrieron la insensibilidad y la crueldad. A Teatro Abierto" (again, to those who suffered insensitivity and cruelty. To Open Theatre [*Teatro*] 125), the play reworks the 1983 version under a new title. Expanding the play adds depth of characterization without modifying the original thrust of this vicious encounter with rampant insensitivity and cruelty. The Germanic ambiance of elegant music, a sense of total absorption in a "cause," a willingness to let suffering go unheeded in order to obey some "higher code" of ethics—all resound of the fascist techniques and attitudes of the Nazi regime during World War II. Rovner's own dedication to good music and his knowledge of technique as a performer enable him to develop a play in which an obsession with Beethoven translates into a powerful central image. The gross neglect of the dying wife, seen earlier in *Cuarteto*, and the boorish behavior of all the principal players reinforces the consistent image of totalitarianism wherever it exists.

In 1992 *Lejana tierra mía* (Distant Land of Mine) was staged by Jorge Petraglia in the Regio Theatre. A brief play, it is perhaps Rovner's most philosophical presentation about the meaning of friendship and life. This simple, tender play (the title comes from a famous Carlos Gardel tango) depends on music by Darius Milhaud (e.g., "Le boeuf sur le toit") with its constant shifts between the melodic and the dissonant. Through the exercise of painting a mural, a father and son share experiences. They work together; they discuss people; they exchange thoughts and dreams. Some items that appear suddenly in the mural (a lighthouse, pasture, etc.) add mystery and intrigue. The message is not the macrocosmic one of trying to save the world but the microcosmic one of the value and beauty of sharing closely with another person. The play contains religious elements, including the Christian symbology of sanctifying the house.

Rovner's most successful play to date is *Volvió una noche* (She Returned One Night), first performed in Montevideo in October of 1993, directed by Jorge Denevi, where it won the Florencio Prize for best play of 1993. Subsequent performances have been scheduled in Buenos Aires, Asunción, São Paulo, Philadelphia, Tel Aviv, Helsinki, and other sites. Virtually Rovner's only piece to date with an overtly Jewish presence, the play depends upon the return of the mother, ten years after her death, to check out her only son's intended bride. Predicated on the concept of the intrusive and protective Jewish mother, the techniques that lead to a humorous development are many and varied, including the restrictive visibility of the dead person, references to the afterlife (a sense of revulsion over worms, for example), and regular theatre activities among the departed (including the staging of "Arrival of a Salesman," an inverse perspective). While the references to Jewish traditions are explicit in both language and action, the play evidently translates well conceptually and has been staged in totally different contexts without the Jewish references.

Carne (Flesh; 1993) is a brief play that presents an obese man, intent on food, whose ample wife approaches him tenderly, only to be rejected by his confusion between her sexual attractions and her physical attractiveness. The play is a simple, non-metaphorical example of Rovner's exquisitely-tuned sense of black humor.

Compañía (Company) was presented as a dramatic reading in the International Theatre Festival of Bogotá in 1994. Composed in 1990, it is perhaps Rovner's most challenging play. In a sense the play is a continuation of his earlier explorations into deep psychological space, attempting to define the parameters of an individual's value system. By introducing a third person (female) within a marriage partnership, he tests the limits of acceptability of the original couple. The play takes sudden turns, leaving the reader/audience startled by each new stage in the development of this unfolding, potential "menage-a-trois." Ultimately, the importance of the play is imbedded in the understanding each person develops about the integrity and compassion of the others.

Tinieblas de un escritor enamorado (Shadows of a Writer in Love), directed by Adelaida Mangani, opened in Buenos Aires in the Liberarte Theatre in 1994. Based on an intertextual frame, a writer, while writing a story about his search for his loved one in death, dies himself or is perhaps trapped in his own fantasy. His search brings him into contact with family and friends who inhabit a world beyond. Like Dante's pursuit of eternal love through Beatrice, the play explores the limits of heroic and romantic behavior through its central venturesome character By staging the play with large puppets, Rovner achieves an aesthetic distance that is at once haunting and effective, and, as in *Sueños de náufrago*, fosters a penetrating intertextual consideration of the relationship between creator and creation.

El otro is a long, unpublished monologue involving two men in a closed hotel room in which one, a compulsive talker, sustains a verbal barrage with/against "the Other," who interacts without speaking. The play provides a classic exploration of obsessive behaviors brought on by an active imagination; the main character's fear of death, leads him to buy a revolver which in turn leads to aggressive action which ironically leads to his death. The Other, in this case, represents death, brings death and perhaps *is* Death. In spite of its closed setting, few props or special techniques, the play succeeds, as Rovner always does, in generating dramatic interest through a series of surprise turns in the action. One of the fundamental premises of the play is that life is ambiguous and constantly offers double perspectives: Do people take on the quality of their possessions—or do they acquire possessions because of the way they are? Rovner plays with similar concepts throughout, at times in a jocular manner, even to the end of the play when Pico, already dead, provides a summary of his feelings. One wonders: Does El Otro exist, or does Pico invent him? Does El Otro kill Pico, or do Pico's obsessions lead him to commit suicide? The play does not provide answers, but it does stimulate consideration of deep psychological and philosophical questions.

Rovner's plays range from very brief one-acts to full-length productions. By exploring profound psychological dimensions of human characterization imbedded within the fabric of Argentine social and political realities, Rovner has not only earned distinction within the panoply of contemporary Argentine playwrights but has achieved, with some plays at least, a universal idiom. His technical range includes plays written in a style of social and moral realism, inspired by and with admiration for Arthur Miller, as well as fantasies with elements of the grotesque and absurd, reminiscent of Armando Discépolo and others. Rovner strives for emotion, tempered by humor, within a context of surprise and wonder. While the Jewish quotient in his plays is minimal, largely because his Jewish heritage and tradition do not play a major role in his personal life, it does appear in a few plays. More important, no doubt, is the fact that his works present a balanced view of the human condition with interesting techniques and important themes.

PRIMARY BIBLIOGRAPHY

Compañía. Ottawa: GIROL Books, 1993. Bound with Mauricio Kartun, *El Partener.*

Cuarteto. Buenos Aires: Torres Agüero, 1992.

¿Una foto. . .?; Concierto de aniversario. In *Teatro: ocho autores.* Buenos Aires: Autores, 1985. 185-203.

El otro. Unpublished manuscript.

Teatro: Una pareja; Una foto. . .?; Ultimo premio; Concierto de aniversario; Sueños de náufrago; Y el mundo vendrá. Buenos Aires: Corregidor, 1989.

Teatro 1: Volvió una noche; Cuarteto; Compañía; Lejana tierra mía. Buenos Aires: Ediciones de la Flor, 1994.

Teatro 2: Y el mundo vendrá; Sueños de náufrago; Ultimo premio; Una pareja; ¿Una foto. . .?; Concierto de aniversario; Carne; La vieja, la joven y el harapiento. Buenos Aires: Ediciones de la Flor, 1996.

Tinieblas de un escritor enamorado. Unpublished manuscript.

Ultimo premio. Buenos Aires: Cinco, 1981.

SECONDARY BIBLIOGRAPHY

Dauster, Frank. "Eduardo Rovner." In *Compañía.* Ottawa: GIROL Books, 1993. ix-xvi.

Pellettieri, Osvaldo. "*Compañía* de Eduardo Rovner o el cuestionamiento simpático." *Primer acto* 248 (1993): 86-88.

—. "La obra dramática de Eduardo Rovner y el sistema teatral argentino." In *Teatro argentino contemporáneo (1980-1990).* Ed. Osvaldo Pellettieri. Buenos Aires: Galerna, 1994. 123-38.

—. "El teatro de Eduardo Rovner." In *Teatro.* Buenos Aires: Corregidor, 1989. 8-44.

Weinstein, Ana E., and Miryam E. Gover de Nasatsky, comps. *Escritores judeoargentinos: bibliografía 1900-1987.* 2 vols. Buenos Aires: Milá, 1994. II. 145-46.

Zayas de Lima, Perla. *Diccionario de autores argentinos 1950-1990*. Buenos Aires: Galerna, 1991. 241-43.

Interviews

Giella, Miguel Angel. "Entrevista con Eduardo Rovner: el triunfo de la imagen sobre la idea." In his *De dramaturgos: teatro latinoamericano actual*. Buenos Aires: Corregidor, 1994. 109-17.

George Woodyard

ROZENMACHER, GERMÁN (Argentina; 1936-71)

German Rozenmacher was born in Buenos Aires on March 27, 1936 into a traditional Jewish household. In his often-quoted self portrait, he described himself in the following manner: "soy feo, judío, rante y sentimental. Nací en el hospital Rivadavia—en el 36—y mi cuna, literalmente, fue un conventillo. . . (I'm ugly, Jewish, poor and sentimental. I was born in Rivadavia Hospital—in 1936—and my crib, literally, was a tenement. . . [the last line refers to a famous sainete; *Cuentos completos* 5]). Rozenmacher earned a degree from the Facultad de Filosofía y Letras (School of Philosophy and Literature) at the Universidad de Buenos Aires. He worked as a professor of Hebrew, a journalist, a theater critic, and he wrote for television. He was considered to be one of the most outstanding Argentine writers to emerge in the 1960s, first earning recognition as a short-story writer, and later proving to be a superb dramatist as well. On August 6, 1971, he was killed, along with his son, in an automobile accident in Mar del Plata, Argentina.

Rozenmacher first entered the national literary scene in 1962 with his short-story collection, *Cabecita negra*. Literally "black-haired person," the term is a synechdotal ethnic slur used to describe the populist supporters, usually of Northern indigenous origen, of Juan Domingo Perón. When used as an invective by anti-Peronists, its most pejorative connotation is roughly equivalent to the word "nigger" in English. The overriding theme that shapes the author's narrative is the impact of Peronism on Argentine society, which Rozenmacher portrays from a variety of perspectives. Many critics have analyzed the incidence of Peronism in Rozenmacher's fiction and consider him to be one of the major proponents of a generation of writers that includes among others David Viñas (1929), Pedro Orgambide (1929), Juan José Saer (1937), and Abelardo Castillo

(1935) whose works are defined by the sociohistorical and political forces of Peronism (Avellaneda; Morello-Frosch; Borello). Rozenmacher officially gained national prominence when his short story "El gallo blanco" (The White Rooster) was selected to be included in an anthology of Argentine fiction, *Crónicas del pasado* (Chronicles of the Past [Buenos Aires: J. Alvarez, 1965]), that showcased such already well-established authors as Ernesto Sabato (1911) and Rodolfo Walsh (1927-?). He published a second volume of short stories, *Los ojos del tigre* (The Eyes of the Tiger) in 1967. This subsequent volume is closely related to *Cabecita negra* in terms of both style, characterized as social or critical realism, and theme. The 1971 *Cuentos completos* (Complete Stories) is a posthumous volume that brings together all of Rozenmacher's short stories save one, "El misterioso Sr. Q" (The Mysterious Mr. Q), also published posthumously in 1972.

The story "Cabecita negra" is without a doubt one of Rozenmacher's most accomplished narratives and the one most analyzed. It recounts the nightmarish experience of a typical middle-class Argentine family man, Lanari, who rather suddenly finds his life and home threatened by the *cabecitas negras* of the lower classes. Ironically, he is largely responsible for the humiliation and pain that he suffers. The story is essentially about the petit-bourgeois attitude—tinged with racism and disdain—toward the populist masses, perceived as being potentially dangerous, in social, political, and economic terms. Other politically charged stories by Rozenmacher include "Los ojos del tigre," "Cochecito" (Little Car), and "Esta hueya la bailan los radicales" (This One's for the Radicals). In other stories, the author creates a more subtle depiction of social reality through the descriptions of the characters. Solitude, loneliness, despair, poverty, desperation, and frustration—all occasioned by social injustices—are part of the emotional baggage that Rozenmacher's protagonists carry with them. "Raíces" (Roots), "El gallo blanco," and "Ataúd" (Coffin) readily come to mind as stories that portray the existential misery experienced by the protagonists who often find themselves living not only on the economic margins of society but also on the geographic fringes, as in "Raíces," which takes place in a northern province on the border with Bolivia.

While Rozenmacher wrote stories that spoke to Argentine society in general, he also penned three stories that deal specifically with the Jewish experience in Buenos Aires. They are narrated from the optic of the aged immigrant who considers himself a stranger in a strange land. "Tristezas de la pieza de hotel" (Hotel Room Sorrows) and "El gato dorado" (The Golden Cat) both from *Cabecita negra*, and "Blues en la noche" ("Blues in the Night") from *Los ojos del tigre* have in common protagonists who were once semirenown artists in their countries of origin, but for whom success in Argentina never came. They are the victims of prejudice from an unaccepting society as well as of their own strict adherence to tradition and nostalgia. Nora Glickman has pointed out the linguistic strategies employed by Rozenmacher to familiarize the non-Jewish reader with the cultural codes of Yiddishkeit that inform the protagonists. Likewise, she underscores the fact that music is central to Rozenmacher's stories as primarily a method to evade the reality of the present while maintaining the fantasy of the past.

"Blues en la noche" revolves around the solitude of a once-great musician, Vasily Goloboff, who sang in the Russian opera, and who had abandoned his Jewish identity. After emigrating to Argentina, he finds work as a music tutor—a humiliating occupation for a renown artist—in order to eke out a living, and he once again embraces his Jewishness. Goloboff lives a miserable existence in a tenement, clinging desperately to his perhaps too idyllic memories of the past. He is befriended by Bernardo, the young son of some acquaintances. They seem to have in common a sense of melancholy and loneliness, although stemming from different sources. Bernardo pleads with Goloboff to give him music lessons, which the latter finally agrees to do. The two share a fondness for jazz music, especially that of North American Jewish jazz artists such as Al Jolson and Aaron Lebedeff. The music speaks to them emotionally, as described by Goloboff: "And he felt as if he were coming down the Mississippi and he was black, and he had lived in 1880, and he was sinking in a river of his own blood, and was howling with all his might" ("Blues in the Night" 80). The story ends on a depressing note as Goloboff frightens his young pupil off. Pleading for him to stay, he finds himself once again abandoned.

Like Goloboff, the *maestro* of "El gato dorado" also cleaves to his past. He is sardonically called *maestro* by his friends, not because he was once a great composer, but because like them he is just a two-bit musician who plays the piano in a basement club. However, he was once part of a band that wandered from town to town entertaining the people before the pogroms that prompted his emigration to Argentina. What is unusual about the story is the element of the fantastic that Rozenmacher weaves into the narration. The *maestro* finds an escape from his doldrums through a magical cat given to him by a neighbor. Nora Glickman likens the cat to a dybbuk that possesses the protagonist. The animal allows the *maestro* to relive his youth as a travelling musician, conversely it keeps his mind from returning to the oppressing reality of his present situation. His escape mechanism is destroyed in the end when the cat is run over by a passing trolley car.

El Gran Félix (Felix the Great), the protagonist of "Tristezas de la pieza de hotel," also lives in the past. He is the typical schlemazl, described as "el solterón, el pariente pobre, el 'kuéntenik' que vagabundea por los boliches y los cafés vendiendo baratijas" (the old bachelor, the poor relative, the salesman who wandered about the bars and cafes selling trinkets [*Cuentos completos* 12]). Likewise, he possesses the "asombrosa habilidad para decir las cosas más lamentables en el momento menos adecuado. Tenía una especie de sentido de la oportunidad al revés" (amazing ability to say the most lamentable things at the least appropriate moment. He had a kind of reverse sense of opportunity [*Cuentos completos* 12]). El Gran Félix lives isolated not only from the Argentine mainstream, but from his Jewish family and community as well. He lives in his hotel room, secluded from the world on the outside, with which he cannot cope.

Saúl Sosnowski argues that these three stories have in common an emphasis on man's solitude. Furthermore, he points out that Rozenmacher utilizes Jewishness as the defining characteristic of that solitude within a society that views the Jew as different and therefore unfit to live alongside the rest of the citizenry. He concludes that Rozenmacher essentially viewed Judaism as incompatible with Argentina (*Revista de crítica* 108).

Rozenmacher is probably remembered best for his dramatic works rather than for his narrative, even though he only wrote four plays. His first play, *Réquiem para un viernes a la noche* (Requiem for a Friday Night) opened on May 21, 1964 at the Idisches Volks Theater (IFT) in Buenos Aires. It played for two years, was produced for television and has been staged numerous times to the present day, most recently at the Teatro Regina in Buenos Aires during the 1994 theater season to commemorate the thirtieth anniversary of the play. *Réquiem* has become a classic of Argentine theater and has been anthologized numerous times. The play is representative of the generation of 1960 to which Rozenmacher belonged and which includes dramatists like Roberto Cossa (1934), Ricardo Talesnik (1935), Ricardo Halac (1935), Griselda Gambaro (1928), and Carlos Somigliana (1932-87). For the most part this generation of dramatists was concerned with creating realist dramatic works on the sociocultural reality of Argentina. Critics have been quick to highlight the realist influence of Arthur Miller's *Death of a Salesman* (1949) on Rozenmacher and the other members of his generation (Zayas de Lima; Fernández; Tirri). *Réquiem* has been studied mainly as a play about generational conflict and cultural identity (Sosnowski; Senkman; Foster). The play brings to the stage the conflict between Sholem and his son David, a first-generation Argentine. Sholem Abramson, a respected chazan at the neighborhood synagogue, and his wife Leie cling to a traditional Jewish way of life steeped in religiosity and adherence to Jewish Law. In direct contrast is David, who finds his parents' unwillingness to adapt to the Argentine way of life too constricting and who in his eagerness to assimilate plans to marry a Catholic girl; an unforgivable act of heresy according to his father. In the middle is Max, Leie's secularized and none-too-serious brother who acts as a mediator between both sides.

It is easy to see why Rozenmacher's play has become part of the mainstream Argentine theatrical tradition. It is a highly developed, moving work, psychologically and emotionally compelling in its portrayal of what was a considerably common problem within the immigrant population, and not only among the Jewish sector. Rozenmacher was not, however, the first playwright to dramatize this generational strife which afflicted the Jewish immigrant family. Thematically, *Réquiem* was preceded by *Hermanos nuestros* (Our Brothers; 1923) by Francisco Defilippis Novoa (1889-1930)—a non-Jewish dramatist—and *El hijo del rabino* (1930) by Bernardo Graiver (1902-83). It is quite clear that Rozenmacher's play reflects many aspects of his own life: his own father was a cantor, Rozenmacher himself married a Catholic, Amelia "Chana" Figueiredo, and he dedicated the play to his parents and to his wife. Significantly, Rozenmacher does not attempt to provide a solution to the conflict presented. Indeed, the force of the work resides in the fact that there can be no reconciliation between the opposing ideological stances father and son represent, and therein lies the "tragedy." Nevertheless, one can also view the play as a representation of the evolutionary nature of Jewish identity—in other words, the process by which each subsequent generation modifies what being Jewish means.

In 1970, Rozenmacher participated in a group effort with fellow dramatists Roberto Cossa, Carlos Somigliana, and Ricardo Talesnik to write *El avión negro* (The Black Airplane). The title comes from the popular myth that Juan Perón, deposed in 1955, would make his triumphant return to Argentina in a black airplane. The play consists of a series of politicized comic sketches that depart from the confines of realism to include elements of the grotesque, the absurd, and even magical realism and epic song (Kaiser-Lenoir; Halac, "La realidad argentina"). The sketches represent the reaction of different sectors of society with regard to Perón's possible return to power.

Rozenmacher's next play, *El Lazarillo de Tormes*, opened in May 1971, also at the IFT Theater. It is based on the anonymous sixteenth-century picaresque novel by the same name. According to Jorge Goldenberg, it was a play aimed at an adolescent audience (*Noaj* 44). Nevertheless, it provides ample material for a critical evaluation of contemporary Argentine society. The play contains no specific Jewish referents, outside the mention of the Inquisition. As David William Foster states, "the Jewish theme is present only by oblique reference through the figure of the Inquisidor and the audience's natural familiarity with the connection between anti-Semitism and the Spanish Empire and the

Inquisition" (*Cultural Diversity* 126). Foster likewise highlights the metaphorical connection between the play and Argentine sociopolitical reality, emphasizing Rozenmacher's assertion that Lazarillo was a Jew (found in the preface to the play; 4).

Simón Brumelstein, el caballero de Indias (*Simón Brumelstein, Knight of the Indies*) was Rozenmacher's last published play, although it was written in 1970 (Zayas de Lima, *Diccionario* 243). Leonardo Senkman notes that it could not be staged at the Teatro Sociedad Hebraica in 1971 because of censorship, though he does not state what the nature or source of the censorship was (Senkman, *La identidad judía* 309). The play finally premiered July 27, 1982 in the Teatro Tabarís of Buenos Aires, but was not published until 1987. *Simón Brumelstein* is Rozenmacher's most daring and accomplished play, both thematically and stylistically. Much like El Gran Félix of "Tristezas de la pieza de hotel," Simón lives enclosed in a room, estranged from his family, a victim of anti-Semitism, and a prisoner to his own fears, doubts, and ineptitude. As an alternative to the real world outside the room he inhabits, Simón creates a fantastic dream world he calls *Chantania* (derived, undoubtedly, as Foster points out, from *chanta/chantaje*, "blackmailer/blackmail" [*Cultural Diversity* 130]). Similar to David of *Réquiem*, Simón takes a non-Jewish lover who also happens to be the wife of Pingitori, from whom he rents his room. As Senkman points out, Simón is a typical luftmensch who exists more in the world of fantasy than reality (*La identidad judía* 310). His psychological plight revolves around his deep desire to assimilate into Argentine society, shedding his Jewishness: "si yo no quiero ser judío. . . quiero ser un hombre, nada más" (but I don't want to be a Jew. . . . I want to be a man, nothing more [20]). Nevertheless, he is constantly reminded that his participation in Argentine society is not only suspect, but that he will never be completely Argentine, as Pingitori tells him: "Judío. . . ¿para qué viniste acá? ¿A alterar el orden de las cosas? ¿Por qué no te mató Hitler, eh? ¿A qué viniste a este país? Si lo hicimos nosotros. . ." (Jew. . . why did you come here? To alter the order of things? Why didn't Hitler kill you, uh? Why did you come to this country? If we're the ones who made it. . . [41]). In an attempt to justify his presence on Argentine soil, Simón creates for himself a noble heritage of Caballeros de Indias who helped to conquer and settle the continent. The action of the play alternates between reality and Simón's dilusional visions. First, Simón's cousin Katz comes to visit and complain that he was left supporting Simón's family after he abandoned them. He tries to convince Simón to at least sell him his jewelry store. Later, Simón's wife also visits in an attempt to win him back. From the fantasy world Simón is visited by his father, who reproaches him for rejecting his Jewish heritage, as well as by his grandmother, who comforts him as she did when he was a child. Ultimately, Simón is taken away to an asylum for the mentally insane. In sum, *Simón Brumelstein* is about the very real clash of cultures, assimilation, anti-Semitism, and crises of identity. Like *Réquiem*, the play offers no facile panacea to ease the pain of being Jewish in Argentina.

One can only wonder what literary heights Rozenmacher would have achieved had his life not been cut short at age thirty-five. His works, however, are and will remain fundamental to the Argentine literary canon and they have left a lasting imprint on Argentine culture. The void created by his absence is eloquently elaborated in the poem "A Germán Rozenmacher" (To Germán Rozenmacher; 1974) written by the Argentine Jewish poet Eliahu Toker (1934) shortly after Rozenmacher's death.

PRIMARY BIBLIOGRAPHY
Creative Writing

El avión negro. (With Roberto Cossa, Carlos Somigliana, and Ricardo Talesnik). Buenos Aires: Talía, 1970.

"Blues in the Night." Trans. by Nora Glickman. In *Tropical Synagogues: Short Stories by Jewish-Latin American Writers.* Edited and with introduction by Ilán Stavans. New York: Holmes & Meier, 1994. 67-82.

Cabecita negra y otros cuentos. Buenos Aires: Anuario, 1962. Also, Buenos Aires: Jorge Alvarez, 1963; Buenos Aires: Centro Editor de América Latina, 1967; 1981 (with prologue by Jorge B. Rivera).

Cuentos completos. Buenos Aires: Centro Editor de América Latina, 1971.

"The Golden Cat." Trans. by Nora Glickman. *Latin American Literary Review* 9.19 (1981) 79-85.

El Lazarillo de Tormes. Buenos Aires: Talía, 1971.

"El misterioso Sr. Q." *Macedonio* 12.3 (1972): 15-31.

Los ojos del tigre. Buenos Aires: Galerna, 1967.

Réquiem para un viernes a la noche. Buenos Aires: Talía, 1964; 2nd ed. 1971. Also in *El teatro argentino.* Vol. I. Comp. by Jorge Lafforgue. Buenos Aires: Centro Editor de América Latina, 1982. 149-95; *Panorama del teatro argentino:* Canillita *y otras obras.* Buenos Aires: Centro Editor de América Latina, 1987. 155-95; *Teatro argentino contemporáneo: antología.* Madrid: Centro de Documentación Teatral, Ministerio de Cultura; Sociedad Estatal Quinto Centenario; Fondo de Cultura Económica, 1992. 807-52.

Simón Brumelstein, el caballero de Indias. Buenos Aires: Argentores, 1987. English version as *Simón Brumelstein, Knight of the Indies.* Trans. by

Nora Glickman and Gloria F. Waldman. In *Argentine Jewish Theatre: A Critical Anthology*. Ed. Nora Glickman and Gloria F. Waldman. Lewisburg: Bucknell UP, 1996. 110-53.

Nonfiction

"Pastillas de dinamita para la memoria." *Noaj* 5.6 (1991): 41-43.

SECONDARY BIBLIOGRAPHY

Avellaneda, Andrés. "El tema del peronismo en la novela argentina." Ph.D. diss., University of Illinois, 1971. (See chapter titled "Narrativa e ideología: lectura de 'Cabecita negra', de Germán Rozenmacher").

Borello, Rodolfo A. "El realismo crítico: Rozenmacher y David Viñas." In his *El peronismo (1943-1955) en la narrativa argentina*. Ottawa: Dovehouse Editions, 1991. 222-48.

Espinosa, Pedro. "*Réquiem para un viernes a la noche*, de Germán Rozenmacher: una ruptura con afecto." *Teatro XX* 1 (1964): 8-9.

Fernández, Gerardo. "Largo viaje de un día hacia la noche." In *Teatro argentino contemporáneo: antología*. Madrid: Centro de Documentación Teatral, Ministerio de Cultura; Sociedad Estatal Quinto Centenario; Fondo de Cultura Económica, 1992. 799-804.

Foster, David William. "Argentine Jewish Dramatists: Aspects of a National Consciousness." *Folio* 17 (1987): 74-103. Expanded treatment of Rozenmacher's work appears in the revised version of this article in Foster's *Cultural Diversity in Latin American Literature*. Albuquerque: U of New Mexico P, 1994. 119-32.

—. "Germán Rozenmacher: escribiendo la experiencia contemporánea judía en Argentina." Trans. by Gustavo Oscar Geirola. In *Teatro y teatristas: estudios sobre teatro argentino e iberoamericano*. Ed. Osvaldo Pellettieri. Buenos Aires: Galerna/Facultad de Filosofía y Letras (UBA), 1992. 129-36. (Essentially the Spanish translation of the material in his *Cultural Diversity*)

Glickman, Nora. "Desarraigo contemporáneo en la narrativa de Germán Rozenmacher." In *Latin American Fiction Today*. Ed. Rose S. Minc. Tacoma Park, MD: Hispamérica; Upper Montclair, NJ: Montclair State College, 1979. 109-17.

Goldenberg, Jorge. "Germán Rozenmacher." *Noaj* 5.6 (1991): 44-48. Also in *El imaginario judío en la literatura de América Latina: visión y realidad*. Ed. Patricia Finzi, Eliahu Toker and Marcos Faerman. Buenos Aires: Editorial Shalom, 1992. 155-61.

Halac, Ricardo. "La realidad argentina, *El avión negro* y el grupo de autores." In *El avión negro*. Buenos Aires: Talía, 1970. 9-12.

—. "El teatro de Germán Rozenmacher y la tensión entre el judaísmo y la revolución." *Los libros* (Argentina) 23 (1971): 24-25.

Kaiser-Lenoir, Claudia. "*El avión negro*: de la realidad a la caricatura grotesca." *Latin American Theatre Review* 15.1 (1981): 5-11. Also in *Revista canadiense de estudios hispánicos* 7.1 (1982): 149-58.

Lafforgue, Jorge. "Germán Rozenmacher: un testimonio." *Macedonio* 12.3 (1972): 39-41.

Miguel, María Esther de. Rev. of *Cabecita negra*. *Señales* 141 (1963): 44-45.

Morello-Frosch, Marta. "La ficción se historifica: Cortázar y Rozenmacher." *Revista de crítica literaria latinoamericana* 3.5 (1977): 75-86.

Paz, Marta Lena. "El exilio y el héroe transgresor como emergentes de la historia en la obra de Germán Rozenmacher." In *Literatura e identidad latinoamericana—siglo XX*. IV Simposio Internacional de Literatura. Ed. Juana Alcira Arancibia. Westminster, CA: Instituto Literario y Cultural Hispánico, 1991. 239-50.

Rosa, Nicolás. "*Cabecita negra*, de Germán Rozenmacher." *Setecientos monos* (Rosario, Argentina) 3.4 (1964): 3-7.

Scotti, María A. "La narrativa de Rozenmacher: testimonio de residencia en la tierra." *Macedonio* 12.3 (1972): 54-59.

Senkman, Leonardo. *La identidad judía en la literatura argentina*. Buenos Aires: Pardés, 1983. 303-16.

—. "Rozenmacher y los malentendidos: una nueva lectura de la obra póstuma de Germán Rozenmacher." *Nueva presencia* 280 (12 Dec., 1982): 8, 24.

Sneh, Simja. "El caballero que no logró abandonar su identidad." *Mundo israelita* 3066 (21 Aug., 1982): 6-7.

Sosnowski, Saúl. "Germán Rozenmacher: tradiciones, rupturas y desencuentros." *Revista de crítica literaria latinoamericana* 3.6 (1977): 93-119. Also as Chapter II of his *La orilla inminente: escritores judíos argentinos*. Buenos Aires: Legasa, 1987. 37-68.

Tirri, Néstor. *Realismo y teatro argentino*. Buenos Aires: La Bastilla, 1973. 113-21.

Toker, Eliahu. "A Germán Rozenmacher." In his *Lejaim*. Buenos Aires: Ediciones de la Flor, 1974. 87-90.

Weinstein, Ana E., and Miryam E. Gover de Nasatsky, comps. *Escritores judeoargentinos: bibliografía 1900-1987*. 2 vols. Buenos Aires: Milá, 1994. I.147-51.

Zayas de Lima, Perla. "Germán Rozenmacher ." In her *Diccionario de autores teatrales argentinos 1950-1990*. Buenos Aires: Galerna, 1991. 243-44.

—. "Germán Rozenmacher: un caballero en busca del *aôr*." In *Teatro argentino de los '60: polémica, continuidad y ruptura*. Ed. Osvaldo Pellettieri. Buenos Aires: Corregidor, 1989. 121-43.

Darrell B. Lockhart

SATZ, MARIO (Argentina; 1944)

Mario Satz was born in Coronel Pringles, Argentina in 1944. He has traveled extensively throughout South America, Europe and the United States. He lived in Jerusalem between 1970 and 1973 where he undertook biblical studies in addition to anthropology, and history of the Middle East. Since 1978 Satz has resided in Barcelona where he received a degree in Hispanic philology. In addition to being a prolific writer, Satz is also a translator, historian, and social critic. His over twenty published books include poetry, narrative, and nonfiction works which deal with the Kabbalah and Jewish history among other topics.

His first collection of poems, *Los cuatro elementos* (The Four Elements; 1964), was published when Satz was twenty years old. It consists of simple elegies to fire, water, earth, and air, and it signals the focus on the natural world that is a constant theme throughout his poetry. *Las frutas* (Fruits; 1970), for example, is a series of poems about different kinds of fruit (apples, oranges, plums, pomegranates, limes, watermelons, pineapples, bananas, coconuts, almonds, cherries, pears). The poems express the power and beauty of nature. Likewise, earth themes of regeneration and fertility create a certain erotic subtone in the poems. Subsequent volumes like *Canon de polen* (Canon of Pollen; 1976), *Los peces, los pájaros, las flores* (The Fish, the Birds, the Flowers; 1976), and *Sámaras* (the botanical term for a seed scales; 1981) continue in this same vein. *Los peces* invokes the creation, while *Sámaras* gives voice to nature through poems that spring from the botanical world of plants and flowers in an erotically-charged poetic blossoming. The collection *Las redes cristalinas* (The Crystalline Nets; 1985) finds its poetic base in the mineral world. It also speaks out strongly against the repression of the military government in Argentina during 1976-83. In a mood of philosophical inquiry, the poet elicits the themes of anti-Semitism in Argentina, particularly in relation to the military. Satz also denounces the ignorance of the Federal Police and the violence of institutionalized Catholicism in the country.

Satz's narrative enterprise is an almost inconceivably vast undertaking. His novels are all grouped under a single literary project titled *Planetarium*. This characterization of his novels as a textual solar system is indicative of the expansive scope of the author's creative vision. The project was initiated with a trilogy that is comprised of *Sol* (Sun, the English translation kept the original Spanish *Sol*; 1976), *Luna* (Moon; 1977), and *Tierra* (Earth; 1978). The subsequent novels *Marte* (Mars; 1980) and *Mercurio* (Mercury; 1990) are part of the *Planetarium*, but they do not continue the narration of the trilogy. It is difficult to identify Satz as an Argentine writer since his works do not take place within the geographic boundaries of his native country, nor do they reveal any close connection to Argentina, thematically or otherwise. Rather, he works on a larger scale with themes that speak to Latin America as a whole. The two principal cities of the trilogy are Jerusalem and Cuzco, Peru; both of which have long histories and are steeped in mythology. Satz utilizes a blend of Latin American history and culture and Jewish tradition, together with the religious beliefs systems of diverse cultures to create his novelistic cosmos. He particularly relies on indigenous Latin American mythology and cosmology and Judaic mysticism and kabbalism to provide the philosophical structure of the texts. Action in the novels alternates primarily between Israel and Latin America. In *Marte*, the author uses Mars not only as an additional planet in his solar system, but more significantly the title refers to the Roman god of war. It revolves around the war in an unnamed South American country, which really serves as a backdrop for the elaboration of a profound mythopoetic representation of Latin American development. Four sections of the novel (Egg, Larva, Chrysalis, Imago) present a kind of metamorphosis that metaphorically is compared to that of a butterfly. Satz's *Planetarium* is a highly complex novelistic endeavor that draws heavily on a variety of cultural belief systems, only one of which is Judaism.

Satz's *Tres cuentos españoles* (Three Spanish Tales; 1988) departs from the narrative immensity of his novels. The book is a collection of three novellas, all of which take place in the tricultural ambience—Christian, Muslim, Jewish—of thirteenth-century Spain. The author has taken painstaking measures in his literary recreation of this period. His attention to historical, linguistic, and sociopolitical detail is astounding. There is such an insistence on including words and phrases in Arabic and Hebrew that it at times encumbers the text, making it difficult for the reader to advance through the linguistic maze. The three separate novellas, "El arco iris del silencio" (The Rainbow of Silence), "El jazmín despierto" (The Flowering Jasmine), and "La unión de los mares" (The Union of the Seas), recall the grandiose and often violent history of Spain, the cooperation and conflict between the three principal cultures, and the flowering of the arts and sciences. Satz mixes fictional characters with historical figures in his stories to create a fascinating glimpse of life in Spain during the period of the Reconquest, prior to the expulsion of the Jews and Muslims from the Iberian peninsula. Satz's nonfiction works reveal his intense interest in Judaica. His books *Arbol verbal: nueve notas en torno a la Kábala* (Verbal Tree: Nine Notes Concerning the Kabbalah; 1983) and *Poética de la Kábala. Senderos en el jardín del corazón* (A Poetics of the Kabbalah. Paths in the Garden of the Heart; 1985) are both detailed studies of the Hebrew alphabet and its kabbalistic meanings. His *Judaísmo: 4,000 años de cultura* (Judaism: 4,000 Years of Culture; 1982) is an all-encompassing history of the Jewish people. In it Satz discusses the influence of other cultures on the development of Judaism, such as Hellenism. Other topics include exile, the Hasidim, the Sephardim, haskalah, and a engaging discussion of Judaism as a temporal and spatial experience.

As one of the more prolific of Latin American Jewish authors, Mario Satz has written a corpus of works that provide fertile ground for literary studies. His texts merit closer critical examination than they have so far received for the way in which he presents his own experience with Jewish tradition into his works, thus creating a Latin American Jewish literary discourse.

PRIMARY BIBLIOGRAPHY
Creative Writing
Canon de polen. Buenos Aires: Sudamericana, 1976.

Los cuatro elementos. Buenos Aires: Montanari, 1964.

Fabulosa historia de Kallima y el árbol que canta. Madrid: Alfaguara, 1987.

Las frutas. Buenos Aires: Rodolfo Alonso, 1970.

Hoja de ruta. Quito: Insurrexit, 1966.

Luna. Barcelona: Noguer, 1977.

Marte. Barcelona: Seix Barral, 1980.

Mercurio. Madrid: Heptada Ediciones, 1990.

Los peces, los pájaros, las flores. Buenos Aires: Sudamericana, 1976.

Quintaesentia. Mallorca: Papeles de Son Armadans, 1974.

Las redes cristalinas. Barcelona: Obelisco, 1985.

Sámaras. Barcelona: Argonauta, 1981.

Sol. Barcelona: Noguer, 1976. English version as *Sol*. Trans. by Helen R. Lane. Garden City, NY: Doubleday, 1979.

Tierra. Barcelona: Noguer, 1978.

Tres cuentos españoles. Barcelona: Sirmio, 1988.

Nonfiction

Arbol verbal: nueve notas en torno a la Kábala. Madrid: Altalena, 1983.
Jesús el nazareno, terapeuta y cabalista. Barcelona: Arcanos Mayores, 1988.
El judaísmo: 4,000 años de cultura. Barcelona: Montesinos, 1982.
El lenguaje de los pájaros. Barcelona: Elfos, 1987.
Poética de la Kábala. Senderos en el jardín del corazón. Madrid: Altalena, 1985.
Umbría lumbre: San Juan de la Cruz y la sabiduría secreta de la Kábala y el Sufismo. Madrid: Hiperión, 1991.

SECONDARY BIBLIOGRAPHY

Criticism

García, Victorino Polo. "La novela argentina contemporánea: aproximación a la narrativa de Mario Satz." *Anales de literatura hispanoamericana* 21 (1992): 457-65.

Gutman, Daniel. "*Sol* de Mario Satz." *Megafón* 5 (1977): 210-11.

Lane, Helen R. "Mario Satz: Cosmic Choreographer." *Review* (New York) 24 (1980): 15-19.

Najenson, José Luis. "Mario Satz: alegoría de una España agónica." *Noaj* 4.5 (1990): 91-92.

Senkman, Leonardo. "Israel en la conciencia e imaginación del judío argentino." *Diálogo* 14 (1982): 41-46.

—. "Jerusalem o el peregrinaje transhistórico al centro del mundo." In his *La identidad judía en la literatura argentina*. Buenos Aires: Pardés, 1983. 400-3.

Interviews

Fingueret, Manuela. "El jardín de los senderos que confluyen." *Nueva Sión* 615 (4 April, 1985): 22.

Darrell B. Lockhart

SCHERSCHENER, EVA (Uruguay; date unknown)

Eva Scherschener is a native of Uruguay who has lived in Israel since 1978. Her works, all of which have been published in Montevideo, have come to occupy "un buen lugar en la literatura nacional" (a good place in national literature), according to Julio Ricci in his prologue to Scherschener's latest book, *La familia Levi* (The Levi Family; 1994).

The author's first work was a collection of short stories titled *La casamentera* (The Matchmaker). This text is mentioned in the prologues to posterior works, yet, at the time of this writing neither the book, nor full bibliographical data for it could not be located. Scherschener's writing, which contains many autobiographical elements, reflects a deep sense of Jewish identity. Her characters confront issues that affect the personal, religious, political, economic, and moral aspects of their lives.

In 1989, Scherschener published *Cuentos de vidas* (Stories of Lives), a collection of four short stories that take place in Latin America—largely Uruguay, but also Argentina and Chile—and Israel. "Las bodas de Anita" (Anita's Wedding) is a story that builds up to the title character's wedding day, but which focuses mainly on the narration of the Kohn family's emigration from Odessa to Argentina and then to Montevideo. The author effectively portrays the forging of an immigrant society in early twentieth-century Montevideo through the juxtaposition of Jewish and Italian families who are learning to cope with different customs, traditions, and religions within the context of a new country. The story "Ibrahim y nosotros" (Ibrahim and Us), takes place in Israel and revolves around a young Jewish-Uruguayan couple who have made aliya and who operate a toilet paper factory. At the core of the story is the couple's friendship with a young Arab employee, Ibrahim. Ultimately, the story is about overcoming stereotypes and the success of Jewish-Arab relations on a personal level, against the backdrop of the political conflict between warring nations. "El candelabro de Kiev" (The Candelabrum of Kiev) is also about a Jewish-Uruguayan woman who has moved to Israel. However, it is told mainly in retrospect with the majority of the story taking place in Chile. The final story, "El libro de Job" (The Book of Job), is about a Holocaust survivor living in New York who must travel to Israel to bury his son who was killed while serving in the Israeli army.

Scherschener situates all the stories of *La montaña roja* in Israel. While the characters are for the most part uninteresting, the dialogue mundane and the story lines fail to intrigue the reader, the author does provide a detailed, at times even tedious, depiction of contemporary Israeli life. What is most engaging about the text is the description of Israeli populace as comprising a multicultural and multiethnic society. In this text as well as in *Cuentos de vidas*, Ethiopian, Yemenite, Iraqi, and Latin American Jews learn to live together, and to co-exist with non-Jews.

La familia Levi is Scherschener's most accomplished text to date in terms of narrative style. The novel seems to be a much expanded version of the story "Las bodas de Anita." It takes place in the Montevideo of the 1930s and 1940s and revolves around the various members of the extended Levi family. Told mostly from the perspective of the adolescent Ita, the book narrates the economic successes and failures, the marriages and divorces, and the generational conflicts of her relatives, as well as depicting more centrally Jewish issues as concerns assimilation and the attenuation of traditional customs and values.

As an author, Eva Scherschener is not on par with fellow Uruguayan writers Cristina Peri Rossi (1941) or Teresa Porzecanski (1945), for example, but she does provide Uruguayan literature with a very fascinating Jewish element. Her works represent the linguistic and cultural hybridization of the Jewish immigrant and the Uruguayan creole, even as it is experienced in Israel.

PRIMARY BIBLIOGRAPHY

Cuentos de vidas. Montevideo: Proyección, 1989.
La familia Levi. Montevideo: Graffiti, 1994.
La montaña roja. Montevideo: Géminis, 1992.

Darrell B. Lockhart

SCHVARTZMAN, PABLO (Argentina; 1927)

Pablo Schvartzman was born in General Campos, a small community in the Mesopotamian province of Entre Ríos. He founded and directed the Haor publishing house in Concepción del Uruguay, Entre Ríos, where he currently resides. He is primarily a poet, but he is also the author of one volume of short stories and a historical essay.

Judíos en América (Jews in America; 1963) is a historical essay on the Jewish presence in Latin America since the time of the Conquest to the twentieth century. The book consists of a very scant survey on the topic and by no means can be considered a comprehensive study of Latin American Jewish history. Nevertheless, the volume does provide some interesting information, largely in anecdotal form. The two main topics discussed by Schvartzman are the Inquisition and a variety of dubious theories that seek to link Latin American indigenous peoples to Jewish history. The rest of the text is dedicated to the discussion of major Jewish historical figures such as Julio Popper, a Rumanian Jewish scientist who did much work in Tierra del Fuego, Mordejai Navarro, a close aid to General Justo José de Urquiza, and Noé Yarcho, the famous doctor of the early agricultural colonies in Entre Ríos.

Schvartzman's collection of short stories, *Cuentos criollos con judíos* (Creole Stories with Jews), was published in 1967. The stories continue the tradition of Alberto Gerchunoff (1883-1950) in *Los gauchos judíos* (*The Jewish Gauchos of the Pampas*; 1910), and other texts that appeal to regionalism and the apparent ease with which Jewish immigrants were able to assimilate into the local rural creole social milieu. The stories in the volume consist of a series of anecdotes that have in common a light-hearted humorous perspective of life in the early Jewish agricultural settlements of the region. What is surprising about such an overly positive recreation of the immigrant experience is the year in which the text was published. The 1960s, particularly the early part of the decade, were years of highly caustic anti-Semitism, and yet the author seems to be summoning up falsely idealistic images of Jewish life in Argentina. Life in the colony is depicted in a highly romanticized fashion. The Jews and the non-Jews in the community get along quite well. There are a number of threatening situations presented in which the safety of individual Jews is put at risk, however, such instances are presented with humor and do not result in any damage being done. Furthermore, the Jews are never threatened by the general population, with whom they hold great community feasts and share a cultural exchange of gastronomic specialties. The problems are always initiated by trouble causing strangers or drunken hooligans. The decline in strict adherence to traditional Jewish custom and religion, as well as in the availability of a Jewish education, is portrayed as being somewhat of a problem. Nonetheless, these situations are again treated with lighthearted humor and resolved quite comically as is the case in the story "Descanso sabático" (Sabbath Rest). In the tale, the local rabbi begins to experience some difficulty filling the synagogue and even gathering enough men together for a minion. The problem lies in the fact that two competing stores refuse to close on Friday evening, each afraid the other will stay open a little longer and steal the other's customers. The rabbi resolves the problem by firing a six-shooter into air in the middle of the street between the two businesses signaling that it is time to close, and everyone obediently begins the Sabbath. Whatever negative aspects may be associated with immigration to Argentina, they are far outweighed by the liberties enjoyed in the new country. Argentina is, in the words of the narrator "un presente de Dios" (a gift from God [11]).

Schvartzman's poetry covers a broad spectrum of topics. His works have remained in relative obscurity in regards to the vast corpus of Argentine poetry in general. The majority of his poetry collections were not published in Buenos Aires, the literary nucleus of the country but in Entre Ríos, in very limited printings. Schvartzman's poetry can be divided into two essential categories: poems of a highly personal nature, and poems of more specifically Jewish content that speak to a wider audience concerning issues such as anti-Semitism and the state of Israel.

In the volumes *Versos a Celia* (Verses to Celia; 1956) and *Antología mínima* (Minimal Anthology; 1962), which contains a section titled "Nuevos versos a Celia" (New Verses to Celia), the poet directs himself mainly toward his wife. The poems contained in these two volumes are simplistic, emotive odes that demonstrate only minimal poetic depth. The verses do, nonetheless, communicate the poet's sincerity of expression. In later collections such as *Década* (Decade; 1965), *Primer hijo* (First Son; 1966), and *Poemas para una muchachita* (Poems for a Little Girl; 1968), the poet reveals a greater poetic intensity, more original and diverse imagery, and a more profound sensibility in his compositions. The poems of the latter two volumes are dedicated to his son and daughter, respectively.

The collection *Versos a Israel y otros versos* (Verses to Israel and Other Verses; 1955) contains poems written by Schvartzman and his wife Celia, in separate sections. Written shortly after the creation of the State of Israel, the volume celebrates the founding of the modern Jewish homeland. The poems express the closure of the past, the joy of the present, and hope for the future. The collection constitutes Schvartzman's most intimate approach to Jewish thematics in his poetry.

It is easy to read *Los mismos* (The Same Ones; 1963) as a response to the anti-Semitic climate of the early 1960s, particularly following the arrest of Adolf Eichmann in Buenos Aires in 1963, which ushered in a new era of overt anti-Semitic activity from Nationalist groups. The volume, therefore, stands in direct contrast to the stance of the posterior *Cuentos criollos con judíos*. The poems in *Los mismos* comprise a series of antinazi verses that brazenly condemn the upsurge of fascist and Nazi ideology in Argentina at the time and compare it with other historical instances both nationally and globally. In the poem "Los mismos," the poet compares an assortment of infamous anti-Semitic historical figures and groups, thereby delineating a continuum of hatred kept alive throughout history by people who are, in essence, one and the same. The recurring figure in the collection is that of what Schvartzman terms the *nazi criollo*, or Creole Nazi, a uniquely Argentine hybrid. In "Retrato" (Portrait), he creates a clear image of the *nazi criollo*: "nublada la mente / cerrados los ojos / Nazi criollo / crimen y violencia / ignominia y odio / nazi criollo (clouded mind / closed eyes / Creole Nazi / crime and violence / ignominy and hate / Creole Nazi [17]). Notwithstanding his apparent despair, the poet does express hope for the future in some of the more optimistic poems of the collection such as "Consejo, quizá inútil, a un Nazi criollo" (Advice, Perhaps Futile, to a Creole Nazi) and "Utopía" (Utopia).

Schvartzman's portrayal of the Jewish experience in Argentina and his concern for and commitment to issues of far-reaching social impact are central to his work. In sum, his literary production represents a significant contribution to Argentine Jewish letters.

PRIMARY BIBLIOGRAPHY
Creative Writing

Antología mínima. Concepción del Uruguay: Haor, 1962.

Cincuenta años y cincuenta versos. Concepción del Uruguay, 1979.

Copledal de cuarta espera. Concepción del Uruguay: Haor, 1972.

Cuentos criollos con judíos. Buenos Aires: Instituto Amigos del Libro Argentino, 1967.

Década. Buenos Aires: Acanto, 1965.

Gurisito del Uruguay. Concepción del Uruguay: Haor, 1969.

Los mismos. Concepción del Uruguay: Haor, 1963.

Poemas para una muchachita. Concepción del Uruguay: Haor, 1968.

Primer hijo. Concepción del Uruguay: Anfora, 1966.

Versos a Celia. Concepción del Uruguay: Haor, 1956.

Versos a Israel y otros versos. With Celia Schvartzman. Concepción del Uruguay: Haor, 1955.

Nonfiction

Judíos en América. Buenos Aires: Instituto Amigos del Libro Argentino, 1963.

SECONDARY BIBLIOGRAPHY

Charosky, Alejandro. "*Primer hijo.*" *Nueva Sión* 433 (2 Sept., 1966): 9.

Furlan, Luis R. "*Década.*" *Davar* 112 (1967): 181-82.

Katz, R. F. "*Década*, poemas de Pablo Schvartzman." *Nueva Sión* 420 (10 Dec., 1965): 9

Rev. of *Cincuenta años y cincuenta versos. Comunidad* (AMIA) 2 (1979): 39.

Rev. of *Los mismos: versos antinazis. Bibliograma* 27 (1964): 31.

Rev. of *Versos a Israel. Mundo israelita* 1686 (26 Nov. 1955): 4.

Sadow, Stephen A. "Judíos y gauchos: The Search for Identity in Argentine-Jewish Literature." *American Jewish Archives* 34.2 (1982): 164-77.

Serfaty, C. "*Primer hijo* de Pablo Schvartzman." *Bibliograma* 39 (1968): 32.

Weinstein, Ana E., and Miryam E. Gover de Nasatsky, comps. *Escritores judeo-argentinos: bibliografía 1900-1987.* 2 vols. Buenos Aires: Milá, 1994. II.174-76.

Darrell B. Lockhart

SCLIAR, MOACYR (Brazil; 1937)

Moacyr Scliar, one of the most acclaimed and widely translated Brazilian authors, was born in 1937 in Porto Alegre, a city which provides the setting for many of his narratives. He defines himself as a cultural mestizo rooted both in Brazilian and Jewish culture, whose deeply entrenched Jewish-Russian heritage gives a special texture to his writings. At the same time, his education in the south of Brazil has imbued his imagination with a distinctive variety of magic realism. Scliar's experience as a public health physician accounts for his naturalistic perspective and complements his approach to literature. His wry, sardonic humor is infused throughout with a gentle sensitivity to human idiosyncrasies.

Scliar is the author of twenty short story collections and novels, ten of which have been published in English translation. He is the recipient of numerous literary prizes, among them the Academia de Letras; Erico Veríssimo; Brasília; Guimarães Rosa; Associação Paulista de Críticos de Arte; Casa de las Américas, the Pen Clube do Brasil.

Scliar can be credited with having given expression to the Jewish-Brazilian novel. His artistic roots are as firmly planted in Jewish tradition and mythology, as they are in the modernism of Mario de Andrade (1893-1945), a Brazilian novelist who in the early thirties advocated the development of artistic forms specially suited to the spirit and language of Brazil.

As Nelson Vieira remarks, Scliar's fiction "portrays a kaleidoscopic Brazilian reality through the magical lens of cultural legends, allegory, myths and folklore" ("Judaic Fiction in Brazil" [43]). His own cultural legacy is founded in biblical parables, legendary tales and humorous Jewish anecdotes, while the Jewish themes that inspire him are recreations of his own experience. All but three of his seventeen books deal with Jewish themes. So Scliar's fiction draws upon history and folklore in order to evoke Brazil's paradoxical realities: gauchos drinking *mate* while conversing in Yiddish; biblical stories intertwined with Indian legends; the rhythm of a *nigun* blending with a *samba*.

Although Scliar deals with panoramic, exotic subjects, his stories never escape the restraints of mundane life. He integrates the magical and the fantastic into the real world, even as he combines Latin American fabulism with Jewish humor. But he doesn't want his readers to think Latin American countries and reality are no more than literary inventions (Garay). Placing fantastic fiction at the service of reality, he applies the concept of magical realism, usually employed to reveal the mystery that pervades reality, to the embodiment of the Jewish condition.

At times Scliar's narratives are reminiscent of the humor found in such Jewish writers as Philip Roth (1933) and Mordecai Richler (1931), though his irony and sadness have been compared to that of Scholem Aleichem (1859-1916), the brilliant fantasy of his creatures to that of Gabriel García Márquez (1928), his mordant satire to that of Jonathan Swift (1667-1745); his intellectual playfulness to Jorge Luis Borges (1899-1986); his animal allegories to George Orwell (1903-1950), his Jewish mysticism to Isaac Bashevis Singer (1904-91). By combining a sense of the absurd with his own kind of Brazilian nationalism, Scliar creates his particular brand of magic to express the marginal condition of being Jewish.

Scliar's style is light, yet incisive. As he sums up his goal as a writer, he considers himself on the one hand, part of the unstable and uneasy Brazilian middle class; on the other, he feels indebted to his Jewish origins for the wonderment that is inherent to the immigrant, and for the cruel, bitter humor that has protected Jews against despair over the centuries. But above all else, Scliar puts his faith in language as a vehicle for aesthetic expression and an instrument for challenging a chaotic world. Scliar tells stories with authenticity and realism. His tales are infused with poetry and ethical substance. His art lies in placing the narration in a perfectly naturalistic setting and then turning the fantastic into something utterly credible.

In 1968 Scliar published his first collection of short stories entitled *O carnaval dos animais* (*The Carnival of the Animals*), which introduces some of his literary postmodernist gallery: animals, comic-strip characters and human beings, all sharing common problems of ecology, sexuality, politics, love, and war. The bestiary that Scliar composes in the manner of Borges, is marked by footnotes and side comments on the text made by the narrator/character. In these fantastic stories animals behave celestially and humans behave bestially, suggesting the Holocaust, which is never far from Scliar's mind.

Scliar's novel *A guerra no Bom Fim* (The War of Bom Fim; 1972), prefigures much of his subsequent fiction in the use of so-called typical Jewish humor and the setting in Porto Alegre. It depicts the rise of a Brazilian Jewish middle class and tells the story of a youth who grows up in Bom Fim during World War II, eventually enlisting in the cause of Israeli Zionism.

Among his most translated works, *O centauro no jardim* (*The Centaur in the Garden*; 1980) is a picaresque novel of fantastic realism that tells the story of Guedali Tartakowsky, a centaur born of Russian immigrants who have fled the pogroms and settled in one of Brazil's rural communities. This mythical creature is brought up as a Jew—circumcised and Bar-Mitzvahed—with devastating consequences. But he is also so down to earth and so universal, that the reader must believe in him. In this existentialist allegory, Scliar contends one can never be free of one's Jewish condition, which begins with the mark of circumcision.

Guedali personifies alienation; desperately lonely and frustrated, he runs away from the protection of his family. After a series of adventures he falls in love, has an operation that turns him into a man, and settles down in the city to a bourgeois, conventional lifestyle. He does not want to be a monstrous freak, but to be accepted. Only then can he confront himself and undertake the most dangerous journey finding his own destiny. In this voyage of self-discovery, Guedali is a metaphor for the outsider— magical and mythological, yet a sentient being. His constant struggle to hide his true identity is an emblem of his handicapped real life as a child and as a Jew. The centaur can be seen as a caricature of man's dualism. A parable about ethnic, psychic and social differences, the novel is also about the intimate duality of man, a hybrid creature.

Scliar's fabulistic, historical novel *A estranha nação de Rafael Mendes* (*The Strange Nation of Rafael Mendes*; 1983), offers a delicate mix of irony, satire, and philosophical speculation. A contemporary story of financial and sexual skullduggery is recounted with a new journalistic matter-of-factness. Rafael Mendes's name is an abbreviation of that of his ancestor Maimonides. Perplexity remains his fate in this tale of misfortune and misadventure. Soon after the protagonist, a successful businessman who professes the Christian religion, learns that his life is in crisis, he discovers a series of genealogical notebooks that allow him to trace his ancestry back centuries.

The strange nation to which the novel owes its title, is on the one hand, the "Jewish nation," a community of people in a continuous state of exile, but it also refers to the Brazil in which Rafael lives as a person in turmoil. From the notebooks, Rafael learns that his ancestors were Jews driven to South America by the Inquisition. Stories within stories provide a magical window into the lives of Sephardic Jews who lived as secret Jews, or as Marranos, to preserve their religion. The wanderings suffered by the Mendes family begin when the prophet Jonah was still inside the whale's intestinal chambers. The novel offers provocative insights on the terrors of the Inquisition, on Rafael Mendes—a cartographer who sailed with Columbus—and on the early pioneers of Brazil. The second notebook reveals to Rafael that he is Jewish, and links the history of the Jewish experience to his present day life.

O exército de um homem só (*The One-Man Army*; 1973), is a novel about Mayer Guinzburg, an absurd Don Quixote figure who moves from being a major real-estate agent in Porto Alegre to designing a utopian city where there will be absolute social equality. As a Jewish emigré, a Marxist fool who loves Stalin and Rosa Luxemburg, Guinszburg founds the People's Republic of New Birobidjan, to which he recruits a variety of animals and social misfits who listen avidly to his anarchist perorations. Yet Guinzburg dies alone, in an awful retirement home.

Max e os felinos (*Max and the Cats*; 1981), an adventure novella written with the intensity of a short story, shares several characteristics with Scliar's other novels: the action takes place between two countries, Germany and Brazil, during and after World War II; the staging displays convergences of Scliar's typical family, including natives, Jews, Nazis, eccentrics, and pragmatists. Here Brazilian and Jew are joined in the immigrant experience. Although the search for identity is Jewish, the theme is very Brazilian: a young man forced to leave Germany for a new life in South America is shipwrecked on the coast of Brazil. He blacks out in his dinghy, only to find himself sitting next to a jaguar, and subsequently is almost devoured by a shark. When he is rescued by a passing ship, Max does not know whether his meetings were real—since the boat the jaguar was on, which was carrying a shipment of animals for the zoo, sank into the ocean—or whether the entire episode was an hallucination.

The strange felines obsessing Max represent conflictive parts of his personality, struggling to express themselves. They are symbols of beastliness and oppression in human relations. Scliar's characters, like those of Isaac Bashevis Singer, are accosted by indomitable forces and tortured by interior demons. Nevertheless, their fantasies live normally alongside their real conflicts. In this sense, there is a great affinity between Jewish tradition and Latin American magic realism, inspired by indigenous cultures. Max's anti-Semitic education is counterbalanced by his friendship with Harald, a Socialist youth persecuted by the Nazis in Berlin. When Harald is assassinated, Max vows to avenge his death. Brazil turns Max into a more tolerant man. Inspired by the romantic novels of José de Alencar (1829-77), Max marries Jaci, a beautiful Brazilian Indian. Ironically, therefore, when he integrates himself into Brazilian society, he has to confront racism against blacks, Mestizos, Indians and foreign minorities. Max is divided between his identification with Germany, as represented by the jaguar, and his solidarity towards the victims of Nazism. Only at the end of his days does he learn to tame his fantasies and discovers that if controlled, the bestiality of fascism that resides within himself can be tamed into an inoffensive cat. Like the rest of Scliar's protagonists, Raquel, of *Os deuses de Raquel* (*The Gods of Raquel*; 1975), is original and wholehearted in her approach to life. Raquel is the daughter of Jewish immigrants who enrole her in a Catholic convent where her identity becomes totally confused. In her search for clarity, she adopts a mentally unbalanced ghetto Jew as her guardian; she marries a Catholic, befriends a Sephardic Jew, and struggles with the gods who tear at her mind, finally taking over.

Scliar's interweaving of tales partakes of a neo-Baroque tradition in Latin America, represented by writers such as Severo Sarduy (1937) and Alejo Carpentier (1904-80). In much contemporary fiction heroes seldom reach their goal, and when they do, it costs them their lives. Scliar's tale *Os voluntários* (*The Volunteers*; 1979) is structured as a journey that succeeds by not coming to its end. Instead, it reworks the effort of the arrival through narrative channels. When the narrator learns that Benjamin, one of his friends, is terminally ill, he and other eccentrics like him embark on a trip to Jerusalem in a tugboat named "Os voluntários." Their mission is to grant the dying Benjamin his last wish—to pray at the Wailing Wall—and in so doing fulfill their own dream. But disaster strikes, with the pilgrims never reaching their destination.

O ciclo das águas (The Cycle of Waters; 1976) offers a natural link between Scliar's background as both doctor and novelist. Here the protagonist tells of an old Jewish woman, now confined to a mental home in Porto Alegre—a victim of the white slave trade from Poland to Brazil in the 1930s—who now recounts her experiences as a prostitute.

One of Scliar's most recent novels, *Cenas da vida minúscula* (Scenes of a Minuscule Life; 1991), is a Brazilian legend that brings together disparate people; ancient Jews (emissaries of King Solomon, sent to find gold in Brazil and bring it to Jerusalem) and contemporary Brazilians. The author explains that this tale is about the crisis of Brazil, and proposes a utopian model of integration as an ideal solution to his country's manifold financial and demographic problems.

Throughout his writing Scliar integrates the Jewish condition into his literature; first, historically and culturally, following the Sephardic and/or Ashkenazi migration that led him to Brazil; second, through the Jewish literary tradition—the Bible, the Sephardic poets, Scholem Aleichem, I.L. Peretz (1852-1915), Franz Kafka (1883-1924), Isaac Babel (1894-1941); and last, through Jewish humor, which blends so wonderfully with Latin American magic realism in the capacity Jews have to laugh at themselves.

Scliar's characters remain an enigma. They are neither typical Jews nor typical Brazilians. They are hybrids, like the centaur. But through them Scliar conveys the synthesis of two rich cultures, Jewish and Brazilian. It may be difficult indeed, to belong to both. Yet for Scliar, "between these two worlds lies a wonderful space for a writer. A space teeming with mysteries, waiting to be discovered" (DiAntonio and Glickman 29).

PRIMARY BIBLIOGRAPHY
Creative Writing

O anão no televisor: contos. Porto Alegre: RBS/Globo, 1979.

A balada do falso mesias. São Paulo: Atica, 1976. English version as *The Ballad of the False Messiah.* Trans. by Eloah F. Giacomelli. New.York: Available Press/Ballantine Books, 1987.

Os cavalos da República. São Paulo: FTD, 1989.

Cavalos e obeliscos. Porto Alegre: Mercado Aberto, 1981.

O carnaval dos animais. Porto Alegre: Movimento, 1968. English version as *The Carnival of the Animals.* Trans. by Eloah F. Giacomelli. New York: Ballantine Books, 1985.

Cenas da vida minúscula. Porto Alegre: L&PM Editores, 1991.

O centauro no jardim. Rio de Janeiro: Nova Fronteira, 1980. English version as *The Centaur in the Garden.* Trans. by Margaret A. Neves. New York: Available Press/Ballantine Books, 1984.

O ciclo das águas. Porto Alegre: Globo, 1976.

Contos reunidos. São Paulo: Companhia das Letras, 1995.

Os deuses de Raquel. Rio de Janeiro: Expressão e Cultura, 1975. Also, Porto Alegre: L&PM Editores, 1978. English version as *The Gods of Raquel.* Trans. by Eloah F. Giacomelli. New York: Ballantine Books, 1986.

[Dez] 10 contos escolhidos. Brasília: Horizonte Editora/Instituto Nacional do Livro/Fundação Nacional Pro-Memória, 1984.

Doutor Miragem. Porto Alegre: L&PM Editores, 1978.

A estranha nação de Rafael Mendes. Porto Alegre: L&PM Editores, 1983. English version as *The Strange Nation of Rafael Mendes.* Trans. by Eloah F. Giacomelli. New York: Ballantine Books, 1987. Also, New York: Harmony Books, 1987.

O exército de um homem só. Rio de Janeiro: Expressão e Cultura, 1973. Also, Porto Alegre: L&PM Editores, 1973. English version as *The One-Man Army.* Trans. by Eloah F. Giacomelli. New York: Ballantine Books, 1985.

A festa no castelo. Porto Alegre: L&PM Editores, 1982.

A guerra no Bom Fim. Porto Alegre: L&PM Editores, 1972.

Histórias da terra trêmula. São Paulo: Vertente, 1977.

Histórias de médico em formação. Porto Alegre: Editora Difusão de Cultura, 1962.

"Inside My Dirty Head—the Holocaust." Trans. by Eloah F. Giacomelli. In *Tropical Synagogues: Short Stories by Jewish-Latin American Writers*. Ed. Ilán Stavans. New York: Holmes & Meier, 1994. 113-16.

Introdução à prática amorosa. São Paulo: Scipione, 1988.

A massagista japonesa. Porto Alegre: L&PM Editores, 1984.

Max e os felinos. Porto Alegre: L&PM Editores, 1981. English version as *Max and the Cats*. Trans. by Eloah F. Giacomelli. New York: Ballantine Books, 1990.

Os melhores contos de Moacyr Scliar. São Paulo: Global, 1984.

Mês de cães danados. Porto Alegre: L&PM Editores, 1977.

Os mistérios de Porto Alegre: coletânea de crônicas publicadas em Zero Hora. Gaúcha Gráfica/Editora Jornalística, 1976.

No caminho dos sonhos. São Paulo: FTD, 1988.

O olho enigmático: contos. Rio de Janeiro: Guanabara, 1986. English version as *The Enigmatic Eye*. Trans. by Eloah F. Giacomelli. New York: Available Press, 1989.

A orelha de Van Gogh: contos. São Paulo: Companhia das Letras, 1989.

Um país chamado infância. Porto Alegre: Sulina, 1989.

Pega pra kapput! [with Josué Guimarães, Luis F. Veríssimo, Edgar Vasques] Porto Alegre: L&PM Editores, 1978.

Um sonho no caroço do abacate. São Paulo: Global, 1995.

Sonhos tropicais. São Paulo: Companhia das Letras, 1992.

O tio que flutuava. São Paulo: Atica, 1990.

Os voluntários. Porto Alegre: L&PM Editores, 1979. English version as *The Volunteers*. Trans. by Eloah F. Giacomelli. New York: Available Press, 1988.

Nonfiction

Caminhos da esperança: a presença judaica no Rio Grande do Sul/Pathways of Hope: The Jewish Presence in Rio Grande do Sul. Porto Alegre: Instituto Cultural Judaico Marc Chagall, 1991.

Cenas médicas: pequena introdução da medicina. Porto Alegre: Editora da Universidade, Universidade Federal do Rio Grande do Sul, 1987.

A condição judaica: das tábuas da lei à mesa da cozinha. Porto Alegre: L&PM Editores, 1985.

Do Edén ao divã: humor judaico. [with Eliahu Toker and Patricia Finzi] São Paulo: Shalom, 1990. Spanish version as *Del Edén al diván.* Buenos Aires: Shalom, 1991.

Do mágico ao social: a trajetória da saúde pública. Porto Alegre: L&PM Editores, 1987.

Mauricio: a trajetória, o cenário histórico, a dimensão humana de um pioneiro da comunicação do Brasil. [On Mauricio Sirotsky Sobrinho] Porto Alegre: Sulina, 1991.

A paixão transformada: história da medicina na literatura. São Paulo: Companhia das Letras, 1996.

Se eu fosse Rothschild: citações que marcaram a trajetória do povo judeu. Porto Alegre: L&PM Editores, 1993.

SECONDARY BIBLIOGRAPHY
Criticism

Barr, Lois Baer. "The Jonah Experience: The Jews of Brazil According to Scliar." In *The Jewish Diaspora in Latin America: New Studies on History and Literature.* Ed. David Sheinin and Lois Baer Barr. New York: Garland, 1996. 33-52.

—. "Navigators without a Compass and Builders without a Plan: Moacyr Scliar." In her *Isaac Unbound: Patriarchal Traditions in the Latin American Jewish Novel.* Tempe, AZ: ASU Center for Latin American Studies, 1995. 33-53.

Bollinger, Rosemarie. "Tres escritores brasileños." *Cuadernos hispanoamericanos* 439 (1987): 85-98.

Baumgarten, Murray. "Urban Life and Jewish Memory in the Tales of Moacyr Scliar and Nora Glickman." *Tradition and Innovation: Reflections on Latin American Jewish Writing.* Ed. Robert DiAntonio and Nora Glickman. Albany: SUNY Press, 1993. 61-72.

Castro Amorim, Beatriz de. "Del mágico realismo de Mario de Andrade hasta el realismo mágico de Moacyr Scliar." *RLA: Romance Languages Annual* 1 (1989): 366-71.

DiAntonio, Robert E. "Aspects of Contemporary Judeo-Brazilian Writing/Moacyr Scliar's *O centauro no jardim*: Ethnicity, Affirmation, and a Unique Mythic Perspective." In his *Brazilian Fiction: Aspects and Evolution of the Contemporary Narrative.* Fayetteville/London: U of Arkansas P, 1989. 113-31.

—. "The Brazilianization of the Yiddishkeit Tradition." *Latin American Literary Review* 17.34 (1989): 40-51.

DiAntonio, Robert, and Nora Glickman, eds. *Tradition and Innovation: Reflections on Latin American Jewish Writing.* Ed. Robert DiAntonio and Nora Glickman. Albany: SUNY Press, 1993. 28-29.

Fonseca, Pedro Carlos L. "O Fantástico no Conto Brasileiro Contemporâneo: Moacyr Scliar e o Reducionismo Fantástico." *Minas Gerais: Suplemento Literário* 14.765 (May 30, 1981): 6-7.

Fraser, Howard, M. "Os Cadáveres Esquisitos de Moacyr Scliar." *Discurso: revista de estudios iberoamericanos* 7.1 (1990): 193-200.

Glickman, Nora. "Los felinos indomables de Moacyr Scliar." *Revista hispánica moderna* 54.1 (1991): 150-51.

—. "*Os Voluntários*: A Jewish-Brazilian Pilgrimage." *Yiddish* 4.4 (1982): 58-64.

Igel, Regina. "Jewish Component in Brazilian Literature: Moacyr Scliar." *Folio* 17 (1987): 111-18.

Lindstrom, Naomi. "Oracular Jewish Tradition in Two Works by Moacyr Scliar." *Luso Brazilian Review* 21.2 (1984): 23-33.

Margarido, Alfredo. "Um Romance Histórico: A Explicação Judaica da História do Brasil." *Jornal de Letras, Artes e Ideias* 5.141 (1985): 4-5.

Marobin, Luiz. "Aspectos lingüísticos de *Os deuses de Raquel*." In his *Painéis da literatura gaúcha.* São Leopoldo, Brazil: UNISINOS [Universidade do Vale do Rio dos Sinos]: 1995. 117-49.

Menton, Seymour. *Latin America's New Historical Novel.* Austin: U of Texas P, 1993. 149-55.

Rubinstein, Zipora. "Quixotismo e picaresca em Moacyr Scliar." In *Ensayos sobre judaísmo latinoamericano.* Proceedings of the V Congreso Internacional de Investigadores sobre Judaísmo Latinoamericano, Buenos Aires, 14-19 August, 1989. Buenos Aires: Milá, 1990. 406-16.

Silverman, Malcolm. "A Ironía na Obra de Moacyr Scliar." *Moderna Ficção Brasileira.* Trad. by João Guilherme Linke. Rio de Janeiro: Civilização Brasileira, 1978. 170-89.

Szklo, Gilda Salem. *O Bom Fim do shtetl: Moacyr Scliar.* São Paulo: Perspectiva, 1990.

Vieira, Nelson H. "Judaic Fiction in Brazil: To Be and Not To Be Jewish." *Latin American Literary Review* 14.28 (1986): 31-45.

—. "Moacyr Scliar: Difference and the Tyranny of Culture." In his *Jewish Voices in Brazil: A Prophetic Discourse of Alterity.* Gainesville: UP of Florida, 1996. 151-92.

SELIGSON, ESTHER 473

—. "Post-Holocaust Literature in Brazil: Jewish Resistance and Resurgence as Literary Metaphors for Brazilian Society and Politics." *Modern Language Studies* 16.1 (1986): 62-70.

—. *Ser judeu e escritor: três casos brasileiros (Samuel Rawet, Clarice Lispector, Moacyr Scliar*. Rio de Janeiro: CIEC [Centro Interdisciplinar de Estudos Contemporâneos, Escola de Comunicação/Universidade Federal do Rio de Janeiro, 1990.

von Brunn, Alberto. "Moacyr Scliar: epopeya judaica en Brasil." *Noaj* 4.5 (1990): 47-50.

Waldman, Berta. "La representación del no judío en la literatura de Moacyr Scliar." In *El imaginario judío en la literatura de América Latina: visión y realidad*. Ed. Patricia Finzi, Eliahu Toker and Marcos Faerman. Buenos Aires: Shalom, 1992. 84-89.

Zilberman, Regina. "A Ficção de Moacyr Scliar." *Minas Gerais: Suplemento Literário* 15.808 (Mar. 27, 1982): 8.

Interviews

Bins, Patricia. "Moacyr Scliar: entrevista a Patricia Bins." *Minas Gerais: Suplemento Literário* 22.1066 (22 Mar. 1987): 6-7.

Catz, Rebecca. "Entrevista com um grupo de escritores gaúchos." *Prismal Cabral: Revista de Literatura Hispánica Caderno Afro-Brasileiro-Asiático-Lusitano* 6 (1981): 108-22.

Espeschit, Antonio. "No mundo de Moacyr Scliar." *Minas Gerais: Suplemento Literário* 15.857 (Mar. 5, 1983): 8.

Garay, René Pedro. "Moacyr Scliar: implicaçoes do fantástico na literatura brasileira contemporânea." *Brasil/Brazil* 3.4 (1990): 93-105.

Nora Glickman

SELIGSON, ESTHER (Mexico; 1941)

Esther Seligson was born October 25, 1941, in Mexico City. She studied French and Hispanic literature at the Universidad Nacional Autónoma de México. She has also studied Art History, as well as Jewish topics in Mexico, Paris, and Israel. She has published her writing in such leading Mexican cultural journals such as *Revista de la UNAM* (Journal of the National Autonomous University of Mexico), *Plural*, *Diálogos* (Dialogues), and *Vuelta* (Turn). Her writing covers a wide spectrum of genres that includes literary essay, studies on the Jewish tradition, poetry, and particularly short stories and poetic prose, all of which is written from a universal and questioning perspective. Some of her essayistic writings have been collected in book form while others have been transformed into novels. Seligson also writes weekly theater critiques.

As an educator, Seligson teaches courses on the history of the theater, theater seminars and workshops, and courses on mythology, comparative religion, and traditional Jewish thought in various educational institutions throughout Mexico City.

Most likely on account of kabbalistic and introspective nature of her writing as well as her poetic language, Seligson's literature has a reduced number of readers, but as J. Ann Duncan comments it also "immediately appeals to the reader through the tenderness and lyricism or her poetic prose, the beauty and sensorial quality of the images, and the pervasive atmosphere of enchantment" (23).

There is practically no trace of Esther Seligson among the principal manuals, dictionaries, encyclopedias, or anthologies of Latin American or Mexican narrative. A possible explanation for this is given by Ilán Stavans who states that "the hard esoteric content of her art, so unpopular and obscure, perpetuates her low profile and elitist appeal" ("Visions" 193-94). This most likely is due to the poetic quality of her fragmentary narrations.

Seligson's texts stand out for their absence of traditional plot lines and realistic characters. The characters in the brief texts share nothing in common with those characters that dominate the literary scene, political struggles, and the cultural establishment. They are better described as voices, dreams, shadows, ghostly murmurs, silences, rhythms, and diverse intertwined sensations that form the themes of an emotional pilgrimage, personal reminiscences, sexual and sensorial knowledge, love and the Western sense of responsibility (Stavans, "Visions" 196). The reader is confronted with a scriptural universe that defines its own evolution, that is to say, Seligson's obsessive words examine a variety of cultural identities that are recreated, sought out, transformed, brought together, and mixed in order to identify the borders of the self. Obsessed by the search for encounters with "la sensación que nos enlaza al Todo" (the sensation that links us to the Almighty [*Luz de dos* 94]), Seligson shuns the immediacy that rules the world. For this reason her characters are not individuals but rather symbolic aspects of the quest that avoid the stereotypes, the mechanization, and the internalization of the traditional scheme of property and family. As Stavans notes, "her creatures are often aesthetes in search of metaphysical truth, most of them Jews in various diasporas, from Spain to Eastern Europe" (196). It is necessary, however, to point out that her stories written during the 1990s contain plots set in Mexico.

The silence on the part of feminists and critics with respect to Seligson's singular work is indicative of the challenge that it presents for the literary canon. This marginality is further complicated by bringing together Judaic tradition with sources of Greco-Latin and Oriental origin. This can be considered a sort of historical alienation for those obsessed with the political Manicheanism that still informs a large part of the official production and reception, external and internal, of Latin American culture. Seligson speaks of universal divinities without ethnocentric preferences. From the biblical and Greco-Latin references utilized in her stories published between 1970 and 1980 she moves on to a reiterated allusion to the Nahuatl language and Aztec gods in her stories united in *Isomorfismos* (Isomorfisms; 1991).

Seligson's first volume of short stories, *Tras la ventana un árbol* (Through the Window a Tree; 1969), consists of fatalist and depressing visions of separation and sad memories of amorous relationships. *Luz de dos* (Light for Two; 1978) continues the same search, but it introduces a medieval environment and themes such as life in the Jewish ghettos of Spain. Critic J. Ann Duncan finds that the light is a way to "abolish contradictions, to re-form a synthesis" and that it represents, not only in these four stories of lights and voices one might add, "an attempt to transcend the human and recreate the divine" (41). This is achieved by depicting the notion of love in its nascent medieval form, the recreation of Renaissance myths, the belief in the founding Word of the biblical tradition, and/or eroticism. In *Luz de dos*, Seligson unites and transform the voices of boys and girls, men and women, anticipation and fears, ghosts and songs, and theater and street fairs in different times and cultures. The first story, "Por el monte hacia la mar" (On the Hill Facing the Sea) the reader is introduced to a family and their memories of a house that had to be sold because of ghostly murmurs that caused the inhabitants to suffer insomnia. The story is reminiscent of the very similar atmosphere in *Pedro Páramo* by Juan Rulfo (1918-86). The second tale, "Distinto mundo habitual" (Different Habitual World), is a circular story narrated by the voice of a neighbor speaking through a window. The third, "Un viento de hojas secas" (A Wind of Dry Leaves), is an intense story in which it is difficult to discern whether one is reading of hallucinations or the dreams of a suicide. The last story of the volume, which gives the book its title, comprises a strange metaphor of Adam and Eve within the context of the Arabic and Sephardic culture of Spain under the rule of Alfonso el Sabio. The story recreates the memories of the love and misfortune of Inés and Pedro. Killed for being a Jew, Inés represents the errant spirit of the lover. Her spirit lingers at the bed where the two lovers' bodies met.

The stories in *De sueños, presagios y otras voces* (On Dreams, Prophecies and Other Voices; 1978), which are included later in *Indicios y quimeras* (Intuitions and Fantasies; 1988), represent a search for identity through dreams and sexuality (Duncan 28).

The collection of prose poetry, *Tránsito del cuerpo* (Voyage Through the Body; 1977), later expanded in *Diálogos con el cuerpo* (Dialogues with the Body; 1981), dispense with individual characteristics to give greater erotic intensity to the words and images as an imperfect reflection of "the search for the ultimate unity of the eternal androgyne" (Duncan 28).

In Seligson's first novel, *Otros son los sueños* (Others Are the Dreams; 1993), the author develops a feminine protagonist of Spanish and Jewish descent who, similar to Héloïse in her passion and commitment, seeks to restore her lost love through memory and intimate feelings.

The majority of critics consider Seligson's novel *La morada en el tiempo* (A Dwelling in Time; 1981) to be her best work and to be representative of the finest of contemporary Mexican narrative. Likewise, it is the author's most specifically Jewish text in content in that it is rich in religious tradition and imagery. The novel must also be read as but one more example of Seligson's incessant search for identity. As J. Ann Duncan states, "shadowy characters, whether named biblical figures or generic personages, are all evidently symbolical aspects of the search rather than individuals" (38). Seligson herself has commented that the novel is part of a process of recovery of her Jewish roots, stating that: "*La morada en el tiempo* fue, es, el intento de reescribir la Torá desde la perspectiva de un Jeremías contemporáneo, pues, modestamente, fue su voz la que guiaba mis escrituras, mis diferentes planos de 'memoria'" (*La morada en el tiempo* was, is, an attempt to rewrite the Torah from the perspective of a modern day Jeremiah, modestly speaking, it was his voice that guided my writing, my different planes of "memory" ("De la memoria y la identidad" 35). The planes of which she speaks are temporal (Jewish tradition) and spatial (Mexican culture), both of which unite in the formation of one identity.

Sed de mar is a brief poetic text that has been characterized as a literary jewel (Menton 369). It is an intense prose poem that presents the diverse voices behind archetypal masks. Instead of weaving strands like a self-sacrificing mother or a devout woman who lives condemned to the absence of her own body, the mythological Penelope weaves with words and writes to overcome her solitude and desperation. Penelope is converted into the clippings of a newspaper that her wet nurse, Euriclea, kept and the fragments of a letter that a messenger gave to Ulysses. Penelope, the metaphor of the woman before the chains that bind her, in the end decides to flee.

Seligson is also the author of a book of essays titled *La fugacidad como método de escritura* (Fleetingness as a Method of Writing; 1988). She writes mainly on the literary works of other authors that have been influential forces in her own writing. Her essays provide key readings of the works of such writers as Clarice Lispector (1926-77), Elena Garro (1920), Virginia Woolf (1882-1941), Samuel Beckett (1906-89), Saul Bellow (1915), Bertolt Brecht (1898-1958), and Franz Kafka (1883-1924), amid a myriad of others. This volume of essays constitutes a reflection on the existential meaning of the word and the author's never-ending search for words.

PRIMARY BIBLIOGRAPHY
Creative Writing

"Desde Jerusalem: tiempos distintos" *Escandalar* 4.4 (1981): 30-31. Also, *Vuelta* 74 (1983): 35-37.

De sueños, presagios y otras voces. México, D.F.: UNAM/Cuadernos de Humanidades 10, 1978.

Diálogos con el cuerpo. México, D.F.: Artífice, 1981.

"En los orígenes." *La mujer por la mujer*. Ed. Juana Robles Suárez. México, D.F.: PEPSA, 1975. 165-80.

Indicios y quimeras (relatos). Colección Molinos de Viento 60. México, D.F.: UNAM/Dirección de Difusión Cultural, 1988.

"Infancia." *Mujeres en espejo I* . Comp. with introduction by Sara Sefchovich. México, D.F.: Folios, 1983. 64-67.

"Infancia," "Requiem." *Cuentistas mexicanas. Siglo XX*. Ed. with introduction by Aurora M. Ocampo. 289-303.

"The Invisible Hour." Trans. by Iván Zatz. In *Tropical Synagogues: Short Stories by Jewish-Latin American Writers*. Ed. with introduction by Ilán Stavans. New York: Holmes & Meier, 1994. 182-88.

Isomorfismos. México, D.F.: UNAM/Textos de Difusión Cultural, 1991.

Luz de dos. México, D.F.: Joaquín Mortiz, 1978.

La morada en el tiempo. México, D.F.: Artífice, 1981.

Otros son los sueños. México, D.F.: Novaro, 1973.

"Palomas mensajeras," "Errantes." *Hispamérica* 20.59 (1991): 115-18.

"Reencuentros." *Diálogos* 19.109 (1983): 20-22.

Sed de mar. México, D.F.: Artífice, 1987.

"El sembrador de estrellas." *Vuelta* 98 (1985): 26-27.

"Sueño de la máscara." *Vuelta* 12 (1977): 30.

"Sueño de una sombra." *Diálogos* 17.97 (1981): 6-7.

"Tampoco diré que llovía." *El cuento erótico en México.* Ed. with prologue by Enrique Jaramillo Levi. México, D.F.: Diana, 1975. 247-52.

Tránsito del cuerpo. México, D.F.: Ediciones de la Máquina de Escribir, 1977.

Tras la ventana un árbol. México: Bogavante, 1969.

"Tres textos" ["Llamado del sueño," "Renuncia del cuerpo," "Aspiración a la presencia"]. *Escandalar* 2.3 (1979): 32-36.

Tríptico. (Contains *Otros son los sueños, Diálogos con el cuerpo, Sed de mar*). México, D.F.: Consejo Nacional para la Cultura y las Artes, 1993.

Nonfiction

"De ciudades santas y tierras prometidas: Jerusalem y Tenochtitlan". *Noaj* 7-8 (1992): 29-30.

"De la memoria y la identidad." *Noaj* 6 (1991): 34-36. Also in *El imaginario judío en la literatura de América Latina: visión y realidad.* Ed. Patricia Finzi, Eliahu Toker and Marcos Faerman. Buenos Aires: Shalom, 1990. 121-23.

La fugacidad como método de escritura. México, D.F.: Plaza y Valdés, 1988.

SECONDARY BIBLIOGRAPHY

Criticism

Cázares, Laura. "Esther Seligson: la luminosa oscuridad de *Luz de dos.*" In *Hacerle al cuento (la ficción en México).* Ed. Alfredo Pavón. México: Universidad de Tlaxcala, 1994. 49-67.

Duncan, J. Ann. "Nostalgia for the Unknown in Esther Seligson." *Ibero-Amerikanisches Archiv* 10.1 (1984): 23-43. Also as "Esther Seligson." in her *Voices, Visions and a New Reality: Mexican Fiction Since 1970.* Pittsburgh: U of Pennsylvania P, 1986. 115-42.

López González, Aralia. "La otra ética: reinterpretación femenina de mujeres míticas." In *Sin imágenes falsas, sin falsos espejos: narradoras mexicanas del siglo XX.* Ed. Aralia López González. México, D.F.: El Colegio de México, 1995. 465-75.

Menassé, Adriana. "*La morada del tiempo.* Esther Seligson." *Diálogos* 21.122 (1985): 40-41.

Menton, Seymour. "Las cuentistas mexicanas en la época feminista, 1970-1988." *Hispania* 73.2 (1990): 366-70.

Robles, Martha. "Esther Seligson." *La sombra fugitiva. Escritoras en la cultura nacional.* 2 vols. México, D.F.: UNAM, 1986. II.279-97.

Schuvaks, Daniela. "Esther Seligson and Angelina Muñiz-Huberman: Jewish Mexican Memory and the Exile to the Darkest Tunnels of the Past." In *The Jewish Diaspora in Latin America: New Studies on History and Literature*. Ed. David Sheinin and Lois Baer Barr. New York: Garland, 1996. 75-88.

Stavans, Ilán. "Esther Seligson y el mito. *Sed de mar*." *Revista de la UNAM* 443 (1987): 43-44.

—. "Visions of Esther Seligson." *Tradition and Innovation. Reflections on Latin American Jewish Writing*. Ed. Robert DiAntonio and Nora Glickman. New York: SUNY Press, 1993. 193-99.

Interviews

Miller, Beth. "Esther Seligson." *26 autoras de México actual*, Beth Miller and Alfonso González. México, D.F.: B. Costa-Amic Editor, 1978. 345-55.

Roberto Forns-Broggi

SEREBRISKY, HEBE (Argentina; 1928-85)

Hebe Serebrisky worked as a journalist and in advertising in Buenos Aires where she was also active in the CGT (Confederación General del Trabajo [General Confederation of Labor]), a powerful workers organization. She is remembered in the literary community for her contributions to Argentine theater in the late 1970s and early 1980s. Like many dramatists who came of age in the 1970s, she studied with Ricardo Monti (1944), one of the most notable of con-temporary Argentine dramatists whose works have profoundly influenced the nature of theater in the country. Serebrisky ended her own life on February 1, 1985.

Serebrisky's theater as a whole is best characterized as pertaining to the tradition of the grotesque (Foster; Zayas de Lima), revealing her formation under Monti. As a theatrical modality, the grotesque—in contrast with the conventions of realism which rely on mimetic gesture—focuses on abstract, but not absurdist, artistic expressionism. The family unit, as a primary social group, often provides the cultural space for the play. This is particularly the case with Serebrisky's works, which often are formulated around mundane situations involving married couples, families, intimate circles of friends, or the environment of the workplace. Such intimate interpersonal relationships provide the necessary environment for the development and representation of the human experience with profound psychological impact. *Redes* (Nets), Serebrisky's first play, is an excellent example of these characteristics and it establishes the foundation for the body of the playwright's subsequent works. It was written in 1978 and won a second-place national award, but it was not performed until 1984, when it opened at the Teatro de la Fábula in Buenos Aires. Although it is a one-act play, *Redes* is a highly complex work that blends well-developed dialogue with sophisticated staging techniques. In fact, the stage scenography as a means of theatrical communication is fundamental to the majority of Serebrisky's plays. This is most obvious in works like *Redes*, *Un fénix lila* (A Lilac Phoenix; 1980), *Finisterre* (1982), and *La cabeza del avestruz* (The Ostrich Head; 1981).

In the plays *Anagrama* (Anagram; 1984), Serebrisky's last, and *Un fénix lila* it is easy to identify a marked emphasis on the articulation of feminine/feminist identity. Nevertheless, it is the nongender-specific nature of the human psyche that Serebrisky seeks to unfold, analyze, and perhaps even exorcise on the stage. *El hipopótamo blanco* (The White Hippopotamus; 1984), for example, utilizes the seemingly benign ambience of a typical office for the unfolding of an intense emotional and violent exchange between two employees that reveals the complexities of the psychological toll modern society takes on the individual.

Serebrisky also participated in the 1983 cycle of Teatro Abierto (Open Theater), a movement that was initiated in 1981 as a direct and daring response to the repression of the military dictatorship that lasted from 1976 to 1983. Her play *Proyecciones* (Projections; 1983) was staged together with three other one-act plays by Susana Torres Molina (1956), Carlos Somigliana (1932-87) and Peñarol Méndez under the joint title *Inventario* (Inventory) at the Teatro Margarita Xirgu in Buenos Aires. The thematic axis of *Proyecciones* is the tragedy of the Malvinas (Falkland Islands) War that occurred toward the end of the dictatorship and which was instigated by the military as a last-ditch tactic to rally populist support in the name of patriotism. The play presents the conflict between the pregnant widow of a young soldier killed in a war he did not support and the members of his family who cannot accept his death and who cling to the ideals of patriotism and duty in spite of it.

Serebrisky's most accomplished play is also that in which she incorporates elements of Jewish identity. In fact, it was the process of writing it that led the author to a reevaluation of her Jewish identity (see her interview with Ploshchuk). *Don Elías, campeón* (Don Elías the Champion) was written in 1979 and received an award from *Argentores*, the Argentine Writers' Guild. It opened on October 22, 1981 at the Teatro Municipal General San Martín, the most technically sophisticated theatrical facility in Argentina, and it received a second-place municipal award the same year. The play revolves around Don Elías and his wife Zulema, an elderly Jewish couple of Rumanian origin who are coping with the tragic death of their only son and his wife. They also assume the responsibility of raising their three grandchildren. The couple runs a general store in a small provincial town in the interior of the country. The "champion" of the title refers to Don Elías's local fame earned for his prowess at the creole dice game *generala*, which is similar to yatze. Indices of Jewish identity are revealed through Don Elías's fondness of the music of Yasha Heifitz or indirectly through anti-Semitic references such as the typical Argentine slur "ruso de mierda" (shitty Jew) that the character Antonio hurls at Don Elías at the end of the play (*Teatro: tomo uno* 79). David William Foster analyzes *Don Elías, campeón* as an illustration of theater as a medium for the expression of cultural integration and/or disintegration and includes Serebrisky's play as one of the principal works in his discussion of Argentine Jewish dramatists.

While Serebrisky was best known as a playwright, she also wrote a collection of short stories. Her *La otra punta* (The Other End) was published in 1985. The stories contain the same insistence on psychological meanderings found in her theater. Many of the stories are so brief as to be characterized as ministories that in an abbreviated space manage to faithfully and concisely portray some aspect of human nature. The stories also vary from the realistic to the fantastic or folkloric in nature. There are only scattered intimations of Jewish identity in the stories; a passing reference to the Pentateuch, for instance. In the story "Any" (Annie) the author uses the figure of her mother to weave a story that hints at the (auto)biographical and also approaches the topic of arbitrary arrests under the rule of military authoritarianism. It is based on the return of the mother, Anita Kirschbaum de Serebrisky, from a trip to Europe. She is detained by the authorities for carrying a large sum of money which the officials, of course, confiscate. The money, she explains, was part of her deceased husband's estate and was destined to be used to construct a cathedral. The story ends with the mother's remandment into the custody of her daughter and the comment "Tu papá hubiera hecho una denuncia ante el Vaticano y otra ante la DAIA" (Your father would have filed a complaint with the Vatican and another with the Delegación de Asociaciones Israelitas Argentinas [Delegation of Jewish Argentine Associations] 49). The story "Primera Dama" (First Lady) is unique in the collection for the subject matter it undertakes. Told from the perspective of Joan Kennedy, the former wife of Senator Edward Kennedy, the story seeks to portray the discord among the members of the Kennedy clan, especially among the women.

In the story the fictional Joan sees herself as an outsider, not wholly accepted as a member of "the Family." It may seem out of place within the context of Argentina, but one must consider the notoriety of John Kennedy in the country and the later connection that Jacqueline Kennedy had with Argentina through Aristotle Onasis.

Serebrisky's works have to date received little critical attention in spite of her talent as a playwright and narrator. Notwithstanding, one cannot overlook her important contribution to Argentine literature, especially in the area of theater.

PRIMARY BIBLIOGRAPHY

Don Elías, campeón. Buenos Aires: Argentores, 1980. 189-248.

La otra punta. Buenos Aires: Celtia, 1985.

Teatro. (Contains *Redes, Don Elías, campeón, El vuelo de las gallinas, Un fénix Lila, La cabeza del avestruz, Finisterre*). Buenos Aires: Ediciones Teatrales Scena, 1982.

Teatro: tomo uno. (Contains *Redes, Don Elías, campeón, El vuelo de las gallinas, Un fénix lila, La cabeza del avestruz*). 2nd ed. Buenos Aires: Ediciones Teatrales Scena, 1985.

Teatro: tomo dos (Contains *Finisterre, Proyecciones, Pura sugerencia* [with Mario Daian], *El hipopótamo blanco, Anagrama*). Buenos Aires: Ediciones Teatrales Scena, 1985.

SECONDARY BIBLIOGRAPHY
Criticism

Foster, David William. "Argentine Jewish Dramatists: Aspects of a National Consciousness." *Folio* 17 (1987): 74-103. Also in his *Cultural Diversity in Latin American Literature.* Albuquerque: U of New Mexico P, 1994. 95-150.

Lorenzo Alcalá, May. "Los cuentos de Hebe Serebrisky." *Cultura de la Argentina contemporánea* 3.11 (1986): 39.

Mallman de López, Elisabeth R. Rev. of *La otra punta. Señales* 187 (1986): 39-40.

Schóó, Ernesto. "La riquísima ambigüedad de Hebe Serebrisky." *Cultura de la Argentina contemporánea* 1.2 (1984): 48-49.

Zayas de Lima, Perla. *Diccionario de autores teatrales argentinos 1950-1990.* Buenos Aires: Galerna, 1991. 253-55.

Interviews

Ploshchuk, Ariel. "Dialogando con Hebe Serebrisky: una obra que me llevó a buscar el reencuentro con mis raíces judías." *Mundo israelita* 3026 (14 Nov., 1981): 5.

Darrell B. Lockhart

SHUA, ANA MARÍA (Argentina; 1951)

The histories and stories of Jewish immigrants lived, remembered, and told by her family have significantly influenced the writing of Ana María Shua, one of the most representative Argentinean writers of her generation. Shua was born in Buenos Aires in 1951 and is the first granddaughter of two Jewish immigrant families; her mother's parents came from Poland and her father's from Lebanon. Her grandparents' homeland memories, their oral tradition, their customs, and their experience living in Argentina as well as the life, memories, and experiences of many other Jewish immigrants have been fused by this writer in a body of work that is truly an accomplished representation of the contemporary Jewish-Argentinean cultural identity.

Shua started her literary career when she was very young. When she was only sixteen years old her collection of poetry, *El sol y yo* (The Sun and I; 1967), earned her the Premio del Fondo Nacional de las Artes y Faja de Honor de la S.A.D.E. (The National Foundation for the Arts Award and the Society of Argentine Writers Banner of Honor). Shua studied education at the Universidad de Buenos Aires. Since graduating, she has continued to write fiction and nonfiction. In 1980, her literary skill was again recognized when she received the first prize in the Concurso Internacional de Narrativa Losada (Losada Publishing House International Narrative Competition) for her novel *Soy paciente* (I am [a] patient; 1980); an auspicious achievement considering the fact that among the members of the jury that awarded the prize were two well-known Argentinean writers, Adolfo Bioy Casares (1914) and Eduardo Gudiño Kieffer (1934). In 1993 she was awarded a Guggenheim Foundation scholarship to finish her novel *El libro de los recuerdos*.

Throughout her career, Shua has proved to be a versatile writer. She has written three novels, three collections of short stories, two books of *blasters*, or sudden fiction, three books for children, one collection of essays, several newspaper and magazine articles as well as humorous books like *El marido argentino promedio* (The Average Argentinean Husband; 1991) and *Risas y emociones de la comida judía* (The Laughter and Emotion of Jewish Cuisine; 1993). This multifaceted writer has also worked as a journalist, advertisement writer, and scriptwriter. Her novels *Soy Paciente* and *Los amores de Laurita* (Laurita's Loves; 1984) have become films. Her latest works include the novel *El libro de los recuerdos* (The Book of Memories; 1994) and the collection of short stories *Cuentos judíos con fantasmas y demonios* (Jewish Short Stories with Ghosts and Demons; 1994).

Unlike other Argentinean writers of her generation, who prefer to experiment with language, Shua prefers to experiment with and invent unexpected anecdotes. Her short stories present unusual turning points and totally unexpected endings as well as unpredictable intertextual references (whether master, oral, and popular narrative intertexts). By means of her intertextual allusions, Shua is able to revise and/or rewrite—humorously most of the time—the traditional master narratives. In her stories, Shua has also shown the ability to decenter the narrative voice in terms of gender identity. Most of her fiction contains conversational simulacrum and multiple fictional voices. This simulacrum, a polyphonic discursive space, allows the narrator and other narrative voices to take turns directing the course of the narrative. Shua's writing style demands an active reading, where the association of thematic, semantic, and discursive isotopies is essential. This type of construction allows the reader to connect different fictional levels which have been carefully interwoven by Shua into her text.

Some recurrent themes in Shua's writing are: (1) the depiction and evaluation of the effects of immigration on the cultural identity of three generations; (2) the exploration of the motherline representation and its subversive discursive properties; (3) the reformulation of traditional concepts such as nationhood, origin, and belonging; and finally, (4) the ironic/witty depiction of the impact of psychoanalysis on the Argentinean middle-class since the sixties. Shua's literary work reflects a constant recreation of the Argentinean social memory registered, preserved, and dynamically transmitted through oral tradition, one generation to another. For Shua, oral tradition represents a form of subversive resistance to the Argentinean official history. This aspect becomes remarkably evident in the author's recreation of the historical events that took place in Argentina during the years of the repressive military dictatorships, 1976-83 ("La época del miedo" [Time of Fear] in *El libro de los recuerdos*).

The aforementioned themes parallel the author's commitment to examine Jewish-Argentinean historical identity. As part of her commitment, Shua explores how the impact of immigration has affected the first generation of Jewish immigrants, how this impact has contributed to their mythic recreation of their homelands, and how it has helped to preserve their traditions, customs, and beliefs in the New Land. Shua also examines how Jewish traditions continually change due to the cultural contact the Jewish community has traditionally maintained with other cultures.

In *Viajando se conoce gente* (You Meet People When Travelling; 1988), one finds two short stories such as "El viejo en el jardín," (The Old Man in the Garden) and "La vida y los malvones," (Life and the Geraniums) that depict how the first generation of Jewish immigrants share their immigration experiences with the new generation of Jewish-Argentineans. In "El viejo en el jardín" a Jewish grandfather tells his grandchild about his homeland. In "La vida y los malvones" a masseuse talks with a woman client about her life in Warsaw before moving to Argentina. All these protagonists convert their homelands into mythic places and comment about Europe during the Second World War. They also revaluate the meaning of nationhood.

In two nonfictional essays from *El marido argentino promedio*, "Recuerdos de la hiper" (Remembering the Hyperinflation) and "Los que vuelven y los que extrañan" (Those Who Come Back, Those Who Miss Their Homeland), Shua highlights the sociohistorical differences between the first generation of Jewish immigrants and the third-generation of Jewish-Argentineans. In an inspiring essay "La patria, la infancia" (Nationhood, Childhood), the writer addresses the traditional concepts of nationhood, origin, and belonging and resemanticizes these concepts according to the vital experience of the first immigrants and their descendants, who have acquired a more multicultural identity. For Shua, childhood symbolically becomes an intense form of nationhood. This symbol reappears in some of her other literary and non-literary discourses.

Another representative symbol used by Shua to refer to the immigrants' rebirth in the New Land appears in the highly poetic essay "Retazos de recuerdos" (Pieces of Memories; *El marido argentino promedio*). In this essay, the author recreates the life of her own Jewish grandparents and relatives. She symbolically uses the vessel which transported her immigrant grandparents from the Old Continent to the Americas to refer to their journey of survival, rebirth, and freedom.

The stereotyping of Jewish and Jewish-Argentinean men and women has also been explored by this writer. In Shua's narratives, the Jewish male is usually presented as conservative and patriarchal. The fatherline representation includes three generations of men—the Jewish immigrant, his children and his grandchildren. Men become the bearers of the Jewish heritage and history as can be perceived in an immigrant grandfather, Gedalia, who initiates the family saga in the novel *El libro de los recuerdos*. However, with uncle Silvestre—Gedalia's first son in the same novel—Shua breaks the aforementioned stereotype and depicts a second generation Jewish-Argentinean character who, when young, used to be a revolutionary Trotskyist.

If the Jewish male is portrayed mainly as traditional and conservative, the Jewish female character in Shua's stories and essays is portrayed as subversive and liberal. As in the case of the fatherline, Shua also explores the representation of motherline in three generations of women: the grandmother, the mother, and the maiden. She places particular emphasis on the depiction of the grandmother in the role of the grandmother or the Jewish *bobe, babuela*. The grandmother's wisdom lies in her vital experience, her ability to interpret reality as well as her ability to adapt herself to different cultural changes. There is a complete chapter in *El libro de los recuerdos*, "La babuela" devoted to the depiction of the grandmother. A particularly interesting aspect in this chapter is the crone's evaluation of contemporary Israel. In the section "Pertenencias" (Belongings) from *El marido argentino promedio*, Shua writes an essay about the life of her own grandmother and grandaunt "Hannah y sus hermanas" (Hannah and Her Sisters).

Shua chooses the role of the aunt to subversively depict the second generation of Jewish-Argentinean women. Humorously outlining the power of memory itself and simulating the rapid flow of oral speech, the writer creates the liberal Aunt Judith in the short story "Tía Judith" (Aunt Judith; *Cien años de narrativa judeo-argentina* [One Hundred Years of Jewish-Argentinean Narratives]; 1990). Aunt Judith is a young defiant woman who runs away from her parents' conventional Jewish home, marries a Christian, and repudiates the old Jewish tradition. Aunt Judith breaks conventions, swears in front of her Jewish parents, and pokes fun at all the beliefs and fears that her brothers and sisters have in life. Shua later included this story in *El libro de los recuerdos*.

Shua represents the third generation of Jewish-Argentinean woman as the maiden. She is portrayed in the novel *Los amores de Laurita*. In this novel, a third generation Jewish-Argentinean woman is represented as liberal, psychoanalyzed, intelligent, and leftist. Shua reworks this stereotype in later writings. This novel also contains three interconnected stories related to the vision of the woman heroine of her own world. These narratives include: Laurita's love stories, Laurita's pregnancy, and a mythical account of a Native woman called Frangipani, an ancient dancer who received the knowledge of her community through her motherline.

The novel *El libro de los recuerdos* constitutes the writer's latest and first work exclusively devoted to surveying Jewish-Argentinean identity. The virtue of this novel lies in the portrayal of a three-generation Jewish-Argentinean family integrated into the Argentinean cultural mainstream. This work evokes intratextual, intertextual, and metatextual referents. Intratextually, the title alludes to the book of memories that serves as a history for the family. Intertextually, the work is thematically linked to earlier works, and metatextually it is linked to the Jewish tradition. In Jewish tradition there has always existed a great reverence for books themselves. In keeping with this tradition, Shua records the family memories in her novel thereby adhering, if only loosely, to the belief that an individual's deeds are recorded in *The Book of Life*.

In conclusion, Ana María Shua's literary and non-literary work is important, because it depicts the complexity of the Argentinean multicultural heritage, one that favors the integration of different cultural identities. This integration serves to avoid any type of cultural supremacy which would create the conditions for cultural assimilation and uprooting. As in Shua's own case, the contemporary Jewish-Latin American writer is no longer in quest of an identity. Her own identity has already been converted into a literary act of resistance and survival. It has become her everyday motivation to represent in literature the dynamic blend of her heritage.

PRIMARY BIBLIOGRAPHY

Creative Writing

Los amores de Laurita. Buenos Aires: Sudamericana, 1984.

Casa de geishas. Buenos Aires: Sudamericana, 1992.

"Cirugía menor." In *Buenos Aires: una antología de nueva ficción*. Ed. Juan Forn. Barcelona: Anagrama, 1992. 119-28.

Cuentos judíos con fantasmas y demonios. Buenos Aires: Grupo Editorial Shalom, 1994.

Los días de pesca. Buenos Aires: Corregidor, 1981.

"Excerpts from Dream Time, "Other/Other," "Fishing Days." Trans. by Regina Harrison and Mary G. Berg. In *Secret Weavers: Stories of the Fantastic by Women of Argentina and Chile*. Ed. Marjorie Agosín. Fredonia, NY: White Pine Press, 1992. 144-63.

"Family Chronicle." Trans. by Norman Thomas di Giovanni and Susan Ashe. In *Hand in Hand Alongside the Tracks and Other Stories*. Ed. Norman Thomas di Giovanni. London: Constable, 1992. 95-104.

"Fiestita con animación." In *El muro y la intemperie: el nuevo cuento latino-americano*. Selección y prólogo de Julio Ortega. Hanover, NH: Ediciones del Norte, 1989. 83-85.

El libro de los recuerdos. Buenos Aires: Sudamericana, 1994.

El sol y yo. Buenos Aires: Pro, 1967.

Soy paciente. Buenos Aires: Losada, 1980.

La sueñera. Buenos Aires: Minotauro, 1984.

"La tía Judith." In *Cien años de narrativa judeoargentina 1899/1989.* Buenos Aires: Milá, 1990. 383-91.

Viajando se conoce gente. Buenos Aires: Sudamericana, 1988.

Children's Literature

La batalla entre los elefantes y los cocodrilos. Buenos Aires: Sudamericana, 1988.

Expedición al Amazonas. Buenos Aires: Sudamericana, 1988.

La fábrica del terror. Buenos Aires: Sudamericana, 1990.

La puerta para salir del mundo. Buenos Aires: Sudamericana, 1992.

Nonfiction

El marido argentino promedio. Buenos Aires: Sudamericana, 1991.

El pueblo de los tontos. Humor tradicional judío. Buenos Aires: Alfaguara, 1995.

"¿Qué erótica? ¿Qué femenina?" In *Mujeres y escritura.* Ed. Mempo Giardinelli. Buenos Aires: Puro Cuento, 1989. 53-55.

"Retazos de recuerdos." In *El imaginario judío en la literatura de América Latina. Visión y realidad.* Ed. Patricia Finzi, Eliahu Toker and Marcos Faerman. Buenos Aires: Grupo Editorial Shalom, 1992. 20-26.

Risas y emociones de la comida judía. Buenos Aires: Grupo Editorial Shalom, 1993.

"Sobre los chicos de los '90: Presente y futuro." In *Jóvenes en los 90. La imaginación lejos del poder.* Ed. Manuela Fingueret. Buenos Aires: Almagesto, 1993. 169-82.

SECONDARY BIBLIOGRAPHY

Criticism

Agosín, Marjorie. "Ana María Shua, Marisa Di Giorgio y Liliana Heker." In her *Literatura fantástica del Cono Sur: las mujeres.* San José: Editorial Universitaria Centroamericana, 1992. 55-66.

Gimbernat González, Ester. "*Los amores de Laurita*: la irreverencia subversiva del cuerpo textual." In her *Aventuras del desacuerdo: novelistas argentinas de los 80.* Buenos Aires: Danilo Albero Vergara, 1992. 277-83.

Pollack, Beth. Rev. of *Los amores de Laurita. Chasqui* 21.1 (1992): 166-68.

—. Rev. of *El marido argentino promedio*. *Chasqui* 22.1 (1993): 105-7.
Rev. of *Soy paciente*. *Comentarios bibliográficos americanos* (Montevideo) 13.3
(1981): 12.

Interviews

Agosín, Marjorie. "Entrevista a Ana María Shua." In her *Literatura fantástica
del Cono Sur: las mujeres*. San José: Editorial Universitaria Centroamericana, 1992. 149-60.
Barone, Roxana. "Ana María Shua." *Puro cuento* 6.36 (1992): 2-6.
Pollack, Beth. "Ana María Shúa." *Hispamérica* 23.69 (1994): 45-54.

Fanny Arango-Keeth

SNEH, SIMJA (Argentina; 1914)

Simja Sneh—writer, poet, journalist—occupies a singular place within
Argentine literature. His vast production (cited in the bibliography), rather than
succumbing to constraint by academic definitions and categorizations, constitutes
the visible mark of an intinerary that not only extends geographically and culturally but includes the transformation of human languages as well.

Sneh is an errant creator among the languages that he treasures, cultivates, and loves: from his native Yiddish and Polish to the Spanish of his adoptive country (Argentina) passing through Hebrew, Russian, English, and German.
This incidence of multilingualism is not foreign to his work given that, we may
say, Sneh is the voice of a tongue murdered by barbarism, but a tongue that can
reappear precisely because he gives it life in another language.

He was born in Pulawy, Poland on October 15, 1914. His father, Menajem (Mendl), was a watchsmith. He received instruction in Hassidic studies by
melamdim (private tutors), especially by his maternal uncle Itzjak Weintraub,
who was well versed in both Hebrew and universal literature. He completed his
secondary education at the gymnasium "Prince Czartorysky" which implemented
a *numerus clausus* policy, that is to say that the number of Jewish students accepted was limited to a very few. He studied history and philosophy at the Free
University of Warsaw (Wschejnitsa). He was an active member of the Socialist
Polish Worker's Party, dedicating himself at that early period to journalism. His
first article, "On Popular and Worker's Theater," was published by the aforementioned organization in 1936.

The Nazi disaster forced him to be a soldier—a circumstance present throughout his works—and to criss-cross the world in the service of various armies (the Red Army, the Polish army in exile commanded by General Anders, the Jewish Brigade of the British Army).

Once having arrived in Argentina, with his previous experience as a newspaperman in Yiddish and Polish, he took up his literary and journalistic endeavors in both Yiddish and Spanish, not only contributing to already existing media, but also creating new sources when the former turned out to be insufficient for him: he founded and directed (together with Aharon Yurkevitch) the journal *Alef* (the first bilingual—Yiddish/Spanish—publication in Argentina), the journal *Undzer Vort* (Yiddish for Our World), and the journal *Raíces: revista judía para el hombre de nuestro tiempo* (Roots: The Jewish Journal for the Man of Our Times), the latter being the first publication of the Jewish community (it came to be under the auspices of the Organización Sionista Argentina [Argentine Zionist Organization]) to reach a massive audience among non-Jewish sectors and to win a separate place in Argentine and Latin American intellectual milieus.

As a professor of Yiddish and Hebrew literature he has worked as a lecturer and educator, and he has held the position of professor of Yiddish literature at the midrasha (School of Higher Studies of the Jewish school system), and giving classes at different schools of the *Vaad Ha'jinuj* (Council of Jewish Education).

In his extensive career he has collaborated with publications such as leading Buenos Aires newspapers *La Nación* (The Nation), *La Prensa* (The Press), *Clarín* (Clarion), *Comunidad* (Community; the journal of the AMIA—the Jewish community of Buenos Aires—that Sneh directed), *Comentario* (Commentary), *Di Presse* (The Press), *Mundo Israelita* (Jewish World; he is responsible for the columns "El rincón del bibliómano" [The Bibliophile's Corner], and "A mi manera de ver" [My Point of View], having published more than one thousand columns in the latter), *Davar*, *Ma'ariv*, *Al Ha'Mishmar* (all three from Israel), and *Di Zait* (Time; as a correspondent in London). His writing has been translated into English, Portuguese, and Hebrew. He directed the journal *Folk un Tzion* (People and Zion, in Yiddish), of the Jewish Agency and collaborated with the journal *Ierushalaimer Almanaj* (Jerusalem Almanac, in Yiddish).

In 1952 Sneh received the Tzví Kessel award for his work *Na Ve'nad*, and in 1979 he was awarded the Fernando Jeno literary prize from Mexico in recognition of his entire literary corpus. Currently he forms part of the Department of Culture for the AMIA. He is a translator of texts written in Russian, Polish, Yiddish, and Hebrew. He is also currently preparing a novel, and the second and third parts of his trilogy *Sin Rumbo* (Aimless) are at press.

The themes that comprise Sneh's writing have a setting and ambiance all their own: the Holocaust, or, as he himself taught me to say (and it is not the only thing he has taught me), the Shoah. However, his work transcends the merely testimonial in the sense of a wealth of historical information about the catastrophe that the Shoah cast down on the world. To write the Holocaust is not simply to remember a scene, a group of facts, or the entire string of events that make up a story in order to remember it—in other words, in order to give it an ending. As Sneh understands it, writing the Holocaust is to write today about its pain and dark threat. It is to point out the helplessness and abandonment not only of those who perished, but of that singular narrator that roams throughout his works: the enigmatic figure of the survivor.

An acute, critical, and pained observer, Sneh witnessed as one after another the lights of the world disappeared from the small Polish village of his childhood, the effervescent Warsaw of his adolescence, the remains of his youthful loves, the voices of his life.

It is this brutal silencing, the silence of death imposed not only on people, but on an entire culture, a language, a unique history, that leads Sneh to refuse to accept the sentence of the assassins and, instead of retreating to the agony, instead of giving in to what George Steiner calls the "temptation of silence" in the face of inhumanity, it is what allows his writing to provide a voice for the silence of the slit throat. Therefore, the fact that multilingualism and the transience of languages (and my reference is not to a mere translation) participate in his creation as a central element.

How will the survivor, he who has returned from the dead, recount what has happened? How will he who speaks a slain language speak? Here, I believe, we find one of the greatest merits of Sneh's literary works: not only does he write in Yiddish, the condemned language, but by making Spanish a language of his own—laboriously and fruitfully adopted by him at a late age—he recreates in Spanish the Yiddish literary universe, transmitting the word of a remote poem that, through his pen, becomes completely contemporary.

The volume of short stories *El pan y la sangre* (Bread and Blood; 1977), distinguished with the Sash of Honor of the Sociedad Argentina de Escritores (Argentine Writer's Guild), is not merely a Spanish version of stories about events that took place in the Yiddish of the Jews "back then," but is remarkable for the way in which this creation is reborn in Spanish.

As Marco Denevi astutely points out, Sneh lies beyond "literary fashion," and by rooting himself in a language that is a testimony of his exile and displacement, he is able to give a name to the unnamable and to give voice to what barbarism tried to annihilate.

The monumental work *Sin rumbo* (Aimless; 1993) proposes once again the impossiblity of resorting to categorizations. It is not strictly speaking a novel, yet it transcends the limits of an autobiography. It is not simply a testimonial record nor a historical compendium (although it may have characteristics of each genre). This work places memory in motion beyond its normal flow. It is, in fact, a narration that moves with the flux of memory and becomes a story through the process of writing. Until then it is only an open wound.

How does one write pain? We can find the answer to this question by looking at the texts themselves, principally, the figure of the narrator in *Sin rumbo*, a possibility Ricardo Feierstein has suggested to us. This narrator appears as "uno" (one), "a uno le parecía que. . ." (it appeared to one that. . .). Yet this "one" is revealed to us as a multiplicity: it vacillates between the first and third person and moves from "we" to "them" almost without any sense of continuity. The verb tenses accompany these changes by introducing a nonlinear temporality, a perspective that is not pure historical past, but a kind of a fold in time. It is difficult to speak from this fold, difficult to maintain oneself in the place of one who has brushed elbows with death in a recurrent and always interrupted romance. This leads us to extend Feierstein's proposal: the subject of the narration in Sneh's work, the "one" to whom things happen, the "one" that becomes "us," that flees with "them," and reappears as "I," precisely through the diverse ways of appearing, signals the unbearable nature of that place, making evident his helplessness and his essential solitude. Because that narrator will never again be one and the same, he remains torn, split, divided between his being a survivor and what, although he survived, he could not survive. Parts of him have remained along the roadside, and each time he crossed death's path it took something from him.

That is the place of this unique narrator, a place that Sneh does not shun, yet he does not wear the emblem of a martyr. He simply travels through it, coming and going tirelessly as one who dives among the wretched, floating remains of a shipwreck. In each passage, each time he submerges himself, the narrator emerges with a new word, some trace, some voice, some scrap of human tenderness. Thus, the horror is not limited to fright or truculence, but becomes visible, more or less announced, among the indescribable colors of the Polish spring, the fog of the steppe, the howl of the jackals, or the memory of an adolescent love.

These voices, these memories, this knot in the throat that appears time and again, much like the icons of that other Jew who painted fiddlers on rooftops, transcend the limits of any ghetto to reach the soul of all feeling men, because all great artists acheive this miracle of universality. Thus, through the words of he who speaks to us **from** Yiddish **in** Spanish, we as humanity comprehend what we hope for, feel, love, and suffer on all parts of the earth.

PRIMARY BIBLIOGRAPHY
Creative Writing
Bleter Oifn Vint (poetry). Buenos Aires: n.p., 1948.

Dos Geshrei in der Najt (theater). Buenos Aires: Undzervort, 1957.

Oif Fremde Vegn (novel). London: Fraieidishe Tribune, 1947.

Na Ve'nad (novel, 1st vol. of trilogy). Buenos Aires: Editorial Undzervort, 1952.

El pan y la sangre. Buenos Aires: Sudamericana, 1977. 2nd ed., 1986.

Sin rumbo. Buenos Aires: Milá, 1993.

Nonfiction
Breve historia del idisch. Buenos Aires: Biblioteca Popular Judía del Congreso Judío Mundial, 1976.

Historia de un exterminio. Buenos Aires: Biblioteca Popular Judía del Congreso Judío Mundial, 1967.

Schmuel Iosef Agnon: premio nobel de literatura 1966. Buenos Aires: Biblioteca Popular Judía del Congreso Judío Mundial, 1967.

SECONDARY BIBLIOGRAPHY
A.P. "*El pan y la sangre*. Lanzamiento de la segunda edición del libro de Simja Sneh." *Mundo israelita* 3245 (14 Feb., 1986): 7.

"Una conducta que es fidelidad al compromiso judío: Simja Sneh y sus 70 fecundos años." *Mundo israelita* 3178 (20 Oct. 1984): 7.

Denevi, Marco. "Nota de presentación a *El pan y la sangre*." Buenos Aires: Sudamericana, 1986.

Invernizzi, Hernán. "*El pan y la sangre*, de Simja Sneh." *Nueva presencia* 458 (April 11, 1986): 24.

Kay, E., ed. *Dictionary of International Biography*. vol. xvi. Cambridge, England: International Biographical Centre, 1980. 785.

Klein, Alberto, ed. *Cinco siglos de historia argentina. Crónica de la vida judía y su circunstancia*. 2da ed. Buenos Aires: n.p., 1980: 78, 119, 120, 125.

Senkman, Leonardo. "Sobrevivir el holocausto: bochorno y culpa." In his *La identidad judía en la literatura argentina*. Buenos Aires: Pardés, 1983. 384-89.

"Simja Sneh premiado por el Fondo Kastner." *Nueva Sión* 144 (15 Feb. 1944): 5.

"Simja Sneh no teme explorar el abismo en *El pan y la sangre*." *Mundo israelita*
2786 (16 April, 1977): 9.

Steiner, George. *Lenguaje y silencio*. México, D.F.: Editorial Gedisa, 1990.

Weinstein, Ana E., and Miryam E. Gover de Nasatsky, comps. *Escritores judeo-
argentinos: bibliografía 1900-1987*. 2 vols. Buenos Aires: Milá, 1994.
II.212-20.

Interviews

Hendel, Noemí. "Develar todas las respuestas posibles: pluralismo e identidad."
Nueva Sión 643 (23 Aug. 1987): 19-23.

Senkman, Leonardo. "Entrevista a Simja Sneh, sobreviviente del atentado." *Noaj*
10 (1995): 38-44.

"Simja Sneh, el periodista-escritor que busca lo judío en el diálogo." *Mundo
israelita* 2973 (8 Nov. 1980): 11.

Ernesto Sabato

STAVANS, ILÁN (Mexico; 1961)

A prolific young Mexican novelist and critic of Eastern European and
Russian descent, Ilán Stavans is the author of the acclaimed experimental narrative *Talia y el cielo* (Talia in Heaven; 1977, rev. 1989), which won the prestigious 1992 Latino Literature Prize, as well as numerous short stories, some of
which were collected in the text entitled *La pianista manca* (The One-Handed
Pianist; 1992), a finalist in the Letras de Oro award in the United States and the
winner of the Gamma Prize in Spain. His essays about literary topics, plagiarism,
and the art of translation, written either in Spanish or in English, have gained
him a solid reputation as an extraordinarily talented new Latin American pen. He
has received grants and honors from the Spanish government, the National Endowment for the Humanities, Poets and Writers, the Latin American Writers
Institute, the New York State Council on the Arts, among other institutions, and
is highly visible in the U.S. and Hispanic American printed media. He currently
teaches comparative literature at Amherst College.

Stavans was born in Mexico City, the son of a professional actor and a
psychotherapist mother and the grandson of rabbis. He attended Yiddish school
since early on and wrote his first play, a musical titled *Genesis 2000*, staged in
1979 and influenced by Antoine de Saint-Exupéry (1900-44), at age seventeen

in the language of Sholem Aleichem (1859-1916) and Isaac Bashevis Singer (1904-91). A passionate filmgoer, in his adolescence he dreamed of becoming a movie director and in 1977 wrote and produced an award-winning Super 8 short film. At the time he also founded a high school film club and wrote film and literary criticism for student magazines.

After graduation, he enrolled in state-run colleges in Mexico's capital, the Universidad Autónoma Metropolitana, and also briefly studied at the Universidad Nacional Autónoma de México, but he interrupted his studies to travel to Spain, France, Africa, and the Middle East. As he puts it in interviews and autobiographical essays, at that point in life he "felt it very difficult to find a link between my Jewish past and my Mexican present, between the two sides of my divided self " (Pakravan, *Literary Review* 43), and thus ran away from home. Thanks to a brief stay in Jerusalem, where he befriended important intellectuals and writers, Stavans discovered he could approach his Judaism from a more intellectual, less emotional perspective. He came to understand his Hebraic identity as the receptacle of an ancient, everlasting collective memory, not in the Jungian sense but in the way explained by Yosef Hayim Yerushalmi in his book *Zahkor* (1982): a metahistorical spirit inhabiting every Jew regardless of time and space.

In 1982 Stavans returned to Mexico to finish his Bachelor of Arts degree and to devote himself to the study of medieval Jewish thought. He became fascinated with Maimonides (1135-1204) and Baruch Spinoza (1632-77), two philosophers who left a deep impression on him. He also committed himself to improving his Hebrew and Yiddish language skills and read Shmuel Yosef Agnon (1888-1970), Mendele Mojer Sforim (1836?-1917), Der Nister (1884-1950), among others in the original.

Talia y el cielo, his only novel, first published in Venezuela in 1977, was rewritten eleven years later and published in its definitive Mexican edition in 1989. Stavans shares credit with Zuri Balkoff, a nonexistent Colombian journalist, who is also, like the Mexican, a main protagonist in the plot. In his 1992 collection of essays, *Prontuario* (Compendium), Stavans explains how he wrote the novel, when and why. He says the manuscript suffered a number of revisions and because of its Hebraic symbolism and its treatment of anti-Semitism, it was difficult to find a publisher in the Spanish-speaking world. Segments of *Talia y el cielo* have been translated into English in several literary publications in the United States. In an autobiographical essay called "Lost in Translation," (1993) Stavans writes about the novel's reception in Mexico, and in particular of the publisher's comments at the reception where the novel was presented: "I no longer remember what he said and why. The only sentence that still sticks in my mind, the one capable of overcoming the passing of time, came at the end of his speech, when he said: 'for centuries Latin America has had Jews living in its basement, great writers creating out of the shadow. And Ilán Stavans is the one I kept hidden until now.' A frightening metaphor" (493-94).

The plot centers around Talia Kahan, a Canadian Jew and the daughter of a concentration camp survivor who, running away from a possessive mother, travels to an imaginary Latin American country called Paranagua. There she meets a queer college professor named Ilán Stabans (note the spelling variation), who both is and is not the book's author, Stabans behaves mysteriously and Talia soon discovers that he has a split personality (the other self is named Igal Balkaff). A tribute to Robert Louis Stevenson's (1850-94) *The Strange Case of Dr. Jekyll and Mr. Hyde* (1886), to Carlos Fuentes's (1928) *Aura* (*Aura*; 1962), and to Oscar Wilde's (1854-1900) *The Portrait of Dorian Gray* (1891), this postmodern narrative has been applauded by numerous renown critics of Latin American literature. The book came about after Stavans wrote columns in two ideologically opposing newspapers in Mexico City: in one he was known as Ilán Stavans, a center-right writer; in the other as Zuri Balkoff, a left-wing polemicist who identified with the Palestinian cause and in general tried to reject his Judaism. Ultimately, Stavans the novelist understood the division of self as the source to two heteronyms in the tradition of Fernando Pessoa (1888-1935): fictional personalities with unique features cohabiting a writer's body.

Besides the above mentioned names, Stavans's major influences are Franz Kafka (1883-1924) and Jorge Luis Borges (1899-1986). The first story in *La pianista manca*, "Un cielo sin cuervos" ("A Heaven Without Crows"), which has been published in English translation, consists of an enchanting fictional letter by Kafka in which a solid bridge between Eastern European and Latin American literatures is masterfully established. The title story of the same volume is dedicated to the Yugoslavian writer Danilo Kiš (1935-89). Stavans has also expressed admiration for the oeuvre of Bruno Schulz (1892-1942) and Milan Kundera (1929). He has written about Henry Roth (1906), Philip Roth (1933), Isaac Bashevis Singer, and Joaquim Maria Machado de Assis (1839-1908), and like Walt Whitman (1819-92), he has written anonymous (or pseudonymous) reviews of his own books and has even published a humorous self-interview.

In 1985 Stavans moved to the United States. In Mexico he had written two long essays, one on Franz Rosenzwieg's (1886-1929) *Star of Redemption* (1921, 1930, 1954) and the other on Bahya Ibn Paquda's (1050-?) *Book of Duties of the Heart* (date unknown), and was offered a scholarship to study for a Masters in Jewish philosophy at the Jewish Theological Seminary in New York City. After finishing, he transferred to Columbia University, where he received a

Doctorate in Letters. Meanwhile, Stavans, writing now under his own name, began publishing on a regular basis in the *New York Times*, *Excelsior*, *Diario 16*, the *Nation*, the *Miami Herald*, *Transition*, and numerous other periodicals in Europe, Hispanic America, and the United States. Some of his collaborations in Spanish have been gathered together in two volumes: *Prontuario*, and *La pluma y la máscara* (The Plume and the Mask; 1993). He is also known as the editor of two acclaimed anthologies, one of Hispanic-U.S. memoirs, *Growing Up Latino: Memoirs and Stories* (1993), and another of Jewish Latin American short fiction, *Tropical Synagogues* (1994). He has translated Yehuda Halevi (1085-1140), Isaac Bashevis Singer, and Leonard Bernstein's (1918-90) *Kaddish* (1963) into Spanish and Juan Goytisolo (1931), Carmen Martín Gaite (1925), Felipe Arau (1902), Manuel Puig, (1929-90), and the Guatemalan fabulist Alcina Lubitch Domecq (1953) into English. His interviews with Joseph Brodsky (1940), John Updike (1932), Isabel Allende (1942), Cynthia Ozick (1928), Oliver Sacks (1933), and other famous personalities have been reprinted time and again. Finally, Stavans has also written a play, *Vals triste* (Sad Waltz), based on stories by Patrick Süskind (1949) and Anton Chekhov (1860-1904), that had a successful Off-Broadway run in 1992.

His full control of English is a result of an obsessive determination to become perfectly bilingual. He has been considered a successor of Joseph Conrad (1857-1924) and Vladimir Nabokov (1899-1977) (cf. Gazarian Gautier; Pakravan) and frequently writes about switching languages. His style is concise, almost mathematical. His recurrent themes are God, identity, time, and human memory. In "La invención de la memoria" (The Invention of Memory; [*La pianista manca*]), a Kundera-like novella written at age twenty-nine, he intertwines these topics and discusses Judaism as a culture devoted to the art of remembrance.

PRIMARY BIBLIOGRAPHY
Creative Writing

"A Heaven Without Crows." Trans. by David Unger. *Michigan Quarterly Review* 32.3 (1993): 380-85.

"The Death of Yankos." *Calypso* 1.1 (1989): 42-46. Also in *Tropical Synagogues: Short Stories by Jewish-Latin American Writers*. Ed. Ilán Stavans. New York: Holmes & Meier, 1994. 193-98.

"The Left-Handed Pianist." Trans. by Harry Morales. *TriQuarterly* 82.2 (1994): 76-80.

La pianista manca. Caracas: Alfadil, 1992.

The One-Handed Pianist and Other Stories. Albuquerque: U of New Mexico P, 1996. (Translations from *Talia y el cielo* and *La pianista manca*).

Talia y el cielo, o el libro de los ensueños. Credit with Zuri Balkaff. México, D.F.: Plaza y Valdés, 1989. Translated fragments by Amy Prince in *Southwest Review* 78.3 (1993): 335-56. *Literary Review* 37.1 (1993): 44-49. *Compass* 14 (Summer 1992): 8-14.

Vals triste. One act play. West Bank Stage, Off-Broadway, 1992.

Nonfiction

"An Appointment with Héctor Belascoarán Shayne, Mexican Private Eye." *Review: Latin American Arts and Literature* 42 (1990): 5-9.

Anti-héroes: México y su novela policial. México, D.F.: Joaquín Mortiz, 1993.

Imagining Columbus: The Literary Voyage. New York: Twayne-Mcmillan, 1992.

"Lost in Translation." *Massachusetts Review* 34.4 (Winter 1993-94): 489-502.

Manual del (im)perfecto reseñista. México, D.F.: Universidad Autónoma Metropolitana, 1989.

La pluma y la máscara. México, D.F.: Fondo de Cultura Económica, 1993.

Prontuario. México, D.F.: Joaquín Mortiz, 1992.

The Hispanic Condition: Reflections on Culture and Identity in America. New York: Harper & Collins, 1994.

"Sam Spade Otra vez." *The Nation* 255.6 (1992): 214-15.

The Stranger Within: Reflections on Hispanic Culture in the United States. New York: Harper Collins, 1994.

Anthologies

Antología de cuentistas judíos. México, D.F.: Porrúa, 1994.

Antología de cuentos de misterio y terror. México, D.F.: Porrúa, 1993.

Growing Up Latino: Memoirs and Stories, (with Harold Augenbraum). Boston: Houghton Mifflin, 1993.

Tropical Synagogues: Short Stories by Jewish-Latin American Writers. New York: Holmes & Meier, 1994.

SECONDARY BIBLIOGRAPHY

Criticism

Albarrán, Jairo Calixto. "Ilán Stavans y los juegos de la literatura." *El buho* (literary supplement of *Excélsior* [Mexico]) 22 March, 1992: 5.

Arenas, Jorge. Rev. of *Prontuario. El Nacional* (Mexico) 6 June, 1992: 7.

F.A. Rev. of *Talia y el cielo. El Universal* (Mexico) 12 January, 1991: 2.

Grumberg, Daniel. "De la mano de la Pianista Manca." *El papel literario* (literary supplement of *El Universal* [Caracas]) 15 March, 1992: 7.

Ponce de León, Juana. "A Fiesta of Mexican Writers." *Washington Post Book World* 3 January, 1993: 15.

Rodríguez, Luis J. "Border States." *Los Angeles Times Book Review* 28 February, 1993: 1, 10.

Schiminovich, Flora. "El lado oscuro de la imaginación." *El papel literario* (literary supplement of *El Nacional* [Caracas]) 31 January, 1993: 7. Also in *Revista hispánica moderna* 46.1 (1993): 222-24.

Interviews

Cuzá Malé, Belkis. "Cuatro preguntas a Ilán Stavans." *La jornada semanal* (Mexico) 2 February, 1993: 7.

Gazarian Gautier, Marie-Lize. "Ilán Stavans: A Character Among His Characters." *Compass* 14 (Summer 1992): 7.

—. "The Man with a Thousand Masks: An Interview with Ilán Stavans." *Confluencia* 10.1 (1994): 141-51.

Guzmán, Patricia. "Ilán Stavans: escribir por culpa de Dios." *Imagen* (Caracas) 2100.89 (May 1992): 4-6.

Pakravan, Saïdeh. "A Writer in Exile: An Interview with Ilán Stavans." *Chanteh* 1.2 (Winter 1993): 28-34. Also in *The Literary Review* 37.1 (19930: 43-55.

Varderi, Alejandro. "Cada día me reconozco menos: Ilán Stavans." *La Opinión* (Los Angeles) 22 December, 1991: 8.

Robert DiAntonio

STEIMBERG, ALICIA (Argentina; 1933)

A denizen of Buenos Aires' cafés, moviehouses, and art nouveau *confiterías*, Alicia Steimberg was born in the capital in 1933 to first generation Argentines of Eastern European Jewish heritage. She remained in Argentina during the period of the repressive military dictatorship called the *Proceso* (1976-83). While she has never actively engaged in politics, her criticism of the current Peronist regime of President Saúl Menem appears in the pages of *Página 12* (Page 12, an opposition newspaper), and the Radical party would like to claim her support. She has supported herself with translations and workshops on fiction writing until 1992 when she won the well-endowed Premio Planeta Biblioteca del Sur prize. Now, her early work, which appeared in small editions from lesser-known publishers, is being reissued by Planeta, a major international press. Best known for her novels, she has also published a collection of short stories, *Como todas las mañanas* (Like Every Morning; 1983) and a humorous guide to cooking for adolescents, *El mundo no es de polenta* (The World's Not Made of Polenta; 1991).

Steimberg's work has a strongly autobiographical vein as the names of her protagonists and narrators—Alicia, Cecilia, Ana, Amatista, Sabina—suggest. These women irreverently satirize every aspect of being Argentine, *porteña* (from the port of Buenos Aires), and Jewish. Set in Steimberg's favorite haunts such as the café Las Violetas, Richmond, and Chacarita cemetery, her fiction explores the hypocrisy and cultural impoverishment of Jewish life as opposed to the seductive aesthetic beauty and order of Catholicism, and the inherent chaos and violence of life in twentieth-century Argentina as refracted through the traumatized psyches of her bourgeois characters.

Her first published work, *Músicos y relojeros* (Musicians and Watchmakers; 1971) deals with the life of Alicia from primary school to adolescence. An orphan at an early age (like most of Steimberg's characters and the author herself) Alicia rebels against the women whose arbitrary rules structure her life. Her connection with Jewish life is mainly negative. Her discomfort arises from her tenuous economic status as represented by her mother's malodorous Jewish cooking and their tenement style apartment. She experiences no Jewish rituals other than the ostentatious weddings of other relatives. Small wonder her classmates' sonorous Latin prayers, omnipresent Christian iconography, and the impressive Gothic architecture of the churches bedazzle yet another rebellious protagonist, Julia in *Su espíritu inocente* (Her Innocent Spirit; 1981). Julia like Alicia has only her father's pen to keep as an inheritance and is very much seduced by the orderly life of Christians, whose nuns are so clean and methodical and whose God is so accessible that he hangs right from the doorframe.

In all of Steimberg's works starting with *Su espíritu inocente*, the characters and the narrators change identity with alacrity. The best example of this technique is *La loca 101* (Madwoman 101; 1973) in which the narrator sometimes calls herself Alicia and finally signs her work as Alicia Steimberg after assuming many identities. This novel also exemplifies another of Steimberg's techniques: the deliberate fragmentation and truncation of the plot. La Loca rudely thrusts fragments of several tales at the reader ranging from the fantastical hatchet murder of Augusto Conrado, the tragic love affair of a tubercular old rake and his beloved Flor de Lujo y Cabaret, a vampire who is the rage of Buenos Aires nightclub life, and the subterranean adventures of Aladdin, to the more prosaic vignettes of the life of a middle-aged, neurotic, petit-bourgeois writer.

But the recurrent nightmarish stories of the crazy woman, asylum inmate number 101, tie the novel together. A violent bloodletting is at the center of this, and Steimberg suggests, all literary work. The artist sucks the blood from life and puts it on a black and white page. But, the cauldron of blood in the garden of the sanatorium also prefigures the concealed and escalating violence of Argentina in the seventies. If the narration has the guise of the disordered ramblings of a madwoman, the chaos in her psyche foreshadows the repression and disorder of the so-called Dirty War in which countless Argentines were disappeared by the military and paramilitary forces. So despite the quirky and humorous tone announced from the cartoon artwork on the front and back covers, the song parodies and childish rhymes, and the flippant allusions to fairytales and folklore, the narrator's lament— "What the hell are we going to laugh about now?" (83)—underlines the serious nature of this book.

El árbol del placer (The Tree of Pleasure; 1986) satirizes the male-dominated world of psychoanalysis Buenos Aires style. Through flashbacks, the narrator Ana reveals how she extricated herself from the autocratic Dr. Alcázar and his devoted coterie of analysands. Alcázar's wealth and old Spanish name dazzle the members of Group O, who are mainly children of immigrants, and when his omnipotence falters, he attempts to seduce them. The novel ridicules the outlandish techniques, the esoteric jargon, arbitrary rules, and the cultish nature of psychotherapy but as in *La loca 101*, Steimberg also critiques her society. Here she indicts an entire generation of pleasure-seeking individuals who ignore the plight of those who starve in the slums which ring their beloved Buenos Aires. These hedonists prefer to submit to a dictator, their psychiatrist, rather than face the difficult social problems which can be sublimated but not erased.

In *Amatista* (Amethyst; 1989) the escape to the senses takes the guise of a course of sex therapy which the *señora* gives to the *doctor*. This novel turns the table on erotic and pornographic works in which males dominate and control females in search of sexual pleasure. Here the woman gives the orders to the man. She tells many fragmented stories in the guise of sexual fantasies used to arouse and to cure the sexual maladies of the lawyer. Eschewing the violence of such writers as the Marquis de Sade, whom she nonetheless parodies, the erotic world of this novel is lavender colored, satin soft, with smells of cologne and freshly roasted coffee and sounds of boleros and tangos. Here the horrors of contemporary life are totally subsumed by pleasures of the flesh.

With *Cuando digo Magdalena* (When I Say Magdalena) the 1992 winner of the Premio Planeta Biblioteca del Sur, Steimberg returns to her old techniques and concerns. This novel deals with psychological order and disorder as well as the disruptive injustice inherent in the social class structure of Argentine life. The seductive security of belonging to the ranks of the Spanish Catholic landowning class obsesses the confused and amnesiac narrator. In the course of the story, the protagonist rejects her name Sabina and chooses Magdalena, Marlene, and finally, Lili Marlene. Although this work has the ingredients for a British detective novel—classmates in a mental control group visit an elegant country estate and a murder occurs—Steimberg, as always, reworks the genre she has chosen. Inserted between uncomfortable dialogues between Magdalena and her doctor Iñaki are her dialogues with Iñaki's wife Flora, with her husband Enrique, with an impudent but imaginary journalist, and her first-person narration of events occurring before, during and after the Christmas time visit to Las Lilas (The Lilacs), her friend Juan Antonio's country estate. Steimberg flaunts authorial freedom by continually disrupting the plot and changing the setting in this exploration of the limits and borders we impose upon ourselves and those imposed by society.

Most of the margins and borders in the novel are social ones. The limits of Juan Antonio's exquisite and prosperous estate are described in great detail. The massive wooden door at the entrance of the ranch and the silver frame around the photo of Juan Antonio and his patrician family obsess the middle-class Jewish narrator. She similarly feels excluded when she contemplates the clearly delineated boundaries of the Christian heaven. Her amnesia stems from a threefold lack of psychological borders and security. As a Jew, she has forgotten her past. As a middle-class Argentine, she forgets where she is and who she came with just as her other classmates forget their spouses in forming brief liaisons with other members of the mental control group. More importantly, she's not sure whether to identify with her patrician friend Juan Antonio or with the impoverished masses. At the center of this novel, just as with *La loca 101*, is an act of violence. Although the mystery within the story is finally resolved, unlike most of Steimberg's fragmented plots, the narrator's sense of resolution is tenuous at best. The novel gives Magdalena's doctor the last word. She asks Iñaki whether she is better and he, no doubt under the influence of his Jewish wife Flora, answers her question with a question, "Better?" (216).

Steimberg's fiction attempts to deflate patriarchal authority with irony, humor, and social satire. Her characters ardently pursue order and security; however, the price for order is subservience, silence, and confinement. In most of her novels violence and social injustice and an arbitrary code of rules prevail. The humor arises when she reveals the arbitrary and absurd nature of language and social behaviors, but underneath lies a more bitter irony about the violence and aggression which structures every human relationship.

PRIMARY BIBLIOGRAPHY

Amatista. Barcelona: Tusquets, 1989.

El árbol del placer. Buenos Aires: Emecé, 1986.

"Cecilia's Last Will and Testament." Trans. by Christopher Leland. In *Landscapes of a New Land: Short Fiction by Latin American Women.* Ed. Marjorie Agosín. Fredonia, NY: White Pine Press, 1989. 102-11. Also in *Tropical Synagogues: Short Stories by Jewish-Latin American Writers.* Ed. Ilán Stavans. New York: Holmes & Meier, 1994. 58-66.

Como todas las mañanas. Buenos Aires: Celtia, 1983.

Cuando digo Magdalena. Buenos Aires: Planeta, 1992.

"Fleur-de-lis." Trans. by Norman Thomas di Giovanni and Susan Ashe. In *Hand in Hand Alongside the Tracks and Other Stories.* Ed. Norman Thomas di Giovanni. London: Constable, 1992. 109-13.

La loca 101. Buenos Aires: Ediciones de la Flor, 1973; Reissued 1995.

"Musicians and Watchmakers." Trans. Miriam Varon. In *Echad: An Anthology of Latin American Jewish Writing.* Ed. Robert and Roberta Kalechofsky. Marblehead, MA: Micah Publications, 1980. 45-54.

Músicos y relojeros. Buenos Aires: Centro Editor de América Latina, 1971. 2nd. ed. with *Su espíritu inocente.* Buenos Aires: Planeta, 1994.

"Sabe que es linda la mar." In *El imaginario judío en la literatura de América Latina: visión y realidad.* Ed. Patricia Finzi, E. Toker and Marcos Faerman. Buenos Aires: Grupo Editorial Shalom, 1990. 10-11.

Su espíritu inocente. Buenos Aires: Pomaire, 1981.

"Viennese Waltz," "García's Thousandth Day," "Segismundo's Better World." Trans. by Lorraine Elena Roses. In *Secret Weavers: Stories of the Fantastic by Women of Argentina and Chile.* Ed. by Marjorie Agosín. Fredonia, NY: White Pine Press, 1992. 221-40.

SECONDARY BIBLIOGRAPHY
Criticism

Agosín, Marjorie. "Alicia Steimberg y Elvira Orphee." In her *Literatura fantástica del Cono Sur: las mujeres.* San José: Editorial Universitaria Centroamericana, 1992. 67-74.

Barr, Lois Baer. "Fighting with Freud, and Other Father Figures: Alicia Steimberg." In her *Isaac Unbound: Patriarchal Traditions in the Latin American Jewish Novel.* Tempe, AZ: ASU Center for Latin American Studies, 1995. 55-84.

—. Rev. of *Amatista. Noaj* 5.6 (1991): 77-78.

Flori, Mónica. "Alicia Steimberg." In her *Streams of Silver: Six Contemporary Women Writers from Argentina*. Lewisburg: Bucknell UP, 1995. 147-84. (Critical essay followed by interview with Steimberg).

——. "Alicia Steimberg y Cecilia Absatz: dos narradoras argentinas." *Chasqui* 17.2 (1988): 83-92.

Gimbernat González, Ester. "*El árbol del placer*: retóricas de enfermedad." In her *Aventuras del desacuerdo: novelistas argentinas de los '80*. Buenos Aires: Danilo Albero Vergara, 1992. 289-94.

Goldberg, Florinda F. Rev. of *Cuando digo Magdalena*. *Noaj* 9 (1993): 110-12.

Heinrich, María E. "*El árbol del placer* de Alicia Steimberg." *Hispamérica* 16.48 (1987): 155-57.

Schneider, Judith Morganroth. "Alicia Steimberg: Inscriptions of a Jewish, Female Identity." *Yiddish* 9.1 (1993): 92-104.

Senkman, Leonardo. *La identidad judía en la literatura argentina*. Buenos Aires: Pardés, 1983. 283-93.

Sosnowski, Saúl. "Alicia Steimberg: enhebrando pequeñas historias." *Folio* 17 (1987): 104-10.

Weinstein, Ana E., and Miryam E. Gover de Nasatsky, comps. *Escritores judeo-argentinos: bibliografía 1900-1987*. 2 vols. Buenos Aires: Milá, 1994. II. 232-34.

Interviews

Agosín, Marjorie. "Entrevista a Alicia Steimberg." In her *Literatura fantástica del Cono Sur: las mujeres*. San José: Editorial Universitaria Centroamericana, 1992. 131-47.

Conde, Susana. "Alicia Steimberg." *Hispamérica* 23.67 (1994): 43-53.

Flori, Mónica. "Conversación con Alicia Steimberg sobre *Amatista*." *Alba de América* 11.20-21 (1993): 433-36.

Lois Baer Barr

SZICHMAN, MARIO (Argentina; 1945)

Mario Szichman, a prolific Argentine writer, journalist, and literary critic was born in Buenos Aires in 1945. He lived in Caracas between 1967 and 1971, where he wrote his first two novels. Upon his return to Buenos Aires in

1971, he assumed the position of editor at an Argentinean news agency for a period of four years. Back in Caracas from 1975 until 1981, Szichman obtained a professorial position at the University of Andrés Bello, and succeeded in publishing the controversial book *Miguel Otero Silva: mitología de una generación frustrada* (Miguel Otero Silva: The Mythology of a Defeated Generation; 1975). Since then he has resided in New York City where he has held several writing positions, for both the United Press International and the Capriles chain of Caracas. Today, he continues his never-ending contribution to the world of Latin American letters.

His novels have centered around the Jewish immigrants' struggle to assimilate into Argentine society, as well as their endless search for a common identity. The author's concern and fascination for Argentine Jewry can be found in four novels that comically and yet grotesquely depict the lives of a Polish Jewish family, the Pechofs, who having escaped a repressive Polish government find themselves struggling to survive day-to-day in early twentieth-century Buenos Aires. The first of these books, *Crónica falsa* (False Chronicles; 1969), attempts to retell the events that took place on the morning of June 9, 1956 which led to the execution of a group of civilians after the attempted Peronist revolution of General Valle. These series of events are, in many ways, closely related to the daily occurrences of the Pechof family. His second novel, *Los judíos del Mar Dulce* (The Jews of the Fresh-Water Sea; 1971), continues the saga of the Pechofs. Szichman cleverly attempts to describe many of the facets in the history of Jewish immigration to Argentina, not only by establishing a parody of Argentine traditions, but also by bringing to the surface the conflicts that have always existed between social groups. This novel "establishes that to rise in competitive, stratified society, immigrants learn to remake their identities" (Lindstrom 157). *La verdadera crónica falsa*; (The Real False Chronicles; 1972) is the third novel in which Szichman confronts once again the difficulties of Jewish immigrant life, and the obstacles that the Pechofs have encountered throughout four generations.

The saga of the Pechof family concludes with the publication of the author's fourth novel *A las 20:25 la señora entró en la inmortalidad* (*At 8:25 Evita Became Immortal*; 1983), winner of the first literary prize from Ediciones del Norte in 1980. Its themes are the importance of assimilation and the search for identity. The novel begins with Evita Peron's death on the evening of July 26, 1952, which left the country in a profound state of paralysis. This national cataclysm coincides with the death of Dora Pechof's daughter, Rifque, and the struggle of the family to secure a death certificate in order to give her a proper

Jewish burial. The only doctor with whom the Pechofs are able to establish contact happens to be a declared anti-Semite, who attempts to force the family to renounce their name, religion, culture and all their traditions. Their plan consists of inventing a family name with a long Argentine past, traceable to the times of the nineteenth-century dictator Juan Manuel de Rosas.

The novel is divided in three parts, each one in turn subdivided into smaller chapters whose titles follow the nomenclature of the Old Testament. As the novel progresses, the circumstances that surround the family complicate the storyline further and further. It is precisely this technique of intercrossing planes, temporal fragmentation, and frenetic dialogues that allows Szichman to create an atmosphere perfectly fit for his purposes (Mathieu 310). The Pechof's attempt at assimilation sadly results in failure due in part to a society that will not allow it, and also to the fact that their Jewish identity is simply indelible. The protagonist's Quixotic dream ends with the failed transformation of the Pechof family, the subsequent murder of the doctor to avoid being reported to the authorities, and the fleeing of the family (Flori 113). Consequently, this open-ended conclusion leaves plenty of room for a new cycle of persecution, death, and exile.

One of Mario Szichman's most interesting characteristics as a writer is his straightforward and sometimes rough style. This can be observed in the aforementioned book *Miguel Otero Silva: mitología de una generación frustrada*, in which Szichman inaugurates a style that is both direct and aggressive. The purpose of the book—to refute Miguel Otero Silva's (1908-1985) fame and grandeur—alone shows the author's unforgiving critical style. In regards to his fiction, Mario Szichman adopts a very colloquial Argentinean vocabulary. The *porteño* (Buenos Aires) slang or *lunfardo* is often mixed with Yiddish words or idiomatic expressions that are common among the Eastern European Jewish immigrants, therefore allowing his novels to reach a greater level of verisimilitude.

In addition to his fiction and nonfiction books, Szichman has published a considerable number of articles on various topics. In addition, he has succeeded in publishing interviews with renowned Latin American writers such as his fellow countryman David Viñas (1929), and the Uruguayan Angel Rama (1926-83).

Mario Szichman is an author whose Jewish identity is directly reflected in his work. His fiction deals primarily with themes that involve assimilation, identity, tradition, immigration and anti-Semitism. Szichman's perseverance and dedication have undoubtedly earned him a special place in the realm of Latin American letters.

PRIMARY BIBLIOGRAPHY
Creative Writing

A las 20:25 la señora entró en la inmortalidad. Hanover, NH: Ediciones del Norte, 1981. English version as, *At 8:25 Evita Became Immortal.* Trans. by Roberto Picciotto. Hanover, NH: Ediciones del Norte, 1983.

"Botín de guerra." *Noaj* 4.5 (1990): 28-36.

Crónica falsa. Buenos Aires: Jorge Alvarez, 1969.

"Cuidado con las imitaciones." *Hispamérica* 3.7 (July 1974): 95-101.

Los judíos del Mar Dulce. Buenos Aires: Galerna, 1971.

"Los papeles de Miranda: en la corte de Catalina de Rusia." *Hispamérica* 24.72 (1995): 77-85.

"La tercera fundación de Buenos Aires." *Noah* 1 (1987): 11-13.

La verdadera crónica falsa. Buenos Aires: Centro Editor de América Latina, 1972.

Nonfiction

Miguel Otero Silva: mitología de una generación frustrada. Caracas: Ediciones de la Biblioteca, Universidad Central de Venezuela, 1975.

Uslar: cultura y dependencia. Caracas: Yadell Hnos., 1975.

SECONDARY BIBLIOGRAPHY

Aizenberg, Edna. "Parricide on the Pampa: Deconstructing Gerchunoff and His Jewish Gauchos." *Folio* 17 (1987): 24-39.

Barr, Lois Baer. "Patriarchy, Parody and a New Authority: Mario Szichman." In her *Isaac Unbound: Patriarchal Traditions in the Latin American Jewish Novel.* Tempe, AZ: ASU Center for Latin American Studies, 1995. 85-105.

Borinsky, Alicia. "Lost Homes: Two Jews in Argentina." *Folio* 17 (1987): 40-48.

Flori, Mónica. "La identidad judío argentina en la ficción de Mario Szichman." *Selecta* 6 (1985): 111-15.

Goldman, Myrna. Rev. of *A las 20:25 la señora entró en la inmortalidad. Latin American Literary Review* 11.22 (1983): 122-25.

Groenewold, Sabine Horl. "Otredad permanente: acerca de la paradoja judía en la novela *A las 20:25 la señora entró en la inmortalidad* de Mario Szichman." In *Ensayos sobre judaísmo latinoamericano.* Buenos Aires: Milá, 1990. 386-93.

Lindstrom, Naomi. "Mario Szichman: A Questioning Eye on Jewish Argentine History." In her *Jewish Issues in Argentine Literature: From Gerchunoff to Szichman.* Columbia: U of Missouri P, 1989. 146-57.

Matamoro, Blas. Rev. of *A las 20:25 la señora entró en la inmortalidad. Cuadernos hispanoamericanos* 381 (1982): 718-19.

Mathieu, Corina. "Mario Szichman como desacralizador de mitos en *A las 20:25 la señora entró en la inmortalidad.*" In *Ensayos de literatura europea e hispanoamericana.* Ed. Felix Menchacatorre. San Sebastián: Universidad del País Vasco, 1990. 307-12.

Morello-Frosch, Marta. "Las caretas de la historia en Mario Szichman." *Folio* 17 (1987): 49-56.

——. "Textos inscritos al margen de la literatura argentina: *A las 20:25 la señora entró en la inmortalidad*, de Mario Szichman." In *El Cono Sur: Dinámica y dimensiones de su literatura. A Symposium.* Ed. Rose Minc. Upper Montclair, NJ: Montclair State College, 1985. 137-45. Also as "Texts Inscribed in the Margins of Argentinian Literature: *A las 20:25 la señora entró en la inmortalidad.*" *Yiddish* 9.1 (1993): 34-43.

Rama, Angel. *Novísimos narradores hispanoamericanos en marcha, 1964-1980.* México, D.F.: Marcha Editores, 1981. 95-109.

Sarlo, Beatriz. "Judíos y argentinos: *A las 20:25 la señora entró en la inmortalidad.*" *Punto de vista* (Buenos Aires) 29 (1987): 47-50.

Senkman, Leonardo. *La identidad judía en la literatura argentina.* Buenos Aires: Pardés, 1983. 269-83.

Sosnowski, Saúl. "Mario Szichman: el mordaz escepticismo ante la des/integración." In his *La orilla inminente: escritores judíos argentinos.* Buenos Aires: Legasa, 1987. 113-53.

Alejandro Meter

SZMULEWICZ, EFRAÍN (Chile; 1911)

There is scant biographical information available on Efraín Szmulewicz Gelbart. His name appears alternately on his books as both Efraím and Efraín with the surname Gelbart appearing only in the second edition of his novel *Un niño nació judío* (A Boy Was Born a Jew; 1940 [2nd ed. 1990]). Since this novel is considered to be highly autobiographical, it is useful in establishing the author's background. Likewise, the prologues to several of his books provide some insight into his life as an immigrant to Chile from his native country of Poland. Though no specific dates are provided, all allude to the fact that he arrived in

Chile as a young man around 1931 and quickly adapted to his new home. Szmulewicz traveled rather extensively throughout Latin America and he was a cultural attache with the Chilean embassy in Argentina. He became active in the literary community of Chile, not only as an author but as a prolific literary critic too. He has published a series of books that he calls "biografías emotivas" (emotive biographies) on a number of renown Chilean authors that include Gabriela Mistral (1889-1957), Pablo Neruda (1903-73), and Vicente Huidobro (1893-1948). He also published the *Diccionario de la literatura chilena* (Dictionary of Chilean Literature) in 1977. It became a leading resource for the study of Chilean literature and a revised and enlarged second edition appeared in 1984. He received three municipal awards in Santiago for his fiction.

Szmulewicz is the author of five works of fiction written over a period of almost fifty years. His first work was a collection of short stories titled *Cuentos y algo más* (Stories and Something More) published in 1937. These stories are also somewhat autobiographical in nature, at least in as much as they draw on the author's own experience as a boy in Poland. He also creates characters that will appear again in later works. The first several stories in the collection take place in Poland and they depict an uneasy environment tinged with anti-Semitism and violence against Jews. The best developed of these Jewish-theme stories is "Job" in which the author presents the conflict between Jewish and Christian students in the school. The protagonist, Stach, is a Christian student who struggles to come to terms with his own anti-Semitic feelings and who eventually speaks out against the harmful attitude and actions of his Christian classmates, for which they severely beat him along with several of the Jewish students. The last five stories of the collection presumably constitute the "something more" referred to in the title since, in reality they are brief, somewhat poetic descriptions rather than cohesive narratives. All revolve around the topic of the Spanish Civil War and each one takes the name of a Spanish city such as "Madrid," "Guernica," or "Badajoz" for its title. The selections present the impact of the war on these places and the destructive force of the fighting that tore Spain apart.

Szmulewicz's second work, the novel *Un niño nació judío*, is also his best known and the one that established him as a writer. The novel boasts a prologue by the famous Peruvian author Ciro Alegría (1909-67), who praises Szmulewicz's work in spite of the ideological differences between the two (2nd ed., 12). It was first published in 1940 with a print run of six thousand copies that quickly sold out. An explanatory note in the second edition (1990) states that Szmulewicz was hesitant to reissue the novel primarily because he felt that it lacked sophistication due to his limited experience with the Spanish language at the time it was first released. The second edition, therefore, is a modified version of the original after having undergone stylistic changes.

Un niño nació judío narrates the life of a young Polish Jew, Josef Grinberg. The novel is divided into two sections titled "Primera etapa" and "Segunda etapa" (First Stage and Second Stage). The first half of the novel narrates Josef's boyhood and establishes from the beginning how his life will be marked by having been born a Jew. Descriptions of family life, Jewish traditions, Josef's adventures with his Christian friend Wacek, his tutelage under Rabí Jaím, and the ever-present threat of anti-Semitism fill the pages dedicated to presenting the first stage in the young protagonist's life. The second stage begins following Josef's thirteenth birthday and his entry into manhood. The psychological development of the character is of primary importance in the second half of the novel as Josef becomes more involved in and influenced by politics and ideology. He experiences a decisive move from religiosity to secular political activism. The novel ends with Josef leaving Poland to start a new life in a new country.

The story of Josef Grinberg continues in Szmulewicz's second novel, *El hombre busca la tristeza* (Man Searches for Sadness; 1950). It begins with the young Polish immigrant struggling to make a new life in Chile. The narrative advances slowly with lengthy descriptive passages and numerous philosophical and political sermons presented mainly in the form of extensive dialogues. The novel presents various stages in Grinberg's life, while at the same time presenting the changing sociopolitical and cultural reality of Chile over the course of time. The author combines the experiences of the protagonist in Chile with his previous history in Poland. He manages to gain his independence, establish a successful bookstore and attain a reasonable sense of belonging in Chile. Yet, he is tormented by events in Europe, the invasion of Poland and the certain loss of his family.

In his third novel, *Forja de hombre* (Forge of a Man; 1978), Szmulewicz narrates the story of an Syrian immigrant family. Ismael Arám, a poor immigrant and father of six children struggles to make a living for his family. The main plot of the novel, however, revolves around Ismael's youngest son Eduardo. As in the previous novel, the author does not focus on the topic of immigration itself, but rather on the difficult process of assimilation into the dominant society. Each chapter in the novel narrates a significant moment or event for the family, which in turn contributes to the forging of Eduardo. *Forja de hombre* is a well-developed narrative that clearly demonstrates the author's literary maturation in comparison to his early works.

Así me lo contaron (That's How They Told It to Me; 1983), a short-story collection, is Szmulewicz's most recent work of fiction. There is very little

Jewish content to the stories which all involve travel to some extent and which depict rather uneventful happenings. They are more concentrated on recreating everyday situations of typical Chileans, with some exceptions. The one story that stands out in the collection is "El demonio pide revisión" (The Devil Requests a Retrial). Narrated by the devil, the story presents the struggle between good and evil in which a trial is held to reevaluate the role of the devil as concerns the creation and God's plan for Humanity.

Szmulewicz also wrote an interesting documentary book on Guillermo Patricio Kelly, the Argentine ex-Secretary General of the Alianza Libertadora Nacionalista (Nationalist Liberation Alliance), a powerful nationalist faction with close ties to Juan Domingo Perón. When Perón was ousted from power in 1955, former Peronista leaders were forced into exile, among them Kelly, who sought political asylum in Chile. The book, *¡Así huyó Kelly!*, is a compilation of newspapers articles, historical documents, official letters, and even maps that trace the "caso Kelly" (Kelly case), which turned into a national embarrassment for Argentina and the source of considerable friction between the two countries.

Even though Szmulewicz's fiction lacks the refined artistic quality to be included in a discussion of Chile's leading literary figures, and his works have received only minimal critical attention, one cannot overlook his pioneering role as one of the relatively few Jewish writers in Chile. If for this reason alone, his works merit a closer examination, which seems to be the sentiment of Ediciones Rumbos, the publishing house that in 1990 reissued his two most important novels. His major contribution to Chilean literature, nevertheless, is undoubtedly in the field of literary criticism.

PRIMARY BIBLIOGRAPHY

Creative Writing
Así me lo contaron: cuentos. Santiago: Nascimento, 1983.
Cuentos y algo más. Santiago: Prensa Cóndor, 1937.
Forja de hombre. Santiago: Rumbos, 1978.
El hombre busca la tristeza. Santiago: Don Quijote, 1950. 2nd ed. Santiago: Rumbos, 1990.
Un niño nació judío. Santiago: Zig-Zag, 1940. 2nd ed. Santiago: Rumbos, 1990.
Nonfiction
Andrés Bello: biografía emotiva. Santiago: Rumbos, 1991.
¡Así huyó Kelly!. Buenos Aires: Andina, 1957.
Diccionario de la literatura chilena. Santiago: Selecciones Lautaro, 1977. 2d ed. rev. and enlarged. Santiago: Andrés Bello, 1984.

Gabriela Mistral: biografía emotiva. Santiago: Atacama, 1958. 7th ed. rev and enlarged. Santiago: Rumbos, 1991.

Meditaciones sobre "La raya en el aire" de Roque Esteban Scarpa. Prologue by Hugo Goldsack. Temuco, Chile: Cielos del Sur, 1984.

Miguel Arteche: biografía emotiva. Santiago: Rumbos, 1992.

Nicanor Parra: biografía emotiva. Santiago: Rumbos, 1988.

Pablo Neruda: biografía emotiva. Santiago: J. Almendros-Orbe, 1975. 2d ed. rev. and enlarged. Santiago: Rumbos, 1988.

Vicente Huidobro: biografía emotiva. Santiago: Editorial Universitaria, 1978.

Editions

Poesía para todos: antología universal. Santiago: Rumbos, 1989.

SECONDARY BIBLIOGRAPHY

Alegría, Ciro. "Prólogo." *Un niño nació judío.* 2nd ed. Santiago: Rumbos, 1990. 9-15.

Jobet, Jorge. "Efraín Szmulewicz, el inmigrante chilenizado." *Forja de hombre.* Santiago: Ediciones Rumbos, 1978. 9-22.

Lassel, Adriana A. *Cambio y permanencia en Szmulewicz.* Santiago: Ediciones Rumbos, 1990.

Sabella Gálvez, Andrés. "Prólogo en traje de calle." *Cuentos y algo más.* Santiago: Prensa Cóndor, 1937. 15-19.

Darrell B. Lockhart

SZPUNBERG, ALBERTO (Argentina; 1940)

Alberto Szpunberg is a poet, journalist, and professor of literature. He was born in Buenos Aires in 1940 and since 1977 he has been part of the vast Argentine diaspora. He worked with Noé Jitrik (1929) teaching Argentine literature at the Universidad Nacional de Buenos Aires from 1965 until the coup d'etat carried out by General Juan Carlos Onganía in 1966, whose intervention in the University provoked a mass exodus of professors. With the return to democracy in 1973, during the so-called "Primavera de Campora" (Spring of Campora), he returned to the university as a professor of Argentine Literature, Media Communication and Literature, and as director of the degree program in Classical Languages and Literatures. He resigned once again following the change in direction that the university took as a result of the political about-face that occurred in the country as a consequence of the events at the Ezeiza International Airport on 20 June, 1973.

As a journalist, Szpunberg was the director of the cultural section of the Buenos Aires daily *La Opinión* from 1975 to May 1976. He was asked to resign when he published a note in the paper that alluded to the disappearance of the writer Haroldo Conti (1925-76?).

As a result of the military repression unleased by the coup d'état of 1976, Szpunberg exiled himself in Barcelona, where he continues to reside. In 1983 he worked as a correspondent for the Nueva Nicaragua (Nicaragua News) agency in Paris. He has participated in two of the international conferences held by the Asociación Internacional de Escritores Judíos en Lengua Hispana y Portuguesa (International Association of Jewish Writers in Spanish and Portuguese): in Jerusalem (1990) and Buenos Aires (1992).

In his first collection of poems, *Poemas de la mano mayor* (Poems of the Greater Hand; 1962), various elements that will later come to characterize his work are already evident. In the words of Eduardo Romano, who writes the prologue to the work, Szpunberg's work demonstrates the author's concern for the inhabitant of the city and the lack of justice that permeates Buenos Aires, in wait of a new social order. Romano also states the originality of Szpunberg's language in cultivating a colloquial rhythm.

In *Juego limpio* (Clean Game; 1963) published the following year, there are two poems about the uprooting of exile ("I. Desarraigo," and "II. Desarraigo" [I. Uprooting; II. Uprooting]). The poems represent the inauguration of a theme on which Szpunberg will have much to say after his exile in 1976. Both poems portray the figure of the immigrant grandfather, in whose gestures one can simultaneously read the land of his past and that of his present. An explicit development of this theme in connection with Judaism can be read in a later text, "A tiro de piedra" (At a Stone's Throw; 1989), a lyrical story about Szpunberg's visit to Jerusalem.

In *El che amor* (Che Love; 1965) a change in the poet's thematics, form, and tone is readily identifiable. The poems move away from the intimate, experiential tone of previous texts to propose a more epic and utopic voice. Szpunberg utilizes poetic prose in the first part of the collection (from which comes the title of the collection), and in "Confabulaciones (Schemes), his poetry reveals a rhythm that is highly original, and in which one can detect the polyphony of dialogue. This volume won a special mention from the Casa de las Américas foundation in 1965; the members of the panel were the poets Nicanor Parra

(1914), Jaime Sabines (1929), Allen Ginsberg (1926), and José Lezama Lima (1912-76).

Su fuego en la tibieza (Your Fire in the Warmth; 1981) won the Alcalá de Henares first prize for poetry in Spain. The text is divided into four sections: "Casa allanada" (Razed House), "Despedidas" (Goodbyes), "Correspondencia Baires-Salzburgo" (Buenos Aires-Salzburg Correspondence), and "Exilio en Masnou" (Exile in Masnou). Each section alludes to the direct experience of the poet with the terror produced in Argentina after the coup d'état of 1976, and with the subsequent consequences of exile. The exquisite poetic quality of the writer unfolds in this collection with uncommon emotional depth.

The poems of *Apuntes (1982-1985)* (Notes [1982-1985]; 1987) were written mostly between 1982 and 1984. The eleven initial texts of the collection received a Honorable Mention from the Mexican literary journal, *Plural*. A number of these poems were transformed into tangos by musician César Strocio and were recorded by the group Cuarteto Cedrón in France (*Faubourg sauvage*, Paris: Polydor, 1983) and by the group Esquina in Italy.

In collaboration with Luis Luchi, and with music by Jorge Sarraute, Szpunberg is the co-author of *A medio hacer todavía* (Still Half-Done; 1978), an album of poems and songs.

His poems also appear in a bilingual (Spanish-French) volume titled *Il nous reste la memoire: poèmes argentines de l'exil* (We Are Left with Memory: Argentine Poems on Exile; 1983), along with poems by Juan Gelman (1930) and Vicente Zito Lema (1939).

In 1993, he won the Antonio Machado International Poetry Prize in France for *Luces que a lo lejos* (Lights That from Afar). This collection of poetry is being translated by the Machado Foundation (Collioure, France), and its publication in Argentina has been announced in the collection Tierra Firme in Buenos Aires.

"Charlas con Ana" (Talks with Ana; 1984) has been defined by the author as one of his fundamental texts, since in it begins his poetic reflection on the Left, his guerrilla militancy and his Jewish humanism. This latter characteristic is also associated with "Conversaciones con Shila" (Conversations with Shila; 1993). The relationship between both texts (published separately in journals) would merit, according to the author, publication as a single volume.

"Conversaciones con Shila" is an essay dedicated to the Palestinian-Israeli conflict seen from the perspective of Jewish humanism. The text was presented at the IV Congreso de Escritores Judíos Latinoamericanos (IV Conference of Latin American Jewish Writers) held in Buenos Aires, 9-12 August 1992.

In the essay Szpunberg proposes a reflection of Judaism whose elements include exile, the condition of wandering, and the promised land. Fragments of the text were published in the journal *Noaj*. Szpunberg has commented the following concerning the text: "Shila was the dog with which I shared, together with my two daughters, the last ten years of my life. She died on 21 January, 1995, on a clear Saturday. I buried her at the foot of a small tree on one of the mountains that are located by Masnou, the town where I live. From the mountains, especially on days as clear as that Saturday, one can see Jerusalem. Whoever doesn't believe it, even if they live with their nose stuck to the Wailing Wall, will never see Jerusalem" (personal interview).

Szpunberg has stated that his writing is born from the impact that events have had on his life. Likewise, the idea of a socially committed literature has never interested him since commitment is just another privilege: have-nots cannot commit themselves (Gilio 214-15).

One can identify in Szpunberg's work a constant reference to his Jewish condition. He maintains that the central issue in Jewish problematics today is the Israeli-Palestinian conflict, together with the resurgence of fascism in the world. Concerning the conflict in the Middle East, Szpunberg has openly declared his support of the right of the Palestinian people to govern themselves. "The conflict puts all Jews to the test as a people, as well as the tradition of Jewish humanism whose ethical truths I believe to be my own. I profoundly reject the idea of private property, a notion that carries with it borders, and therefore, both offensive and defensive violence. I strongly support an Israeli-Palestinian dialogue that places peace, equal rights, and human life above all else" (personal interview).

PRIMARY BIBLIOGRAPHY
Creative Writing
Apuntes (1982-1985). Buenos Aires: Libros de Tierra Firme, 1987.
El che amor. Buenos Aires: Editora Nueve 64, 1965.
Il nous reste la memoire: poemes argentines de l'exil. Paris: La Decouverte/Maspero, 1983.
Juego limpio. Buenos Aires: Nueva Expresión, 1963.
Poemas de la mano mayor. Buenos Aires: Gente del Sur, 1962.
Su fuego en la tibieza. Madrid: Alcalá Poesía, 1981.
Nonfiction
"Charlas con Ana." *Hispamérica* 13.38 (1984): 47-56.
"Conversaciones con Shila." *Noaj* 9 (1993): 75-82.
"A tiro de piedra." *Noaj* 3.3-4 (1989): 50-53.

SECONDARY BIBLIOGRAPHY
Criticism
Barros, Daniel. Rev. of *Juego limpio*. *El barrilete* 7 (1964): 22.
Brodsky, Marcelo. "Alberto Szpunberg y el violinista de Chagall." *Nueva presencia* 370 (3 Aug. 1984): 5.
Muleiro, Vicente. Rev. of *Apuntes*. *Crisis* 54 (1987): 86.
Perrone, Alberto. "Poesía ciudadana sin pintoresquismo: *El Che amor*, por Alberto Szpunberg." *Hoy en la cultura* 25 (1965): 24.
Sverdlik, Oded. "*Poemas de la mano mayor*, por Alberto Szpunberg." *Nueva Sión* 349 (17 Nov. 1962): 6.
Vásquez, Rafael. "*Juego limpio*, de Alberto Szpunberg." *Vigilia* 6 (1964): 7.
Interviews
Fonderbrider, Jorge. "La historia nos pisa los talones." *Mascaró* 7 (1987): 53-56.
Gilio, María Esther. "Alberto Szpunberg, 'Olí la huelga en el aire y corrí a alimentarme'." In her *EmerGentes*. Buenos Aires: Ediciones de la Flor, 1986: 213-19.

Claudia Ferman

TALESNIK, RICARDO (Argentina; 1935)

Born in Buenos Aires in 1935, Ricardo Talesnik began his long career in the arts as a child actor at the age of two. He studied piano for five years, but his formal education ended after the second year of high school. As the only child of a middle-class family, he helped his father sell bananas in the Mercado de Abasto Proveedor, later selling on his own, and eventually, with his father's help, buying a truck to transport cargo, especially bananas, from the port to market. Talesnik did his military service in the Escuela Superior Técnica as a member of the clean-up crew.

Because of his aversion to regular work governed by a time clock, Talesnik pursued his artistic interests. Fascinated by film, he took courses in *cineclubes* (movie clubs) where he studied directing, and he worked in public relations for an evening newspaper, *La Razón*. Obligated to learn typing, which he managed with two fingers, he began to write jokes and sketches. His first professional work dates from 1964 when he wrote segments of a TV show ("Show 90") with Enrique Wernicke (1915-68). In 1965 he scripted the Show

Standard Electric for television, and in 1966 wrote several chapters for *Historias de jóvenes* (Stories of Youth), one of which was selected to open the series. His first two plays, one untitled, the other called *Cómo se hace una fiesta* (How to Make a Party; 1966), are from the same period.

Talesnik's career has been characterized by an irrepressible sense of humor that led him into comedy and comedy sketches for theatre, television, and clubs. The humor represents a mixture of his Jewish ancestry, North American silent films, British and Italian films, the *sainete argentino* (Argentine comedy), the *revista porteña* (Buenos Aires musical review), and all the other influences that have impinged upon his life—his family, his schooling, his phobias and anxieties. Even though a serious or critical vein lies beneath the surface, the presentation is always underscored by humor, both in dialogue and action.

Talesnik's first play, *La fiaca* (the word is a Buenos Aires slang expression that translates roughly as "The Doldrums"), was an instant and enduring success. First performed in Santiago de Chile by ICTUS (a major theater group) in September of 1967, it was staged in Buenos Aires only a few days later, going on to win the Argentores Prize for best play of the year. It has subsequently played in virtually every country in the Americas as well as many European nations, translated into several languages. *La fiaca* deals with a middle-aged, middle-class businessman who, one Monday morning, simply decides not to go to work. His wife and mother are delirious with anguish and resort to subterfuge, bribery, threats, and coercion to convince him otherwise.

Divided into two acts of four and two scenes, respectively, the play functions basically as a farce with an alternating internal rhythm that borders on the tragicomic. With a light tone and jocular language, the first three scenes establish Nestor's decision and his family's reactions. The contrast in the fourth scene between Nestor and Peralta, his friend from work, portends a more serious dimension because of Peralta's inability to follow Nestor's example. The farcical tone returns in the second act, set several days later, as Nestor's wife decides to leave him, but the situation turns serious again in the sixth and final scene when Nestor, near starvation, becomes the object of special interests, including those of his friend Peralta, who sees opportunistic possibilities in this impasse. The interplay of the humorous and the serious sustains the dramatic interest throughout this popular play.

This first play catapulted Talesnik into the artistic spotlight, bringing him fame and money, but it did not assuage his own inner fears about the prophecies of a "one-play author." He adapted the script for the movie, *Yo también tengo fiaca* (I Am Also Down), which was filmed in Argentina in 1969 and won an Argentores prize (1978). Later he wrote another filmscript in collaboration with Jorge García Alonso, *La guita* (Money; 1970), which also won an Argentores prize.

In 1970 Talesnik had two new plays. *El avión negro* (The Black Airplane), written in collaboration with Roberto Cossa (1934), Germán Rozenmacher (1936-71), and Carlos Somigliana (1932-87), dealt at a critical juncture in Argentine history with the projected mythical return from exile of General Juan Perón in a black airplane—at the time it was prohibited to even speak the name Perón in Argentina. The episodic structure provides for various perspectives, including the *neo-peronistas* (new supporters of President Perón), who are seen to be hypocritical and generally incompetent, as opposed to the special interests represented by the oligarchy, intelligentsia, clergy, professionals, and the working class. Even though the scenes are not identified by author, the humor that permeates the play is characteristic of Talesnik's style and indicates his involvement in this unusual four-way collaborative project.

The same year, 1970, Talesnik premiered *Cien veces no debo* (A Hundred Times I Should Not; a reference to the school child who does penance by writing in his notebook), a modern-day version of a Armando Discépolo (1887-1971) *sainete* (comedy) with all the twists and turns of a fast-paced comedy. A loving, middle-class family discovers that their only daughter, eighteen and unmarried, is pregnant. From their original position of decent and moral individuals of high values, scandalized by their daughter's behavior, they paradoxically show themselves to be willing accomplices in various forms of trickery designed to protect their sense of status. Their own behavior includes violence, both verbal and physical, entrapment, lies, and other deceptions. The play exhibits a mixture of farce and tragicomedy analogous to that of *La fiaca* through the clever dialogue, the abrupt turns of phrase, and the manipulation of three suitors, individually and collectively. The play followed on Talesnik's anonymous work with *Maipo*, which represented the pinnacle of the music hall variety show, an outlet for daring and racy language. With this work he confirmed his craft with dialogue.

In 1972 Talesnik wrote a piece for *café-concert* (night club show) called *Solita y sola* (Alone and Lonely); the same year he wrote another filmscript, *Las venganzas de Beto Sánchez* (The Vengeance of Beto Sánchez) and finished a piece begun in 1971, *Los japoneses no esperan* (The Japanese Don't Wait). Both premiered in 1973. *Los japoneses no esperan* is a curious title for a play about the dangers of marital infidelity. Under the guise of signing a contract with the Japanese in Lima, the central character, Miguel, arranges an assignation with his lover, but his wife locks him in their Buenos Aires apartment. A change in Talesnik's own marital status, now separated from his first wife and involved in a second relationship, and the influence of Julio Cortázar's (1914-84) *Rayuela* (*Hopscotch*; 1963) and Federico Fellini's (1920-93) *8 1/2*, in which each author himself relates a work of fiction, inspired Talesnik to write this play which depends on a series of metatheatrical turns involving the central character's wife and lover. This comedy has a happy ending as Miguel comes to realize the importance of his vows to his wife and time with his child. The women's discussion, without homosexual overtones, of having babies without husbands was avant-garde for 1973, anticipating developments of some 20 years later. The play provides a clever and comic setting for a lesson in morality with the underlying serious message about male responsibility and the need for truth in one's life.

In 1972-73 Talesnik wrote *Traylesnik*, a comedy piece designed to showcase his talents as well as those of his wife. Premiered in Kingsville, Texas, the spectacle depended on music, dance and movement, and little language. A second spectacle, *El Chucho* (1976-77), contained more spoken material and involved music, scenography and costume changes.

Cómo ser una buena madre (How to Be a Good Mother) was a theatrical spectacle presented more than a thousand times between 1977 and 1983 in the US and various countries of Latin America. Predicated on the concept of the over-protective mother who cares for her son to the point of paralysis, the work was enormously entertaining and successful for its presentation of guilt and other complexes.

Nunca más una sola mujer (Never Again Just One Woman; 1992) continued the farcical episodes of male/female relationships within a metatheatrical framework. The divorced and lonely Miguel interacts directly with his audience while consorting with five different women—Reina, Carola, Mónica, Luciana, and Teresa—one at a time, each one with her special qualities. Miguel aspires to have a "harem" (actually the first working title, but one that was already registered with Argentores) in which each woman (lover, cook, cleaning woman, companion, psychologist) can attend to his needs. In the second structural part, the women all converge on him at once, discussing this relationship. The third part requires Miguel to meet with each one individually to consider their special characteristics. Talesnik provides his usual twists, leading us from one surprise to another, until the women all abandon Miguel at the end, at which point he calls his ex-wife to inquire about the children. The play provides yet another vision of the foibles of the male ego, the use and abuse of others in order to enhance one's own position, power, or sense of security and well-being. The situation is humorous and the interaction between the women and Miguel provides comedy. The language is less jocular than in other plays and the bottom line is that this is serious business.

In *Cómo se hace una fiesta* (How to Throw a Party), Talesnik's first full-length play, later revised and updated with contemporary references, he utilized techniques that are familiar from other works. The unexpected visitor and the element of surprise, combined with the absurdist technique of putting people in a room together to see what will happen, characterize this farce, again with overtones of tragicomedy. In this long, one-act play, Talesnik develops a three-part structure: in the first segment a modern couple (from the year 2000) accepts the sexual vagaries of their insatiable young daughter who brings a virtual parade of men to their home. The second segment introduces Luisito, the party organizer, whose mission in life is to help people celebrate *anything*. In the third segment when the two couples can not agree on the party logistics, the message about the value of human relationships becomes clear. The elements of farce are obvious, including many sexual references and innuendos, but under the surface of humor and joking, one perceives the concepts of loving another (not sexually but spiritually), fidelity, and living life to the fullest without the sarcasm and abuse that characterize many relationships.

In *Ensayo de pareja* (Rehearsal for Matrimony; 1994) Talesnik uses the technique of a couple in rehearsals for a play that deals with male/female relations. The dichotomy between their exterior and interior roles enhances the different dimensions of tension, conflict and, curiously, emotion. The incorporation of music, song and dance enhances the movement as Talesnik questions all the stereotypes and traditions underlying a successful relationship. The language is racy (including a special segment on "the male member"), typical of Talesnik, as he maintains his usual standards of humor in scenes that are both original and familiar. Talesnik keeps reminding us, in different formats, that males and females have basic needs—physical, sexual, social, psychological—and that the business of taking care of them is complicated. He is a versatile individual with multiple talents. In addition to writing, no doubt his most enduring legacy, he has also been an actor in several shows, including *Traylesnik, Cómo ser una buena madre, El Chucho* and *En camiseta* (In T-Shirt; 1985-91). As a director he staged *La fiaca* in Rio de Janeiro (1970) and Mar del Plata, Argentina (1985), *Los japoneses no esperan* in Caracas in 1980 (with a domestic tour of Argentina in 1981 and New York in 1993), and *Nunca más una sola mujer* in Mexico (1992). In 1987 he offered workshops in Buenos Aires on humorous expression in acting and writing. He adapted Neil Simon's (1927) *Plaza Suite* (1969) for staging in Buenos Aires (1988), and in 1993 he wrote weekly television programs called "programas unitarios" (weekly television programs that played without continuity of plot or story) for Televisa in Mexico. In mid-1994, on the death of Oscar Viale (1932-94), Talesnik was commissioned to script the weekly television show *Mi cuñado* (My Brother-in-Law).

In 1994 Talesnik opened a new one-person show titled *Bueno para la risa* (Good for a Laugh) in the Picadilly Theatre. As expected, the work plays with familiar concepts—women, sex, relatives and relationships, language, animals, sound effects. The work incorporates music, costume changes, and stage effects in order to entertain the public. One of the funniest segments reproduces the sounds of males reaching orgasm in different countries and cultures. Talesnik is a master craftsman in the business of humor.

His Jewish heritage is, as he describes it, of only relative importance. His parents were both born in Argentina and totally adapted to their culture. Ricardo had no religious education; the family did not observe Jewish customs or cuisine. His parents were partial to tango and to gambling; the bouts of poker games put him into houses of friends with some exposure to Jewish food. Talesnik does not feel integrated into the Jewish community in Buenos Aires; although he maintains relations and contacts. On the other hand, neither is he aware of any discrimination against him. His plays and theatrical spectacles contain, at most, only oblique references to Jewish traditions or cultural phenomena. In Israel in 1993, his film *Las venganzas de Beto Sánchez* was re-filmed with the title *Las venganzas de Isaac Finkelstein*. The new version won seven Israeli awards and was selected to represent Israel in the Oscar competitions in Hollywood in the category of best foreign film. All in all, Talesnik is, at this writing, still a boyish individual with a quick smile and quick wit. Now with his third wife, he is full of life and vigor and as of November 1994 became a father again.

PRIMARY BIBLIOGRAPHY

El avión negro. (with Roberto Cossa, Germán Rozenmacher and Carlos Somigliana). Buenos Aires: Talía, 1970.

Cien veces no debo. Buenos Aires: Talía, 1972.

La fiaca. Buenos Aires: Talía, 1967.

Teatro: La fiaca. Cien veces no debo. Ed. Miguel Angel Giella and Peter Roster. Ottawa: Girol Books, 1980.

Talesnik's other plays mentioned in the text exist only as unpublished manuscripts.

SECONDARY BIBLIOGRAPHY
Criticism

Campanella, Hebe. "El hoy y el aquí en el teatro argentino de los últimos veinte años." *Cuadernos hispanoamericanos* 78.234 (1969): 673-93.

Castagnino, Raúl. "Tendencias actuales del teatro argentino." *Revista interamericana de bibliografía* 20.4 (1970): 435-52.

Dubatti, Jorge. "Ricardo Talesnik y el realismo: *La fiaca.*" In *Teatro argentino de los '60: polémica, continuidad y ruptura.* Comp. Osvaldo Pelletieri. Buenos Aires: Corregidor, 1989. 157-68.

Kaiser-Lenoir, Claudia. "*El avión negro*: de la realidad a la caricatura grotesca." *Revista canadiense de estudios hispánicos* 7.1 (1982): 149-58.

Martínez, Marta. "Seis estrenos del teatro argentino en 1976." *Latin American Theatre Review* 11.2 (1978): 95-101.

Previdi Froelich, Roberto. "Crimen y castigo en *La fiaca* de Ricardo Talesnik." *Rocky Mountain Review of Language and Literature* 43.1-2 (1989): 61-73.

Ramos Foster, Virginia. "The Buenos Aires Theatre, 1966-67." *Latin American Theatre Review* 1.2 (1968): 54-61.

Roster, Peter. "Biobibliografía selecta." In *Teatro: La fiaca. Cien veces no debo.* Ottawa: Girol Books, 1980. 189-94.

Sosonowski, Saúl. "Desmantelamientos, rebeldías chicas e inoperancia: los escenarios de Ricardo Talesnik." In *Teatro: La fiaca. Cien veces no debo.* Ottawa: Girol Books, 1980. 7-21.

Tirri, Néstor. *Realismo y teatro argentino.* Buenos Aires: La Bastilla, 1973. 123-31, 167-71.

Tschudi, Lilian. *Teatro argentino actual (1960-1972).* Buenos Aires: García Cambeiro, 1974. 70-74.

Weinstein, Ana E., and Miryam E. Gover de Nasatsky, comps. *Escritores judeo-argentinos: bibliografía 1900-1987.* 2 vols. Buenos Aires: Milá, 1994. II. 256-58.

Zayas de Lima, Perla. *Diccionario de autores teatrales argentinos 1950-1990.* Buenos Aires: Galerna, 1991. 265-67.

Interviews

Giella, Miguel Angel. "Ricardo Talesnik: el teatro en el escenario." In *Teatro: La fiaca. Cien veces no debo.* Ottawa: Girol Books, 1980. 23-40.

George Woodyard

TARNOPOLSKY, SAMUEL (Argentina; 1908)

Samuel Tarnopolsky, a medical specialist in rheumatic diseases, is also adept at social commentary and criticism. While Tarnopolsky's early works shared the theme of the conquest of the desert (Senkman 349, n.18), he is probably best known for the novel *La mitad de nada* (Half of Nothing; 1969), which reflects the affronts to the liberal Argentine Jewish conscience conveyed through dialogue between the novel's two major protagonists, Braunstein and Michaelson—the former, who despite Argentine anti-Semitism, still identifies strongly with Argentina and the latter, a Zionist youth, who decides to make aliyah. This conflict in attitude is a theme throughout the novel from which may be traced the profound fractures of the liberal conscience prompted by the anti-Semitic murders of Daniel Grinblat in 1962 and Raúl Alterman in 1964. *La mitad de nada* thus transcends the genre of the novel as Tarnapolsky's prose reflects his own torment in the face of an outbreak of anti-Semitic incidents which gripped Argentina from 1959 to 1964, largely attributable to the rightwing organization known as Tacuara. This explosion of anti-Semitic violence shook the belief in democracy held by Argentine liberal Jews like Tarnopolsky. According to Leonardo Senkman, Tarnopolsky's was the most straightforward and "honest testimony that has been written not only on Argentine anti-Semitism, but rather on the disappointment of liberalism: to learn, through violence, what it means to be a Jew in Argentina" (320).

This disillusionment of the liberal vis-à-vis the hypocrisy of the democratic-friend-of-the-Jew extended to another book by Tarnopolsky entitled *Los prejuiciados de honrada conciencia* (Prejudiced Men of Honorable Conscience; 1971), in which he clearly explained all the hidden mechanisms of the Argentine liberal who conceals an odious prejudice against the Jew for being different. Examples discussed by Tarnopolsky included writers like Silvina Bullrich (1915), Ricardo Rojas (1882-1957), Roberto Jorge Payró (1876-1928), Enrique Larreta (1875-1961), and Manuel Mujica Láinez (1910-1984) (Senkman 327, n.5). Singled out for attention were also Roberto F. Giusti (1887-?) and Alfredo A. Bianchi (1882-?), editors of the liberal journal *Nosotros* (Us). Giusti and Bianchi had been "anti-Nazi combatants," who had great insight into the world's political and social problems. They publicly defended the Jewish cause at a time when the Jews did not have many friends because it was fashionable to be anti-Semitic. While Giusti and Bianchi had defended Jewish immigration in 1919, they seemed to reverse their position in an editorial in *Nosotros* entitled "A New and Dangerous Invasion," which Tarnopolsky characterized as "the most violent diatribe which had been published in Spanish," reminiscent of militant Nazism. They maintained that the involuntary exodus of Jewish artists from Germany had repercussions in Argentina, where they practiced their art and thereby restricted what opportunities had existed for native Argentines prior to this influx. This was a very serious problem according to Giusti and Bianchi. They also asserted that this Jewish influence perverted Argentine artistic and aesthetic expression, which constituted a "crime" of cultural and national offense and could "justify any violent reaction. . ." (60-62).

This prejudice against Jews was shared across the Argentine political spectrum as reflected in Tarnopolsky's observations on Argentine socialists such as Alfredo L. Palacios (1879-1965), Alicia Moreau de Justo (1885-1986), and Juan B. Justo (1865-1928), the leader of the Socialist Party. A 1939 survey conducted by the socialist magazine *Claridad* (Clarity) provided insight into the attitudes of Argentine socialists toward Jews around that time. Tarnopolsky noted that socialist responses to questions on Nazi persecution of the Jews and the possibility of anti-Semitism in democratic countries contradicted the image of socialists as progressives and defenders of the oppressed. For example, Tarnopolsky observed that while Jews were perishing in concentration camps, Moreau de Justo's only solution was to call for the disappearance of the myths of race and religion, reflecting socialist ambivalence of the Jew (116). As Tarnopolsky quoted Jean-Paul Sartre (1905-1980): "'The Jews have passionate enemies and defenders without passion'" (50-51). Tarnopolsky frankly discussed socialist prejudice and misgivings about Jews as well as leftist calls for Jewish assimilation. He noted that there were anti-Semites who were "philosemites of the individual, [but] anti-Semites of the group. Their solution is that the group disappears and the individual remains". Tarnopolsky believed that socialist leader Justo always held this view while Palacios temporarily did so. In a reflection that anti-Semitic prejudice transcended political ideology, Tarnopolsky toward the end of his book describes the overcoming of prejudice by two Argentines different in practically all respects—Palacios and Father Gustavo Juan Franceschi (1871-1957 [113-17]). The latter, especially in the 1930s, wrote anti-Semitic commentaries in his capacity as editor of the influential Catholic publication *Criterio* (Criterion).

With the novel *La mitad de nada* followed by *Los prejuiciados de honrada conciencia*, Tarnopolsky distinguished himself from other writers of his generation who would not have thought to publicly doubt the prevailing optimism of their contemporaries. The questioning and pessimism of this liberal writer who wrote such effusive books on the Conquest of the Desert (*Rastrillada en Salinas Grandes*, [Trail to Salinas Grandes; 1944], for example) eloquently symbolized the extent to which confidence in the process of the country's harmonious integration had been shaken by the end of the 1960s (Senkman 464). Thus, while Tarnopolsky was a physician by profession, he certainly made his mark on Argentine intellectual life as both a writer and social/political commentator by offering keen insight into what it meant to be Jewish in Argentina as largely defined by the dominant non-Jewish culture.

PRIMARY BIBLIOGRAPHY
Creative Writing
Alarma de indios en la frontera sud: novela. Buenos Aires: S. Rueda, 1941.
La mitad de nada. Buenos Aires: Candelabro, 1969. Reissued, Buenos Aires: Milá, 1988.
Los prejuiciados de honrada conciencia. Buenos Aires: Candelabro, 1971.
La rastrillada de Salinas Grandes; novela inspirada en la famosa expedición al desierto dirigida por el coronel Pedro Andrés García pocas semanas después de la Revolución de Mayo. Buenos Aires: Ediciones Feria, 1944.
Nonfiction
Los curanderos, mis colegas. 2a ed. Buenos Aires: Galerna, 1984.
Libros con indios pampas y conquistadores del desierto. Buenos Aires: Expansión Bibliográfica Americana, 1958.

SECONDARY BIBLIOGRAPHY
Jofré Barroso, Haydeé M. "Confesiones de una lectora." Prologue to *La mitad de nada.* Buenos Aires: Milá, 1988. 5-9.
Senkman, Leonardo. *La identidad judía en la literatura argentina.* Buenos Aires: Pardés, 1983. 142, 320-22, 346, 464, 465.
Soifer, Bernardo. "*La mitad de nada,* por Samuel Tarnopolsky." *Comentario* 73 (1970): 92-93.

Allan Metz

THÉNON, SUSANA (Argentina; 1937-90)

Susana Thénon was born May 7, 1937 in Buenos Aires, Argentina and passed away in 1990 in the same city. She completed her studies at the National University of Buenos Aires, where she received her degree in Literature with an emphasis in Classical languages. She was employed as a professor in areas related to her specialty and was a researcher under the auspices of the Consejo de Investigaciones Científicas y Técnicas de la Argentina (Council of Scientific and Technical Investigations of Argentina). She co-directed two literary journals which where fundamental to the poetic development of her generation: *Airón* (Heron; 1-, 1957-), and *Agua viva* (Living Waters; 1-, 1960). Her poetry was fragmentarily published in these and other Argentine journals such as *Bibliograma* (Bibliogram), *Empresa poética* (Poetic Enterprise), *Encuentro* (Encounter), and *Sur* (South). Five books appeared between 1958 and 1987 which comprise her poetic production; numerous poems, both published and unpublished, were likewise included on a regular basis in the best anthologies of the 1960s and in literary journals in Holland, France, Italy, and England. Beginning in 1970 she also dedicated herself to photography, participating in numerous exhibitions and obtaining various honorable mentions in Argentina and abroad.

Susana Thénon's work is unified by her interest in exploring language as a central resource for poetry. Her texts—published at a time when newer Argentine poetry emphasized colloquial language, conversational diction, and an ideological tone of social commitment—proposed an alternative that added variety to the intense, although at times too uniform, poetic production of the decade. Thénon used poems, and the pages of *Airón* and *Agua viva* to promote a voice whose roots were to be found as much in the Argentine and European vanguardism of the 1920s (Oliverio Girondo [1891-1967], Macedonio Fernández [1874-1952], André Breton [1896-1966]), as in classical Greco-Roman, Spanish, medieval, and Renaissance traditions, both popular and high culture. Many of her technical resources (parallelisms, alliteration, and anaphora on a syntactic level, chaotic enumeration, the use of envoi and other formulas of closure) owe much to that rich inheritance and its subsequent elaboration in the development of Spanish-language literature; likewise, the iconic use of symbols in emblematic style (the rose, the bridge, the open field), or the presence of a deliberately exogenous/exotic lexicon (litters, rudderless ship bows, mistletoe, ravens, funeral urns, birch trees).

Thénon's personal trademark was from the outset the practice of a humorous bent of parody and mocking expertly exercised on the phonetic, morphologic, syntactic, and semantic levels of the text. This style, linked in her poetry to surrealist sources as well as medieval goliardery, little by little came to define the intrinsic originality of her poetry: sentimentality or poignancy controlled by linguistic surprise, plays on words, the deconstruction of meaning. *Ova completa* (Complete Ova; 1987—the title conveys multiple plays on words, its figurative meaning within Argentine culture means "fed up," more irreverently "busted balls") is her last work, and in this sense a true *summa*. These texts bring together parodic mixtures of styles and languages: pluri-compound sequences, symmetries, and chaotic oppositions typical of the Baroque; parallelisms extracted from the medieval ballad (or its Lorquian reelaboration); the inclusion of classical and pig Latin; Peninsular and American Spanish, English, and Spanish; refined, popular, and slang Spanish. In this conglomeration of uses, imitations, quotations, deformations, and parodies become intertwined. A systematic deconstruction of master symbols is practiced while at the same time some of them are elevated to a position central to diction: death as a cryptic sign; truth as a circular lie; poetry (language) as confusion and subversive dispersion. Thénon's poetry is thus gradually constructed as a proposal of language inserted into the Baroque tradition, in line that stretches from the Spaniard Francisco de Quevedo (1580-1645) to Chilean Nicanor Parra (1914), or Argentines like Nicolás Olivari (1900-66), Raúl González Tuñón (1905-74), and Oliverio Girondo. The poet corrects emotion with delirium and free will made operant through language. The following explanatory note to the poem that gives the book its title, a text about the impunity of the corrupt, is quite telling: "OVA: sustantivo plural neutro latino. Literalmente: huevos. COMPLETA: participio pasivo plural neutro latino en concordancia con huevos. Literalmente: colmados. Variantes posibles: rellenos, repletos, rebosantes, henchidos" (OVA: neutral Latin plural noun. Literally: eggs/balls, testicles. COMPLETE: neutral Latin plural passive participle in agreement with eggs. Literally: filled to the brim. Possible variants: stuffed, replete, overflowing, swollen [32] = fed up, busted balls). *Ova completa* is thus a volume of "complete works" whose ultimate meaning refers to the impossiblity of enduring/bearing boundaries drawn, while laughing in a democratic, ferocious, and uproarious guffaw.

PRIMARY BIBLIOGRAPHY

"Al atardecer, las muchachas." In *Suma de poesía argentina 1538-1968. Crítica y antología*. 2 vols. Comp. Guillermo Ara. Buenos Aires: Guadalupe, 1970. II.243.

De lugares extraños. Buenos Aires: Carmina, 1967.

Distancias. Buenos Aires: Torres Agüero, 1984.

distancias / distances. Translated with an introduction and afterword by Renata Treitel. Epilogue by Ana María Barrenechea. Los Angeles: Sun & Moon Press, 1994.

Edad sin tregua. Buenos Aires: Cooperativa y Distribuidora Argentina, 1958.

"Fundación," "Zombie," "Juego," "Círculo," "Mundo." In *Selección poética femenina 1940-1960*. Comp. Marta Giménez Pastor and José Daniel Viacaba. Buenos Aires: Ediciones Culturales Argentinas, 1965. 261-65.

Habitante de la nada. Buenos Aires: Thiriel, 1959.

Ova completa. Buenos Aires: Sudamericana, 1987.

"Para el que amó," "Porque la memoria...," "Fuera del hecho natural," "Dame libertad...," "Algún instante vuelve..." In *Los nuevos*. Comp. Josefina Delgado and Luis Gregorich. Buenos Aires: Centro Editor de América Latina, 1968. 141-42.

"Poema." In *El 60*. Comp. Alfredo Andrés. Buenos Aires: Editorial Dos, 1969. 139.

SECONDARY BIBLIOGRAPHY

Andrés, Alfredo. *El 60*. Buenos Aires: Editorial Dos, 1969. 232.

Barrenechea, Ana María. "Disyunción, conjunción, constelación de voces en *Distancias* de Susana Thénon." *Kanina: revista de artes y letras de la Universidad de Costa Rica* 9.2 (1985): 57-59.

—. "El español de América en la literatura del siglo XX a la luz de Bajtin." *Lexis: revista de lingüística y literatura* (Lima, Peru) 10.2 (1986): 147-67.

—. "El texto poético como parodia del discurso crítico: los últimos poemas de Susana Thénon." *Dispositio* 12.30-32 (1987): 255-72.

Cambours Ocampo, Antonio. *El problema de las generaciones literarias*. Buenos Aires: Peña Lillo, 1963. 135, 150, 151, 209.

McGuirk, Bernard. "Back to the Suture: Patriarchal Discourse and Susana Thénon's *Ova completa*." In *Carnal Knowledge: Essays on the Flesh, Sex, and Sexuality in Hispanic Letters and Film*. Ed. Pamela Bacarisse. Pittsburgh: Ediciones Tres Ríos, 1991. 163-81.

Reisz de Rivarola, Susana. "Poesía y polifonía: de la 'voz poética' a las 'voces' del discurso poético en *Ova completa* de Susana Thénon." *Filología*, 23.1 (1988): 177-94.

Treitel, Renata. "Translating Susana Thénon." *Translation Review* 17 (1985): 25-26.

Weinstein, Ana E., and Miryam E. Gover de Nasatsky, comps. *Escritores judeoargentinos. Bibliografía 1900-1987*. 2 vols. Buenos Aires: Milá, 1994. II.266-68.

Andrés Avellaneda

TIEMPO, CÉSAR (Pseud. of Israel Zeitlin; Argentina; 1906-80)

Israel Zeitlin, better known as César Tiempo, expressed through his writings and his life the conflictive nature of the Jewish experience in Argentina. He became a well known figure in the literary circles of Buenos Aires due not only to his numerous contributions to the newspapers and journals of the time, but also to the controversial content of his work, in which he advocates the idea of an Argentina without religious or racial barriers. His extensive writings are not, however, limited to providing a panoramic view of intellectual life in Argentina. He transcends the boundaries of time and space in order to interview and write about famous politicians and artists, present and past, from all over the world.

Born in Ekaterinoslav, Ukraine, on 3 March, 1906 he emigrated with his family to Buenos Aires nine months later. His life spanned a politically chaotic period, characterized by profound anti-Semitism and xenophobia which started with the fall of President Yrigoyen in 1930 and continued through the following military regimes and the Peronist era. Tiempo endeavored to bring about an idyllic and peaceful coexistence among Jews and Christians, an attempt that often backfired, since he was accused of trying to bridge a gap which some felt should not and could not be bridged. The fact that he felt it was necessary to change his name reveals a great deal about the nature of the controversy. The intrinsic ambivalence of his feelings is reflected in his work, where he expresses both his love for his adopted land and for the culture of his forefathers. Tiempo was not, however, the only Argentinean writer to dream of a harmonious state between the races and to view reality with an apologetic eye. Many writers of the so-called Generation of 1922, who witnessed events such as the pogrom of the Semana Trágica (Tragic Week) of January 1919 in Buenos Aires, were still able to deflect the fault away from the people of Argentina and blame the military regimes instead, as Tiempo did in his pamphlet titled *La campaña antisemita* (The Anti-Semitic Campaign; 1935).

In the literary world of the time, Tiempo identified himself with the writers of Boedo Street, a left-wing revolutionary group. The opposition was represented by the writers of Florida Street, which formed the Vanguard movement, an elitist group that unfortunately became identified with fascist and chauvinistic elements. Although Tiempo himself felt that the division was rather artificial, it served to stir up some invigorating literary sparring among the members. The publication of Tiempo's first collection of poems, *Versos de una. . .* (Poems of a. . . ; 1926), constituted one of the most accomplished deceptions of the time. The poems were submitted anonymously and were purported to be the work of a Jewish prostitute named Clara Beter. To add to the confusion, they were published with an introduction by Elías Castelnuovo, the editor of the Claridad publishing house, under the pseudonym of Ronald Chaves. The publication delighted the writers of Boedo who immediately saw in the touching words of the prostitute the tragedy of the lower class exploited by society. In 1977, Estelle Irizarry published the poems with a critical study which included a commentary written by Clara Beter's supposed daughter. In it she established the links between the writer and the imaginary figure, who in fact exhibited much of the biographical and ideological characteristics of its creator. The poems were more than a prank. In them Tiempo had sown the seed of themes which he would elaborate throughout his poetry and drama: the alienation of the immigrant and other oppressed groups, the suffering of the poor and social responsibility, and the integration of Jews and Christians into a melting pot. To express this ideal he made extensive use of religious symbolism taken from both faiths. Thus we hear echoes from both the Old and the New Testament, the resurrection and the cross together with the Song of Songs and the Sabbath, the latter having particular importance throughout as a symbol of peace and harmony for all men.

In *Versos de una. . .* Tiempo establishes biblical links between the poetry of Clara Beter and the Song of Songs while also comparing her to Mary Magdalene. This work served to highlight a social problem prevalent at the time, the trade of women brought over from Eastern Europe under false pretenses to become prostitutes in the New World. Clara Beter, the protagonist of Tiempo's poems, expressed the despair of these women's lives, the indifference and scorn of a society that in itself could have been considered guilty of other forms of prostitution. Like Mary Magdalene she redeems herself through her suffering and undergoes a sort of spiritual resurrection and from her bitterness a message of messianic hope for the future brotherhood of men rises brightly.

Nowhere is this wish for unity and harmony more apparent than in Tiempo's well known series of poems dedicated to the Sabbath. The first collection was published in 1930 under the title *Libro para la pausa del Sábado* (A Book for the Sabbath Pause), which won the First Municipal Prize for Poetry. This was followed by *Sabatión argentino* (Argentinean Sabation) in 1933 and *Sabadomingo* (Saturdaysunday) in 1938. The latter reflects clearly Tiempo's philosophy, as observed in the oxymoron he created by the fusion of the names of the two sacred days. The actual printing of the title offers a clever visual interpretation of the idea, since from the last two letters of *sábado*, written horizontally, hangs suspended vertically the word *domingo*. Tiempo seemed to enjoy this type of visual message, since he uses it again at the end of the text by writing the name of the editorial and the year of publication, Hebrew year 5699, in the shape of a menorah.

His poems describe scenes of Jewish life in Argentina, the historic suffering of the Jewish race and the hope imbedded in the creation of a Jewish state. The Sabbath acts as a social equalizer in that it embodies joy and peace for both rich and poor, and Tiempo transforms it into a universal symbol for Argentineans of both creeds. He personifies the sacred day as it appears in Jewish prayers, describing it as a queen or a bride of great beauty who ushers in a day of rest. Tiempo forges the Sabbath into a link for Argentineans of all races, much as the Lacroze—the street car which figures in his poems—serves to link the Jewish ghetto with the rest of the city or as a river such as the legendary Sabation, whose current changes direction on the Sabbath. His poems describe the betrothal of the Jewish bride, the Sabbath, to the Christian Sunday, in a union which carries a messianic message. The Sabbath remains the feminine element in his poetry, the moon, the biblical mistress from the Song of Songs, while Sunday is the virile and carefree Argentinean lover, the sun, who woos her and earns her love.

His poems are not, however, lyrics without a social conscience. He repeatedly chastises the society he lives in, and he addresses himself to both the Christian and the Jewish population, making use at times of well-known and repugnant Jewish stereotypes. The latter brought on critical comments from his countrymen who felt that there was no need to fuel the already prevalent misconceptions about the Jewish race. What must be kept in mind is that the butt of his criticism is the bourgeoisie and religious hypocrisy, neither of which he endured very well, be it Jewish or Catholic. He expressed a great disdain for the upper classes, the wealthy Jew, the materialism and indifference of the lawyers and the doctors, the zeal in arranging marriages for money, the prayers offered for the wrong reasons in ornate temples while the poor wait for food at the People's Kitchen. In a poem that he composed in honor of Hayyim Bialik (1873-1934), he expressed bitterness about the indifference with which the Jewish community received the news of the death of the famous Hebrew poet, an event barely mentioned in the Jewish press, otherwise concerned with social events and other such frivolous issues. Concerning his mocking of some of the physical characteristics of Jews, it must be noted that the same ones, such as the crooked nose, are at other times described with a sense of pride, as when he writes about his father. Here the well known Jewish nose becomes a symbol of an ancestry to which he is honored to belong. Certainly he gives credit to innumerable members of the Jewish race in his other writings, dedicating short and long essays to famous

Jewish writers, entertainers, musicians, and a whole collection to the very well known Jewish writer Sholem Aleichem (1859-1916).

Tiempo's concern with the underprivileged and the exploited is evident in his dramatic work as well. He entered the world of the theater in 1933 with the production of *El teatro soy yo* (I Am the Theater), written as a farce in the popular Pirandelian style of the day, a play within a play. Here the author presents two characters who have been alienated from society, a Jewish woman and a black man, both playwrights and both victims of discrimination either by virtue of their sex, their race or religion, and even their profession. In the midst of competitive jealousy they turn against each other revealing a deep seated antagonism with racial overtones which they strive to overcome with tragic consequences. The play was not as well received as it deserved to be, perhaps because the Argentinean public was not ready to admit that there actually existed any discrimination in their land, and although Tiempo criticized directly only events that took place outside of the country, it was perhaps perceived to be too close for comfort. His Jewish critics again found the unfortunate descriptions of Jewish stereotypes, aggravated by less than flattering references to blacks as well. However, the nature of the remarks is so blatantly obvious that it seems valid to assume that the express purpose of the author is in fact to highlight the prejudice that engenders this type of characterization and that the purpose of the play is in reality to invalidate such prejudice.

In Tiempo's work the frontiers between theater and life, as well as art and reality are permeable and fluid. His characters are endowed with a will of their own as they appear and reappear throughout his work, free to leap even from one genre to the other. Thus we see Clara Beter reappearing to introduce a play titled *Alfarda* (*The Tithe*; 1935) and later on as the main protagonist in the play *Quiero vivir* (I Want To Live; 1941), where she surfaces to act out the rest of her life. In the same manner we find that a play written by an imaginary author in *El teatro soy yo* serves as the underlying theme for another play by Tiempo entitled *Pan criollo* (Creole Bread). Written in 1937, it was itself an elaboration of the earlier and shorter *Alfarda*, which did not achieve the same degree of success. *Pan criollo* went on to win the National Prize for Drama and was made into a musical. Both plays deal with the sensitive subject of intermarriage, a topic which was sure to awaken strong emotions in a Jewish audience. In *Alfarda* we meet once more the greedy, wealthy and distrustful Jew in the figure of a father who loses his daughter and declares her dead rather than accepting a non-Jewish son-in-law. The play ends with the old man mourning his loss, which is the *alfarda*, or price he has to pay for his intransigence. The second version of the play *Pan criollo* featured a much more acceptable ending, at least for the gentile audience. Also transformed was the previously unappealing father who becomes a wise and noble Jewish judge performing his duty in an Argentinean court in an efficient manner by judiciously applying his knowledge of both the Bible and the customs of the townspeople with whom he lives in great harmony. The initial negative reaction to his daughter's relationship with a gentile gives way eventually to a quiet acceptance of the facts, thus bringing peace to himself and to his family. This takes place in the country, where he has retired to find comfort by working close to the earth and in the company of farmers who lack the deceit and meanness of spirit characteristic of sophisticated city people. Whether the ending reflects a total capitulation is debatable. There is in the resigned attitude of the protagonist a note of defeat which overshadows the joyful and harmonious ending. There is also the fact that the character's name, Lefanejo, forms the words included in one of the Jewish prayers for Yom Kippur, asking for forgiveness of one's sins. It seems that Tiempo did not advocate assimilation unconditionally, but more as an *alfarda*, or payment in exchange for a peaceful coexistence either between members of a family or among his countrymen.

Pan criollo represents the mixture of elements that enter into the formation of the Argentinean people, and it is in fact the theatrical version of his poetry as reflected in the title *Sabadomingo*. The symbolism associated with the bread in this play is borrowed from the New and the Old Testament. It is the source of Christian charity, the origin and sustenance of life, man's basic food, and an essential part of the celebration of the Sabbath, an offering of peace. Thus, the bread represents not only the ideal racial mixture but also helps to highlight the ever present concern Tiempo felt for the hungry and poor masses regardless of religion.

This play describes in detail typical scenes of life in the streets of Lavalle, Junín and Corrientes and contains humorous skits presenting characters and situations which were sure to amuse audiences of both creeds. Tiempo borrows Talmudic quotations and words of wisdom from the New Testament, sprinkling "creolisms" and Yiddish phrases all around, proving that he had a good understanding of and felt truly at home with both cultures. Jewish audiences found it hard to accept not only the assimilative message, but also the actual physical appearance of God, which takes place in the play. The latter, however, must be interpreted as a hallucination born from the inflamed imagination of the overwrought father and not as a true attempt at rendering an image of God, which would indeed violate Jewish dogma. Nevertheless, the reactions from the audiences were predictable. The play proved to the Jewish critics that Tiempo wrote mostly for a gentile audience, nationalists embraced it and the fascist elements that controlled the Commission of National Culture did not find it inconsistent to award the National Prize to Tiempo, a Jewish writer. The fact that there were actually two versions of the play, and the subtitle which Tiempo himself provided, "Comedia gravemente cómica o lo que a Ud. le parezca" (A gravely funny comedy or whatever), serve to illustrate the author's true ambivalence.

The reach of Tiempo's message was universal. He left innumerable journalistic articles, collections of interviews, some real and some imagined, short biographies, reports, essays and movie scripts, even trying his hand at acting. He blended fiction and reality with impressive poetic license in plays and novels dedicated to Carlos Gardel, Berta Singerman, Sarah Bernhardt, Parravicini, Paganini and other famous artists. His invaluable legacy is a detailed document of the society of the time, its vibrant artistic life, the stimulating intellectual atmosphere, and especially the portrait of a people, some of universal fame, others an unknown part of the history of a country who owe their small measure of immortality to this author's writings.

Tiempo's work reflects a witty, gently critical human being whose desire for a peaceful coexistence was so intense that he was willing to offer his own personal *alfarda* in payment. He attempted to reconcile nationalistic fervor with love for his Jewish heritage, a courageous task at a time in history when nothing short of undivided allegiance would suffice.

PRIMARY BIBLIOGRAPHY
Creative Writing

Alfarda, drama. Buenos Aires: Columna, 1935. English version as *The Tithe*. Trans. Nora Glickman and Gloria F. Waldman. In *Argentine Jewish Theatre: A Critical Anthology*. Ed. Nora Glickman and Gloria F. Waldman. Lewisburg: Bucknell UP, 1996. 82-105.

Así quería Gardel, novela. Buenos Aires: Bell, 1955.

El becerro de oro. Buenos Aires: Paidós, 1973

Los camellos. Unpublished.

El canto del cisne. Unpublished.

El caudillo. With Ulyses Petit de Murat. Unpublished.

La dama de las comedias. With Arturo Cerretani. Buenos Aires: Argentores/Carro de Tespis, 1971.

Libro para la pausa del sábado. Buenos Aires: Manuel Gleizer, 1930.

El lustrador de manzanas. Buenos Aires: Ediciones Dintel/Argentores/Carro de Tespis, 1958.

La macacha. Musical in collaboration with U. Petit de Murat. Unpublished.

Mi tío Scholem Aleijem y otros parientes. Buenos Aires: Ediciones Corregidor, 1978.

Moravia, Vivian Wilde y Compañía: retratos intempestivos. Buenos Aires: Argos, 1953.

Orozco te desconozco. Unpublished.

Pan criollo: comedia gravemente cómica o lo que a Vd. le parezca, en cuatro estampas y dos desenlaces. Buenos Aires: Porter, 1938. Reissued, Buenos Aires: Ediciones Dintel, Argentores, Carro de Tespis, 1968.

Poesías completas. Buenos Aires: Stilman Editores, 1979.

Quiero vivir: drama increíble en tiempo de fuga, un prólogo, cuatro actos y un epílogo superpuesto. Buenos Aires: Porter, 1941.

Sabadomingo. Buenos Aires: Porter, 1938. Reissued, Buenos Aires: Centro Editor de América Latina, 1966.

Sábado pleno: Libro para la pausa del sábado. Sabatión argentino. Sábadomingo. Nuevas devociones. Buenos Aires: Manuel Gleizer, 1955.

Sabatión argentino: antiguas y nuevas dones para la pausa del sábado. Buenos Aires/Montevideo: Sociedad Amigos del Libro Rioplatense, 1933.

El teatro soy yo. Buenos Aires: Anaconda, 1933.

El último romance de Gardel, novela. Buenos Aires: Quetzal, 1975.

Versos de una . . . [published under the name Clara Béter]. Buenos Aires: Claridad, 1926. Reissued with commentary and notes by Estelle Irizarry. Buenos Aires: Rescate, 1977.

Yrigoyen. With Ulises Petit de Murat, 1973. Unpublished.

Nonfiction

André Spire. Buenos Aires: Congreso Judío Latinoamericano, 1968.

La campaña antisemita y el director de la Biblioteca Nacional. Buenos Aires: Mundo Israelita, 1935.

Capturas recomendadas. Buenos Aires: Librería del Jurista, 1978.

Cartas inéditas y evocación de Quiroga. Montevideo: Biblioteca Nacional, 1970.

Clara Beter y otras fatamorganas. Buenos Aires: A. Peña Lillo, 1974.

Evocación de Quiroga. Montevideo: Biblioteca Nacional, 1970.

Exposición de la actual poesía argentina (1922-1927). Ed. with Pedro-Juan Vignale. Buenos Aires: Minerva, 1922-1927 (In collaboration with P.J.Vignale)

Florencio Parravicini. Buenos Aires: Centro Editorial de América Latina, 1971.

Manos de obra. Buenos Aires: Corregidor, 1980.

Máscaras y caras. Dialogues. Buenos Aires: Arrayán, 1943

Protagonistas. Buenos Aires: Guillermo Kraft, 1954.

Sábado y poesía. Rosario, Argentina: Escuela Normal de Rosario, 1935.
La vida romántica y Pintoresca de Berta Singerman. Buenos Aires: Sopena, 1941.
Yo hablé con Toscanini. Buenos Aires: Anaconda, 1941.

SECONDARY BIBLIOGRAPHY

Barrera, Trinidad. "Testimonio de la vanguardia: la *Exposición de la actual poesía argentina (1922-1927)*." *Río de la Plata: Culturas* 4-6 (1987): 133-39.

Blasi, Alberto. "Vanguardismo en el Río de la Plata: un diario y una exposición." *Revista iberoamericana* 48.118-119 (1982): 21-36.

Del Saz, Agustín. "La tragedia de los prejuicios raciales: *El teatro soy yo* de César Tiempo." In his *Teatro social hispanoamericano. Farsa y Grotesco Criollo.* Barcelona: Labor, 1967. 94-98.

Dym, Sabina. "Religión y sociedad en las obras de César Tiempo." Ph.D. diss., Georgetown University, 1991.

Fingueret, Manuela. "César Tiempo, el poeta de la judería porteña." In *El imaginario judío en la literatura de América Latina: visión y realidad.* Ed. Patricia Finzi, Eliahu Toker, and Marcos Faerman. Buenos Aires: Shalom, 1992. 151-54.

Foster, David William. "Argentine Jewish Dramatists: Aspects of a National Consciousness." *Folio* 17 (1987): 74-103.

—. "César Tiempo y el teatro argentino-judío." In *El Cono Sur: dinámica y dimensiones de su literatura. A Symposium.* Ed. Rose S. Minc. Upper Montclair, NJ: Montclair State College, 1985. 43-48. Also as "César Tiempo and Jewish-Argentine Theater." In his *The Argentine Teatro Independiente, 1930-1955.* York, SC: Spanish Literature Publishing Company, 1986. 110-16.

Hiriart, Rosario. "Un estudio sobre las bromas literarias." *Insula* 37.432 (1982): 12.

Irizarry, Estelle. "El argentino César Tiempo y sus *Versos de una . . . .*" In *Versos de una . . .* Buenos Aires: Rescate, 1977. 47-86.

—. *La broma literaria en nuestros días.* New York: Eliseo Torres, 1979.

Karduner, Luis. "Carta abierta a César Tiempo." *Judaica* (Buenos Aires) 4.45 (1937): 99-104.

Lindstrom, Naomi. "César Tiempo: Worldly Lyricization of the Urban Jewish Experience." In her *Jewish Issues in Argentine Literature. From Gerchunoff to Szichman.* Columbia: U of Missouri P, 1989. 61-78.

—. "Proletarian/Avant-Garde Proletarian/Jewish/Christian Balances in Two Poems by Cesar Tiempo." *Hispanic Journal* 4.2 (1983): 85-98.

—. "*Sabatión argentino*: Poetry of Jewish Cultural Possibilities." *Revista de estudios hispánicos* 20.3 (1987): 81-95.

Méndez Calzada, Enrique. Preface to *Sabatión argentino*. Buenos Aires/Montevideo: Sociedad Amigos del Libro Rioplatense, 1939. 23-31.

Nesbit, Louis. "The Jewish Contribution to Argentine Literature." *Hispania* 33.4 (1950): 313-20.

Orgambide, Pedro. "César Tiempo." In *Enciclopedia de la literatura argentina*. Ed. Pedro Orgambide and Roberto Yahni. Buenos Aires: Sudamericana, 1970. 595-96.

Pinto, Juan. *Pasión y suma de la expresión argentina: literatura, cultura, región*. Buenos Aires: Huemul, 1971. 121-24, 135-36, 202-4.

Sadow, Stephen. "Judíos y Gauchos: The Search for Identity in Argentine-Jewish Literature." *American Jewish Archives* 34.2 (1982): 167-77.

Senkman, Leonardo. "César Tiempo: la integración judeo-argentina." In his *La identidad judía en la literatura argentina*. Buenos Aires: Pardés, 1983. 153-95.

Walsh, Donald D. "La misión poética de César Tiempo." *Revista iberoamericana* 10 (1945): 99-106.

Wapnir, Salomón. "Los protagonistas de César Tiempo." In his *Imágenes y letras*. Buenos Aires: Insituto Amigos del Libro Argentino, 1955. 101-8.

Weinstein, Ana E., and Miryam E. Gover de Nasatsky, comps. *Escritores judeo-argentinos: bibliografía 1900-1987*. 2 vols. Buenos Aires: Milá, 1994. 2:269-91.

Winter, Calvert. "Some Jewish Writers of the Argentine." *Hispania* 19.4 (1936): 431-436.

Sabina Dym

TIMERMAN, JACOBO (Argentina; 1923)

Jacobo Timerman was born in the Ukraine in 1923 and emigrated with his family to Argentina in 1928. Although he was a most successful journalist for years, Jacobo Timerman rose to international prominence with the publication of *Prisoner Without a Name, Cell Without a Number* (1981), his account of illegal imprisonment carried out by Argentine military officers during the so-called Dirty War of the late 1970s. At that time, Timerman was editor of the liberal newspaper *La Opinión* (Opinion) during the years of social and political tumult which characterizedthe second presidency of Juan Domingo Perón (1973-74) and the regimes of Perón's civilian and military successors. Timerman and his fellow journalists on the paper and even *La Opinión* itself were subject to intimidation and attacks during this period in which the respect for human rights sank to its nadir when the government confiscated the paper and Timerman was imprisoned in 1977.

Suspended above the turgid atmosphere of authoritarianism and violence which permeates this tale as well as the subjects of his other books, *The Longest War: Israel in Lebanon* (1982), *Chile, Death in the South* (1987), and *Cuba: A Journey* (1992), hover inexplicable mysteries. One of the most baffling of these concerns is the lack of communication in contemporary political life. In each of these four published reports, Timerman asks why governments have sought to control their citizens' access to the truth, both in their deceptive pronouncements of policies and goals as well as their distrust of a free press as the most appropriate avenue for citizens to exercise their right to know. Timerman also struggles to understand how the kind of authoritarianism he has observed in Hispanic military regimes is heir to European fascism in ideology, strategy, and tactics.

There is no self-evident or obvious answer to these gnawing concerns in Timerman's books. Rather, the presentation of these inexplicable mysteries is designed to disquiet the reader who must strive to study the seeming universality of inhumanity as portrayed in Timerman's narratives. Although each of his books has a national focus, Timerman's narrative voice functions as humanity's conscience in a universalized campaign against silence and deception waged over four crucial fronts: Argentina, Israel, Chile, and Cuba. His mission, although he never proclaims his motive for publishing these memoirs as such, is to serve as a conscience of the body politic, defender of the faith of true democracy in order to bring the truth to light and give voice to the deceived and downtrodden.

Timerman's work captures social strife and dissent on various fronts. As an observer and a victim of injustices such as torture, war, and political repression, Timerman sounds his voice against violence in four critical moments of contemporary history: the oppression of Argentina's military of the 1970s, Israel's protracted occupation of Lebanon during 1982, Chile's uncharacteristic involvement with military rule and the establishment of a state of constant fear during the mid 1980s, and the mythification of Fidel Castro as the salvation of a Cuban nation on the brink of extinction.

For all of the attention to autobiographical detail, Timerman's narratives are strikingly modern in their pacing and structure. While his departure from strict chronology is atypical of traditional autobiographies, the disjointed treatment of time in *Prisoner Without a Name, Cell Without a Number* is wholly appropriate to the subject matter. For six months, Timerman was held incommunicado in clandestine prisons in and around Buenos Aires. When he mixes recollections of this period with historical reportage and general considerations of the continuation of the Holocaust in modern-day Argentina, he conveys the sense of his individual plight as well as the feeling of being caught in a web of intolerance which characterize this period. The fluctuations or oscillations between the personal, national, and international themes, then, provide an overview of Timerman's state of mind and of his relationship with time itself during the traumatic events of his incarceration. Most appropriate as well is the sense of being lost in time, without touchstones to the causes and effects of his imprisonment.

In its organization of time, *Prisoner Without a Name, Cell Without a Number*, captures the narrator's sense of alienation as he is beset by unknown tormentors. The voice of the narrator fluctuates between in medias res passages which vividly describe his imprisonment, and discursive critiques of Argentina under military rule. As is also evident from its title, the book captures the anonymity of Timerman, the namelessness of others who have disappeared, as well as that of his captors and interrogators. As such, these memoirs serve as a tribute to all nameless victims of isolation and torture. In keeping with the anonymity and euphemistic distortion of language during the Holocaust, while the captives have been deprived of their personal identities through language, they live in a world of rich euphemistic creativity. Torture sessions are linguistically transformed into "conversations with Susana," and his interrogators are called "doctors on duty" who routinely appear in disguise in order to disorient their "patients."

Clearly, the touchstone of Timerman's work is the Jewish tradition and its uprootedness brought about by centuries of wandering in the diaspora. *Prisoner Without a Name* sketches a family history which begins in the Ukraine, in the town of Bar. This place is a suitable genesis for his family, in view of its longstanding suffering through pogroms and invasions by Cossacks and then Nazis. As Timerman states, "It was, most likely, an enlightened, combative community" (vii). In the Foreword, he sets the principal theme of the book, that is the ideological link between the assault upon human rights in modern-day Argentina with special reference to anti-Semitism and the long tradition of anti-Semitism in Europe and the convulsion of injustices which erupted during the Holocaust. Even though we know that Timerman's travails in Argentina are brought to an end with his exile in Israel at the end of the book, the final chapter of *Prisoner*

Without a Name has a tension typically reserved for detective stories or novels of espionage and intrigue. Here is the last-minute diplomatic wrangling over Timerman's future, the race to the airport and escape from the counterforce of army officers intent on kidnapping Timerman yet again.

On numerous occasions in this memoir, Timerman attempts to drive home his principal thesis: that the widespread anti-Semitism of these years has ideological roots in Nazi Germany. In support of this thesis, it must be noted that anti-Semitism re-emerged in Argentine society with renewed vigor in the mid 1970s, and was nurtured by a resurgence of interest in Nazi and fascist literature including works by Mussolini, Goebbels, and Hitler. Over 1500 Jews were among thousands of Argentines who were abducted during the "dirty war," and Timerman, as other Argentine Jews, was subjected to additional suffering and torture due to his ethnicity. Trumped-up charges of "subversion" and vague accusations of participation in "Zionist conspiracies" were used as rationalizations for his unjust treatment in the military's misguided attempt to save Argentina from what it perceived as the dangers of Communism.

This updated Holocaust story begins in medias res, written from within the cellblock and the spare surroundings of his individual cubicle. This place represents the spiritual point of departure to oblivion, a mental space from which he can never fully escape. Timerman provides vivid details about the conditions of his confinement. Dark and damp, lacking toilet facilities, ventilation, and the opportunity for human contact to soften his anonymity, the cells where he is detained set the stage for the horrors he experiences. Poorly fed, unable to communicate with either his captors, jailers, or fellow prisoners, Timerman endows the most insignificant moments and events with transcendental importance: a mere glance from another prisoner across a vacant corridor, the opportunity to trace a few steps across his miniscule cell, trivial verbal exchanges at mealtime with whoever delivers his food, and rolling up his mattress to fight the dampness during sleep.

As a journalist who has been concerned with the longstanding popularity of authoritarian regimes in Argentina, Timerman summarizes the rise of organized violence on the part of the Argentine government in the twentieth century. Modern-day violence stems from the Argentines' flawed understanding of and distrustful response to turn-of-the-century immigration, according to Timerman. Suspicion over the materialistic motives of the new Argentines and the immigrants' perceived threat to traditional values are at the root of the country's inability to embrace diversity and its penchant to seek violence as a solution.

In a sense, twentieth-century violence is also a natural outgrowth of the cultural dichotomy known as "Civilization and Barbarism" according to Timerman. This expression was coined in the last century by author and statesman Domingo Faustino Sarmiento (1811-88) as a broadly descriptive metaphor of the geographic and social divisions and cultural rifts in Argentine society. Torn by the inevitable conflicts between the educated and progressive populace in the nation's capital city on the one hand and the more primitive dwellers of the vast and desolate pampas on the other, Argentina continues to reflect a disparate and fundamentally divided culture, whose response to political and cultural change is the rule of terror.

If the traumatic events of the past provide a painful background to *Prisoner Without a Name*, the sufferings of the Jews in ancient and modern times are touchstones of *The Longest War: Israel in Lebanon* (1982). Timerman's Jewish identity is a cultural substratum which underlies his compassion and anguish for the human destruction around him in the Middle East. The setting for Timerman's second book is Israel, where he was deported at the end of *Prisoner Without a Name*. Unlike the sub-rosa detainment and trial without a jury, violence erupts in overt military conflict while public opinion and diplomatic debates from around the world accompany each aspect of the campaign. The source of international discord emanates from the fact that Israeli General Ariel Sharon's "first war launched by the state of Israel" (11) is no swiftly waged seven-day skirmish. The war lingers on for weeks and becomes Israel's "longest war" to the protest and uproar of sabras and foreigners alike.

In a sense, these two works, though vastly different in their settings and basic themes, are directly linked by Timerman's affinity to the victims of violence. While tracing the path of destruction, Timerman considers the anonymity of those caught in its path, and for a moment he senses a kinship with the nameless dead and wounded, and their families who attempt to locate them. He imagines their hopelessness and anguish, and recalls verses of Chilean Nobel laureate Pablo Neruda's (1904-73) *Las alturas de Machu Picchu* (*The Heights of Machu Picchu*; 1950) in which the poet strolls through the ancient indigenous fortress, now abandoned, seeking signs of the disappeared, "Man, where is he?"

Another connection between Timerman's narratives can be seen in the climate of political unrest in the two countries. Support for the war is not unanimous in Israel, which Timerman hastens to show. He compares the clash between opposing forces within the country to Argentina under Perón, where the most militant citizens were among the nation's poorest and least educated. So it is in Israel where the Ashkenazis, descendants of European Jews, favor withdrawal from Lebanon and creation of a Palestinian state on the West Bank whereas Sephardic Jews from Asia Minor and Africa crow for the fight to wage on. As the war becomes more protracted, public criticism of Israel's involvement in

Lebanon increases and receives added impetus from adverse reactions to reports from troops returning from the front, some of whom feel deceived by an apparent shift in the government's stated mission in Lebanon.

According to Timerman, the lessons of the Holocaust emerge as a motive for this conflict which underscore some of the deception the people sense. The Holocaust is used as the rationale for all involvements of self-defense, real or imagined, and is even mirrored in examples of graveyard humor in this joke: "we have no more blood left in our veins because Begin has spilled it all in his speeches" (38).

As in his earlier book, Timerman is unrestrained in his condemnation of violence and also shows how Israelis can successfully reverse the results of its devastation. He writes vividly of both the abstract and concrete effects of violence, the anguish of continued civil unrest caused by the conflict as well as the sight and smells of decomposing flesh from the front lines. In this war diary, he takes issue with the opinion expressed by some Israelis that war at this time and in this place is inevitable. Instead he criticizes the somewhat self-fulfilling prophecy offered by excessively optimistic combatants who tout victory as though it were inevitable: "When an army is convinced of victory, its capacity for transmitting this conviction is overwhelming. Nothing can stop it" (7).

But the war being waged here is an ideological and emotional conflict, one in which many Israelis express their sense of guilt for destruction of their neighbor. Timerman records Israeli citizens' awe and shame over the army's destruction of civilian targets and the demolition of cities in air force bombings. In an attempt to atone for mass destruction visited upon Lebanon, Timerman shows how groups of youth on kibbutzim and other Israeli volunteers immediately set out to rebuild Lebanon once the conflict is over. This impulse to rebuild and restore is the hallmark of Jewish tradition, as reflected in Jorge Luis Borges's (1899-1986) poem "Israel" cited in the text:

> You will forget your father's tongue
> and learn the tongue of Paradise.
> You shall build a country on wasteland,
> making it rise out of deserts. (144)

Resonances of the Nazi subjugation of Europe reverberate in *Chile: Death in the South*. What makes this sequel to Argentina's experience with militarism so unusual is that, unlike the Argentine experience, Chile's authoritarianism has no historical precedent. For Timerman, a circumstance akin to Argentina's civilization and barbarism has spread to its more politically placid neighbor following the coup against President Salvador Allende in 1973 with understandably disastrous results. Furthermore, what brings back the sense of a Nazi presence is the atmosphere of Prussian rule. Chilean generals exercise their fantasies of empire with impunity, as their influence pervades all levels of Chilean life: schools, factories, publishing and journalism, local government and cultural life.

Timerman is careful to note that the professed goals of the military regime are artfully distorted linguistic paradoxes (in harmony with the welcome posted at Auschwitz, "Arbeit macht Frei"). In this update of Nazi linguistic subversion, Pinochet and the military perform their duty to protect and fortify democracy in order to preserve a "democracy that is worth living." Of course, in many other ways the Pinochet years recapitulate the sorry tale of the Holocaust. Although less routine than in Argentina where 20,000 disappeared from a population of 32 million, kidnapping and clandestine murder claim hundreds of civilians and keep Chile's population in a state of constant fear. Timerman describes the nightmarish displays of random violence to which Chile is subjected due to the arbitrary massacres, assassinations, and unprovoked killings by the military squads and vigilantes.

Remarkably, the intellectual atmosphere in Chile during the Pinochet years or, more aptly, the lack of intellectual activity, appears in sharp contrast with the cultural life of the ghetto during the period of Nazi dominance in Europe. Side by side with the inhumanity of Nazism, the rich cultural life in the ghettos permitted Jews to create an alternative intellectual life, which Timerman finds completely different from life in Chile where artists, writers, and performers are subject to a sense of national denial regarding the stultification of their lives under military rule. As in the case of the Germans during the Holocaust, many Chileans cannot acknowledge that they are pawns of the Pinochet regime.

Rather than an inconvenience to which Chileans must accommodate themselves, Timerman views the effect of the regime upon the nation's artistic and literary creativity as a cultural crisis which Chileans fear to admit. "Few intellectuals and artists live fully the profundity of the crisis, with all its madness and its anxiety" (16). Timerman resorts to military metaphors as he attempts to capture the magnitude of the crisis, referring to Chile's cultural life as a "cultural blackout" during Pinochet's regime. He notes the lessening of productivity, even an extinction of cultural activity, during the military dictatorship. Timerman exposes the intellectual paradox of Chile's living amidst the drama of current events without this drama finding its way into its literary creation.

Cuba: A Journey, Timerman's most recent book, renews his zeal to understand the daily lives of people living in crisis. It is evident that Cuba holds a different set of challenges than the Argentine, Israeli, and Chilean circumstances. Nonetheless, despite the luxury of not needing to cope with daily eruptions of overt violence as outlined in Timerman's earlier narratives, the ideological and economic forces which affect Cubans are reminiscent of the problems he has posed elsewhere. Because, as Timerman is careful to note, his visit in 1987 is not in any sense official, he has the freedom to travel throughout Cuba and to speak with ordinary people, unencumbered by an "official story" he or they must uphold.

To be fair, Timerman credits the Castro regime with ameliorating the lot of Cubans. Nonetheless, despite some successes of the Castro regime such as improvements in literacy, education, standard of living for the rural masses, and betterment of health care as outward signs of social progress, Timerman concludes that the lives of numerous *cubanos* are imperiled by some of the same problems he has exposed in other countries: the cult of personality surrounding the Chief of State; asphyxiating political atmosphere; human rights violations (e.g., the well-known cases of Heberto Padilla and Armando Valladares among others), infringement upon personal privacy and the freedom of expression through gathering of information by local reporting networks; and lack of religious freedom (in particular intolerance shown to Jehovah's Witnesses). The government's distrust of adverse criticism to its motives and policies has distorted language as a manifestation of its defensive posture, which recalls the use of propaganda, euphemism, and hyperbole in other authoritarian regimes he has decried.

Regarding religion and the climate surrounding Judaism, Cuba presents a situation rather unique in Timerman's narratives. To judge from this Cuban journey, no one persecutes Jews living in Cuba. Nor, unfortunately, is the uniqueness of Jewish culture a part of Cuban cultural or intellectual life. More lamentable is the fact that this absence is symptomatic of an even greater deficiency in Cuba today, according to Timerman, the appreciation of probing inquiry which has characterized Jewish culture and which has shaped Timerman's own sense of drive and even elan in investigative journalism. In an offhand joke, a remark which can easily serve as a key to his motivation in this and his other books, Timerman suggests that Cuba would profit from the importation of Jewish journalists, which could be put to great use in this nation which has suffered from an inability to examine itself critically: "Jews have brought to our profession two elements—part of Jewish culture—without which journalism can't function: irony and skepticism. Might this not be the antidote to the spirit of complacency and intellectual subjugation characteristic of the profession on the island" (81)?

True to this goal in support of muckraking inquiry in which he has engaged throughout his career, Timerman has expressed here the importance of his role as dissident in order to offer a perspective which runs counter to the official self-serving pronouncements of a government, its official story. In all of his books, Jacobo Timerman wages his own war against the injustices, official deceptions, and the "conspiracy of silence" which undergird the cases of state violence he has described. In his writings and his personal sense of mission to undo injustice, he has uncovered something akin to the great convulsion of the twentieth century, the defining moment of Nazism. The work of Timerman can serve as a reminder of the Nazi period and can serve as a conscience for those who might forget.

PRIMARY BIBLIOGRAPHY

Chile, Death in the South. Trans. by Robert Cox. New York: Knopf, 1987. Spanish version as *Chile: el galope muerto.* Buenos Aires: Planeta, 1988.

Cuba: A Journey. Trans. by Toby Talbot. New York: Knopf, 1990. Spanish version as *Cuba hoy, y después.* Barcelona: Muchnik, 1990.

The Longest War: Israel in Lebanon. Trans. by Miguel Acoca. New York: Knopf, 1982. Spanish version as *Diario de la guerra más larga.* Knopf: New York, 1982; Madrid: Mondadori, 1983; Barcelona: Muchnik, 1983.

Prisoner Without a Name, Cell Without a Number. Trans. by Toby Talbot. New York: Knopf, 1981. Spanish version as *Preso sin nombre, celda sin número* (cover title: *El caso Camps, punto inicial*). Barcelona: El Cid, 1981.

SECONDARY BIBLIOGRAPHY

Chile, Death in the South

Bouvier, Virginia M. "The Impenetrable Pinochet." *Commonweal* 115:8 (April 22, 1988): 249-50.

Coetzee, J. M. "They Wanted to Terrify." *New York Times Book Review* (January 10, 1988): 10.

Cumming, Don. "A Chilean Nightmare." *Macleans* 101:12 (March 14, 1988): 50.

Hougland, Kenneth. *Christian Century* 105:26 (September 14, 1988): 815-16.

Lowenthal, Abraham F. *Foreign Affairs* 66:4 (Spring, 1988): 879.

—. "Police State." *Progressive* 52:3 (March, 1988): 31.

Rosenberg, Tina. *Washington Monthly* 19:12 (January, 1988): 58.

Stuttaford, Genevieve. *Publishers Weekly* 232:20 (November 13, 1987): 62.

Cuba: A Journey

Black, George. "The Long Goodbye." *The Nation* 252:5 (February 11, 1991): 165-68.

Brzezinski, Steve. *Antioch Review* 49:2 (Spring, 1991): 296-97.

Hollander, Paul. *Problems of Communism* 40:3 (May, 1991): 116-23.

Horowitz, Irving Louis. *The American Spectator* 24:6 (June, 1991): 35-36.

Radu, Michael. *Orbis* 35:1 (Winter, 1991): 158

Steif, William. "On Old Havana." *The Progressive* 55:8 (August, 1991): 42-43.

White, Robert E. "A Miss and a Hit on Cuba." *Commonweal* 118:3 (February 8, 1991): 108-09.

The Longest War: Israel in Lebanon

Elon, Amos. "Dissent in Israel." *The New York Times Book Review* (December 12, 1982): 1, 30-31.

Varon, Benno Weiser. "Jacobo Timerman: The Controversial Author's Second Coming." *The Jewish Week* (February 4, 1993): 2, 40.

Wieseltier, Leon. "Have Conscience Will Travel." *Harper's* (January, 1983): 64-68.

Prisoner Without a Name, Cell Without a Number

Herman, Donald. *The Latin American Community of Israel.* New York: Praeger, 1984. 16-21.

Leonard, John. *The New York Times* (May 7, 1981): C23.

Lewis, Anthony. "The Final Solution in Argentina." *The New York Times Book Review* (May 16, 1981): 1, 30-32.

Neilson, James. "The Education of Jacobo Timerman." *Encounter* 57.4 (1981): 74-85.

Russell, George. "Face of Fascism." *Time* 117.24 (June 15, 1981): 79-80.

Howard M. Fraser

TOKER, ELIAHU (Argentina; 1934)

Eliahu Toker, Argentine poet, translator, and architect, has produced an astonishingly diverse body of work. In addition to penning five volumes of poetry, he has compiled and translated numerous collections of poetry from Yiddish into Spanish, written essays on everything from Jewish spiritual resistance to the poetics of petty things, edited various literary magazines, and designed and constructed several edifices in and around Buenos Aires.

Toker was born and raised in the *barrio del Once*, then a predominantly Jewish neighborhood located a few blocks from downtown Buenos Aires. From a very early age, Toker was acutely sensitive to the differences of the Yiddish and Spanish languages. For the young Toker, Yiddish was his first language, the mother tongue, the language that surrounded and sustained him. Conversely, Spanish was the other tongue; it was public and what was spoken on the outside, in the city, in school. But as a young poet struggling to find his own voice, Toker would learn to cultivate his dual linguistic and cultural roots, nourished from Yiddish literature as well as Spanish and Latin American literature. It was his seminal cross readings of, among others, the prophets Amos and Isaiah, and Federico García Lorca (1898-1936), and Pablo Neruda (1904-73) that would sow, as Toker calls it, a harvest of five collections of poetry: *Piedra de par en par* (Wide Open Stone; 1972), *Lejaim* (To Life; 1974), *Homenaje a Abraxas* (Homage to Abraxas; 1980), *La caja del amor* (Box of Love; 1986), and *Papá, Mamá y otras ciudades* (Papa, Momma and Other Cities; 1988).

In a general sense, Toker's literary project is, to appropriate a term of his, one of transcreation. In addition to five collections of poetry, he has translated and compiled anthologies of Yiddish poetry, including *El resplandor de la palabra judía: antología de la poesía ídish del siglo XX* (Splendor of the Jewish Word: Anthology of 20th Century Yiddish Poetry; 1981) and *Poesía de Avrom Sútzkever* (The Poetry of Avrom Sutzkever; 1983). For Toker, writing poetry and translating poetry are two paths that do not fork, but rather twin, and quite often tangle. He has described both experiences similarly as violent and affectionate struggles with the word, much like Jacob wrestling with the angel.

For Toker, a poem is the product of a somatic reaction, an urge and a surge sparked by a glimmer in the darkness and the mystery that constitute the poet. The process is akin to a wakeful dreaming, a sober drunkfest where words and images spill forth. In this stage, the pen becomes an extension of the arm, the body. And the poet, in a strange doubling, observes himself writing. But writing a poem is a dual process as well; part intuition and part craft, poetry for Toker becomes an exercise in montage, in construction. To recapture that initial coruscation, the poet tweaks and prunes, polishes and smooths out the text to the point of verbal translucence, and even of verbal transparency. For Toker, as he writes in "Entretanto" (Meanwhile [*Lejaim*]), the ideal poem is replete with windows where the reader can peek in and where the poet's emotions can filter out.

If for Toker to write is to translight, then to translate is to transplant. To translate a poem is for the translator to take a poetic text soaking in the amniotic liquids of another culture and language, plunge his hands into the poem's entrails, extricate them and reconfigure them in the host language. But like the act of writing poetry, to translate poetry entails a loss, in this case of the original poem's initial ambiguities and richness. But the transmuted text is newly incorporated, submerged in linguistic and cultural liquids and thus acquiring another life in another context.

The act of translation for Toker has a vital consequence. Yiddish is a deterritorialized language spoken by a fractured minority. It is a language that is not dead, but dying out. Yiddish, Toker's visceral language, the language of tradition, then, gets translated into Spanish, Toker's creative language, the language of traduction. In effect, to translate is to share the mother tongue, in this case Yiddish, a language that has produced a great amount of quality literature but which has remained largely unknown and undiscovered, at least in the Spanish-speaking world. One might say, then, that for Toker, to translate is to transloot, to untrove the encrusted poetic gems of the Yiddish language, to pour what he calls the poetic treasures of Jewish culture into the Spanish language.

While Toker's poetry shades from the quotidian ("Las manos de mi padre [My Father's Hands [*Papá, Mamá y otras ciudades*]), to the reflexive ("Poemas de borrador" [Poems in the Rough; [*Papá, Mamá*]), to the erotic (*La caja del amor*), to the historically concrete ("25 de mayo de 1973" [25 of May, 1973 [*Lejaim*]), his poetry is generally one of introspection and retrospection. In effect, one of the antimonies that his poetry cultivates is the contradiction of what it means for him to be "born abroad" in Israel and to live "exiled among friends" in his native Buenos Aires. But in Toker's case the line of exile is not altogether clear. Toker was born in Argentina and never left Argentina. His uprooting, then, is not necessarily a topographical one, but an existential one. As one critic has put it, Toker's existential state is not exile, but dual exile: exiled from a familial past he never really knew and an inner exile in his native Buenos Aires, where he happens to feel like a stranger (cf. Goldberg, "The Complex Roses").

Consequently, many of Toker's poems are spatially all over the map, so to speak. They are, in effect, atopias that shift between memory and actuality, between an *allá* (Israel) and an *acá* (Buenos Aires). Structurally, Toker's poems seek to pour foundations, to lay down and cultivate his Jewish roots, however ramified they may be. His poems are essentially houses of words that might resemble that imaginary house in *Piedra de par en par*, one which he should like to erect in another continent as an ideal solution to erase the line of exile. Indeed, reading Toker's poems one finds that his architecture privileges intimate spaces: patios, bedrooms, doors, porches, portals and windows open both ways;

walls and dusty books and old photo albums limn thresholds to a past, one which has been burnished in history, obscured in forgetfulness and in the swales of memory.

But it is these intimate and insular spaces that serve as bulwarks against the brutal exterior, usually represented in the form of the city. Unlike the warm confines of his family's house, or the immutable walls that bounded his childhood, the city immures him in chaos, tragedy, and isolation. In "Buenos Aires" (*Papá, Mamá*), for example, the poet knows a lot about the city; he walks the streets, but nevertheless he feels foreign (*ajeno*). The speaker is, to use Toker's own neologism, an *espectagonista* (part spectator, part protagonist). To live in Buenos Aires, he writes, must be something different than what he is doing. In "Agosto de 1972" (August 1972 [*Lejaim*]), Buenos Aires is agitated, peopled with evaporating hands, fleeting faces, and pummeled bodies being dragged down the streets. It is the city where the poet's dreams and nightmares take place, where familiar street corners of his childhood have receded into photo albums, where the city is either a crumbling palimpsest of memories devoured by modernity or a very real concentration camp run by the brutal military dictatorship.

But Toker's relationship with the city, whether it be his native Buenos Aires, or the Warsaw of his mother, or the Ratne of his father is ambivalent. In the case of his parents' cities, the past is almost mythical, unknown to the poet although he attempts to fill in the gaps, at least topographically, by naming the streets as he talks of the need to wander down those streets of that old Jewish barrio, to pass by the house of his grandfather, or to pay a visit to Tlomatzke 13, home of the Society of Jewish Writers in Warsaw. But warm, nostalgic images melt into images of resistance and destruction. The city's ruins throb, its buildings burn, and its steaming pavement has been trowled with screams that the new Warsaw conceals. And as in many of Toker's poems, photographs and desiccated pages from books are the only access to this past and while they do preserve it, they also distort it, their borders effectively keeping the poet from gaining access to their patios.

In "Kadish" (*Lejaim*) Toker writes that everything can be explained except his existence, but nothing is explained without his existence. This existential chiasmas could very well describe Toker's own relationship with Israel and Argentina. If one critic calls Toker's situation an open-ended existential problem (cf. Goldberg, "The Complex Roses"), then Toker's open-ended solution to his displacement is not a geographic one, but a graphic one. Toker's broad writerly itinerancy seeks out points of conjunction and disjunction between Jewish, Argentine, and Latin American culture as manifested in their respective literatures as well as in the Yiddish and Spanish language. In effect, text and translation bridge distance. For Toker, writing and translation, indeed the act of transcreation forms a discursive crossroads from where he can, in fact, purvey his dual roots.

PRIMARY BIBLIOGRAPHY
Creative Writing
La caja del amor. Buenos Aires: Arte y Papel, 1986.
Homenaje a Abraxas. Buenos Aires: Nueva Presencia, 1980.
Lejaim. Buenos Aires: Ediciones de la Flor, 1974.
Papá, Mamá y otras ciudades. Buenos Aires: Contexto, 1988.
Las picardías de Hérshele. (With Manuela Fingueret) Buenos Aires: Ediciones Colihue, 1989.
Piedra de par en par. Buenos Aires: J. L. Trenti Rocamora, 1974.
Nonfiction
H. Leivik. Buenos Aires: Congreso Judío Latinoamericano, 1972.
Editions
Comp. *A mi viejo.* Buenos Aires: Arte y Papel, 1985.
Comp. *En sí: antología poética de Jacobo Glatstein.* Buenos Aires: Diálogo, 1968.
Comp. *Muestra de la poesía ídish del siglo XX.* Caracas: Arbol de Fuego, 1976.
Comp. *Poesía de Avrom Sútzkever.* Buenos Aires: Pardés, 1983.
Comp. *El pueblo judío por si mismo.* Buenos Aires: Sociedad Hebraica Argentina, 1987.
Comp. *Refranero judío.* Buenos Aires: Pardés, 1986.
Comp. *El resplandor de la palabra judía: antología de la poesía ídish del siglo XX.* Buenos Aires: Pardés, 1981. (trad. y selección de E. Toker).

SECONDARY BIBLIOGRAPHY
Criticism
Goldberg, Florinda. "The Complex Roses of Jerusalem: The Theme of Israel in Argentinian Jewish Poetry." *Tradition and Innovation: Reflections on Latin American Jewish Writing.* Ed. Robert DiAntonio and Nora Glickman. Albany: SUNY Press, 1993. 73-87.
—. Rev. of *Papá, mamá y otras ciudades. Noaj* 3.3-4 (1989): 194-96.
Kovadloff, Santiago. "El péndulo incesante: lo judío en la poesía de Eliahu Toker." *El imaginario judío en la literatura de América Latina: visión y realidad.* Ed. Patricia Finzi, Eliahu Toker, and Marcos Faerman. São Paulo: Shalom, 1992. 90-97.
Tiempo, César. "Toker en la poesía." *Mundo Israelita* 2945 (26 April, 1980): 6.

Weinstein, Ana E. and Miryam Gover de Nasatky, comps. "Eliahu Toker." *Escritores judeo-argentinos: bibliografía 1990-1987*. 2 vols. Buenos Aires: Milá, 1994. Vol. II, 292-300.

Interviews

Platkin, Abraham. "Poesía igual a provocación." *Nueva presencia* 207 (19 June, 1981): 15, 18.

Safranchik, Graciela. "Poesía: esa palabra inoportuna: una triple entrevista al poeta Eliahu Toker." *Plural* 26 (1980): 6-8.

Tenembaum, Ernesto. Nuestra civilización no tiene una rima musical." *Nueva Sión* 659 (6 June, 1987): 20-21.

David E. Davis

VARSAVSKY, PAULA (Argentina; 1963)

Trained in English, Varsavsky works as a journalist, both with the literary supplement of the Buenos Aires daily *La Nación* (The Nation) and with the French *Vogue*. She has unpublished texts in the areas of movie and theater scripts. Her single published book is the novel *Nadie alzaba la voz* (No One Raised His Voice; 1994).

In a minimalist (but not colloquial) fashion, Luz Golman recounts the death of her father who died suddenly on the plane carrying him from New York to Buenos Aires. Golman had been an important professor of physics at the University of Buenos Aires until his dismissal by the military dictatorship in 1969; Luz's life corresponds to the period of the dictatorship (significantly, her father dies at the time of the democratic elections in 1983), and it is clear that her separation from her father, who decides to pursue his career in New York, is her principal understanding of the consequences on society of the de facto government. Although raised in settings of considerable material comfort—ample town houses, country retreats, luxurious summer spas, international vacations in the United States, Brazil, and Europe—Luz's life is one of spiritual desolation.

The title of Luz's account is both ambiguous and ironic. It is ironic because she is surrounded by people who do raise their voices, loudly and persistently, her family as well as her friends, her elders as well as her peers, the authorities as well as her intimates, all in the frantic scramble to assert the validity of their point of view and the primacy of their needs. But the title is also ambiguous in that, while it can refer to tone and volume of voice in the process of human intercourse, it also refers to speaking out against the social structures of family, education, and institutional authority that produce the spiritual desolation Luz experiences. Her family is composed of secular or cultural Jews who also have firm political commitments. But these commitments, which are never really very much in evidence (her father professes to hate Argentina, but he ends up making a considerable amount of money representing in New York the business interests of crass Argentines who became wealthy during the dictatorship) are inadequate to the task of alleviating Luz's alienation. Indeed, the only voice that would appear to have been raised in an acceptable fashion is her own, in the form of the narrative.

Varsavsky's inaugural novel invites comparison with Enrique Medina's *Con el trapo en la boca* (1983), which deals with a young woman of approximately Luz's age who is described as a "girl of the dictatorship." However, despite the fact that both novels provide a first-person unsentimental portrait of coming of age in Argentina under the generals, Medina's novel is characterized by dirty realism colloquiality, a socially marginal perspective, and a trenchant homologization between male authoritarianism and military dictatorship, with a pronounced dimension of lesbianist feminism. Luz by contrast is upper middle-class, naively homophobic, and convinced that there is a difference between the authoritarian structures (the dictatorship, but her family as well, and specifically her mother, her grandmother, and her stepmother) that have separated her from her father and the unmediated ideal of her father's love for her. Undoubtedly, Varsavsky's narrator is deluded in her adherence to this ideal, but her novel shows a level of consciousness for her protagonist quite starkly alien to Medina's.

While the Jewish elements in the novel are relegated to the general cultural ambiance (and Luz is embarrassed when her father is given a generic Jewish burial), Freudian Oedipalism constitutes the crucial narrative core, shaded by Argentinian versions of Lacan and the Law of the Father. Luz's desolation is as much her stifling existence in the Buenos Aires of the dictatorship as it is the lack of any parameters—and, crucially, no consciousness, despite the privilege of her narrative act—to question the ways in which she must enact and enforce the will of her father. Luz is depressingly as much a nonfeminist as is possible, and Varsavsky's text only opens itself up to a feminist reading to the extent that the reader can assess the ironic gaps in Luz's account.

PRIMARY BIBLIOGRAPHY
Nadie alzaba la voz. Buenos Aires: Emecé, 1994.

David William Foster

VERBITSKY, BERNARDO (Argentina; 1907-79)

The son of Russian immigrant parents, Bernardo Verbitsky was born in Buenos Aires, and much of his work chronicles a span of more than forty years in the life of that city. Much can be learned about this writer's life from his essentially autobiographical novel *Hermana y sombra* (Sister and Shadow; 1977) the title of which came from a euphemistic expression often used by his mother to describe the family's abiding poverty. "La hermana Pobreza" she would say, "no nos deja nunca. Es como la sombra... pertenecemos a su familia, o ella es parte de la nuestra" (Sister poverty never leaves us. She's like a shadow... we belong to her family, or she is part of ours; 20). In this novel, Verbitsky describes his family's poverty, the kindness of friends from the old country who allowed his family, newly arrived in the city, to share their rented apartment free while his father sought work. Bernardo's father, incapable of making a false sales pitch, proved to be a less than successful salesman. Similarly, his mother, who augmented the family's income as a midwife, earned far less than she could have because her moral rectitude led her to adamantly refuse to perform abortions.

Despite their poverty, Verbitsky's parents, hungry for the cultural activities that had been part of their life in Russia, created a cultural ambiance for their children by acting out Russian plays in their home and attending open air concerts to hear the classical music they hungered for. Determined that their children would have an education, though it meant borrowing the books they could not afford to buy, the writer's parents saved money by dressing the family in second-hand clothing and begging an uncle for textbooks and occasional assistance. The family's interaction with the Argentine ambiance; their struggles between tradition and progress, Judaism and assimilation; his parent's moral intensity, their determination to escape the past and make a future for themselves and their children all are chronicled in Verbitsky's works.

Rich in personal observation and autobiographical elements, Verbitsky's portrayals of specific *porteño* (Buenos Aires) settings, his frequent allusions to real people, actual political events, radio programs, popular movies and music, current cinema stars and tango artists all work to preserve the moral and social milieu of his era. Immersed in this ambiance, the reader comes to understand the problems the author and the youth of his era faced as individuals adapting to, growing up, and living in Argentina's port city, a city whose types and characters are the unique product of their own concrete environment.

Because of his humane, observant understanding of the lives and outlook of the city's poor, as well as because of the unapologetic autobiographical elements of his work, Verbitsky early earned the title "Chronicler of the City" as critics everywhere came to consider him the foremost exponent of Argentine literature on the problems of life in the city.

Able to read the works of Maksim Gorky (1868-1936), Fyodor M. Dostoyevsky (1821-81) and Leo Tolstoy (1828-1910) in their original Russian, Verbitsky was greatly influenced by their realism. He in turn, with his essentially journalistic style (logical since he was a news writer for over twenty years), became the inspiration of the generation of Argentine writers who came after him which included authors such as David Viñas (1929).

During the depression years Verbitsky was an active member of the Boedo group of writers which cultivated the novel of social consciousness and political protest rather than of the Florida group headed by Jorge Luis Borges (1899-1986) which preferred aesthetic expression and metaphysical analysis, (both groups were named for the streets where they held their *tertulias* or literary meetings rather than for their leaders or ideals). Altogether, Verbitsky authored some fourteen novels, several collections of stories, and one collection of poems. He also served for many years as editor of *Davar*, a Jewish journal.

Although Verbitsky considered himself essentially Jewish, he seldom wrote explicitly Jewish stories or novels but seemed, rather, to be most Jewish when least conscious of it—when, for example, his characters clearly reflected his own personal sentiments and consciousness.

Es difícil empezar a vivir, the author's first novel, is an interesting study of adolescent psychology. Its protagonist, Pablo Levinson, is portrayed as a typically curious and critical young man attending classes at the medical school, meeting classmates in cafes to discuss books, politics, philosophy, and literature. As he describes Pablo's daily life Verbitsky chronicles his entire milieu, the Buenos Aires of the Uriburu years with its impresarios and adventurers, its political, social, university, and hospital circles, its press and literary groups. He ably conveys Pablo's distress and bewilderment when some of his more radical classmates are arrested and beaten and when, reflecting European fascism, swastikas and graffiti appear on his university's walls vilifying Jews. Son of a non-observant Jewish family Pablo feels rootless, belonging neither to mainstream (Christian) Argentine society nor (because of his unfamiliarity with many Jewish customs and traditions) at home in the Jewish community. He admires his friend Leo whose family does observe Jewish customs, and yearns to be like him, believing in and belonging to something. When Pablo attends services on Yom Kippur, his inhibiting lack of religious training causes him to resent Leo's ability to "fit in."

This novel, which won the Ricardo Güiraldes award for its depiction of middle-class life in Buenos Aires during the Uriburu period of the 1930s, is both an interesting study of adolescent psychology and an observant chronicle of a specific historical milieu. It established the concept that a novel need not necessarily be rooted in the pampa to be essentially Argentine but could portray another, equally authentic perspective of Argentine life—that of life in the city—specifically the capital, port city. It also establishes Verbitsky as the quintessential chronicler of that life in the city.

In *Una pequeña familia* (A Small Family; 1951) Verbitsky depicts the ordinary life of the typical married young white-collar worker of his day. He introduces the reader to Eduardo and Luisa and their children Tucho and Lila when they first move into a small house with a garden on the outskirts of Buenos Aires and then chronicles Eduardo's continuing efforts to rise above mediocrity and provide a better life for his family. Although he is repeatedly frustrated in these attempts, either by his own timidity or the failure of others he depends on, Eduardo eventually does succeed with the loyal support of his dedicated wife and a few good friends. Luisa's dedication as a wife and mother are well detailed in the novel as she observes and nurtures her children's development through their childhood games, discoveries, and adventures. The lower middle-class neighborhood ambiance of the Buenos Aires of the times is clearly delineated against a background of contemporary events as we follow Verbitsky's characters from work to the bars and cafes they frequent or into their homes and intimate family life sharing their discussions about rising prices and land values, political events and current movies, their hopes and dreams, problems, concerns and anxieties.

Vacaciones (Vacations; 1953) is a short novel describing a teen-ager's development in the course of a summer vacation at his grandmother's house by the sea. Oscarcito, the novel's protagonist, symbolically dons his first long pants and begins to emerge from adolescence as he experiences his first love, his first sexual encounter and his first close experience with death. By presenting that time of adolescence when sexual change and awareness are most evident and overwhelming from the viewpoint of Oscar and his young female cousins, Verbitsky makes the reader aware of the tremendous psychological pressures these changes bring and helps him realize how unaware most adults are of the crises their adolescent relatives are experiencing. When Oscar's mother asks, "Y el chico, cómo lo pasa"? (And the boy, how is he?), his grandmother, unaware of all that he has experienced internally or otherwise, replies with cheerful ignorance, "Lo pasa divinamente. . . debe haber aumentado por lo menos dos kilos" (He's having a wonderful time. . . he must have gained at least five pounds; 90).

In *La esquina* (The Corner; 1953) Verbitsky presents yet another study of adolescent psychology by introducing us to a group of youths who go from adolescence to maturity together, hanging out first on the corner of the title, then later, at a favorite cafe. Eventually, one of them goes into the army, another into business, a third marries, a fourth goes to jail and only three remain in the group at the story's end. Sadly they realize that their group will never again come together completely as they were before, that time has changed everything.

The author's compassionate understanding of adolescent psychology is evident throughout the work in his portrayal of the youths' frustrations, insecurities, aggressiveness, and in their attempts to seem macho and adult, despite sometimes feeling like frightened or timid children inside. His characters are essentially sincere and decent boys who, although considered bad by some, are merely poor, weak, naive, inexperienced, or uneducated. He understands their adolescent insecurities, and need to belong to the group, explaining, "Sólo en la esquina se les abría el mundo. . . la esquina les cobijaba en ese rebullir de las primeras audacias. . ." (It was only on the corner that the world opened before them. . . the corner sheltered them in their first audacious steps; 81-82).

Un noviazgo (A Courtship; 1956) seems almost mistitled, for rather than dwelling on Emilio's interrupted relations with his sweetheart, Carmen, it is a detailed and somewhat autobiographical description of an ordinary journalist's experiences in the bustling political and social ambiance of Buenos Aires in the 1930s. Verbitsky draws verbal portraits of the city's physical aspects and its political and psychological climate as he describes Emilio's routine and ordinary life. The author names and thereby preserves specific streets, monuments, cinemas, cafes, bars, restaurants and hotels of his beloved Buenos Aires. He also introduces us to the city's moral and psychological ambiance as we follow Emilio into the city's middle-class apartments and cafes, its slums and girlie bars, its police stations and its newsrooms. We share the young journalist's encounters with the yellow press, police brutality and government attempts to distort public opinion until finally, in a contrived and unlikely conclusion, Emilio, having had his fill of such adventures, returns to Carmen, seemingly prepared to settle down to a more mundane, but peaceful existence.

In *Villa miseria también as América* (The Slum Too Is America; 1957), which won the Alberto Gerchunoff Prize for fiction, Verbitsky describes what happens when over one thousand people live huddled together in a small, dense slum area. An excellent study of social conditions and human behavior as well as psychological study of the effects of poverty on its victims, *Villa miseria* presents slum dwellers as they really are, with their good side and bad, their petty jealousies and noble deeds, their kindness and vengefulness, problems and dreams, humor, grief and ever-ready *chispa* (wit). He shows how all of them, old and young, children and parents, dream of having something better someday and how it was that same dream that brought them all—immigrant farmers from the provinces and Bolivian, Paraguayan and Easter European immigrants escaping poverty or political persecution—to Buenos Aires.

Verbitsky describes how even in these slums a few public-minded citizens form so-called committees for community action motivating others to share, help, or get involved. He also describes the small-minded people who interpret such initiatives as attempts to control others or keep them from getting ahead. His objective descriptions help the reader understand how, despite being hardworking and hopeful, most slum dwellers have too many children, too little education, and too little earning power to ever get ahead. Lost in the city, they yearn nostalgically for the provinces from whence they came but find no turning back. Dominga, for example who has idealized the province of her youth, succeeds in returning home at great sacrifice only to learn that there, too, life has become equally insecure and difficult.

Verbitsky skillfully uses a variety of events to show the different aspects of life and problems in the Villa. He shows how, when the Villa is flooded during heavy rains, firemen evacuate reluctant "home owners" from their shacks and homes; when their only pump breaks down leaving the Villa without water, people work together to raise money to replace it; how the unions' efforts to obtain benefits for their workers meet with repression, intimidation, violence and assassinations.

It is only after fire destroys forty shacks in the Villa that newspaper publicity brings commissions to investigate conditions and people from outside to offer food, clothes, and blankets. Although they see the fire as their big chance to obtain government aid and attention, people are wary that offers of temporary housing in police barracks and warehouses will preclude the long-term help they so badly need. When Benítez, an opportunistic disaster victim, takes over as leader of the *damnificados* (the affected victims) he undercuts the committee that had worked hard to improve the *barrio*, or neighborhood, and makes himself the virtual arbiter of those who will and won't receive aid. As some of the fire victims try to prevent others from meeting officials or getting aid, hostilities grow and a series of injustices are perpetrated.

Overall, *Villa miseria* projects Verbitsky's fundamental values as it stresses the importance of human dignity and shows that despite some occasional baseness, humanity is essentially worthy and able to overcome all odds to improve the quality of life.

Un hombre de papel (Paper Man; 1966) is a long novel in which Ríos, the protagonist, serves as spokesman for Verbitsky's own comments and observations as he searches for a rational basis for social order. Ríos, like Verbitsky, is a writer conscious of his need to express his reactions to the horrors of World

War II and contemporary politics and the various levels of human folly and degradation. The novel reflects the author's very personal awareness that the individual—sensitive, creative, intelligent though he may be—is nothing more than a helpless witness to life—one whose only comfort is that of hearing his own voice in the wilderness. This work partially focuses on the danger of an all-out nuclear holocaust—the same thing which runs through Verbitsky's collection of poems entitled *Megatón* (1959). Ríos, Verbitsky's alter ego throughout, feels compelled to express his horror of war. He centers his writing on the large and small events of human misery: the poverty-ridden lives of Buenos Aires's slum dwellers; the shocked victims of a Chilean earthquake; the threatening cold war crises of the super powers. More universal in theme than his previous works, this novel is somehow also more personal in its expression of the author's awareness that the individual, or writer, can be no more than a helpless witness to his time.

Trying his hand at a stream-of-consciousness novel in *La neurosis monta su espectáculo* (Neurosis Mounts a Spectacle; 1969) Verbitsky presents a character who, following the advice of his psychoanalyst, plans to confess an illicit love affair to his wife. As he mentally reviews the minute details of the affair's progression he guiltily admits, "Soy una persona con un gusano adentro" (I'm a person with a worm inside; 217). He yearns for others to know him as he really is, not so they may justify or absolve him, but merely so that they may totally accept him, with all his flaws.

Etiquetas a los hombres (Labels for Men; 1972) is a didactic work in which a thin novelistic thread connects long philosophical essays on topics as disparate as Judaism, Israel, the reactions of a traveler in Paris, Russia, socialism, and even the possibility of world holocaust. Its characters speak in long, theoretical or philosophical monologues rather than dialogue. Of Verbitsky's fourteen novels, it is his least novelistic work. Considered by some his most "Jewish" work, it deals nonetheless, with themes of basic concerns to all men.

More truly novelistic in style, *Enamorado de Joan Baez* (In Love with Joan Baez; 1975) seems designed simply to chronicle the new sexual freedom of the 1970s. Eugenio, the novel's protagonist, is incurably in love with a cousin whom everyone expects him to marry. She, however, runs off with another admirer when Eugenio balks at fathering the child she's determined to have. After bearing the child, Mausi asserts her freedom by abandoning her husband, leaving her mother to raise the child, and embarking on a series of lovers. Although the contrite Eugenio repeatedly offers to marry her and adopt her child as his own, the erratic and sometimes suicidal Mausi rejects him. Her own father, a doctor who had seduced numerous patients throughout his long medical career, confides to Eugenio that he is repelled by the provocative dress and excessive sexual liberty of his four young daughters and their whole generation. Eugenio meets and eventually enters into a relationship with another woman, only to return to Mausi when she again attempts suicide. After spending weeks at her bedside he is once more disillusioned when she again rejects him. Throughout the novel Eugenio finds solace in listening to Joan Baez records, following the star's career, rejoicing at her marriage, suffering her divorce, and always identifying with her lyrics about personal freedom. Overall this work is interesting, but somewhat moralistic with its repetitive comments about the changing mores of the time, and the liberated young folks' ostentatious public displays of affection, provocative clothing, and blatant sexuality. At times, too, the narrative, with no apparent purpose abruptly switches from first to third person, leaving the reader groping for continuity. The characters, although more developed than in many of Verbitsky's works, nevertheless remain stereotypical, drawn to represent types rather than individuals and embody the themes the author has chosen to address.

In addition to his novels and numerous newspaper and journal articles, Verbitsky also wrote a number of short stories which he published in a series of collections. *Café de los angelitos* (Café of Little Angels; 1949), appeared first, followed by *La tierra es azul* (The Earth Is Blue; 1961), *Calles de tango* (Tango Streets; 1966), *Cuatro historias de Buenos Aires* (Four Stories of Buenos Aires; 1978), *Octubre maduro* (Ripe October; 1976), and *A pesar de todo* (In Spite of Everything; 1978). Immensely varied in theme and style some of Verbitsky's stories center on people as types, while others present the commonplace small tragedies of daily life among the poor, the small traumas of adolescence, the timid first stirrings of sexual awareness or the loneliness caused by loss or betrayal. His topics are endlessly varied and his characters run the gamut from young to old, from innocent to jaded from lonely to loving, from ordinary to eccentric.

The reader meets a youthful prostitute, so anxious to be a decently wed *señora*, or lady, that she knowingly marries a widower accused of brutally abusing his dead wife; a servant who is a "bad" girl because that's what everyone expected of her; a cast-off mistress humbly begging shelter outside her former lover's home; a young mother, tenderly caring for her deformed child or a group of people whose lives briefly coincide in the course of an ordinary subway ride; a group of newspaper reporters flying to New York on a company-sponsored trip to a special conference; a reporter lamenting the bombing of Nagasaki and another reporting on Gagarin's first flight in space. We meet a black musician who mysteriously appears and reappears in critical moments of the narrator's life, a juggler who, despite the loneliness of his own life brings joy to countless children as he takes his traveling carousel to various locations around the outskirts of the city; a belligerent drunk who deliberately tries to pick a fight by bullying a Negro bartender or a journalist saddened by the dawning realization of how little he knows of the lives of all his colleagues who are retiring.

There are also a variety of adolescent protagonists who Verbitsky presents with accuracy and astute observation as he draws authentic and compassionate psychological descriptions of the traumas they experience as an inevitable part of growing up. One fantasizes about his first kiss; another anguishes over the loss of his best friend; a third steals money from the collection plate to take his girlfriend to a movie. A teenage girl is distraught by the discovery that her mother has a lover, while another teenager manfully struggles to conceal his hurt upon encountering his dream girl petting with an older man.

Presented without comment and without resolution these stories, rich in their everyday use of *lunfardo* (slang) words and expression authentically capture the tone, cadence, and color of Argentina's ordinary people. Much as Toulouse Lautrec used oils to paint his famous scenes of Paris, Verbitsky used words and his unfailingly gift of keen observation to chronicle and present the rich variety of human types he met each day as he went about his very ordinary life in Buenos Aires. In perusing these stories, the reader is moved not so much by the action as by the atmosphere. It is not so much what happens as the authentic sensation of being there that makes Verbitsky's stories memorable.

Several stories stand out from all the rest because of their specifically Jewish themes. "Llovizna sobre la desdicha" (Raining Misfortune [*Café de los angelitos*]) narrates the trials of a young woman who was fired from various jobs where Jews weren't wanted, and reduced to dependence on the Jewish Beneficent Society to pay her family's room and board. The story provides an example of the kind of unnecessary hardships endured by many immigrant Jews in Buenos Aires. Two more notably Jewish stories, "La visita" (The Visit [*Café de los angelitos*]) and "La culpa" (The Sin [*A pesar de todo*]) are very different in style and theme.

"La visita," one of Verbitsky's few short stories written in an uncharacteristically humorous vein, describes what happens when a Jewish grandmother comes from the old-folks home one day to visit her nonobservant daughter's family. She manages in this, as in previous visits to lay a blanket of guilt over all the family. When the old lady surprises them in the non-kosher killing of the chicken intended for supper the sharpness of her verbal scoldings and the ineptness of her intimidated family are handled with both sensitivity and humor. Here, Verbitsky compassionately presents some of the everyday crises of conscience occasioned by the generational and cultural gaps that Argentina's Jewish immigrants experienced.

"La culpa" differs so greatly in theme and style from all his other work that it is hard to identify with Verbitsky. An allegorical tale written with a mordant humor which cleverly parodies history's purist purges of Jews, the story takes place in an unnamed place and undefined time when, by chance someone happens to notice that some people are different from others because they have two bones in the foot joined at the metatarsal. When the supposed deformity becomes an object of conversation and intense study, the nation's dictator, El Absoluto, determined to have only perfect citizens, issues yellow cards to the "defectives" and green cards to all "normal" citizens. Eventually all yellow card holders are persecuted, rounded up, starved, and exterminated. At first, many compliantly surrender to their fate. Later, more aware or forewarned, others resist, but all eventually succumb overpowered by arms and numbers.

Longer than his other stories but shorter than a novel, "La culpa" is Verbitsky's most significant work on a Jewish theme. It is in this work that Verbitsky most vigorously speaks out against the inherent senselessness of any and all kinds of anti-Jewish or anti-minority purges wherever and whenever they might take place.

Essentially a journalist, Verbitsky inevitably also wrote several books or collections of essays. *Hamlet y Don Quijote* (1964) for example, is a lengthy essay affirming the similarities between the characters born almost contemporaneously in the minds of their creators. He considers both authors men of their time and transfers the similarities he sees between them to their characters. Verbitsky sees Hamlet, like Don Quijote, as a man with a different kind of sensibility, one whose actions are not always understood.

Literatura y conciencia nacional (Literature and National Conscience; 1975), another collection of essays, is based on the thesis that each nation has its own literary consciousness. Here Verbitsky reviews several major Argentine works and authors; Ricardo Güiraldes's (1886-1927), *Don Segundo Sombra* (*Don Segundo Sombra: Shadows on the Pampas*; 1926), Eduardo Gutiérrez's (1851-89), *Juan Moreira* (1879-80), Lucio V. Mansilla's (1831-1913) *Una excursión a los indios ranqueles* (Excursion to the Ranquel Indians; 1870), José Hernández's (1834-86) *Martín Fierro* (1872, 1879), Leopoldo Marechal's (1900-70) *Megafón* (Megaphone; 1959) and *Adán Buenosayres* (1948). His basic thesis in this work is that "A través de la literatura. . . un país encuentra su verdadera imagen y la conocen sus gentes como miembros de esa particular comunidad y en su condición más general y más honda de seres humanos" (Through literature. . . a country finds its true image and its people are recognized as members of that particular community and in a deeply and more general way human beings; [42]). Verbitsky also theorizes that, in addition to economic underdevelopment, countries can also be spiritually underdeveloped. Through essays such as this Verbitsky continuously reaffirms his appreciation of Argentina's national character and language. In the preface to *Octubre maduro*, one of his collections of short stories, Verbitsky wrote a sort of self-interview, apparently responding to the questions he had most encountered. To the question "¿Cómo se define como escritor?" (How does one define a writer?) he responded "un novelista es cronista. . . es decir, el que da testimonio. . . Escribir es la forma de actuar del escritor como pintar lo es la del pintor" (a novelist is a chronicler . . . that is to say, one who gives testimony. . . Writing is the writer's form of acting just as painting is the artist's [9]. To the question "¿Cómo define su literatura" (How do you define your work?) he responded, "Algunos me califican de escritor social. En mi opinión, toda literatura digna de ese nombre es social. . . Creo que soy un individualista absoluto, que no es, sin embargo, indiferente o insensible a nada de lo que ocurre en su entorno" (Some classify me as a social writer. In my opinion all literature worthy of the name is social. . . I believe I'm an absolute individualist, who is not however, indifferent or insensible to anything that occurs around him [13].

Overall, there seem to be two abiding aspects to Verbitsky's work: he is essentially Argentine and he is essentially Jewish. Conscious of this dual tradition, he neither attempted to synthesize the two nor to explicitly portray "Jewishness." He quite simply set himself to chronicle his own experiences and those of the people around him whose lives he knew. In doing so, Bernardo Verbitsky created for readers everywhere a powerful testimonial to life in Buenos Aires in the first half of this century.

PRIMARY BIBLIOGRAPHY
Creative Writing

A pesar de todo. Caracas: Monte Avila, 1978.

Atila, el rey de los hunos. (Published under the pseudonym Bernardo Metz) Buenos Aires: Abril, 1945.

Café de los angelitos y otros cuentos porteños. Buenos Aires: Ediciones Siglo Veinte, 1949.

Calles de tango. Buenos Aires: Centro Editorial de América Latina, 1966.

Una cita con la vida. Buenos Aires: Platina, 1958.

Cuatro historias de Buenos Aires. Buenos Aires: Rayuela, 1970.

En esos años. Buenos Aires: Futuro, 1947.

Es difícil empezar a vivir. Buenos Aires: Losada, 1941. Also, Compañía General Fabril, 1963.

Enamorado de Joan Baez. Barcelona: Planeta, 1975.

La esquina. Buenos Aires: Sudamericana, 1953.

Etiquetas a los hombres. Barcelona: Planeta, 1972.

Hermana y sombra. Buenos Aires: Planeta, 1977. Also, Buenos Aires: Planeta, 1993.

Megatón. Buenos Aires: Platina, 1959.

La neurosis monta su espectáculo. Buenos Aires: Paidós, 1969.

Un noviazgo. Buenos Aires: Goyanarte, 1956. Also, Buenos Aires: Sudamericana, 1966; Buenos Aires: Planeta, 1994.

Octubre maduro. Buenos Aires: Macondo, 1976.

Una pequeña familia. Buenos Aires: Losada, 1951.

La tierra es azul. Buenos Aires: Losada, 1961.

Vacaciones. Buenos Aires: Instituto Argentino Amigos del Libro Argentino, 1953. Also, Buenos Aires: Ediciones de la Flor, 1967.

Villa miseria también es América. Buenos Aires: G. Kraft, 1957. Also, Buenos Aires: Paidós, 1967; Buenos Aires: Contrapunto, 1987.

Nonfiction

Hamlet y Don Quijote. Buenos Aires: Jamcana, 1964.

Literatura y conciencia nacional. Buenos Aires: Paidós, 1975.

El teatro de Arthur Miller. Buenos Aires: Siglo Veinte, 1959.

SECONDARY BIBLIOGRAPHY

Aguinis, Marcos. "Bernardo Verbitsky también es América." In his *El valor de escribir.* Buenos Aires: Sudamericana-Planeta, 1985. 39-45.

Alonso, Fernando Pedro, and Arturo Rezzano. "Bernardo Verbitsky." In their *Novela y sociedad argentina.* Buenos Aires: Paidós, 1971. 150-61.

Barcia, José. "Bernardo Verbitsky." In *Encyclopedia de la literatura argentina.* Ed. Pedro Orgambide and Roberto Yahni. Buenos Aires: Sudamericana, 1970. 616-18.

Bazán, Juan F. "Bernardo Verbitsky." In his *Narrativa paraguaya y latinoamericana.* Asunción, 1976. 215-21.

Bonet, Carmelo M. "La novela." In *Historia de la literatura argentina.* Ed. Rafael Alberto Arrieta. Buenos Aires: Peuser, 1959. Vol. 4, 211-13.

Escardó, Florencio. Rev. of *Enamorado de Joan Baez. Hispamérica* 16 (1977): 115-16.

—. "Una novela de nuestro tiempo" (*Villa miseria también es América*). *Raíces* 7 (1969): 84-85.

—. "Visión de América en una novela" (*Villa miseria también es América*). *Cuadernos americanos* 154 (1967): 223-29.

Fernández, Javier. "Tres novelistas argentinos (Mallea, Verbitsky, Anderson Imbert)." *Oeste* 14 (1952): n.p.

Foster, David William. "Bernardo Verbitsky." In *A Dictionary of Contemporary Latin American Authors.* Comp. D. W. Foster. Tempe, AZ: Center for Latin American Studies/ASU, 1975. 106.

——. "The Formation of a Critical Argentine Consciousness in Bernardo Verbitsky's *En esos años.*" In his *Social Realism in the Argentine Narrative.* Chapel Hill: North Carolina Studies in the Romance Languages and Literatures/UNC Department of Romance Languages, 1986. 73-89.

Freitas, Newton. "*Es difícil empezar a vivir* de Bernardo Verbitsky." In his *Ensayos americanos.* Buenos Aires: Schapire, 1942. 181-85.

Lichtblau, Myron I. "The Young Jew in Buenos Aires: Bernardo Verbitsky's 'It's Hard to Begin Living.'" *Yiddish* 5.4 (1984): 82-86.

Lindstrom, Naomi. "Bernardo Verbitsky: Toward a Critical Discussion of Jewish Argentine Issues." In her *Jewish Issues in Argentine Literature: From Gerchunoff to Szichman.* Columbia: U of Missouri P, 1989. 79-87.

Lipp, Solomon. "Jewish Themes and Authors in Contemporary Argentine Fiction." In *El Cono Sur: dinámica y dimensiones de su literatura.* Ed. Rose Minc. Upper Montclair, NJ: Montclair State College, 1985. 49-55.

Mallea Abarca, Enrique. "Dos novelistas jóvenes (Verbitsky y Juan Carlos Onetti)." *Nosotros* (2a época) 66 (1941): 307-17.

Martini Real, Juan Carlos. "Los libros de Bernardo Verbitsky." *Macedonio* 6-7 (1970): 65-77.

Mastrángelo, Carlos. "Bernardo Verbitsky." In *El cuento argentino.* Buenos Aires: Hachette, 1963. 78-82.

——. Bernardo Verbitsky: novelista porteño." *Ficción* 10 (1957): 52-60.

Pak-Artsi, Diana I. "Aportes de cuatro autores judíos a la literatura argentina: Gerchunoff, Espinoza, Verbitsky y Eichelbaum." Ph.D. diss., Arizona State U, 1989.

Sadow, Stephen A. "Judíos y gauchos: The Search for Identity in Argentine-Jewish Literature." *American Jewish Archives* 34.2 (1982): 164-77.

Sánchez Sivori, Amalia. "Un argentino de primera generación: Pablo Levinson, personaje de Verbitsky." *Comentario* 46 (1966): 33-40.

Senkman, Leonardo. "Verbitzky [sic], o la crispación de la identidad judía." In his *La identidad judía en la literatura argentina.* Buenos Aires: Pardés, 1983. 365-74.

——. "El judío del Holocausto: sobreviviente del ser humano." q.v., pp. 375-82.

Soler Cañas, Luis. "Ansiedad por fijar lo porteño: las dos últimas novelas de Verbitsky." *Capricornio* 4 (1954): 31-33.

Weinstein, Ana E., and Miryam E. Gover de Nasatsky, comps. *Escritores judeo-argentinos: bibliografía 1900-1987*. 2 vols. Buenos Aires: Milá, 1994. II.306-18.

Rita Gardiol

VIÑAS, DAVID (Argentina; 1927)

David Viñas was born in Buenos Aires in 1927. He is considered one of the most prominent Latin American writers of his generation. In addition to his works of fiction, which include novels, short stories and several plays, Viñas has written numerous books of criticism that deal with Latin America's social and political problems. Until recently, Viñas was a professor of Latin American literature at the Universidad del Litoral in Buenos Aires and director of the magazine *Contorno*. He also has been a visiting professor at Freie Universitat, Berlin; the University of Rome; the University of California; and the University of Salamanca. He has written articles for newspapers such as *Les Temps Modernes*; *New Left*; *Rinascita*, and many others in Europe and Latin America.

His first novel entitled *Cayó sobre su rostro* (It Fell On His Face) was written in 1955 and reveals, through the use of irony, the social standoff of the Latin American intellectuals in society. Other works followed later which likewise are representative of the continual repression, corruption and social dissatisfaction of the Argentinian establishment of the times.

In general, Viñas's works are well known for portraying social ideas and strong political convictions. The typical Viñas scenario sheds light upon the primitive conscience and selfishness of individuals through the characters of his fiction. Some of his novels are focused on a re-evaluation of the early immigrant's reality, and particularly that of the Jewish groups who arrived in Argentina at the turn of the century. Their presence in Argentinian society and specifically their settlement in Buenos Aires is described by Viñas with expressive and elaborate allusions to a time in history when the identity of Argentina as a nation took shape with the help of these groups.

In this case, his complete collection reflects his own perspective of Argentina. By incorporating into his fiction historical referents, the author's main objective is to represent the class consciousness and powerlessness of the individual in such societies. Thus, according to Viñas, the individual's potential is blocked by a culture that places race and class as conditions of social and political hierarchy.

Viñas's characteristic fiction reveals, for the most part, the complexity of power relations throughout history. Aggressiveness and violence are shown to be marks of a society that is ruled by the attitudes and values of the social classes. The collective conflicts of Argentina, caused by military regimes and iconic political structures such as Peronism, are themes that reveal an individual and socio-ethical responsibility. Thus, the author's vision of the middle class is embedded with critical remarks, with the intellectuals being the group that is most condemned by Viñas because of their adopted messianic attitude and their inability to face the concrete aspects of social conflicts. These issues are well represented in his sociopolitical analysis entitled *Literatura argentina y realidad política* (Argentinian Literature and Political Reality) published in 1964.

Aside from his political ideologies, Viñas's concerns go far beyond that of undermining the roles of the establishment and they indicate in his discourse a sense of identification with undercurrent references to Jewishness.

Being of a Russian Jewish background, Viñas is aware of the historical contributions and developments of this group yet is bearer of a strong Latin America identity. In fact, themes of Jewish identity often function as a backdrop to most of his novels, and particularly, the repeated references to their struggle to survive the victimization and their adaptation to society.

The insight of Jewish identity is presented in Viñas's characters as a contradictory awareness of the difference that being a Jew implies; an Other, lost in a system that excludes him/her from the social process.

Thus, Jewishness is seen as either raising questions and always looking for an answer, or being a nuisance, features that are depicted by some of the characters such as Bernardo Carman in *Dar la cara* (Making A Stand; 1962).

On the other hand, the racial conflicts they cause and their struggle to assimilate ironically emphasize their principles and their social mission as a group, allowing the author to create a realistic representation of sociohistorical conditions often neglected by Latin American historians.

Viñas's objective, therefore, seems to be to present Argentina's past as a documentary, where values and interests are shown to be spaced between reality and chaos, identity and meaning. Therefore, his fictional characters stand in society as builders of a present that is only possible by re-evaluating the past.

When considered as an added process to the sociohistorical component of Argentina, Jewishness in Viñas's works focuses on the significance of ethnic traditions and values. His novels are rich in ideological expressions and linguistic variants voiced through characters who are often searching for existential meaning and self-autonomy.

Los dueños de la tierra (The Land Owners), published in 1958, is an early production that traces the development of social consciousness in the Patagonian region of Argentina and the struggle of the proletarian class against oppression. Jewish identity in this novel is portrayed through the image of Yuda, a Russian Jew who resents the treatment and the social condition of her race. She analyzes her role as a woman considering herself an outsider, alienated and disillusioned with a system that allows the continuation of pogroms. Thus to Yuda, Jewishness implies exclusion and segregation. Her forceful voice in the novel reflects a complex perspective of exile as an escape to freedom, an issue that becomes a matter of asserting an identity that reclaims its place from history.

Dar la cara (Making A Stand) focuses on the cultural complexities of Jewish immigration to Argentina. This phenomenon is reflected in the Jewish latecomers whose expectations surpass their determination to assimilate in a new culture. A central issue to this novel is shown through the testimony of the anticlericalism exhibited by Jewish characters, who by putting aside their difference as such, join the laicization that took place in the late 1950s. Thus, in his fiction Viñas elaborates strategic and grotesque ways of showing the anti-Semitism which is concealed under secularization. The author's optimistic view of this conflict, moreover, is shown through the main characters who by not being aware of their difference become involved in the anticlerical movement.

Perhaps one of the most representative novels written by Viñas is that of the ethnic conflicts that took place in Buenos Aires in January 1919. *En la Semana Trágica* (In The Tragic Week; 1966) is a fictionalized chronicle about a national labor strike that reveals social unrest and class struggle as part of the country's history. What makes this work interesting is a well elaborated reference to the anti-Jewish pogrom that took place that week. Implicitly, Viñas allows the voice of the narrator to anticipate *la caza del ruso* (the hunting of the Russian), paralleling the bourgeoisie and aristocratic persecution of the proletarian Jews. He sends a concise message through the narrative voices of the strike's participants who stand together despite their ideological differences. In fact, the author's objective in *En la Semana Trágica* is the portrayal of ritual of violence where the victim's identity becomes important even though a common grave is one for all.

Although some of Viñas's works focus on Jewishness more than others, the author seems to warn his readers that when immigrants' expectations are confined by cultural oppression their identities become fragmented. On the other hand, Viñas's strong message of the Argentinian quest for identity is shown through the insecurities and paranoia of some of the characters in the novel and in their attitudes toward new cultures.

Interest in Viñas's writings increased during the 1970s and the 1980s. Today, the author continues to be studied as one of the most influential authors and critics of Argentina. His works offer a central aspect of the cultural conflicts and identity of immigrants in Latin America and are a significant source of history and social reality.

PRIMARY BIBLIOGRAPHY
Creative Writing

Los años despiadados. Buenos Aires: Letras Universitarias, 1956; Buenos Aires: Ediciones de la Flor, 1967.

Cayó sobre su rostro. Buenos Aires: Jorge Alvarez, 1964; Buenos Aires: Centro Editor de América Latina, 1967.

Claudia conversa. Buenos Aires: Planeta, 1995.

Cosas concretas. Buenos Aires: Tiempo Contemporáneo, 1969.

Cuerpo a cuerpo. México, D.F.: Siglo XXI, 1979.

Dar la cara. Buenos Aires: Cooperativa Poligráfica Editora, 1962; Buenos Aires: Jamcana, 1966; Buenos Aires: Centro Editor de América Latina, 1967.

Un dios cotidiano. Buenos Aires: Centro Editor de América Latina, 1968; 1981.

Dorrego; Maniobras; Tupac-Amaru. Buenos Aires: Carlos Pérez, 1974.

Dorrego; Tupac-Amaru. Buenos Aires: Galerna, 1985.

Los dueños de la tierra. Buenos Aires: Losada, 1958; Buenos Aires: Shapire, 1964; Buenos Aires: Sudamericana, 1966; Buenos Aires: Galerna, 1970; Buenos Aires: Librería Lorraine, 1974; Madrid: Orígenes, 1978; Buenos Aires: Contrapunto, 1987.

En la Semana Trágica. Buenos Aires: Jorge Alvarez, 1966; Buenos Aires: Ediciones Siglo XX, 1975.

Los hombres de a caballo. 2d. ed. Buenos Aires: Siglo XXI, 1968; Barcelona: Bruguera, 1981.

Jauría. México, D.F.: Siglo XXI, 1979.

Lisandro. Buenos Aires: Merlín, 1971.

Lisandro; Maniobras. Buenos Aires: Galerna, 1985.

Las malas costumbres. Buenos Aires: Jamcana, 1963.

Maneuvers. Trans. by Flaurie S. Imberman. *Modern International Drama* 15.1 (1981): 49-85.

Prontuario. Buenos Aires: Planeta, 1993.

Ultramar. Madrid: Edascal, 1980.

Nonfiction

Contrapunto político en América Latina: Siglo XX. México, D.F.: Instituto de
Capacitación Política, 1982.

Grotesco, immigración y fracaso: Armando Discépolo. Buenos Aires: Corregidor,
1973.

Indios, ejército y frontera. México, D.F: Siglo XXI, 1982.

Laferrère: del apogeo de la oligarquía a la crisis de la ciudad liberal. Rosario:
U.N.L., 1965.

*Literatura argentina y política I: de los jacobinos porteños a la bohemia anar-
quista.* Buenos Aires: Sudamericana, 1995.

Literatura argentina y política II: de Lugones a Walsh. Buenos Aires: Sudamericana, 1996.

Literatura argentina y realidad política: apogeo de la oligarquía. Buenos Aires:
Siglo XX, 1973.

Literatura argentina y realidad política: de Sarmiento a Cortázar. Buenos Aires:
Siglo XX, 1971.

Literatura argentina y realidad política: la crisis de la ciudad liberal. Buenos
Aires: Siglo XX, 1973.

Qué es el fascismo en Latinoamérica. Barcelona: La Gaya Ciencia, 1977.

SECONDARY BIBLIOGRAPHY
Criticism

Agosti, Héctor P. "Viñas: política y literatura." *La milicia literaria.* Buenos
Aires: Sílaba, 1969. 163-66.

Alonso, Fernando Pedro, and Arturo Rezzano. "David Viñas." *Novela y sociedad
argentina.* Buenos Aires: Paidós, 1971. 193-209.

Borello, Rodolfo A. "El realismo crítico: Rozenmacher y David Viñas." *El peronismo (1943-1955) en la narrativa argentina.* Ottawa Hispanic Studies.
Ottawa: Dovehouse Editions Canada, 1991. 222-48.

Campos, Julieta. "*Los hombres de a caballo.*" *Oficio de leer.* México, D.F.:
Fondo de Cultura Económica, 1971. 21-24.

Cano, Carlos José. "Epica y misión en *Los hombres de a caballo.*" *Revista iberoamericana* 96-97 (1976): 651-65.

Castillo, Abelardo. "*Dar la cara*: David Viñas o Martínez Suárez." *El escarabajo
de oro* (Buenos Aires) 15 (1962): 19-20.

Foster, David William. "David Viñas." In *A Dictionary of Contemporary Latin
American Authors.* Comp. David William Foster. Tempe: ASU, Center
for Latin American Studies, 1975. 107.

—. "David Viñas: lecturas desconstructivas y correctivas de la historia socio-cultural argentina." *Ideologies and Literatures* 2.2 (1987): 159-67.

Glickman, Nora. "Viñas's *En la Semana Trágica*: A Novelist's focus on an Argentine Pogrom." *Modern Jewish Studies Annual (Yiddish)* 5.4 (1984): 64-71.

González Echeverría, Roberto. "David Viñas y la crítica literaria: De Sarmiento a Cortázar." In his *Isla a su vuelo fugitiva: ensayos sobre literatura hispanoamericana*. Madrid: José Porrúa Turanzas, 1983. 103-22.

Herrera, Francisco. "David Viñas." In *Enciclopedia de la literatura argentina*. Ed. Pedro Orgambide and Roberto Yahni. Buenos Aires: Sudamericana, 1970. 625-26.

Jarkowski, Aníbal. "Sobreviviente en una guerra; enviando tarjetas postales." *Hispamérica* 21.63 (1992): 15-24.

Jitrik, Noé. "David Viñas." *Seis novelistas argentinos de la nueva promoción*. Mendoza: Cuadernos de Versión, 1959. 68-72.

Kerr, Lucille. "La geometría del poder: *Los hombres de a caballo* de David Viñas." *Revista de crítica literaria latinoamericana* (Lima) 5.9 (1979): 69-77.

Lindstrom, Naomi. "David Viñas: The Novelistics of Cultural Contradiction." In her *Jewish Issues in Argentine Literature: From Gerchunoff to Szichman*. Columbia: U of Missouri P, 1989. 88-101.

Lyon, Ted. "El engaño de la razón: Quiroga, Borges, Cortázar, Viñas." *Texto crítico* 4 (1976): 116-26.

Rassi, Humberto Mario. "David Viñas, novelista y crítico comprometido." *Revista iberoamericana* 95 (1976): 259-65.

Rodríguez Monegal, Emir. "David Viñas en su contorno." *Narradores de esta América*. 2nd ed. Montevideo-Buenos Aires: Alfa, 1969-1974. 2.310-13.

Rosa, Nicolás. "Sexo y novela: David Viñas." *Crítica y significación*. Buenos Aires: Galerna, 1970. 7-99.

—. "Viñas: la evolución de una crítica." *Los libros* (Buenos Aires) 18 (1971): 10-14.

Rubio, Isaac. "*Tupac-Amaru*, de David Viñas: una propuesta de teatro materialista." *Revista canadiense de estudios hispánicos* 7.1 (1982): 131-39.

Senkman, Leonardo. *La identidad judía en la literatura argentina*. Buenos Aires: Pardés, 1983. 103-6, 288-95, 317-20.

Sosnowski, Saúl. "*Los dueños de la tierra*, de David Viñas: cuestionamiento e impugnación del liberalismo." *Caravelle* 25 (1975): 57-75.

—. "*Jauría*, de David Viñas: continuación de un proyecto desmitificador." *Revista de crítica literaria latinoamericana* (Lima) 7-8 (1978): 165-72.

Tealdi, Juan Carlos. "David Viñas: materializar lo espiritual." In his *Borges y Viñas (literatura e ideología)*. Madrid: Orígenes, 1983. 91-161.

Valverde, Estela. "Una bibliografía en busca de un autor." *Chasqui* 17.2 (1988): 110-28.

—. *David Viñas: en busca de una síntesis de la Historia argentina*. Buenos Aires: Plus Ultra, 1989.

Vásquez Rossi, Jorge. "David Viñas y la crítica literaria argentina." *El lagrimal trifurca* (Rosario, Argentina) 2 (1968): 39-43.

Villanueva-Collado, Alfredo. "Política y sexualidad en *Jauría* de David Viñas." *Explicación de textos literarios* 16.2 (1987-88): 22-33.

Weinstein, Ana E., and Miryam E. Gover de Nasatsky, comps. *Escritores judeo-argentinos: bibliografía 1900-1987*. 2 vols. Buenos Aires: Milá, 1994. II.322-33.

Zubieta, Ana María. "La historia de la literatura: dos historias diferentes." *Filología* (Buenos Aires) 22.2 (1987): 191-213.

Interviews

"David Viñas." In *Encuesta a la literatura argentina contemporánea*." Buenos Aires: Centro Editor de América Latina, 1982. 499-503.

Kraniauskas, John. "Setting the Table in Argentina." *Index on Censorship* 18.9 (1989): 28-31.

Speranza, Graciela. "David Viñas." In her *Primera persona: conversaciones con quince narradores argentinos*. Buenos Aires: Norma, 1995. 235-51.

Spiller, Roland. "La cara de la identidad (Conversación con David Viñas)." In *La novela argentina de los años 80*. Ed. Roland Spiller. Frankfurt am Main: Vuervet Verlag, 1991. 315-24.

Szichman, Mario. "David Viñas (entrevista)." *Hispamérica* 1.1 (1972): 61-67.

Edith Dimo

VOLOCH, ADÃO (Brazil; 1914-91)

Adão Voloch was born on March 9, 1914 in Philipson, one of the farms subsidized by the Jewish Colonization Association (ICA) in the southern Brazilian region of Rio Grande do Sul. He died February 21, 1991 in Rio de Janeiro.

His father, Nathan Voloch, was from Bessarabia and immigrated via England to Argentina before finally arriving in Brazil. After having settled in Brazil he met Tânia, who became his common-law wife and the mother of Adão and his four siblings. The elder Voloch was a man of strong social-political views and a supporter of the anarchist regime. Because of his reformist ideas toward Western societies and his outspoken attitudes toward politics he was constantly at odds with his fellow expatriates wherever he went. The younger Voloch inherited, or perhaps emulated, some of these traits from his father according to the semi-autobiographical description provided mostly in the first book of a trilogy that fictionalizes his life story. In the trilogy Adão Voloch deals equally with the experiences of Jewish immigrants on the ICA farms and in the cities where the author later established residence.

His trilogy of novels is composed of *O colono judeu-açu* (The Grand Jewish Peasant; 1984), *Os horizontes do sol* (The Horizons of the Sun; 1987), and *Um gaúcho a pé* (A Gaucho on Foot; 1987). Other books penned by Voloch include *Ben Ami um homem louco pintor* (Ben Ami, a Deranged Man and Painter; 1988), a biography of his older brother; *Sob a chuva nasceu Nucleary* (Nucleary Was Born Under the Rain; 1989), a collection of short stories and chronicles; *Os desgarrados de Nonoai* (The Desperate of Nonoai; 1989), a fictional account of the suffering of Indians who fled capture and slavery from the Portuguese during colonial times.

When he was ten years old Voloch and his family moved from Philipson to the Quatro Irmãos farm. There, the author spent the remainder of his childhood and adolescence working on the plantations and raising cattle. He attended school in the neighboring town of Cruz Alta, but his formal education was interrupted when his help was needed in the chores related to the fields. The leading theme of the trilogy are the experiences of the Litvinoff family whose itinerary coincides with the route taken by his father from Bessarabia to Latin America. They are, nonetheless, fictional characters to whom Voloch attributed aspects of the real lives of some members of his family. The name Litvinoff was the author's mother's maiden name and Voloch himself is represented by the character of Arturo Litvinoff. His life story coincides temporally with the time the writer spent working in the fields, followed by his political involvements, prison terms, escapes, flights, and his disillusionment with the people whom he expected to be the supporters of the Communist ideal in Brazil.

Voloch left the farm in 1934, settling in Porto Alegre, the state's capital, where he experienced an entirely different way of life from the one he had lead until then. At age twenty he became a blue-collar worker, supporting himself with a variety of occupations that ranged from being a carpenter to a salesman to a handyman. A self-educated man, he was a devoted, impassioned, and vehement defendant of the ideology of Communism which became his great political passion for life. His ideological fervor would overcome even his disillusions over the divisions within the Brazilian Communist Party that took place when he was in his seventies.

The author later settled in Campos, in Rio de Janeiro, where he married a young Brazilian teacher of French of the local upper-middle class, but the couple separated a few years later. In 1944 he officially became a proud member of the Brazilian Communist Party. By 1949 he was elected *suplente de vereador* (vice-councilman), a position on the city council that thrust him into the middle of controversial personal and political situations. He was incarcerated many times, mainly during the military regime (1964-1985), when he was considered a threat by the local Rio police.

Eventually, Voloch became involved in the trade of agricultural machinery and began to prosper economically. Toward the end of his life he owned, along with his second wife, a medium-sized store that carried items for tourists, especially precious stones, located in the back of the Copacabana Hotel in Rio de Janeiro. Upon his death he was survived by two married sons, Marcio Viveiros—who carries his mother's maiden name due to Voloch's fear of persecution against the Jews in Brazil during World War II—and José Felipe Voloch, a step-daughter, three grandchildren, and his widow, Riva Wacks Voloch.

Along with his activities within the spheres of politics and commerce he kept in contact with his Jewish roots. He was an avid reader of novels in Yiddish, and with what he could remember of this language he would communicate with some fellow Jews. In literature his Jewishness emerges mostly in the trilogy of novels that deal with his family and himself. Only a few passages of the biographical account of his brother refer to his Judaic roots, probably because of the painter's own estrangement from Judaism. In the volume of short stories some of the narratives resume the topic of experiences of the Jewish immigrants on the ICA farms.

Adão Voloch's bibliography, though rather modest in number, contributes significantly to Brazilian literature mainly for its first-hand account of the initial Jewish settlements in southern Brazil. His skillfulness in dealing with the diversity of the characters' psychological turns and behavioral moods also emerges in his semi-autobiographical and fictional stories. Though somewhat naive in terms of literary structure, and in spite of some erratic spelling of proper names, Voloch's works encompass a world of human activities in such global terms that Jewish or non-Jewish readers might find them exquisite and intriguing.

PRIMARY BIBLIOGRAPHY
Creative Writing
O colono judeu-açu: romance da colônia Quatro Irmãos, Rio Grande do Sul. São Paulo: Novos Rumos, 1984?

Os desgarrados de Nonoai. Rio de Janeiro: Revista da Cidade, Gráfica e Editora Ltda., 1989.

Um gaúcho a pé. Rio de Janeiro: Novos Rumos, 1987.

Os horizontes do sol. Rio de Janeiro: Novos Rumos, 1987.

Sob a chuva nasceu Nucleary. Rio de Janeiro: Novos Rumos, 1989.

Nonfiction
Ben Ami um homem louco pintor: uma biografia do pintor Ben Ami. Rio de Janeiro: Novos Rumos, 1988.

SECONDARY BIBLIOGRAPHY
Igel, Regina. "Surcos literarios e ideológicos en la trilogía novelística de Adão Voloch: *El colono judeu-açu, Los horizontes del sol, Un gaucho de a pie.*" In *El imaginario judío en la literatura de América Latina: visión y realidad.* Ed. Patricia Finzi, Eliahu Toker and Marcos Faerman. Buenos Aires: Grupo Editorial Shalom, 1990. 34-37.

Regina Igel

WECHSLER, ELINA (Argentina; 1952)

Elina Wechsler was born in Buenos Aires, Argentina where she lived until 1977. She is a psychoanalyst by profession. Following the disappearance of her sister at the hands of the military government she emigrated to Madrid. She has written poems, short stories, and essays since her early adolescence. Aside from professional articles on psychoanalysis, she has published three poetry collections: *El fantasma* (The Apparition; 1983), *La larga marcha* (The Long March; 1988), and *Mitomanías amorosas* (Mythomanias of Love; 1991). Together with Daniel Schoffer (1953) she published a volume of essays titled *La metáfora milenaria: una lectura psicoanalítica de la Biblia* (The Millennial Metaphor: A Psychoanalytic Reading of the Bible; 1993). She has also completed an unpublished novel titled *El exilio de las mujeres* (The Exile of Women). Wechsler recognizes the influence in her discourse of such Latin American poets as Jorge

Luis Borges (1899-1986), Mario Benedetti (1920), and Juan Gelman (1930), as well as the European novelists Milan Kundera (1929), Robert Musil (1880-1940), Simone de Beauvoir (1908-86), Marguerite Duras (1914), and Doris Lessing (1919).

Wechsler never published any texts in Argentina; the poems included in her books were written beginning at the time of her exile-asylum in Spain. Her poetry explores and elaborates the conditions of permanence and the consolidation of an "I" in spite of the mutilations, and the violent and unnatural changes provoked by mourning and exile. At its first stage this "I" discovers itself to be (with certain astonishment) whole, and later it continues trying deliberately to affirm and enrich its integrity. In *El fantasma*, the lyrical "I" is presented at the beginning of the volume in the poem "Curriculum," as precisely what the title of the book invokes, a ghostly apparition; its self-identity erased by the rupture produced by mourning and exile. However, toward the end of the volume with the poem "Inventario" (Inventory) the "I" has reaffirmed itself and has recovered the dimension of the future. This consolidation is more evident in *La larga marcha* in which the "I" feels capable not only of surviving, but of acting and growing. The tone of the texts combines nostalgia, resignation, and a resolute decision toward vital and active continuation. In *Mitomanías amorosas* that maturity becomes the central theme. The challenges of exile, love found and lost, the passing of the years, are understood as an existential condition that, confronted with relentless wakefulness, is converted into wisdom and the spirit to fight.

The dimensions of space and time, granted painful relevance through exile, are affected by a similar dialectic. This dialectic is situated between two spaces: the original and natural one, and the one adopted by force. "Poseo algunas virtudes, no la de entender los espacios" (I Possess Several Virtues, Not That of Understanding Spaces) is the title of a poem included in *La larga marcha*. The aforementioned spaces are superimposed in *El fantasma* and *La larga marcha* with two different time frames: that which in youth was believed to be eternal ("Nosotros los de allá" [We the Ones from There]), and the present in which a forced maturity demands rebuilding (Papeles en orden" [Papers in Order]). Both dimensions intersect, and as a consequence the "here" is also the "not-then," and the "now" the "not-there." The present, be it explicit or implicit in the enunciation is made up, significantly, of the rupture between the preterite of paradise lost, and the future whose uncertainty is discovered in the condition of exile. In *Mitomanías* the here and now have also achieved a harmony which is simultaneously active and resigned to the losses. After all, the valid space is the interior, in which the exterior spaces overcome their distances and differences, in the Derridean double entendre of *différance*.

Like space and time, love is thematized in a reiterative dynamic of encounters, losses, and recoveries. The painting by René Magritte that illustrates the cover of *Mitomanías* shows two lovers kissing beneath the covers that completely envelope them. What is at issue is not a statement on the impossibility of or insistence in spite of, but rather a dialectic of attempts reinitiated with obstinacy and bravery. Illustrative of this instance is "Legado" (Legacy), the poem that ends *Mitomanías*, Wechsler's last collection of poetry to date, in which the poet reunites her four central themes: space, time, love, and the consolidation of her "I" as woman.

Jewish identity permeates her lyrical "I" as an intimate component tied to the dynamic of exile and belonging. The landscape covered by the traveler/wanderer in search of lost space includes the "Tierra Prometida" (Promised Land) and its sites of strong symbolic and even mystic connotation: Jerusalem, Safed, the Dead Sea, the Red Sea. Likewise, her lyrical treatment of biblical feminine figures and Jewish legends suggests a level of identification with bold women who managed to persist in spite of actual defeat (Eve, Lot's wife) or of textual displacement (Lilith, erased from the biblical canon but surviving in legend). This aspect, obviously, has to do with her psychoanalytic reading of the Bible as developed in her *La metáfora milenaria*.

In addition, on a personal level, Wechsler participates actively in specific Jewish spheres. She is a member of the Grupo de Reflexión Judía de Madrid (Madrid Group on Jewish Reflection). She participated in the III Encuentro de Escritores Judíos Latinoamericanos (III Congress of Latin American Jewish Writers) in Israel (1989). Also, she is a member of the Asociación Internacional de Escritores Judíos en Lengua Hispana y Portuguesa (International Association of Jewish Writers in Spanish and Portuguese), and contributes to *Noaj*, the journal published by the Asociación.

PRIMARY BIBLIOGRAPHY

Creative Writing

El fantasma. Madrid: Monte Negro, 1983.

La larga marcha. Madrid: Playor, 1988.

Mitomanías amorosas. Madrid: Verbum, 1991.

"Palabras exiliares" (three poems). *Noaj* 3.3-4 (1989): 174-77.

"Los pequeños paraísos," "Buenos Aires atrás," "Tradiciones." *Noaj* 2.2 (1988): 83-84.

"Poemas." *Hispamérica* 17.49 (1988): 61-64.

Nonfiction

"Dejarlo ser." *Noah* 1.1 (1987): 76.

"Exilio y creación poética." *Noaj* 2.2 (1988): 82.

La metáfora milenaria: una lectura psicoanalítica de la Biblia. (With Daniel Schoffer). Buenos Aires: Paidós, 1993.

SECONDARY BIBLIOGRAPHY

Arias, Juan. "Explorando el gran libro: una lectura psicoanalítica de la Biblia." *El País* Jan. 8, 1994: n.p.

Beguiristáin, Fabián. Rev. of *La metáfora milenaria. Clarín Cultura* (Buenos Aires) 2 Sept. 1993: n.p.

Goldberg, Florinda F. "Elina Wechsler: *El fantasma* y *La larga marcha.*" *Hispamérica* 18.53-54 (1989): 216-18.

Lapuerta Amigo, Paloma. "Elina Wechsler, *Mitomanías amorosas.*" *Cuadernos hispanoamericanos* 529 (1994): 320-21.

Mahler, Simón. Rev. of *La metáfora milenaria. Página 12* (Buenos Aires) 27 Sept., 1993: n.p.

Seligson, Esther. "Elina Wechsler: *Mitomanías amorosas.*" *Noaj* 7-8 (1992): 171-72.

Florinda F. Goldberg

WEIL, CLARA (Argentina; 1924-85)

Clara Rosenbaum de Weil was born to a traditional Jewish household in Monfalcone, Italy in 1924. She emigrated to Argentina, along with her family in 1938, in an effort to escape the growing Jewish persecution which had spread from Nazi Germany. The oldest of three sisters, Clara quit high school in order to help her parents who had opened a store in Buenos Aires. Even amongst Argentine Jewry, Clara and her family were outsiders. The majority of Jewish emigres were Yiddish speakers who were largely unaware of the existence of Italian Jews.

Two months after her marriage at age twenty-two, Clara was bedridden by a serious illness for more than a year. Biographical information about the exact nature of this illness is inconclusive, however, it is known that it was coupled with a severe mental crisis. These factors nurtured the creative spirit necessary for her to begin writing. Her first attempt was a composition of childrens' stories which were never published. Her subsequent efforts produced two books which are both compilations of short stories. *Una cruz para el judío* (A Cross for the Jew) was published in 1982, followed by *Del amor y la condena* (Of Love and the Conviction) in 1984. She was in the process of writing a third novel when she died in 1985.

Weil's writings portray the daily contradictions she faced as an immigrant Jew in Argentine society. Each story is a particular embodiment of different fundamental human feelings. The stories posess a dramatic cogency which causes the reader to yield to the narrative and confront the position which Clara occupied as a woman and a Jew caught in Argentina's move toward modernity. Immigrant women and ethnic minorities, as well as creole and indigenous groups, were viewed as a threat to the existing order. Entangled in the demoralizing ideological positions associated with the Nationalist revival movement, Clara Weil was a true target of repression. Her vocations, first as an employee in her parent's shop and then more specifically as a writer, defied the subordinate place of women and other subalterns in society.

Her first book, *Una cruz para el judío*, is a collection of seventeen short stories which focus mainly upon the Jewish experience. The characters deal with the stark, basic human emotions of frustration, oppression, and nostalgia. These emotions resound through all humankind, fusing the events which occur with the incompatibilities of all individuals who battle the orderly mechanisms of social decorum. The title story stands as a strong reminder of how language and in particular letters function in patriotic discourse as an inimical force, restraining subalterns to their limited roles, which remain effectively unchallenged. It relates the misfortunes of a Jew who escapes Nazi Germany because his father has paid a Gestapo official to omit the letter "j" from the word Jew on his passport. Ironically the French imprison him precisely for being a German and ship him off to Marrakesh where he dies of cholera. A wooden cross which marks his grave, bears testimony to his mistaken identity.

Weil's second compilation of stories, *Del amor y la condena*, further affirms the confusion of identity suffered by the Argentine Jewry. Drawing from numerous sociohistoric sources, she expresses the dilemas of integration and assimilation through the words of Jewish scholars including Alberto Gerchunoff (1884-1950) and Abraham J. Heschel (1907-72), aptly blending them with the strong influences of North American films and music, as well as French and Italian politics.

Clara Weil's writings continue to merit recognition in an Argentine society which is still struggling towards democracy. Her works are an important record of ideological impulses which persist in the modern cultural climate of Argentina today.

PRIMARY BIBLIOGRAPHY

Una cruz para el judío. Buenos Aires: Mantícora, 1982.
Del amor y la condena. Buenos Aires: Corregidor, 1984.

Susan Romain Speirs

YURKIEVICH, SAÚL (Argentina; 1931)

Saúl Yurkievich was born November 27, 1931 in La Plata, Argentina.
He is the author of five books of poetry and several books of criticism that deal
with contemporary Latin American poetry. His academic career began in Argentina in the 1960s. During that period he emigrated to France and since then has
been teaching at the University of Paris-Vincennes. He also has been a visiting
professor at various universities in Europe and the United States, including the
University of Maryland, Harvard University, the University of Chicago, and the
University of Pittsburgh. In addition, he collaborated with the international journal *Change* as an editorial member and was president and vice-president of the
Instituto Internacional de Literatura Iberoamericana during the 1980's. In 1987,
he was awarded a Guggenheim Fellowship to do research on the works of his
friend and colleague Julio Cortázar (1914-84). Yurkievich's works have been
translated into several languages including French, German, Italian, and English.

Although Saúl Yurkievich is well known in Latin America as an influential critic, mainly because of his inquisitive essays on modernism, avant-garde
and issues of modernity, he is also an accomplished poet with experimental
profile, an effusive effect on the reader, and an exceptional style.

His initial works on poetry appeared during the 1960s. In such works,
far from elaborating an antipoetic representation of the social conflicts of the
times, Yurkievich symbolizes through poetic verse the human nature of such
conflicts. In 1961, he published his first book, *Volanda linde lumbre* (Flying on
Shiny Limits); then followed another three books that end his initial period of
production: *Cuerpos* (Bodies; 1965), *Ciruela la loculira* (Crazy Plum and Lyre;
1965), and *Berenjenal y merodeo* (Dirty Business and Theft; 1965). All of these
books appeared together in a later volume entitled *Fricciones* (Frictions), published in 1969. Yurkievich's most recent work is a collection of stories called *A
imagen y semejanza* (In the Image and Likeness) which appeared in 1993. In this
text, Yurkievich strays away from the traditional poetic cut of the sixties to

create a derivative collage of poetry and prose with a personal touch that reflects his own view of art and creativity.

In general, the works of Yurkievich can be characterized as a selection of a continuous struggle for a very subjective and esthetic view of the world and its situation. His preoccupation with existential matters goes beyond his personal experience and it turns into a collective mission. Within this context, the significance of historical and social matters are placed well above his metaphorical representation. Therefore, his poetry is extremely absorbed by everyday conflicts.

As an Argentinian of Jewish descent, Yurkievich has been able to incorporate his identity into his works by developing a style that focuses on the multiple challenges of being different. This style encompasses a resourceful repertoire of language that points out precisely the discontinuity and the fragmentation of the human being. For Yurkievich, the poetic word is *acto y signo* (an act and a sign), therefore, he inscribes in his lyrics, images and symbolic references that are part of a multiple identity, that of himself.

Within this fragmentary vision of himself, Yurkievich inscribes the history of the world. Accompanying this viewpoint is the perceptive intuition of a child that sees his father as being "un David olvidado" (a forgotten David) by the world and by society. This father is a victim of exile and the social manipulations of his country, Argentina.

Perhaps his book *Fricciones* best represents his entire poetic collection. This text, rather than containing an idealistic framework of verses, is an example of the author's concern about the real world. The poetry in this book is a wide kaleidoscope of words that allows all possibilities of language to come into being. By using this kind of incoherent game of words, Yurkievich inscribes in his verses the catastrophic nature of our contemporary world, the social problems, the conflicts of the megalopolis, the genocides, and all those human situations governed by aggression and war.

In the collection *Ciruela la loculira*, there is an experimental nature where the traditionality of poetic language is put into question. The ludic process is used purposefully to communicate something; it's a message with a dual intention that is hidden behind the simple advertisement, a culinary recipe, funny riddles, tongue twisters, colloquial language or bureaucratic formulas that are utilized by the government. Yurkievich's game is semantic and constitutes a "pastel de palabras" (pie of words) that he creates according to the circumstances he encounters.

At the same time in the selection, *Berenjenal y merodeo*, chaos is reflected on through the use of sarcasm and irony. The author's dissatisfaction is expressed through such words as *hemorragia* (hemorrhage), *muerte* (death), *golpes* (bumps), *temor* (fear), *vómitos de sangre* (to vomit blood), *aniquilamiento* (annihilation), and *pájaros descuartizados* (dismembered birds). The use of these images, according to the author's view, are signs of today's consumer society and the political systems that are authoritative and wasteful.

Yurkievich's concern for the well-being of society is exhibited in his allusion to the painful events of war. The description of concentration camps is reflected in some of the pieces of his poetry, and it is expressed through the images of the children that are left behind, homeless. These children *vagan solitarios* (wandering in loneliness) will soon be taken away by the train that carried their parents. Yurkievich reminds us in these verses that hate is not an alternative to the injustice of the Holocaust, but neither is forgiveness, because this only can lead us to indifference. Therefore, in Yurkievich's works Jewish identity not only appears implicitly in the poems, but also manifests itself as a historical and cultural process.

In 1993, Yurkievich initiated an innovative trend of writing that encompassed a new prose constructed with some remains of poetry. Though he had been concerned with language and social issues in his poetry, his book entitled *A imagen y semejanza* promises to be an exceptional analysis of creativity and art. The book is divided into two parts: the first part *Figuraciones* (Figurations), contains three texts that are related to painting. This particular prose focuses on the perspective of a painter, Francisco de Goya, whose passion for his muse turns into creativity. At the same time, the language utilized in this text exhibits some of the avant-garde poetry and the ludic elements typical of Julio Cortázar. The second part of the book is of various themes and subjects and it deals with descriptions of places with the use of adjectival phrases and the reflection of art that is expressed in the creative experience of Kurt Schwiters and his "collage." The preponderant self-reflexion and irony as individual and collective elements contained in this creative production are also part of an assertive way of the artist to reach perfection.

Over the last decade, there has been an increasing interest in Yurkievich's works beyond that of his books of criticism. His creative ability in experimenting with new forms of poetry and prose has led some editorials such as Ediciones de Tierra Firme in Buenos Aires to publish a complete anthology of his poetry entitled *A la larga: antología poética* (At the End: Poetic Anthology, 1993). On the other hand, some of his poetry and creative prose have been translated and have appeared in various literary journals in France, Italy, Germany, England, Canada, and the United States. Currently, translations of his poetic selections into English are being done by Cola Franzen who has elaborated on a systematic and thorough project without losing sight of the complex cultural traits that are embedded in Yurkievich's works.

PRIMARY BIBLIOGRAPHY
Creative Writing
Acaso acoso. Valencia: Pre-Textos, 1982.

A imagen y semejanza. Madrid: Anaya-Muchnik Editores, 1993.

A la larga: antología poética. Buenos Aires: Ediciones de Tierra Firme, 1993.

Berenjenal y merodeo. La Plata, Argentina: Asterisco, 1965.

Ciruela la loculira. La Plata, Argentina: Asterisco, 1965.

Cuerpos. Buenos Aires: Wien 1965.

De plenos y de vanos. México, D.F.: Artífice Ediciones, 1984.

Fricciones. México, D.F.: Siglo XXI Editores, 1969.

Retener sin detener. Barcelona: Ocnos, 1973.

Rimbomba. Madrid: Hyperión, 1978.

Trampantojos. Madrid: Alfaguara, 1987.

El trasver. México: Fondo de Cutura de México, 1988.

Volanda linde lumbre. Buenos Aires: Altamar, 1961.

Nonfiction
A través de la trama: sobre vanguardias literarias y otras concomitancias. Barcelona: Muchnik, 1984.

Carlos Mastronardi. Buenos Aires: ECA, 1962.

Celebración del modernismo. Barcelona: Tusquets, 1976.

La confabulación con la palabra. Madrid: Taurus, 1978.

Fundadores de la nueva poesía latinoamericana: Vallejo, Huidobro, Borges, Neruda, Paz. Barcelona: Barral Editores, 1971.

Julio Cortázar: al calor de tu sombra. Buenos Aires: Legasa, 1981.

Modernidad de Apollinaire. Buenos Aires: Losada, 1968.

Valoración de Vallejo. Resistencia, Argentina: Universidad Nacional del Nordeste, 1958.

SECONDARY BIBLIOGRAPHY
Criticism
Acín, Ramón. "El poder de la palabra." *Heraldo de Aragón*. Feb. 18, 1993: n.p.

Carignano, Dante. "*Fricciones*: entre el rechazo y la atracción." *Rio de La Plata: Culturas* (France) 7 (1988): 93-102.

Marco, Joaquín. Rev. of *A imagen y semejanza*. *ABC Literario* Feb. 5, 1993: n.p.

Salanova, E. *A imagen y semejanza*, de Saúl Yurkievich." *El* Feb. 22, 1993: n.p.

Sosa, Víctor. Rev. of *A imagen y semejanza*. *Vuelta* 198 (199

Zapata, Miguel Angel. "Saúl Yurkievich: la omniposibilidad ve *de literatura hispánica* 26-27 (1987-88): 363-72.

Interviews
Cohen, Marcelo. "Entrevista con Saúl Yurkievich: el terrorisn está acabado." *Quimera* 4 (1981): 19-22.

Fondebrider, Jorge. "Saúl Yurkievich: vigencia de la vanguardi *ciones con la poesía argentina*. Comp. Jorge Fondebrid Libros de Tierra Firme, 1995. 277-85.

Fischer, María Luisa, and Roberto Castillo Sandoval. "Saúl Yurk lador con la palabra." *Revista chilena de literatura* 37

Tenreiro, Salvador. "Conversación con Saúl Yurkievich." *Zona f* la) 6.34 (1983): 20-26.

NOTES ON CONTRIBUTORS

DARRELL B. LOCKHART is Assistant Professor of Spanish at North Carolina A&T State University. He completed his Ph.D. at Arizona State University and wrote his dissertation on Argentine Jewish essayists. He is the author of *Latin American Jewish Literature*, forthcoming 1997. Other research interests include Latin American theater and narrative, science-fiction literature in Latin America, and translation.

JOSÉ B. ÁLVAREZ IV is Assistant Professor of Spanish at the University of Georgia in Athens. He received his Ph.D. from Arizona State University specializing in contemporary Cuban literature and film.

FANNY ARANGO-KEETH was born in Lima, Peru. She is a professional translator and she is currently finishing her Ph.D. in Spanish at Arizona State University where she teaches translation theory. Arango-Keeth has published literary translations in a variety of literary and translation journals. Her research is oriented around her interests in Hispanic and Latin American avant-garde movements, popular culture, resistance literature, Native and diglossic literatures, nineteenth-century Panamerican women's literature, and children's literature.

ANDRÉS AVELLANEDA teaches Spanish American literature at the University of Florida. He is the author of two books on Spanish American literature and culture, one of them dealing with censorship in Argentina, and many articles published in academic journals of Latin America, the U.S., and Europe. Between 1974 and 1976 he worked as a journalist for Jacobo Timerman's Argentine newspaper *La Opinión*, both in its cultural section and literary supplement, and as chief editor of *La Opinión Semanal*.

LOIS BAER BARR has taught Spanish language and literature at Northwestern University and she is currently Assistant Professor of Spanish at Lake Forest College. She has written a book entitled *Isaac Unbound: The Patriarchal Tradition in the Latin American Jewish Novel* (1995), and she is the co-editor with David Sheinin of *The Jewish Diaspora in Latin America* (1996). She has published many articles and reviews on the works of numerous Spanish and Latin American authors. She has served on the board of the Latin American Jewish Studies Association since 1987.

DAVID E. DAVIS resides in Los Angeles and works as a translator. His scholarly interests include Argentine and Chilean vanguard literature and Latin American crime fiction.

ROBERT DIANTONIO is the author of *The Admissions Essay* (1987), *Brazilian Fiction: Aspects and Evolution of the Contemporary Narrative* (1989), and he is co-editor of *Tradition and Innovation: Reflections on Latin American Jewish Writing* (1993). He has received four National Endowment for the Humanities grants and one Fulbright fellowship. He is a regular contributor to *The Jerusalem Post*, *The Kansas City Star*, *Hadassah Magazine*, and the *St. Louis Post Dispatch*. His twenty studies on Brazilian and Hispanic literature have appeared in various journals around the world.

EDITH DIMO is an Assistant Professor at California State University, Northridge. She received her Ph.D. from the University of California, Riverside in 1995 with a dissertation on "Culture and Repression: The Construction of Gender in the Chilean Narrative." Her scholarly interests deal primarily with twentieth-century Latin American narrative, especially the literature of the Southern Cone and the Caribbean. She has published articles, reviews and several interviews in a variety of professional journals and she has contributed essays to various anthologies. She is currently editing an anthology of Venezuelan women writers entitled *Escritura y desafío: narrativa venezolana escrita por mujeres*.

SABINA DYM was born in Kattakurgan, Russia in 1944. Dr. Dym emigrated to Bogotá, Colombia, where she lived for fourteen years. In 1969, she moved to Montreal, Canada and obtained a B.A. and M.Sc. in Speech and Hearing at McGill University. She then obtained a Ph.D. in Spanish Literature and Linguistics at Georgetown University, Washington, D.C. where she taught Spanish for ten years. Dr. Dym is presently an Assistant Professor at Gallaudet University in Washington, D.C. where she teaches Spanish language and culture to the deaf student population. Her Ph.D. dissertation, written in 1989, was titled "Religión y sociedad en las obras de César Tiempo."

CLAUDIA FERMAN was born in Buenos Aires. She is currently teaching at the University of Richmond. Her book *Política y posmodernidad: hacia una lectura de la anti-modernidad en Latinoamérica* won the Letras de Oro First Prize 1993. A revised and augmented version was published in Buenos Aires in 1994. She is the editor of *The Postmodern in Latin and Latino American Cultural Narratives* (1996).

ROBERTO J. FORNS-BROGGI was born in Lima, Peru in 1962. He has taught literature in Peruvian high schools and universities, and he has published a book and articles about reading and creative writing. He received his Ph.D. in Spanish at Arizona State University. He is currently a professor of Spanish at Mesa State College in Grand Junction, Colorado.

DAVID WILLIAM FOSTER is Regents' Professor of Spanish at Arizona State University. He is the author, co-author, or editor of over forty books and one-hundred-fifty articles on Latin American and Peninsular literature. His publications include *Alternate Voices in the Contemporary Latin American Narrative* (1985), *Gay and Lesbian Issues in Latin American Literature* (1991), *Contemporary Argentine Cinema* (1992), the second edition of the *Handbook of Latin American Literature* (1992), and *Mexican Literature: A History* (1994).

COLA FRANZEN is the translator of creative works by Alicia Borinsky, Saúl Yurkievich, Juan Cameron, and Marjorie Agosín, among others. Twelve volumes of her translations have been published; recent books include *The Challenge of Comparative Literature* (1993) by Claudio Guillén, and *Si regreso/If I Go Back* (1993), a bilingual volume of poetry by Juan Cameron.

HOWARD M. FRASER is N.E.H. Professor of Modern Languages and Literatures at the College of William and Mary in Williamsburg, Virginia where he has been teaching both Spanish and Portuguese for the past twenty years. He has written two books, including *In the Presence of Mystery: Modernist Fiction and the Occult* (1993), over two dozen articles, and twenty reviews covering the fields of Spanish, Portuguese, and Latin American literature.

EDWARD H. FRIEDMAN is Professor of Spanish and Comparative Literature at Indiana University. His major research field is Spanish Golden Age literature, and his publications include *The Unifying Concept: Approaches to Cervantes' Comedias* and *The Antiheroine's Voice: Narrative Discourse and Transformations of the Picaresque*. He is editor of the *Indiana Journal of Hispanic Literatures* and a book review editor of *Cervantes* and the *Yearbook of Comparative and General Literature*.

JOAN FRIEDMAN was born in China of German and Russian parents, and she grew up in Venezuela. She has taught at Harvard and the University of Wisconsin, and she is currently a faculty member in the Department of Modern Languages and Literatures at Swarthmore College, where she teaches Spanish. The focus of her current research is Venezuelan Jewish literature. She is presently working on a translation of Alicia Freilich Segal's novel *Claper*.

RITA GARDIOL is Chairperson of the Department of Spanish, Italian and Portuguese at the University of South Carolina, Columbia. During a sabbatical leave from Ball State University, where she served for twenty-three years (thirteen as department chair in Foreign Languages and one as Interim Provost), she became interested in Argentine Jewish authors. Her publications include *Argentina's Jewish Short Story Writers* (1986), *Ramón Gómez de la Serna* (1974), and numerous articles on Argentine Jewish literature and contemporary Latin American literature.

GUSTAVO GEIROLA is Assistant Professor of Spanish at Whittier College. He was born in Buenos Aires and graduated as a Professor of Modern Literatures from the University of Buenos Aires. He obtained his Ph.D. in Spanish at Arizona State University and his dissertation was on Latin American theater during the 1960s. As a literary and political dramatist and critic, he has published articles on theater, narrative, and gay and popular culture. He is also author of *El tatuaje invisible: ensayos sobre la escritura del horror en Hispanoamérica*, a forthcoming book on marginal Latin American texts.

NORA GLICKMAN was born in La Pampa, Argentina in 1944. She is the author of two collections of short stories, *Uno de sus Juanes* (1983) and *Mujeres, memorias, malogros* (1991). Her play *Suburban News*, performed in New York at the Theatre for the New City, received the Jerome Foundation Award (1993). She is also the author of *La trata de blancas* (1984), a study on the white slave trade in Argentina, and she is the co-editor of *Tradition and Innovation: Reflections on Latin American Jewish Writing* (1993), and *Argentine Jewish Theatre: A Critical Anthology* (1996). Her critical essays and her short stories have appeared in numerous journals and anthologies. She is Associate Professor of Spanish at Queens College CUNY.

FLORINDA FRIEDMANN GOLDBERG was born in Buenos Aires in 1943. She currently lives in Israel, where she teaches in the Department of Spanish and Latin American Studies at the Hebrew University of Jerusalem. She has published essays dealing with, among other subjects, Latin American literature, Jewish Latin American writers, and Ibero-American literature in Hebrew translation. She is assistant editor of the literary review *Noaj*, and editorial advisor of *Reflejos*. In 1994 she published *Alejandra Pizarnik: "Este espacio que somos"* and she is currently working on her Ph.D. dissertation on "Poeticity in the Works of Alejandra Pizarnik."

MAGGI SALGADO GORDON received her Ph.D. in Spanish Language and Literature from the University of Maryland, College Park. Between degrees, she accompanied her husband on diplomatic assignments to Japan, Paris, Korea, Argentina, Taiwan, and Hong Kong, with extensive travel throughout Latin America, Asia, and Europe. She became interested in and did research on Alberto Gerchunoff and Samuel Eichelbaum as a result of her studies at La Universidad del Salvador during her tour of Buenos Aires. They became the subjects of her doctoral dissertation as precursors of the continuing effort to define the Judeo-Argentine identity in Latin American literature.

CRISTINA GUZZO was born in Argentina, where she has been a professor of literary criticism and Latin American literature at a variety of Argentine universities including the Universidad del Salvador (Buenos Aires), the Universidad de Buenos Aires, and the Universidad Nacional de Salta. She prepared a critical edition of Manuel Prado's *La guerra al malón* (1983), and she prepared the *Enciclopedia de la Lengua y la Literatura* (1986-87). She has also written journalistic pieces for the Buenos Aires paper *Clarín* and *Los Andes* (Mendoza). She is currently a doctoral candidate in Spanish at Arizona State University.

ELIZABETH HORAN is Associate Professor of English at Arizona State University, where she directs the graduate program in Comparative Literature. She has published articles on Emily Dickinson, Gabriela Mistral, and lullabies, in addition to translations and a monograph on Gabriela Mistral.

REGINA IGEL is a professor of Brazilian and Portuguese literatures at the University of Maryland, College Park. Her research interests include women as authors and characters in Brazilian literature, fiction by and on immigrants in Brazil, and Brazilian Jewish fiction. Her publications include, *Imigrantes Judeus/ Escritores Brasileiros (O Componente Judaico na Literatura Brasileira* (1996), *Osman Lins, Uma Biografia Literária* (1988), as well a numerous articles on Brazilian literature. Professor Igel is contributor-editor of "Brazilian Novels," *Handbook of Latin American Studies* (a publication of the Library of Congress). She is also Affiliate Faculty at the Rebecca and Joseph Meyerhoff Judaic Center at the University of Maryland.

DENNIS A. KLEIN is Professor of Spanish in the Department of Modern Languages at the University of South Dakota. He has been widely published on the subjects of Hispanic and British drama. Dr. Klein is the author of three books on Peter Schaeffer and of *Blood Wedding, Yerma, and The House of Bernarda Alba: García Lorca's Tragic Trilogy*. He served as contributing editor for *García Lorca: An Annotated Primary Bibliography* and *García Lorca: A Selectively Annotated Bibliography of Criticism*, both edited by Francesca Colecchia; and contributed articles to *Peter Schaeffer: A Casebook*, edited by C. J. Gianakaris and *Israel Horovitz: A Collection of Critical Essays*, edited by Leslie Kane. Dr. Klein is head bibliographer in Spanish for the Modern Language Association's *International Bibliography*.

MILAGRO LARSON has a Masters degree in Spanish from the University of New Mexico and a Ph.D. in Spanish from Arizona State University. Her areas of interest are language-teachingmethodology, contemporary Latin American and Spanish theater, Spanish and Latin American literature of the nineteenth century, and contemporary Venezuelan literature. She has taught at Columbus College (Georgia), Arizona State University, and is currently a professor of Spanish at Estrella Mountain Community College in Arizona.

NAOMI LINDSTROM is Professor of Spanish and Portuguese at the University of Texas at Austin and Director of Publications at the Institute of Latin American Studies. Her recent books are *Jewish Issues in Argentine Literature: From Gerchunoff to Szichman* (1989), *Women's Voice in Latin American Literature* (1990), *Jorge Luis Borges: A Study of the Short Fiction* (1990), and *Twentieth-Century Spanish American Fiction* (1994).

MELISSA FITCH LOCKHART is a professor of Spanish at the Arizona International Campus of the University of Arizona in Tucson. She received her Ph.D. from Arizona State University where she completed her dissertation on Latin American women authors writing during the return to democracy in Southern Cone nations. She has published articles on Spanish American and Brazilian writers.

ESTELA ZAMORA McGLADE was born in Iraputo, Mexico in 1967. After completing her coursework in Public Accounting at the University of Guanajuato in 1990. She completed her coursework in Latin American literature at Arizona State University in 1994 and wrote her thesis on satire in the novel *Los pasos de López* by Jorge Ibargüengoitia.

ALEJANDRO METER was born in Buenos Aires in 1971. He has lived in the United States since the age of fourteen. In 1988 he received a Bachelor's degree in Spanish from California State University at Northridge. He is currently a graduate student at the University of Nebraska, Lincoln. His research interests include Jewish writers of the River Plate region.

ALLAN METZ is Periodicals/Reference Librarian at Drury College in Springfield, Missouri. While he continues to be interested in Latin American topics, his primary research focus is currently on the Clinton presidency. Metz is compiler of *Bill Clinton's Pre-presidential Career: An Annotated Bibliography* (1994) and has compiled a book-length annotated bibliography on NAFTA as well as article-length bibliographies regarding assessments of the Clinton administration at its various stages. Current projects include planned annotated book-length bibliographies on national service, community service, and eventually, Bill Clinton and the Clinton presidency.

ROSE MINC was born in Buenos Aires and completed her university studies in the United States, earning a BA degree from Douglass College and a MA and Ph.D. from Rutgers University. She is the author of *Lo fantástico y lo real en la narrativa de Juan Rulfo y Guadalupe Dueñas* and has edited *The Contemporary Short Story*, *Latin American Fiction Today*, and *Requiem for the Boom: Premature?* She has also edited a variety of special issues of professional journals, published numerous articles, reviews, and translations, and she has participated in prestigious national and international conferences. She is now Professor Emeritus of Montclair State College, where she taught for many years.

SALVADOR OROPESA studied at the University of Granada (Spain) and Arizona State University, where he received his Ph.D. His currently teaches Spanish literature and civilization at Kansas State University. He is the author of *La obra de Ariel Dorfman: ficción y crítica* (1992) and of articles on Spanish and Mexican literature and culture, especially on women writers that include Martín-Gaite, Rosa Montero, María Teresa León, Laura Esquivel, Angeles Mastretta, and Carmen Boullosa. He has also written on Salvador Novo.

MARIANA D. PETREA is Assistant Professor of Spanish at the University of Portland. Dr. Petrea received her Ph.D. in Latin American Studies from the University of Oregon (Eugene). She is the author of the book *Ernesto Sabato: la nada y la metafísica de la esperanza* (1986).

NANCY POSNER is currently Assistant Professor of Spanish at Shippensburg University of Pennsylvania. Her doctoral dissertation (University of California, Santa Barbara) explores the ideological implications in the portrayal of New World Jews in the Spanish playwright Lope de Vega's work *El Brasil restituido*.

MARIO ROJAS is Associate Professor at The Catholic University of America, Washington, D.C. He is the co-editor of *Aproximaciones a la sintaxis del español*, *Pedro Lastra o la erudición compartida*, and *De la colonia a la postmodernidad: teoría teatral y crítica sobre teatro latinoamericano*. He served as guest editor of a special volume of *Dispositio* on the semiotics of theater. He has published several articles on narratology, semiotics of theater, and on Spanish American narrative and theater.

ERNESTO SABATO is one of the foremost novelists and intellectuals in Argentina. His works include *El túnel* (1952), *Sobre héroes y tumbas* (*On Heroes and Tombs*; 1962), and *Abaddón el exterminador* (*Angel of Darkness*; 1974), as well as several collections of essays. Following the return to democracy, after eight years of brutal military repression, Sabato headed the National Commission on the Disappearance of persons. The resulting volume *Nunca más* (Never Again; 1984-85) documents the atrocities committed by the military government.

STEPHEN A. SADOW is Associate Professor of Modern Languages at Northeastern University in Boston. With J. Kates, he has translated Ricardo Feierstein's poetry and is working on the translation of the novel *Mestizo*. These translations appear in a bilingual edition entitled *We, the Generation of the Wilderness* (1989) as well as in numerous anthologies and little magazines. He has written on Latin American Jewish subjects for *The American Jewish Archives*, *Revista Interamericana de Bibliografía*, and *Raíces: Judaísmo contemporáneo* (Buenos Aires).

SILVIA E. SAUTER is Associate Professor of Spanish at Kansas State University. Her major areas of research are contemporary Spanish American narrative, critical theory, and psychocritical approaches to literature. She has published articles in journals such as *Confluencia*, *Letras femeninas*, *Revista canadiense de estudios hispánicos*, *Revista iberoamericana*, and in several editions on the works of Argentine novelists and women poets. Currently she is working on a book-length manuscript titled *Theory and Practice of the Visionary Creative Process*.

FLORA SCHIMINOVICH was born in Argentina and is now a citizen of the United States. She is the author of *Macedonio Fernández: una lectura surrealista* (1986) and editor of the anthology *La pluma mágica* (1994). She has written numerous articles about female writers and poets, politics, cinema, fantastic and detective fiction in Latin America. Her most recent contributions include studies for the collections *Gender and Genre: Redefining Women's Autobiographies* (1991), *Tradition and Innovation: Reflections on Latin American Jewish Writing* (1993), and *España en América y América en España. Actas del Congreso Argentino de Hispanistas* (1994). She teaches at Barnard College.

DANIELA SCHUVAKS was born in Argentina in 1967. She attended Montclair State University in New Jersey where she completed her Bachelors degree. She received her Masters degree in Latin American literature at Arizona State University where she wrote her thesis on Jewish Mexican literature. Currently she is working on her Ph.D. at the University of Maryland, College Park.

RENÉE SCOTT is Associate Professor of Spanish at the University of North Florida. She received her Ph.D. from the University of California, Berkeley. Her research interests include Latin American literature, women's writing, and Spanish language teaching methodology. She is the author of *Javier de Viana: un narrador del Novecientos* and her articles have appeared both in the United States and Latin America.

STACEY D. SKAR is a graduate student at the University of Wisconsin-Madison. She is writing her doctoral dissertation on the problematics of the representation of torture in Latin American literature. She has published articles on Rigoberta Menchú and Diamela Eltit.

DORIS SOMMER is Professor of Romance Languages at Harvard University. She is author of *One Master for Another: Populism as Patriarchal Rhetoric in Dominican Novels* (1984), *Foundational Fictions: The National Romances of Latin America* (1991), as well as a variety of essays on North and South American literature. Currently, with support of a Guggenheim Foundation grant, and a grant from the ACLS, she is completing a book of "Resistant Texts and an Ethics of Reading."

SUSAN ROMAIN SPEIRS received her Masters degree from Arizona State University. Her thesis consisted of an examination of the works by several Argentine Jewish women writers.

GILDA SALEM SZKLO holds a Ph.D. in Brazilian literature and is she a professor at the Universidade Federal do Rio de Janeiro. She conducted postdoctoral studies in 1993 with Jacques Leenhardt at the Ecole en Sciences Sociales, Groupe de Sociologie de la Littérature, in Paris. She has published several essays on Brazilian modern poetry and on Jewish culture in Brazilian prose. She is the author of *O bom Fim do Shtetl: Moacyr Scliar* (1990), which has been translated into French, and *Baudelaire e Carlos Drummond de Andrade: Um Estudo das Afinidades Espirituais* (1994).

CARMEN DE URIOSTE is currently Assistant Professor of Spanish at Arizona State University. She has published numerous articles on contemporary Spanish literature and film, focusing on questions of popular culture, canonicity, and marginality. Her book *Culturas de España* is forthcoming.

JASON WEISS is the author of *Writing at Risk: Interviews in Paris With Uncommon Writers* (1991). His writing—both creative and critical—has appeared widely. He is presently completing a novel, and he is writing a book on Latin American writers in Paris.

MARCELO WILLCHAM, a native of Argentina, received his Masters degree in 1994 from California State University. He is currently a doctoral candidate at Arizona State University where he is completing his dissertation, "Literary Narrative and Film Narrative: Representation of the Point of View in the Work of Beatriz Guido and Leopoldo Torre Nilsson."

GEORGE WOODYARD is Professor of Spanish and Dean of International Studies at the University of Kansas. The founder of *Latin American Theatre Review* in 1967 (a journal devoted to the study of theatre in Spanish and Portuguese America and recipient of the Ollantay prize [1979] in Caracas), he has published numerous critical studies, anthologies, editions, and bibliographies in the field of Latin American theatre.

CLARK ZLOTCHEW is Professor of Spanish, SUNY at Fredonia, and he is the author of *Libido into Literature: The "Primera época" of Benito Pérez Galdós*, *Estilo literario: análisis y creación*, and *Voices of the River Plate: Interviews with Writers of Argentina and Uruguay*, as well as numerous articles on Spanish and Latin-American literature. His translations, including works of Nobel laureates Juan Ramón Jiménez and Pablo Neruda, have appeared in book form and in journals.

INDEX

Bold indicates the page numbers for the entry on the author.